SOCIAL MARKETING
Perspectives and viewpoints

SOCIAL MARKETING
Perspectives and viewpoints

WILLIAM LAZER, Ph. D.
Professor of Marketing
Graduate School of Business Administration
Michigan State University

EUGENE J. KELLEY, Ph. D.
Research Professor of Business Administration
The Pennsylvania State University

1973

RICHARD D. IRWIN, INC. Homewood, Illinois 60430
IRWIN-DORSEY INTERNATIONAL London, England WC2H 9NJ
IRWIN-DORSEY LIMITED Georgetown, Ontario L7G 4B3

First Printing, April 1973
Second Printing, March 1974

ISBN 0-256-00284-3
Library of Congress Catalog Card No. 72–92419

Printed in the United States of America

To Joyce and Dorothy

PREFACE

Marketing is an evolving discipline subject to continued reassessment, redirection, and restructuring. During the 1950s and 1960s, marketing thought underwent a major conceptual revision. A managerial orientation emerged; the marketing management concept with its emphasis on policies, analysis, strategies, and planning was well received in both marketing education and practice. The influence of this period has had an enduring effect evidenced by an internalization of the marketing concept and the managerial approach to marketing in literature and business practice.

New theories and approaches to marketing thought are emerging in the 1970s. Social marketing and related developments have attracted considerable attention from every sector of the economy. Once again some of the fundamental concepts and dimensions of marketing are being challenged, resulting in a further reorientation of marketing thought.

The companion volumes, *Managerial Marketing: Policies, Strategies, and Decisions* and *Social Marketing: Perspectives and Viewpoints*, are designed to reflect these changes. Both books provide a realistic and comprehensive orientation to the study, analysis, and management of change in marketing. Both managerial marketing and social marketing are necessary complements to an understanding of business in contemporary society. The volume, *Managerial Marketing: Policies, Strategies, and Decisions*, is designed to present the most current perspectives on marketing management while highlighting the changing environmental forces influencing and shaping marketing policy and strategy. The companion volume, *Social Marketing: Perspectives and Viewpoints*, treats the evolving societal approach to marketing. The marketing management and social marketing volumes, however, are complete and self-sufficient. They are designed for use as independent learning units or as an integrated package at both undergraduate and graduate levels. When read together, they provide an integrated overview of both social and managerial focuses. Moreover, the contents and material in both volumes have been carefully selected and coordinated to reflect an integrated overview and learning approach to contemporary marketing.

The articles included in *Managerial Marketing: Policies, Strategies, and Decisions* and *Social Marketing: Perspectives and Viewpoints* were selected for their fundamental contributions, forward-looking insights, and effectiveness in stimulating marketing thought and understanding. Several manuscripts were developed especially for these volumes by leading marketing authorities. The coverage of these volumes has been extended to give more emphasis to emerging marketing topics.

Both volumes evolved from previous editions of *Managerial Marketing: Perspectives and Viewpoints.* The first edition, published in 1958, reflected the new managerial directions of that time. The readings in that volume emphasized problem solving and decision making, a managerial focus, and an interdisciplinary approach. Readings in theory were included to challenge, extend, and perhaps excite some students. The materials on managerial marketing and marketing theory emphasized the need of making the innovations and adjustments necessary to adapt the firm to a continuously changing environment.

The second edition of *Managerial Marketing: Perspectives and Viewpoints,* published in 1962, focused on the basic elements of managerial marketing. It included, in addition, an emphasis on quantitative methods and models, consideration of behavioral science-based marketing contributions, attention to the impact of systems thinking on marketing thought and practice, the development of the managerial functions of marketing, and greater stress on the marketing consequences of innovation and change. The majority of the articles appearing in this second edition did not appear in the first edition. Several manuscripts were developed or reworked specifically for the second edition.

Published in 1967, the third edition of *Managerial Marketing: Perspectives and Viewpoints* likewise featured the managerial approach to the study of marketing. The majority of the articles in this edition were also new to the book. Four major topics received greater coverage in this edition. First, the systems approach to the study of marketing was featured. The systems approach was identified as a promising area in the first edition. At the time of the third edition, the systems approach was receiving increasing emphasis. Second, the international dimension of marketing was considered in a separate section containing coverage of both its impact on the multinational firm and its contribution to economic development. Third, greater emphasis was given to the decision-making developments—including mathematical models and computers—and the new technology that were shaping marketing strategy. Fourth, attention was directed to the societal dimensions of marketing—the area of marketing beyond the profit motive. At the time it was stated that the public policy area would be receiving increasing attention by marketing scholars and practitioners. We are now devoting an entire volume to the developing area of social marketing.

We are grateful that the three previous editions were well received and used widely as teaching vehicles in marketing management courses, seminars, and executive development programs. We owe a deep debt of thanks to the teachers and students who used the three editions and whose acceptance made these new volumes possible.

Four major topics are presented in the first new volume, *Managerial Marketing: Policies, Strategies and Decisions.* First, a systems-oriented conceptual framework for managerial marketing is developed. Second, the expanding area of consumer behavior is appraised in terms of the changing demographics and life styles and values of the consumer market. Third, the systems approach is focused on marketing management activities, both domestic and international. Fourth, the book closes with a series of articles on various elements of the marketing mix, i.e., products and services, distribution and communications.

The managerial orientation of this volume extends and clarifies, rather than alters, the fundamental focus and objectives of previous editions of *Managerial Marketing: Perspectives and Viewpoints.* The selections emphasize the dynamic aspects of marketing management, including developments in marketing theory that underlie and ultimately influence the practice of marketing. Consideration of the behavioral sciences, quantitative-based marketing contributions, and the interdisciplinary focus are featured.

Currently, a new stream of marketing thought and action which is characterized by the term "social marketing" is evolving. Social marketing is concerned with the application of marketing knowledge, concepts, and techniques to enhance social as well as economic ends. It is also concerned with analysis of the social consequence of marketing policies, decisions, and activities.

The second new volume, *Social Marketing: Perspectives and Viewpoints,* considers this "new marketing" in its initial stages of development. The articles presented in this volume reflect the newness of the concept. However, this very newness provides an opportunity to students and scholars to develop in these areas. The definitive statement on social marketing is yet to be written. This volume, however, does attempt to position the subject in marketing thought at this point in time.

First, a conceptual framework for social marketing is presented and marketing's social role is appraised. Second, consumers, consumerism, and marketing are discussed from a social perspective. Next, specific marketing activities are appraised from the viewpoints of social responsibility, the quality of life issue, and governmental and business impact on the marketplace. The volume closes with a section illustrating the social interfaces of the marketing mix.

The selections in both volumes are intended to be used in educating students and administrators to analyze problems in an environment of increasing business and social change. The thrust of the selections is toward the frontiers of marketing knowledge. Many of the selections in the books invite careful study and rigorous analysis. However, understanding a discipline which proposes to explain and predict human action in the modern marketplace requires substantial intellectual effort. It requires a desire and capacity to continue learning. It is to those with such desire and capacity that these books are addressed.

It is hoped that students and managers of marketing will form their own framework and priorities concerning the societal implications and responsibilities of marketing. In this way, present and future marketing people can reflect this thinking in those decisions which concern each firm's market opportunities, plans, programs, organizations, and control.

We are greatly indebted to several groups of people in preparing these volumes. We wish to thank the authors and publishers who gave us permission to reproduce their articles and the authors who prepared original contributions for these volumes. Without their cooperation these books would not have been possible. These companion volumes have become a reality because of the complete cooperation of contributors and publishers.

We are grateful to our wives for their encouragement and assistance during the preparation of these volumes. We also wish to acknowledge the assistance of several graduate students for their valuable aid in the technical preparation of the manuscripts. Those graduate students to whom we are particularly indebted include: Peter Bambic, Philip Cooper, Rebecca Gould, James Harvey, Priscilla LaBarbera, Lawrence Lepisto, Scott Luley, Ronald Socha, Daniel Toy, Lewis Tucker, and Mitsuo Wada. We also wish to thank Mrs. Brenda N. Grenoble for her many secretarial contributions to the development of the manuscripts.

We shall feel well rewarded if these companion volumes bring further clarity to the marketing management approach and to the study of social marketing, and if they can convey some of the challenge and excitement of marketing to the university classroom and to executive development programs.

April 1973

William Lazer
Eugene J. Kelley

CONTENTS

1 SOCIAL MARKETING: A CONCEPTUAL FRAMEWORK

a.

Marketing's changing social role: Conceptual foundations

THERE ARE many approaches to the study of marketing. The institutional, functional, and commodity approaches—the traditional focuses—have been complemented by such emphasis as the historical, cost, and managerial. This book emphasizes the social approach to marketing. It stresses the study of marketing from a total social systems perspective. It deals with an emerging discipline, the discipline of social marketing.

During the 1950s and 1960s marketing witnessed a development of its traditional bases that shaped and structured curriculums, courses, corporate activities, and governmental activities. This development, resulting from a mixture of changing philosophies, concepts, and the climate of the times led to the marketing management thrust. Marketing management concepts, approaches, and topics characterized the marketing literature of the 1950s and the 1960s. *Managerial Marketing: Perspectives and Viewpoints,* a companion volume of this book, played a role in shaping the development of the marketing management discipline.

During the 1970s a complementary thrust seems to be emerging. It is evidenced by a concern for such areas as the impact of marketing on the quality of life; marketing and community affairs; marketing and social problems; the reduction of poverty; the opportunity to develop human capital to its fullest potential; the provision of good health care, education, and training; the development of better communities; the reduction of pollution and the protection of environments; the provision of ample jobs and opportunities; and greater consideration for one's fellow man. The result is a movement from the consideration of profits or sales only, to a consideration of the societal implications and dimensions of marketing decisions and actions.

Marketing management is now involved in significant social changes. The most relevant of these changes for marketing are allied to the impact of shifting environmental forces. Trends in each of them and their effect on marketing can be noted. Marketing is faced with increasingly new *social* considerations; previously, the considerations were mainly managerial and profit oriented. The result is the evolution of the discipline of social marketing, which includes extending marketing to embrace nonprofit institutions.

SOCIAL MARKETING DESCRIBED

Social marketing is that branch of marketing concerned both with the uses of marketing knowledge, concepts, and techniques to enhance social ends as well as with the social consequences of marketing policies, decisions, and actions. The purview of social marketing is, therefore, broader than that of managerial marketing. It refers to the study of markets and marketing activities within a total social system.

In countries of abundance, social marketing is a necessary complement to managerial marketing. It indicates the extended nature of marketing responsibility in a broader sphere of interest. It highlights the fact that a company interfaces with society in many ways other than the economic. It indicates that marketing decisions have an impact on factors other than corporate sales and profits. Social marketing gets to the very root of the functions and contributions of marketing in our total system.

The definitive statement on social marketing is yet to be written. Nevertheless, the intent of social marketing seems clear. It involves sets of social expectations that arise from the interfaces between the marketing activities of businesses and the many publics that surround business. Included in the publics are competitors, governments, consumers, employees, shareholders, business, and labor.

The boundaries of social marketing are as yet ill-defined, and the areas of study that comprise its province are only now being investigated. This book attempts to highlight some of the areas and to bring organization and structure to the field. The selections included reflect the fact that certain aspects of social marketing, such as consumerism, are currently being developed. However, other aspects, such as the social aspects of distribution, are not; they present good opportunities for future research and writing.

What distinguishes social marketing from other approaches to marketing? While social marketing emphasizes the macrodimensions, macromarketing is not the equivalent. Social marketing has micro- as well as macrodimensions. Perhaps the major distinguishing characteristic is the

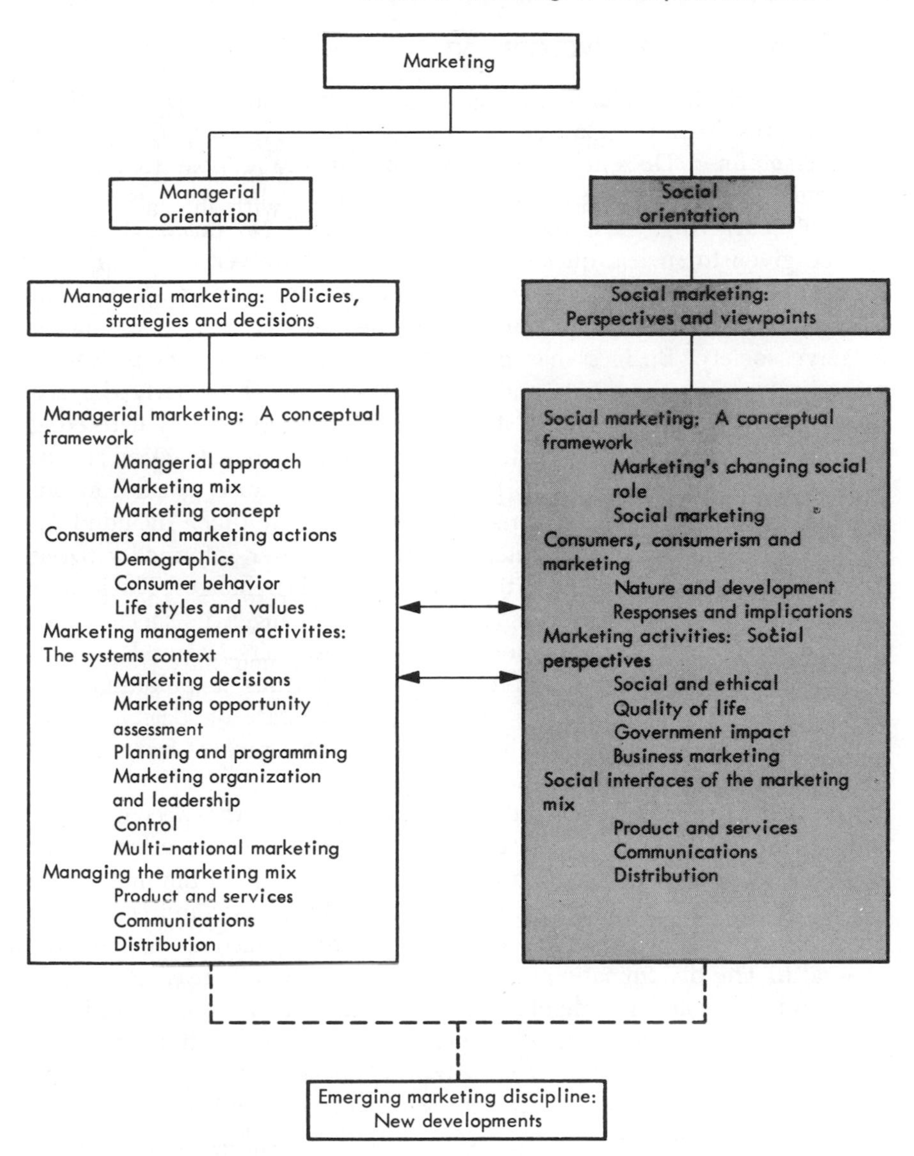

The illustration indicates relationships between the managerial and social orientations to marketing. The shaded area covers the social marketing elements treated in this book.

independent variable used as the fulcrum or basic perspective in pursuing a topic. In managerial marketing the independent variables may be such factors as the firm, profits, sales, costs, personal selling, advertising effectiveness, and related factors. In social marketing the independent variables may be society, social costs, social values, social products, and social benefits.

REASONS FOR THE DEVELOPMENT

Why should the social marketing discipline arise at this point in time? Is it the result of the natural evolution or the unfolding of marketing as a discipline? Does it stem from a moral and ethical root that is now emerging and taking precedence over some of the economic dimensions of marketing? Is it the result of affluence? No definitive answer can be given to such a question. It is evident, however, that marketing in our era is a major thrust of business. The marketing system does allocate scarce resources in our society. Business is created by society to serve society. Business has provided a very efficient mechanism for meeting some of the wants and needs of society, particularly the economic ones. But business, and that part of business that is marketing, has not been as successful in allocating scarce resources to social means.

Social marketing now seems to be emerging because of the convolution of several factors and forces at this point in time. Included are affluence, technology, communications media, better informed citizens, increased educational opportunities, and social value changes. The latter is among the most powerful single influences. Changes in social values are reflected in new environmental sensitivities—physical and esthetic, national and international. For example, sensitivities to pollution, consumer protection, utilization of resources, the welfare of society, human capital, and ecology have been heightened. These represent frontier areas for the marketing discipline.

Ours is currently a postindustrial society with the accompanying higher standard of living. The result is the rise of service-oriented and knowledge-oriented industries and the relative decline of the importance of manufacturing. Greater gaps exist between businesses and consumers. Changes are occurring where education is recognized as a generator of wealth. The dissemination of information becomes increasingly important. and the role of technology and productivity assumes a different status. In such a society there seems to be a redistribution of power. More power seems to flow to groups such as citizens and consumers. This ultimately shapes the structures of society's institutions, values, and perceptions, as seems to be occurring now. It is shaping and restructuring marketing, with one result being the development of social marketing.

In our postindustrial society it is necessary to make better applications of technology. The management of technology brings with it not only beneficial but also detrimental effects. Technology has brought with it problems of pollution, congestion, waste, the use of resources, and so on. However, it also has provided the high standard of living so many now enjoy. Unfortunately, most analysts and research efforts have focused only on the short run, such as the short-run consequences of the application of technology. Now, however, it is the long-run social consequences that are receiving greater attention. We are analyzing not merely positive economic costs but also negative social costs—both long- and short-run. Thus, there is a redirection of marketing management skills and technology to projects that have greater social significance.

The forces stimulating the evolution of social marketing at this time include the following:

1. Given a society of affluence and abundance, people can afford to pay increasing attention to social goals and social needs. Thus, it is likely that as other countries emerge from less developed economic situations, they too shall adopt a social perspective. It is also evident that currently many of the developing countries are more concerned with the economic than the social aspects of marketing.

2. Many of the younger members of society seem to be more idealistic and humanistic, on the surface at least. They express greater concern with social aspects. At certain times they appear to be less concerned with the economic and business aspects. Idealistic youth are in the vanguard of some of the social developments, including those in marketing.

3. A number of citizens and groups have accepted more responsibility for furthering activities that interface with social marketing. Many citizen groups exist in various areas of social concern. The whole consumer movement has a social dimension. Such individuals as Ralph Nader and Rachel Carson have focused on some of the societal problems. The institutionalization of consumerism by the establishment of governmental agencies such as the Office of Consumer Affairs and the proposed National Institute of Marketing and Society results in increasing attention being paid to social aspects of marketing.

4. The communications focus, particularly that provided by television and newspapers, has increased the educational awareness of the nation. The result is a climate that is riper for the acceptance of social marketing.

5. The fact that consumers have increasing leisure, travel more, and become exposed to a wider variety of people and lifestyles results in more cosmopolitan consumers. They are broader in perspective and more socially aware. Such factors, coupled with affluence, mean that these new cosmopolites can indulge in more societal activities. Thus it appears that the climate is right at the present time for the development of social marketing in our highly industrialized society. Redefinition of the role of business marketing in society is, therefore, appearing.

BUSINESS CONTRIBUTIONS

Throughout the discussion up to this point is an implied feeling on the part of society that business is not consumer oriented. There is the feeling that business has not really been sensitive to the needs of a major part of society. The so-called consumer orientation has been partially amiss. Business has not protected, nor considered, the environments in which it functions. Such goals as the rebuilding of ghettos, training of the poor, and provision of adequate educational opportunities and health facilities for all have not been handled effectively.

In essence, a large segment of the public seems to feel that business has not contributed enough to meeting socially desirable goals. Thus, there is a change in the directions of marketing—the responsibilities are extending well beyond the economic domains. They include more than just the profit goals of marketing management. There is now a sense of awareness of social needs, and social problems that can be handled by marketing; that are caused, created, and affected by marketing. Emerging is the new social responsibility on the part of the firm and hence the development of social perspectives.

Underlying the demands of society in marketing is an implication that marketing possesses the know-how and capabilities to have an impact. In addition, society is implying that the performance on the part of government and of social work agencies is inadequate. The result is that marketing managers who have the confidence and capabilities of solving risky problems, of dealing with economic uncertainty, and of handling unstructured situations in business are being called on to do so in the social domain. If this know-how is applied to the solution of social problems, it is evident that the rules and roles of marketing will change. Whether such carryover from business to society will be effective is another matter.

MARKETING FROM A SOCIAL PERSPECTIVE

Marketing as a business activity functions by the consent of the public. Its basic purpose is indicated by the marketing philosophy—the satisfaction of consumers' wants and needs. Obviously, it is impossible to totally satisfy society. Consumers do not form a homogeneous group with agreement on desirable means and ends. It is the existence of conflicting values, desires, and expectations, that adds a very difficult dimension to the performance of the tasks of social marketing.

While marketing may satisfy some consumers or the majority of them, it can, nevertheless, be criticized. However, despite the criticism and the necessity of improving marketing performance, it is obvious that marketing has some creditable social accomplishments. Marketing has contributed significantly to the continuously rising standard of living. It has resulted in consumers less fettered socially and economically. It has provided the most open society of all, along with better jobs, products, and services. The level of purchasing power that has been made available indicates that at least by some criteria marketing has performed fairly well for society.

However, according to other criteria, marketing has not performed effectively. The problems of the cities and of the poor, of the congestion of highways, of pollution of the air result in difficulties for society. A major problem for social marketing is: Who is to provide the social standards and criteria? What are the values that should be adopted? What are the criteria by which marketing should be judged?

The adoption of a social perspective should not be interpreted to mean that marketplace conflicts will be thereby eliminated. Conflicting desires, objectives, and priorities occur among the many publics. They are evidenced in the approaches adopted by various business executives. One of the reasons for conflict is the assumptions which vary among people depending upon the perspectives adopted. The assumptions of an economic man or a marketing man might be different than those of a social man. In appraising the desirability and benefits of products, innovations, promotions, policies, or decisions each might come to different conclusions.

For example, it is entirely likely that marketing men will support activities that lead to economic growth, provide employment, and satisfy consumer wants and needs that are not deemed significant by social activists. A social man might consider the waste of resources over the long run, the resulting impact on environments, or the benefits to society as a whole, and arrive at different conclusions. Marketing has as one of its basic assumptions the fact that growth per se is desirable. Some of the more socially concerned might question this assumption. Marketing, however, might point to the fact that science and technology lead to new products, that these products will satisfy consumers' wants and needs, that productivity must continue to increase in order to raise the standard of living of all. The marketing man may choose not to make a moral judgment about whether the new products are good or bad. He might leave that to the determination of individual consumers in the marketplace as they exercise their freedom of choice.

A social critic might emphasize other aspects. He might be more willing to make value judgments. He might desire a redistribution of the allocation of resources in a manner other than that determined by the marketplace. Therefore, a social man might attach entirely different weights to economic activity.

One result of such different perspectives, approaches, and values is the existence of a set of conflicting statements concerning how well marketing has done in our society. From a social perspective, marketing is criticized for many aspects such as wasting resources, adding to pollution, confusing and misleading consumers, and for additional negative impacts on the quality of life. But it could also be complimented for the high standard of living that it has created as compared with the rest of the world, and for the existence of the great opportunities that have been provided by our open society through the marketplace.

WHY SHOULD MARKETING BE INVOLVED IN SOCIAL ACTIVITIES?

The question of why marketing should be involved in activities related to the profit motive may evoke a host of responses. At one extreme are those who claim that the business of marketing is profits and sales and that any assumption to broaden responsibility will destroy the marketing activities in our society. At the other extreme is the altruistic notion that marketing is an institution of society which must pay attention to the social problems and contribute to the well-being of society beyond the economic boundaries.

It is evident that the marketing management actions and decisions intertwine with society. Marketing management depends upon the goodwill and resources of society including air, water, communication facilities, transportation, and so on. Marketing management must earn the approval of society for the use of these resources and evaluate the social opportunity costs. One way of doing this is through the development of its social dimensions.

A cogent argument can be made that it is in marketing's own self-interest to be involved actively with the solution of social problems. If these problems are solved, then better satisfied customers, better markets, and an improved environment will ensue.

Essentially, two streams of thought seem to be most relevant for the acceptance of social responsibilities of marketing. The first is that it is in marketing's own self-interest that it pay attention to social problems. If it does not, the reactions of society may be rather severe. Legal and other restrictions may abound. Hence, the resolution of the conflict of increasing profits, sales, and productivity with social values, human concerns, and the host of other social problems must receive increasing attention.

Second, it can be cogently argued that many aspects of social problems such as those concerned with pollution, consumer discontent, the quality of life, environmental degradation, unemployment, better products, and so on are problems that rightly fall in the area of marketing. Marketing management created some of them, and marketing concepts and approaches should be used to solve them.

But it would be rather naïve to think that marketing alone can solve most of society's problems, that social conflicts do not exist, or that perfect solutions can be reached. Realistically, marketing is a fundamental institution of the American society, an important part of American business. Thus, marketing does have a stake in the welfare of this nation and it should accept its responsibilities in society and become more intimately involved with societal concerns. As a result, it is necessary to develop further marketing theory, facts, concepts, models, and ideas that interface with such problems. This is grist for social marketing.

Unless marketing develops its social awarenesses and implements social actions that are acceptable, government will be forced to do that which marketing has not been willing to do voluntarily, thereby circumscribing the boundaries of marketing management.

CONSUMER AND MARKETING INTERESTS

The interests of consumers are not merely economic interests. The justification of the marketplace need not lie with only the lowest price or the lowest cost producer. Marketing's task lies not only in providing for expressed consumer wants and needs in a convenient manner; but also exists for providing new goods and services including housing, education, transportation, urban development, pollution abatement and manpower development. They may even require higher prices for products and services. Moreover, they require a scheme for prioritizing. The marketplace may not be the most appropriate mechanism to establish all priorities. Hence, in social marketing the values of the market system may be reconsidered, extended, and reordered.

It is also evident that the objectives of the profit and social pursuits may not always be complementary. It is entirely possible that they might be in conflict. Therein lies a very difficult kind of problem for business to resolve.

The market mechanism has been a very efficient allocator of products and services. It has performed effectively in the economic domain. Now it is necessary to adopt this organization mechanism in the social domain. This is the social challenge of marketing. As yet, we are not sure what is the best way to meet this challenge. However, we are moving toward the self-actualizing society described by Maslow or toward the humanistic and person-centered society where man uses resources for noble aspirations. The result is that we are witnessing an extension of the traditional boundaries of marketing.

Among the important questions which may be raised that reflect social marketing's directional approach in pursuing these tasks are:

1. Can marketing's organizational effectiveness be applied directly to social problems?
2. Should activities be undertaken by marketing where no financial profit exists?
3. What activities can the government perform best and which of these should remain in the domain of the public sector?
4. How can important social markets be made economically attractive?
5. What is the appropriate balance between economic goals and social goals for marketing management?
6. Who should determine the weight of marketing social responsibility?

7. What is the appropriate mix between the public and private involvement in solving social marketing problems?
8. What is the appropriate organizational arrangement of institutions such as education, labor, and others that will result in efficient social marketing?
9. What changes are required in governmental regulation to optimize social marketing approaches?
10. How can the social performance of marketing be evaluated?
11. How much social responsibility can a marketing group endure under current market conditions?
12. What are the appropriate short-run and long-run standards by which to evaluate marketing management with respect to social roles?

In an economy of abundance, marketing is more than a technology of the firm. The evaluation of new consumption patterns and social values requires a marketing perspective beyond that of traditional economic analysis. What, then, are the boundaries for marketing in modern society? Is it necessary for marketers to extend beyond the realm of profit? Does marketing have a social responsibility? If so, what is it?

---

1. MARKETING'S CHANGING SOCIAL RELATIONSHIPS*

William Lazer†

Marketing is not an end in itself. It is not the exclusive province of business management. Marketing must serve not only business but also the goals of society. It must act in concert with broad public interest. For marketing does not end with the buy-sell transaction—its responsibilities extend well beyond making profits. Marketing shares in the problems and goals of society and its contributions extend well beyond the formal boundaries of the firm.

The purpose of this article is to present some viewpoints and ideas

* Reprinted from "Marketing's Changing Social Relationships," *Journal of Marketing*, Vol. 33 (January 1969), pp. 3–9.

† Michigan State University.

on topics concerning marketing's changing social relationships. The author hopes to stimulate discussion and encourage work by others concerned with the marketing discipline, rather than to present a definitive set of statements. He first presents a brief discussion of marketing and our lifestyle, and marketing's role beyond the realm of profit. This is followed by the development of some ideas and viewpoints on marketing and consumption under conditions of abundance, with a particular focus on changing consumption norms. The last section is concerned with changing marketing boundaries and emerging social perspectives.

MARKETING AND LIFESTYLE

Recent developments in such areas as consumer safety and protection, product warranties, government investigations, and a host of urban issues, including air and water pollution, and poverty, are stimulating thoughtful executives and academicians to pay increasing attention to marketing's fundamental interfaces with society. They highlight the fact that marketers are inevitably concerned with societal norms and lifestyles of both our total society and societal segments. Since the American economy is a materialistic, acquisitive, thing-minded, abundant market economy, marketing becomes one of the cores for understanding and influencing lifestyles; and marketers assume the role of taste counselors. Since American tastes are being emulated in other parts of the world such as Europe, Japan, and Latin America, the impact of our values and norms reverberate throughout a broad international community.

Yet a basic difference exists between the orientation of the American lifestyle, which is interwoven with marketing, and the lifestyle of many other countries, particularly of the emerging and lesser-developed countries, although the differences are blurring. American norms include a general belief in equality of opportunity to strive for a better standard of living; the achievement of status and success through individual initiative, sacrifice, and personal skills; the provision and maintenance of a relatively open society with upward economic and social movement; the availability of education which is a route for social achievement, occupational advancement, and higher income. Yet, there are contradictory and conflicting concepts operating within this value system. One contradiction is seen in the conflict between concepts of equality for all on the one hand and the visible rank and status orderings in society. Another conflict much discussed today concerns the conflicts between the coexisting values of our affluent society and the pockets of poverty in the United States.

In their scheme of norms the majority of Americans, even younger Americans, exude optimism in the materialistic productivity of our society. They feel confident that the economic future will be much better than the present, that our standard of living and consumption will expand and increase, that pleasures will be multiplied, and that there is little need to curb desires. They are certain that increasing purchasing power will be made available to them.

This is not to deny the existence of discontent in our economy of plenty, or the challenging and questioning of values. There is evidence that some younger members are critical of our hedonistic culture, of our economic institutions and achievements. Questions have been raised about priorities of expenditures, and authority has been challenged. Various marketing processes and institutions have been attacked. But, by and large, there exists a general expectation of increasing growth, the availability of more and more, and a brighter and better future. As a result of this perspective, economic opportunities and growth are perceived not so much in terms of curbing consumer desires as is the case in many other societies, particularly in underdeveloped economies, but in increasing desires; in attempting to stimulate people to try to realize themselves to the fullest extent of their resources and capabilities by acquiring complementary goods and symbols. Whereas other societies have often hoped that tomorrow will be no worse than today, we would certainly be dismayed if present expectations did not indicate that tomorrow will be much better than today. Similarly, the emerging nations now have rising economic expectations and aspiration levels, and their lifestyle perspectives are changing. They expect to share in the economic abundance achieved by highly industrialized economies.

The growth orientation which reverberates throughout the American society has its impact on our norms and on marketing practices. It is reflected in such marketing concepts and techniques as product planning, new product development, installment credit, pricing practices, advertising campaigns, sales promotion, personal selling campaigns, and a host of merchandising activities.

BEYOND THE REALM OF PROFIT

One of the next marketing frontiers may well be related to markets that extend beyond mere profit considerations to intrinsic values—to markets based on social concern, markets of the mind, and markets concerned with the development of people to the fullest extent of their capabilities. This may be considered a macro frontier of marketing, one geared to interpersonal and social development, to social concern.

From this perspective one of marketing's roles may be to encourage increasing expenditures by consumers of dollars and time to develop themselves socially, intellectually, and morally. Another may be the direction of marketing to help solve some of the fundamental problems that nations face today. Included are such problems as the search for peace, since peace and economic progress are closely intertwined; the renewal of our urban areas which is closely related to marketing development and practices, particularly in the area of retailing; the reduction and elimination of poverty, for marketing should have a major role here; the preservation of our natural resources; the reshaping of governmental interfaces with business; and the stimulation of economic growth. To help solve such problems, in addition to its current sense of purpose in the firm, marketing must develop its sense of community, its societal commitments and obligations, and accept the challenges inherent in any institution of social control.

But one may ask whether social welfare is consonant with the bilateral transfer characteristics of an exchange or market economy, or can it be realized only through the unilateral transfer of a grants economy? This is a pregnant social question now confronting marketing.

Business executives operating in a market economy can achieve the degree of adaptation necessary to accept their social responsibilities and still meet the demands of both markets and the business enterprise. At the very least, the exchange economy will support the necessary supplementary grants economy. Currently we are witnessing several examples of this.[1] The National Alliance for Businessmen composed of 50 top business executives is seeking jobs in 50 of our largest cities for 500,000 hard-core unemployed; the Urban Coalition, composed of religious, labor, government, and business leaders, as well as several individual companies, is actively seeking ways of attacking the problem of unemployment among the disadvantaged; and the insurance companies are investing and spending millions for new housing developments in slum areas. It even seems likely that business executives, operating in a market environment, stimulated by the profit motive, may well succeed in meeting certain challenges of social responsibility where social planners and governmental agencies have not.

Governmental agencies alone cannot meet the social tasks. A spirit of mutual endeavor must be developed encompassing a marketing thrust. For marketing cannot insulate itself from societal responsibilities and problems that do not bear immediately on profit. Marketing practice must be reconciled with the concept of community involvement, and marketing leaders must respond to pressures to accept a new social role.[2]

The development of the societal dimensions of marketing by industry

[1] For a discussion of this point see Robert J. Holloway, "Total Involvement in Our Society," in *Changing Marketing Systems,* Reed Moyer (ed.) (Washington, D.C.: American Marketing Association 1967 Winter Conference Proceedings, December 1967), pp. 6–8; Robert Lekachman, "Business Must Lead the Way," *Dun's Review,* Vol. 91 (April 1968), p. 11; and Charles B. McCoy, "Business and the Community," *Dun's Review,* Vol. 91 (May 1968), pp. 110–11.

[2] Among the recent articles discussing management's new social role are "Business Must Pursue Social Goals: Gardner," *Advertising Age,* Vol. 39 (February 1968), p. 2; B. K. Wickstrum, "Managers Must Master Social Problems," *Administrative Management,* Vol. 28 (August 1967), p. 34; and G. H. Wyman, "Role of Industry in Social Change," *Advanced Management Journal,* Vol. 33 (April 1968), pp. 70–4.

and/or other institutions is necessary to mold a society in which every person has the opportunity to grow to the fullest extent of his capabilities, in which older people can play out their roles in a dignified manner, in which human potentials are recognized and nurtured, and in which the dignity of the individual is accepted. While prone to point out the undesirable impact of marketing in our lifestyle (as they should), social critics have neglected to indicate the progress and the contributions that have been made.

In achieving its sense of broad community interest and participation, marketing performs its social role in two ways. First, marketing faces social challenges in the same sense as the government and other institutions. But unlike the government, marketing finds its major social justification through offering product-service mixes and commercially unified applications of the results of technology to the marketplace for a profit. Second, it participates in welfare and cultural efforts extending beyond mere profit considerations, and these include various community services and charitable and welfare activities. For example, marketing has had a hand in the renewed support for the arts in general, the increasing demand for good books, the attendance at operas and symphony concerts, the sale of classical records, the purchase of fine paintings through mail-order catalogues, and the attention being given to meeting educational needs. These worthy activities, while sometimes used as a social measure, do not determine the degree of social concern or the acceptance of social responsibility.

A fundamental value question to be answered is not one of the absolute morality or lack of problems in our economic system and marketing activities, as many critics suggest. Rather, it is one concerning the *relative* desirability of our lifestyle with its norms, its emphasis on materialism, its hedonistic thrust, its imperfections, injustices, and poverty, as contrasted with other lifestyles that have different emphases. Great materialistic stress and accomplishment is not inherently sinful and bad. Moral values are not vitiated (as many critics might lead one to believe) by substantial material acquisitions. Increasing leisure time does not automatically lead to the decay and decline of a civilization. In reality, the improvement of material situations is a stimulus for recognition of intrinsic values, the general lifting of taste, the enhancement of a moral climate, the direction of more attention to the appreciation of arts and esthetics. History seems to confirm this; for great artistic and cultural advancements were at least accompanied by, if not directly stimulated by, periods of flourishing trade and commerce.

MARKETING AND CONSUMPTION UNDER ABUNDANCE

American consumers are confronted with a dilemma. On the one hand, they live in a very abundant, automated economy that provides a surplus of products, an increasing amount of leisure, and an opportunity for a relative life of ease. On the other hand, they have a rich tradition of hard physical work, sweat, perseverance in the face of adversity, earning a living through hard labor, being thrifty, and "saving for a rainy day." There is more than token acceptance of a philosophy that a life of ease is sinful, immoral, and wrong. Some consumers appear to fear the abundance we have and the potential lifestyle that it can bring, and are basically uncomfortable with such a way of life.

Yet, for continued economic growth and expansion, this feeling of guilt must be overcome. American consumers still adhere to many puritanical concepts of consumption, which are relevant in an economy of scarcity but not in our economy of abundance. Our society faces a task of making consumers accept comfortably the fact that a lifestyle of relative leisure and luxury that eliminates much hard physical labor and drudgery, and permits us to alter unpleasant environments, is actually one of the major accomplishments of our age, rather than the indication of a sick, failing, or decaying society. Those activities resulting in the acquisition of more material benefits and greater enjoyment of life are not to be feared or automatically belittled, nor is the reduction of drudgery and hard physical tasks to be regretted.

Some of the very fundamental precepts underlying consumption have changed. For example, consumption is no longer an exclusive home-centered activity as it once was; consumption of large quantities of many goods and services outside the home on a regular basis is very common. Similarly, the hard work and drudgery of the home is being replaced by machines and services. The inherent values of thrift and saving are now being challenged by the benefits of spending and the security of new financial and employment arrangements.[3] In fact, the intriguing problems of consumption must now receive the attention previously accorded to those of physical production.

In essence, our consumption philosophy must change. It must be brought into line with our age of plenty, with an age of automation and mass production, with a highly industrialized mass-consumption society. To do so, the abundant lifestyle must be accepted as a moral one, as an ethical one, as a life which can be inherently good. The criteria for judging our economic system and our marketing activities should include opportunity for consumers to develop themselves to the fullest extent, personally and professionally; to realize and express themselves in a creative manner; to accept their societal responsibilities; and to achieve large measures of happiness. Abundance should not lead to a sense of guilt stemming from the automatic declaration of the immorality of a comfortable way of life spurred on by marketing practices.

[3] Some aspects of the economic ambivalence of economic values are discussed by David P. Eastburn, "Economic Discipline and the Middle Generation," *Business Review*, Federal Reserve Bank of Philadelphia (July 1968), pp. 3–8.

In our society, is it not desirable to urge consumers to acquire additional material objects? Cannot the extension of consumer wants and needs be a great force for improvement and for increasing societal awareness and social contributions? Is it not part of marketing's social responsibility to help stimulate the desire to improve the quality of life—particularly the economic quality—and so serve the public interest?

In assessing consumption norms, we should recognize that consumer expenditures and investments are not merely the functions of increased income. They stem from and reflect our lifestyle. Thus, new consumption standards should be established, including the acceptance of self-indulgence, of luxurious surroundings, and of nonutilitarian products. Obviously, products that permit consumers to indulge themselves are not "strict necessities." Their purchase does not, and should not, appeal to a "utilitarian rationale." For if our economic system produced only "utilitarian products," products that were absolute necessities, it would incur severe economic and social problems, including unemployment.

Yet some very significant questions may be posed. Can or should American consumers feel comfortable, physically and psychologically, with a life of relative luxury while they are fully cognizant of the existence of poverty in the midst of plenty, of practice of discrimination in a democratic society, the feeling of hopelessness and despair among many in our expanding and increasingly productive economy, and the prevalence of ignorance in a relatively enlightened age? Or, on a broader base, can or should Americans feel comfortable with their luxuries, regular model and style changes, gadgetry, packaging variations, and waste while people in other nations of the world confront starvation? These are among the questions related to priorities in the allocation of our resources, particularly between the public and private sectors and between the national and international boundaries that have been discussed by social and economic commentators such as Galbraith[4] and Toynbee.

These are not easy questions to answer. The answers depend on the perspective adopted (whether macro or micro), on the personal philosophy adhered to (religious and otherwise), and on the social concern of individuals, groups, and nations. No perfect economic system has or will ever exist, and the market system is no exception. Economic and social problems and conflicts will remain, but we should strive to eliminate the undesirable features of our market system. And it is clear that when abundance prevails individuals and nations can afford to, and do, exercise increasing social concern.

Toynbee, in assessing our norms and value systems (particularly advertising), wrote that if it is true that personal consumption stimulated by advertising is essential for growth and full employment in our econ-

[4] John K. Galbraith, "The Theory of Social Balance," in *Social Issues in Marketing*, Lee E. Preston (ed.) (Glenview, Ill.: Scott, Foresman and Company 1968), pp. 247–52.

omy (which we in marketing believe), then it demonstrates automatically to his mind that an economy of abundance is a spiritually unhealthy way of life and that the sooner it is reformed, the better.[5] Thus, he concluded that our way of life, based on personal consumption stimulated by advertising, needs immediate reform. But let us ponder for a moment these rather strong indictments of our norms and the impact of marketing on our value systems and lifestyle.

When economic abundance prevails, the limitations and constraints on both our economic system and various parts of our lifestyle shift. The most critical point in the functioning of society shifts from physical production to consumption. Accordingly, the culture must be reoriented: a producers' culture must be converted into a consumers' culture. Society must adjust to a new set of drives and values in which consumption, and hence marketing activities, becomes paramount. Buckminster Fuller has referred to the necessity of creating regenerative consumers in our affluent society.[6] The need for consumers willing and able to expand their purchases both quantitatively and qualitatively is now apparent in the United States. It is becoming increasingly so in Russia, and it will be so in the future among the underdeveloped and emerging nations. Herein lies a challenge for marketing—the challenge of changing norms and values to bring them into line with the requirements of an abundant economy.

Although some social critics and observers might lead us to believe that we should be ashamed of our lifestyle, and although our affluent society is widely criticized, it is circumspect to observe that other nations of the world are struggling to achieve the stage of affluence that has been delivered by our economic system. When they achieve it, they will be forced to wrestle with similar problems of abundance, materialism, consumption, and marketing that we now face.

CONSUMPTION ACTIVITIES AND NORMS

The relative significance of consumers and consumption as economic determinants has been underemphasized in our system.[7] Consumption should not be considered an automatic or a happenstance activity. We must understand and establish the necessary conditions for consumption to proceed on a continuing and orderly basis. This has rich meaning for marketing. New marketing concepts and tools that encourage continuing production rather than disruptive production or the placement

[5] "Toynbee vs. Bernbach: Is Advertising Morally Defensible?" *Yale Daily News* (Special Issue 1963), p. 2.

[6] Buckminster Fuller, *Education Automation: Freeing the Scholar to Return to his Studies* (Carbondale, Ill.: Southern Illinois University Press, 1961).

[7] George Katona, "Consumer Investment and Business Investment," *Michigan Business Review* (June 1961), pp. 17–22.

of consumer orders far in advance, or new contractual obligations, must be developed.[8] To achieve our stated economic goals of stability, growth, and full employment, marketing must be viewed as a force that will shape economic destiny by expanding and stabilizing consumption.

To date the major determinant of consumption has been income. But as economic abundance increases, the consumption constraints change. By the year 2000 it has been noted that the customer will experience as his first constraint not money, but time.[9] As time takes on greater utility, affluence will permit the purchase of more time-saving products and services. Interestingly enough, although time is an important by-product of our industrial productivity, many consumers are not presently prepared to consume time in any great quantities, which in turn presents another opportunity for marketing. The manner in which leisure time is consumed will affect the quality of our lifestyle.

In other ages, the wealthy achieved more free time through the purchase of personal services and the use of servants. In our society, a multitude of products with built-in services extend free time to consumers on a broad base. Included are such products as automobiles, jet planes, mechanized products in the home, prepared foods, "throw-aways," and leased facilities. Related to this is the concept that many consumers now desire the use of products rather than mere ownership. The symbolism of ownership appears to take on lesser importance with increasing wealth.[10]

We live in a sensate culture, one which stresses materialism and sensory enjoyment. Consumers desire and can obtain the use of products and symbols associated with status, achievement, and accomplishments. Material values which are visible have become more important to a broader segment of society, and marketing responds to and reinforces such norms. But our basic underlying value system is not merely the result of the whims of marketers—it has its roots in human nature and our cultural and economic environments.

The concept of consumption usually conjures a false image. Consumption generally seems to be related to chronic scarcity. It is associated with hunger, with the bare necessities of life, and with the struggle to obtain adequate food, shelter, and clothing.[11] It is associated with the perception of economics as the "dismal science," with the study of the allocation of scarce resources.

But, it has been noted that in the future consumption and consuming

[8] Ferdinand F. Mauser, "A Universe-in-Motion Approach to Marketing," in *Managerial Marketing—Perspectives and Viewpoints,* Eugene J. Kelley and William Lazer (eds.) (Homewood, Ill.: Richard D. Irwin, Inc., 1967), pp. 46–56.

[9] Nelson N. Foote, "The Image of the Consumer in the Year 2000," Proceedings, Thirty-Fifth Annual Boston Conference on Distribution, 1963, pp. 13–18.

[10] F. F. Mauser, "A Universe-in-Motion Approach . . ."

[11] N. N. Foote, "The Image . . ."

activities will occur in a society suffering from obesity and not hunger; in a society emerged from a state of chronic scarcity, one confronting problems of satiation—full stomachs, garages, closets and houses.[12] Such an environment requires a contemporary perspective and concept of consumption and consumers. It requires a recognition and appreciation of the importance of stimulating the consumption of goods. For consumers will find that their financial capabilities for acquiring new products are outstripping their natural inclinations to do so.

But what happens to norms and values when people have suitably gratified their "needs"? What happens after the acquisition of the third automobile, the second color television set, and three or four larger and more luxurious houses? Maslow has noted that consumers then become motivated in a manner different from that explained by his hierarchy of motives. They become devoted to tasks outside themselves. The differences between work and play are transcended; one blends into the other, and work is defined in a different manner. Consumers become concerned with different norms and values reflected in metamotives or metaneeds, motives or needs beyond physical love, safety, esteem, and self-actualization.[13]

The tasks to which people become dedicated, given the gratification of their "needs," are those concerned with intrinsic values. The tasks are enjoyed because they embody these values. The self then becomes enlarged to include other aspects of the world. Under those conditions, Maslow maintains that the highest values, the spiritual life, and the highest aspirations of mankind become proper subjects for scientific study and research. The hierarchy of basic needs such as physical, safety, and social is prepotent to metaneeds. The latter, metaneeds, are equally potent among themselves.

Maslow also makes a distinction between the realm of being, the "B-realm," and the realm of deficiencies, the "D-realm,"—between the external and the practical. For example, in the practical realm of marketing with its daily pressures, executives tend to be responders. They react to stimuli, rewards, punishments, emergencies, and the demands of others. However, given an economy of abundance with a "saturation of materialism," they can turn attentions to the intrinsic values and implied norms—seeking to expose themselves to great cultural activities, to natural beauty, to the developments of those "B" values.

Our society has reached the stage of affluence without having developed an acceptable justification for our economic system, and for the eventual life of abundance and relative leisure that it will supply. Herein lies a challenge for marketing: to justify and stimulate our age of consumption. We must learn to realize ourselves in an affluent life and

---

[12] Ibid.

[13] Abraham Maslow, "Metamotivation," *The Humanist* (May-June 1967), pp. 82–84.

to enjoy it without pangs of guilt. What is required is a set of norms and a concept of morality and ethics that corresponds to our age. This means that basic concepts must be changed, which is difficult to achieve because people have been trained for centuries to expect little more than subsistence, and to gird for a fight with the elements. They have been governed by a puritanical philosophy, and often view luxurious, new, convenient products and services with suspicion.

When we think of abundance, we usually consider only the physical resources, capabilities, and potentialities of our society. But abundance depends on more than this. Abundance is also dependent on the society and culture itself. It requires psychological and sociological environments that encourage and stimulate achievement. *In large measure, our economic abundance results from certain institutions in our society which affect our pattern of living, and not the least of these institutions is marketing.*

Advertising is the institution uniquely identified with abundance, particularly in America. But the institution that is actually brought into being by abundance without previous emphasis or existence in the same form is marketing.[14] It is marketing expressed not only through advertising. It is also expressed in the emphasis on consumption in our society, new approaches to product development, the role of credit, the use of marketing research and marketing planning, the implementation of the marketing concept, the management of innovation, the utilization of effective merchandising techniques, and the cultivation of mass markets. Such institutions and techniques as self-service, supermarkets, discount houses, advertising, credit plans, and marketing research are spreading marketing and the American lifestyle through other parts of the world.

Marketing is truly an institution of social control in a relatively abundant economy, in the same sense as the school and the home. It is one of the fundamental influences of our lifestyle. It is a necessary condition of our high standard of living. It is a social process for satisfying the wants and needs of our society. It is a very formative force in our culture. In fact, it is impossible to understand fully the American culture without a comprehension of marketing. But, unlike some other social institutions, marketing is confronted with great conflicts that cloud its social role.

CHANGING MARKETING BOUNDARIES

We may well ask, what are the boundaries of marketing in modern society? This is an important question that cannot be answered simply.

[14] David M. Potter, "People of Plenty" (Chicago, Ill.: The University of Chicago Press, 1954), p. 167.

But surely these boundaries have changed and now extend beyond the profit motive. Marketing ethics, values, responsibilities, and marketing-government relationships are involved. These marketing dimensions will unquestionably receive increasing scrutiny by practitioners and academicians in a variety of areas, and the result will be some very challenging and basic questions that must be answered.

We might ask, for example, can or should marketing, as a function of business, possess a social role distinct from the personal social roles of individuals who are charged with marketing responsibilities?[15] Does the business as a legal entity possess a conscience and a personality whose sum is greater than the respective attributes of its individual managers and owners? Should each member of management be held personally accountable for social acts committed or omitted in the name of the business? Answers to such questions change with times and situations, but the trend is surely to a broadening recognition of greater social responsibilities—the development of marketing's social role.

Few marketing practitioners or academicians disagree totally with the concept that marketing has important social dimensions and can be viewed as a social instrument in a highly industrialized society. Disagreement exists, however, about the relative importance of marketing's social dimensions as compared to its managerial or technical dimensions.

The more traditional view has been that marketing management fulfills the greater part of its responsibility by providing products and services to satisfy consumer needs profitably and efficiently. Those adopting this view believe that as a natural consequence of its efficiency, customers are satisfied, firms prosper, and the well-being of society follows automatically. They fear that the acceptance of any other responsibilities by marketing managers, particularly social responsibilities, tends to threaten the very foundation of our economic system. Moot questions about who will establish the guidelines, who will determine what these social responsibilities should be, and who will enforce departures from any standards established, are raised.

However, an emerging view is one that does not take issue with the ends of customer satisfaction, the profit focus, the market economy, and economic growth. Rather, its premise seems to be that the tasks of marketing and its concomitant responsibilities are much wider than purely economic concerns. It views the market process as one of the controlling elements of the world's social and economic growth. Because marketing is a social instrument through which a standard of living is transmitted to society, as a discipline it is a social one with commen-

[15] For a discussion of the social responsibilities of executives see James M. Patterson, "What are the Social and Ethical Responsibilities of Marketing Executives?" *Journal of Marketing*, Vol. 30 (July 1966), pp. 12–15, and K. Davis, "Understanding the Social Responsibility Puzzle," *Business Horizons*, Vol. 10 (Winter 1967), pp. 45–50.

surate social responsibilities that cannot merely be the exclusive concern of companies and consumers.

Perhaps nowhere is the inner self of the populace more openly demonstrated than in the marketplace; for the marketplace is an arena where actions are the proof of words and transactions respresent values, both physical and moral. One theologian has written, "the saintly cannot be separated from the marketplace, for it is in the marketplace that man's future is being decided and the saintly must be schooled in the arts of the marketplace as in the discipline of saintliness itself."[16]

In this context, marketing's responsibility is only partially fulfilled through economic processes. There is a greater responsibility to consumers and to the human dignity that is vital to the marketplace—the concern for marketing beyond the profit motive.

Academicians and executives will be forced to rethink and reevaluate such situations in the immediate future just by the sheer weight of government concern and decisions if by nothing else.[17] In the last year, there have been governmental decisions about safety standards, devices for controlling air pollution, implied product warranties, packaging rules and regulations, the relationship of national brands to private labels, pricing practices, credit practices, and mergers. There have been discussions about limiting the amount that can be spent on advertising for a product, about controlling trading stamps, about investigating various promotional devices and marketing activities. Such actions pose serious questions about marketing's social role. If we do not answer them, others will; and perhaps in a manner not too pleasing, or even realistic.

There need be no wide chasm between the profit motive and social responsibility, between corporate marketing objectives and social goals, between marketing actions and public welfare. What is required is a broader perception and definition of marketing than has hitherto been the case—one that recognizes marketing's societal dimensions and perceives of marketing as more than just a technology of the firm. For the multiple contributions of marketing that are so necessary to meet

[16] Louis Finkelstein in Conference On The American Character, Bulletin Center for the Study of Democratic Institutions (October 1961), p. 6.

[17] The reader can gain some insight into government concern from such articles as "Consumer Advisory Council: First Report," in *Social Issues in Marketing,* Lee E. Preston, editor (Glenview, Ill.: Scott, Foresman and Company, 1968), pp. 282–94; Betty Furness, "Responsibility in Marketing," in *Changing Marketing Systems . . . ,*" Reed Moyer, editor (Washington, D.C.: American Marketing Association 1967 Winter Conference Proceedings, December 1967), pp. 25–27; Galbraith, same reference as footnote 4; Richard H. Holton, "The Consumer and the Business Community," in *Social Issues in Marketing,* Lee E. Preston, editor (Glenview, Ill.: Scott, Foresman and Company, 1968), pp. 295–303; George H. Koch, "Government-Consumer Interest: From the Business Point of View," in *Changing Marketing Systems . . . ,*" Reed Moyer, editor (Washington, D.C.: American Marketing Association 1967 Winter Conference Proceedings, December 1967), pp. 156–60.

business challenges, here and abroad, are also necessary to meet the nation's social and cultural problems.

Marketing is being widely criticized for its lack of social sensitivity. Marketers who are sincerely concerned about the impact of their actions and inactions on society will have no shortage of challenges during the next decade. The author introduces and discusses specific areas in which marketing has a responsibility to serve society.

---

2. THE GROWING RESPONSIBILITIES OF MARKETING*

Robert J. Lavidge†

Marketing is being widely criticized for its failure to contribute more to the solution of social as well as economic problems. This is a new phenomenon. Until recently, the expectation that marketing should, or could, contribute to society in a significant way was held by few.

AREAS OF GROWING RESPONSIBILITY

As a result of changes in both marketing and its environment, it is likely that marketing people will have an expanding opportunity, *and responsibility,* to serve society during the 1970s. Examples relate to:

1. Consumerism.
2. The struggle of the poor for subsistence.
3. The marketing of social and cultural services.
4. The day-to-day functioning of the economy.
5. The use and pollution of society's resources.

Efficiency and social justice

Marketing has a key role to play in the drive for increased efficiency within our economy. It also has an opportunity to play a significant role

---

* Reprinted from "The Growing Responsibilities of Marketing," *Journal of Marketing,* Vol. 34 (January 1970), pp. 25–28.

† Elrick and Lavidge, Inc.

in the drive for social justice which is replacing the drive for security or affluence among many members of our society. There is a need for more vigorous action in both of these areas, efficiency and social justice. There also is a need, which is likely to grow during the 1970s, for truly responsible marketing practitioners and educators to vigorously resist action proposed in the cause of either efficiency or social justice which is likely to damage the economy and to do more harm than good in the long run.

Consumerism

The "social concerns" of marketing men and women have been focused primarily on sins of commission—especially on fraudulent or deceptive advertising, packaging, pricing, and credit practices. Although some progress is being made, marketing leaders must do a more effective job during the next decade, of identifying and reducing these practices. Moreover, history suggests that standards will be raised. Some practices which today are generally considered acceptable will gradually be viewed as unethical, then immoral, and will eventually be made illegal. Rather than resisting such changes, marketing leaders have a responsibility to provide intelligent guidance in bringing them about. But that is not enough.

"Consumerism" related to sins of omission, as well as those of commission, will continue to grow during the 1970s. There will be further expansion in the demand for more useful information to help consumers decide what to buy. Both consumers and marketers will increasingly be concerned with warranties and guaranties, with the handling of consumer complaints, and with product performance testing. Marketing men and women also have a responsibility to provide intelligent *leadership* in this movement rather than to stand aside, to cast themselves in the role of obstructionists, or to go to the other extreme and lend support to actions in the name of social justice are well-intentioned but reflect a lack of understanding of marketing.

The struggle for subsistence

For much of the United States' population the struggle for material subsistence no longer provides direction. But the subsistence struggle will continue during the 1970s throughout most of the world. Socially concerned marketing men and women will not be content with their role in satisfying other needs while a large share of the world's population struggles with hunger and starvation. With vastly improved communications and increased education, we will become increasingly conscious of the unsatisfied needs of people in the economically underdeveloped nations of the world and in the poverty areas of the United

States. Growing recognition of these unsatisfied needs will continue to provide ammunition to those who think of marketing activities primarily in terms of stimulating selfish desires rather than satisfying both physical and psychological needs. Marketing people must work simultaneously in cultures of affluence and of poverty during the 1970s. The dual culture problem will pose difficulties because actions appropriate for one culture could be very inappropriate for the other.

More than a decade ago, Peter Drucker noted marketing's opportunity in connection with the ". . . race between the promise of economic development and the threat of international world-wide class war. The economic development is the opportunity of this age. The class war is the danger. . . . And whether we shall realize the opportunity or succumb to danger will largely decide not only the economic future of this world—it may largely decide its spiritual, its intellectual, its political and its social future. Marketing is central in this new situation. For marketing is one of our most potent levers to convert the danger into the opportunity."[1]

Walt Rostow, while serving as chairman of the Policy Planning Council of the Department of State, told the members of the American Marketing Association: "I can tell you—without flattery—that I believe the skills this organization commands and represents are going to prove critical in the generation ahead to the development of countries and regions which contain a clear majority of the world's population."[2] The opportunity and the challenge about which Drucker and Rostow spoke remain to be met in the 1970s.

Social and cultural services

The coming decade also will witness an expansion of the role of marketing in connection with ". . . markets based on social concern, markets of the mind, and markets concerned with the development of people to the fullest extent of their capabilities."[3] Kotler and Levy have pointed out that the work of marketing people is contributing to the enrichment of human life through improved marketing of educational, health and religious services, better utilization of natural resources, and enjoyment of the fine arts.[4] Marketing people are helping the institutions

---

[1] Peter F. Drucker, "Marketing and Economic Development," *Journal of Marketing*, Vol. XXII (January 1958), pp. 252–59, at pp. 254 and 255.

[2] Walt W. Rostow, "The Concept of a National Market and its Economics Growth Implications," in *Marketing and Economic Development*, Peter D. Bennett, ed. (Chicago, Ill.: American Marketing Association, September 1965), pp. 11–20, at p. 11.

[3] William Lazer, "Marketing's Changing Social Relationships," *Journal of Marketing*, Vol. 33 (January 1969), pp. 3–9, at p. 4.

[4] Philip Kotler and Sidney J. Levy, "Broadening the Concept of Marketing," *Journal of Marketing*, Vol. 33 (January 1969), pp. 10–15, at p. 10.

which provide such social and cultural services to improve the tailoring of their services to their "customers" and to improve the "distribution," "pricing," and "promotion" of them.

The day-to-day functioning of the economy

During the coming decade, marketing people will be responsible for helping bring material rewards to more members of society. Ethical, creative, efficient day-to-day marketing activities help the economy function more effectively to serve mankind. And, as William Lazer noted in a recent *Journal of Marketing* article, ". . . it is clear that when abundance prevails individuals and nations can afford to, and do, exercise increasing social concern."[5] It is when basic needs are met that men can turn attention to other needs and values, to the higher aspirations of mankind.[6] Nevertheless, it is likely that marketing people will find themselves increasingly under fire and working in what seems to be a hostile environment during the coming decade. There are likely to be continued increases in the importance of noneconomic values with growing resistance to competitive activity and resultant attacks on marketing. This may be intensified during the latter part of the decade by movement toward the checkless, cashless society. This could result in changes affecting marketing institutions which make the distribution revolution of the 1950s and 60s seem like a period of relative stability. The resultant dislocations may lead to attacks on marketing from within, as well as outside, the marketing community.

Marketing leaders will have to respond to broader attacks on marketing, as well as to issues related to consumerism. The marketing leaders who truly serve society will be those who search for, seize, and act on opportunities for improvement rather than merely defend themselves or take popular actions in the name of social justice regardless of their impact on society.

The use and pollution of society's resources

During the 1970s, marketing men and women will become increasingly concerned with the pollution of our air, water, and land (by others as well as by business firms). With greater emphasis on business ecology, there will be expanding opportunities for marketing people to assist in the adoption and use of new techniques for preserving and improving the environment.

Marketing teachers and practitioners have a responsibility to play a role in discouraging activities which are generally agreed to be harmful to society. During the next decade, marketing leaders also will be much

[5] W. Lazer, "Marketing's Changing . . . ," at p. 6.

[6] A. H. Maslow, *Motivation and Personality* (New York: Harper and Row, 1954).

more concerned with the impact of their actions and inactions on society in connection with a host of goods and services which cannot be clearly labeled either good or bad. The automobile, for example, has contributed enormously to economic development and to the enrichment of human life during the past half-century. But this contribution has not been without cost. The automobile is a major factor in the pollution of our air. It contributes to a staggering number of accidental deaths and injuries, and its land utilization cost has reached significant levels in many urban areas. Marketing people will become increasingly involved in questions of the type to which this inevitably leads. In evaluating the opportunities for new products and services, for example, the role of marketing people heretofore has focused largely on the question: Can it be sold? During the 1970s there will be increasing attention to: *Should* it be sold? Is it worth its cost to society?

THE CHANGING NATURE OF MARKETING

The areas in which marketing people can, and must, be of service to society have broadened. In addition, marketing's functions have been broadened. Marketing no longer can be defined adequately in terms of the activities involved in buying, selling, and transporting goods and services. The role of marketing in determining what goods and services will be offered now is also widely, although not universally, accepted. In addition, the coordinating and integrating roles of marketing are being given more attention. Increasingly, we are recognizing that the organization—business, educational, governmental, religious, or other—functions to serve people, its "customers." This, of course, is the essence of the "customer concept" (a term I prefer to "marketing concept").

Planning and the systems approach

The next decade is likely to witness a significant increase in the use of marketing planning, with emphasis on integrating coordinated marketing activities into the total fabric of the organization. There will be greater use of the systems approach, with planning based on the "customer concept" to solve both business and nonbusiness problems and to take advantage of opportunities for improvement. This offers much that is good. Marketing people must be prepared to play a central role in this important advance. But in doing so, they must be alert to the danger of introducing rigidities which strangle our economy in the interest of efficiency. The type of problem which can be created was illustrated by J. B. McKitterick in "Planning the Existential Society."[7] He

[7] J. B. McKitterick, "Planning the Existential Society," in *Marketing and the New Science of Planning*, Robert L. King, ed. (Chicago, Ill.: American Marketing Association, August 1968), pp. 3–9, at p. 3.

cited the person who chose the right course in school in order to gain admission to the right college where he could study the right subjects and move on to the right graduate school in order to work in the right career—only to discover that it really wasn't the right career for him. This, of course, is an argument for liberal education. It also illustrates the danger of commitment to a plan or a system which does not provide for revision of goals and the roads to them in the light of changing objectives and changing environmental factors. This is a danger to which marketing leaders must be alert in the 70s as planning based on the customer concept is adopted more widely by both business and nonbusiness organizations.

Moreover, marketers must avoid letting their desire for more and better information on which to base their plans blind them to the dangers to society which lie in the *improper* use of data banks and new surveillance techniques. Marketing men and women have a clear responsibility to provide leadership in avoiding the threats that George Orwell envisioned in *1984*,[8] as well as in making proper use of such tools.

CONCLUSIONS

Marketing practitioners and marketing educators who are sincerely concerned about the impact of their actions and inactions on society will have no shortage of challenges during the 1970s. Facing the kinds of changes which can be anticipated plus those we do not now foresee, marketing people will have an opportunity to make a significant contribution to society in their day-to-day activities—influencing decisions about what goods and services are offered, as well as helping bring them efficiently to their end users in a climate which is increasingly hostile to competitive activity and to many of the functions of marketing. At the same time, socially concerned marketing men and women will strive during the 70s: (1) to reduce marketing abuses and upgrade standards; (2) to help mitigate and ultimately eliminate the effects of poverty; (3) to aid in improving the marketing of social and cultural services; (4) to reduce the pollution of our environment; and (5) to develop international marketing institutions which will contribute to improved utilization and distribution of the world's resources and, hopefully, as a result, to world peace. In all these efforts, the truly responsible marketing leader will vigorously resist actions which would damage the economy that serves society imperfectly but increasingly well—whether those actions are proposed in the interests of profits, efficiency, or social justice.

It has been said that the ". . . social responsibilities of businessmen arise from the amount of social power they have. The idea that responsi-

[8] George Orwell, *1984* (New York: Harcourt, Brace & World, Inc., 1949).

bility and power go hand-in-hand appears to be as old as civilization itself."[9] As it matures, as it broadens in function and scope, marketing will become increasingly relevant during the 1970s to the fulfillment of man. And as the impact of marketing on society increases, so does the social responsibility of marketing people.

Marketing is a pervasive societal activity that reaches considerably beyond the selling function. The opportunity is currently present for marketers to broaden their perspectives and to apply their skills to a greater dimension of social activity. Is the marketing discipline capable of accepting this broader social responsibility, or will it remain an activity limited solely to business? The authors succinctly discuss the transferability of marketing theory and techniques to nonbusiness organizations, individuals, and ideas.

---

3. BROADENING THE CONCEPT OF MARKETING*

Philip Kotler
and
Sidney J. Levy†

The term "marketing" connotes to most people a function peculiar to business firms. Marketing is seen as the task of finding and stimulating buyers for the firm's output. It involves product development, pricing, distribution, and communication; and in the more progressive firms, continuous attention to the changing needs of customers and the development of new products, with product modifications and services to meet these needs. But whether marketing is viewed in the old sense of "pushing" products or in the new sense of "customer satisfaction engineering," it is almost always viewed and discussed as a business activity.

[9] Keith Davis, "Understanding the Social Responsibility Puzzle," *Business Horizons,* Vol. 10 (Winter 1967), pp. 45–50, at p. 48.

* Reprinted from "Broadening the Concept of Marketing," *Journal of Marketing,* Vol. 33 (January 1969), pp. 10–15.

† Both of Northwestern University.

It is the authors' contention that marketing is a pervasive societal activity that goes considerably beyond the selling of toothpaste, soap, and steel. Political contests remind us that candidates are marketed as well as soap; student recruitment by colleges reminds us that higher education is marketed; and fund raising reminds us that "causes" are marketed. Yet these areas of marketing are typically ignored by the student of marketing. Or they are treated cursorily as public relations or publicity activities. No attempt is made to incorporate these phenomena in the body proper of marketing thought and theory. No attempt is made to redefine the meaning of product development, pricing, distribution, and communication in these newer contexts to see if they have a useful meaning. No attempt is made to examine whether the principles of "good" marketing in traditional product areas are transferable to the marketing of services, persons, and ideas.

The authors see a great opportunity for marketing people to expand their thinking and to apply their skills to an increasingly interesting range of social activity. The challenge depends on the attention given to it; marketing will either take on a broader social meaning or remain a narrowly defined business activity.

THE RISE OF ORGANIZATIONAL MARKETING

One of the most striking trends in the United States is the increasing amount of society's work being performed by organizations other than business firms. As a society moves beyond the stage where shortages of food, clothing, and shelter are the major problems, it begins to organize to meet other social needs that formerly had been put aside. Business enterprises remain a dominant type of organization, but other types of organizations gain in conspicuousness and in influence. Many of these organizations become enormous and require the same rarefied management skills as traditional business organizations. Managing the United Auto Workers, Defense Department, Ford Foundation, World Bank, Catholic Church, and University of California has become every bit as challenging as managing Procter and Gamble, General Motors, and General Electric. These nonbusiness organizations have an increasing range of influence, affect as many livelihoods, and occupy as much media prominence as major business firms.

All of these organizations perform the classic business functions. Every organization must perform a financial function insofar as money must be raised, managed, and budgeted according to sound business principles. Every organization must perform a production function in that it must conceive of the best way of arranging inputs to produce the outputs of the organization. Every organization must perform a personnel function in that people must be hired, trained, assigned, and promoted in the course of the organization's work. Every organization must perform a purchasing function in that it must acquire materials in an efficient way through comparing and selecting sources of supply.

When we come to the marketing function, it is also clear that every organization performs marketing-like activities whether or not they are recognized as such. Several examples can be given.

The police department of a major U.S. city, concerned with the poor image it has among an important segment of its population, developed a campaign to "win friends and influence people." One highlight of this campaign is a "visit your police station" day in which tours are conducted to show citizens the daily operations of the police department, including the crime laboratories, police lineups, and cells. The police department also sends officers to speak at public schools and carries out a number of other activities to improve its community relations.

Most museum directors interpret their primary responsibility as "the proper preservation of an artistic heritage for posterity."[1] As a result, for many people museums are cold marble mausoleums that house miles of relics that soon give way to yawns and tired feet. Although museum attendance in the United States advances each year, a large number of citizens are uninterested in museums. Is this indifference due to failure in the manner of presenting what museums have to offer? This nagging question led the new director of the Metropolitan Museum of Art to broaden the museum's appeal through sponsoring contemporary art shows and "happenings." His marketing philosophy of museum management led to substantial increases in the Met's attendance.

The public school system in Oklahoma City sorely needed more public support and funds to prevent a deterioration of facilities and exodus of teachers. It recently resorted to television programming to dramatize the work the public schools were doing to fight the high school dropout problem, to develop new teaching techniques, and to enrich the children. Although an expensive medium, television quickly reached large numbers of parents whose response and interest were tremendous.

Nations also resort to international marketing campaigns to get across important points about themselves to the citizens of other countries. The junta of Greek colonels who seized power in Greece in 1967 found the international publicity surrounding their cause to be extremely unfavorable and potentially disruptive of international recognition. They hired a major New York public relations firm and soon full-page newspaper ads appeared carrying the headline "Greece Was Saved From Communism," detailing in small print why the takeover was necessary for the stability of Greece and the world.[2]

An anticigarette group in Canada is trying to press the Canadian

---

[1] This is the view of Sherman Lee, Director of the Cleveland Museum, quoted in *Newsweek*, Vol. 71 (April 1, 1968), p. 55.

[2] "PR for the Colonels," *Newsweek*, Vol. 71 (March 18, 1968), p. 70.

legislature to ban cigarettes on the grounds that they are harmful to health. There is widespread support for this cause but the organization's funds are limited, particularly measured against the huge advertising resources of the cigarette industry. The group's problem is to find effective ways to make a little money go a long way in persuading influential legislators of the need for discouraging cigarette consumption. This group has come up with several ideas for marketing antismoking to Canadians, including television spots, a paperback book featuring pictures of cancer and heart disease patients, and legal research on company liability for the smoker's loss of health.

What concepts are common to these and many other possible illustrations of organizational marketing? All of these organizations are concerned about their "product" in the eyes of certain "consumers" and are seeking to find "tools" for furthering their acceptance. Let us consider each of these concepts in general organizational terms.

Products

Every organization produces a "product" of at least one of the following types:

Physical products. "Product" first brings to mind everyday items like soap, clothes, and food, and extends to cover millions of *tangible* items that have a market value and are available for purchase.

Services. Services are *intangible* goods that are subject to market transaction such as tours, insurance, consultation, hairdos, and banking.

Persons. Personal marketing is an endemic *human* activity, from the employee trying to impress his boss to the statesman trying to win the support of the public. With the advent of mass communications, the marketing of persons has been turned over to professionals. Hollywood stars have their press agents, political candidates their advertising agencies, and so on.

Organizations. Many organizations spend a great deal of time marketing themselves. The Republican Party has invested considerable thought and resources in trying to develop a modern look. The American Medical Association decided recently that it needed to launch a campaign to improve the image of the American doctor.[3] Many charitable organizations and universities see selling their *organization* as their primary responsibility.

Ideas. Many organizations are mainly in the business of selling *ideas* to the larger society. Population organizations are trying to sell the idea

[3] "Doctors Try an Image Transplant," *Business Week*, No. 2025 (June 22, 1968), p. 64.

of birth control, and the Women's Christian Temperance Union is still trying to sell the idea of prohibition.

Thus the "product" can take many forms, and this is the first crucial point in the case for broadening the concept of marketing.

Consumers

The second crucial point is that organizations must deal with many groups that are interested in their products and can make a difference in its success. It is vitally important to the organization's success that it be sensitive to, serve, and satisfy these groups. One set of groups can be called the *suppliers*. *Suppliers* are those who provide the management group with the inputs necessary to perform its work and develop its product effectively. Suppliers include employees, vendors of the materials, banks, advertising agencies, and consultants.

The other set of groups are the *consumers* of the organization's product, of which four subgroups can be distinguished. The *clients* are those who are the immediate consumers of the organization's product. The clients of a business firm are its buyers and potential buyers; of a service organization those receiving the services, such as the needy (from the Salvation Army) or the sick (from County Hospital); and of a protective or a primary organization, the members themselves. The second group is the *trustees* or *directors,* those who are vested with the legal authority and responsibility for the organization, oversee the management, and enjoy a variety of benefits from the "product." The third group is the active *publics* that take a specific interest in the organization. For a business firm, the active publics include consumer rating groups, governmental agencies, and pressure groups of various kinds. For a university, the active publics include alumni and friends of the university, foundations, and city fathers. Finally, the fourth consumer group is the *general public*. These are all the people who might develop attitudes toward the organization that might affect its conduct in some way. Organizational marketing concerns the programs designed by management to create satisfactions and favorable attitudes in the organization's four consuming groups: clients, trustees, active publics, and general public.

Marketing tools

Students of business firms spend much time studying the various tools under the firm's control that affect product acceptance: product improvement, pricing, distribution, and communication. All of these tools have counterpart applications to nonbusiness organizational activity.

Nonbusiness organizations to various degrees engage in product improvement, especially when they recognize the competition they face from other organizations. Thus, over the years churches have added a host of nonreligious activities to their basic religious activities to satisfy members seeking other bases of human fellowship. Universities keep updating their curricula and adding new student services in an attempt to make the educational experience relevant to the students. Where they have failed to do this, students have sometimes organized their own courses and publications, or have expressed their dissatisfaction in organized protest. Government agencies such as license bureaus, police forces, and taxing bodies are often not responsive to the public because of monopoly status; but even here citizens have shown an increasing readiness to protest mediocre services, and more alert bureaucracies have shown a growing interest in reading the user's needs and developing the required product services.

All organizations face the problem of pricing their products and services so that they cover costs. Churches charge dues, universities charge tuition, governmental agencies charge fees, fund-raising organizations send out bills. Very often specific product charges are not sufficient to meet the organization's budget, and it must rely on gifts and surcharges to make up the difference. Opinions vary as to how much the users should be charged for the individual services and how much should be made up through general collection. If the university increases its tuition, it will have to face losing some students and putting more students on scholarship. If the hospital raises its charges to cover rising costs and additional services, it may provoke a reaction from the community. All organizations face complex pricing issues although not all of them understand good pricing practice.

Distribution is a central concern to the manufacturer seeking to make his goods conveniently accessible to buyers. Distribution also can be an important marketing decision area for nonbusiness organizations. A city's public library has to consider the best means of making its books available to the public. Should it establish one large library with an extensive collection of books, or several neighborhood branch libraries with duplication of books? Should it use bookmobiles that bring the books to the customers instead of relying exclusively on the customers coming to the books? Should it distribute through school libraries? Similarly the police department of a city must think through the problem of distributing its protective services efficiently through the community. It has to determine how much protective service to allocate to different neighborhoods; the respective merits of squad cards, motorcycles, and foot patrolmen; and the positioning of emergency phones.

Customer communication is an essential activity of all organizations although many nonmarketing organizations often fail to accord it the importance it deserves. Managements of many organizations think they have fully met their communication responsibilities by setting up advertising and/or public relations departments. They fail to realize that *everything about an organization talks.* Customers form impressions of an organization from its physical facilities, employees, officers, stationery, and a hundred other company surrogates. Only when this is appreciated do the members of the organization realize that they all are in marketing, whatever else they do. With this understanding they can assess realistically the impact of their activities on the consumers.

CONCEPTS FOR EFFECTIVE MARKETING MANAGEMENT IN NONBUSINESS ORGANIZATIONS

Although all organizations have products, markets, and marketing tools, the art and science of effective marketing management have reached their highest state of development in the business type of organization. Business organizations depend on customer goodwill for survival and have generally learned how to sense and cater to their needs effectively. As other types of organizations recognize their marketing roles, they will turn increasingly to the body of marketing principles worked out by business organizations and adapt them to their own situations.

What are the main principles of effective marketing management as they appear in most forward-looking business organizations? Nine concepts stand out as crucial in guiding the marketing effort of a business organization.

Generic product definition

Business organizations have increasingly recognized the value of placing a broad definition on their products, one that emphasizes the basic customer need(s) being served. A modern soap company recognizes that its basic product is cleaning, not soap; a cosmetics company sees its basic product as beauty or hope, not lipsticks and makeup; a publishing company sees its basic product as information, not books.

The same need for a broader definition of its business is incumbent upon nonbusiness organizations if they are to survive and grow. Churches at one time tended to define their product narrowly as that of producing religious services for members. Recently, most churchmen have decided that their basic product is human fellowship. There was a time when educators said that their product was the three R's. Now most of them define their product as education for the whole man. They try to serve the social, emotional, and political needs of young people in addition to intellectual needs.

Target groups definition

A generic product definition usually results in defining a very wide market, and it is then necessary for the organization, because of limited resources, to limit its product offering to certain clearly defined groups within the market. Although the generic product of an automobile company is transportation, the company typically sticks to cars, trucks, and buses, and stays away from bicycles, airplanes, and steamships. Furthermore, the manufacturer does not produce every size and shape of car but concentrates on producing a few major types to satisfy certain substantial and specific parts of the market.

In the same way, nonbusiness organizations have to define their target groups carefully. For example, in Chicago the YMCA defines its target groups as men, women and children who want recreational opportunities and are willing to pay $20 or more a year for them. The Chicago Boys Club, on the other hand, defines its target group as poorer boys within the city boundaries who are in want of recreational facilities and can pay $1 a year.

Differentiated marketing

When a business organization sets out to serve more than one target group, it will be maximally effective by differentiating its product offerings and communications. This is also true for nonbusiness organizations. Fund-raising organizations have recognized the advantage of treating clients, trustees, and various publics in different ways. These groups require differentiated appeals and frequency of solicitation. Labor unions find that they must address different messages to different parties rather than one message to all parties. To the company they may seem unyielding, to the conciliator they may appear willing to compromise, and to the public they seek to appear economically exploited.

Customer behavior analysis

Business organizations are increasingly recognizing that customer needs and behavior are not obvious without formal research and analysis; they cannot rely on impressionistic evidence. Soap companies spend hundreds of thousands of dollars each year researching how Mrs. Housewife feels about her laundry, how, when, and where she does her laundry, and what she desires of a detergent.

Fund raising illustrates how an industry has benefited by replacing stereotypes of donors with studies of why people contribute to causes. Fund raisers have learned that people give because they are getting something. Many give to community chests to relieve a sense of guilt because of their elevated state compared to the needy. Many give to medical charities to relieve a sense of fear that they may be struck by a disease whose cure has not yet been found. Some give to feel pride. Fund raisers have stressed the importance of identifying the motives operating in the marketplace of givers as a basis for planning drives.

Differential advantages

In considering different ways of reaching target groups, an organization is advised to think in terms of seeking a differential advantage. It should consider what elements in its reputation or resources can be exploited to create a special value in the minds of its potential customers. In the same way Zenith has built a reputation for quality and International Harvester a reputation for service, a nonbusiness organization should base its case on some dramatic value that competitive organizations lack. The small island of Nassau can compete against Miami for the tourist trade by advertising the greater dependability of its weather; the Heart Association can compete for funds against the Cancer Society by advertising the amazing strides made in heart research.

Multiple marketing tools

The modern business firm relies on a multitude of tools to sell its product, including product improvement, consumer and dealer advertising, salesman incentive programs, sales promotions, contests, multiple-size offerings, and so forth. Likewise nonbusiness organizations also can reach their audiences in a variety of ways. A church can sustain the interest of its members through discussion groups, newsletters, news releases, campaign drives, annual reports, and retreats. Its "salesmen" include the religious head, the board members, and the present members in terms of attracting potential members. Its advertising includes announcements of weddings, births and deaths, religious pronouncements, and newsworthy developments.

Integrated marketing planning

The multiplicity of available marketing tools suggests the desirability of overall coordination so that these tools do not work at cross purposes. Over time, business firms have placed under a marketing vice president activities that were previously managed in a semiautonomous fashion, such as sales, advertising, and marketing research. Nonbusiness organizations typically have not integrated their marketing activities. Thus, no single officer in the typical university is given total responsibility for studying the needs and attitudes of clients, trustees, and publics, and undertaking the necessary product development and communication programs to serve these groups. The university administration instead includes a variety of "marketing" positions such as dean of students, director of alumni affairs, director of public relations, and director of development; coordination is often poor.

Continuous marketing feedback

Business organizations gather continuous information about changes in the environment and about their own performance. They use their salesmen, research department, specialized research services, and other means to check on the movement of goods, actions of competitors, and feelings of customers to make sure they are progressing along satisfactory lines. Nonbusiness organizations typically are more casual about collecting vital information on how they are doing and what is happening in the marketplace. Universities have been caught off guard by underestimating the magnitude of student grievance and unrest, and so have major cities underestimated the degree to which they were failing to meet the needs of important minority constituencies.

Marketing audit

Change is a fact of life, although it may proceed almost invisibly on a day-to-day basis. Over a long stretch of time it might be so fundamental as to threaten organizations that have not provided for periodic reexaminations of their purposes. Organizations can grow set in their ways and unresponsive to new opportunities or problems. Some great American companies are no longer with us because they did not change definitions of their businesses, and their products lost relevance in a changing world. Political parties become unresponsive after they enjoy power for a while and every so often experience a major upset. Many union leaders grow insensitive to new needs and problems until one day they find themselves out of office. For an organization to remain viable, its management must provide for periodic audits of its objectives, resources, and opportunities. It must reexamine its basic business, target groups, differential advantage, communication channels, and messages in the light of current trends and needs. It might recognize when change is needed and make it before it is too late.

IS ORGANIZATIONAL MARKETING A SOCIALLY USEFUL ACTIVITY?

Modern marketing has two different meanings in the minds of people who use the term. One meaning of marketing conjures up the terms selling, influencing, persuading. Marketing is seen as a huge and increasingly dangerous technology, making it possible to sell persons on buying things, propositions, and causes they either do not want or which are bad for them. This was the indictment in Vance Packard's *Hidden Persuaders* and numerous other social criticisms, with the net effect that a large number of persons think of marketing as immoral or entirely self-seeking in its fundamental premises. They can be counted on to resist the idea of organizational marketing as so much "Madison Avenue."

The other meaning of marketing unfortunately is weaker in the public mind; it is the concept of sensitively *serving and satisfying human needs.* This was the great contribution of the marketing concept that was promulgated in the 1950s, and that concept now counts many business firms as its practitioners. The marketing concept holds that the problem of all business firms in an age of abundance is to develop customer loyalties and satisfaction, and the key to this problem is to focus on the customer's needs.[4] Perhaps the short-run problem of business firms is to sell people on buying the existing products, but the long-run problem is clearly to create the products that people need. By this recognition that effective marketing requires a consumer orientation instead of a product orientation, marketing has taken a new lease on life and tied its economic activity to a higher social purpose.

It is this second side of marketing that provides a useful concept for all organizations. All organizations are formed to serve the interest of particular groups: hospitals serve the sick, schools serve the students, governments serve the citizens, and labor unions serve the members. In the course of evolving, many organizations lose sight of their original mandate, grow hard, and become self-serving. The bureaucratic mentality begins to dominate the original service mentality. Hospitals may become perfunctory in their handling of patients, schools treat their students as nuisances, city bureaucrats behave like petty tyrants toward the citizens, and labor unions try to run instead of serve their members. All of these actions tend to build frustration in the consuming groups. As a result some withdraw meekly from these organizations, accept frustration as part of their condition, and find their satisfactions elsewhere. This used to be the common reaction of ghetto Negroes and college students in the face of indifferent city and university bureaucracies. But new posssibilities have arisen, and now the same consumers refuse to withdraw so readily. Organized dissent and protest are seen to be an answer, and many organizations thinking of themselves as responsible have been stunned into recognizing that they have lost touch with their constituencies. They had grown unresponsive.

Where does marketing fit into this picture? Marketing is that function of the organization that can keep in constant touch with the organization's consumers, read their needs, develop "products" that meet these needs, and build a program of communications to express the organization's purposes. Certainly selling and influencing will be large parts of organizational marketing; but, properly seen, selling follows rather than precedes the organization's drive to create products to satisfy its consumers.

[4] Theodore Levitt, "Marketing Myopia," *Harvard Business Review,* Vol. 38 (July-August 1960), pp. 45–56.

CONCLUSION

It has been argued here that the modern marketing concept serves very naturally to describe an important facet of all organizational activity. All organizations must develop appropriate products to serve their sundry consuming groups and must use modern tools of communication to reach their consuming publics. The business heritage of marketing provides a useful set of concepts for guiding all organizations.

The choice facing those who manage nonbusiness organizations is not whether to market or not to market, for no organization can avoid marketing. The choice is whether to do it well or poorly, and on this necessity the case for organizational marketing is basically founded.

What are a banker's opinions concerning the emerging discipline of social marketing? Is there more to the case for "social responsibilities" than simply minimizing the pressure of government regulations and of consumer advocates? Long-term social benefits and economic profits can accrue to business and society as a result of the adoption of socially responsible business policies by corporate enterprise.

---

4. ECONOMIC MAN vs. SOCIAL MAN*

David P. Eastburn†

With so much attention focused on violence in many of our city streets, there is danger of losing sight of a desperate conflict underlying much of the violence. This is the conflict between Economic Man and Social Man.

Each of us, of course, is both Economic and Social Man. Each of us is concerned with making a living and with living with his fellows, but the mix varies, and it is there that the source of conflict lies. Those who are 90 percent Economic Man see today's world differently from those who are 90 percent Social Man. Many, in whom the proportions more nearly approach 50–50, are torn apart by conflicting beliefs. And

* Reprinted from "Economic Man vs. Social Man," *Series for Economic Education*, Federal Reserve Bank of Philadelphia, 1970.

† Federal Reserve Bank of Philadelphia, President.

so we have a kind of national schizophrenia which is both divisive and debilitating.

It is easy, of course, to overdraw the contrast between economic and social values, but as a first approximation, consider the following shorthand list of characteristics and concerns:

Economic man	*Social man*
Production	Distribution
Quantity	Quality
Goods and services	People
Money values	Human values
Work and discipline	Self-realization
Competition	Cooperation
Laissez-faire	Involvement
Inflation	Unemployment

Economic Man tends to be concerned primarily with producing goods and services, with quantitative problems. He is largely responsible for the doubling in the nation's real output over the past quarter of a century. Ironically, however, his very success has made it possible for Social Man to gain a sympathetic hearing for his concerns about the *distribution* of output and the *quality* of life. The turning point for many was the appearance of J. K. Galbraith's *The Affluent Society* in the late 1950s. Galbraith made a persuasive argument that the problem of production in this nation has been solved. It is no coincidence that the war on poverty followed in the 1960s and concern for the environment promises to be the issue of the 1970s.

Economic Man embodies many of the values of the Establishment which youth today finds so distasteful. He believes that a relatively free pursuit of self-interest has served this nation well; that self-interest in a market economy is expressed largely in monetary terms; that monetary rewards are directed by competition to the efficient and enterprising; and that the Puritan Ethic of hard work and self-discipline is still a major guidepost to the good life.

Social Man sees quite a different route to the good life. He stresses people rather than things; human rather than monetary values; and freedom not to pursue one's self-interest but to realize one's true individuality by involvement in a cooperative way in solving society's problems.

Obviously, these are caricatures, not carefully toned portraits. Yet it is precisely because such black-and-white conceptions exist that much of the current conflict is possible. . . . It is a truism to say that the only reliable road to lasting domestic peace is through understanding. It may well be, however, that controversy between races and generations contains such a large component of emotion that a frontal attack will only produce more discord. Better understanding of underlying economic and social issues may promise quicker results. A question of considerable significance, therefore, is what can Economic Man and Social Man learn from each other?

Social Man must convince Economic Man that this nation cannot prosper unless action is taken to solve social ills. A great deal of progress has already been made. Indeed, historians may note some day that one of the most outstanding achievements of the twentieth century was the softening of a harsh and inhuman economic philosophy, a process which has yielded unprecedented economic as well as social dividends. It is impossible, for example, to visualize anyone today seriously subscribing to Herbert Spencer's philosophy of 1850:

> . . . The poverty of the incapable, the distresses that come upon the imprudent, the starvation of the idle, and those shoulderings aside of the weak by the strong, which leave so many "in shallows and in miseries," are the decrees of a large, far-seeing benevolence.

Social action taken in the 1930s and since has brought us a great distance.

Tacked on to the end of this long-run trend has been a new awareness on the part of corporations in the past decade of their social responsibilities. Motivations behind this latest development are varied, but for the most part they are perfectly consistent with the traditional forces of self-interest that drive Economic Man. Looking to the longer run, businessmen see growing markets among Negroes, a supply of manpower from the ghetto, and goodwill from efforts to improve the environment.

All this has become the conventional wisdom as far as Economic Man is concerned. He may be less aware, however, of an equally valuable benefit from social action: it can enhance the possibility that public authorities might achieve a stable economy. Unemployment compensation and minimum income maintenance provide buffers between the disadvantaged and recession. Better training and education make it possible for those who are presently disadvantaged to hold their own in recession. If public authorities could gain more assurance that their actions will not bear down unfairly on the poor and greater confidence that their economic policies will not have severe social side effects, they could move with more vigor and effectiveness against inflation whenever it threatened. Social action, in short, promises Economic Man not only expanding markets in which to sell his wares but a more stable economy in which to produce *his* order of priorities, to giving him a bigger slice of the pie, the more effective he will be in solving social problems.

In the longer run, it is possible to meet rising social needs without sacrificing material comforts; the slices may be the same, but the pie can be bigger. Social Man's best hope is to work with Economic Man toward the kind of dynamic economy that will make such a happy solution possible.

Possibilities of cooperation are greater now that there is common recognition of a pressing need to clean up the environment. The environment is something tangible that Economic Man can understand; and it is free of difficulties which the Puritan Ethic poses for him in accepting such social programs as minimum income maintenance. At the same time, Social Man can find in efforts to improve the environment many opportunities to better the lives of those who are socially deprived. The danger in the environmental issue is that it could divert attention from the needs of people. The hope is that it may provide a common ground for Economic Man and Social Man to come together to work for their mutual interests.

Both have a vital role to play. Social problems cannot be solved without a strong and growing economy, and we cannot prosper economically if we continue to have large parts of the population not sharing in the fruits of production.

b.

The development of social marketing

THE INCREASE in social awareness and social responsibility concerns has different meanings for various groups in society. For the marketing professional one manifestation is the emergence and development of the social marketing area. In conjunction with traditional orientations to marketing, the development of the social marketing approach is leading to a reevaluation of the marketing concept. The "new" marketing concept is a customer-focused orientation guiding all functions within an organization toward the profitable achievement of organizational objectives by providing benefits which fulfill the economic and social needs of the consumer-citizen.

In the first article in this section, Lazer discusses some of the dimensions of social marketing. Kotler and Zaltman describe the possibilities of achieving social objectives through the application of marketing principles. Browne and Haas next discuss two principal questions involved with the social responsibility issue. Concluding this section, Kotler presents the generic concept of marketing, the broadest conception of marketing to date.

What concepts are now being used to evaluate marketing decisions? How will the development of social marketing influence marketing theory and practice? What is the relative importance of the social dimensions of marketing as compared to the managerial and technical dimensions? The following article discusses these major areas of concern.

5. DIMENSIONS OF SOCIAL MARKETING*

William Lazer†

SOCIAL MARKETING AS A DISCIPLINE

A major change in the direction of the marketing development of the discipline occurred during the 1960s. In the previous period, the late 1940s and 1950s the main and sometimes sole orientation was the managerial thrust. The discipline of marketing management evolved with its focus on company sales and profits. The major view was that the marketing manager fulfills his responsibilities by providing products and services that satisfy consumers in an efficient manner while achieving its corporate goals such as sales, profits, image, and share of market. The perspective was an internal one.

A different perception of marketing and its responsibilities, however, has currently emerged. The justification of marketing is now sought in a social context as well as a corporate one. Pluralistic marketing objectives are evolving and becoming more explicit. Executives are being asked to act at least with partial disregard for the single criterion of profit in arriving at marketing decisions. Marketing's responsibilities in such areas as urban development, education and training, health and welfare, quality of life, reduction of pollution, and civil rights are being investigated. The fundamental reason for this emphasis is not altruistic or noneconomic. Rather it is based on long-run enlightened self-interest of marketing with direct, long-run economic consequences.

In the past, marketing decisions have been justified solely on the basis of cost-revenue relationships. Now, however, the concepts of social costs, social profits, social audits, and social benefits are being introduced. Mention is made of social products, social capital, and social wealth. The result is evidenced in the emergence of the discipline of social marketing.

Social marketing complements the discipline of managerial marketing of the 1960s. It has a parallel in the development of such disciplines as social psychology and social anthropology. It is a hybrid discipline resulting from the meld of two perspectives—that of the marketing viewpoint with its approaches, concepts, models, tools, and concerns; and that of the social viewpoint with its roots in society, groups of human

* Presented at the World Congress of Sales and Marketing Executives International, Puerto Rico (May 1972).

† Michigan State University.

beings, social problems, the poor, our declining cities, and that which is "good for all."

Will social marketing result in improved social problem solving? Will it provide more effective approaches to the study of society? What the results of the social thrust will be is not yet clear. Nevertheless, the directions of the current social emphasis are leading marketing into fundamentally new areas of concern for business. One effect will be a change in scope, standards, and goals of the discipline.

Social marketing suggests that marketing decisions cannot be justified on economic costs and profits alone. It indicates that some products and services should be marketed where there is little or no economic profit. It holds that marketing has dimensions that extend beyond the profit motive. It maintains that management know-how must be applied to the solution of society's problems. It is in marketing's best enlightened self-interest to do so, for the alternative consequences of society's negative reaction, governmental regulations, administrative rulings, and an expanded posture are not desirable alternatives.

With this new posture many intriguing questions remain to be answered by the discipline. Who owns the roads, the waterways, the airways? What are they worth? What contribution should be made by individuals and companies that use them? Given conflicting social goals and limited resources, who should establish the social guidelines? Who will determine what the social responsibilities of a particular marketing company should be? Who will enforce departure from established standards? Are social responsibilities consonant with the profit motive and with the effective competition? Are such marketing activities as advertising, product development, personal selling, and merchandising consonant with social responsibilities? Will social well-being and increasing social responsibility mark decline in the important motivations all necessary for the maintenance of our way of life?

APPLICATION OF MARKETING APPROACHES

Relatively few marketing practitioners or academicians now seem to disagree totally with the concept that marketing has important social dimensions. Disagreement exists, however, about the relative marketing importance of social dimensions as compared to managerial and technical dimensions. There are conceptual gaps that have not been bridged between individual self-interest on the one hand and social welfare on the other, between the energizing impact of self-motivation and the leveling effect of social welfare. In fact, it seems that the social adversaries and protagonists of our market system are not communicating since each bases his discussions on different conceptual foundations.

It is a challenge for the marketing discipline to redefine and reevaluate the assumptions and conceptual foundations of marketing and so develop more meaningful constructs, models, and theories. However, this requires a change in orientation. For marketing, as a set of forces, activities, and as an institution that has been so aggressive in developing products and services, and in expanding consumption, is now being challenged to become aggressive in the social field in helping to achieve social objectives. It will be evaluated on this basis.

Many pertinent questions can be formulated about marketing applications in the social domain. Is idealism and social impact a valid concern for a firm? Do heavy social responsibilities tend to debilitate the firm and lead it into areas that it does not belong? What is the appropriate hierarchy of marketing executives' responsibility in consideration of self, family, management, customers, government, society, the world? Is social welfare consonant with the bilateral transfer characteristics of an exchange of market economy, or can social welfare be realized only through the unilateral transfer of a grant economy?

There is also a question about the relevancy of marketing concepts as they are applied to broad social issues. Can we directly transpose our concepts as they are applied to managerial issues in the firm to broad social issues? Can we directly transpose our models, data, and findings? Do we have the justification and the data base for this? Much of the literature concerned with marketing and society seems to suggest in a very simplistic manner that if we look at social problems from the perspective of the wants and needs of various groups of patrons, clients, or customers, if we gather information about them, and if social programs are so shaped and promoted progressively, then we have applied marketing in the broader sense. Is this truly so?

It has also been implied and directly suggested that marketing managers will succeed in solving social problems. There are not now hard facts to support the contention that business executives operating in marketing environments, stimulated by profit models, may well succeed in meeting certain social challenges and in solving social problems where social workers, governmental managers, and agencies have not. I hope this will be the case, and would like to think so, but I am not sure.

In a way, marketing practitioners and academicians are confronted with a crisis of legitimacy. Our discipline power does not emanate from a coherent body of accepted social thought, as in the case for sociology, medicine, theology, or social work. Gaps exist between marketing with its aim, thrust and quests for profit, and society with its aims, thrusts, and goals. In trying to bridge this gap, and assume greater societal responsibility by applying its know-how to social ends, marketing may gain increasing social approval of its position and thereby legitimacy of the discipline.

SOCIAL INDICATORS

Currently there are many questions being raised about the impact of marketing approaches and activities on the quality of life. How does a corporation determine the impact of its products, marketing policies, and decisions and strategies. We are just beginning to raise such questions and seek answers.

Currently in marketing people are involved in defining social indicators, trying to operationalize them and obtain measurements, prioritize them for use in individual businesses and planning models. The fact that American business must now factor social impact into plans and decisions will have a great influence on the discipline which will require a reconsideration of current marketing constructs and theories. It could result in a new way of assessing marketing performance.

To date we do not have the methodology to conduct social audits. Some progress has been made. But most of the opinions, ideas, and concepts of the social impact of marketing actions are being left to spokesmen outside the discipline. Yet marketing which is largely managerially oriented is being held accountable. Note the recent hearings on the effect of television programs on children, or of advertising on our lifestyle. Evidence exists that emphasis on the reporting of social statistics—emphasis on areas of social marketing—is overdue.

Questions will be raised about discipline responsibility in educating people who are able to perform social audits. Several marketing consulting companies now offer this service. Will we eventually have the parallel of CPA's—CSA's (Certified Social Auditors)? Will corporations develop management teams charged with performing such internal audits? What will the government's role be? These are among the operating questions that remain to be answered.

MARKETING AND GOVERNMENTAL INTERFACES

There has been a change in the marketing-governmental interfaces. A noticeable shift is occurring from government in marketing being inherently labeled undesirable, to the recognition of the necessity of government and its significant roles in marketing as a regulator, arbitrator, stimulator, customer, and even as a partner in modern society. In fact, there seems to be a feeling today among many young people that government and not marketing is where the action is.

It is curious to note, however, that some governmental actions and laws may not foster the acceptance of social obligation by marketing. For example, socially responsible action often requires concerted cooperation by several competing companies. This can result in a violation of antitrust laws. Thus, what may be in the social interest, may in reality prove to be illegal.

Governmental impact on marketing is evident by the sheer weight of governmental regulations at federal, state, and local levels if by nothing else. In the last few years, for example, there have been governmental decisions about safety standards, devices for controlling air pollution, implied product warranties, packaging rules and regulations, of national and private bands, pricing practices, advertising and promotional tactics, credit arrangements, and the formation of mergers and conglomerates.

It is evident that new challenges are being presented to our discipline in these developments. Former Secretary of Commerce Maurice H. Stans pointed out the necessity of developing early warning systems in marketing to discern and handle the host of consumer problems before the government is required to act. We should be able to develop the theoretical bases and models for more responsive marketing systems.

One of the critical spheres of marketing activity in the coming decade will be that of reformulating the relationship between the public and private sectors of concern. In the area of antitrust, the marketing discipline faces several developments and opportunities. The discipline faces the important task of analyzing marketing factors influencing court cases and establishing governmental guidelines about such variables as market concentration, market share, and market power. They are practical considerations leading to many marketing questions not being handled effectively by current economic precepts. We should develop the theories, extend the discipline, based on the analysis of specific marketing cases and data which do not fit partial equilibrium analysis.

Public policy issues to date even when rooted in the marketing domain have been left as tasks for economists and lawyers. Their resolution has not been the most effective for either the public or private sectors. New concepts and approaches by those rooted in the marketing discipline should prove beneficial.

NEW AREAS OF CONCERN

What are the major areas of concern of social marketing? How will they differ from managerial marketing? Perhaps a good indication may be gleened from the list of concerns developed by the Committee on Economic Development[1] in discussing the social responsibilities of business. Included are:

1. Economic growth which is the assumed traditional responsibility.
2. Education and training in the broad sense which includes more than schools and universities.
3. Employment and the provision of opportunities for people to realize themselves vocationally and professionally.
4. Civil rights and equal opportunity for all, including minority groups.
5. Urban renewal and development.
6. Pollution abatement, including air, water, house, food, and temperature.
7. Culture and the arts so necessary for a total society.

[1] Committee for Economic Development, "Social Responsibilities of Business Corporations," a statement by the Research and Policy committee, (June 1971).

8. Conservation and recreation which focus on the use of parks and natural resources.
9. Health care, including preventative as well as curative.
10. Government relationships which extend well beyond antitrust laws and other regulations.

Such issues carry marketing activities well beyond the usual bounds of marketing management action. They raise a host of interesting questions and challenges for investigation by marketing academicians and practitioners. The results of the applied and theoretical approaches and findings will mold social marketing as a discipline. It will be a counterpart to managerial marketing in the unfolding of the body of marketing knowledge.

Marketers traditionally have depended upon the proper development of product, promotion, place, and price policies to design a successful marketing campaign. The authors define these concepts and show their applicability to social causes. They also present a definition and theory of social marketing. The concept is positioned as a bridging mechanism linking the behavioral scientist's knowledge of human behavior with the socially useful implementation of that knowledge.

---

6. SOCIAL MARKETING: AN APPROACH TO PLANNED SOCIAL CHANGE*

Philip Kotler
and
Gerald Zaltman†

In 1952, G. D. Wiebe raised the question "Why can't you sell brotherhood like you sell soap?"[1] This statement implies that sellers of com-

---

* Reprinted from "Social Marketing: An Approach to Planned Social Change," *Journal of Marketing*, Vol. 35 (July 1971), pp. 3–12.

† Both of Northwestern University.

[1] G. D. Wiebe, "Merchandising Commodities and Citizenship on Television," *Public Opinion Quarterly*, Vol. 15 (Winter 1951–52), pp. 679–91, at p. 679.

modities such as soap are generally effective, while "sellers" of social causes are generally ineffective. Wiebe examined four social campaigns to determine what conditions or characteristics accounted for their relative success or lack of success. He found that the more the conditions of the social campaign resembled those of a product campaign, the more successful the social campaign. However, because many social campaigns are conducted under quite un-market-like circumstances, Wiebe also noted clear limitations in the practice of social marketing.

A different view is implied in Joe McGinniss's best-selling book *The Selling of the President 1968.*[2] Its theme seems to be "You can sell a presidential candidate like you sell soap." Once Nixon gave the word: "We're going to build this whole campaign around television . . . you fellows just tell me what you want me to do and I'll do it," the advertising men, public relations men, copywriters, makeup artist, photographers, and others joined together to create the image and the aura that would make this man America's favorite "brand."

These and other cases suggest that the art of selling cigarettes, soap, or steel may have some bearing on the art of selling social causes. People like McGinniss—and before him John K. Galbraith and Vance Packard—believe everything and anything can be sold by Madison Avenue, while people like Wiebe feel this is exaggerated. To the extent that Madison Avenue has this power, some persons would be heartened because of the many good causes in need of an effective social marketing technology, and others would despair over the spectre of mass manipulation.

Unfortunately there are few careful discussions of the power and limitations of social marketing. It is the authors' view that social marketing is a promising framework for planning and implementing social change. At the same time, it is poorly understood and often viewed suspiciously by many behavioral scientists. The application of commercial ideas and methods to promote social goals will be seen by many as another example of business's lack of taste and self-restraint. Yet the application of the logic of marketing to social goals is a natural development and on the whole a promising one. The idea will not disappear by ignoring it or rallying against it.

This article discusses the meaning, power, and limitations of social marketing as an approach to planned social change. First, this will require delineating the generic nature of marketing phenomena and some recent conceptual developments in the marketing field. This will be followed by a definition of social marketing and an examination of the conditions under which it may be carried out effectively. The instruments of social marketing are defined, followed by a systems view of the application of marketing logic to social objectives.

---

[2] Joe McGinniss, *The Selling of the President 1968* (New York: Trident Press, 1969).

WHAT IS MARKETING?

The following statement testifies that there is no universal agreement on what marketing is.

It has been described by one person or another as a business activity; as a group of related business activities; as a trade phenomenon; as a frame of mind; as a coordinative, integrative function in policy making; as a sense of business purpose; as an economic process; as a structure of institutions; as the process of exchanging or transferring ownership of products; as a process of concentration, equalization, and dispersion; as the creation of time, place and possession utilities; as a process of demand and supply adjustment; and many other things.[3]

In spite of the confusing jumble of definitions, the core idea of marketing lies in *the exchange process. Marketing does not occur unless there are two or more parties, each with something to exchange, and both able to carry out communications and distribution.* Typically the subject of marketing is the exchange of goods or services for other goods or services or for money. Belshaw, in an excellent study of marketing exchange and its evolution from traditional to modern markets, shows the exchange process in marketing to be a fundamental aspect of both primitive and advanced social life.[4]

Given that the core idea of marketing lies in exchange processes, another concept can be postulated, that of marketing management, which can be defined as:

Marketing management is the analysis, planning, implementation, and control of programs designed to bring about desired exchanges with target audiences for the purpose of personal or mutual gain. It relies heavily on the adaptation and coordination of product, price, promotion, and place for achieving effective response.[5]

Thus marketing management occurs when people become conscious of an opportunity to gain from a more careful planning of their exchange relations. Although planned social change is not often viewed from the client's point of view, it involves very much an exchange relationship between client and change agent.[6]

The practice of marketing management as applied to products and services has become increasingly sophisticated. The responsibility of

---

[3] Marketing Staff of the Ohio State University, "A Statement of Marketing Philosophy," *Journal of Marketing*, Vol. 29 (January 1965), p. 43.

[4] Cyril S. Belshaw, *Traditional Exchange and Modern Markets* (Englewood Cliffs, N.J.: Prentice-Hall, Inc., 1965).

[5] Philip Kotler, *Marketing Management: Analysis, Planning and Control* (2d ed.; Englewood Cliffs, N.J.: Prentice-Hall, Inc., 1972).

[6] Arthur H. Niehoff, *A Casebook of Social Change* (Chicago: Aldine, 1966); Warren G. Bennis, Kenneth D. Benne and Robert Chin, *The Planning of Change* (New York: Holt, Rinehart & Winston, 1969).

launching new products on a national basis involving the investment and risk of millions of dollars and the uncertainties of consumer and competitor responses, has led to an increased reliance on formal research and planning throughout the product development and introduction cycle. Marketing management examines the wants, attitudes, and behavior of potential customers which could aid in designing a desired product and in merchandising, promoting, and distributing it successfully. Management goes through a formal process of strategy determination, tactical programming, regional and national implementation, performance measurement, and feedback control.

There has been a shift from a sales to a marketing orientation in recent years. A sales orientation considers the job as one of finding customers for existing products and convincing them to buy these products. This sales concept is implicit in *The Selling of the President 1968*, since one is actually not developing a new "product" for the job, but rather trying to sell a given one with a suggestion that it is somewhat "new and improved." The marketing concept, on the other hand, calls for most of the effort to be spent on discovering the wants of a target audience and then creating the goods and services to satisfy them. This view seems privately and socially more acceptable. In private terms, the seller recognizes that it is easier to create products and services for existing wants than to try to alter wants and attitudes toward existing products. In social terms, it is held that this marketing philosophy restores consumer sovereignty in the determination of the society's product mix and the use of national resources.

In practice, since at any time there are both products in existence and new products being born, most marketing efforts are a mixture of selling and marketing; that is, a change strategy and a response strategy. In both cases, marketing management is becoming a sophisticated action technology that draws heavily on the behavioral sciences for clues to solving problems of communication and persuasion related to influencing the acceptability of commercial products and services. In the hands of its best practitioners, marketing management is applied behavioral science.

SOCIAL MARKETING

An increasing number of nonbusiness institutions have begun to examine marketing logic as a means to furthering their institutional goals and products. Marketing men have advised churches on how to increase membership, charities on how to raise money, and art museums and symphonies on how to attract more patrons. In the social sphere, the Advertising Council of America has conducted campaigns for social objectives, including "Smokey the Bear," "Keep America Beautiful," "Join the Peace Corps," "Buy Bonds," and "Go to College." In fact, social advertising has become an established phenomenon on the American scene. Sandage says:

True, (advertising's) communication function has been confined largely to informing and persuading people in respect to products and services. On the other hand, it can be made equally available to those who wish to inform and persuade people in respect to a city bond issue, cleaning up community crime, the "logic" of atheism, the needs for better educational facilities, the abusive tactics of given law and enforcement officers, or any other sentiment held by any individual who wishes to present such sentiment to the public.[7]

Social advertising has become such a feature of American society that it is no longer a question of whether to use it, but how to use it. It has been very successful in some cases and conspicuously unsuccessful in others. At fault to a large extent is the tendency of social campaigners to assign advertising the primary, if not the exclusive, role in accomplishing their social objectives. This ignores the marketing truism that a given marketing objective requires the coordination of the promotional mix with the goods and services mix and with the distribution mix. Social marketing is a much larger idea than social advertising and even social communication. To emphasize this, the authors define social marketing in the following way:

Social marketing is the design, implementation, and control of programs calculated to influence the acceptability of social ideas and involving considerations of product planning, pricing, communication, distribution, and marketing research.

Thus, it is the explicit use of marketing skills to help translate present social action efforts into more effectively designed and communicated programs that elicit desired audience response. In other words, marketing techniques are the bridging mechanisms between the simple possession of knowledge and the socially useful implementation of what knowledge allows.

THE REQUISITE CONDITIONS FOR EFFECTIVE SOCIAL MARKETING

Some clues concerning the difference between social advertising and social marketing are contained in early papers by Lazarsfeld and Merton and by Wiebe which attempt to explain the limitations of social advertising.[8]

[7] C. H. Sandage, "Using Advertising to Implement the Concept of Freedom of Speech," in *The Role of Advertising*, C. H. Sandage and V. Fryburger, eds. (Homewood, Ill.: Richard D. Irwin, Inc., 1960), pp. 222–23.

[8] Paul F. Lazarsfeld and Robert K. Merton, "Mass Communication, Popular Taste, and Organized Social Action," in *Mass Communications*, William Schramm, ed. (Urbana, Ill.: University of Illinois Press, 1949), pp. 459–80, and Wiebe, "Merchandising Commodities . . ."

Lazarsfeld and Merton's analysis

Lazarsfeld and Merton took exception with the view of many people that mass media can easily be used to control people's minds: "It is our tentative judgment that the social role played by the very existence of the mass media has been commonly overestimated."[9] They believed that the effectiveness of mass media for propaganda purposes depended on three conditions, one or more of which is lacking in most propaganda situations. The first condition is real or psychological *monopolization* by the media; that is, a condition marked by the absence of counter-propaganda. This characterizes the totalitarian state and accounts for the greater effectiveness of these regimes in molding public opinion through mass media. It is found occasionally in free societies under special circumstances, such as a wartime effort. For example, Kate Smith's effectiveness in selling war bonds over the radio during World War II was partially due to the marathon nature of the event and the fact that everyone believed in the cause; i.e., there was no counterpropaganda. However, most campaigns in a free society in peace time compete with so many other causes and everyday distractions that the monopoly condition is lacking, and this condition reduces the effectiveness of such campaigns.

Lazarsfeld and Merton said the second condition required for effective mass propaganda is *canalization*, the presence of an existing attitudinal base for the feelings that the social communicators are striving to shape. They asserted that typical commercial advertising is effective because the task is not one of instilling basic new attitudes or creating significantly new behavior patterns, but rather canalizing existing attitudes and behavior in one direction or another. Thus, the seller of toothpaste does not have to socialize persons into new dental care habits, but rather into which brand of a familiar and desired product to purchase. If the preexisting attitudes are present, then promotional campaigns are more effective, since canalization is always an easier task than social reconditioning.

The authors accept this idea but would add that many business marketing situations also involve the task of reshaping basic attitudes rather than canalizing existing ones. For example, consider business efforts to influence farmers to change time-honored farming practices, doctors to try out new drugs, and males to dress with more fashion and flair. Canalization is always easier, but the authors would like to emphasize that business marketers, like social marketers, often try to diffuse fundamentally new products and services which require major attitudinal reorientations.

Lazarsfeld and Merton call the third condition *supplementation* by

[9] Lazarsfeld and Merton, Ibid., p. 462.

which they mean the effort to follow up mass communication campaigns with programs of face-to-face contacts. In trying to explain the success of the rightist Father Coughlin movement in the thirties, Lazarsfeld and Merton observe:

This combination of a central supply of propaganda (Coughlin's addresses on a nationwide network), the coordinated distribution of newspapers and pamphlets and locally organized face-to-face discussions among relatively small groups—this complex of reciprocal reinforcement by mass media and personal relations proved spectacularly successful.[10]

This approach is standard in many closed societies and organizations and suggests another key difference between social advertising and social marketing. Whereas a social advertising approach contrives only the event of mass media communication and leaves the response to natural social processes, social marketing arranges for a stepdown communication process. The message is passed on and discussed in more familiar surroundings to increase its memorability, penetration, and action consequences. Thus supplementation, monopolization, and canalization are critical factors influencing the effectiveness of any social marketing effort.

Wiebe's analysis

An additional contribution was made by Wiebe in his attempt to understand the differential effectiveness of four social campaigns.[11] He explained the relative effectiveness of these campaigns in terms of the audience member's experience with regard to five factors:

1. *The Force.* The intensity of the person's motivation toward the goal as a combination of his predisposition prior to the message and the stimulation of the message.
2. *The Direction.* Knowledge of how or where the person might go to consummate his motivation.
3. *The Mechanism.* The existence of an agency that enables the person to translate his motivation into action.
4. *Adequacy and Compatibility.* The ability and effectiveness of the agency in performing its task.
5. *Distance.* The audience member's estimate of the energy and cost required to consummate the motivation in relation to the reward.

To show how these factors operate, Wiebe first analyzed the Kate Smith campaign to sell bonds during World War II. This campaign was eminently successful, according to Wiebe, because of the presence

[10] Lazarsfeld and Merton, same reference as footnote 8.

[11] Same reference as footnote 1.

of force (patriotism), direction (buy bonds), mechanism (banks, post offices, telephone orders), adequacy and compatibility (so many centers to purchase the bonds), and distance (ease of purchase). In fact, extra telephone lines were installed on the night of the campaign at 134 CBS stations to take orders during her appeal. The effort to buy bonds

> . . . was literally reduced to the distance between the listener and his telephone. Psychological distance was also minimized. The listener remained in his own home. There were no new people to meet, no unfamiliar procedures, no forms to fill out, no explanation, no waiting. . . .[12]

In the case of a campaign to recruit Civil Defense volunteers, many of the same factors were present except that the social mechanism was not prepared to handle the large volume of response, and this reduced the campaign's success. Teachers, manuals, equipment, and registration and administration procedures were *inadequate,* and many responding citizens were turned away and disappointed after they were led to believe that their services were urgently needed.

The third campaign, a documentary on juvenile delinquency, did not meet with maximum success because of the *absence of a mechanism.* Instead of being directed to an existing agency, people were urged to form neighborhood councils themselves. This certainly takes far more effort than simply picking up the phone to buy a war bond, or "stopping in" to register at the nearest Civil Defense unit.

The fourth campaign revolved around the goal of the Kefauver committee hearings to arouse citizens to "set their house in order." This campaign met with a notable lack of success, however, because citizens were not *directed* to an appropriate mechanism despite the fact that one existed in principle in the political party organizations. Political party organizations apparently left much to be desired in terms of availability and compatibility. The skepticism prevalent at the time concerning the chances of anything beneficial happening as a result of the hearings was ample evidence that considerable psychological distance existed between the audience and the mechanisms for action.

The social marketing approach

The Lazarsfeld and Merton conditions and the Wiebe factors provide a useful background for viewing the conceptual framework used by marketing strategists. Marketers view the marketing problem as one of developing the right *product* backed by the right *promotion* and put in the right *place* at the right *price.* These key variables in the marketing mix have been named the four P's by McCarthy.[13] The authors

[12] Ibid., p. 633.

[13] E. Jerome McCarthy, *Basic Marketing: A Managerial Approach* (3d ed.; Homewood, Ill.: Richard D. Irwin, Inc., 1968), pp. 31–33.

shall examine each of these variables, designated control variables, in terms of some well-known social issues.

Product. In business marketing, sellers study the needs and wants of target buyers and attempt to design products and services that meet their desires. If well-designed and affordable, these products will be purchased. In social marketing, sellers also have to study the target audiences and design appropriate products. They must "package" the social idea in a manner which their target audiences find desirable and are willing to purchase. This corresponds to Wiebe's idea of a mechanism.

Product design is typically more challenging in the social area than it is in the business area. Consider the problem of marketing "safer driving." The social objective is to create safer driving habits and attitudes in the population. There is no one product that can accomplish this. Various products have to be designed that will make partial contributions to the social objective. A public education media campaign providing tips on safe driving is one such product; the offering of "defensive driving courses" is another; the creation of insurance policies which reduce premiums for safer drivers is still another product. In general, the social marketer remains aware of the *core product* (safer driving) and tries to create various tangible products and services which are "buyable" and which advance the social objective.

Identical reasoning is required by those who market *altruistic causes* (e.g., charity giving, blood donation), *personal health causes* (e.g., nonsmoking, better nutrition), and *social betterment causes* (e.g., civil rights, improved housing, better environment). In each case, the social marketer must define the change sought, which may be a change in values, beliefs, affects, behavior, or some mixture. He must meaningfully segment the target markets. He must design social products for each market which are "buyable," and which instrumentally serve the social cause. In some social causes, the most difficult problem will be to innovate appropriate products; in other cases it will be to motivate purchase.

Promotion. The marketing man's second control variable is promotion. It is the communication-persuasion strategy and tactics that will make the product familiar, acceptable, and even desirable to the audience. Wiebe's counterpart to promotion is "force." The social campaign strategist will tend to think of this as mass media communication, but promotion is actually a much larger idea. To the marketing man, promotion includes the following major activities:

Advertising: Any paid form of nonpersonal presentation and promotion of products, services, or ideas by an identified sponsor.

Personal selling: Any paid form of personal presentation and promotion of products, service, or ideas by an identified sponsor.

Publicity: Any unpaid form of nonpersonal presentation and promotion of products, services, or ideas where the sponsor is unidentified.

Sales promotion: Miscellaneous paid forms (special programs, incentives, materials, and events) designed to stimulate audience interest and acceptance of a product.

Each of these promotional tools involves complex issues in strategy and tactics. With respect to advertising, the marketer has to determine the size of the total advertising budget, the choice of appeals, the development of attention-getting copy, the selection of effective and efficient media, the scheduling of the advertising inputs, and the measurement of overall and segment-level results. With respect to personal selling, the marketer must determine the size of the total sales force, the development of sales territory boundaries and assignments, the development of personal presentation strategies, the degree and type of salesforce motivation and supervision, and the evaluation of salesforce effectiveness. Publicity necessitates arranging for significant news about the product to appear in various media. Sales promotion calls for developing special display, premiums, programs, and events that might be useful in stimulating interest or action.

Each of these activities is a specialty in which the experts have achieved sophisticated levels of knowledge and techniques. This is especially apparent when one examines social campaigns developed by amateurs where the appeals and copy seem very naive. Even behavioral science consultants to social campaign organizations often fail to make a maximum contribution because of their inability or reluctance to view the issue in broad marketing terms instead of in strictly social or ethical terms.

Recently Nathaniel Martin criticized the Indian government for failing to handle family planning as a marketing problem.

> Selling birth control is as much a marketing job as selling any other consumer product. And where no manufacturer would contemplate developing and introducing a new product without a thorough understanding of the variables of the market, planners in the highest circles of Indian government have blithely gone ahead without understanding that marketing principles must determine the character of any campaign of voluntary control. The Indians have done only the poorest research. They have mismanaged distribution of contraceptive devices. They have ignored the importance of "customer service." They have proceeded with grossly inadequate undertrained staffs; they have been blind to the importance of promotion and advertising.[14]

This is not to deny that the Indian government has undertaken some innovative promotional approaches. Referral fees are paid to salesmen, barbers, and others who bring in consenting males for sterilization. The consenting male is given a transistor radio or a small payment to cover his costs of being absent from work. Women have been offered gifts

[14] Nathaniel A. Martin, "The Outlandish Idea: How a Marketing Man Would Save India," *Marketing/Communications,* Vol. 297 (March 1968), pp. 54–60.

for consenting to use intrauterine contraceptive devices. But Martin feels that the total program lacks the qualities of an organized, well-planned, and continuous marketing effort.[15]

An example of careful promotional planning for a social objective is found in the American Cancer Society efforts to raise money for cancer research. In their brochure directed to local units, they attempt to educate the volunteer and professional chapters on the handling of newspapers, pictures, company publications, radio and television, movies, special events, and controversial arguments. For example, in terms of special events:

Dramatic special events attract attention to the American Cancer Society. They bring color, excitement, and glamour to the program. Well planned, they will get excellent coverage in newspapers, on radio and TV, and in newsreels. . . . A Lights-on-Drive, a one-afternoon or one-night House-to-House program have such dramatic appeal that they stir excitement and enthusiasm . . . keep in mind the value of bursts of sound such as fire sirens sounding, loud-speaker trucks, fife and drum corps. . . . A most useful special event in the ringing of church bells to add a solemn, dedicated, note to the launching of a drive or education project. This should be organized on a Division or community basis, and the church bell ringing may be the signal to begin a House-to-House canvass. Rehearsals of bell ringing, community leaders tugging at ropes, offer good picture possibilities.[16]

Some readers might be critical of this approach to a worthwhile social objective, but two things should be mentioned. The first is that this should not be identified as the *marketing approach to social objectives.* Many persons mistakenly assume that marketing means hard selling. This is only a particular style of marketing, and it has its critics both inside and outside the profession. There are many firms that market their products with taste and sensitivity; examples include Xerox, Container Corporation, and Hallmark. It is important to recognize that this is not nonmarketing but rather a style of marketing that was chosen in the belief of its greater effectiveness in accomplishing the goals of the organization.

Second, the issue is not whether a particular approach suits one's personal taste, but whether it works. If a "hard" marketing style raises substantially more money for cancer research than a "soft" marketing style, it must be respected by those who think cancer research is more important than personal aesthetics.

---

[15] For two analyses of the marketing issues and opportunities in the family planning issue, see Julian L. Simon, "A Huge Marketing Research Task—Birth Control," *Journal of Marketing Research,* Vol. 5 (February 1968), pp. 21–27; and Glen L. Urban, "Ideas on a Decision-Information System for Family Planning," *Industrial Management Review,* Vol. 10 (Spring 1969), pp. 45–61.

[16] *Public Information Guide* (New York: American Cancer Society, Inc., 1965), p. 19.

Place. The third element of the marketing approach to social campaigns calls for providing adequate and compatible distribution and response channels. Motivated persons should know where the product can be obtained. Place is equivalent to two of Wiebe's five conditions for an effective mass communication campaign (direction, and adequacy and compatibility). The poor results of many social campaigns can be attributed in part to their failure to suggest clear action outlets for those motivated to acquire the product. The current campaign to interest people in the pollution problem may suffer from this defect. It is succeeding in making everyone not only aware of environmental pollution but also fearful of it. People want to do something about it. But for the most part they cannot act because there is not a clear product to "buy" (such as a petition to sign, an election in which to choose an antipollution candidate, or a pending piece of national legislation). Nor does the average person have a clear picture of the alternative channels of action for expressing his interest in the issue. There are so many ad hoc organizations working without coordination and at times with cross-purpose, that the average person is likely to "tune out" from further messages because of personal frustration. Saturation campaigns unaccompanied by the provision of adequate response channels may result in "interest overkill."

The importance of place has been recognized in several campaigns. The most notable example is the Kate Smith bond-selling campaign and its imaginative establishment of telephone order channels during the broadcast. Strategists of anticigarette campaigns have recognized the need for action channels by setting up smoker's clinics in many large cities. They could even go further and provide telephone advice and even social calls if the economics would justify these additional channels. An advertising agency is planning a campaign called "Pick Your Issue" in which several different social issues would be individually featured. The point would be made that because the busy citizen does not have time to become involved in all issues, this should not be an excuse to remain uninvolved in any issues. The good citizen should "pick an issue." Each issue advertisement will contain information on the organizations active in that area and inform the citizen about where to write for further information.

Thus, place means arranging for accessible outlets which permit the translation of motivations into actions. Planning in this area entails selecting or developing appropriate outlets, deciding on their number, average size, and locations, and giving them proper motivation to perform their part of the job.

Price. The final control variable that must be planned is price. Price represents the costs that the buyer must accept in order to obtain the product. It resembles Wiebe's concept of distance and incorporates some aspects of adequacy and compatibility. Price includes money costs, opportunity costs, energy costs, and psychic costs. Thus, the cost to persons asked to appear for immunization shots includes any possible money charge, any opportunities foregone, the expenditure of energy, and the psychological concerns aroused by inoculation. The cost of giving up smoking is largely psychological, since there is actually a financial saving in breaking the habit. The cost of using seat belts is the charge for buying them, the effort to lock and unlock them, and the psychological cost of not being completely sure one is better off in an accident wearing them or not wearing them.

The functioning of this concept can also be illustrated in terms of an interesting phenomenon in health care services where many poor patients prefer to patronize unlicensed practitioners and pay a fee instead of going to the free hospital. In Caracas, Venezuela, for example, although there is a free hospital for the indigent, many of them patronize private clinics which cost them 20 bolivares for consultation. Why? Because while there is no charge at the free hospital, there is a substantial cost to the patient in terms of energy and psychological abuse. When a patient arrives at the hospital, he has to wait to see a social worker first. When he is finally interviewed, the social worker asks many questions about his income to determine whether he is really indigent. Then he sees a number of other hospital staff members for various tests, and again is asked about his income. Finally, he sees the doctor who might discover that he really needs to see a specialist who will not be available for several weeks. Throughout the experience, the person is made to feel inferior and a nuisance. Therefore, it is not surprising that he wishes to avoid these energy and psychological costs even if it means paying for the services.

But even monetary charges may play a useful role in leading the poor back to free hospital services. In private correspondence, a social psychologist suggested:

> It is a surprising discovery that even free medical care presents a marketing problem. Maybe we should apply dissonance theory and introduce such medical care at a high price to make it look more desirable. Then let us apply a cents-off special introductory offer to make the service attractive.

The marketing man's approach to pricing the social product is based on the assumption that members of a target audience perform a cost-benefit analysis when considering the investment of money, time, or energy in the issue. They somehow process the major benefits and compare them to the major costs, and the strength of their motivation to act is directly related to the magnitude of the excess benefit. This type of conceptualization of behavior is found not only in the economist's model of economic man, but also in behavioristic theory with its emphasis on rewards and costs, in Gestalt theory with its emphasis on positive and negative valences, and in management theory with its emphasis on incentives and constraints. The marketer's approach to selling a social product is to consider how the rewards for buying the product can be increased relative to the costs, or the costs reduced relative to the rewards, or trying to find a mix of product, promotion, place, and price that will simultaneously increase the rewards and reduce the costs. The main point is that social marketing requires that careful thought be given to the manner in which manageable, desirable, gratifying, and convenient solutions to a perceived need or problem are presented to its potential buyers.

THE SOCIAL MARKETING PLANNING PROCESS

The "four P's" of marketing management are integrated in an administrative process framework in Figure 1. Continuous information is collected from the *environment* by the *change agency. Plans and messages* are created and sent through *channels* to *audiences,* and the results are monitored by the *change agency.*

The change agency operates a research unit and a planning unit. The research unit collects several types of information. It monitors the environment—economic, political, technological, cultural, and competi-

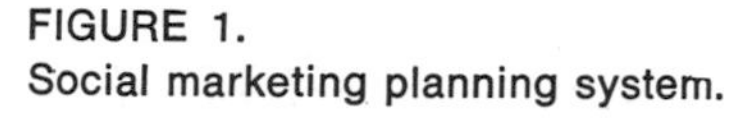
FIGURE 1.
Social marketing planning system.

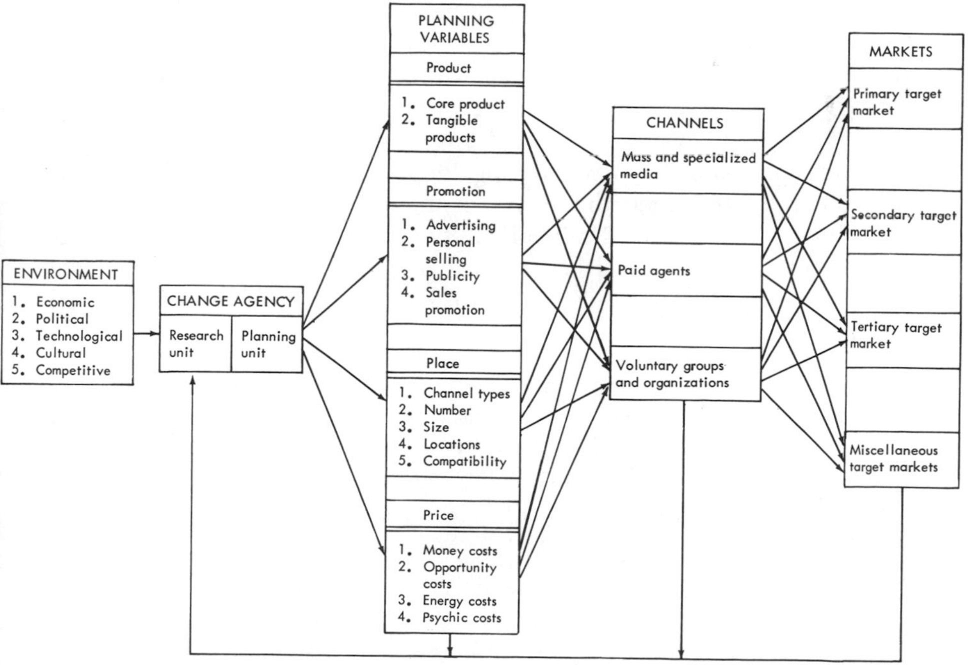

tive influences—for important developments affecting its social policies and objectives. For example, a family-planning agency would monitor economic-demographic developments (income and population trends), political developments (liberalization of birth control information), technological developments (new birth control techniques and devices), cultural developments (attitudinal changes toward birth control), and competitive developments (actions of similar and competing groups). The research unit also collects information on the past effectiveness of various programs as well as information on audience attitudes, desires, and behavior.

The change agent's planning unit formulates short- and long-range social marketing plans on the basis of this information. For example, the family-planning organization carefully considers the role of different products, promotions, places, and prices. It would identify the major channels of communication and distribution, such as mass or specialized media, paid agents, and volunteer groups. It would differentiate the programs intended for its primary target market (large and low-income families), secondary target market (other child-bearing families), tertiary target market (sources of funds and additional volunteer efforts), and miscellaneous target markets (politicians and church groups). Finally, it would continuously gather effectiveness measures on these programs for recycling its planning.

This approach represents an application of business marketing principles to the problem of marketing social change. It is already manifest in some of the larger social change agencies. For example, consider the work of the National Safety Council. Its staff includes an advertising manager, a sales promotion management, an Advertising Council of America coordinator, a research director, and a program director. One of its products is a defensive driving course. Figure 2 shows the various channels through which this course is marketed along with the promotional tools its uses. The National Safety Council reaches potential prospects through business firms, service organizations, schools, and the police and court system. For the 1970s, the National Safety Council has adopted

> . . . a four point marketing program. . . . One of the first objectives is to increase the sales effectiveness of our existing 150 state and local safety council cooperating agencies. . . . The second part of the program is to create 500 new training agencies in communities not now served by safety councils. . . . A third part of the marketing program will be aimed at selling big industry on adopting DDC as a training course for all employees or selected categories of employees in plant-run training programs. . . . The fourth part of the marketing plan deals with a nationwide promotional effort built around a series of community special-emphasis campaigns running from February 1 through Memorial Day each year of the decade.[17]

[17] Chris Imhoff, "DDC's Decisive Decade," *Traffic Safety Magazine*, Vol. 69 (December 1969), pp. 20 and 36.

FIGURE 2.
Marketing channels and tools: Defensive driving course.

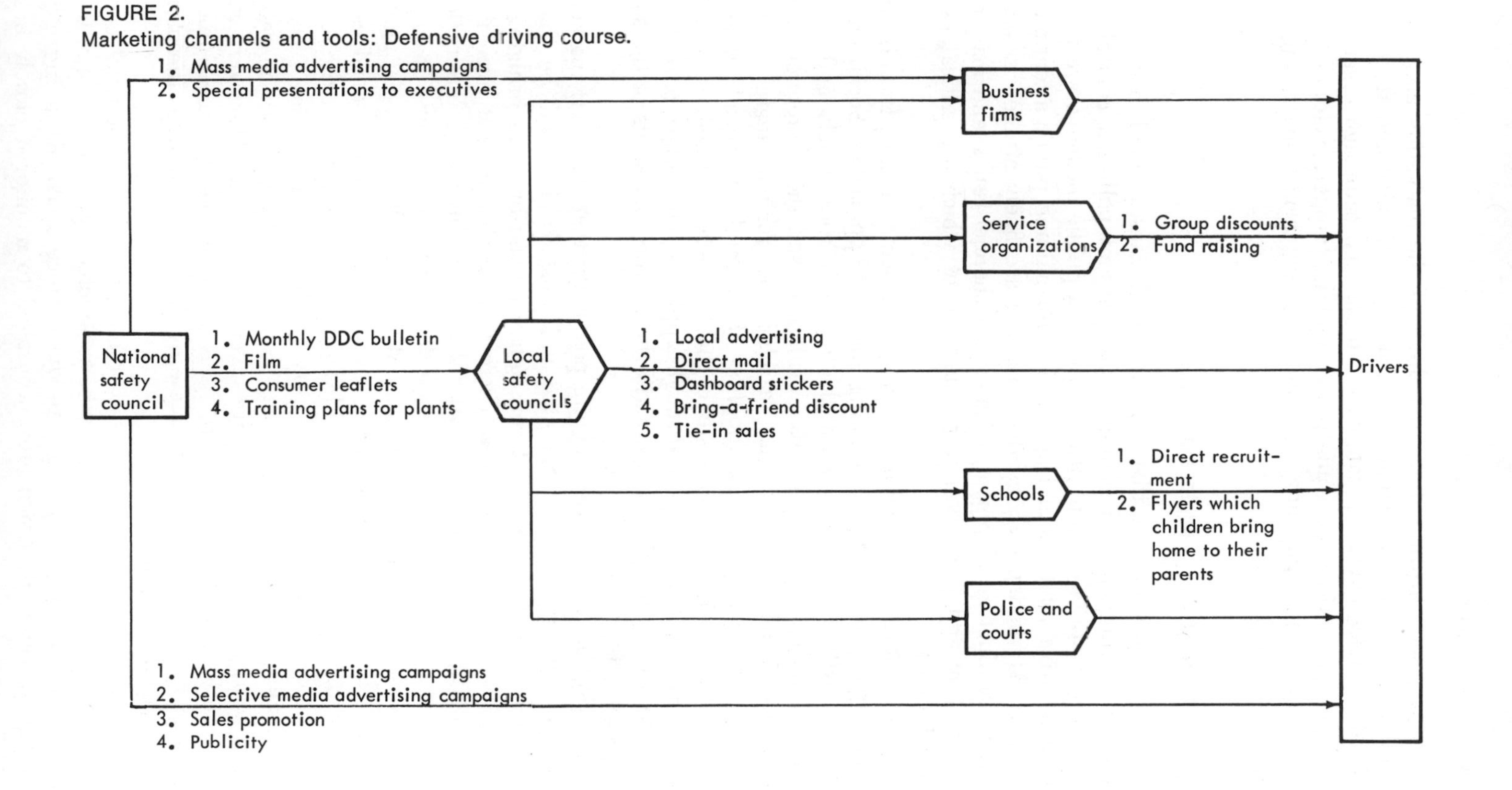

This example illustrates the possibilities of the marketing approach for furthering social causes. The National Safety Council and several other social agencies have graduated from occasional campaign organizations to full-time marketing organizations which go through cycles of information gathering, planning, product development, measuring, and reprogramming.

Social implications of social marketing

The authors believe that specific social causes could benefit from marketing thinking and planning. Problems of pollution control, mass transit, private education, drug abuse, and public medicine are in need of innovative solutions and approaches for gaining public attention and support. Marketing men by their training are finely attuned to market needs, product development, pricing and channel issues, and mass communication and promotion techniques, all of which are critical in the social area.

At the same time, social marketing is sufficiently distinct from business marketing to require fresh thinking and new approaches. Social marketing typically has to deal with the market's core beliefs and values, whereas business marketing often deals with superficial preferences and opinions. Social marketing must search harder for meaningful *quid pro quos* to gain acceptance or adoption of its products. Social marketing has to work with channel systems that are less well-defined and less pecuniarily motivated. Only through applying marketing concepts and tools to a large number of cases will the powers and limits of the social marketing approach be learned.

In addition, there is the definite possibility that the overt marketing of social objectives will be resented and resisted. There will be charges that it is "manipulative," and consequently contributes to bringing the society closer to Orwell's 1984. There will be charges that even if not manipulative, social marketing will increase the amount of "promotional noise" in the society, which is found distasteful both because it emphasizes "trivial differences" and because it is "noise." Finally, social marketing will be accused of increasing the costs of promoting social causes beyond the point of a net gain either to the specific cause or the society as a whole. In the charities industry, professional marketing increases the absolute cost of raising money, but it usually succeeds in raising more money after these costs are taken into account. However, when one considers the entire picture, it is possible that the total amount donated to charities may not increase by the same amount as the professional marketing costs.

The authors are concerned with these possible dysfunctional consequences, and they must obviously be subtracted from the potential benefits that social marketing might produce. Since social marketing is just emerging, those concerned are encouraged to monitor it closely in the same dispassionate spirit that business marketers have so ably analyzed and documented the many manifestations of business marketing practice over the years.

SUMMARY

This article considered the applicability of marketing concepts to the problem of promoting social causes. Social marketing was defined as the design, implementation, and control of programs calculated to influence the acceptability of social ideas and involving considerations of product planning, pricing, communication, distribution, and marketing research.

Too often, social advertising rather than social marketing is practiced by social campaigners. Lazarsfeld and Merton attributed the failure of many social advertising campaigns to the frequent absence of conditions of monopolization, canalization, and supplementation in the social arena. Wiebe, in his examination of four campaigns, concluded that a campaigns effectiveness depended on the presence of adequate force, direction, an adequate and compatible social mechanism, and distance. To the marketer, the success of the campaign depends on the proper development of product, promotion, place, and price considerations. These concepts were defined and were shown to have applicability to social causes. The social marketing process calls for marketing research and the subsequent development of a well-conceived product and appeals moving through mass and specialized communication media and through paid agents and voluntary groups to reach targeted audiences. The marketing style may be hard or soft, depending on which is deemed most effective in accomplishing the social objectives.

A marketing planning approach does not guarantee that the social objectives will be achieved, or that the costs will be acceptable. Yet social marketing appears to represent a bridging mechanism which links the behavioral scientist's knowledge of human behavior with the socially useful implementation of what that knowledge allows. It offers a useful framework for effective social planning at a time when social issues have become more relevant and critical.

The preceeding article considered the application of traditional marketing analysis to social causes. The next article questions the underlying tenets of the concept of social responsibility as it relates to market performance. The following questions are considered. Is the distinction between private and public institutions a meaningful one for marketing students? What mechanism would insure that corporate managers are accountable to the public in the same sense as are governmental representatives?

---

7. SOCIAL RESPONSIBILITY AND MARKET PERFORMANCE*

M. Neil Browne
and
Paul F. Haas†

In our contemporary world, production processes are complex and individual members of the community are dependent upon one another for the supply of goods and services. Man is also dependent, in a somewhat different manner, upon society and its institutions for the provision of necessary social goods and services, and this dependence is currently in a state of flux as a result of evolving attitudes toward the proper relationship between business and society. American corporations are increasingly being asked to assume a positive role in solving our pressing social problems. Business firms are responding to this demand amidst the sometimes agonizing realization that the distinction between private and public institutions is becoming less clear.

Corporate concern about their social responsibility is evident in a statement by Richard Gerstenberg, vice chairman of General Motors Corporation:

> More and more, our people demand that business resolve the great social and environmental problems that bedevil our society and contract our prosperity. Business is being judged every day in the press and in the public mind. In the past, the test was principally profits. But today it is also how well a business responds to social and environmental responsibilities. The profit motive must be explained. People are being told that profit is earned at the expense of progress. We must demonstrate that profit and progress go hand in hand—that without profit there can be no progress.

This concern is not unique with GM. In Camden, New Jersey, RCA and Campbell Soup Company have combined efforts to help rebuild the city, and Chase Manhattan Bank has instituted a special environmental division to search for projects to which it can lend money.

This demand for social responsibility on the part of private firms requires analysis and evaluation. The issue of whether certain expenditures are most appropriately made by private institutions or by some

* Reprinted from "Social Responsibility and Market Performance," *MSU Business Topics*, Vol. 19 (Autumn 1971), pp. 7–10 (footnotes omitted).

† Both of Bowling Green State University.

level of government frequently is lost in the quest for any action which improves the general environment. In an attempt to stimulate concern over the propriety of private provision of public goods, this article explores the consequences of accepting social responsibility as an additional performance norm for the business sector.

The structure-conduct-performance framework used by industrial organization economists predicts that an industry which has a competitive structure in terms of the size and distribution of its firms and a conduct that is within the bounds of the antitrust laws will perform well in light of the goals of society. Generally, these goals include efficiency, utilization of capacity, and progressiveness. Much current literature appears to add social responsibility to this list of performance criteria, but the legitimacy of this addition should be evaluated.

THE MEANING OF SOCIAL RESPONSIBILITY

The concept of social responsibility is one of those which, no matter how ill-defined, is embraced by all sectors of the economy, at least at first glance. Certainly businesses and other capable institutions should play some role in solving problems common to all, but social responsibility on the part of large corporations has quite different implications depending on the precise nature of the problem-solving role they assume.

In any attempt to cope with social problems several distinct functions can be identified. The most important of these include: (1) deciding which problem is most significant; (2) determining who is to pay for the solution, and how much money is to be allocated for this purpose; (3) administration of the social action; and (4) evaluation of the resulting impact on the problem. Socially responsible behavior by corporations could conceivably encompass any or all of these elements of the problem-solving process.

Those who analyze the social responsibility of business rarely indicate precisely which of these possible meanings of socially responsible behavior they have in mind. As a result, the controversy concerning social responsibility continues, while the real nature of the disagreement remains obscure. For example, if corporations are demonstrating their social responsibility when they solicit government contracts, then social responsibility is hardly revolutionary. The fundamental purpose of any business firm is the profitable production of some good or service for a customer. Social responsibility in this sense of the word would be a euphemism for normal business activity in which some level of government plays the role of consumer. Surely, few would question the propriety or urgency of business assuming this responsibility. The actual administration of many solutions to social problems must be handled by large corporations because only they possess the organizational and technical capacities to provide large quantities of a required good or service. Therefore, the remainder of this article assumes that social responsibility is not being used in this noncontroversial sense.

When the social responsibility of business refers to either identification of social priorities, acquisition and allocation of funds to pay for the social action, or evaluation of program results, its implications become more complex, and its democratic legitimacy is called into question. For example, what right does a large corporation have to accumulate revenue from the sale of its products and appropriate these funds for social actions which its management selects? Consequently, the prime issue of this article is whether social responsibility as just defined is a proper criterion for evaluation of industry performance.

FINANCING SOCIAL RESPONSIBILITY

Economists have assumed at least since the *Wealth of Nations* that capitalism, through its reliance on private greed, could under certain structural conditions yield highly efficient resource allocation. Profit-hungry economic units would provide what the public desires not because the businessman is altruistic, but because he wishes to enrich himself. This justification of private economic behavior and the assumption that government has neither the information nor the incentive to carry out this task efficiently have been strong enough to force the burden of proof to be on any governmental incursion into the economy. However, students of capitalism are relatively unprepared for coping with the participation of some contemporary corporations in activities which are intrinsically unprofitable, except in some ambiguously long-run sense. The private corporation which produces social goods in addition to its normal private function must be analyzed within the same framework as is any other institution which claims to act in the public interest.

When a large private corporation engages in social activities which are generally unprofitable, one must be curious as to the means of paying for this allegedly altruistic behavior. When government provides social goods, such as pollution control or manpower policies, tax revenue is used to finance them under the principle that the public in general will benefit. What similar type of mechanism has the private firm whereby it can pursue its social responsibilities? Two possibilities exist. First, the firm may be producing social goods as a means of increasing or perpetuating the demand for its products. If consumers perceive socially responsible behavior and, as a result, purchase the firm's product more frequently, the corporation is merely incurring another cost of promotion and advertising. Consequently, the cost of selling the product increases. In addition, the firm is congratulated for its socially responsible behavior—behavior which was motivated more by selfish interests than by a concern for the general public. Second, the firm may be financing its social expenditures from the greater than normal profit which it is earning. To the extent that this taxation is the source of funds for expenditures on social responsibility, such behavior by private firms provides prima facie evidence of market power.

The justification for capitalism and consumer sovereignty is that *if* prices truly reflect the relative costs of producing products, consumers are led to channel their purchases along lines reflecting the actual availability of resources. Firms are similarly led to channel their production along the lines of consumer desires. But if the firm is engaging in socially responsible behavior, this system of incentives breaks down. Either the customer pays a price greater than that necessary to call the good into the market or the firm's product-mix provides less consumer satisfaction. In either case there has been a distortion of the allocative mechanism of the marketplace.

If the firm is capable of raising the price of the product to cover the cost of providing social goods, the firm has sufficient market power to force the consumer to pay for goods or services which he did not request. The choice of which social goods are to be provided has been determined by the corporation in a manner it has deemed desirable. If the firm is willing to accept lower profits to pay for social goods, the firm must have greater than normal profits in order to make that decision. If the company were experiencing competitive pressures, the additional economic cost of financing social activities would endanger its existence. Thus, the firm is unlikely to provide social goods unless its greater than normal profit position is sufficiently strong to survive the loss of any immediate return it could gain through the sale of its products. If the company simply uses its greater than normal profits to finance the supply of social goods, it appears to gain the best of two worlds; it receives community approval for its alleged community spirit, and at the same time antitrust authorities and academic critics may relax their vigilance because profit rates are reduced.

An example of this process is provided by an illustration Joseph McGuire uses to depict social responsibility. McGuire asserts that

> there are many instances where the corporation is trying to act as a "good" citizen and in doing so is performing functions which seem to be detrimental to its profits—even in the long run. For example, some corporations have not moved to more profitable locations, because their management has felt that their present town would go bankrupt should they move.

Although this behavior appears desirable to the people within the community, the consumers of that company's products are probably confronted with an unnecessarily high-priced product resulting from the firm's need to raise the price of the product to finance social goods.

In addition, the consumers have little or no representation with respect to the particular social goods that the firm purchases. The individual consumer has no direct way of influencing the corporate decisions on social goods comparable to that available to citizens when they select their political representatives.

CONCLUSION

Society needs some agency to provide social goods, but because of their nature social goods are not compatible with the market mechanism. If social responsibility is to be raised to the level of an economic performance goal, such as efficiency, utilization of capacity, and progressiveness, certain assumptions are implicit:

1. Adverse effects of market power are offset by the provision of social goods.
2. The corporate conscience is sufficiently representative of the public mind to allow the corporation to make public decisions without consulting directly with that public.

If either of these assumptions are not met, the concept of social responsibility may be more of a threat than a boon to society. For example, market power within the United States results in a substantial loss of economic welfare to the consumer. If the corporate expenditures on social goods do not equal this excess revenue generated by the firm, a covert redistribution of income has transpired. If the corporation supplies social goods on which society as a whole places a low priority, the consumers lose their central role in determining allocative efficiency. Finally, higher prices resulting from the purchase of social goods are a form of secret tax for which the firms are not held accountable. In summary, the central issues surrounding the social responsibility of business firms are (1) the extent to which the distinction between private and public institutions is a meaningful one, and (2) a search for mechanisms which would insure that corporate managers were accountable to the public in the same sense as are governmental representatives.

Generic marketing is a logic available to all organizations facing problems of market response. The author contends that the substance of marketing does not belong solely to the business area, but is applicable to all areas in which organizations attempt to relate to customer and other publics.

---

8. A GENERIC CONCEPT OF MARKETING*

Philip Kotler†

One of the signs of the health of a discipline is its willingness to reexamine its focus, techniques, and goals as the surrounding society changes and new problems require attention. Marketing has shown this aptitude in the past. It was originally founded as a branch of *applied economics* devoted to the study of distribution channels. Later marketing became a *management discipline* devoted to engineering increases in sales. More recently, it has taken on the character of an *applied behavioral science* that is concerned with understanding buyer and seller systems involved in the marketing of goods and services.

The focus of marketing has correspondingly shifted over the years. Marketing evolved through a *commodity focus* (farm products, minerals, manufactured goods, services); an *institutional focus* (producers, wholesalers, retailers, agents); a *functional focus* (buying, selling, promoting, transporting, storing, pricing); a *managerial focus* (analysis, planning, organization, control); and a *social focus* (market efficiency, product quality, and social impact). Each new focus had its advocates and its critics. Marketing emerged each time with a refreshed and expanded self-concept.

Today marketing is facing a new challenge concerning whether its concepts apply in the nonbusiness as well as the business area. In 1969, this author and Professor Levy advanced the view that *marketing is a relevant discipline for all organizations insofar as all organizations can be said to have customers and products.*[1] This "broadening of the concept of marketing" proposal received much attention, and the 1970 Fall Conference of the American Marketing Association was devoted to this theme.

Critics soon appeared who warned that the broadening concept could divert marketing from its true purposes and dilute its content. One critic did not deny that marketing concepts and tools could be useful in fund raising, museum membership drives, and presidential campaigns, but he felt that these were extracurricular applications of an intrinsical business technology.[2]

* Reprinted from "A Generic Concept of Marketing," *Journal of Marketing*, Vol. 36 (April 1972), pp. 46–54.

† Northwestern University.

[1] Philip Kotler and Sidney J. Levy, "Broadening the Concept of Marketing," *Journal of Marketing*, Vol. 33 (January 1969), pp. 10–15.

[2] David Luck, "Broadening the Concept of Marketing—Too Far," *Journal of Marketing*, Vol. 33 (July 1969), pp. 53–54.

Several articles have been published which describe applications of marketing ideas to nonbusiness areas such as health services, population control, recycling of solid wastes, and fund raising.[3] Therefore, the underlying issues should be reexamined to see whether a more generic concept of marketing can be established. This author concludes that the traditional conception of marketing would relegate this discipline to an increasingly narrow and pedestrian role in a society that is growing increasingly post-industrial. In fact, this article will argue that the broadening proposal's main weakness was not that it went too far but that it did not go far enough.

This article is organized into five parts. The first distinguishes three stages of consciousness regarding the scope of marketing. The second presents an axiomatic treatment of the generic concept of marketing. The third suggests three useful marketing typologies that are implied by the generic concept of marketing. The fourth describes the basic analytical, planning, organization, and control tasks that make up the logic of marketing management. The fifth discusses some interesting questions raised about the generic concept of marketing.

THREE STAGES OF MARKETING CONSCIOUSNESS

Three different levels of consciousness can be distinguished regarding the boundaries of marketing. The present framework utilizes Reich's consciousness categories without his specific meanings.[4] The traditional consciousness, that marketing is essentially a business subject, will be called *consciousness one*. Consciousness one is the most widely held view in the mind of practitioners and the public. In the last few years, a marketing *consciousness two* has appeared among some marketers holding that marketing is appropriate for all organizations that have customers. This is the thrust of the original broadening proposal and seems to be gaining adherents. Now it can be argued that even consciousness two expresses a limited concept of marketing. One can propose *consciousness three* that holds that marketing is a relevant subject for all organizations in their relations with all their publics, not only customers. The future character of marketing will depend on the particular consciousness that most marketers adopt regarding the nature of their field.

Consciousness one

Consciousness one is the conception that marketing is essentially a business subject. It maintains that marketing is concerned with *sellers, buyers,* and *"economic" products and services*. The sellers offer goods

[3] *Journal of Marketing,* Vol. 35 (July 1971).

[4] Charles A. Reich, *The Greening of America* (New York: Random House, 1970).

and services, the buyers have purchasing power and other resources, and the objective is an exchange of goods for money or other resources.

The core concept defining marketing consciousness one is that of *market transactions.* A market transaction involves the transfer of ownership or use of an economic good or service from one party to another in return for a payment of some kind. For market transactions to occur in a society, six conditions are necessary: (1) Two or more parties; (2) a scarcity of goods; (3) concept of private property; (4) one party must want a good held by another; (5) the "wanting" party must be able to offer some kind of payment for it; and (6) the "owning" party must be willing to forego the good for the payment. These conditions underlie the notion of a market transaction, or more loosely, economic exchange.

Market transactions can be contrasted with nonmarket transactions. Nonmarket transactions also involve a transfer of resources from one party to another, *but without clear payment by the other.* Giving gifts, paying taxes, receiving free services are all examples of nonmarket transactions. If a housekeeper is paid for domestic services, this is a market transaction; if she is one's wife, this is a nonmarket transaction. Consciousness one marketers pay little or no attention to nonmarket transactions because they lack the element of explicit payment.

Consciousness two

Consciousness two marketers do not see *payment* as a necessary condition to define the domain of marketing phenomena. Marketing analysis and planning are relevant in all organizations producing products and services for an intended consuming group, whether or not payment is required.

Table 1 lists several nonbusiness organizations and their "products"

TABLE 1
Some organizations and their products and customer groups

Organization	*Product*	*Customer group*
Museum	Cultural appreciation	General public
National Safety Council	Safer driving	Driving public
Political candidate	Honest government	Voting public
Family Planning Foundation	Birth control	Fertile public
Police department	Safety	General public
Church	Religious experience	Church members
University	Education	Students

and "customer groups." All of these products, in principle, can be priced and sold. A price can be charged for museum attendance, safe-driving lessons, birth control information, and education. The fact that many of these services are offered "free" should not detract from their character as products. A product is something that has value to someone. Whether a charge is made for its consumption is an incidental rather than essential feature defining value. In fact, most of these social goods are "priced," although often not in the normal fashion. Police services are paid for by taxes, and religious services are paid for by donations.

Each of these organizations faces marketing problems with respect to its product and customer group. They must study the size and composition of their market and consumer wants, attitudes, and habits. They must design their products to appeal to their target markets. They must develop distribution and communication programs that facilitate "purchase" and satisfaction. They must develop customer feedback systems to ascertain market satisfaction and needs.

Thus consciousness two replaces the core concept of *market transactions* with the broader concept of *organization-client transactions.* Marketing is no longer restricted only to transactions involving parties in a two-way exchange of economic resources. Marketing is a useful perspective for any organization producing products for intended consumption by others. *Marketing consciousness two states that marketing is relevant in all situations where one can identify an organization, a client group, and products broadly defined.*

Consciousness three

The emergence of a marketing consciousness three is barely visible. Consciousness three marketers do not see why marketing technology should be confined only to an organization's transactions with its client group. An organization—or more properly its management—may engage in marketing activity not only with its customers but also with all other publics in its environment. A management group has to market to the organization's supporters, suppliers, employees, government, the general public, agents, and other key publics. *Marketing consciousness three states that marketing applies to an organization's attempts to relate to all of its publics, not just its consuming public.* Marketing can be used in multiple institutional contexts to effect transactions with multiple targets.

Marketing consciousness three is often expressed in real situations. One often hears a marketer say that his real problem is not *outside marketing* but *inside marketing;* for example, getting others in his organization to accept his ideas. Companies seeking a preferred position with suppliers or dealers see this as a problem of marketing themselves. In addition, companies try to market their viewpoint to congressmen in Washington. These and many other examples suggest that marketers see the marketing problem as extending far beyond customer groups.

The concept of defining marketing in terms of *function* rather than *structure* underlies consciousness three. To define a field in terms of function is to see it as a process or set of activities. To define a field in terms of structure is to identify it with some phenomena such as a set of institutions. Bliss pointed out that many sciences are facing this choice.[5] In the field of political science, for example, there are those who adopt a structural view and define political science in terms of political institutions such as legislatures, government agencies, judicial courts, and political parties. There are others who adopt a functional view and define political science as the study of *power* wherever it is found. The latter political scientists study power in the family, in labor-management relations, and in corporate organizations.

Similarly, marketing can be defined in terms of functional rather than structural considerations. Marketing takes place in a great number of situations, including executive recruiting, political campaigning, church membership drives, and lobbying. Examining the marketing aspects of these situations can yield new insights into the generic nature of marketing. The payoff may be higher than from continued concentration in one type of structural setting, that of business.

It is generally a mistake to equate a science with a certain phenomenon. For example, the subject of *matter* does not belong exclusively to physics, chemistry, or biology. Rather physics, chemistry, and biology are logical systems that pose different questions about matter. Nor does *human nature* belong exclusively to psychology, sociology, social psychology, or anthropology. These sciences simply raise different questions about the same phenomena. Similarly, traditional business subjects should not be defined by institutional characteristics. This would mean that finance deals with banks, production with factories, and marketing with distribution channels. Yet each of these subjects has a set of core ideas that are applicable in multiple institutional contexts. An important means of achieving progress in a science is to try to increase the generality of its concepts.

Consider the case of a hospital as an institution. A production-minded person will want to know about the locations of the various facilities, the jobs of the various personnel, and in general the arrangement of the elements to produce the product known as health care. A financial-minded person will want to know the hospital's sources and applications of funds and its income and expenses. A marketing-minded person will want to know where the patients come from, why they appeared at this particular hospital, and how they feel about the hospital care and services. Thus the phenomena do not create the questions to be asked;

[5] Perry Bliss, *Marketing Management and the Behavioral Environment* (Englewood Cliffs, N.J.: Prentice-Hall, Inc., 1970), pp. 106–8, 119–20.

rather the questions are suggested by the disciplined view brought to the phenomena.

What then is the disciplinary focus of marketing? The core concept of marketing is the *transaction. A transaction is the exchange of values between two parties.* The things-of-values need not be limited to goods, services, and money; they include other resources such as time, energy, and feelings. Transactions occur not only between buyers and sellers, and organizations and clients, but also between any two parties. A transaction takes place, for example, when a person decides to watch a television program; he is exchanging his time for entertainment. A transaction takes place when a person votes for a particular candidate; he is exchanging his time and support for expectations of better government. A transaction takes place when a person gives money to a charity; he is exchanging money for a good conscience. *Marketing is specifically concerned with how transactions are created, stimulated, facilitated, and valued.* This is the generic concept of marketing.

THE AXIOMS OF MARKETING

The generic concept of marketing will now be more rigorously developed. Marketing can be viewed as a *category of human action* distinguishable from other categories of human action such as voting, loving, consuming, or fighting. As a category of human action, it has certain characteristics which can be stated in the form of axioms. A sufficient set of axioms about marketing would provide unambiguous criteria about what marketing is, and what it is not. Four axioms, along with corollaries, are proposed in the following section.

Axiom 1. *Marketing involves two or more social units, each consisting of one or more human actors.*

Corollary 1.1. The social units may be individuals, groups, organizations, communities, or nations.

Two important things follow from this axiom. First, marketing is not an activity found outside of the human species. Animals, for example, engage in production and consumption, but do not engage in marketing. They do not exchange goods, set up distribution systems, and engage in persuasive activity. Marketing is a peculiarly human activity.

Second, the referent of marketing activity is another social unit. Marketing does not apply when a person is engaged in an activity in reference to a *thing* or *himself*. Eating, driving, and manufacturing are not marketing activities, as they involve the person in an interactive relationship primarily with things. Jogging, sleeping, and daydreaming are not marketing activities, as they involve the person in an interactive relationship primarily with himself. An interesting question does arise as to whether a person can be conceived of marketing something to himself, as when he undertakes effort to change his own behavior. Normally, however, marketing involves actions by a person directed toward one or more other persons.

Axiom 2. *At least one of the social units is seeking a specific response from one or more other units concerning some social object.*

Corollary 2.1. The social unit seeking the response is called the *marketer,* and the social unit whose response is sought is called the *market.*

Corollary 2.2. The social object may be a product, service, organization, person, place, or idea.

Corollary 2.3. The response sought from the market is some behavior toward the social object, usually acceptance but conceivably avoidance. (More specific descriptions of responses sought are purchase, adoption, usage, consumption, or their negatives. Those who do or may respond are called buyers, adopters, users, consumers, clients, or supporters.)

Corollary 2.4. The marketer is normally aware that he is seeking the specific response.

Corollary 2.5. The response sought may be expected in the short or long run.

Corollary 2.6. The response has value to the marketer.

Corollary 2.7. *Mutual marketing* describes the case where two social units simultaneously seek a response from each other. Mutual marketing is the core situation underlying bargaining relationships.

Marketing consists of actions undertaken by persons to bring about a response in other persons concerning some specific social object. A social object is any entity or artifact found in society, such as a product, service, organization, person, place, or idea. The marketer normally seeks to influence the market to accept this social object. The notion of marketing also covers attempts to influence persons to avoid the object, as in a business effort to discourage excess demand or in a social campaign designed to influence people to stop smoking or overeating.[6] *The marketer is basically trying to shape the level and composition of demand for his product.* The marketer undertakes these influence actions because he values their consequences. The market may also value the consequences, but this is not a necessary condition for defining the occurrence of marketing activity. The marketer is normally conscious that he is attempting to influence a market, but it is also possible to interpret as marketing activity cases where the marketer is not fully conscious of his ends and means.

Axiom 2 implies that "selling" activity rather than "buying" activity is closer to the core meaning of marketing. The merchant who assembles

[6] See Philip Kotler and Sidney J. Levy, "Demarketing, Yes, Demarketing," *Harvard Business Review,* Vol. 49 (November-December 1971), pp. 71–80.

goods for the purpose of selling them is engaging in marketing, insofar as he is seeking a purchase response from others. The buyer who comes into his store and pays the quoted price is engaging in buying, not marketing, in that he does not seek to produce a specific response in the seller, who has already put the goods up for sale. If the buyer decides to bargain with the seller over the terms, he too is involved in marketing, or if the seller had been reluctant to sell, the buyer has to market himself as an attractive buyer. The terms "buyer" and "seller" are not perfectly indicative of whether one, or both, of the parties are engaged in marketing activity.

Axiom 3. *The market's response probability is not fixed.*

Corollary 3.1. The probability that the market will produce the desired response is called the *market's response probability.*

Corollary 3.2. The market's response probability is greater than zero; that is, the market is capable of producing the desired response.

Corollary 3.3. The market's response probability is less than one; that is, the market is not internally compelled to produce the desired response.

Corollary 3.4. The market's response probability can be altered by marketer actions.

Marketing activity makes sense in the context of a market that is free and capable of yielding the desired response. If the target social unit *cannot respond* to the social object, as in the case of no interest or no resources, it is not a market. If the target social unit *must respond* to the social object, as in the case of addiction or perfect brand loyalty, that unit is a market but there is little need for marketing activity. In cases where the market's response probability is fixed in the short run but variable in the long run, the marketer may undertake marketing activity to prevent or reduce the erosion in the response probability. Normally, marketing activity is most relevant where the market's response probability is less than one and highly influenced by marketer actions.

Axiom 4. *Marketing is the attempt to produce the desired response by creating and offering values to the market.*

Corollary 4.1. The marketer assumes that the market's response will be voluntary.

Corollary 4.2. The essential activity of marketing is the creation and offering of value. Value is defined subjectively from the market's point of view.

Corollary 4.3. The marketer creates and offers value mainly through configuration, valuation, symbolization, and facilitation. (Configuration is the act of designing the social object. Valuation is concerned with placing terms of exchange on the object. Symbolization is the association of meanings with the object. Facilitation consists of altering the accessibility of the object.)

Corollary 4.4. *Effective marketing* means the choice of marketer actions that are calculated to produce the desired response in the market. *Efficient marketing* means the choice of *least cost* marketer actions that will produce the desired response.

Marketing is an approach to producing desired responses in another party that lies midway between *coercion* on the one hand and *brainwashing* on the other.

Coercion involves the attempt to produce a response in another by forcing or threatening him with agent-inflicted pain. Agent-inflicted pain should be distinguished from object-inflicted pain in that the latter may be used by a marketer as when he symbolizes something such as cigarettes as potentially harmful to the smoker. The use of agent-inflicted pain is normally not a marketing solution to a response problem. This is not to deny that marketers occasionally resort to arranging a "package of threats" to get or keep a customer. For example, a company may threaten to discontinue purchasing from another company if the latter failed to behave in a certain way. But normally, marketing consists of noncoercive actions to induce a response in another.

Brainwashing lies at the other extreme and involves the attempt to produce a response in another by profoundly altering his basic beliefs and values. Instead of trying to persuade a person to see the social object as serving his existing values and interests, the agent tries to shift the subject's values in the direction of the social object. Brainwashing, fortunately, is a very difficult feat to accomplish. It requires a monopoly of communication channels, operant conditioning, and much patience. Short of pure brainwashing efforts are attempts by various agents to change people's basic values in connection with such issues as racial prejudice, birth control, and private property. Marketing has some useful insights to offer to agents seeking to produce basic changes in people, although its main focus is on creating products and messages attuned to existing attitudes and values. It places more emphasis on preference engineering than attitude conditioning, although the latter is not excluded.

The core concern of marketing is that of producing desired responses in free individuals by the judicious creation and offering of values. The marketer is attempting to get value from the market through offering value to it. The marketer's problem is to create attractive values. Value is completely subjective and exists in the eyes of the beholding market. Marketers must understand the market in order to be effective in creating value. This is the essential meaning of the marketing concept.

The marketer seeks to create value in four ways. He can try to design the social object more attractively (configuration); he can put an attractive term on the social object (valuation); he can add symbolic significance in the social object (symbolization); and he can make it easier for the market to obtain the social object (facilitation). He may use these activities in reverse if he wants the social object to be avoided. These four activities have a rough correspondence to more conventional statements of marketing purpose, such as the use of product, price, promotion, and place to stimulate exchange.

The layman who thinks about marketing often overidentifies it with one or two major component activities, such as facilitation or symbolization. In *scarcity economies*, marketing is often identified with the facilitation function. Marketing is the problem of getting scarce goods to a marketplace. There is little concern with configuration and symbolization. In *affluent economies*, marketing is often identified with the symbolization function. In the popular mind, marketing is seen as the task of encoding persuasive messages to get people to buy more goods. Since most people resent persuasion attempts, marketing has picked up a negative image in the minds of many people. They forget or overlook the marketing work involved in creating values through configuration, valuation, and facilitation. In the future post-industrial society concern over the quality of life becomes paramount, and the public understanding of marketing is likely to undergo further change, hopefully toward an appreciation of all of its functions to create and offer value.

TYPOLOGIES OF MARKETING

The new levels of marketing consciousness make it desirable to reexamine traditional classifications of marketing activity. Marketing practitioners normally describe their type of marketing according to the *target market* or *product*. A *target-market classification* of marketing activity consists of consumer marketing, industrial marketing, government marketing, and international marketing.

A *product* classification consists of durable goods marketing, nondurable goods marketing, and service marketing.

With the broadening of marketing, the preceding classifications no longer express the full range of marketing application. They pertain to business marketing, which is only one type of marketing. More comprehensive classifications of marketing activity can be formulated according to the *target market, product,* or *marketer.*

Target market typology

A *target-market classification* of marketing activity distinguishes the various *publics* toward which an organization can direct its marketing activity. *A public is any group with potential interest and impact on an organization.* Every organization has up to nine distinguishable publics (Figure 1). There are three *input publics* (supporters, employees,

FIGURE 1.
An organization's publics.

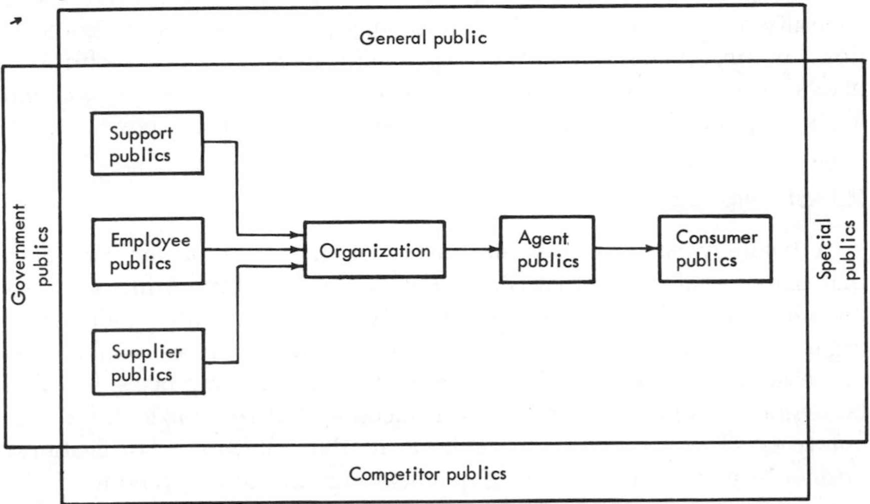

suppliers), two *output publics* (agents, consumers), and four *sanctioning publics* (government, competitors, special publics, and general public). The organization is viewed as a resource conversion machine which takes the resources of supporters (e.g., stockholders, directors), employees, and suppliers and converts these into products that go directly to consumers or through agents. The organization's basic input-output activities are subject to the watchful eye of sanctioning publics such as government, competitors, special publics, and the general public. All of these publics are targets for organizational marketing activity because of their potential impact on the resource converting efficiency of the organization. Therefore, a *target-market classification* of marketing activity consists of supporter-directed marketing, employee-directed marketing, supplier-directed marketing, agent-directed marketing, consumer-directed marketing, general public-directed marketing, special public-directed marketing, government-directed marketing, and competitor-directed marketing.

Product typology

A typology of marketing activity can also be constructed on the basis of the *product* marketed. Under the broadened concept of marketing, the product is no longer restricted to commercial goods and services. An organization can try to market to a public up to six types of products or social objects. A product classification of marketing consists of goods marketing, service marketing, organization marketing, person marketing, place marketing, and idea marketing.

Goods and service marketing, which made up the whole of traditional marketing, reappear in this classification. In addition, marketers can specialize in the marketing of organizations (e.g., governments, corporations, or universities), persons (e.g., political candidates, celebrities), places (e.g., real estate developments, resort areas, states, cities), and ideas (e.g., family planning, Medicare, antismoking, safe-driving).

Marketer typology

A typology can also be constructed on the basis of the *marketer,* that is, the organization that is carrying on the marketing. A first approximation would call for distinguishing between business and nonbusiness organization marketing. Since there are several types of nonbusiness organizations with quite different products and marketing tasks, it would be desirable to build a marketer classification that recognizes the different types of organizations. This leads to the following classifications: business organization marketing, political organization marketing, social organization marketing, religious organization marketing, cultural organization marketing, and knowledge organization marketing.

Organizations are classified according to their primary or formal character. Political organizations would include political parties, government agencies, trade unions, and cause groups. Social organizations would include service clubs, fraternal organizations, and private welfare agencies. Religious organizations would include churches and evangelical movements. Cultural organizations would include museums, symphonies, and art leagues. Knowledge organizations would include public schools, universities, and research organizations. Some organizations are not easy to classify. Is a nonprofit hospital a business or a social organization? Is an employee credit union a political or a social organization? The purpose of the classification is primarily to guide students of marketing to look for regularities that might characterize the activities of certain basic types of organizations.

In general, the purpose of the three classifications of marketing activity is to facilitate the accumulation of marketing knowledge and its transfer from one marketing domain to another. Thus political and social organizations often engage in marketing ideas, and it is desirable to build up generic knowledge about idea marketing. Similarly, many organizations try to communicate a program to government authorities, and they could benefit from the accumulation of knowledge concerning idea marketing and government-directed marketing.

BASIC TASKS OF MARKETING MANAGEMENT

Virtually all persons and organizations engage in marketing activity at various times. They do not all engage in marketing, however, with equal skill. A distinction can be drawn between *marketing* and *marketing management*. *Marketing* is a descriptive science involving the study of how transactions are created, stimulated, facilitated, and valued. *Marketing management* is a normative science involving the efficient creation and offering of values to stimulate desired transactions. Marketing management is essentially a disciplined view of the task of achieving specific responses in others through the creation and offering of values.

Marketing management is not a set of answers so much as an orderly set of questions by which the marketer determines what is best to do in each situation. Effective marketing consists of intelligently analyzing, planning, organizing, and controlling marketing effort.

The marketer must be skilled at two basic analytical tasks. The first is *market analysis*. He must be able to identify the market, its size and location, needs and wants, perceptions and values. The second analytical skill is *product analysis*. The marketer must determine what products are currently available to the target, and how the target feels about each of them.

Effective marketing also calls for four major planning skills. The first is *product development*, i.e., configuration. The marketer should know where to look for appropriate ideas, how to choose and refine the product concept, how to stylize and package the product, and how to test it. The second is *pricing*, i.e., valuation. He must develop an attractive set of terms for the product. The third is *distribution*, i.e., facilitation. The marketer should determine how to get the product into circulation and make it accessible to its target market. The fourth is *promotion*, i.e., symbolization. The marketer must be capable of stimulating market interest in the product.

Effective marketing also requires three organizational skills. The first is *organizational design*. The marketer should understand the advantages and disadvantages of organizing market activity along functional, product, and market lines. The second is *organizational staffing*. He should know how to find, train, and assign effective co-marketers. The third is *organizational motivation*. He must determine how to stimulate the best marketing effort by his staff.

Finally, effective marketing also calls for two control skills. The first is *market results measurement*, whereby the marketer keeps informed of the attitudinal and behavioral responses he is achieving in the marketplace. The second is *marketing cost measurement*, whereby the marketer keeps informed of his costs and efficiency in carrying out his marketing plans.

SOME QUESTIONS ABOUT GENERIC MARKETING

The robustness of the particular conception of marketing advocated in this article will be known in time through testing the ideas in various situations. The question is whether the logic called marketing really helps individuals such as educational administrators, public officials, museum directors, or church leaders to better interpret their problems and construct their strategies. If these ideas are validated in the marketplace, they will be accepted and adopted.

However, academic debate does contribute substantially to the sharpening of the issues and conceptions. Several interesting questions have arisen in the course of efforts by this author to expound the generic concept of marketing. Three of these questions are raised and discussed below.

(1) *Isn't generic marketing really using influence as the core concept rather than exchange?*

It is tempting to think that the three levels of consciousness of marketing move from *market transactions* to *exchange* to *influence* as the succeeding core concepts. The concept of influence undeniably plays an important role in marketing thought. Personal selling and advertising are essentially influence efforts. Product design, pricing, packaging, and distribution planning make extensive use of influence considerations. It would be too general to say, however, that marketing is synonymous with interpersonal, intergroup, or interorganizational influence processes.

Marketing is a particular way of looking at the problem of achieving a valued response from a target market. It essentially holds that exchange values must be identified, and the marketing program must be based on these exchange values. Thus the anticigarette marketer analyzes what the market is being asked to give up and what inducements might be offered. The marketer recognizes that every action by a person has an opportunity cost. The marketer attempts to find ways to increase the person's perceived rate of exchange between what he would receive and what he would give up in *freely* adopting that behavior. The marketer is a specialist at understanding human wants and values and knows what it takes for someone to act.

(2) *How would one distinguish between marketing and a host of related activities such as lobbying, propagandizing, publicizing, and negotiating?*

Marketing and other influence activities and tools share some common characteristics as well as exhibit some unique features. Each influence activity has to be examined separately in relation to marketing. *Lobbying*, for example, is one aspect of government-directed marketing. The lobbyist attempts to evoke support from a legislator through offering values to the legislator (e.g., information, votes, friendship, and favors). A lobbyist thinks through the problem of marketing his legislation as carefully as the business marketer thinks through the problem of marketing his product or service. *Propagandizing* is the marketing of a political or social idea to a mass audience. The propagandist attempts to package the ideas in such a way as to constitute values to the target audience in exchange for support. *Publicizing* is the effort to create attention and interest in a target audience. As such it is a tool of marketing. *Negotiation* is a face-to-face mutual marketing process. In general, the broadened concept of marketing underscores the kinship of marketing with a large number of other activities and suggests that marketing is a more endemic process in society than business marketing alone suggests.

(3) *Doesn't generic marketing imply that a marketer would be more capable of managing political or charitable campaigns than professionals in these businesses?*

A distinction should be drawn between marketing as a *logic* and marketing as a *competence*. Anyone who is seeking a response in another would benefit from applying marketing logic to the problem. Thus a company treasurer seeking a loan, a company recruiter seeking a talented executive, a conservationist seeking an antipollution law, would all benefit in conceptualizing their problem in marketing terms. In these instances, they would be donning a marketer's hat although they would not be performing as professional marketers. A professional marketer is someone who (1) regularly works with marketing problems in a specific area and (2) has a specialized knowledge of this area. The political strategist, to the extent he is effective, is a professional marketer. He has learned how to effectively design, package, price, advertise, and distribute his type of product in his type of market. A professional marketer who suddenly decides to handle political candidates would need to develop competence and knowledge in this area just as he would if he suddenly decided to handle soap or steel. Being a marketer only means that a person has mastered the logic of marketing. To master the particular market requires additional learning and experience.

SUMMARY AND CONCLUSION

This article has examined the current debate in marketing concerning whether its substance belongs in the business area, or whether it is applicable to all areas in which organizations attempt to relate to customers and other publics. Specifically, *consciousness one marketing* holds that marketing's core idea is *market transactions,* and therefore marketing applies to buyers, sellers, and commercial products and services. *Consciousness two marketing* holds that marketing's core idea is *organization-client transactions,* and therefore marketing applies in any organization that can recognize a group called customers. *Consciousness three marketing* holds that marketing's core idea is *transactions,* and therefore marketing applies to any social unit seeking to exchange values with other social units.

This broadest conception of marketing can be called *generic marketing.* Generic marketing takes a functional rather than a structural view of marketing. Four axioms define generic marketing. *Axiom 1:* Marketing involves two or more social units. *Axiom 2:* At least one of the social units is seeking a specific response from one or more other units concerning some social object. *Axiom 3:* The market's response probability is not fixed. *Axiom 4:* Marketing is the attempt to produce the desired response by creating and offering values to the market. These four axioms and their corollaries are intended to provide unambiguous criteria for determining what constitutes a marketing process.

Generic marketing further implies that marketing activity can be classified according to the *target market* (marketing directed to supporters, employees, suppliers, agents, consumers, general public, special publics, government, and competitors); the *product* (goods, services, organizations, persons, places, and ideas); and the *marketer* (business, political, social, religious, cultural, and knowledge organizations).

Marketers face the same tasks in all types of marketing. Their major analytical tasks are *market analysis* and *product analysis.* Their major planning tasks are *product development, pricing, distribution,* and *promotion.* Their major organizational tasks are *design, staffing,* and *motivation.* Their major control tasks are *market results measurement* and *marketing cost measurement.*

Generic marketing is a logic available to all organizations facing problems of market response. A distinction should be drawn between applying a marketing point of view to a specific problem and being a marketing professional. Marketing logic alone does not make a marketing professional. The professional also acquires competence which, along with the logic, allows him to interpret his problems and construct his marketing strategies in an effective way.

Bibliography

1. Business Leadership in Social Change. The Conference Board, Inc. New York, 1971.
2. DAWSON, LESLIE M. "The Human Concept: New Philosophy for Business," *Business Horizons,* December 1969, pp. 29–38.
3. DAWSON, LESLIE M. "Marketing Science in the Age of Aquarius," *Journal of Marketing,* July 1971, pp. 66–72.
4. FELDMAN, LAWRENCE P. "Societal Adaptation: A New Challenge for Marketing," *Journal of Marketing,* July 1971, pp. 54–60.
5. GELB, BETSY D., AND BRIEN, RICHARD H. "Survival and Social Responsibility: Themes for Marketing Education and Management," *Journal of Marketing,* April 1971, pp. 3–9.
6. HACKETT, J. T. "Corporate Citizenship: The Resolution of Dilemma," *Business Horizons,* October 1969, pp. 69–74.
7. LODGE, GEORGE C. "Top Priority: Renovating Our Ideology," *Harvard Business Review,* September 1970, pp. 43–55.
8. LODGE, G. C. "Why an Outmoded Ideology Thwarts the New Business Conscience," *Fortune,* October 1970, pp. 106–7.
9. LUCK, DAVID J. "Broadening the Concept of Marketing—Too Far," *Journal of Marketing,* July 1969, pp. 66–72.
10. McDONALD, JOHN. "How Social Responsibility Fits the Game of Business," *Fortune,* December 1970, pp. 164–66.
11. MACY, JOHN W. "The Future—Management in the Public Interest," *Academy of Management Journal,* June 1968, pp. 147–51.
12. NATIONAL GOALS RESEARCH STAFF. A *Report toward Balanced Growth: Quantity with Quality.* Washington, D.C.: Superintendent of Documents, July 4, 1970.
13. "Progress in Areas of Public Concern," General Motors Corporation. Milford, Mich.: General Motors Corp., 1971.
14. STIGLER, GEORGE J. The *Intellectual and the Marketplace,* Vol. 3. Chicago: University of Chicago Press, 1967.

Bibliography

2 CONSUMERS, CONSUMERISM, AND MARKETING

PROVIDING CONSUMER SATISFACTIONS has been a guiding tenet for marketing practitioners. It was felt that if a product "satisfied a need," it would be acceptable to the consumer and profitable for the firm. The consumerism movement has sharpened the reality that consumers are not satisfied with many of today's products and/or marketing practices.

To explain this phenomenon, the concept of satisfaction must be more broadly defined and applied. A product must be capable of providing satisfaction not only on the day of purchase, but as long as the consumer uses it. Other variables accompanying the product such as service, warranties, safety, and quality influence the degree of satisfaction. Satisfaction can also be determined by such marketing practices as advertising, pricing, packaging, and labeling. A host of factors determine long-run consumer-citizen satisfactions with market offerings.

It must be recognized that many consumer demands will be met. The only question is who will act to accommodate these demands—business or government? Antagonism, apathy, or delay all increase the probability of government filling this void with regulation and restriction. Business must act quickly and with responsibility to meet consumers' needs, if not on moral grounds, for self-protection.

Although many businessmen view consumerism as a threat or nuisance, it has a positive side. Perceptive marketers can see multiple opportunities where new products and practices are necessitated by a changing marketing environment.

The consumer movement is one result of businesses' failure to respond to increased consumer-citizen demands. The first section of this chapter is concerned with the *nature* and *development* of this movement. Kotler begins by arguing that consumerism is inevitable, enduring, beneficial, promarketing, and profitable. Next, Buskirk and Rothe present a study of the causes, development, and implications for organizational change of the consumerism movement. McGuire concludes this section by pointing out the accompanying marketing opportunities resulting from the consumerism movement.

Consumers do not necessarily desire governmental regulation of business and marketing activity; however, increased intervention will result from unresponsive business policy. The following articles present corporate *responses* to consumer problems and the possible *implications* of a lack of response by the business community. Leighton describes the possibility of increased governmental involvement in the market system as a result of business' delayed response to consumerism. As an alternative to increased governmental regulation, Weiss discusses the necessity of adopting new practices and attitudes to accommodate consumer desires. Following this, Virginia Knauer points out that consumerism is, after all, only an appeal to sound marketing practice. Concluding this section, Lazer discusses the effect of consumerism on public policy development.

a.

Nature and development

What factors are contributing to the rise of consumerism? Will consumerism prove to be enduring, beneficial and promarketing as the author maintains? How does consumerism promise to provide profitable opportunity to business in the long-run? The societal marketing concept is described as an advance over the original marketing concept.

9. WHAT CONSUMERISM MEANS FOR MARKETERS*

Philip Kotler†

In this century, the U.S. business scene has been shaken by three distinct consumer movements—in the early 1900s, the mid-1930s, and the mid-1960s. The first two flare-ups subsided. Business observers, social critics, and marketing leaders are divided over whether this latest outbreak is a temporary or a permanent social phenomenon. Those who think that the current movement has the quality of a fad point to the two earlier ones. By the same token, they argue that this too will fade away. Others argue just as strongly that the issues which flamed the

* Reprinted from "What Consumerism Means for Marketers," *Harvard Business Review,* Vol. 50 (May-June 1972), pp. 48–57.

† Northwestern University.

Author's note: I wish to thank Professor Fred Allvine for his helpful and incisive comments during the writing of this article.

latest movement differ so much in character and force that consumerism may be here to stay.

In retrospect, it is interesting that the first consumer movement was fueled by such factors as rising prices, Upton Sinclair's writings, and ethical drug scandals. It culminated in the passage of the Pure Food and Drug Act (1906), the Meat Inspection Act (1906), and the creation of the Federal Trade Commission (1914). The second wave of consumerism in the mid-1930s was fanned by such factors as an upturn in consumer prices in the midst of the depression, the sulfanilamide scandal, and the widely imitated Detroit housewives strike. It culminated in the strengthening of the Pure Food and Drug Act and in the enlarging of the Federal Trade Commission's power to regulate against unfair or deceptive acts and practices.

The third and current movement has resulted from a complex combination of circumstances, not the least of which was increasingly strained relations between standard business practices and long-run consumer interests. Consumerism in its present form has also been variously blamed on Ralph Nader, the thalidomide scandal, rising prices, the mass media, a few dissatisfied individuals, and on President Lyndon Johnson's "Consumer Interests Message." These and other possible explanations imply that the latest movement did not have to happen and that it had little relationship to the real feelings of most consumers.

In this article, I shall discuss the current phenomenon and what it portends for business. In so doing, I shall present five simple conclusions about consumerism and largely focus my discussion on these assessments. Consider:

1. *Consumerism was inevitable.* It was not a plot by Ralph Nader and a handful of consumerists but an inevitable phase in the development of our economic system.
2. *Consumerism will be enduring.* Just as the labor movement started as a protest uprising and became institutionalized in the form of unions, government boards, and labor legislation, the consumer movement, too, will become an increasingly institutionalized force in U.S. society.
3. *Consumerism will be beneficial.* On the whole, it promises to make the U.S. economic system more responsive to new and emerging societal needs.
4. *Consumerism is promarketing.* The consumer movement suggests an important refinement in the marketing concept to take into account societal concerns.
5. *Consumerism can be profitable.* The societal marketing concept suggests areas of new opportunity and profit for alert business firms.

These assessments of consumerism are generally at variance with the views of many businessmen. Some business spokesmen maintain that consumerism was stirred up by radicals, headline grabbers, and politicians; that it can be beaten by attacking, discrediting, or ignoring it; that it threatens to destroy the vitality of our economic system and its benefits; that it is an antimarketing concept; and that it can only reduce profit opportunities in the long run.

WHAT IS CONSUMERISM?

Before discussing the foregoing conclusions in more depth, it is important to know what we mean by "consumerism." Here is a definition:

Consumerism is a social movement seeking to augment the rights and power of buyers in relation to sellers.

To understand this definition, let us first look at a short list of the many traditional rights of sellers in the U.S. economic system:

Sellers have the right to introduce any product in any size and style they wish into the marketplace so long as it is not hazardous to personal health or safety; or, if it is, to introduce it with the proper warnings and controls.

Sellers have the right to price the product at any level they wish provided there is no discrimination among similar classes of buyers.

Sellers have the right to spend any amount of money they wish to promote the product, so long as it is not defined as unfair competition.

Sellers have the right to formulate any message they wish about the product provided that it is not misleading or dishonest in content or execution.

Sellers have the right to introduce any buying incentive schemes they wish.

Subject to a few limitations, these are among the essential core rights of businessmen in the United States. Any radical change in these would make U.S. business a different kind of game.

Now what about the traditional *buyers' rights?* Here, once again, are some of the rights that come immediately to mind:

Buyers have the right not to buy a product that is offered to them.

Buyers have the right to expect the product to be safe.

Buyers have the right to expect the product to turn out to be essentially as represented by the seller.

In looking over these traditional sellers' and buyers' rights, I believe that the balance of power lies with the seller. The notion that the buyer has all the power he needs *because he can refuse to buy* the product is not deemed adequate by consumer advocates. They hold that consumer sovereignty is not enough when the consumer does not have full information and when he is persuasively influenced by Madison Avenue.

What additional rights do consumers want? Behind the many issues stirred up by consumer advocates is a drive for several additional rights. In the order of their serious challenge to sellers' rights they are:

Buyers want the right to have adequate information about the product.

Buyers want the right to additional protections against questionable products and marketing practices.

Buyers want the right to influence products and marketing practices in directions that will increase the "quality of life."

Consumer proposals

The "right to be informed," proposed by President Kennedy in his March 1962 directive to the Consumer Advisory Council, has been the battleground for a great number of consumer issues. These include, for example, the right to know the true interest cost of a loan (truth-in-lending), the true cost per standard unit of competing brands (unit pricing), the basic ingredients in a product (ingredient labeling), the nutritional quality of foods (nutritional labeling), the freshness of products (open dating), and the prices of gasoline (sign posting rather than pump posting).

Many of these proposals have gained widespread endorsement not only from consumers but also from political leaders and some businessmen. It is hard to deny the desirability of adequate information for making a free market operate vitally and competitively in the interests of consumers.

The proposals related to additional *consumer protection* are several, including the strengthening of consumers' hands in cases of business fraud, requiring of more safety to be designed into automobiles, issuing of greater powers to existing government agencies, and setting up of new agencies.

The argument underlying consumer protection proposals is that consumers do not necessarily have the time and/or skills to obtain, understand, and use all the information that they may get about a product; therefore, some impartial agencies must be established which can perform these tasks with the requisite economies of scale.

The proposals relating to *quality-of-life* considerations include regulating the ingredients that go into certain products (detergents, gasoline) and packaging (soft drink containers), reducing the level of advertising and promotional "noise," and creating consumer representation on company boards to introduce consumer welfare considerations in business decision making.

The argument in this area says that products, packaging, and marketing practices must not only pass the test of being profitable to the company and convenient to the consumer but must also be life-enhancing. Consumerists insist that the world's resources no longer permit their indiscriminate embodiment in any products desired by consumers without further consideration of their social values. This "right" is obviously the most radical of the three additional rights that consumers want, and the one which would constitute the most basic challenge to the sellers' traditional rights.

CONSUMERISM WAS INEVITABLE

Let us now consider in greater depth the first of the five conclusions I cited at the outset of this article—namely, that consumerism was inevitable. Consumerism did not necessarily have to happen in the 1960s, but it had to happen eventually in view of new conditions in the U.S. economy that warranted a fresh examination of the economic power of sellers in relation to buyers.

At the same time, there are very good reasons why consumerism did flare up in the mid-1960s. The phenomenon was not due to any single cause. Consumerism was reborn because all of the conditions that normally combine to produce a successful social movement were present. These conditions are structural conduciveness, structural strain, growth of a generalized belief, precipitating factors, mobilization for action, and social control.[1] Using these six conditions, I have listed in Exhibit 1 the major factors under each that contributed to the rise of consumerism.

Structural conduciveness refers to basic developments in the society that eventually create potent contradictions. In the latest consumer movement, three developments are particularly noteworthy.

First, U.S. incomes and educational levels advanced continuously. This portended that many citizens would eventually become concerned with the quality of their lives, not just their material well-being.

Second, U.S. technology and marketing were becoming increasingly complex. That this would create potent consumer problems was noted perceptively by E. B. Weiss: "Technology has brought unparalleled abundance and opportunity to the consumer. It has also exposed him to new complexities and hazards. It has made his choices more difficult. He cannot be chemist, mechanic, electrician, nutritionist, *and* a walking computer (very necessary when shopping for fractionated-ounce food packages)! Faced with almost infinite product differentiation (plus contrived product virtues that are purely semantic), considerable price differentiation, the added complexities of trading stamps, the subtleties of cents-off deals, and other complications, the shopper is expected to choose wisely under circumstances that baffle professional buyers."[2]

Third, the environment was progressively exploited in the interests

[1] These conditions were proposed in Neil J. Smelser, *Theory of Collective Behavior* (New York: The Free Press, 1963).

[2] "Marketers Fiddle While Consumers Burn," *HBR* (July-August 1968), p. 48.

of abundance. Observers began to see that an abundance of cars and conveniences would produce a shortage of clean air and water. The Malthusian specter of man running out of sufficient resources to maintain himself became a growing concern.

These developments, along with some others, produced major *structural strains* in the society. The 1960s were a time of great public discontent and frustration. Economic discontent was created by steady inflation which left consumers feeling that their real incomes were deteriorating. Social discontent centered on the sorrowful conditions of the poor, the race issue, and the tremendous costs of the Vietnam war. Ecological discontent arose out of new awareness of the world population explosion and the pollution fallout associated with technological progress. Marketing system discontent centered on safety hazards, product breakdowns, commercial noise, and gimmickry. Political discontent reflected the widespread feelings that politicians and government institutions were not serving the people.

Discontent is not enough to bring about change. There must grow a *generalized belief* about both the main causes of the social malaise and the potent effectiveness of collective social action. Here, again, certain factors contributed importantly to the growth of a generalized belief.

First, there were the writings of social critics such as John Kenneth Galbraith, Vance Packard, and Rachel Carson, that provided a popular interpretation of the problem and of actionable solutions.

Second, there were the hearings and proposals of a handful of Congressmen such as Senator Estes Kefauver that held out some hope of legislative remedy.

Third, there were the Presidential "consumer" messages of President Kennedy in 1962 and President Johnson in 1966, which legitimated belief and interest in this area of social action.

Finally, old-line consumer testing and educational organizations continued to call public attention to the consumers' interests.

Given the growing collective belief, consumerism only awaited some *precipitating factors* to ignite the highly combustible social material. Two sparks specifically exploded the consumer movement. The one was General Motors' unwitting creation of a hero in Ralph Nader through its attempt to investigate him; Nader's successful attack against General Motors encouraged other organizers to undertake bold acts against the business system. The other was the occurrence of widespread and spontaneous store boycotts by housewives in search of a better deal from supermarkets.

These chance combustions would have vanished without a lasting effect if additional resources were not *mobilized for action*. As it turned out, three factors fueled the consumer movement.

First, the mass media gave front-page coverage and editorial support to the activities of consumer advocates. They found the issues safe,

EXHIBIT I.
Factors contributing to the rise of consumerism in the 1960s

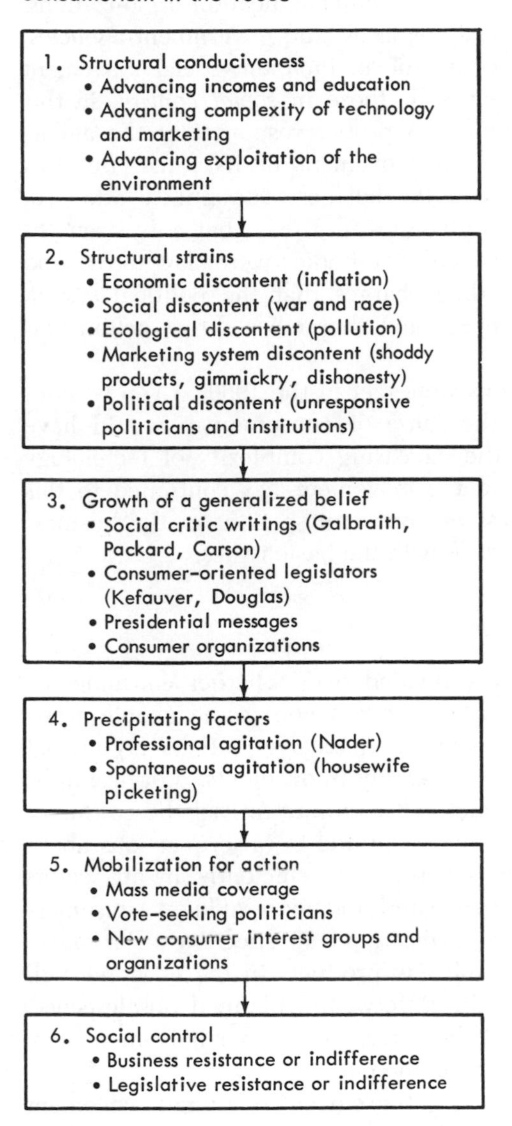

dramatic, and newsworthy. The media's attention was further amplified through word-of-mouth processes into grass-roots expressions and feelings.

Second, a large number of politicians at the federal, state, and local levels picked up consumerism as a safe, high-potential vote-getting social issue.

Third, a number of existing and new organizations arose in defense of the consumer, including labor unions, consumer cooperatives, credit unions, product testing organizations, consumer education organizations, senior citizen groups, public interest law firms, and government agencies.

Of course, the progress and course of an incipient social movement depends on the reception it receives by those in *social control,* in this case, the industrial-political complex. A proper response by the agents of social control can drain the early movement of its force. But this did not happen. Many members of the business community attacked, resisted, or ignored the consumer advocates in a way that only strengthened the consumerist cause. Most legislative bodies were slow to respond with positive programs, thus feeding charges that the political system was unresponsive to consumer needs and that more direct action was required.

Thus all the requisite conditions were met in the 1960s. Even without some of the structural strains, the cause of consumerism would have eventually emerged because of the increasing complexity of technology and the environmental issue. And the movement has continued to this day, abetted by the unwillingness of important sections of the business and political systems to come to terms with the basic issues.

IT WILL BE ENDURING

As we have seen, observers are divided over whether consumerism is a temporary or a permanent social phenomenon: some people argue that the current consumer movement will pass over; others argue that it differs substantially from the two earlier movements. For example, the ecology issue is here to stay and will continue to fuel the consumer movement. The plight of the poor will continue to raise questions about whether the distribution system is performing efficiently in all sectors of the economy. There are more educated and more affluent consumers than ever before, and they are the mainstay of an effective social movement. The continuous outpouring of new products in the economy will continue to raise questions of health, safety, and planned obsolescence. Altogether, the issues that flamed the current consumer movement may be more profound and enduring than in the past.

No one can really predict how long the current consumer movement will last. There is good reason to believe, in fact, that the protest phase of the consumer movement will end soon. The real issue is not how long there will be vocal consumer protest but rather what legacy it will leave regarding the balance of buyers' rights and sellers' rights.

Each of the previous consumer movements left new institutions and laws to function in behalf of the consumer. By this test, the victory already belongs to consumers. Sellers now must operate within the new constraints of a Truth-in-Lending Law, a Truth-in-Packaging Law, an

Auto Safety Law, an Office of Consumer Affairs, an Environmental Protection Agency, and a greatly strengthened Federal Trade Commission and Federal Food and Drug Administration.

It is no accident that such laws and institutions come into being when the demonstration and agitation phase of the consumer movement starts to dwindle. It is precisely the enactment of new laws and creation of new institutions that cause the protest phase to decline. Viewed over the span of a century, the consumer movement has been winning and increasing buyers' rights and power. In this sense, the consumerist movement is enduring, whether or not the visible signs of protest are found.

IT CAN BE BENEFICIAL

Businessmen take the point of view that since consumerism imposes costs on them, it will ultimately be costly to the consumer. Since they have to meet more legal requirements, they have to limit or modify some of their methods for attracting customers. This may mean that consumers will not get all the products and benefits they want and may find business costs passed on to them.

Businessmen also argue that they have the consumer's interests at heart and have been serving him well, and that customer satisfaction is the central tenet of their business philosophy. Many sincerely believe that consumerism is politically motivated and economically unsound.

The test of beneficiality, however, lies not in the short-run impact of consumerism on profits and consumer interests but rather in its long-run impact. Neither consumerism nor any social movement can get very far in the absence of combustible social material. Protest movements are messages coming from the social system that say that something is seriously wrong. They are the body politic's warning system. To ignore or attack protest signals is an invitation to deepening social strains. Protest movements are social indicators of new problems which need joint problem solving, not social rhetoric.

The essential legacy of consumerism promises to be beneficial in the long run. It forces businessmen to reexamine their social roles. It challenges them to look at problems which are easy to ignore. It makes them think more about ends as well as means. The habit of thinking about ends has been deficient in U.S. society, and protest movements such as consumerism, minority rights, student rights, and women's rights have a beneficial effect in raising questions about the purposes of institutions before it is too late.

Beyond this philosophical view of the beneficial aspects of protest movements may lie some very practical gains for consumers and businessmen. Here are four arguments advanced by consumerists:

1. Consumerism will increase the amount of product information. This will make it possible for consumers to buy more efficiently. They may

obtain more value or goods with a given expenditure or a given amount of goods with a lower expenditure. To the extent that greater buying efficiency will result in surplus purchasing power, consumers may buy more goods in total.

2. Consumerism will lead to legislation that limits promotional expenditure which primarily affects market shares rather than aggregate demand. Consumer games, trading stamps, and competitive brand advertising in demand-inelastic industries are largely seen as increasing the costs of products to consumers with little compensating benefits. Reductions in the level of these expenditures, particularly where they account for a large portion of total cost, should lead to lower consumer prices.

3. Consumerism will require manufacturers to absorb more of the social costs imposed by their manufacturing operations and product design decisions. Their higher prices will decrease the purchase of high social cost goods relative to low social cost goods. This will mean lower governmental expenditures covered by taxes to clean up the environment. Consumers will benefit from a lower tax rate and/or from a higher quality environment.

4. Consumerism will reduce the number of unsafe or unhealthy products which will result in more satisfied, healthier consumers.

These arguments are as cogent as contrary arguments advanced by some business spokesmen against responding to consumerism. This is not to deny that many companies will inherit short-run costs not compensated by short-run revenues and in this sense be losers. Their opposition to consumerism is understandable. But this is not the basis for developing a sound long-run social policy.

IT IS PROMARKETING

Consumerism has come as a shock to many businessmen because deep in their hearts they believe that they have been serving the consumer extraordinarily well. Do businessmen deserve the treatment that they are getting in the hands of consumerists?

It is possible that the business sector has deluded itself into thinking that it has been serving the consumer well. Although the marketing concept is the professed philosophy of a majority of U.S. companies, perhaps it is more honored in the breach than in the observance. Although top management professes the concept, the line executives, who are rewarded for ringing up sales, may not practice it faithfully.

What is the essence of the marketing concept?

The marketing concept calls for a *customer orientation* backed by *integrated marketing* aimed at generating *customer satisfaction* as the key to attaining long-run profitable volume.

The marketing concept was a great step forward in meshing the actions of business with the interests of consumers. It meant that consumer wants and needs became the starting point for product and market planning. It meant that business profits were tied to how well the company succeeded in pleasing and satisfying the customer.

Peter F. Drucker suggested that consumerism is "the shame of the total marketing concept," implying that the concept is not widely implemented.[3] But even if the marketing concept as currently understood were widely implemented, there would be a consumerist movement. Consumerism is a clarion call for a *revised marketing concept.*

The main problem that is coming to light rests on the ambiguity of the term *customer satisfaction.* Most businessmen take this to mean that *consumer desires* should be the orienting focus of product and market planning. The company should produce what the customer wants. But the problem is that in efficiently serving customers' desires, it is possible to hurt their long-run interests. Edmund Burke noted the critical difference when he said to the British electorate, "I serve your interests, not your desires." From the many kinds of products and services that satisfy consumers in the short run but disserve or dissatisfy them in the long run, here are four examples:

1. Large, expensive automobiles please their owners but increase the pollution in the air, the congestion of traffic, and the difficulty of parking, and therefore reduce the owner's long-run satisfaction.

2. The food industry in the United States is oriented toward producing new products which have high taste appeal. Nutrition has tended to be a secondary consideration. Many young people are raised on a diet largely of potato chips, hot dogs, and sweets which satisfy their tastes but harm their long-run health.

3. The packaging industry has produced many new convenience features for the American consumer such as nonreusable containers, but the same consumers ultimately pay for this convenience in the form of solid waste pollution.

4. Cigarettes and alcohol are classic products which obviously satisfy consumers but which ultimately hurt them if consumed in any excessive amount.

These examples make the point that catering to consumer satisfaction does not necessarily create satisfied consumers. Businessmen have not worried about this so long as consumers have continued to buy their products. But while consumers buy as *consumers,* they increasingly express their discontent as *voters.* They use the political system to correct the abuses that they cannot resist through the economic system.

The dilemma for the marketer, forced into the open by consumerism, is that he cannot go on giving the consumer only what pleases him without considering the effect on the consumer's and society's well-being.

[3] "The Shame of Marketing," *Marketing/Communications* (August 1969), p. 60.

On the other hand, he cannot produce salutary products which the consumer will not buy. The problem is to somehow reconcile company profit, consumer desires, and consumer long-run interests. The original marketing concept has to be broadened to the societal marketing concept:

The *societal marketing concept* calls for a *customer orientation* backed by *integrated marketing* aimed at generating *customer satisfaction* and *long-run consumer welfare* as the key to attaining long-run profitable volume.

The addition of long-run consumer welfare asks the businessman to include social and ecological considerations in his product and market planning. He is asked to do this not only to meet his social responsibilities but also because failure to do this may hurt his long-run interests as a producer.

Thus the message of consumerism is not a setback for marketing but rather points to the next stage in the evolution of enlightened marketing. Just as the *sales concept* said that sales were all-important, and the original *marketing concept* said that consumer satisfaction was also important, the *societal marketing concept* has emerged to say that long-run consumer welfare is also important.

IT CAN BE PROFITABLE

This last assessment is the most difficult and yet the most critical of my five conclusions to prove. Obviously, if consumerism is profitable, businessmen will put aside their other objections. It is mainly because of its perceived unprofitability that many businessmen object so vehemently.

Can consumerism be profitable? Here my answer is "yes." Every social movement is a mixed bag of threats and opportunities. As John Gardner observed, "We are all continually faced with a series of great opportunities brilliantly disguised as insoluble problems." The companies that will profit from consumerism are those in the habit of turning negatives into positives. According to Peter F. Drucker:

> Consumerism actually should be, must be, and I hope will be, the opportunity of marketing. This is what we in marketing have been waiting for.[4]

The alert company will see consumerism as a new basis for achieving a differential competitive advantage in the marketplace. A concern for consumer well-being can be turned into a profitable opportunity in at least two ways: through the introduction of needed new products and through the adoption of a company wide consumerist orientation.

---

[4] Ibid., p. 64.

NEW OPPORTUNITIES

One of the main effects of consumerism is to raise concerns about the health, safety, and social worthiness of many products. For a long time, *salutary criteria* have been secondary to *immediate satisfaction criteria* in the selection of products and brands. Thus when Ford tried to sell safety as an automobile attribute in the 1950s, buyers did not respond. Most manufacturers took the position that they could not educate the public to want salutary features but if the public showed this concern, then business would respond.

Unfortunately, the time came but business was slow to respond. Consumer needs and wants have been evolving toward safety, health, and self-actualization concerns without many businessmen noticing this. More and more people are concerned with the nutritiousness of their foods, the flammability of their fabrics, the safety of their automobiles, and the pollution quality of their detergents. Many manufacturers have missed this changing psychological orientation of consumers.

Product reformulations

Today, there are a great many opportunities for creating and marketing new products that meet consumer desires for both short-term satisfaction and long-term benefits.

Exhibit II suggests a paradigm for thinking about the major types of new product opportunities. All current products can be classified in one of four ways using the dimensions of immediate satisfaction and long-run consumer interests. As this exhibit shows, *desirable products* are those which combine high immediate satisfaction and high long-run benefit, such as tasty, nutritious breakfast foods. *Pleasing products* are those which give high immediate satisfaction but which may hurt consumer interests in the long run, such as cigarettes. *Salutary products* are those which have low appeal but which are also highly beneficial to the consumer in the long run, such as low phosphate detergents. Finally, *deficient products* are those which have neither immediate appeal nor salutary qualities, such as a bad tasting patent medicine.

The manufacturer might as well forget about deficient products because too much work would be required to build in pleasing and salutary qualities. On the other hand, the manufacturer should invest his greatest effort in developing desirable products—e.g., new foods, textiles, appliances, and building materials—which combine intrinsic appeal and long-run beneficiality. The other two categories, pleasing and salutary products, also present a considerable challenge and opportunity to the company.

The challenge posed by pleasing products is that they sell extremely

EXHIBIT II.
Classification of new product opportunities

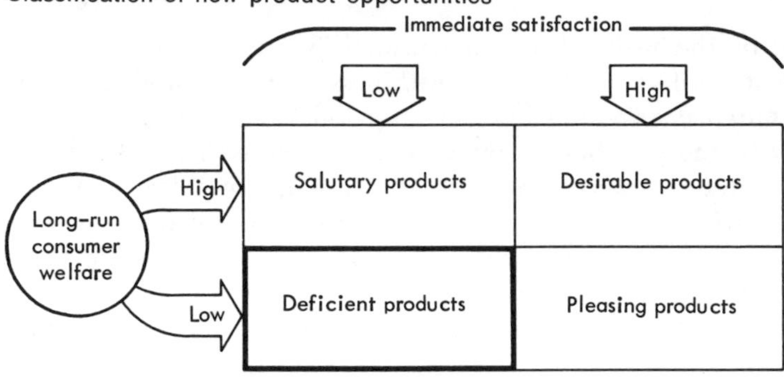

well but they ultimately hurt the consumer's interests. The product opportunity is therefore to formulate some alteration of the product that adds salutary qualities without diminishing any or too many of the pleasing qualities. This type of product opportunity has already been seized by a number of companies:

Sears has developed and promoted a phosphate-free laundry detergent which has become a big selling brand.

American Oil and Mobil Oil have developed and promoted no-lead or low-lead gasolines.

Pepsi-Cola has developed a one-way plastic soft drink bottle that is degradable in solid waste treatment.

Various automobile manufacturers are redesigning their engines to reduce their polluting levels without reducing their efficiency.

Various tobacco firms are researching the use of lettuce leaf to eliminate the health hazards of tobacco leaf in cigarettes.

Not all of these product reformulations will be successful. The new product must incorporate the salutary qualities without sacrificing the pleasing qualities. Thus new low-phosphate detergents must continue to wash effectively, or almost as effectively, as the former high-phosphate detergents. New low-lead or no-lead gasolines must continue to give efficient mileage and performance.

In addition, the company must be skilled at marketing the new products. The company faces difficult questions of what price to set, what claims to make, and what to do with the former product. In the case of low-lead gasoline, initial sales have been disappointing because of several factors, not the least of which is that it was priced at a premium and discouraged all but the most devoted environmentalists from buying it. The environmental appeal is strong, provided that the new product performs about as well as the old product and is not priced higher.

Salutary products, such as noninflammable draperies and many health foods, are considered "good for the customer" but somehow lack pleasing qualities. The challenge to the marketer is to incorporate satisfying qualities in the product without sacrificing the salutary qualities. Here are examples:

Quaker Oats has been reviewing desirable nutrients and vitamins, and formulating new breakfast cereals around them.

Some food manufacturers have created new soybean-based products, in each case adding pleasing flavors that appeal to the intended target groups.

Fabric manufacturers are trying to create attractive draperies out of new synthetic noninflammable materials.

Thus new product opportunities may be found by starting with appealing products and trying to add salutary qualities, or starting with salutary products and trying to add appealing qualities. This will become more important as more people show a concern for their environment and demand desirable products. There is already a sizable market segment made up of environmentalists who are ready to buy any product that has a salutary stamp. The alert company can even specialize in this market by committing itself to creating and assorting products of high environmental appeal.

Consumerist orientation

A second way to respond profitably to consumerism is to become one of a growing number of companies that adopt and implement a thoroughgoing concern-for-the-consumer attitude. This goes beyond the occasional introduction of a few new products that combine pleasing and salutary qualities. It goes beyond an enlarged public relations campaign to appear as a "we care" company. To be effective, it involves management commitment, employee education, social actions, and company investment. A few companies have moved into a total consumerist orientation and have earned high consumer regard in the process. Here are two illustrative examples:

Giant Food, Inc., a leading supermarket chain in the Washington, D.C. area, actively introduced unit pricing, open dating, and nutritional labeling. According to a spokesman for the company. "These actions have improved Giant's goodwill immeasurably and have earned the admiration of leaders of the consumer movement."

Whirlpool Corporation has adopted a large number of measures to improve customer information and services, including a toll-free complaint service and improved product warranties. According to Stephen E. Upton, Whirlpool Vice President, "Our rate of increase in sales has tripled that of the industry. Our interest in the consumer has to be one of the reasons."

Obviously, such companies believe that these measures will increase their consumer goodwill and lead in turn to increased profits. The companies in each industry that adopt a consumerist orientation are likely to earn the early advantage and reap the rewards. If the profits are forthcoming, others will rush in and imitate the innovators. But imitation is often not as effective as innovation. Consumerism may well turn out to be an opportunity for the leaders and a cost for the laggards.

CONCLUSION

Consumerism was born for the third time in this century in the middle 1960s as a result of a complex combination of circumstances, not the least of which was increasingly strained relations between current business practices and long-run consumer interests. To many businessmen, it came as a shock because they thought the economic machinery, creating the highest standard of living in the world, was beyond consumer complaint. But the movement was inevitable, partly because of the success of the economic machinery in creating complex, convenient, and pleasing products.

My assessment is that consumerism will be enduring, beneficial, pro-marketing, and ultimately profitable. Consumerism mobilizes the energies of consumers, businessmen, and government leaders to seek solutions to several complex problems in a technologically advanced society. One of these is the difference between serving consumer desires efficiently and serving their long-run interests.

To marketers, it says that products and marketing practices must be found which combine short-run and long-run values for the consumer. It says that a societal marketing concept is an advance over the original marketing concept and a basis for earning increased consumer goodwill and profits. The enlightened marketer attempts to satisfy the consumer *and* enhance his total well-being on the theory that what is good in the long run for consumers is good for business.

What does the consumerism movement mean to the business executive? Who will pay the price for consumerism? How can the socially responsible businessman react to the growing challenge of the consumer movement? The authors attempt to provide an answer to these questions by studying the causes and development of consumerism. They conclude by offering guidelines for corporate policy.

10. CONSUMERISM—AN INTERPRETATION*

Richard H. Buskirk†
and
James T. Rothe‡

Consumerism has received much attention in recent business literature.[1] Most articles and editorials dealing with the topic have commented on its importance, its underlying causes, its implications, or what interested parties (consumer, government, firms) should do, but most discussions have failed to deal with the topic in a total sense. This article attempts to (1) determine what consumerism is, (2) reveal what has caused it, (3) study its implications and potential dangers, and (4) develop guidelines for corporate policy in dealing with consumerism.

Peter Drucker offers the following definition of consumerism: "Consumerism means that the consumer looks upon the manufacturer as somebody who is interested but who really does not know what the consumers' realities are. He regards the manufacturer as somebody who has not made the effort to find out, who does not understand the world in which the consumer lives, and who expects the consumer to be able to make distinctions which the consumer is neither willing nor able to make."[2]

Another definition of consumerism has been developed by Mrs. Virginia H. Knauer, special assistant to the President for Consumer Affairs. She stated that the watchword for the new militant mood among American consumers is simply, "Let the seller beware," in comparison to the age-old *caveat emptor* or, "Let the buyer beware."[3]

Both of these definitions provide some insight into this current phenomenon referred to as *consumerism.* Perhaps it would be most relevant to relate consumerism to what has been popularly accepted as the marketing concept for the past 20 years. The marketing concept, simply

* Reprinted from "Consumerism—An Interpretation," *Journal of Marketing,* Vol. 34 (October 1970), pp. 61–65.

† California State College, Fullerton.

‡ University of Colorado.

[1] "Business Responds to Consumerism," *Business Week,* Vol. 2088 (September 6, 1969), pp. 94–108. "And Now, a Message From the Consumers," *Fortune,* Vol. 80 (November 1969), p. 103. "Buckpassing Blues," *Wall Street Journal,* Vol. CLXXIV (November 3, 1969).

[2] Peter Drucker, "Consumerism in Marketing," a speech to the National Association of Manufacturers, New York, April 1969.

[3] "The Consumer Revolution," *U.S. News & World Report,* Vol. LXVII (August 25, 1969), pp. 43–46.

stated, suggests that the purpose of a business is to provide customer satisfaction. Thus, it is anticipated that the firm will maximize long-term profitability through customer orientation. The marketing concept is primarily a post-World War II development, produced largely by economic conditions which changed a seller's market to a buyer's market. The marketing concept was hailed as being the essential fulcrum with which business resources could be allocated to best enhance profitability for the firm in a buyer's market. Consequently, much has been written and said about the marketing concept—how it can be utilized and what it means. However, the marketing concept and the forces labeled *consumerism* are incompatible. If consumerism exists, the marketing concept has not worked. It may be that consumerism actually is the result of prostitution of the marketing concept, rather than a malfunction of it.

Examples of customer dissatisfaction are not difficult to find. For example, a recent article in *The Wall Street Journal* noted that roofs leak, shirts shrink, toys maim, mowers do not mow, kites do not fly, television sets burn up, service is difficult or impossible to obtain, and warranties are not honored.[4]

Certainly each of us, as a consumer, has experienced the cumulative frustration associated with products that do not conform to expectations. It is this sense of frustration and bitterness on the part of consumers who have been promised much and have realized less, that may properly be called the driving force behind consumerism. Accordingly, consumerism is defined as *the organized efforts of consumers seeking redress, restitution and remedy for dissatisfaction they have accumulated in the acquisition of their standard of living.*

CAUSE OF CONSUMERISM

There are two major opposing theories about the role of the consumer in the market place of a free enterprise system. One theory suggests that the consumer is "king." It is his dollar choice in the market which decides success or failure of producers; consequently, the consumer plays a decisive role in the entire process. This concept is referred to as "consumer sovereignty."

A completely opposite approach suggests that the consumer is a pawn in the entire process. The brilliance of Madison Avenue, sparked by research conducted by skilled behavioral scientists, has been used to deceive the consumer to the extent that he is incapable of intelligent selection. His dollar vote does not come across in any rational manner to decide who should be producing what; consequently, the consumer is not playing a decisive role in the process.

According to the marketing concept, the first of these two theoretical

[4] "Caveat Emptor," *The Wall Street Journal,* Vol. CLXXIII (June 26, 1969), p. 1.

approaches would be correct: the consumer is viewed as the dominant force since his purchases determine market success for competing firms.

There is some truth in both theories. This can best be explained by relating purchase behavior to the type of product purchased. When consideration is given to the importance of the product purchased, the frequency of the purchase, and the information sources used, both theories are partially correct. For example, if a product is purchased frequently, the consumer has an outstanding information source—his previous experience with it. In such a situation he is capable of judging the product's effectiveness and how well it has lived up to his expectations, both physically and psychologically. Thus, the consumer is capable of exhibiting more rational behavior when buying frequently purchased products than when acquiring "once-in-a-lifetime" items. Collective consumer behavior of this type results in the market process being served appropriately. Competition for the consumer's choice is then the determinant which leads to congruity between perceived and received quality on the part of the buyers. This is, in essence, a fulfillment of the marketing concept and accurately reflects a situation in which the consumer plays a major role in deciding who is successful in the market place.

On the other hand, the situation in which the consumer purchases a product he has not bought before (or at best, infrequently) and which is of sufficient importance, often finds his attempt at rational behavior stymied by the lack of information. Since he has not previously purchased this product, his own experience is negligible. Another possible source of information is his peer group, but the limited accuracy of this type of information reduces its role in the transaction. Also, independent concerns' ratings of products are not widely used. This leaves the consumer with a basic information source—the company's marketing program. Evidently many marketing programs are not providing the information necessary for rational purchase behavior. This may be the result of short-term orientation on the part of management whose performance is judged on an annual basis. Top management's insistence on quarterly and annual budgeting performance may force operational management to make short-run decisions detrimental to the consumer because the impact of such decisions will not be reflected during operational management's tenure in that position. Consequently, when a product revision is needed, the response may be increased advertising and promotion expenditures rather than the more appropriate effort.

CATALYSTS IN CONSUMERISM MOVEMENT

The current wave of consumerism is not unprecedented in the history of business.[5] However, this time consumerism is enhanced by several

[5] Stuart Chase and F. J. Schlink, *Your Money's Worth* (New York: The Macmillan Company, 1934).

major factors which were not evident in earlier expressions of consumerism. First, increased leisure time, rising incomes, higher educational levels, and general affluence have tended to magnify and intensify the forces of consumerism. The consumer's expectations with respect to the products he purchases are founded in a quest for individuality; yet, the market provides mass-consumption products with which the individual is not completely satisfied.

Second, inflation has made purchase behavior even more difficult. Rising prices have led consumers to increased quality expectations which are not achieved; thus, again contributing to the frustration of consumers.

Third, unemployment has been low. Therefore, the marginal laborer has been employed even though he has fewer skills. Such workers reduce output quality.

Fourth, demands for product improvement have led to increased product complexity. Further, this complexity has been stimulated by the emergence of new technology. This has led to increased service difficulties as well as performance and reliability problems. Moreover, society has been thoroughly conditioned to expect perfection from its technology. Moon landings, miracle drugs, organ transplants, and jet transportation make the housewife wonder why zipper manufacturers cannot make one that will not jam. The high degree of perfection that has been reached in recent years in a few fields only serves to disguise the higher *average* level of technical proficiency of present-day manufacturing. Yet, it is apparent that the consumer is demanding better products than those presently available, regardless of the economic and technical ability of the firm to provide it.

Finally, the popular success achieved by individuals such as Ralph Nader, in his crusade for consumerism, and the political support now developing for the forces of consumerism certainly reinforce the fact that this entire area must become a more important factor in business policy.

IMPLICATIONS OF CONSUMERISM

It seems apparent that consumerism will affect industries, firms, governments, and, if it is effective, the consuming public.

The consumerism movement will develop more power as its forces become more coordinated and as it develops more leadership and organization. This will be partly manifested in legal remedies, such as class suits, that the consumer will seek.

At present, it appears the success of consumerism will depend largely on governmental involvement, the beginnings of which are already evident. For example, truth in lending, truth in packaging, product safety standards, and other recent legislative efforts, as well as a great number of consumer protection and awareness bills, indicate that the role of government will be much greater. (Over 100 "consumer protection" bills have already been introduced in the 91st Congress since January 1969.)[6]

The role of the federal government in consumerism was first set forth by President John F. Kennedy's directive to the Consumer Advisory Council in March of 1962. He said:

> Additional legislative and administrative action is required, however, if the federal government is to meet its responsibility to consumers in the exercise of their rights. These rights include: (1) the right to safety; (2) the right to be informed; (3) the right to choose; and (4) the right to be heard.[7]

It is apparent that the right to be informed, as well as the right to be heard, is of major importance. In fact, if all consumers were informed and were heard, this would then represent the fulfillment of the marketing concept as it was initially developed. The responsibility President Kennedy mentioned above should be industry's in a free society, not the government's. However, consumerism rightly claims industry has neglected its responsibility.

The relative role the government will play, and that which industry should play, is a critical aspect in the resolution of the consumerism issue. Given industry's traditional negative or complacent reaction to such issues, the result may be a coalition of consumer and government forces versus industry, which could lead to federal standards for industry. The resulting standardization and bureaucracy may stifle the economic process. It is imperative that industry recognize the message and seriousness of the consumer movement and take positive action *now* rather than having to live with legislation that may not be in the long-run best interest of society.

The basic premise is that consumerism is primarily the result of a lack of information on the part of consumers which hinders their ability to buy certain products. This reflects itself in an ever-increasing gap between product expectations and product performance. Moreover, consumers must be heard, which indicates the need for an industry or company *ombudsman*. An excellent example of the *ombudsman* concept in action is that of the Whirlpool Corporation which has established a "cool line." The "cool line" enables owners to call the customer service director at all times.[8] A direct communication contact of this nature will greatly enhance consumer-company relationships; it represents the first step toward solution of owner problems.

---

[6] "The Rush to Help Consumers," *U.S. News & World Report,* Vol. LXVII (August 25, 1969), p. 47.

[7] *Consumer Advisory Council, First Report,* Executive Office of the President (Washington, D.C.: United States Government Printing Office, October 1963), pp. 5–8.

[8] "Appliance Maker Comes Clean," *Business Week,* Vol. 2088 (September 6, 1969), p. 100.

The owner problem is not fraudulent or deceptive practices for the most part; rather, the problem is improper or nonexistent communication. This seems to be incongruous since communication efforts—primarily advertising—exist in great abundance. However, communications between the firm and the consumer emphasize *imagery* at the expense of *information.*

Consumerism is attempting to tell industry something their research has not found, or that management has rejected or ignored. Appropriate information flow from the firm to the market in the form of product performance characteristics, simple-language warranty specifications, and safety standards will improve the basic customer-firm relationship, particularly for the infrequently purchased item where long, low service life is a major objective of the consumer. Product performance characteristics must be improved for competitive success if communication is predicated on an information basis. Thus, the poor product quality problem will be largely eliminated.

The other link in this communication structure, that of the consumer to the firm, should be explored. It is imperative that some mechanism be developed which will enable the consumer to communicate more directly with management. The consumer *does* have something to say, but management must learn to listen and translate this information into action.

FALLOUT FROM CONSUMERISM—LOCUS OF LIABILITY

While it is easy for consumers' advocates to talk about "class suits" against manufacturers, it is not completely clear how these would work. If consumers as a group were damaged by an automobile made by General Motors, then General Motors would be the defendant in the class suit, and if it lost the case there would be some hope of collecting the resulting judgment.

But let us examine several other cases. Suppose consumers are damaged by an automobile produced by a small foreign automobile manufacturer. Who would be sued if the parent corporation did not do business in the United States, but rather operated through an independent agent, a corporate front set up to absorb such liabilities?

What about situations in which the manufacturer of a product is not apparent? Suppose a sales agency imports a product made by an unknown manufacturer. The sales agent takes the product and sells it. Later, a class suit is levied against the sales agent, who has taken care to have his corporate entity contain few assets.

It would seem that if class suits became a great risk businessmen would take steps to limit their personal liability and leave successful plaintiffs with judgments against nothing. Class suits strongly discriminate against the large, reputable American manufacturers to the benefit of the fly-by-night operator who is, from a practical standpoint, beyond the reach of such judgments. It is conceivable that a successful class suit against a significant U.S. corporation could bankrupt it. Who would benefit from such a development—competitors or consumers? Is this legal situation in the consumer's best interests? It is doubtful. Clearly, the class suit must be examined closely by all parties before being used.

WHO PAYS THE PRICE?

State and federal governments now pay more than half the cost of a class suit, because the defense costs and judgments are legitimate business expenses. The remainder comes from earnings. The economic facts of life indicate that if class suits and other costs of consumerism become a fact of corporate life, then management will have to budget for such costs because those costs must be covered by the price obtained for the products the company sells. The result of imposing more stringent legal and quality control regulations on industry will be to raise prices. This should not be underestimated. Evidence from the space industry indicates that the marginal costs of increased quality are high. The consumer has been conditioned to expect perfection from technology but not to the price this perfection costs.

A valid question can be asked concerning the economic wisdom of consumerism: Is it socially wiser to accept the present market-determined rate of consumer dissatisfaction than to pay the marginal costs that will be incurred in reducing consumer dissatisfaction by government decree? Is the market willing to pay for these consumer recommendations? It may not be.

Only the well-established, reputable firm that fully intends to meet its costs and obligations under consumerism would be forced to raise its prices. Again, fly-by-night operators who are beyond the reach of the law from a practical standpoint would not have to include the costs of consumerism in their prices; therefore, such operators may become competitively stronger if consumers fail to discriminate between the reputable firm and the fly-by-night operation. Further, this problem will become increasingly acute in private label situations where the producing firm is unknown.

GUIDELINES FOR CORPORATE POLICY

Consumerism is here, and businesses should respond thoughtfully and rationally to the issues rather than react negatively or not at all. Several guidelines are developed below which businesses should follow in their response to consumerism.

Establish a separate corporate division for consumer affairs. This division would participate in all corporate decisions that have consumer implications. It would participate in research and design, advertising, credit, pricing, quality assurance, and other similar decisions.

It would respond to all consumer inquiries and complaints and would have the authority to make appropriate adjustments.

It would be responsible for the development and dissemination of factual product and service information.

It would work with industry or trade associations in the development of a consumer education program.

The division must be given the status and power necessary for it to fulfill its mission. It should not be placed in a position in which either marketing or production forces could dilute its effectiveness. Possibly the wisdom of placing all quality assurance programs in this division should be carefully examined.

Change corporate practices that are perceived as deceptive. The consumer affairs division should identify corporate practices that are perceived as deceptive and/or antagonistic by consumers. These practices should be reviewed and a viable resolution of the problem developed. Examples of such corporate practices include packaging, credit, advertising, warranties, and the like.

Educate channel members to the need for a consumerism effort throughout the channel system. Recognition of the need for a consumerism effort by all members of the channel will aid in the development of an industry consumerism program which will enhance performance of the channel system and provide better customer satisfaction. Moreover, a firm must be willing to eliminate an organization from its overall channel system if that organization is unwilling or unable to work within the constraints of corporate policy.

Incorporate the increased costs of consumerism efforts into the corporate operating budget. Unless the consumer affairs division is budgeted sufficient money to carry out its mission, it will be little more than a facade and its effectiveness will be hampered. These costs will be reflected either in higher prices or lower margins unless the consumer program affects sales sufficiently to lower costs commensurately. To date little or no research exists to document the market responses to such programs. However, it does seem apparent that substantial costs will be incurred by firms not meeting their responsibilities to the consumer because of both governmental and legal actions.

An analysis of the above guidelines suggests that an effective consumerism program will be directed primarily at the communications problem between firms and consumers. The main purpose of the consumerism program will be to enhance the quality of communications between the consumer and the firm and to incorporate valid complaints into corporate decisions.

The corporate leader has two basic options: He may take positive action in this matter, or he may ignore it. If he ignores it, he must be prepared for a government program. It would seem that the corporate decision maker should prefer to develop a consumerism program of his own. The alternative course of action, with its attendant governmental regulation and bureaucracy, would not be in the best interest of either the consumer or the firm because of its impact upon competition, prices, and consumer satisfaction.

The time has come for marketers to replace the outmoded and unequal principle of "caveat emptor" with the more equitable rule of "doceatur emptor"—let the buyer be informed. Many businessmen view the increasing demands of the consumerism movement as resulting in only more regulation and more problems. But the perceptive marketer should be able to analyze this new thrust as presenting expanded business opportunities for his firm as well as an opportunity to enhance our social and physical environment.

---

11. NEW OPPORTUNITIES IN CONSUMERISM*

E. Patrick McGuire†

"Sue the bastards" is said to be the credo of 29-year-old consumer advocate John H. Banzhaf, III. Banzhaf will be remembered as the young attorney who toppled tobacco advertising from the nation's airwaves. While Banzhaf, along with consumer stalwarts such as Ralph Nader, might be considered by some as "extreme" in their approach, there is impressive evidence that consumer activism has achieved a broad base of popular support. And consumer advocates are receiving comfort and assistance from an increasing number of private and governmental agencies.

At The Conference Board's recent Marketing Conference, spokesmen even for such nonlitigious groups as Consumers Union of the United States, Inc., indicate that they expect to enter the courts to allay consumer grievances.

"We can, we have, and we will use the courts to force government

---

* Reprinted from "New Opportunities in Consumerism," *Conference Board Record* (December 1970), pp. 41–43.

† Conference Board.

and business to act responsibly," stated Consumers Union's Washington representative David A. Swankin.

Consumer militancy seems to well up from a broad stratum of marketplace inadequacies. Buyers are concerned over premature product failures, useless warranties, and advertising claims that subtly distort product attributes. Many consumers are comparing notes and what they find is disturbing them.

"For years," noted New York State's Consumer Protection Director Betty Furness, "we were so delighted and overwhelmed with the fruits of the industrial revolution that we approached every consumer problem on the defensive. It took a while to discover that a sick appliance was a universal experience rather than an individual operation." Furness went on to point out, "There is no longer that easy acceptance of corporate reliability. Consumers are growing more and more suspicious and more and more questioning. The myth that just because a product is on the market means that it has been tested and proven to be safe has been exploded."

The plain fact is that many consumers, perhaps a majority, do not believe that the marketplace is being operated for their benefit. Edward L. Bond, Jr., chairman of Young & Rubicam, Inc., pointed out that a 1969 study by Opinion Research Corporation revealed that fully 68 percent of Americans feel that new consumer protection laws are vitally needed. Of a similar group tested only two years earlier, only 55 percent felt the need for such corrective legislation.

In part, consumer frustration arises from what some consumers regard as a one-sidedness in the marketplace. They feel powerless to communicate their frustrations and anxieties to manufacturers. Some feel as if no one at all is listening. "Consumers want to be taken seriously," Federal Trade Commissioner Mary Gardiner Jones reminded businessmen. "They do not want to be treated as if they have a mentality of twelve, concerned only about romance, social status, interpersonal success and the acquisition of material well-being. They do not want to be solely dependent upon the goodwill and honesty of the merchants and manufacturers with whom they deal."

Many consumer advocates believe that business could do a much better job of listening to its customers and caring about their problems. "It's extremely difficult," Furness noted, "for a corporate entity to take the cotton out of its ears."

PERFORMANCE RESPONSIBILITIES

At the root of many consumer complaints is the simple fact that the product purchased either is not as it was advertised or has broken down and represents a vexing repair problem. When a manufacturer brings a product to the marketplace, and subsequently advertises and describes its features to an interested public, he *implies* that the product is suitable for the use intended. In order to assure the prospective buyer, who is perhaps worried because of previous experiences, the manufacturer *warrants* that the product will perform in a specified manner for a stated period of time.

However, as Professor Corwin D. Edwards of the University of Oregon suggested, "No matter how well a product is designed or how carefully it is made, some end products will still be defective and the frequency of such defects is likely to increase with the complexity of the design and the number of parts." Thus, it is inevitable that products will require adjustments, repairs, and in some cases replacement. But some observers believe that manufacturers may be focusing entirely on in-plant quality controls while ignoring out-of-plant product service requirements. Instead, the manufacturer may push off service requirements on a dealer organization that is ill-equipped or motivated to perform such service.

Manufacturers may also be underestimating the ingenuity of consumers in misusing their products. This miscalculation is especially evident in the field of product safety. Swankin noted that "the product must be adapted to the idiosyncrasies of the consumer to whatever extent is feasible. If people *will* stand on the shelf of a ladder, it should be made strong enough to support them. Autos should be made with the certain knowledge that people will drive them into objects and into each other."

Some panelists felt that manufacturers compound their consumer relations problems by not providing sufficient information on how to use their products. Consumers approach the purchase of a new product with open-ended expectation levels. They may have only a vague idea of how long the product should last and are often uninformed about the limits of product use and necessary maintenance.

The danger to the business community comes not from the well-informed buyer; quite the opposite. "The danger to business," Secretary of Commerce Maurice H. Stans pointed out, "is the *uninformed* consumer whose rage is directed at all business when he discovers that he has bought a third-rate product that does not measure up and may be backed by a warranty which promises much in the big print and takes it away in the fine print. This person is business' worst enemy and can hardly be expected to applaud the system."

A CHANCE FOR RELIEF

Both industry and government officials agree that the consumer must be better informed about the products he purchases and uses. Traditionally, the government, through various elements of the public education system, has been vested with the responsibility for consumer education. But the magnitude and complexity of the task makes it unlikely that the educational establishment alone can accomplish this feat. "We've got to get consumer education into public education on a required basis," Whirlpool Corporation Chairman Elisha Gray, II, stated. "We've also got to help educators develop useful consumer education courses, because only business has both the practical experience and resources needed to do this."

It would appear that if industry is unable—or unwilling—to provide the consumer with sufficient product information, it may discover government taking a much more aggressive role in closing the information gap. Stans said that it is time for marketers to replace the outmoded and unequal principle of *caveat emptor* with the more equitable rule of *doceatur emptor*—let the buyer be informed.

Some panel members felt that industry may well be facing its last opportunity for self-regulation. Steven L. Osterweis, president of Associated Merchandising Corporation, noted that self-regulation is certainly in the long-range self-interest of industry, but acknowledged that in some fields such regulation is extremely difficult. For example, Osterweis said, "Voluntary regulation in the area of public interest (pollution abatement, etc.) does not seem reasonable to expect." Where environmental or general public interest considerations are involved Osterweis believes that "self-interest would be best served by working with government to achieve the prompt development of appropriate statutory or regulatory limitations."

Certain kinds of self-regulation are also inhibited by the very nature of the modern business corporation. The structure of the corporation, according to Osterweis, places many operating executives in a position where they must be primarily concerned with short-term product objectives rather than the long-range economic implications inherent in their decision-making powers.

Industry self-regulation, because of previously less-than-successful examples, comes under questioning scrutiny by legislators and media alike. Many businessmen, like Osterweis, also feel that self-regulation, particularly in the public interest sector, is difficult to obtain. Arjay Miller, dean of Stanford's School of Business, reminded his audience that "the costs of meeting society's demands for clean air and clean water are so great that any individual company acting unilaterally puts itself at an extreme cost disadvantage with its competition. For any program to be fully effective, compliance must not be a matter of option."

ACTION AND REACTION

The thesis that consumerism can be a valid and useful movement will find few opponents among the responsible business community. There are some, however, who are concerned over possible excesses that could ultimately prove self-defeating. Stans warned that "all of us have seen various movements or causes go overboard, and in the long run have the very opposite effect from that intended."

There is some fear that the fires of the consumer movement may generate more smoke than light. "Attacking is not solving," Bond commented, "and complaining is not thinking. Ridiculing is not reasoning." Simplistic consumer solutions, it was said, have great appeal but the realities are such that these remedies seldom possess enough muscle and depth to resolve the problems.

During the next several years businessmen may discover that it is not enough to simply adhere to the *letter* of the law if in the process they violate the *spirit* of the law. For example, Robert S. Marker, president of McCann-Erickson, Inc., pointed out that certain "legal clearances," which might be provided by the networks, ad agencies, or client's legal staff, are "worthless" if the advertising message is not telling the consumer what he needs to know about the product. Marker felt that most consumers "search for honest merchants, but there are not enough around." If some advertisers do not become more responsive to consumer information needs, and government agencies thus accelerate their regulatory intervention, ad agencies could become so "citation-shy" that they would lose much of the creative spark which has been a major factor in the successful launching of a parade of new products.

Consumerism is a movement of economic interdependence, as noted by Furness. "None of us can survive without the other. We're locked together in a remarkable struggle. The outcome may depend on just how honest we can learn to be with each other, and that may be the real consumer revolution."

There is abundant evidence that businessmen, if somewhat late in first appreciating consumerism's implications, are now awakening to the promise and perils of aroused consumers. Several panelists described newly created "consumer advisor" positions within their own and other corporate structures. Some have created unique consumer communication systems, such as Whirlpool Corporation's "Cool-Line"—a nationwide toll-free telephone system that allows Whirlpool customers to speak directly to factory-based customer service representatives. Gray, in relating the success of the Whirlpool innovation, declared that the communications device is one of the "single best marketing mechanisms we have ever encountered."

But most of all, businessmen are approaching the consumer with a changed attitude. Keynote speaker Lee A. Iacocca, president of Ford Motor's North American Automotive Operations, best summed it up by stating that "consumers in a complicated world do need a lot of protection, but more and more they are also going to want their money's worth. As businessmen, unless you're thinking of early retirement, you and I better see that they get it!"

b.

Responses and implications

An educator discusses appropriate responses to the consumerism issue by describing his perceptions concerning the social responsibility of the advertising industry. Ignoring the consumerism movement will not reduce its pressure on business. What is in store for consumerism during the coming decade? The executive's response, or lack of it, to these coming pressures may indicate the degree of governmental involvement in our competitive system.

12. RESPONDING TO CONSUMERISM*

David S. R. Leighton†

Professor Robert Holloway has pointed out that the responses one prescribes for consumerism depend on your diagnosis of the causes. He listed the causes of consumerism as politics, technology, population, affluence, and the failure of the business system itself. And these are clearly all factors of considerable importance in explaining the growth of consumerism.

From the outset, we have a paradox. The growing, more insistent voice of consumers has been largely a product of the decade of the 60s, a decade of unparalleled growth of prosperity in most of the coun-

* Reprinted from "Responding to Consumerism," *Distinguished Lectures in Marketing Series,* York University.

† Banff School of Fine Arts and Centre for Continuing Education.

tries of the Western world. I remember standing on a platform in this city 12 years ago, one of a panel on the outlook for the "Soaring Sixties." All of us on the panel pointed to the nirvana that lay ahead, with rising population, education, leisure time, affluence, and the like. Not one foresaw the growth of the consumer movement that is so strong today. And anyone who might have predicted it would have been hooted off the stage. We just didn't expect to have protest in the midst of plenty.

A second factor. The consumer movement is by no means exclusively confined to Canada, not even to North America. It is a tidal wave, sweeping the Western world. It has swept through Britain, through France, through Scandinavia, through Holland. Two years ago, I was in Israel, which was then as now in the shadow of Arab guns. And the chief topic of conversation among businessmen there was not the Six-Day War, or the threat of the Fedayeen, but the proposed new Consumer Protection Law.

CAUSES OF CONSUMERISM

A movement as widespread as this must clearly have deep roots. Consumerism is not something dreamed up by politicians as a ready means of picking up votes, although the politicians have been much quicker to sense the public mood than have businessmen, and many have successfully ridden the wave. It is not something promoted by a bunch of woolly-headed, antibusiness academics who haven't anything better to do with their time. And it is not something that comes from a few upper middle-class, do-gooder ladies who don't understand the complexities of the modern business world. This movement is something else again.

It would be a great mistake to think that consumerism will, if left to itself, quietly go away. For better or worse, conditions have changed for keeps. The cause of consumerism is merely one manifestation of the social unrest that has burst upon us in the last half decade. It is no coincidence that consumerism has emerged at the same time as separatism, racial unrest, women's liberation, and a host of other revolutionary movements. Their roots are the same: In its own way, consumerism too is a revolutionary movement. It is not understood by reading Consumer Reports or Vance Packard, but by reading Herbert Marcuse and Rap Brown.

Not only is the consumerism movement a manifestation of the basic social malaise that permeates our society, but there are factors within the consumer movement itself that seem certain to maintain the momentum and propel us far beyond the traditional confines of consumer concern. I would like to return to this point later in my paper.

In examining the causes of consumerism, one must go back to the market system itself. The market system, according to the theory, is one in which the free interplay of consumer choices will result, over time, in the best product or service winning out in the competitive struggle for the consumer's favor. In this battle, the producer who best meets the needs of the consumer will be rewarded with success, and the producer of inferior goods will lose out. The consumer casts his ballot in the form of his purchases, and the seller woos his vote by improving his products or services by attractive packaging, by offering more value for money.

Some observers of our economic system, notably Karl Polanyi in his book *The Great Transformation,* have pointed out that the free market system, as we know it, has been in a long period of decline for virtually all of this century—that free enterprise reached its peak in terms of unrestrained freedom for the seller at about the turn of the century, and that the period of long decline set in with the passage of the Sherman Antitrust Act and parallel measures in Canada. In this view, the history of this century has been one of constant erosion of business' powers.

This marketing system as developed in the United States and in Canada is still the envy of the world. The drive and initiative released by this system of distribution has without any doubt been one of the principal factors that have given the United States its preeminence in standard of living. The system has been honed to a fine edge by developments in marketing research, in marketing organization, new product development, and communication methods. All this is recognized by even the most militant critics of the system. But this system, magnificent as it has been in terms of economic performance, has not been without its faults. It has, the critics point out, led to an overemphasis on material values and hence has contributed to the hollowness and emptiness of much of life today. In our disillusionment with nirvana, we have turned against the system that brought us there.

Others have said that this system, effective as it is in raising the overall standard of living, has not only failed to solve the problem of disparities in living standards, it has in fact accentuated it. In our world of middle-class affluence, in our trumpeting of material values, we have made life increasingly intolerable for the weak and the castoffs of the social system. The fittest have indeed survived, but so have the weak. They have found it less and less possible to live on government handouts and welfare vouchers when a large part of the society around them is driving two cars. They have found it harder just to exist in a society where the powerful and the organized, in both labour and business, have used market power to increase their share of the national pie at the expense of those who have no means of organization and no power. They have found it increasingly difficult to live in a society which promotes prosperity by maintaining an annual increment in inflation for the principal benefit of those who are better organized to capitalize on such growth.

It is from here that the roots of today's consumerism spring—not from the May Court Club, the Junior League, and the Consumers Association. Nor from the politicians and the academics. What we are seeing is a revolt of the poor against a system that has been seen as passing them by, keeping them and others like them in perpetual bondage and dependence.

What is at stake here is nothing less than the market system itself. And in the battle that is shaping up for its preservation, the odds are heavily against the status quo, due to the appearance of one major new factor.

What is new in the picture is the entry of government into the marketing system, on the side of the consumer, in a really significant way. In this process, there is no turning back. It is not, in my opinion and contrary to Professor Holloway's, a matter of the pendulum swinging back and forth. It is, to use playwright N. B. Simpson's term, a one-way pendulum in which the freedom of business managers in the marketplace has been, and will continue to be, eroded.

In Canada, we have had since 1967 a federal Department of Consumer and Corporate Affairs with a minister of cabinet rank charged with representing the consumer interest at the highest political level. In three and a half years, this department has become one of the most active and vigorous proponents of new legislation in the entire federal government, and in the process has accumulated a large and competent staff. Does anyone really think that this body is somehow going to wither away when current legislation now in the pipeline is passed into law? In the United States, 1971 will almost certainly see the office of the Special Assistant to the President, currently occupied by Mrs. Virginia Knauer, become an independent consumer protection agency with statutory status. This bill, the spearhead of the consumer legislative thrust last year, lost out by the very narrowest of margins in the Congress, and many government officials are confidently predicting its passage into law in 1971. Once such a body exists in the United States, does anyone seriously predict a diminution in legislative activity at the federal level?

Indeed no. Everything we know from past history of such organizations leads one to conclude that while we may see consumer activity take a different direction, we will certainly not see it die down. Quite the contrary.

THE FUTURE OF CONSUMERISM

With the entry of governments into the field in a big way, we are seeing the beginning of a new phase. At the moment, these relatively new governmental bodies are busy trying to catch up with many of the traditional bêtes noires of the consumer groups—shoddy merchandise, hazardous products, phony advertising claims, high-pressure selling, credit disclosure, deceptive packaging. But it is my thesis that when these are cleaned up, we will see the organization built up to deal with these specific abuses shift its direction into hitherto unexplored aspects of the "quality of life." Indeed, many consumer activists will privately admit today that the increased pace of legislation of the last few years has left little room for further activity in the traditional areas. They are looking much wider afield. Some of these trends have started already: it requires no crystal ball to see the way things are developing.

I believe the next decade of consumerism will follow these lines:

1. We will see a renewed attack on big business, focused on obtaining consumer representation on corporate boards of directors. Ralph Nader and others have already made G.M. their target, and in the process have wrung significant concessions from the world's largest corporation in the face of what can only be described as incredibly inept opposition. Other boards will move into the gunsights, and will be pressured not only into appointing consumer representatives, but also more women, more blacks, more French-Canadians.

2. We will see a very strong pressure to exert more public control over such publicly-sanctioned monopolies as medical associations, legal societies, teachers' associations and others. Consumer representatives will demand a voice in the rate setting and professional standards committees of such bodies.

3. There will be a strong movement towards more active consumer representation in the collective bargaining process. Consumers are tired of being made the patsies for labour and management, and will insist that their voice be heard, directly or indirectly, through government representatives.

4. Government-sponsored marketing boards will also come under consumer scrutiny. Most such bodies are designed primarily with the producer interest in mind, and in some cases have resulted in the preservation of inefficient operations and high prices to consumers.

5. Government agencies themselves will increasingly come under the gun. Ralph Nader has already almost singlehandedly brought about a reorganization and revitalization of the Federal Trade Commission, and we can expect a vigorous program of action from this quarter in future.

6. Penalties against offenders, in the form of class action and treble damage provisions, will be substantially stiffened, and prosecution will be increasingly vigorous.

7. In Canada, there will be a strong movement away from virtually exclusive reliance on the criminal law, with its rigorous requirements for evidence, towards civil law and the creation of government tribunals with

considerable flexibility and injunctive powers. Such a tribunal has already been proposed for the regulation of competitive practices under the new Combines Law expected this year, and a great deal of the uproar over the new Packaging and Labelling Bill centers around the discretionary power which it gives to the federal government.

8. Consumer groups will increasingly focus their attention on broader issues that have traditionally been seen as being outside the sphere of consumer interests—fields like tariffs, pollution, poverty, and the welfare system, and, indeed, on the process of government itself.

In this sense, consumerism becomes a manifestation of "direct democracy" in action—a means of making the political system more responsive to the needs of all its members. Its movement into these broader areas is symptomatic of at least partial breakdown of our political system, in its inability to cope with the rapid changes of the last decade or two.

APPROPRIATE RESPONSES

If my diagnosis as to the causes of consumerism is correct, then the central challenge of consumerism to business is to help solve the problem of inequities in the distribution of wealth. For until this is done, the marketing system will remain under attack. And the longer the situation remains, the more the system will come under attack.

The facile solution is to redistribute wealth. But surely, after a half century or more of attempts to do just that, we have accumulated enough evidence to show that it won't work. Peter Drucker has said that we used to think that the problem was one of making the poor wealthy; we are beginning to realize that the challenge is to make the poor productive. Not only do our existing welfare schemes fail to make the poor productive, but in many respects they penalize their attempts to become productive.

The challenge of making the poor productive is a challenge for businessmen as well as for governments. For it is undeniably true that no system can exist for long when there are great disparities in the system. The world of the poor is another world, little understood by businessmen. There are instead two solitudes living side by side, but not communicating with each other. To solve the problem is an enormous task. It will not be solved in our generation, or even in the next. There may be no solution, but we must surely make the effort.

The appropriate response to consumerism must start with the individual. A manager without values, without a social conscience, without a personal philosophy of life on which he is prepared to stand, cannot complain when standards of conduct are imposed on him from without. An essential first step is to turn the mirror on oneself.

Organizations and systems create conflicts for the individual and his values. The pressure of meeting short-term profit or sales yardsticks can frequently pose a dilemma for the individual. Exclusive reliance on ROI or profitability yardsticks in evaluating performance forces individuals to cut corners to survive. The organization itself must clearly have something more in view than making the greatest possible ROI in the shortest possible time.

Much can be done within the firm itself. There are many firms today who have clearly spelled out their ideals and who sincerely attempt to live by them. Most are leaders in their industries.

Industry self-regulation is a further step. This is clearly preferable to legislation from a social point of view. While there are potential abuses, a self-regulated industry can eliminate abuses before they start, before there are victims. From a cost-benefit point of view, this approach should yield the greatest social benefit for the least cost. But bad actors will always exist, and self-regulatory bodies often become self-protective bodies, so there will always be a need for outside regulation.

Legislation is, almost by definition, unwieldy and inflexible. The good get swept up in the net along with the bad. It is expensive and cumbersome, and its administration may create more inequities than it was intended to solve. Nevertheless, the responsible businessman must realize that there must be some regulation, and should work to support soundly based regulation and oppose that which is not. He should not get caught in the trap of blindly opposing all regulation, as many do.

In discussing appropriate responses to consumerism, I would like to take as an example one specific industry, as more meaningful than a lot of moral generalizations, that we all can either accept too readily or shrug off as easily. I would like to discuss the responses made by the Canadian advertising industry.

This is an industry I know very well. I once worked, albeit very briefly, for Canada's largest agency. I have consulted with many of the leading advertisers, agencies, and media. I have taught a course on advertising. And I have the greatest respect for the potential of advertising in making our economy function as it should. In my view, what we need in this country is not less advertising, but less *bad* advertising.

I say all this because I do not want my remarks to be misconstrued. I come as a friend of advertising, but as one who is sincerely and deeply concerned about its future. For I believe that the advertising industry in this country is in trouble, and I think that its troubles from consumerism are just beginning.

In many ways, I think the advertising industry is being made the whipping boy for the faults of the entire marketing system. And while this may be unfair, it should not surprise us in view of the pervasive and intrusive nature of advertising; almost by definition, we are all experts on advertising, and it is an obvious first target for someone with a gripe against the system.

I would like to make my argument in a series of very simple propositions:

1. I submit that advertising and marketing in any free exchange system are based on the faith and trust of the consumer. That is, the consumer must be able to assume that he will get what he has paid for, and that it will do what the seller says it will do. Otherwise, the system breaks down.

2. From both direct conversation with a large number of consumer groups, and from surveys and other evidence, I believe that the credibility of advertising in this country is at a dangerously low level. There is a widespread cynicism about advertising; consumers have "turned it off" in growing numbers. A whole generation of youngsters is being raised with an undiscriminating distrust of any advertising they see on their TV screens, hear on their radios, or read in their newspapers and magazines.

3. If this is the case—and I'd like to be convinced otherwise—there will be a growing willingness by the public to see not only the content of advertising regulated, but also the amount of it as well. We have already seen some rumblings in this direction in the wake of Mr. Basford's Boston speech last fall.

4. The honest advertiser has the most to lose in this process. The legitimate operator must submit to regulations designed to catch the fringe operator. The effectiveness of a dollar invested in advertising declines as the level of credibility declines, and it becomes more expensive to communicate a product or brand advantage, or to introduce a new product. So I believe there is considerable and legitimate cause for concern among the large and reputable firms that form the bulk of the industry.

What has been the response?

Some have attacked the qualifications and veracity of those who have expressed concern, avoiding direct discussion of the issues themselves. This type of response is not only irrelevant, it is irresponsible.

Some others have dismissed the whole matter as being vastly overstated, and it may be. But in this case, the argument should be capable of resolution by appeal to facts derived from research. And if the facts bear out the concern, then some more positive response by the industry is clearly called for.

Some have reacted by calling for a countercampaign—"advertising makes good things happen." The naïvety of such a response makes one wonder whether those advocating it have the slightest understanding of the device they are dealing with every day.

In fact, a very constructive start has been made by the advertising industry in setting up the Canadian Advertising Advisory Board, publication of a code of advertising standards, and in encouraging consumers with complaints to contact C.A.A.B., which will then follow up the complaints with the alleged offender. The board has also taken the initiative in sponsoring basic research in the advertising process, and approaches have been made to governmental authorities to cooperate in researching and resolving key public issues. This is all to the good.

At the same time, I think it should be said that some skeptics have claimed that the C.A.A.B.'s efforts have been far too modest, that these efforts have been used to provide a protective shield over its members, and that it has no teeth with which to punish any offenders. In short, it is claimed by some that C.A.A.B. is designed primarily to protect the club, and not the consumer. Justified or not, these same criticisms may be, and are, applied to most industry efforts at self-regulation. There exists a large measure of skepticism concerning any industry's ability to regulate itself effectively.

In the final analysis, this means some measure of government regulation and/or legislation. Declaiming about the evils of government intrusion into free enterprise will accomplish nothing. What is required under the circumstances is a more positive approach, suggesting the lines that regulation should take for the good of all concerned, and developing a relationship with government policy makers as an adviser who is to be trusted. It means active collaboration with, and education of, consumer groups and legislators as to the facts of economic life, and the complications that inevitably beset any attempt at regulation.

Above all, it means a willingness to support truly independent research through third parties who have no axe to grind, even though some of this research may not turn out to support the industry's position.

Let me close with a quotation from Kahlil Gibran's *The Prophet:*

> And a merchant said, Speak to us of Buying and Selling.
>
> And he answered and said:
>
> To you the earth yields her fruit, and you shall not want if you but know how to fill your hands.
>
> It is in exchanging the gifts of the earth that you shall find abundance and be satisfied.
>
> Yet unless the exchange be in love and kindly justice, it will but lead some to greed and others to hunger.
>
> When in the market place you toilers of the sea and fields and vineyards meet the weavers and the potters and the gatherers of spices—
>
> Invoke then the master spirit of the earth, to come into your midst and sanctify the scales and the reckoning that weighs value against value.
>
> And suffer not the barren-handed to take part in your transactions, who would sell their words for your labour.
>
> To such men you should say,
>
> Come with us to the field, or go with our brothers to the sea and cast your net;
>
> For the land and the sea shall be bountiful to you even as to us.

And if there come the singers and the dancers and the flute players,—buy of their gifts also.

For they too are gatherers of fruit and frankincense, and that which they bring, thought fashioned of dreams, is raiment and food for your soul.

And before you leave the market place, see that no one has gone his way with empty hands.

For the master spirit of the earth shall not sleep peacefully upon the wind till the needs of the least of you are satisfied.

Will corporations respond in time to the growing demands of consumerism? Or, will it become necessary for government to intervene and impose strict regulations on marketers? Corporations are on trial. To avoid an unfavorable verdict, the author feels that business must adopt new attitudes and develop new organizations to accommodate consumer demands.

---

13. MARKETERS FIDDLE WHILE CONSUMERS BURN*

E. B. Weiss†

It was in 1962 that President John F. Kennedy proclaimed the consumer's four-pronged Magna Charta:

1. The right to safety.
2. The right to be informed.
3. The right to choose.
4. The right to be heard.

These four "rights" symbolized—and heralded—consumerism. They became the basis for auto and tire safety legislation, the truth-in-packaging bill, and truth-in-credit regulations. And they will spawn six to ten additional consumer bills over the next several years.

In 1962, industry tended to shrug off consumerism as a political gambit that would soon fizzle out. During the six ensuing years, each industry affected by proposed legislation has tended, on balance, to

* Reprinted from "Marketers Fiddle While Consumers Burn," *Harvard Business Review,* Vol. 46 (July-August 1968), pp. 45–53.

† Doyle, Dane, Bernbach, Inc.

oppose uncompromisingly each new legislative proposal on behalf of consumerism. The food industry fought truth-in-packaging bills for five years. Truth-in-credit legislation was opposed by the credit industry for seven years. The meat packers' initial posture was one of confrontation; reluctant collaboration came only toward the end of the debate.

Clearly, industry has been unwilling to accept the philosophy that what is good for the public is good for business. That is why few corporate managements have directed the organizational changes necessitated by consumerism, why even fewer managements have charted an imaginative course to guide present consumer legislation to beneficial socioeconomic ends, and why few managements have ordered a study of impending consumer legislation so as to have an appropriate marketing program ready in advance.

In short, after six years of tuning up, Washington is literally racing toward additional consumerism legislation, regulation, and organization. State governments are doing the same thing, and so are many city governments. But industry's attitude tends to remain a mixture of confrontation, lamentation, and pious posturing. The marketing fraternity, especially, is almost united in its opposition. Marketing conventions resound with wails of anguish, of frustration, of bewilderment. Thunderous applause is reserved for the speaker who ties Communism and consumerism into an unholy alliance.

This is the road to a quasi-utility status for marketing. I do not predict that corporate marketing departments will be supervised in the minute way that railroads or power companies are. But I do foresee a future in which, rightly or wrongly, marketing will be regulated by law far more than it has ever been before. Most marketing leaders have only themselves to blame if they do not like this prospect.

THE "SMUGLY" AMERICANS

I will concede that at the very top management level, consumerism is tending to be accepted as part of the new dimensions of corporate social responsibility. But at the marketing level, fanatical and tearful defense of the status quo remains typical. For instance, here is how the Washington Bureau of *Advertising Age* described a February 1968 meeting of the American Advertising Federation (AAF):

> Much of AAF's annual government-business relations meeting was keyed to a current issue: Consumer legislation—do we need more or less? . . . [The] dialog failed to materialize. Government people feel the spotlight tended to focus on spokesmen from industry (and Republican Congressmen) who imply that the whole "consumerism" issue will go away if everyone puffs hard enough.
>
> One speaker from advertising told how government "Paternalism" had crushed the creative spark in the American Indian. . . .

How was AAF's cause advanced by the speaker who belittled "consumerism" by arguing that the issues which really worry the public are Vietnam, crime in the streets, taxes . . . ?[1]

At the same meeting a very high-ranking advertising executive unquestionably spoke for the majority of marketing officials when he complained that the government was using consumerism "as a divisive issue." He admitted "confusion" over the "dissension" existing between government and business. Striking the pious pose typical of too many marketing men, he said, "The business people I know feel they are trying their best to make a meaningful contribution to the welfare of the country, and they are hurt when the government portrays them as hawks and consumers as doves requiring protection." He warned that this situation will lead to "severe damage" to the economic and social structure of the country. With supreme irony,—remember that this was a meeting presumably called to develop collaboration between government and marketing—he added that there was "need for more humility on the government's part" and called on the government to "remedy the damage" done to business!

Fortunately, voices from another direction are also being heard. For example:

"Beyond question, the emerging ethics are challenging business orthodoxy," said A. N. McFarlane, the chairman of the board of Corn Products Company, recently.

"What concerns me is how the business community may respond to these ethical changes. It would be a grave error to view them only as a threat, as something to resist. As I see it, they are an expression of public thinking which we attack or disregard only at great peril. . . .

"Putting it another way, we have to decide whether, in the marketplace for ideas, we will allow ourselves to become alienated from the mainstream of public thought. . . .

"We can respond to the new emphasis on the quality of life—as opposed to the quantity of things—not only by modifying our product mix, but by more sensitive handling of business actions and communications—advertising included. . . ."[2]

"In our kind of society, there are times when government *has* to step in and help people with some of their more difficult problems," according to Thomas J. Watson, IBM board chairman. "If we businessmen insist that free enterprise permits us to be indifferent to those things on which people put high value, then the people will quite naturally assume that free enterprise has too much freedom."[3]

---

[1] February 19, 1968, p. 16.

[2] Address before the Better Business Bureau of Metropolitan New York, Inc., October 10, 1967.

[3] *A Business and Its Beliefs* (New York: McGraw-Hill Book Company, Inc., 1963), pp. 88, 90.

It is probable that the top managements of many companies will direct their marketing departments to adopt policies and practices more responsive to the public's desires. If this happens, it will help. But in view of marketing's abysmal record to date, I am dubious that it can save itself in time from substantial extensions of government regulation.

Who needs 1,000 eyes?

The Chinese say the buyer needs a thousand eyes—the seller but one. Marketing wants to keep it that way. However, consumerism now says the *seller* needs a thousand eyes—the buyer but one.

The buyer will never be protected to that degree, but he will need fewer than 1,000 eyes in the future. Years ago, when the employer became legally responsible for reasonable diligence in providing safe working conditions for his employees, and when workmen's compensation laws emerged, both the incidence and the severity of on-the-job injuries were sharply reduced. Is it unreasonable to conclude that new legal concepts of the seller's responsibilities and liabilities could accomplish similar results for the general public?

Consumer exploitation has been replacing labor exploitation as the real problem of our times. *We would not permit the things to be done to people as workers that we allow to be done to them as shoppers!* A more intelligent society, especially its younger generation, insists this must change.

But the market is self-policing, argues the marketing man, because the shopper is sovereign. This is true in a legalistic sense, perhaps—and it may check with the precepts of classical economics. But to the U.S. public of today it sounds more and more like pure poppycock.

No marketing man hissed (but hundreds applauded) when the former president of a large publishing enterprise declared:

> Freedom of shopping decision is a fundamental prerogative—even the freedom to be wrong, to make a wrong choice. No one has to buy anything, at any price, at any time. . . . Some degree of responsibility must rest on and with the consumer. He cannot be regarded as a pitiable imbecile. He cannot be wholly protected in every move and every purchase he makes, every day of his life.

Now, there is an interesting combination of truth and misjudgment in this argument. Who could disagree that "no one has to buy anything, at any price, at any time"? Who could disagree that "some degree of responsibility must rest on and with the consumer"? Who could disagree that it is foolish to regard the consumer as a "pitiable imbecile"? Who wants the consumer to be "wholly protected in every move and every purchase he makes, every day of his life"? Yet we err in going on (as so many businessmen seem to do) to insist not only that the consumer has a *right* to be wrong, but that marketing must make sure he exercises that right! I rather doubt that a sophisticated, affluent society—especially the properly critical younger generation—will offer much of a mass market for products that cater to the public's right to be *wrong*.

BEWILDERED BUYERS

The fact is that technology is expanding at such an unprecedented rate and spawning such a torrent of new products that it is difficult for the trade, not to mention consumers, to keep fully informed about them. Should shoppers be expected to be able to differentiate between a latex foam mattress and a urethane foam mattress? How many consumers can be expected to understand the difference between a transistorized and a solid-state radio or TV?

Technology has brought unparalleled abundance and opportunity to the consumer. It has also exposed him to new complexities and hazards. It has made his choices more difficult. He cannot be chemist, mechanic, electrician, nutritionist, *and* a walking computer (very necessary when shopping for fractionated-ounce food packages)! Faced with almost infinite product differentiation (plus contrived product virtues that are purely semantic), considerable price differentiation, the added complexities of trading stamps, the subtleties of cents-off deals, and other complications, the shopper is expected to choose wisely under circumstances that baffle professional buyers. His job is not made easier by the fact that prices tend *not* to be uniform in different stores even of the same food chain, and may vary daily. Moreover, if he is like most of us, he has to decide in a hurry.

Let us suppose he stops to buy a can opener. He finds there are hand, wall, and table models, manually operated or electrically powered. Some are combined with knife sharpeners. They are finished with various materials. They come in a range of colors. Some differences are functional and practical; others are merely for appearance or for promotion. Moreover, he must usually choose the can opener without the aid of a salesclerk. (If a clerk is present, he is apt to be as confused and unknowing as the customer!)

Flunking the shopping test!

Several years ago, California's Consumer Counsel decided to conduct a test to see how a shopper might fare in a typical unarmed encounter with a supermarket. According to a then current survey by Du Pont, the average shopper on an average visit bought 13.7 items in an average time of 27 minutes. Accordingly, a list of 14 items was drawn up. These were all packaged products—common staple foods and household necessities. Then a typical supermarket in the Sacramento area was selected.

In the case of the 14 items, the store offered a total of *246 possible choices.*

Five housewives were selected to participate in the test. Though picked at random, they were not average shoppers; each had had some college training as well as considerable family-marketing experience. Their instructions were simple: to make their selections solely on the basis of quality and cost—i.e., get the most possible for their money.

Each of the five women was given $10 and sent into the supermarket to buy the 14 items. They were clocked from the time they entered the store till they reached the checkout counter.

Only one of the women finished in less time than the average found in the Du Pont survey; she completed her shopping in 25 minutes. The other four women took, respectively, 35, 40, 55, and 60 minutes.

How did they fare? All five succeeded in picking the lowest-priced package of one item, cheddar cheese. But that was their only triumph. In the case of 2 of the 14 products, all five were baffled by the maze of prices and package sizes. For instance, there were 14 different packages of white rice; not one was in a one-pound package! The same was true of the 6 packages of salt, which ran a confusing range from $\frac{4}{10}$ ounce to 5 pounds. Toilet tissue was packed in rolls of 650, 800, and 1,000 sheets—some single-ply, some double-ply. Of the 10 cans of tuna, none was one pound or one half pound; 7 were fractional ounces.

In summary, possessing better-than-average educations, and spending more than the average amount of time, the five housewives as a group succeeded 36 times and failed 34 times to pick the most economical items.

The resulting confusion must have been what Marya Mannes had in mind when she stated, "Most of us are simply too busy or too tired or too harassed to take a computer, a slide rule, and an M.I.T. graduate to market. . . ."[4]

Caveat venditor

I am not arguing that prices should not fluctuate, that various package sizes should not be offered, or that different models, brands, and colors should not be displayed. My point is simply that the shopper is dazed—and understandably so. U.S. marketers should be taking far more responsibility than they have thus far to help the customer make decisions. Just how much protection does he or she need? That is a question about which reasonable and sincere men differ; but the need for offering *much more* than at present is, in my opinion, beyond dispute.

A free economy depends on rational consumer choice. If consumers cannot choose wisely, if they regularly reach their decisions in a state

[4] Quoted in Jeremy Main's article, "Industry Still Has Something to Learn About Congress," *Fortune* (February 1967), p. 129.

of wonder and perplexity, if they make their choices on the basis of meaningless and irrelevant claims, a free economy suffers.

Just as a rational voting procedure is necessary to a free political system, so a rational shopping system is necessary to a free market. The marketplace displays more irrationality than rationality. The better educated, more sophisticated shopper of today is beginning to rebel. Politicians are paying heed; marketers are not.

CAN SELF-REGULATION SUCCEED?

Marketing men regularly advance the contention that the device of self-regulation should be attempted and exhausted before resorting to legislative remedies. It is beyond dispute that our whole political and economic system fares better if regulation of industry takes place voluntarily by business itself. The sad fact, however, is that marketing has an especially poor record of self-regulation, even in areas where its self-interest is most obvious. The list of consumer legislation (ranging from auto safety laws and product warranties to meat controls and truth-in-lending regulations) is obviously a damning indictment of the failure of marketing to regulate itself. So are the scores of fair practice codes voluntarily drawn up by industry under Federal Trade Commission supervision—and then blithely ignored by industry.

Dr. William Haddon, Jr., Administrator of the National Highway Safety Agency, reminded the auto industry of the inherent futility of self-regulation: "Voluntary standards failed to produce the degree of safety that could be well afforded through the more universal application of modern technology."[5] Because Detroit lacked the foresight to act with statesmanship on matters of the greatest public urgency, safety standards for automobiles are now being established by government.

"Can we get away with it?"

Some marketing men ask, "Wouldn't industrial self-regulation be a lot more effective if the antitrust laws were repealed to allow better enforcement of codes of ethics?" Unfortunately, nothing in the present or in the past history of business conduct in the face of competition justifies any real confidence that self-regulatory power would not be abused by business. Perhaps no function of business has indicted itself more severely in this respect than marketing. The marketing practices that are regulated in most consumer legislation seldom involve out-and-out fraud (which is susceptible to some degree of effective self-regulation). Instead, they embrace marketing practices in the gray areas. This

[5] Quoted in *Freedom of Information in the Marketplace* (Columbia, Missouri, School of Journalism, University of Missouri), December 1966.

is the crux of consumer legislation—not fraud, but dubious ethics, dubious morality.

There is a decided tendency in marketing to use the words "legal" and "honest" interchangeably. When the marketing executive says that most marketing programs are "honest," what he really means is that most marketing programs operate within the law. His too-common tendency is to ask, "Is it legal?" If the answer is affirmative, then he presumes he has demonstrated his responsibility to society. In short, the philosophy of the day, in considering borderline cases involving public taste, fair dealing, and full and accurate information, too often seems to be, "This is the deal: Can we get away with it?"

This attitude may have sufficed in a previous age, but a more sophisticated society, especially the younger and better educated segments, is now beginning to say, "That is not a modern concept of social responsibility." It is saying that marketing must observe standards of morality and good taste. It is even saying, at this very moment, that the business community definitely and specifically has a legal obligation to protect the user *against his own carelessness!* It wants to hold the manufacturer accountable for harm to the careless, as well as the careful, user.

The burden of proof will increasingly be on the seller. The trend will be to hold him strictly liable without requiring proof of negligence or culpability. This view has already become law in several states.

ADVERTISING ON TRIAL

Advertising is the "goldfish bowl" phase of marketing. It has more visibility, and is even more omnipresent in time and space than packaging is. If marketing becomes a quasi-utility, advertising will hurry it along the final laps. This conclusion seems inescapable in view of the stubborn, unresponsive, outdated posture of the advertising fraternity. All too typical is this gem of fossilized self-defense, which I heard at a recent ad club meeting:

> Some people complain that advertising is repetitious. Others think it is often in bad taste. But the people spend thousands of hours reading and listening to advertising and buying billions of dollars of advertised products. They obviously don't disapprove of it.

Don't they really? If advertising were anywhere near as convincing and acceptable to people as the quotation suggests, one would think brand loyalty would be at an all-time high. Actually, though, brand loyalty is at an all-time *low;* private labels have more acceptance than ever. Is this a testimonial to advertising's effectiveness—or the reverse?

And is it true that no one is bothered by misleading, deceptive ads? A major oil company featured the fact that its gasoline contained Platformate, the obvious implication to the lay consumer being that this was a unique ingredient. The ads did not reveal that practically all gasoline sold for automobile use contains Platformate. Do Americans approve of this? Consider the many ads implying that this food or that treatment will keep the user healthy, vigorous, and/or good-looking—when any nutritionist or doctor knows that it will not. Do Americans approve of this practice? Surely advertising cannot disregard the portentous implications of the Public Broadcast Laboratory two-hour television program, backed by a $10 million grant from The Ford Foundation, which is offering "commercials" attacking the credibility of TV commercials.

Aside from the problem of misleading advertising, there is the question of good taste and appropriateness. When so much advertising is deceptive, vulgar, unattractive, and greedy, can we be surprised if the public moves on to the assumption that marketing in toto is deceptive, vulgar, unattractive, and greedy? When so much advertising is unbelievable, is in bad taste, involves so much excessive puffery, and is boorish and boring, can it ever hope, in a sophisticated, critical society, to make a favorable impression on the 85 percent *on whom it does not now register at all?* How much damage continues to be done to advertising by its enormous emphasis on cigarette sales—especially when television, with its penetration of the family, is employed?

During the decade of the 1970s, advertising will come under more criticism, and more intelligent criticism, than ever before in its history. A more aware young generation makes this inescapable. It will be dealing with a public which (especially at the younger levels) is more sophisticated, aware, critical. Will the same old claims that defenders of advertising have been using for at least 30 years—with an obvious lack of success—mount an effective counterattack? I doubt it. What is needed is intelligent, critical self-analysis, not self-righteousness and self-pity. I recommend the kind of approach recently taken by the management of the Pillsbury Company:

The occasion was the company's second Consumer Forum, a week-long series of lectures and workshops planned to focus attention on the problems of taste in consumer communication. "Our object was to intensify the sensitivity of Pillsbury employees to matters of taste," explained Thomas Mulcahy, Pillsbury's director of public affairs. "And I think the forum succeeded quite effectively in doing this."

In announcing the second forum, Pillsbury's president, Robert J. Keith, observed that consumer protection had moved well beyond such basic considerations as sanitation and honest representation. "The modern consumer accepts these as minimum commitments from a food manufacturer," he said, "and now judges us by the more complex standard of quality in our products and the way we talk about them."

In opening the forum, Keith advised: "Just as we would not try to conduct our business with outdated equipment or methods, let us use this week to make certain that we do not try to conduct it with outdated attitudes."[6]

"Do-nothing" defenders

Even though advertising has been under attack for many years, it has never felt much need to research its side of the case. It is shocking that only one truly objective analysis of the economics of advertising has ever been made—and that one was done 26 years ago![7] (I am ruling out, of course, many thinly researched publications which *purport* to be highly analytical.) As a result, great gaps exist in our factual knowledge of advertising—gaps that need not exist at all. For instance, we do not know:

— whether advertising, which originally was presumed to lower prices, may not now tend, on balance, to increase prices.
— the extent to which advertising creates monopolies, or something akin to monopolies (especially as the Supreme Court now defines them).
— the extent to which advertising (especially on TV) gives competitive advantages to giant corporations and "bars entry" to some other enterprises.

On the one hand, there is no doubt in my own mind of the following propositions:

1. The foregoing and related charges against advertising are not entirely unfounded.
2. These charges have *never* been *objectively* studied by advertising's protagonists (or by its critics, I must add).
3. These charges will not be buried by fervent "free enterprise" pleas, by slanted studies, or by angelic poses.

The lackluster attitude of most advertising practitioners seems to be matched by a large number of teachers and writers. W. Allen Wallis, the president of the University of Rochester, recently wrote:

> Passages on advertising in our college textbooks of economics present a rather appalling collection of disorganized chatter. Analysis is superficial. Crucial terms are undefined. "Facts" are mere conjectures. There is a written conformity to current patterns of "group-think."[8]

To date, the advertising fraternity's response has tended to "admit nothing" and to strike a posture that combines piety with unyielding confrontation. It has apparently learned nothing from the sad experience

---

[6] Minneapolis, Minnesota, April 17, 1967.

[7] Neil H. Borden, *The Economic Effects of Advertising* (Chicago, Richard D. Irwin, Inc., 1942).

[8] Introduction to *Advertising—A New Approach,* by Walter Taplin (Boston, Little, Brown & Company, 1963), p. xiii.

of the past. Not long ago its stubborn refusal to give an inch led to near disaster in connection with truth in packaging. As Jeremy Main pointed out in his article in *Fortune:*

> Industry's strategic mistake in battling truth in packaging was to adopt an attitude of intransigent opposition. The companies concerned denied any need for the bill, challenged the right of the federal government to interfere, and attempted to kill the legislation. They thereby lost a number of opportunities to come to terms with Congress on an early compromise.[9]

NEEDED: VPs OF CONSUMERISM

How must corporations be restructured, in philosophy and in organization, to conform with and profit from the consumerism trend? The logical starting points would seem to be:

1. The formulation of an up-to-date "consumerism code" that summarizes top management's philosophy and provides a practical framework of policy for line executives.
2. A staff and line reorganization.
3. A program to facilitate implementation of the code.

Arjay Miller, Ford Motor Company's vice chairman, puts it this way:

> The corporation must go beyond its traditional role of business enterprise and seek to anticipate, rather than simply react to, social needs or problems. This may require the establishment of a long-range planning function to make sure a firm will be able to respond to what society wants it to do. It may involve not only changed "product," but also changed internal organization.[10]

Miller's new post at Ford was described by Henry Ford II as "recognition of the need for a senior officer to concentrate on the company's external affairs—to maintain better relations with government and with the public." For similar reasons, I propose that companies establish the position of *vice president–consumerism.* The executive holding this position would function at the staff level. He would be concerned with the corporation's external affairs and with the internal functions that have implications for consumerism. It would be his responsibility to:

— develop an organizational structure and procedures that would ensure more consideration of ethical issues in decision making.

— work out strategic and tactical plans for keeping the company abreast of its responsibilities to consumerism.

— spell out the duties and responsibilities to the buying public of each department and function in the company, along with precise

[9] J. Main, "Industry Still . . . ," *Fortune,* p. 128.

[10] From a speech delivered at a University of Illinois Symposium, April 21, 1967.

objectives and methods of measuring performance in accomplishing these objectives.

The vice president–consumerism would review marketing programs regularly. Policies must be periodically reexamined and, if necessary, their objectives redefined in order for the company to keep in step with the volatile demands of a more sophisticated and therefore more critical and demanding marketplace. He would also collaborate with:

1. Congress (as well as state legislatures and local civic authorities) in drafting new consumer legislation and regulations—and in drafting changes in existing consumer legislation and regulations.
2. The regulatory and enforcement departments and officials of government.
3. The various public consumer organizations—national, state, and local.

Further steps

The next organizational step might be the establishment of a task force which would report to the vice president–consumerism and represent him at meetings of line executives. This task force would also report on profit opportunities in existing and future consumer legislation.

The vice president–consumerism might organize a panel consisting of representatives of the public and of the trade. The purpose of the panel would be to provide management with a continuing playback on consumerism programs. It would also provide a listening post that would help management to anticipate potential consumerism trends.

The legal department would, of course, be closely aligned with the department headed by the vice president–consumerism. A practical resolution of this departmental kinship will obviously require a high degree of corporate statesmanship. (The strictly legal approach to the requirements of a "consumeristic" society is sterile and self-defeating.) In addition, the legal department should be restructured to include specialists in consumerism legislation and even specialists in certain aspects of consumer legislation that particularly affect the corporation.

Moreover, communications between the legal department and other departments on matters that affect consumerism must be reexamined. The tendency is for the legal department's conclusions to prevail—and that, too often, can be poor policy in our present-day society.

It would also appear advantageous to arrange for closer collaboration between the new department and the legal and marketing departments during the discussion stage of certain marketing programs so as to lessen the likelihood of a negative conclusion being reached later by the legal department.

The vice president–consumerism would, of course, maintain the closest liaison with the marketing department.

TRADE ASSOCIATION ACTION

Trade associations, too, should make changes in their philosophy, organization, programs, and personnel budgets to meet the needs of consumerism. On balance, our trade associations, over the last several decades, have been immobilized by fears, made impotent by legal counsel, and operated with utterly inadequate budgets. Most of them have been slow to reorganize and to reorient themselves so as to provide government and industry members with the leadership and guidance called for by consumerism. And where they have recognized the gathering forces of consumerism, their typical posture has been annoyance, aggravation, frustration, resentment—and a fierce determination to defend the status quo to the last detail.

Recently a few trade associations have taken a different approach. If their example were followed by others, and if this trend were to gather momentum, U.S. industry would benefit greatly. Here are some cases in point:

In August 1966 the Washington Bureau of *Advertising Age* reported:

> We have already pointed out editorially how the food industry bungled truth in packaging. There was diligent reform by many individual companies, but no concerted industry effort to create machinery to deal with consumer complaints. Would the truth in packaging bill, with all its pitfalls, have mustered such strength if the food industry had acted a year or two ago to form its own committee on labeling and packaging standards?[11]

Apparently, the food industry has profited from that experience. Aware that moves will be made to add to truth in packaging, it has been developing a compliance program.

A most significant and enlightened forward step has been announced by Donald L. Peyton, the managing director of the U.S.A. Standards Institute:

> In constituting the U.S.A. Standards Institute, the [Institute] assured consumer input by changing the basic structure of the organization to provide for the interface of three operating councils . . . member body council, consumer council, and company member council. The consumer council, which has the primary responsibility of representation and protection of the interests of the consuming public, will provide the mechanism for initiation, review and coordination of consumer standards. . . .
>
> Government representation at the policy-making level of the Institute was one of the recommendations of the consumer advisory council. Provision has been made in the constitution and bylaws for government representation on the board of directors, which is the governing body of the Institute. The director of the National Bureau of Standards, if willing to serve, becomes a director of the Institute. . . .

[11] August 22, 1966, p. 100.

At least one group of manufacturers has *anticipated* the government in its effort to promote safer use of its product. For the past few years, the Outdoor Power Equipment Institute, in conjunction with the Public Health Service, has waged a public campaign to acquaint users with the hazards and proper use of power mowers.

The American Gas Association maintains two laboratories where appliances and equipment are subjected to exhaustive tests for compliance with U.S. standards. Each manufacturer who wishes his product to bear the certification mark of these laboratories must submit a prototype which can meet their stringent requirements. Moreover, even after acquiring the certification mark, the manufacturer is subjected to periodic unannounced inspection in his plant by laboratory personnel.

The Architectural Aluminum Manufacturers Association established a quality certification labeling program for aluminum windows and sliding glass doors which has resulted in a renewal of consumer confidence in these products. Few building products had offered a more variable and uncertain quality than aluminum windows. Now, however, there are carefully drawn standards, a program for effective policing, and a seal to attest to quality.

The textile industry has organized its own "care labeling" committee. This group, formed by industry leaders, agreed to identify causes of consumer complaints and to see what could be done to lessen these complaints. Its report was highly praised in Washington.

In anticipation of truth-in-servicing legislation, manufacturers of appliances (individually, as well as through their association) are:

1. Stepping up their programs to train servicemen.
2. Working on product development to increase reliability and ease service access.
3. Developing criteria against which service performance can be measured and rewarded.
4. Providing a stronger voice for service generally in management.

CONCLUSION

As I review the events and experience of recent years, several conclusions stand out:

First, technological progress will continue to require that marketing provide more guidance to the consumer.

Second, additional consumerism legislation is inevitable—and for years to come.

Third, marketing can avoid becoming a new type of quasi-utility only if it collaborates with government. However, its response to date has involved more confrontation than collaboration. The question seems to be *how much* utility-type regulation marketing will let itself in for, not *whether* it will become more controlled.

Fourth, the new generation of corporate executives (e.g., the new members of the Committee for Economic Development, who have shown an extraordinary grasp of the expanding opportunities and responsibilities of corporate citizenship) will insist on new and higher levels of marketing integrity. Under their enlightened direction, marketing will find profit, as well as other satisfactions, in greater public service.

Fifth, I believe 1968 will mark marketing's turning point in its attitude toward consumerism. And none too soon. The time is already late.

How can one account for the growing impact of consumerism? The author discusses examples of some corporate and governmental responses, many of which are simple and straight-forward, yet surprisingly effective. Consumerism is, after all, only an appeal to sound marketing practice and high standards of business. Marketing students should understand that the growing impact of consumerism on marketing-government relationships offers an exceptional opportunity for business renewal.

---

14. THE GROWING IMPACT OF CONSUMERISM ON MARKETING-GOVERNMENT RELATIONSHIPS*

Virginia Knauer†

Consumerism is increasing government's role in marketing. That may sound ominous, but it is not necessarily so. Nor need it be. Whether the increasing role will be directed towards stimulating workable competition, competition which meets the goals and values of society or simply directed toward greater restriction of marketing practices, is in large part dependent upon how marketers and students of marketing view consumerism. To understand consumerism is to explore questions of responsiveness posed by consumers both to government and business.

A common viewpoint of consumerism is that it is synonymous with

---

* Not previously published.

† Special assistant to President Nixon for Consumer Affairs and Director, Office of Consumer Affairs.

government regulation. That conception is not correct. Fortunately it is a view which is changing. With this change one can perceive reassurance of the future for workable competition rather than merely increased government regulation.

I feel that business and government can agree that consumers are entitled to safe products with accompanying product information to facilitate value comparisons. Moreover, it is reasonable for consumers to expect a responsiveness on the part of government and business, a responsiveness which manifests itself in expeditious handling of consumers' requests for information and consumers' complaints. Yet it is curious to note that while government and business can agree that such aims of consumerism are in the national interest, business in large part still regards consumerism as antagonistic. An increasingly better educated American consumer with more leisure time and resources available, with greater economic and social security, with more interest in the characteristics of the products and services purchased by his dollar, stands ready to be an ally of the efficient marketer. Why then should the advocates of consumerism sometimes be described as enemies of the free enterprise system?

The simplistic conception of the situation is as follows. Laws and regulations designed to protect consumers in the marketplace restrict competition. They affect advertising, packaging, selling, pricing, grading and labeling, as well as the sale of drugs, foods, cosmetics, and consumer durables. They were enacted in whole or in part to promote the ends of the consumer at a time when consumers were not vigorously advocating and lobbying for such enactments, or even demanding greater responsiveness of government and industry. Therefore, what can business expect other than more regulation when consumers are actively advocating their interests before legislative hearings and tribunals as well as in company board rooms.

The rationale contains heavy elements of validity. In the past the unorganized and poorly represented consumer viewpoint had to await a national tragedy or a scandal before action by either government or industry could be expected. The literature of the decades signaling the turn of the century describe the robber barons. In response, "the representatives of the people" enacted the Sherman Antitrust Act, the Federal Trade Commission Act, and other legislation to preclude unfair competition. Upton Sinclair, in his novel *The Jungle,* described the unsanitary conditions in the food industry and the Congress reacted with the 1906 Pure Food Act. The Kefauver-Harris Drug Amendments to the Federal Food, Drug, and Cosmetic Act were brought about almost solely through the tragedy of thalidomide. Consumer legislation and regulation of the past was not a testimony to the ballot box or marketplace muscle of consumers. It was a response to crises.

Lobbies for private interests in state capitols and in Washington have long known that consumerism did not really offer effective opposition. Therefore lobbying strategy did not have to be prepared to deal with an onslaught of public clamor advocating the consumers' point of view or interest. However, with the advent of consumer representatives in government, voluntary consumer organizations at the state and local level, public interest lay firms, and other spokesmen and advocates of consumer interests, it is perhaps to be expected that representatives of business and lobbyists for private interests will look upon consumerism of the 70s with considerable concern and, even in some cases, with outright fear.

Certainly administrators of independent and old-line regulatory agencies recognize consumerism as the "new boy in town." Not too long ago, consumers and their representatives were, for the most part, unaware of the many proposed regulations, policies, and edicts issued by the regulators of business in such agencies as the Federal Trade Commission, Food and Drug Administration, the Civil Aeronautics Bureau. These proposals and policies would simply be issued in an obscure governmental document (the Federal Register), absorb comments from the regulated industry, perhaps be modified somewhat before being issued in final form to be codified, and included in the countless books making up the code of federal regulation. All that, however, has now changed. As a matter of fact, consumers and their representatives no longer even wait for government to issue a proposed regulatory sanction. Rather direct and immediate action is taken. The Federal Trade Commission is petitioned to require prior proof of advertising claims. The U.S. Department of Agriculture is petitioned and then used by consumer groups on the kind of labeling and advertising permitted for USDA-inspected meat products. In short, government administrators know that regulations whose statutory base is the promotion of honesty and fair dealing in the interest of consumers will be followed closely and even challenged by consumers. President Nixon in fact has recognized the obligation of government to inform consumers and involve them in the creation of rules and regulations designed to protect or enhance the consumer's interest.

The last few years have seen consumer advisory councils and consumer representatives established in many agencies of the federal government, including the establishment by executive order of President Nixon of an Office of Consumer Affairs in the White House. The organization of government will continue to reflect the growing impact of consumerism. In the future this impact will take on more of an activist character. Consumers and their representatives will obtain a keener understanding of the processes and procedures of the legislative and regulatory forum. They will master the budgetary processes which underlie the effective enforcement of all consumer protection statutes. They will challenge elected officials and administrators on their record of promoting the consumers' interest. They will become much more knowledgeable regarding the economics of consumer markets. This is an awareness perhaps most significantly registered in the field of antitrust enforcement by the courts, the Federal Trade Board, and the Justice Department.

What is the significance of this activism for marketers? It may carry with it a call to the barricades. Or, it may be regarded as one of the greatest long-term and short-term opportunities for marketing in the history of the republic. Let us consider a few examples of opportunities in consumerism.

In 1968, a leading manufacturer of major home appliances broke with the traditional defensive posture of business toward consumerism. It announced in full-page advertisements that upon examining its own warranties for the full product line, it had come to a sobering conclusion: consumers had been correct in criticizing the company's warranty. The company's president declared that their warranties were confusing, legalistic, and, in short, a disgrace to a company perfectly willing to stand behind the quality of its product. The company announced a simplification and liberalization of its warranties, and immediately introduced and benefited from an aspect of what is called "enterprise competition." The company also introduced several highly imaginative techniques, illustrating its responsiveness to consumers and consumerism in the last few years. The sales and market position of the company has been increasing.

The company's president established another precedent by indicating his willingness to man the company's hotline (direct-action phone) with consumers. Competition caught on, as competition always has a way of doing. Company after company brought changes in warranty language and content, compensation for inwarranty repairs and handling of consumer complaints. Most of the competition, however, waited until these changes were recommended by a presidentially appointed government task force.

Pressures of consumerism have increased government interest in matters related to packaging and labeling of consumer product. The major food chains, almost without exception, have recognized irritating packaging and labeling problems of the consumers, and acted upon them voluntarily, as a direct and positive response to consumerism. Consumers and consumer advocates complained of the inability of the Fair Packaging and Labeling Act to facilitate value comparisons through limitation of package sizes. The chains have voluntarily moved to unit pricing. There were complaints about the inability to determine the age of the food product, so the chains have increasingly moved towards open code dating of food products. Other chains have insisted on carrying on labeling experiments, gauged to test the best means of conveying nutritional information to consumers through labeling and advertising. If regulation is needed in any of these areas, I believe the chains will make the first move to call for uniform regulation in the name of economy and compliance. The canning industry has already asked for mandatory percentage labeling of juice products as a means of stimulating product improvement through competition based on informed consumer choice.

Of course, one ought not to conclude that marketers either have or are in a position to preempt governmental action on issues brought to the government by consumers or their advocates. A review of the legislative and regulatory activity in the field of consumer protection in the last 10 years would quickly dispell that conception. We have seen legislation to require premarket proof of efficiency of drugs, mandatory inspection of all meat and poultry products traveling in interstate commerce, legislation covering package sizes, package fill, package labeling and product representations, legislation to ban unsafe toys, poison prevention packaging requirements, prohibition of certain types of advertising, special labeling and prohibitions covering hazardous household substances, credit disclosure legislation, requirements covering credit reporting companies, and so on. The list is a lengthy one.

Regulatory agencies, pressured by executive and consumer initiatives, have also been busy. The Federal Trade Commission has required premarket proof of advertising claims, of conformitive disclosures of the quality and durability of light bulbs, and the mandated permanent care labeling, to list but a few of their immediate activities. The Securities and Exchange Commission has brought multilevel distributorships under the requirements of FCC regulations. The Food and Drug Administration has banned hundreds of drugs from the market on the basis of lack of proof of efficiency or safety. The Justice Department has been especially active in the field of competitive drug pricing. National advertising has been especially vulnerable to regulatory activities of government agencies in the late 60s and early 70s. Thus, it is not surprising that representatives of business frequently view consumerists and consumer advocates as competitors in dealings with government. But there are a growing number of marketers beginning to perceive consumers as allies rather than competitors in dealings with government.

Mentioned above was a proposal made to the government by the citrus industry to require percentage labeling of juice content for diluted juice products. The proposal, if finalized, would result in the establishment of a standard of identity and quality under the Federal Food, Drug, and Cosmetic Act. Although there have been hundreds of standards established under this act, this voluntary standard-making procedure marks a significant departure from the past. The citrus industry was convinced that its proposed percentage labeling requirement represented the best move in the interests of consumers, and therefore perceived consumers and consumer groups across the country as allies rather than as potential competitors. The citrus industry, therefore, corresponded with over 3,000 consumer groups across the country, supplied each one with a brief explaining the proposal put forward by the industry, and urged consumer groups to provide the government agency, the Federal Food and Drug Administration, with their views on the proposed rule-making procedure. The results indicate that consumer groups have in fact urged the government agency to enact the proposed regulatory requirement put forward by citrus marketers.

The casualty insurer whose television commercials attempt to educate consumers about the relationship between drinking and driving, cosmetic automobile bumpers, and the rising cost of insurance certainly views consumers as potential allies, in an overall effort to sway legislature action.

As government provides more representation to consumers, and more assistance to consumer groups informing and working with government, marketers must recognize consumers as persistent and increasing factors in the government-industry equation. The point has been made by many writers that government administrators frequently substitute government judgment for consumer judgment in the regulation of marketers. Marketers then should welcome the opportunity to bring their cases to consumers in the regulatory proceedings required to reflect the best interests of the public. Marketers ought not to assume that the aim of consumerism is more regulation and more restriction of business. For example, actions against fair-trade laws by state courts and state legislatures have been met with applause from consumers. Consumers were the first to approve efforts by the U.S. Department of Justice to promote state action against laws which prohibit the advertising of prescription drug prices. As consumers become more aware of laws actually enacted for the protection of special interest groups, and passed in the name of consumer protection or the promotion of competition, and as they become more aware of regulations which from their inception represented poor compromises between competing economic interests, the consumer may play a decisive role in creating a marketplace with less regulation rather than increased regulation.

Government as the largest customer of business is expected to share its purchasing knowledge with consumers. Government contractors will be expected to provide lists of products which correspond to the specifications established under government contracts. This and other information was ordered compiled by President Nixon in 1971. He also forwarded to Congress a product testing methods bill. Under it marketers would be encouraged to make reference in their advertising and labeling to the fact (if true) that their products passed tests certified by the government as indicative of important product characteristics. Marketers can anticipate increasing government interest in the stimulation of more effective markets through providing the consumer, from government and business sources, with relevant information about product and service characteristics. Recently we have seen the emergence of firms whose sole function is that of facilitating the consumer's value comparisons through improved product information.

The creation, by executive order of the president in 1971, of the National Business Council for Consumer Affairs formalized the efforts of top management to work with government in the promotion of consumers' interests. The Office of Consumer Affairs in the White House has worked with industry on various programs in the interests of consumers for some time. Government does not have the function to exacerbate irritations that exist between producer and consumer. Rather, it is a legitimate function of government to promote voluntary action by business in the interest of consumers. The interest of government and the response of business are perfectly compatible with workable competition.

Consumerism as a movement should not be feared by marketers or students of marketing. Consumerism, in fact, does not have the earmarks or characteristics of historical movements in our country. It has not enjoyed an effective lobby over the years to promote its legislative desires. State and local consumer groups are just now beginning to organize themselves properly.

Consumerism does not have a national fund or war chest to finance its program. It is not assisted by highly efficient law firms to wage its battles. Its priorities, in fact, are often poorly articulated. Yet government has begun to pay serious heed to the aims and aspirations of consumers as a block.

How then can one account for the growing impact of consumerism? The truth is that the influence exerted by consumerism on government and business stems from the appeal of consumerism to logic and to high ethical values.

I have reviewed selected cases of marketers who have seized upon various facets of consumerism and have gained consumer groups as allies in efforts to improve competition through regulation. This trend will grow. I believe we will see more marketers cast aside their previous defensive attitudes and postures adopted when working with consumer representatives and consumer goods.

It is true that consumerism through government action and through the collective impact of buying power asks business to cast aside the "buyer beware" philosophy. The consumer wants to act and be treated as an intelligent, respected purchaser. The consumer desires to be highly prized as a repeat purchaser. This is after all only an appeal to sound marketing practice and high standards of business. Students of marketing should understand that the growing impact of consumerism on marketing-government relationships offers an exceptional opportunity for business renewal.

The author explores several areas relating to public policy, its development, and its relationship with the consumer movement. Can self-regulation be developed to a satisfactory level to significantly reduce pressures for new legislation? The future of the traditional free-enterprise system hangs in the balance.

15. THE CONSUMER MOVEMENT AND PUBLIC POLICY DEVELOPMENT* †

William Lazer‡

INTRODUCTION

This session is organized around four questions:

1. To what extent is there a cause and effect relationship between the consumer movement and public policy considerations?
2. Has the consumer movement preceded the enactment of laws and constraints of the business system in the past?
3. Was the consumer movement of the 1960s of such an intensity to presage the passage of major legislation affecting marketing?
4. Can self-regulation be developed to a satisfactory level to significantly reduce pressures for new legislation?

These questions are of course impossible to answer unequivocally. Yet that is exactly why they are good grist for the minds assembled here today. Permit me to illustrate with a few general comments about them.

Determining the extent of the existence of the consumer movement as a cause and public policy as the effect, can only be a matter of speculation. Hard data do not exist to establish "the statistical facts." While one might speculate about a number of the correlates, it is important to be aware that the reverse could also be true with public policy as a cause and the consumer movement as effect.

---

* Northwestern University Symposium.

† The author is deeply indebted to Mr. Frank McLaughlin, Director of Industry Relations, Office of Consumer Affairs, The White House, who so willingly and ably shared insights that shaped the development of this paper. Appreciation is also due to the 1971 American Marketing Association White House Interns, Mr. Alvin Katzman, Miss Priscilla LaBarbera, Mr. Richard Rose, and Mr. Morris Shapero, for their research into consumer inputs in the federal rule-making procedures. Some of their findings are reflected herein.

‡ Michigan State University.

Or to illustrate the situation in another manner, suppose an observer assumes that the climate of the times of the late 1960s had within it ingredients nurturing the seeds of general discontent and unrest. Suppose in addition that one aspect of that unrest was in the consumer domain. Such a climate could naturally stimulate changes in public policy. This might occur with or without consumerism and the changes, then, might be the effects, not the causes, resulting from the climate of the times. Note that in such a situation after certain changes occur, including public policy developments, some of them may be titled consumerism. Can an observer at a later date unambiguously deduce that consumerism caused changes in public policy?

I suspect that conclusions about whether the consumer movement preceded the enactment of laws and constraints of the business system in the past is at least partly determined by how one defines the consumer movement, and which laws constraining the business system are selected.[1] I am not clear on the unambiguous parameters of the consumer movement, nor whether consumer reactions and dissatisfaction recorded at the turn of the century, or during the 1920s, are basically similar to today's consumer movement.

The question can self-regulation be developed to a satisfactory level that will reduce pressures for new legislation significantly has a simple theoretical answer. Yes it can. Whether it will be or not, is, I suspect, the more relevant issue for us to examine and it is not handled so readily.

But regardless of such caveats, let us delve into the issues in a more penetrating manner. And since this is a workshop, my paper is merely intended as a draft of some perspectives and ideas to facilitate your thinking and discussion.

SOME PERSPECTIVES ON CONSUMERISM AND THE CONSUMER MOVEMENT

Everyone here recognizes that there is no one accepted definition of consumerism. A variety of definitions focusing on different emphases now exist. Some refer to consumerism as evidence of the failure of the marketing concept. Others emphasize the power of rights of consumers as contrasted with the influence of middlemen, manufacturers, and other business interests—the caveat venditor concept. Still others highlight the organized efforts of sellers seeking to get their money's worth and to gain remedies for dissatisfaction. Consumerism has also

[1] Morton H. Broffman, "Is Consumerism Merely Another Marketing Concept?" *MSU Business Topics* (Winter 1971), pp. 15–21; Richard H. Buskirk and James T. Rothe, "Consumerism—An Interpretation," *Journal of Marketing* (October 1970), pp. 61–65; Robert O. Herrmann, "Consumerism: Its Goals, Organizations and Future," *Journal of Marketing* (October 1970), pp. 55–60.

been envisaged in the broader context of sociopolitical developments that go beyond the concerns of the marketplace and encompass various aspects of social unrest.

The manifestations of consumerism are numerous and varied including, Ralph Nader and his Raiders, Virginia Knauer and her Office of Consumer Affairs, Rachael Carson's writings, consumer boycotts, consumer pressure groups, consumer action programs, government legislation, school and union education programs, and consumer publications. It is worth noting that not only are the manifestations numerous and varied, but the points of view of interested parties are not consonant. The viewpoint of housewives, labor, business, and government on a particular consumer issue, and in fact their very viewpoints on consumerism per se, may be divergent.

Nevertheless, consumerism does imply an undercurrent, a feeling of dissatisfaction, a need for change and improvement in our marketing system, a need for greater consumer concern. The movement has high visibility, achieved largely through mass communications media—particularly television. As a movement, it has credibility, broad general acceptance, and even a sort of charisma.

Consumerism in the minds of business executives is sometimes equated with governmental regulation. As such it is seen as the substitution of the will of government for the will of the market on business. The result, the reasoning goes, is a suppression of competition, and of businesses' ability to contribute economically as well as socially.

The fact that consumerism increases government's role in marketing has been regarded as an ominous sign by some businessmen. Fortunately this perception is changing. Businessmen now are more willing to admit some market regulation makes good sense, that laws protecting consumers can offer new business opportunities, and that consumerism itself can be profitable.[2]

In our age it is reasonable for consumers to expect responsiveness on the part of both government and business. Responsiveness by government often manifests itself in terms of laws. Responsiveness by business may manifest itself in terms of self-regulation, new decisions, policies, and organizational adjustments. In any case the result is an increasing awareness of consumer benefits and of public policies and issues.

Yet, some businessmen seem to regard consumers as antagonists of

---

[2] For a discussion of market regulations see J. T. Connor, "Changing Pattern of Business-Government Relations," *Conference Board Record* (May 1971), pp. 23–26; M. J. Etzel, and D. L. James, "Can Government Regulations Replace Market Orientation?" *Journal of Retailing* (Winter '71–72), pp. 14–23; A. Kapor, "Business-Government Relations Become Respectable," *Columbia Journal of World Business* (July 1970), pp. 27–32; J. C. Narver, "Some Observations on the Impact of Antitrust Merger Policy on Marketing," *Journal of Marketing* (January 1969), pp. 24–31; L. W. Stern, "Perspective on Public Policy: Comments on the Great Debate," *Journal of Marketing* (January 1969), pp. 24–31.

business. But while doing so they are often willing to agree that consumer requests for information, consumer complaints, and consumer desires for better products and services are reasonable. Thus it is often difficult for advocates of consumerism to understand why they are depicted as antagonists of our market system.

The antagonists of consumerism often present a simplistic rationale which takes the following general mold. Consumerism is based on laws designed to protect consumers. These laws regulate marketplace activity such as packaging, labeling, pricing, grading, selling, and advertising. They restrict freedom of business action and competition, and therefore are undesirable.

It is obvious, however, that consumerism need not automatically mean more government regulation. Sometimes consumer groups oppose regulations. The fair-trade laws may be cited as an example. Laws to ban the advertising of prescription drug prices are another. Consumer groups in fact might be willing to promote action against certain laws. They may prefer self-regulation by industry.

The point is that as consumer groups become more sophisticated, more informed, and more aware, they will look at the implications both of laws that are now on the books and those that are being proposed. They will be better able to evaluate the impact of laws passed in the name of consumer protection or to promote competition. Sometimes such laws are actually designed to protect special interest groups. Other times they seek to block activities that are actually in the consumers' best interest. Consumer advocates in the future may present their ideas on the facts to the public, and so influence public policy. A recent case in point is the proposed no-fault insurance which is being opposed quite actively and avidly by special interest groups such as the trial lawyers. Consumer advocates, however, are countering the trial lawyers' opposition.

As consumer groups mature and become better informed, they will become more cognizant of existing and proposed regulations. Thus the consumer movement may well play a rather important role in creating a marketplace that has not merely more regulation, but regulation designed to benefit consumers, while enhancing the competitive climate.

In reality consumerism as a movement does not have the inherent characteristics of many other historical movements of our country. Consumerism, even though it has reportedly been noted in other decades, has never had an effective lobby. It has not had an active power to promote its legislative demands in Congress. Consumer groups are only now beginning to organize themselves.

The consumer movement is not a movement that has been well financed. It does not have the funds available to underwrite desired actions. Consumerism is not supported by highly efficient corporate law firms. It does not have an accepted list of national priorities. Its objectives and goals are often poorly articulated, if at all. Yet despite this, progress has been made. Congressmen, senators, state and federal governments are now paying heed. Serious attention is being given to the general aims and desires of the consumer movement.[3]

The consumer movement in the literature, sometimes appears to be portrayed as a unified movement with nonconflicting interests and objectives. Traditional economic thought supports this by indicating that all interests are satisfied or maximized in the marketplace. In reality, however, some consumer interests are satisfied at the expense of other consumers. Inconsistency exists among consumers in their various roles such as performing inadequately on the production line and complaining about the quality of products; demanding more jobs and higher wages along with higher dividends and pensions; expecting higher than normal wage increases coupled with less inflation and less expensive goods.

THE CONSUMER MOVEMENT AND PUBLIC POLICY

To what extent does a cause and effect relationship seem to exist between the consumer movement and public policy developments? Have consumer movements preceded the enactment of laws restraining the business system? Was the consumer movement of the 1960s of such an intensity to presage the passage of major legislation confronting marketing? Let me share a few opinions.

There is little doubt that the consumer movement has had an impact on some laws that were proposed and passed. When the so-called "consumer bill of rights" was in essence endorsed by Presidents Kennedy, Johnson, and Nixon, one might reasonably have expected some of the kinds of governmental and legislative activity that occurred.

However, it is also interesting to note that many of the laws designed to protect the consumer were not demanded by consumer activists. They were brought into being at a time when the consumer movement may not even have been a recognized force. They did not stem from actions of groups of consumer advocates or the lobbying actions of consumerists. Rather, they stemmed from administrative decisions that had been made, or the pressures from particular interest groups, including professional and business interests.

Some interesting questions for this workshop to consider relate to what will happen as the consumer movement unfolds, develops a more active voice and political clout. What will happen when consumer activists start advocating their interests and flexing their muscles before various hearings and regulatory agencies as well as before company boards

[3] For a historical perspective of the consumer movement see Ralph Nader, "Consumer Protection and Corporate Disclosure," *Business Today* (Autumn 1968), p. 20; and footnotes 4, 5, and 6.

of directors? Will there be even more regulation and greater restrictions of self-initiative and our market system?

A thorough investigation of the interface between the consumer movement and public policy should include a consideration of the nature of business constraints, how they are initiated, and what role consumer inputs play. Permit me to make a few brief comments.

Most of the rules governing the conduct of our nation's daily business activities are not legislatively proposed nor enacted. Rather they are both proposed and executed by federal administrative agencies. These agencies base their decisions on their own administrative expertise, and on public response received to proposed legislation. Public response may consist both of business and consumer opinions. In reality, however, consumer viewpoints are usually lacking.

Last year the American Marketing Association initiated a White House Internship Program for undergraduate students. Four White House interns working in the Office of Consumer Affairs during the summer investigated in detail the nature of consumer representation in this rule-making process. They determined that there is little consumer involvement in federal agency rule making. The interns also investigated methods of broadening consumer response to proposed regulations to make federal administrative decision making more responsive to the interests of consumers.

THE FEDERAL RULE-MAKING PROCESS

The federal agency rule-making process includes such important activities as setting regulations, governing labeling of products, quantity and quality of products, product safety, packaging of products, advertising, pricing and product warranties, and so on. Yet the process is not at all well understood by consumers. In reality, the consumer sector is practically excluded from this decision-making process.

The federal agency decision process revolves around the publication of the Federal Register. It is the instrument by which federal agencies are required to convey to the public, including consumers, legal notices of proposed rules that are awaiting final action. Under the Administrative Procedures Act, the particular federal agency concerned sets a time limit for the receipt of comments on proposed rules. Frequently the agency does not allow enough time for consumer comments. All the letters and briefs received, however, are put into a file which is open to the public. In this manner comments received by the agency may eventually be incorporated into the final rule. In theory, the final regulation is to reflect the consideration of all comments submitted by the public—consumer and business alike—as well as the expertise of the particular agency.

But it is obvious that consumers up to now have not participated actively. Had they tried to respond, consumers would have faced difficulties in interpreting the legal and technical language used in the Federal Register. The Federal Register has been termed as being incomprehensive to almost anyone.

The AMA White House interns investigated several of the files resulting from notices placed in the Federal Register. The actions concerned proposals to raise standards on imported tomatoes, standards on peanut butter, statements in the advertising of nonprescription systemic analgesics, and the grades for limes and avocados. The interns concluded that small business interests are not represented in the federal agency rule-making process. Large business interests, such as the interests of growers and agriculture suppliers, are well represented. Consumers generally are nonparticipants, yet this occurred at a time when there is a great influx of new regulations being promulgated on behalf of consumers.

The Federal Register is virtually unnoticed by general consumers. Consumers' voices are not heard in making the rules which are supposed to reflect their interest. Consumers do not comprehend what is being proposed nor the implications of rules. The system of making comments on the proposals in the Federal Register usually allows little time for individual consumers to represent opinions to the proper agency. The Federal Register is not widely publicized and I would guess that most advocates of consumerism, or members of the consumer movement, do not even know that it exists. While businessmen may have trouble reading the Federal Register, through their lawyers, they are well aware of the limitations and implications of proposed actions. They are represented.

The major item of concern for our session, however, is the fact that consumerism and the consumer viewpoint does not seem to be well represented in public policy developments. A consumer perspective does not appear to have proceeded the enactment of various federal agency roles and constraints on the business system of the past.

The above is just one area of public policy concern. Public policies have taken at least two general developmental directions. Some have developed as a direct response to consumer pressures and complaints as our program description might suggest. Others, however, have emerged without great concern for what the consumer may seem to prefer at a point in time. For example, the policies and rules that "largely protect consumers from themselves," even though not explicitly sought, worked for, or even desired by consumer groups, have been implemented and may be highly desirable.[4] They may be surrounded by a hedge of ethical implications and implementation problems.

Also it should be noted that while I shall not deal at all with the

[4] Ralph Nader, "Consumer Protection . . . ," p. 20.

public policy alternatives to governmental rules and regulations, they include a host of viable alternatives. The education of consumers, the use of financial policies to control the consumers, the emphasis on social responsibility, and the use of fiscal control over business practice are examples. In implementing such alternatives, it may be easier in general to use fiscal policy to control business than it is to educate consumers. For in so doing there are fewer entities to deal with and there are positive political benefits for some politicians.[5]

THE CHANGING SCENE

It is not clear whether "consumer movements" preceded the enactment of laws constraining the business and market system in the past. It may be argued that we had consumer movements at the turn of this century, or during the 1920s.[6] But in reality, I do not believe that there is much comparability among them. To draw conclusions about the impact of consumerism in the past and to assume that parallel situations exist today is very dangerous.

If nothing else has changed, certainly the climate of the times, the characteristics of consumers, their very outlooks, educational perspectives and expectations, the practices of businesses, the nature of business and political response and mass communications are vastly different. The consumer perspectives in times past were even more unorganized, even more poorly represented, and far less institutionalized on state and federal government levels. The consumer viewpoint had far fewer advocates. Consumers themselves were more fettered both socially and economically. The result was that the consumer viewpoint, in order to be focused and congealed, seemed to be more dependent on a crisis, tragedy, or scandal before actions benefiting the consumer on the part of either government or business could be expected.

This is supported by some of the events that led to the enactments of the Sherman Antitrust Act, the Federal Trade Commission Act, or the Clayton Act which were designed to preclude unfair competition and unfair competitive practices. Upton Sinclair's novel *The Jungle,* for example, set forth in a very dramatic fashion the existence of a crisis. It caused great reactions and stimulated the enactment of the Pure Food Act of 1906.

One could also argue, however, that to an extent the consumer movement still requires a crisis as a rallying point. This was the case with the Kefauver-Harris Amendment to the Food, Drug, and Cosmetic Act. The amendment was stimulated by the tragedy of the thalidomide

[5] *The Challenge of Consumerism,* The Conference Board, 1971.

[6] Patrick McGuire, "New Opportunities in Consumerism," *The Conference Board Record* (December 1970), pp. 41–43.

babies. But I think the consumer movement is now less dependent on such crisis issues. It is becoming less reactive and more active.

In a similar vein, it is difficult to accept the proposition that the consumer movement of the past resulted from the political impact of potential votes. For it was not the reaction of the consumers in the marketplace, nor even the threat at the ballot boxes sensed by politicians, that led to consumer regulation at the turn of this century or during the 1920s and 30s. That is at least partially the case today. I think that prior to the 1960s politicians and lobbyists were well aware that there really was no effective consumer interest or point of view.

Contrast this with the current situation on the Washington scene and in state and local governments. There are now consumer representatives in various governmental agencies. A Federal Consumer Protection Agency is being proposed. Numerous voluntary consumer organizations exist. Consumer advocates, public interest law firms, and other spokesmen are regularly featured on mass media. Business representatives, their lobbyists in Washington, governmental administrators, and politicians perceive of the consumer movement of the 1970s much differently than was the case previously. Thus the impact upon public policy appears to be much greater, more immediate,[7] and to have a more lasting impact.

Another difference is notable. Consumers are now becoming more aware of some proposed regulations and edicts issued by governmental agencies that affect them. This has not been the case for very long, and certainly was not so during the 1920s. In fact, consumerists have been regarded as novices in government circles. They did not have the contacts with the various federal regulatory agencies that many other pressure groups had. They were not aware of developments that affected them. Recently, however, the proclamations of such groups as the Food and Drug Administration, Federal Trade Commission, Justice Department, Department of Agriculture, and Civil Aeronautics Bureau, which have consumer implications, are being surveyed by many including volunteers, consumer groups, public interest lawyers, student groups, and representatives of mass media.

Consumer groups no longer merely wait for the government to take the appropriate legislative action. They have begun to petition agencies asking that certain actions be taken on issues such as warranties, advertising, and insurance. They follow proposed regulations designed to protect them and seek to improve the flaws and overcome loopholes and limitations. Certainly the movement is more aware, sophisticated, and coordinated.[8]

---

[7] George S. Day, and David Aaker, "A Guide to Consumerism," *Journal of Marketing* (July 1970), pp. 12–19.

[8] Virginia Knauer, *The Growing Impact of Consumerism on Marketing.*

How can one account for the growing impact of the consumer movement in the 1960s as contrasted with previous decades? I am not sure. Perhaps it is based on the climate of the times including affluence, technology, depersonalization of society, and bigness. Perhaps it is a movement whose time has simply arrived. Perhaps it results from the charisma of some of its leaders. Perhaps it is rooted in the fundamental "goodness" of its appeal that it represents what is ethical, moral, and right.[9]

It seems evident that the consumers movement will gain increasing power in the near future. It will have greater impact on public issues. The movement will grow and become even more organized. As such, it will become more aware of both business and government interests and actions on many issues. In some ways business will stand to benefit.[10] It is obvious that marketing people must reject some of their postures and work with consumer representatives within the boundaries and public policy constraints established by consumer groups.

SELF REGULATION

Can self regulation be developed to a satisfactory level to significantly reduce pressures for new legislation? I am assuming we are referring to self regulation on the part of a whole industry or across industries, and not on the part of one company. There are several recent examples of self regulation.

The New York Movers Association presents one interesting example. Movers were the target of an exceptionally large number of consumer complaints. Many of them were warranted. The New York association became serious and established a mandatory arbitration system. An impartial chairman was established who receives complaints and can arbitrate—his decisions are binding. The association also had standards designed to preclude deceptive practices written directly into their labor agreements. The association, being serious about self-regulatory attempts, has teeth and seems to work. The result has been a dramatic reduction in consumer complaints.

A different approach to self regulation is that adopted by the National Association of Home Builders, which, however, poses a legal problem. The association has a Registered Builders Program. Contractors who pass a screen of the association by meeting certain standards can use the Registered Builders Logo. The program includes a full year's warranty for purchasers of homes and an arbitration program. But con-

[9] William Lazer and Eugene J. Kelley, *Social Marketing: Perspectives and Viewpoints*, (Homewood, Ill.: Richard D. Irwin Inc., 1973). See especially Section II, pp. 93–169.

[10] E. B. Weiss, "Consumerism and Marketing," an eight-part series appearing in *Advertising Age* from May 8 to July 3, 1967.

tractors gaining use of the Logo must meet certain standards. They must in essence "open their books." If this program really works for the industry and contractors are screened, then there might well be a question of restraint of trade on the part of those excluded.

Sometimes to prevent additional regulation an industry will work with and through government agencies to establish rules and standards. The cosmetic industry met with the Food and Drug Administration to do so. The industry did not want to list ingredients on packages and labels, or to provide adverse reaction data. They were willing, however, to supply information about ingredients to the government on registering and filing applications. To protect consumers, particularly allergic consumers, data about ingredients are desirable. The Office of Consumer Affairs was able to gain a commitment from a few of the cosmetic manufacturers to list all ingredients. By giving favorable publicity to those companies cooperating and so benefiting consumers, some of the other manufacturers are being influenced to follow suit. Perhaps appropriate self-regulation will be achieved.

The citrus industry adopted an interesting approach to self regulation. The industry is concerned with percentage labeling of juice contents for diluted juice products. They requested that the federal government establish a standard of quality for juice under the Food, Drug, and Cosmetic Act. The industry corresponded with over 3,000 consumers and consumer groups across the country and urged them to provide the Federal Food and Drug Administration with consumer viewpoints on proposed rules. Thus consumers were encouraged to become a force in establishing standards by citrus marketers themselves.

The American Home Appliance Manufacturers developed a widely publicized and successful program of self-regulation. The program covered a new point of sale information system that included information about installment and maintenance costs, as well as a consumer complaint system. The latter involves public spirited citizens who serve as members of "the jury." The action seems to have helped the industry.

In a similar manner two associations, the Home Furnishings Manufacturers and Home Furnishings Retailers, have gotten together to set up a consumer dispute system that lessens the "ping pong" effect on consumers seeking remedy from members of one group or the other. Many additional programs are starting to emerge in a variety of formats including those of the Better Business Bureaus.

The Council of Better Business Bureaus is trying to improve consumer-business relations by setting up voluntary arbitration systems in every major city. The programs would require that businessmen agree in advance to binding arbitration in disputes with consumers. The arbitrators would be nonlegal volunteers from the community. Decisions reached would have the impact of law. About 35 pilot arbitration programs are now in operation. While this appears to be an effective and economical way of handling many grievances, it does not seem to have received the enthusiastic support and acclaim of consumer groups.

A number of supermarket chains are conducting their own basic research and experimentation. They are trying to assess the best ways of presenting information to consumers so that consumers can act on a rational basis. They are studying the impact of unit pricing. Based on the findings, chains may call upon the government to pass regulations that will permit chains to act in the best interests of the consumers and also in the interests of the food chains themselves. The important fact is that they are gathering scientific data and not merely countering consumer demands on an emotional basis.

Self regulation can result in conflicts on the part of industry or association segments. For example, the Federal Food and Drug Administration is urging food processors to adopt nutrient labeling plans that will list food values. Some members of the industry are willing to implement such plans immediately. The National Canners Association, however, is definitely opposed. Thus the traditional perspective of the existence of a solid antigovernment front by industry does not seem to correspond with reality.

Government agencies can play the role of stimulator in gaining self regulation. The packaging of bacon is one case in point. Consumers have complained widely about bacon packaging over an extended period of time. The industry held that the problem was caused by technical packaging complications which consumer complainants did not understand. A governmental agency contacted the paperboard industry about the possibility of solving the packaging problem. The paperboard industry offered several feasible alternatives for improving the packaging of bacon. One bacon manufacturer saw a competitive advantage in adopting the new package and did so. This was publicized by the Office of Consumer Affairs with the result that other members voluntarily adopted the new packaging.

Permit me to venture a few opinions about self regulation. First, to date self regulation including arbitration has not had great impact but it is a promising alternative. Second, in the near future the thrust in the development of self regulation will not replace the need for new legislation. Third, over the next decade the state and federal governments will continue to play the major role in regulating industries to protect consumers. There are several reasons for this. It is difficult, if not impossible, to gain agreement and financial commitments on the part of all of the members of an industry—particularly the worst offenders. It is even more difficult to persuade consumers that industry actions alone will be enough. It is also impossible to convince some politicians, who will recognize publicity opportunities, that further legislation is not required. Fourth, there will be new roles for both government agencies and consumer groups in the self regulation process, and a more cooperative stance will develop on the part of both government and business. Fifth, self regulation as an activity will expand and with it there will be an increase in both consumer satisfaction and the effective functioning of our market system.

ADDITIONAL OBSERVATIONS

Permit me to close with a few general observations concerning consumerism and public policy developments. The role of consumers in the federal government is being institutionalized. A number of the federal governmental agencies have established consumer advisory councils, others have consumer representatives. The White House Office of Consumer Affairs, established by executive order of President Nixon in 1971, was a signal event. A Federal Consumer Protection Agency may soon be approved. The result will be that the federal government will indeed continue to reflect the growing impact of consumerism which makes itself felt in public policy.

In the future, the consumer groups and their representatives will be even more active. Through time they will obtain a much better understanding of governmental processes and will be more keenly aware of the procedures involved in achieving their objectives in legislation and public policy. They will begin to master the budgetary aspects involved in the effective enforcement of consumer protection statutes. They will learn where the sensitive pressure points are in government. They will become more organized and able to challenge the various congressmen, senators, and federal administrators on their records in order to promote the public interest. They will become better equipped with data and will be more knowledgeable about the pragmatics of the marketplace.

There seems to be a curious phenomenon operating in consumer regulation. The major thrust is not now occurring at the federal level. In the last few years, federal regulation has been slowed. This often is obscured by statistics quoted on the 400 or 500 consumer bills that have been proposed at federal level. The current action in consumer legislation, however, is at the state and not the federal level. Even though far fewer bills are proposed at state levels, a much higher proportion are passed. For example, state legislation has been enacted on class action suits, unit pricing, advertising, merchandising schemes, and no-fault insurance.

The thrust of consumerism at the state level, however, has created an interesting phenomenon. Given minute variations in each of the state laws, businessmen and industry associations are sometimes unduly handicapped. It is difficult to conduct business effectively when a host of minor variations exist in regulations dealing with essentially the same matter. Thus, it is quite possible, although perhaps ironic, that businessmen may on their own accord actively seek federal preemptive statutes to regulate them. Should this occur, consumerism at the state level could lead to federal action, which in turn might be the coup de grace for state consumer regulation.

Has the consumer movement led to increased governmental intervention in business? Indeed it has. One need only consider such matters as truth in lending, truth in advertising, product dating, unit pricing, and nutrient labeling. A glance about a major supermarket will indicate that food chains have been responding to a number of labeling, pricing, coding, and packaging practices that consumers found irritating. Businessmen recognize that further legislation will be pending unless action is taken, which is itself a stimulus for voluntary action. Thus a very direct and positive posture has been adopted in response to some consumer pressures.

As you know, some supermarkets have moved to unit pricing. They may not prefer it. Perhaps it is bothersome and costly. However, consumer advocates still complain about the inability to make rational decisions based upon price comparisons. Unit pricing is an issue to which the Public Policy and Issues Division of the American Marketing Association has addressed itself. The American Marketing Association has just approved a statement supporting unit pricing.

In the future government is going to provide more representation to consumers and their advocates. They will give consumer groups greater assistance. Consumerism will be recognized as a more significant force in government-industry relationships. The consumer viewpoint will be brought more directly into the federal government and industry equation. Regulatory procedures will be adjusted to reflect better the best interests of consumers. In the past, the voice of federal administration has frequently been substituted for the voice of business administrators under the guise of furthering consumer welfare and gaining consumer benefits by regulations.

The federal government in the future, will share more knowledge with consumers. It can be expected to provide lists of products that meet prescribed standards. President Nixon in 1971 ordered a compilation of such information. He also forwarded a product methods testing bill to Congress under which marketers would be encouraged to make reference in their communications, and on their labels, to the fact that their products met tests certified by the government. It may be that government approval and certification might be given to products. At any rate, consumers will be obtaining more government information to help them compare products and services.

A specific outcome of the consumerism movement was the creation of the National Business Council for Consumer Affairs, created by executive order of the president in 1971. It institutionalized and formalized the efforts to top business leaders to work with government to promote consumer interests. The results will probably be several programs within government, as well as more self-regulation by business that will benefit consumers.

What will the role of marketers be in all of this? On the one hand they might prefer to lead an active charge to counter consumers forces and measures. That in general would, I believe, be a very short-sighted and unsuccessful activity. Hopefully marketers will recognize the many opportunities that exist within consumerism. Obviously, some marketing practices will be altered.

What has been the impact of consumerism on public policy issues? What will it be? Will it mean much heavier restrictions on marketing, greater government regulation of marketing activities, increased self-regulation, or all of these? Will it result in suppressed markets, or a more keenly competitive marketing environment and more workable competition? As the discussion indicates at this juncture, unequivocal answers do not exist. The important activity is to consider the issues, share insights and opinions, and become better informed. Regardless of specific outcomes, developing trends indicate that we shall realize increasing responsiveness on the part of both government and business to consumers, their wants, needs, and expectations. In turn this should result in a decrease in the need for the kinds of consumer programs now being demanded and perhaps the emergence of a new role for the consumer movement.

Bibliography

1. Aitken, J. L. "Implications for Marketing in Current U.S. Social Trends," *The Conference Board Record,* December 1970, pp. 37–40.
2. Broffman, Morton H. "Is Consumerism Merely Another Marketing Concept?" *MSU Business Topics,* Winter 1971, pp. 15–21.
3. Day, George S., and Aaker, David. "A Guide to Consumerism," *Journal of Marketing,* July 1970, pp. 12–19.
4. Drucker, Peter. "The Shame of Marketing," *Marketing/Communications,* August 1969, pp. 60–64.
5. Herrmann, Robert O. "Consumerism: Its Goals, Organizations, and Future," *Journal of Marketing,* October 1970, pp. 55–60.
6. Hopkinson, Thomas G. "New Battle Ground—Consumer Interest," *Harvard Business Review,* September-October 1964, pp. 97–104.
7. McGuire, E. Patrick. "New Opportunities in Consumerism," *Conference Board Record,* December 1970, pp. 41–43.
8. Nader, Ralph. "Consumer Protection and Corporate Disclosure," *Business Today,* Autumn 1968, p. 20.
9. Stover, Carl F. "The Corporation and the Public Good," *The Conference Board Report,* December 1970, pp. 33–36.
10. Weiss, E. B. "Consumerism and Marketing," An eight-part series appearing in *Advertising Age* from May 8 to July 3, 1967.

3 MARKETING ACTIVITIES: SOCIAL PERSPECTIVES

MARKETING ACTIVITIES are examined from a social perspective in this chapter. The social and ethical dimensions of marketing, quality of life issues, and governmental and business impacts on marketing are considered as they relate to a modern society. Management is increasingly aware that business has a social responsibility. The major concern is becoming one of translating social consciousness into business practice.

One issue is how to reward socially conscious behavior throughout the organization. Managers have traditionally been rewarded on a short-term financially oriented basis. If the entire organization is to develop a social consciousness, it will be necessary to reward those in the organization based on longer-term behavior which serves to enhance consumer-citizen as well as business interests. Reconciling corporate and consumer-citizen interests involves discussion of such questions as: Are profit considerations the only moderating factors determining company policy and market offerings? What is the ethical responsibility of the firm to provide products that are "good" for society even if these are not products necessarily wanted by all consumers—automobile safety devices being an example.

Scholars, businessmen, government officials, and consumer advocates are debating the extent and viability of business involvement in many areas of social responsibility. In this chapter, this issue is examined in terms of societal implications of a firm's marketing activities. Thus, the social responsibility and ethical dimensions, quality of life considerations, and government and business impact are considered as they relate to business and marketing activities in modern society.

What do these social perspectives mean to the individual businessman? Is it possible for him to be a businessman during the day and assume other roles at night? Why are some advocating the meshing of these two roles? Why insist that a firm be interested in more than just the generation of profits? Must a firm involve itself in ethical considerations when considering what suppliers to deal with, what products to manufacture, what markets to sell to, and what future consequences present actions will lead to?

In addition to questions about the expanded role of business and the businessman within the social system, questions arise concerning the assessment of these activities. Should the firm initiate self-audits of its and its employees social performance? Should it await consumer or government outcries? Or, should it wait for government regulation? These and other questions must be answered by the individual firm and individual businessman. However, discussion of the "correct solution" for all firms and businessmen will remain topics for debate for many years.

a.

Social and ethical responsibilities of marketing

CONSUMER-CITIZENS are pressuring business to achieve higher levels of social and ethical responsibility. Why should corporations, and especially marketers, respond to these new demands? Part of the answer lies in business concern with the "threat" of more governmental regulation. This is the argument which goes, "If we don't, government will." But part of the reason why business is moving to higher levels of social performance is to be found in consideration of the ethics of the situation. Socially responsible behavior on the part of the firm can be justified by standards of rightness as well as of economics and the law. It may be sound business practice, as well as morally right, for a marketer to attempt to meet socially responsible performance standards.

What implications does the trend to higher standards of ethical responsibility have for marketing managers? The pressures imply the development of rules and standards by which business actions may be judged as "right" or "wrong". In other words, ethical decisions under free enterprise are "moral decisions", impelled by social sanctions, but modified by economics and environmental requirements. The growing professionalism in marketing is also stimulating the development and acceptance of pervasive "socially conscious" standards of ethics. In this section some insights into the changing social and ethical responsibilities of marketing are explored.

In the first article Lipson, Kelley, and Marshak discuss the use of social performance objectives and measurement by corporations. Clasen concludes that effective channels of communications are essential for the development of ethical marketing practice. Next, Bartels proposes a model for analyzing ethics in marketing. Patterson then provides insight on how marketing executives can develop some guidelines for the social and ethical responsibilities. Anshen describes alterations being made in the social contract between the business community and society. Concluding this section, Grether discusses the prerequisites for long-run, effective social involvement.

Answers to questions of social accomplishment are expected by consumers, community action groups, social critics, and other publics. If business does not provide this information, other groups will. The starting point for socioindustrial progress can only be accomplished through the meshing of corporate and national goals. The authors posit one manner in which social performance can be improved—by extending the sociobusiness planning horizon.

16. INTEGRATING SOCIAL FEEDBACK AND SOCIAL AUDITS INTO CORPORATE PLANNING*

Harry A. Lipson,†
Eugene J. Kelley,‡
and Seymour Marshak§

How are General Motors' contributions to society *measured?* How is Lockheed's *social impact evaluated*—or that of a product like the SST? How does the Bank of America *audit* specific policies to meet public interest criteria tests? How does Procter and Gamble know if its products are beneficial to the *consumer-citizen?* How does General Electric assess what it *contributes* to improving the human condition—or the *quality of life* for its employees and its customers?

Corporate presidents and board members of the largest and most powerful firms confronted by these questions do not have acceptable answers. Unless socially acceptable answers to these quality of life questions are forthcoming, there will be yet another chapter written in the "Why Business Always Loses" book. In this article, the essentials of a corporate strategy for confronting and meeting the quality of life issue is presented.

There are two basic reasons a major firm must invest time and resources in finding answers to such questions and developing policies which will improve social performance.

1. Total corporate planning requires confronting *quality of life* questions.

* Not previously published.
† University of Alabama.
‡ Pennsylvania State University.
§ Ford Motor Company.

2. Answers to social accomplishment questions are expected by customers, legislative committees, investors, community action groups, employees, social critics, and other publics. *If business does not provide this information, other groups will.*

Expenditure of time and resources on such issues is still regarded by some managers as wasteful or as time spent on peripheral issues. However, allocating resources to such issues is no longer a matter of option. These questions are not on the periphery of corporate planning, but an inescapable part of corporate planning and concern.

The partial answers existing in accounting-economics terms do not satisfy growing concern with the corporation as a means to a social end—improving the quality of life. The *quality of life* issue is the major problem confronting U.S. business now. Meeting the issue will require management commitment and time, will be costly, and frustrating, but necessary.

Corporate presidents can expect to spend more time on the quality of life issues—on consumer/environmental and social concerns—than their predecessors. Management's new task is to balance traditional profit and rate of returns on investment criteria with new definitions of social costs, social purpose, and social conscience. The president of General Motors stated he spent more time in one year on matters of this type than all of past presidents did over the entire life of the corporation! Time of this sort will be spent; the question is how wisely will the time be invested and how successful will the firm be in answering social performance questions raised by the groups shown in the following illustration?

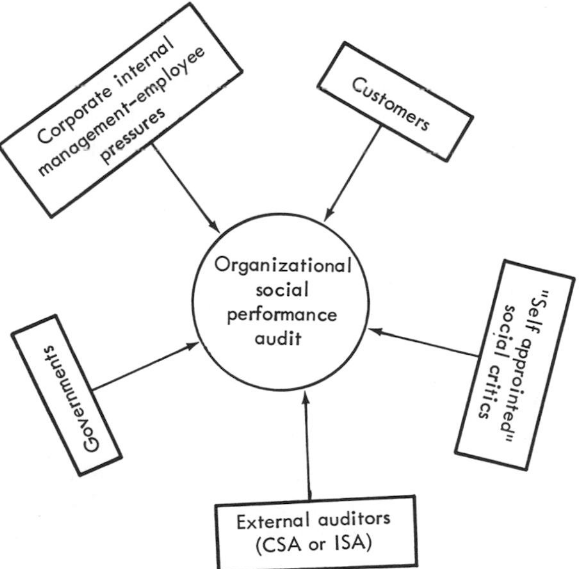

In this article we will indicate what some companies are doing now to meet the quality of life issue and what they could be doing to manage these problems of social concern.

The following problems facing management must be assessed and planned for. Each of these is discussed in this article.

1. Identification of relevant problems, present and emerging, of social concerns relating to corporate mission and operations. (National Social Goals)

2. Development of baseline concepts and measures of social performance and social impact of individual corporation and organizational units. (Sociobusiness Concept and Audit)

3. Routinization of social performance objectives and measurement into total corporate planning and action. (Organizational Changes)

4. Investment of corporate talent and resources in specific prioritized programs for change designed to achieve specified results on a scheduled basis in areas of social concern. Changes in the magnitude and direction of programs are indicated by management/auditor assessment of baseline measures. (Sociobusiness Planning)

SELECTIVE CONVERSION OF NATIONAL SOCIAL GOALS INTO CORPORATE OPPORTUNITIES

Meshing of corporate and national goals

The starting point for socioindustrial progress analysis is not to be found in corporate traditions or corporate history or even industrial history. The starting point is to relate social progress of the corporation to national goals and to the social indicators being developed to evaluate the attainment of these goals. This approach sounds like socialism to some. It is not. Social progress was once considered to be a national by-product of economic progress. Society believed that social progress was achieved through continued economic growth and progress. The accumulation of material wealth and affluence is no longer automatically equated with social progress by a growing number of influential Americans. Public policy sees social progress as a goal to be achieved in itself and not necessarily the same as economic progress. With the new parity between social progress and economic progress, social progress is seen as a goal to be deliberately sought—by business and other social groups.

Here is where national goals and governmental programs can be useful as indicators of major areas of social concern. National goals have business relevance as we move toward a social industrial complex. In a social industrial society national goals are increasingly relevant to business policy. A classification of national goals follows.

NATIONAL SOCIAL GOALS

1. Health and safety
   - Personal and environmental health
   - Public and environmental safety
2. Education, skills, and income
   - Basic schooling and higher education
   - Skills and jobs
   - Amount, adequacy, and continuity of incomes
3. Human habitat
   - Housing
   - Quality of neighborhood
   - Access to the area
   - Recreational opportunities
   - Quality of larger environments
4. Finer things
   - Arts and sciences
   - Nature and beauty
5. Leisure and production
   - Interrelationships between economic growth and availability of discretionary time
6. Freedom, justice, and harmony
   - Concerns with liberty
   - Concerns with democratic values
   - Quality of social environment

Specialists concerned with social indicators are now developing tools and measures to appraise progress towards such goals.

Social indicators are tools to be used to measure progress in quality of life areas. They are, as Bauer defined them, statistics, statistical series, and all other forms of evidence that enable us to assess where we stand and are going with respect to our values and goals, and to evaluate specific programs and determine their impact. A social indicator is a describable trait/characteristic/attitude which either is applicable to a substantial segment of the population or has shown evidence of recent change in magnitude or intensity. Over a period of time, it should show changes in magnitude or intensity of the trend being measured and identify the population groups most involved with the change. Hopefully, it should show how the trend being measured interacts with other trends.

We are at a low level of theoretical and statistical sophistication in responding to such events. The present state of the art of measuring life quality factors limits our ability to use social indicators. However, this means that a great deal of work is required, not that we ignore the present intangibles.

Various primary indicators are in each grouping of national goals (except freedom, justice, and harmony). For example, primary indicators in health and safety include:[1]

1. Average life expectancy in years at birth.
2. Number of persons with major disabilities.
3. Number of violent crimes per 100,000 persons per year.

In the human habitat area, indicators include:[2]

1. Percent of persons living in adequate housing.
2. Percent of persons living in satisfactory neighborhoods.
3. Total travel and freight cost to the public index of costs.
4. Number of persons exposed to bothersome pollution.
5. Percent persons regularly taking part in recreation.

No business enterprise can be expected to devote itself to all social goals in profit or service terms. Rather, each firm must prioritize these goals in order of need for its stockholders, community, employees, and customers. Thus, the business relevancy of these goals may include in the area of health and safety:

Business Relevancy:
Health and Safety National Goals

1. Correction of past infractions in the environmental pollution area.
2. Abandonment of company policies which cause pollution.
3. Refusal to deal with suppliers damaging the environment.
4. Abandonment or correction of products which pollute the environment or which are hazardous to personal health.
5. Abandonment or correction of products which are hazardous to public safety.
6. Employee dispensary and physical checkups.

In the area of education, skills, and income:

1. Company sponsored continuing education for employees.
2. Monetary contributions to various institutions of learning.
3. Help with training or retraining skills programs.
4. Income policies.
   a. Adequacy of income.
   b. Disability income, which includes maternity benefits disability, and continuance of seniority during disability periods for both male and female.
   c. Pension policies.

In the area of finer things:

1. Monetary support of arts.
2. Monetary support of sciences.

---

[1] Nestor E. Terleckyj, "Measuring Possibilities of Social Change," *Looking Ahead* (National Planning Association, 1970), pp. 1–11.

[2] Ibid.

3. Sponsorship of concerts for public.
4. Free cultural events for employees.
5. Maintenance or support of recreational facilities for employees and/or public.
6. Esthetically pleasing company facilities.

It is difficult to quantify these measures given the current state of the art. Premature attempts at quantification can lead to various methodological problems and policy failures as in the McNamara Fallacy. Yankelovich has described what happens when what he describes as the McNamara discipline is applied too literally:

> The first step is to measure whatever can be easily measured. This is okay as far as it goes. The second step is to disregard that which can't be easily measured or give it an arbitrary quantitative value. This is artificial and misleading. The third step is to presume what can't be measured easily really isn't important. This is blindness. The fourth step is to say that what can't be easily measured really doesn't exist. This is suicide.[3]

Business confronting quality of life issues is reacting not only to statistics but to not easily measured social value changes. The danger is that business perceives social value changes as another short-term crisis, not as a situation requiring fundamental change in management.

One starting point for corporate analyses is to relate its efforts to thinking about national social goals and about the fundamental shifts in the relationships between economic progress and social progress as perceived by influential Americans.

The common element in the new demands upon business is the departure from strictly economic considerations which have been regarded as appropriate criteria to determine the allocation and use of private resources. This is a direct challenge to the thesis that decisions taken with intent to maximize profits also maximize public benefits.

SOCIOBUSINESS: A NEW CONCEPT

Some chief executives think that the issue is whether or not business should give a little more or less money to solving some nonbusiness social problems or hiring more hard-core minorities. This interpretation assumes that the decisions are optional and that they don't have much to do with the nitty-gritty of running a profitable business. Nothing could be further from the truth. Increasingly, the decisions demanded are not optional but are a matter of tough government legislation and enforcement. Increasingly, the demands conflict directly with traditional methods of achieving profits, growth, and market share.[4]

---

[3] Daniel Yankelovich, "The New Odds," presented at the Eleventh Annual Marketing Strategy Conference of the Sales Executives Club of New York (October 15, 1971).

[4] Yankelovich, "The New Odds," p. 7.

Adoption of a sociobusiness concept is no longer a matter of option for our major enterprises if the business is to be relevant to the new social progress concerns and social value changes. The sociobusiness concept offers a conceptual framework for integrating the firm's relationship to its ultimate environment. The sociobusiness concept is an extension of traditional management and marketing concepts with redefinitions of mission, service, consumer, product, and profit. The sociobusiness concept has six major elements:

Mission 1. *The corporate mission is defined in social system terms of long-run profitable service to the consumer-citizen.* Sociobusiness issues are seen as critical and urgent, impacting not only on profits but also being relevant to the survival of the enterprise in society.

Societal service 2. *Management recognizes that service to the consumer-citizen requires fulfilling societal and environmental concerns as well as the satisfaction of traditional economic goods and services.* Therefore, business programs are evaluated and tested in terms of societal impact as well as traditional balance sheets and profit and loss statements.

Products 3. *Products are defined as sociobusiness products, not just as economic goods.* Analysis of sociobusiness product policies considers the social effects on the individuals within the corporate system—in larger systems within which the firm operates and with customers. The firm is aware of its role as a molder of social values for both employees and consumer-citizens.

Profits 4. *Profit concepts are recognized in their full complexity.* Sociobusiness firms are concerned with redefining profit to reflect contemporary values and needs. For example, the concept of social profit might provide for more efficient resource management and rehabilitation over the long run instead of simply being a monetary sum or accounting figure accumulated during the fiscal year.

Actions priorities 5. Management commitment is reflected in prioritized action programs in each area of sociobusiness performance. A company can't do everything at once and still stay in business. Priorities are required in order to change attitudes, organization, and corporate performance.

Audits 6. *The firm acknowledges its sociobusiness performance is now, or will be, evaluated by external groups.* Examples include Nader, the Council on Economic Priorities, student groups, and governmental agencies. Sociomarketing firms are auditing their societal as well as economic performance, partly in anticipation of the time when such audits may be legislatively mandated.

ORGANIZATIONAL AND MANAGERIAL ACTIONS

Attitude changes must be made in order for the firm to utilize the new sociobusiness concept in its planning. The importance of social value issues to the survival of the corporation and society must be accepted from the board of directors, through the president's office, down through all levels of the firm. This attitude change is manifested in two major ways, adoption of a new definition of the business in sociobusiness terms and organizational changes.

Major changes in the organization structure are being made. In January 1972 the Bank of America, the country's largest bank, announced the creation of a new post, executive vice president in charge of social policy. This is believed to be the first time a major bank has created such a high post solely for the direction of corporate social responsibility. Specific responsibility areas include, but are not limited to, programs in the fields of consumerism, aspirations of minority groups, and the environmental crisis. The vice president will also chair a committee of key senior officers whose functional responsibilities have a major impact in the bank's social performance.[5]

This type of appointment will be much more common in the next few years—not only with banks which have been fire-bombed, or manufacturers who have been the special targets of critics, but other firms recognizing it is not altruism but tough-minded management and good business to reconcile profits and social performance in these days of the consumer-citizen. In fact, major companies not now considering such senior appointments are suffering a form of "social myopia" potentially more harmful to long-run corporate welfare than the "marketing myopia" of the 1960s. The answer is not simply to broaden the role of the public relations director but to create a new definition of a position of corporate leadership.

In another attempt to close the gap between corporate decision making and the new social demands, corporations have utilized "movement" spokesmen such as Giant Food Inc.,'s use of Mrs. Esther Peterson to advise on unit pricing and open dating. More such use of consumer oriented spokesmen can be anticipated.

Another approach which has worked well in the insurance industry has been The Travelers establishment of an Office of Consumer Information. This office has been set up to answer questions about insurance and has handled over 40,000 letters and telephone calls. A more formal arrangement is to have "consumer ombudsmen in residence," as the automobile companies and the insurance companies did with "your man in the home office."

The placement of "movement" spokesmen on the board of directors

[5] *Wall Street Journal* (January 19, 1972), p. 25.

will come more slowly. However, to this point in time the success of Reverend Leon Sullivan as a General Motors director will probably encourage more minority group-social critic representation on boards.

Such organizational changes should and will have impact on the annual planning process including the audit of the ultimate performance achieved within the annual planning period. The integration of policy and organization into the planning format is the next phase of corporate response.

Extending the sociobusiness planning horizon

The sociobusiness orientation is a long-term one. However, the orientation ultimately involving attitude change at all management levels can be reduced to the annual planning cycle. The annual planning process should begin by looking at the desired kind, quality, and quantity of sociobusiness transactions desired by corporate management. Using the marketing function as an example, there are seven steps in the annual sociobusiness planning process.

1. Identify and forecast annual sales for each item in the product line to each target market segment by taking into account the impact upon the annual sales of the changes in the physical environment requirements, the consumer-citizen welfare needs, and the social accomplishment measures being monitored (analysis of market opportunities).
2. Set dollar and unit sales volume, dollar profit, return on investment percentage, market share percentage, number of customers with a favorable perception of the business by the end of 1973, the number of dollar value of resources to be accumulated by the end of 1973, the amount of pollution of various types which will be acceptable by the end of 1973, the number of hard-core unemployed who will be trained by the business by the end of 1973, the number of housing units for those over 65 which will be available in the community by the end of 1973, and/or the number of hospital beds which will be available in the community by the end of 1973, etc. (establishment of marketing goals).
3. Match jobs, machines, and people by means of organization charts and job descriptions so that the necessary task will be performed to achieve the planned goals for 1973 (development of organization relationships).
4. Carry out the stages and steps of the buying process to acquire the men, money, machines, materials, and information which are needed for the performance of the tasks which must be performed in order to achieve the 1973 goals (procurement of resources).
5. Create the marketing mix for each item in the product line for each target marketing segment by putting together all of the ingredients

which will make up the market offerings of the business for 1973 (formulation and implementation of market offerings).

6. Periodically compare actual results reported for the business with the planned 1973 goal figures in order to make adjustments during 1973 and later for 1974 (evaluation and control of marketing performance).
7. Compare the 1973 performance of the operations of the business with the promise/performance and revenue/cost results achieved by other competitive organizations in order to determine possible threats to the continued success of the business, and recycle to (1) for 1974.

The figure illustrates the process. Firms that follow this seven-step procedure will be able to move to their own consumer-citizen welfare/environmental/social performance audits. These firms will be ready when social audits are commonplace or required.

In a 1971 survey of the goals planned by large U.S. industrial corporations for 1970, it was found that these large corporations were planning

The corporate sociomarketing planning process

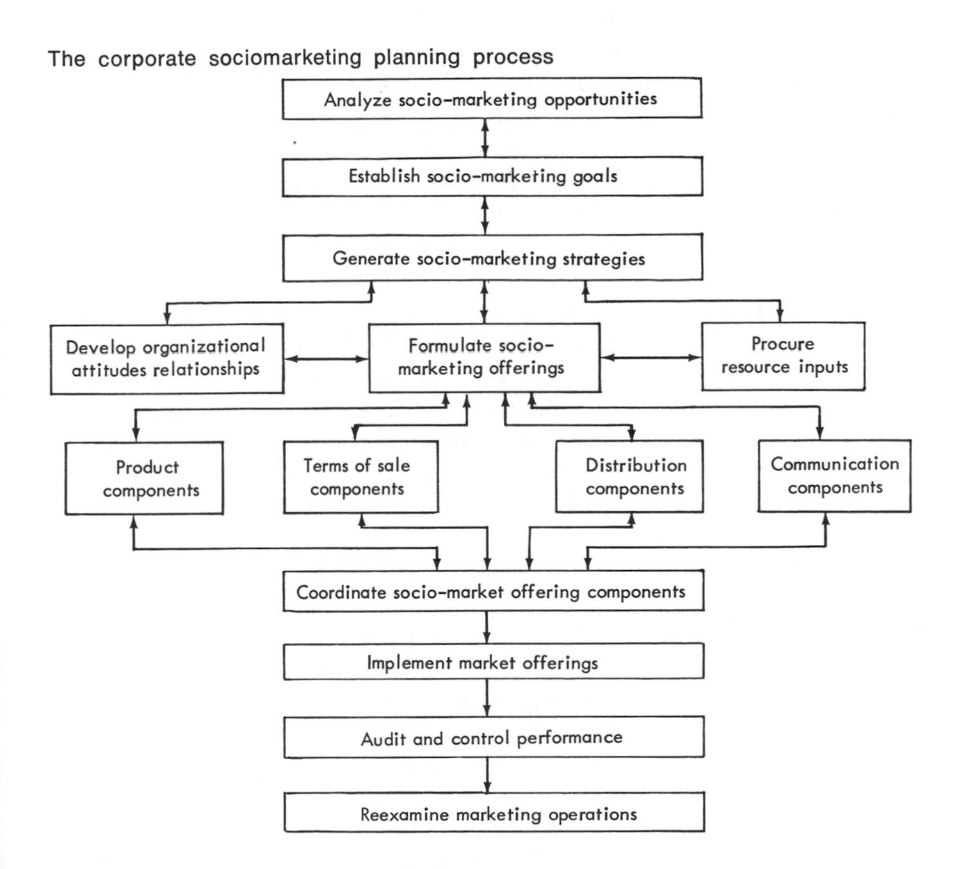

to achieve multiple goals. The number planning "social goals" was lower than those planning any of the other following numerical goals: sales volume, profit, return on investment, market share, image, and resource accumulation. However, the very fact that some firms included social goals in their planning process indicates that social goal formulation is becoming a part of the total planning process of these firms.

Evidence of the importance of social goal planning and achievement as a part of the total planning and control program is found in the fact that of the 38 percent of those firms including social goals in their planning process, 22 percent reviewed social goal performance monthly, 36 percent checked it quarterly, 67 percent checked it semiannually, and all reviewed it annually.

Forty-two percent of the respondents reported that one individual was in charge of matters of social concern. The title of this executive was quite varied and about equally spread between senior vice president, vice president, vice president—public relations and urban affairs, director—corporate communications, director—community relations, and director—urban affairs. One fifth of these individuals were members of the corporate board of directors and two thirds were members of top internal policy committees. Sixteen percent of the executives in charge of matters of social concern were on a higher level than the executive in charge of manufacturing or marketing; 66 percent were on the same level. Thirty-two percent of the corporations had a committee handling matters of social concern while 25 percent had no specific assignment of responsibility for matters of social concern.

Thirty-three percent of the respondents reported on social goal plans and the degree of achievement to internal management committees, 18 percent reported on these matters to their boards of directors, and 8 percent reported on selected social items of goal achievement to stockholders. Quantitative measures of performance were used by nearly two thirds of those corporations planning 1970 social goal performance.

No two firms agreed upon the identical social goals or worded their specific social goals in the same way. There was an apparent lack of agreement as to which social goals to include in the planning process. However, the following social goals and indicators were listed as having the highest priority: (1) increase in the proportion of minority employment measured by change in percentage, (2) hard-core training program measured by number trained, (3) equal opportunity for minorities measured by numbers and percentages, (4) closer personnel relationships with employees measured by employee attitudes, and (5) environmental control measured by decrease in amount of pollution. The goals and indicators ranked in the second highest priority listing are: (1) eliminate pollution measured by compliance with legal requirements, (2) upgrading black employees measured by numbers and percentages, (3) work toward eradication of organized crime measured by fewer crimes,

(4) equal opportunity measured by compliance with government requirements, (5) product safety measured by meeting government requirements.

The findings of this study clearly show that 38 percent of the large U.S. corporations are responding to the demand for business to include social goals in their annual planning process. Therefore, one must conclude at this point in time that social goals are going to be measured by more large industrial corporations as they prepare for the time when social performance accomplishment audits become commonplace or required. The seven numerical goals that large U.S. industrial corporations are planning for and using as measures of annual accomplishment are: (1) sales volume, (2) profit, (3) return on investment, (4) market share, (5) resource accumulation, (6) image, and (7) social goals.

Ford's corporate planning office

Beyond annual planning the sociobusiness concept has to be integrated into long-term corporate strategy. One organizational device is to assign specific sociobusiness responsibilities to the corporate planning office.

Ford Motor Company has an Urban Affairs Office and a Corporate Planning Office reporting directly to Mr. Henry Ford II. Both of these groups also make presentations to the Operating Policy Committee. The Ford management is concerned; it wants information, and wants good information. It recognizes that the propensity to overreact is there, and that the cost of overreaction can be devastating. The Ford Planning Office is organized to help management to respond early and positively, rather than late and defensively, to emerging changes in public expectations.

Fords' Corporate Planning Office is staffed by people from various disciplines; their job is "futures planning." They are concerned with determining the magnitude, intensity, and direction of social change so management can make sound current decisions on matters with complex, long-range social implications. They serve as a sort of early warning system. Aside from reams of governmental, institutional, educational, and other data, the office subscribes to the studies being conducted by the Hudson Institute, Yankelovich, Gallup, Opinion Research, Stanford University, and the University of Michigan.

The biggest problem for this group is to organize all the data they collect in a way that permits them to screen and determine what is relevant. They deal daily with ideas, events, issues, and trends, some of which impact on the social form and structure, and some of which are trivial or transitory in nature. They look at forces for change and stability—the church, family, ideology, community. They look at power groups and coalitions—lobbies, financial institutions, the new media.

They examine the high-visibility social issues—discrimination against minority groups, poverty, crime, women's lib, etc. and they look at potential catastrophes—antitrust suits, class action suits, mandated product changes that disregard cost-effectiveness. Then they try to assess the interaction of these pressures for change within a time frame.

The next step, then, is to make management aware of the existence of such information and studies so the company's leadership can assess the cost, the penalties, and the rewards that may flow from decisions to meet or ignore new demands.

Simply stated, Ford management wants to know about each of the following issues.

Its level of awareness.
Peoples' stated concern.
How this concern is being registered by behavior.
Relative concern among various issues.
Whose responsibility is it perceived to be?
Costs of attacking the issue.
Potential for success within a time frame.
Prioritization.
Recommended action.

One problem is to dramatize the work of such a group. Ford developed an eight-minute film which was presented to the board of directors. This film depicts the impact of social trends in a combination of facts seasoned with emotions. The feeling of frustration and even violence of reaction to automobile companies came through loud and clear.

That film, when shown to the Ford board and to the various executives around the company, made the problems and the feelings of the customers real. It bridged the gap between the isolation of the board room and the realities of the marketplace—and led to the establishment of the "We Listen" campaign, the new Ford Customer Service Division, and numerous new product considerations. There is reason to believe that the film did help to change attitudes.

Need for social selectivity

Each firm has to decide which of the major areas of social concern might be relevant as "social" goals for the company. Each management has to decide for itself how and what it has been doing in each of these areas, how and what it should be doing in each of these areas in the future, and how important it is to their survival that they commit their resources to the achievement of specific improvements in their performance in these areas during the next year and period of years.

No business can be expected to devote itself to all sociobusiness goals. Rather, each firm must set priorities in order of need for its community, employees, consumers, and itself. Therefore they might decide, for example, that the relevant firm goals relating to the national goals of health and safety include: (1) correction of past infractions of land, air, water, solid waste, and noise pollution; (2) dropping or modifying products which pollute the environment or are harmful to health; (3) elimination of products hazardous to public safety; and (4) preventive health programs for employees and preventive inspections for housing and plant areas. The same type of goals could be developed for other major areas of social concern.

SOCIOBUSINESS AUDIT AND PRIORITIZED ACTIONS

The board of directors of major firms could have a public policy or social audit committee. This committee could audit the societal impact of the corporation in the following areas: environmental quality, consumer-citizen welfare, sociomarketing product, personnel policies, military contracting, and sociopolitical influence, and to provide recommendations for future performance. This committee could be composed of both company and public or outside members, and also have a staff of resource people to audit the company's performance in its ultimate environment. More firms will add more minority group representation to the board of directors—including directors charged with representing the consumer interest. Last year the Board of Directors of General Motors established a public policy committee.

The board of directors' committee could be reinforced by a parallel permanent committee of corporate officers. A Department of Social Affairs may also be a possibility for some of the largest corporations. However, most corporations are at such an elementary stage in this area that a committee approach may be more appropriate. Some firms just getting into this area may be advised to begin with the task force approach and then move to a permanent committee.[6]

New board committees, vice presidents of social policy, and senior management committees will find that, in most cases, the statistics they come up with do not tell too much, that the figures in the sociomarketing area are fuzzy. We really do not understand the arithmetic of social responsibility, but do understand that work must be done in this area.[7]

The second phase of attitude change implementation is in social goal definitions. These goal definitions should follow the pattern of economic goal definitions which includes the desired performance level, determination of responsibility to achieve these goals, the delegation of authority to achieve these goals, and the measurement of goal achievement at the end of the period. The sociobusiness concept may be useful here.

An important part of the attitude problem is in changing both business

---

[6] Michael Mazis and Robert Green, "Implementing Social Responsibility," *MSU Business Topics*, vol. 19 (Winter 1971), pp. 68–76.

[7] Ibid., p. 10.

and governmental attitudes about cooperative attempts to solve social problems. This cooperation can take place in three areas. The first is the utilization of managerial talent for community purposes. This may involve using company personnel to plan a fund drive, to help with volunteer training programs, or to help with community planning and developing.

A second aspect of this cooperation is the voluntary participation by business in the establishment of public-private corporations. These corporations would combine the best of government, that is, public accountability, political capacity, and funding, and the best of business which includes systems analysis, technology, and managerial implementation. These corporations could then work in such problem areas as communications and transportation.[8]

The third aspect of this cooperation is government contracting of certain responsibilities at a fair price. In this way, the government would be accountable for business actions, the possibility of future hidden costs for consumers would be avoided, and business ability to solve particular problem areas would be utilized.

Sociobusiness performance audit

The objectives of the sociobusiness performance audit are to position the company over a time period in each of the following areas of sociobusiness performance, and to provide a base for the measurement of the social costs of doing business. Lets assume a firm divides its social performance examination into these six areas.

Sociobusiness performance audit

	Numerical measure of performance
1. Environmental quality	
Air pollution—Water—Land—Noise—Solid waste	
2. Consumer-citizen welfare	
Income and poverty	
Health and illness	
Public order and safety	
3. Sociomarketing product	
Information—Warranties—Service—Obsolescence improvements	
4. Personnel policies	
Recruiting—Training—Advancement social mobility	
5. Military contracting	
Scale of contracting—Scope of contracting	
6. Sociopolitical influence	
Employee participation in social programs	
Management talent utilization for community purposes	

[8] F. A. Lindsay, "Management and the Total Environment," *Columbia Journal of World Business*, Vol. 5 (January-February 1970), pp. 19–25.

The general areas of public concern to the firm are identified when the social performance audit is divided into these components. The items listed under the components are suggestive of the kinds of things which a management should want to examine. The numerical measures to be selected for each item would not be too difficult to select—for example, the number of pollutant particles in the air or water per standard unit of measurement as determined by the Environmental Protection Agency. In the case of income and poverty, it might be by increasing the number of underincomed and underskilled employees who are to be recruited and trained during the coming year. It might also include a planned number of house management talent to be devoted to support of public programs established to improve low-income neighborhoods.

Once a social performance audit has been carried out by a firm in order to get ready for outside auditors, and once it has become part of the annual planning and review of performance process, then there will be a demand for some way to compare how the management of the firm sees its social performance and how the outside auditor sees its performance. Both the firm's management and the auditor will have the benefit of measurement against planned goals this year as well as the trend in performance over a series of years. The auditors might bring a knowledge of the industry to the audit and be able to compare the performance with the other firms making up the industry.

A social performance index based upon a market promise/market performance analysis is a way to provide an overall measure to compare the social performance of one corporation with another. The auditor would report the results from an instrument that would measure management's perception of the impact of its market offerings upon each component and each item to be included in the social performance audit.

The auditor would also report on the results from an instrument that would measure the public's perceptions of the impact of the firm's market offerings upon each component and each item. The instruments that would measure these results might include attitude and opinion questions that would require answers that the respondents would scale 1–9. One way the questions might be developed would be to deal with beliefs about specific expectations and performance. If measurements are made of the management's perceptions and the public's perceptions, then correlation analysis could be used to determine the similarities and differences in perceptions.

The ideas above would have to be worked out with a very broad brush since the objective is to determine the attitudes of large segments of the population. By use of this very broad brush, an overall index number might then be computed to show the market promise/market performance rating for the corporation.

Business will confront social audits in the future. David Rockefeller (chairman of the Chase Manhattan Bank) told the Advertising Council of New York that he foresees the day when, in addition to the annual financial statement, certified by independent accountants, corporations may be required to publish a social audit similarly certified. There are a few groups now making such audits. However, the social audit, or audit of sociobusiness performance should not wait until the concept is legally imposed. Social audit information must be built into decision making today.

The best way to prepare for the day when the CSA (Certified Social Auditor) or ISE (Independent Social Auditor) may be as common as the CPA is to begin to build social audit concepts into current operations.

The problems of a social performance audit are real. The audit requires objectivity, detachment, tough-mindedness, and persistence. These attitudes may be more important than specific techniques.

The alternatives to corporate progress in auditing its own social performance are dismal. It's the old "if we don't, government will" debate. Right now a lot of multimillion dollar decisions in societal areas are being made on the basis of $2.98 statistics.

Difficulties abound when attempting to put numerical values on a company's sociomarketing performance. Should a three-point, five-point, or ten-point scale be used? What standards should the corporation compare itself against: the leading offender in that particular sociomarketing area, its immediate competitors, or governmental standards if they exist? How is the corporation going to change its position over time; what is its direction of progress to be? And, is the corporation going to boast of its accomplishments in this area or is it accepting the fact that these actions were long overdue and even now may be inadequate?

Whatever the rating scale, tough-minded objectivity is required. The social audit should not be performed by company personnel alone, but by both inside and outside people. Perhaps the forecast that external audits of corporate social performance will be required or performed, just as external economic, legal, and accounting audits are now performed, is wrong. However, it might be prudent to assume it sound and to begin to get ready for such audits now.

Outside input in social auditing is desirable because the audit must be conducted in terms relevant to the consumer-citizen not just to the corporation. More firms would be well advised to begin gaining experience with consumer consultants, consumer representatives, and with consumer ombudsmen. The idea is now to generate internal initiative for improved social performance.

Every organization has its traditions, its established patterns of performance, its sacred cows in societal policies. Many of these policies have remained for years without serious questioning inside the corporation. All performance areas in the sociomarketing realm must be subjected to searching, critical, systematic, and continuing examination in terms relevant to society, not just to the corporation. In the process, long accepted policies will have to change. Outside auditing is necessary to bring about the changes on the scale required by a society in which the issues are in a survival context. Each aspect of sociobusiness performance should be audited separately.

In summary, why should a business spend the money and time to develop socially relevant performance measures? What are the potential benefits to a business in identifying and using such measures in new planning models? Why should management spend the money integrating social feedback into corporate planning? The six major benefits are:

Business Benefits of Social Audits

1. Result in a corporate social accomplishment statement; a social accomplishment balance sheet.
2. Identify areas or problems requiring corporate confrontation and correction for social accomplishment purposes; help in setting priorities.
3. Serve as a benchmark of corporate contributions to social progress over time periods.
4. Identify present market, products, and appeals to sociomarket segments.
   - Purchase motivations.
   - Purchase behavior.
5. Identify new social requirements and future markets.
6. Provide a new scale of achievement on which to measure management and the corporation.

The corporate sociobusiness audit offers the starting point for action. That audit must reflect the views of many groups beyond the executive suite. It is going to be expensive and time-consuming to make progress. Just as growing old is not a particularly attractive idea—until you consider the alternative; corporate survival, even at unusual costs and lowered short-term profits, may be better than the alternatives to which continued corporate social myopia might lead.

What is the role of personal conscience in corporate decision making? Does managerial craftsmanship and professional expertise provide an important source for ethical judgments? The following article develops an ethical hypothesis for corporate decision making, and provides insight into how one firm has responded to its definition of ethical responsibility.

---

17. MARKETING ETHICS AND THE CONSUMER*

Earl A. Clasen†

If you are like many U.S. executives, your upbringing included regular attendance at Sunday school or church. You learned the Ten Commandments and the Golden Rule, and you have attempted to apply these precepts in your daily life. You absorbed the formal expressions of our moral tradition in your youth. Today you strive to exemplify them in your business decision making.

If this briefly describes your ethical experience—and I think for many of us it does—and if solely on the basis of this experience you undertake to control marketing behavior in a large corporation, then God help you!

This was the conclusion which several of my colleagues and I arrived at in a recent discussion of ethical behavior in marketing. We agreed that there was no fundamental conflict between personal morality and business purpose. None of us felt himself forced to violate his principles in order to succeed. But we had to admit that these principles were simply not adequate to guide us in many of the decisions we had to make. We found them almost everywhere applicable, and almost nowhere sufficient in themselves to resolve the kinds of ethical problems we faced.

This conclusion—so startling when first it dawned on us—beckoned us on to further exploration. As the general managers of a national consumer products company, we felt that the quality of marketing behavior in our organization was an appropriate subject for our concern. Aside from our personal feelings in the matter, an objective glance at current public interest in some of the effects of mass marketing was enough to convince us of the necessity to examine our practices. With all of us involved in one way or another with marketing at Pillsbury, it was inevitable that our conversations should center around specific experiences which each had encountered in the course of his marketing career. We determined to find out, if we could, the real source of those ethical principles which we were all convinced played so important a role in our decisions.

---

* Reprinted from "Marketing Ethics and the Consumer," *Harvard Business Review*, Vol. 45 (January-February 1967), pp. 79–86.

† Pillsbury Company.

Our discussions continued over a period of several weeks. We found ourselves asking questions such as these:

What is the role of personal conscience in business decision making?

What are the functions of the law and corporate policy in framing ethical decisions?

What of the marketplace itself? Does it exert its own ethic?

How about our customer, the U.S. housewife? What does she expect of us—what kinds of values and at what price?

How about our craftsmanship, our professional expertise? Isn't this an important source of our ethical judgments?

TRADITIONAL WELLSPRINGS

Our objective seemed clear to us. It was to discover the source of those principles which, if consistently applied, would ensure that all of our marketing decisions would be ethical and would, in fact, contribute to the public welfare. But the path to this objective seemed murky indeed. We probed many of the traditional well springs from which business ethics are supposed to flow, and in which the public welfare is supposed to find its protection. From this examination emerged an approach to business ethics which we would like to propose as a working hypothesis for marketing executives. The purpose of this section of the article is to build up the hypothesis through retracing the route by which we arrived at it.

Our first step was to examine those sources which, it seemed to us, most often contributed the ethical content of our marketing decisions. We were able to identify six primary sources:

1. Personal conscience, molded and formed by the ethical traditions of our society, this in combination with high personal standards, was quickly singled out as exerting a major influence on the marketing behavior of a large corporation.

2. The law and its corollary—an articulated corporate philosophy and explicit statements of policy.

3. Organization structure and procedures that ensure the interjection of the ethical component into decision making through a system of checks and balances.

4. The marketplace, which in the terms of Adam Smith exerts its own ethic on buyer and seller alike.

5. Professional knowledge—the business and technical expertise which allows one to know what is good for someone else, even when the other is unaware of the factors and ethics involved.

6. Consumer wants and acceptance; full, free, and open communication between buyer and seller, which in itself represents a kind of ethic.

The identification of these primary sources of ethical control leads to a natural question: What are the adequacies and the limitations of each of these sources for the marketing executive? Let us move in for a closer look.

Personal conscience

This is a wonderful and sacred thing, but not all consciences are alike. As most marketers of consumer products learn early in their careers, consciential difference is a fact of life with which they must deal almost daily. Consider these two decisions:

> Recently my company purchased a Sunday morning network television show for children. Are we commercially encouraging that element of our population which prefers to stay home rather than go to church on Sunday? A raft of consumer letters will tell us so. Their writers will solemnly affirm that they will not purchase our products again until the offending show is dropped.
>
> Do you enjoy a cocktail at day's end? We are currently test marketing a product called Tart 'n Tangy. It is a citric, noncaloric, presweetened drink mix available in three flavors. The product was conceived to satisfy adult and teen-age tastes. The point here, however, is that it mixes well with gin or vodka to make an unusually good summer cooler. For ten cents you can have four glasses. We believe that there is no other product on the market which compares in quality or economy with Tart 'n Tangy as an alcoholic mixer. Yet we are preventing any reference in our advertising, publicity, or promotion to use of the product with alcoholic beverages. The policy is set. Our marketing department, our advertising agencies, and our publicity people know it. We will miss a large sales volume as a result of our decision.

Now, to the cynical these decisions may seem trivial and arbitrary. Would the alternates have been ethical, unethical? Philosophers and theologians may debate consciential difference in matters of high import. The businessman must act. And often, in acting, he may be surprised at the range of subjects which are viewed by some segment of the U.S. public as having important ethical implications. My associates and I concluded that the individual conscience is absolutely essential to ethics in marketing behavior, but it is by no means adequate to serve as a guide. For which individual conscience would you follow? And how would you sustain it against all of the individual consciences in the marketplace?

At Pillsbury we have developed a technique which at least partially answers the question of how to engage effectively a range of individual consciences in our decision making. An offshoot of our manpower development program, this technique uses a derivative of the T-group to broaden the spectrum of conscience which is brought to bear on a marketing decision.[1] Theoretically, members of a T-group relate to each other in a completely unstructured situation. The process and its objective are identical.

Assisted by our industrial psychologist, we have applied T-group theory to marketing decision making. Our technique differs from the traditional T-group approach in that our group members are given a specific marketing problem to consider. The essential element of the process is to create an atmosphere of openness in which people feel free to express their moral commitments and ethical viewpoints. They must feel free to interact with one another in healthy conflict. Our approach is speculative and experimental. But we have found on occasion that, out of the clashings and collisions of individual consciences, a group consensus can emerge which cuts broader and deeper in its search for an ethical decision than would any individual conscience working in isolation. As a means for controlling marketing behavior, this approach substitutes personal involvement for coercion, and individual commitment for external control.

Law and policy

Many writers on business ethics view public law and the private law of the corporation, which is articulated in statements of philosophy and policy, as the primary source of ethical decision making. My associates and I concluded that the law, both public and private, plays a significant role in our marketing decisions. We have come to view it as a valuable, but not totally adequate, contributor to ethical decisions.

When a man assumes responsibility for managing the marketing behavior of a large corporation, he is dealing with every business law of the land, from antitrust to post office regulations. In these circumstances he needs adequate interpretation of the law from his legal counsel. Beyond this, he needs a working knowledge of the law deep down in his organization and a feel for potential problems—a sixth sense—on the part of the managers who report to him. But none of these conditions, even if fully attained, will obviate the need for a further source of marketing ethics.

Where the law is clear, he has no problem. But ultimately the marketing executive will face a situation in which the law is open to interpretation. If his competitors interpret it differently from the way he does, the pressure can be severe. Therefore, it is in this continuing gray area of interpretation that he has the greatest need for a source of ethical judgment which reaches out beyond the law, beyond corporate policy, and beyond even personal conscience or group consensus.

Few industries are subjected to a body of law and regulation which

[1] See Chris Argyris, "T-Groups for Organizational Effectiveness," *HBR* (March-April 1964), p. 60.

is as historic, well developed, and effective as that of the food industry. And yet the marketing executive in a food company is continually faced with making ethical decisions in areas where neither law nor policy can supply him with a definitive answer. The law proscribes conduct in terms which the trained lawyer can apply. Is the action discriminatory, false, or misleading? Is there misrepresentation or deceit? Is another's product or service disparaged? Is the promotion a lottery? Words such as these are terms of art, capable of application to marketing situations as varied as tire advertising and cents-off deals. My lawyer can tell me with considerable particularity what the law means by "unfair trade practices." However, legal compliance does not ensure ethics in marketing. The businessman whose boundaries of conduct are drawn by the law poses an ethical problem to his competitors. Perhaps an example which came up in the course of our discussions will illustrate this point:

We market a product called Buttermilk Pancake mix, which contains 9.3 percent buttermilk solids. This is approximately equivalent to a pint of buttermilk in each one-pound package. It is so rich a mix that the housewife need only add water to prepare it. The product competes directly with one which contains only half as much buttermilk, to which the housewife must add whole milk. Our product obviously costs more to manufacture. And obviously the pressure is great to cheapen it. Neither law nor corporate policy tells us whether the product should contain 5 percent, 8 percent, or 15 percent buttermilk.

When we analyzed our decision to maintain the quality of this product, we realized that we had relied on our technical expertise as an experienced baking mix manufacturer. Our formulators, working in conjunction with our commercial research people, had recommended the 9.3 percent formulation as being within the range which produced optimum consumer quality. Figuratively, this was a case in which we took our ethics from a test tube, rather than from law or policy.

Checks and balances

Another specific example led us to consider the function of organizational structure in promoting ethical decisions. To illustrate:

We market a product called Nut Bread mix. Our market research indicates that consumer acceptance of the product is optimum when it contains a mixture of 50 percent filberts and 50 percent almonds. When the price of filberts increased sharply, we were under pressure to convert to a 100 percent almond product, thus protecting our profit margins. However, as the responsible general manager, I decided not to do this. I also made a decision not to pass on our increased cost to the consumer, despite pressures from our accounting, procurement, and marketing departments. These were proper pressures, I might add, based on sound technical judgments.

In analyzing this example, my discussion partners and I concluded that decisions of this type must be made at the general management level. Obviously, not all decisions can, or should, flow through the top levels. But we believe that ethical decisions should be shared upward, and that it is a part of our function as general managers to examine continually our organizational structure to assure this upward sharing.

At Pillsbury we operate on the principle that no man should be forced to act as both executor and judge on the same issues. The reason for this is that the pressure on a subordinate manager to "short-term" a product can be very severe. Our plant managers, for example, neither establish our product quality standards nor audit plant production performances against them. The standards are set by general management, in consultation with our technical and commercial research people. Production performance is audited by an organizationally separate quality-assurance department.

Ethical problems arise when a man's assignment forces him to emphasize a single job objective—say, maintaining the profit margin on a particular product. But suppose that in order to meet this objective his only alternative is to sacrifice quality. In blunt terms, when the man's choice is between profit margins and ethics, which is going to give? Choices of this kind must be forced upward in the corporation; for—as one assumes increased obligations toward employees and stockholders—profit itself represents an ethical standard.

This conclusion led us directly to consider the case of the general manager who must make ethical decisions which balance profit and product quality. To what set of ethical guideposts does he turn? Organizational structure, with its system of checks and balances and built-in auditing functions, becomes a less effective control device as you move up the ladder of responsibility. Like personal conscience and personal standards, and like the law and corporate policy, it is an important, but not totally adequate, source of ethical control for the corporate manager. It does not supply all of the answers to all of the questions he must face.

Technical knowledge

At this point one of our group, referring to the example of our Buttermilk Pancake mix, pointed out that our general managers relied heavily on the company's technical resources in framing marketing decisions. A combination of technical knowledge and expertise as a manufacturer can be an important contributor to ethical decision making. In this sense you apply for the consumer the kinds of tests and standards which she cannot apply for herself. This example was quickly brought up:

> We manufacture a product called Apricot Nut Bread mix. The product enjoyed a high level of consumer acceptance and was moving well in the

market. But we continued to experiment with its formulation and concluded that the product was improved by a higher ratio of apricots to other ingredients. We moved to this new formulation, which cost us more to produce, and were gratified to find that sales of the product increased.

This is not always the case with product improvements. Many improvements which affect a product's total performance go unnoticed by the consumer. The temptation to label such products as "new and improved" is very great. It may have to be resisted. Thus:

About two years ago, an internal task force assigned to criticize our consumer relations recommended that we limit the appellation "new and improved" to those instances where product improvements were perceived as such by the consumer. The recommendation was adopted by general management and continues today as a binding marketing policy.

Consumer wants

This brought us to a consideration of the marketplace itself, and the role played by consumer wants and preferences in determining marketing behavior. What does the consumer want? What values at what price? As managers, we decided that the ethical control of marketing behavior required us to have a deep understanding of the demographic changes which are occurring in our society. We need to maintain a contemporary view of market segmentations which are developing at an ever increasing rate.

To continue to rely solely on one's own standards of quality and value may be tantamount to serving an ever decreasing slice of a growing and changing market. Let me illustrate this point with two examples:

For many years, my company produced an angel food cake mix of high quality. Few housewives could prepare as good a cake from their own ingredients as from our mix. But its two-step preparation proved a stumbling block to that growing segment of the market which places a tremendous premium on ease, speed, and convenience. To meet the needs of these modern housewives, we developed a one-step angel food cake mix which requires just one minute from package to baking pan. Our tests showed that it did not equal the old-fashioned quality of our regular angel food mix. Yet, for millions of U.S. housewives, it became the preferred product. Our general management made a judgment that if we were to insist on maintaining the old quality standard, at the sacrifice of the consumer's ease and convenience, we would not satisfy those increasing millions who found that the new mix better suited their needs.

The group in charge of marketing our Brownie mix wanted to use the phrase "loaded with nuts" in the product's advertising. Consumer research showed that 50 percent of all consumers would agree with this claim; 25

percent would think the product contained too many nuts; and a significant 25 percent would think that there were not enough nuts in the product. On this basis, management eliminated the claim from the promotional copy.

There are many types of consumers in the marketplace. Among them is the "weights and measures type" (which is represented by Consumers Union), to whom the most important fact about a product label is the net weight, preferably evened off to avoid fractional ounces. Another type is the harried husband left at home with three kids, to whom the most important fact is how many servings he can expect to get from a can of beef stew. He could care less about net weight or fractions of ounces.

What consumer standard do you follow? Our one-step angel food cake mix fits the standards of one consumer group exactly, but offends the standards of another. You have to have data on the market. You have to know what consumers want—in the matter of servings, for example. You cannot put out a product that meets every standard in the marketplace. Nor can a package direction fit every user.

The need to meet consumer wants exerts a powerful control on marketing behavior. But, as business becomes more adept at defining consumer wants through market research, our ethical problems become increasingly complex. With so many audiences to serve, how is it possible to suit one group without offending another? For example, companies like mine are now dealing with a generation which has a new frame of reference in which to judge food-product quality. For them the "homemade" standard of quality no longer applies. This is a generation which has never eaten a homemade cake or tasted fresh orange juice.

Under these circumstances, what is to prevent a kind of Gresham's law[2] from operating in the marketplace to bring about a continuing erosion of product quality? With no absolute standard as a reference, what is to prevent products of inferior quality from driving their superiors off the market? All that is required is a sufficient number of consumers who can be persuaded by price, or by advertising—or by plain lack of exposure to anything better!

Can we use consumer acceptance as an ethical standard in marketing? Is "what the market will bear" truly the limit of our ethical commitment? And, even if it is, does not the very relativity of consumer standards imply a relativity—and absolute confusion—in the application of this most permissive of ethical principles? I think that if our ethical standards are based solely on consumer acceptance, we cannot escape a relativity that renders all concern with marketing ethics meaningless.

[2] The tendency, when two or more coins are equal in debt-paying power, but unequal in intrinsic value, for the one having the least intrinsic value to remain in circulation and for the other to be hoarded. It is often stated more briefly as, "Cheap money drives out dear."

TOWARD A HYPOTHESIS

This, then, seemed to lead us to the horns of our dilemma—or, perhaps I should say, stretched us upon the antlers of a poly-lemma. Consider:

We had examined the individual conscience and the role played by high personal standards in the control of marketing behavior in the large corporation. But the dictates of personal conscience, even in a society informed by a common ethical tradition, are relative and individual.

We had examined the law and the role of corporate policy in the control of marketing behavior. But the law and corporate policy merely push back the frontiers of ethical decision to new, gray areas of interpretation.

We had looked at organizational structure and at procedures which can function as a system of checks and balances, analogous to those of our political institutions. But, as critical issues ascend through this system, it ultimately evolves on one man to make final decisions without further recourse.

We had considered professional knowledge—the state of the art—as a source of ethical judgment, as indeed it is. But the standards of the craftsman must be continually checked and modified to conform with the real needs of a fast-changing marketplace.

We had looked to the marketplace itself—to consumer wants and needs—as a source of ethical decisions. But consumer wants and consumer acceptance yield the most relative of variables.

Where then do we look for our ethical system? System aside, where even do we look for some source of those touchstones which can supply a working basis for ethical decision making in marketing?

At this point we broke off the search for what ought to be the case and turned to a discussion of what we believe *is* the case in most large marketing organizations. We concluded that most marketing executives do in fact rely on each of these ethical sources in their day-to-day decision making. Depending on situation and circumstance, they may rely more heavily on one than on the others in a particular instance.

In examining our own experience, however, we could not recall a single instance in which the entire ethical content of a decision derived solely from one of these sources. In every instance in which any of us had been personally involved, it appeared that he had had recourse to two or more of these sources in framing what he hoped was an ethical decision.

Conscience, policy, organizational procedure, consumer acceptability, technical expertise—each contributes its standards, its demands, and its responsibilities to the marketing decision maker.

At this point, our group disbanded for further individual reflection on the ground we had covered. None of us, I suspect, felt that we had accomplished our objective of defining some kind of working hypothesis which could serve our daily ethical needs.

Later, in thinking over our discussion while I was making marketing decisions, I was tempted to single out those ethical sources which seemed particularly pertinent to me. This became a kind of daily exercise in decision analysis. It ultimately bore fruit in the framing of an ethical hypothesis which my colleagues and I are willing to accept, at least until it stimulates a better one.

Prime sources

It seemed to me that there were two sources of ethical standards which predominated in my daily decision making—that is, they were always present, regardless of whichever other sources also contributed their moral imperatives. Furthermore, they seemed to me to be interrelated in a way which gave rise to a further, and underlying, ethical principle.

Professional expertise. The first of these sources was knowledge, which I have variously defined as the state of the art, craftsmanship, or that professional and technical expertise which allows one to know what is good for someone else even when the other is unaware of the factors and the ethics involved. If you think about the foods which you personally will consume today, you will realize the degree to which you are staking your welfare on the professional expertise of persons totally unknown to you. Those of us who control the marketing behavior of a national foods company are dealing with massive trust. The scale of our technology has made a vast difference in the consumer's "ability to know" and to choose. Our attitude has got to be one of love and of service. Of course, this is also true of an airline, of a manufacturer of drugs and medicines, and in varying degrees of a host of other products.

Now, this massive trust implies a relationship between buyer and seller which demands that they engage in a dialogue. How does this dialogue come about? In simpler times it was a rudimentary dialogue—literally carried on through the medium of the marketplace. The baker produced his bread or cake and put it up for sale in the marketplace. When the consumer purchased it, he or she in effect gave an assent to the question asked by its producer: "Does this product fulfill your standards of quality and price? Does it provide you with the benefits you expect of it?"

This dialogue is still at the base of all marketing transactions in a free economy. But it has become vastly more complex as a result of mass production, mass communication, and mass consumption. We who deliver our promotional messages daily, in what are literally millions of impressions, know that we are influencing the consumer's choice through this action—at least as much as we do through the intrinsic merits and qualities of our products. We must assure ourselves that the consumer believes what we say about our products; that our claims are perceived as accurate and truthful.

How do we get this assurance? By a careful testing of consumer attitudes and responses. By listening to and heeding those consumer voices which tell us, for example, that the claim "loaded with nuts" will be disbelieved by 25 percent of all housewives, even though another 25 percent will think we put too many nuts in the brownies.

Consumer acceptance. Thus I came to recognize consumer wants and consumer acceptance as being the second major source of the ethical standards which I was applying in my daily marketing decisions. In my view professional expertise and consumer acceptance became the two poles of a vast ethical dialogue carried on between buyer and seller.

As manufacturers it is our responsibility to bring to the marketplace an expert point of view. Our decisions must in fact constitute what the consumer would do or choose (*a*) if she had the best technical education, or (*b*) if she had the most modern tools for testing and evaluating. We must apply, for the average consumer, the kinds of tests and standards she cannot apply for herself.

Then we must continually check back and forth with her. We must create an interchange of our special knowledge and technical resources with her expression of her wants and needs.

Media control

In the course of this interchange, we must never forget that we control the media of its expression. It is we who produce, label, and advertise the product. This is a one-way street. The consumer's response is limited to a decision to buy or not to buy. Such distortions as occur in this channel of communication are of our own making.

But there is another channel, also within our control, which allows the consumer to respond more adequately and more fully with respect to her wants, needs, and unformed wishes. This is the channel of consumer research—of attitudinal and market analysis. Through the application of consumer research—and marketing-oriented companies like Pillsbury are in a very real sense vast radar antennas attuned to the consumer—we are able to pinpoint and define, for example, consumer interest in a simpler, easier-to-make angel food cake mix. We are able to confirm the levels of ingredients—whether buttermilk solids, apricots, or filberts—which most nearly suit her taste.

It seems to me that such distortions as usually occur in this channel of communication are less the result of ethical lapse than of technical inadequacy—the state of the art. It is true that marketing men do not always heed the consumer voices picked up by their radar systems. (You may recall that the problem at Pearl Harbor lay not in our primitive radar sets, but in a decision to disregard the data which they reported.) However, the costs of adequate consumer research today are so great that it is difficult to conceive of a marketing executive consciously skewing his intelligence system so as to produce distorted results.

A greater source of distortion, I think, lies in the inadequacy of our present research techniques to reflect truly and fully consumer wants and desires. In the realm of practical ethics, our mandate is clear—continuing refinement of technique.

Adequate communication

Obviously, both we and the consumer have a major stake in the adequacy of our channels of communication. And the requirements of adequate communication, in fact, impose their own ethic. Granted the ethical dialogue which I have proposed—between professional expertise and consumer acceptance—the purity, efficacy, and efficiency of our channels of communication become all important. To the extent that we in marketing control these channels—and we alone control them—a major source of our ethic is clear. We have a moral responsibility to cherish them, to develop and improve them, and, above all, to guard and protect their integrity.

CONCLUSION

This ethical hypothesis has some very practical consequences. On the one hand, we communicate to the consumer through (*a*) the quality of our products, (*b*) our packaging and labeling, and (*c*) our advertising and promotion. On the other hand, the consumer communicates to us through (*a*) repeat purchase of our products (or the lack thereof), and (*b*) the myriad techniques of commercial research—controlled perception tests for appearance and flavor, label and price tests, retail store tests, and full-scale market tests.

Any distortion which we consciously or willfully introduce in this two-way communication process becomes, in my view, a violation of marketing ethics. Some of these distortions are obvious and are often commented on—inaccurate labeling, deceptive packaging, and false or misleading advertising. Not so obvious, perhaps, are the distortions which erode the channels of communication themselves—threats of economic boycott brought to bear on the mass media for the purpose of influencing editorial policy, economic pressures exerted through trade channels to force the distribution of products for which there is clearly no consumer demand, and inadequate or willfully misinterpreted research data which deny to the consumer the right to be heard as fully and truly as possible.

We need strong, clear channels of communication both to and from the consumer. We must guard the integrity of our media, whether these are a national television network or a field researcher's work sheet. Our goal is in view, although we may but imperfectly realize it—namely, full and free and open communication between buyer and seller.

Have business practices become less ethical, or has business consciousness become more ethically sensitive? Are ethics relative to time, place, and circumstances? The author presents a schematic plan for analyzing the variables inherent in the ethics of decision making and proposes a framework for the development of social and personal ethics.

---

18. A MODEL FOR ETHICS IN MARKETING*

Robert Bartels†

Interest expressed in business ethics has not always been identified as a concern for ethics alone. Thus, demands for standards of ethics have grown up in defense of various rights—of labor, of competitors, of the community.

Emerging social consciousness in defense of rights was indicated in legislation such as the Sherman Antitrust Act and the Pure Food and Drug Act. Direct concern for business ethics appeared strongly during the 1920s. The business literature of that period contains many titles dealing with ethics per se, such as "Adventures on the Borderlands of Ethics," "The Ancient Greeks and the Evolution of Standards in Business," "Book of Business Standards," "The Ethics of Business," and "Christian Ideals in Industry."

Each recurrence of interest in ethics has raised the question: Have business practices become *less ethical*, or has business consciousness become *more ethically sensitive?*

Whichever it may be at this time, several aspects of the present interest are symptomatic of our times. First, tests of ethics are applied to problems of our day: to price-fixing and to price-cutting, to deceptive labeling and to advertising, to coercive trade practices, and to conflicts of interest in a pluralistic society. Second, concern is shown for ethics

* Reprinted from "A Model For Ethics in Marketing," *Journal of Marketing*, Vol. 31 (January 1967), pp. 20–26.

† Ohio State University.

in both operational and administrative marketing problems. Third, responsibility for ethics in marketing is attributed increasingly to individuals on the higher management levels.

A review of what is currently said about business or marketing ethics reveals it to have several distinguishing characteristics:

Emphasis has been given to subjective factors, action, and the performer's viewpoint, more than to objective factors, interaction, and the relationships between individuals. In other words, emphasis has been given to lists of actions regarded as ethical or unethical, rather than to the determinants which place an action on the list.

Specific rather than general concepts of ethics usually have been expressed. The ethics of management-customer relations has not been integrated with the ethics of management-employee relations. The standards of one company have not been conceptually integrated with those of other companies, except perhaps through agreements.

The absolute rather than the relative character of ethics has been emphasized. Once determined, the universality of ethical standards has been assumed. Exceptions have been dealt with as deviations from a general principle, rather than as the conflict of actions stemming from two perhaps valid principles.

Conflicts of this sort have increased as the growing volume of international business has multiplied the frequency of cross-cultural marketing situations.

Inasmuch, therefore, as marketing ethics is part of general ethics in business, there is merit in an attempt to construct a model for ethics in marketing. A model in this sense is a logical framework in terms of which two basic questions might be asked and answered: *How are ethical standards set? How are ethical decisions made?*

ELEMENTS OF A MODEL

A model represents an attempt to explain the nature and behavior of some phenomenon, to show causes and effects in related variables. If a sufficiently credible theory of behavior can be built, it may serve as a basis for behavior in specific situations. Preliminary to model-building, however, some basic premises must be laid down. The following assumptions, therefore, are made:

1. It is assumed that "ethics" means a standard by which *business action may be judged "right" or "wrong."*

Where judgment is involved, there is always a standard. However, standards differ, and so actions regarded "right" by one standard may be in conflict with and judged unethical from the standpoint of another standard. Then an understanding of the standard in terms of which action is made may be more useful than a mere appraisal of the action itself.

The ethics of another society, or of our own society at an earlier time, may differ from what we regard to be "right" today. If so, inasmuch as we cannot always change other people but must deal with them as they are, we can at least *understand* the reasons for their actions and view ethical conflict objectively, in terms of its bases.

2. It is assumed that ethics is a standard for judging the rightness not of action per se, but of *action of one person relative to another.*

Ethics is a basis for judgment in personal interaction. It pertains to the fulfilment or violation of *expectations.* Simply to make an untrue statement about a product is in itself not unethical, nor to make a shoddy product—that may be bad management, but it is not necessarily unethical.

Neither is it unethical to make the false statement to a person who does not expect to be told the truth—that may be the level of trade practice.

However, if a customer *expects* to receive truthful information and a product of specified quality, and if he does not, and if his expectation is a general expectation sanctioned by society, failure of the other party to fulfill these expectations is an unethical act. Furthermore, if a particular customer expects little or does not know what he is entitled to expect, and if society makes this determination for him, such a failure is also unethical. Ethics is a concern for *people,* not just for acts or things.

3. It is assumed that *business is primarily a social process,* within which it is an economic process, and that, within the latter, marketing is a specialized process involving role relationships and interactions.

Marketing is something that people do *as people,* not merely as buyers and sellers, nor even just as economic men. Marketing is a process engaging whole men, social entities, who have commitments both within and without the marketing process, and whose marketing behavior reflects their total institutional involvement.

To grasp the full import of the social standard of ethics in marketing, one must recognize the orientation of marketing in society. Marketing is a function of the economy, which is but one of seven identified major social institutions: the family, the church, the school, the economy, the government, the military, and leisure. Each fulfills certain needs of mankind, the economy providing for the material or consumption needs of people, acquiring and creating products, distributing them, and regulating consumption processes.

As a social institution consists of relationships among participants in roles essential to the performance of the needed function, each institution has myriad sets of expectations and obligations among these participants. Thus, in each institution are evolved *ethics* peculiar to the relationships and activities involved. In turn, the norms of behavior in each or all institutions are the product of the general cultural characteristics of the society, which differ among societies, producing dissimilar standards, codes, and patterns of behavior among men in their role relationships.

As marketing is part of the economic process, participants in this process occupy distinct role positions; and their interactions constitute the personal aspect of marketing—the part of marketing in which ethical considerations arise. Ten role positions are identifiable—four may be thought of as inside the technical organization of the business enterprise; four are outside private participants; and two are outside public sectors of the marketing economy:

1. Managers
2. Employees
3. Owners
4. Other financiers
5. Consumers
6. Intermediate customers
7. Resources
8. Competitors
9. Government
10. Community

4. It is assumed that the *expectations* of the participants in the respective marketing roles are known.

The fact is that many of the marketing role expectations are known, but that they are subject to change as society evolves. Actually, the number of roles engaged in the marketing process has increased over the years, and their expectations have become more clearly articulated.

In this connection, consider the monolithic and quite autonomous character of the business enterprise from the time of the Industrial Revolution throughout most of the 19th century. The owner-manager was typically one individual, representing a single interest. Management-government relationships were minimized by the philosophy of laissez-faire; management-consumer relationships, by the philosophy of caveat emptor; management-employee relationships, by the dominance of entrepreneurial interests; and management-competitor relationships, by the philosophy of rugged individualism.

Gradually, throughout the 19th century and thereafter, the expectations of economic participants other than managers became more clearly formulated and sanctioned by society in general. Employees were among the first to achieve recognition of their demands for reasonable working hours, humane treatment, and safe working conditions. These demands were voiced through the countervailing institution of the labor union.

Expectations of competitors gave rise to trade regulation; and when competitors themselves were not sufficiently vocal, the government, on behalf of the society's general interest in the economy, represented the interests of competitors. The Sherman Act and the Federal Trade Commission Act and their amendments followed.

Expectations of the public in the role of consumers were expressed, feebly at first in enactments prohibiting sale of harmful and adulterated products, later in the "Consumer Movement," and more recently in the entrepreneurial philosophy known as The Marketing Concept.

5. It is assumed that *ethics is a matter of social sanction,* not of mere technical appraisal.

Not every expectation has the social sanction which makes it a matter of ethical significance. Many expectations are purely technical, expressing the expectation of technical competence, conformity to job requirements, etc.

If a sales manager sets a high quota for a salesman, that expectation may have no ethical implications. Whether the salesman fails or succeeds in meeting the quota may be of no ethical importance. However, if the sales manager puts such pressure on the salesman to meet a quota that the salesman must resort to reprehensible practices to accomplish this, or must neglect personal obligations and health, then ethical implications of the sales manager's expectations appear.

Likewise, to be expected to make a profit, even a large profit, for owners is not an ethical expectation; but if it is at the expense of other managerial obligations, the ethical considerations are involved.

The following concepts have now been incorporated into the model:

1. Ethics as a standard of rightness in behavior.
2. Social interaction as the realm in which ethical judgment is made.
3. Noneconomic and economic institution influences upon personal behavior through role participation.
4. Role expectations constituting ethical obligations through social sanction.
5. Social sanction, rather than technical requirement, as the basis of ethical judgment.

MODEL MATRICES

The model by which the above elements are related, as a means of explaining how ethical standards are determined and how decisions are made in compliance with ethical standards, consists of a series of matrices relating sets of variables.

Three pertain to the influence upon ethical standards of cultural values, noneconomic role expectations, and expectations of roles involved in the economic processes. A fourth matrix provides an explanation of the manner in which decisions are made in compliance with ethical standards.

Culture influences

Matrix #1 in Table 1 illustrates the influence of the cultural characteristics of society upon all of its major institutions. In it are related, along the horizontal axis, the distinguishing culture characteristics of a society and, along the vertical axis, the major institutions of the society.

TABLE 1
Matrix #1
Culture characteristic classified by social institutions

Social institutions	*Culture characteristics*					
	A	*B*	*C*	*D*	*E*	*F*
1. Family						
2. Church						
3. School						
4. Economy						
5. Government						
6. Military						
7. Leisure						

This suggests the influence of such basic cultural factors as law, respect for individuality, nature of power and authority, rights of property, concept of deity, relation of the individual to the state, national identity and loyalty, values, customs, and mores, state of the arts, etc., upon each of the institutions.

Thus are found in the characteristics of our own society sanctions for the following ethical expectations, among others: that personal integrity should not be destroyed or compromised; that checks and balances are essential to general welfare in a pluralistic society; that the state is subordinate to persons; that preservation of competition is laudable; that freedom of initiative is essential; and that economic entrepreneurship is rewarded by profit.

From these generalizations, marketing actions may be judged unethical on the basis of fundamental humanistic social expectations. Competitors derive from this logic their expectations of fair play in competition. Consumers derive their expectations of honest representation. Employees derive their expectations of humane treatment.

Contrasting cultures of different societies produce different expectations and become expressed in the dissimilar ethical standards of those societies.

Noneconomic factors

A second aspect of the model is shown in Matrix #2 in Table 2, where the noneconomic influences upon economic behavior are suggested.

TABLE 2
Matrix #2
Noneconomic influence upon economic behavior

Economic roles of participants	*Noneconomic social institutions*					
	Family	*Church*	*School*	*Government*	*Military*	*Leisure*
1. Manager						
2. Employees						
3. Owners						
4. Other financiers						
5. Consumers						
6. Intermediate customers						
7. Resources						
8. Competitors						
9. Government						
10. Community						

The influence of culture characteristics upon business ethics is felt through their effects upon behavior in both the economic and noneconomic activities. General concepts of rightness imbue an individual with ethical standards which, if consistent, he applies in all of his role relationships. Attitudes nurtured in family relationships influence behavior in business relationships, as between manager and employee. Religious concepts of brotherhood, individualism, and the dignity of man influence management relations with customers, competitors, and resources.

Matrix #2 represents the possibility that standards developed in each of the six noneconomic institutional relationships determine ethical standards for behavior in each of the ten economic roles and influence behavior among these economic role participants. In this matrix, six noneconomic institutions are shown along the horizontal axis and ten roles of economic participation along the vertical axis. At each of the 60 resulting coordinate points is suggested the influence upon economic behavior of that participant's activities and relationships outside the economy.

For example, family organization and solidarity in some cultures result in exclusion or discrimination against nonrelatives employed in business. In church-dominated societies, numerous prescriptions are set forth for consumption. Under socialistic governments, competitive interaction is highly restricted. Thus may be observed some of the influences upon managerial decisions that lie outside the realm of purely economic motivation. In other words, in matters of business ethics men do not act entirely as "economic men" but as social beings.

Role expectations

In the two matrices previously shown, the influence of general cultural factors and of noneconomic expectations is shown. In addition to that, ethical standards are created by the expectations which arise *within* the behavior patterns of the economy itself—among the ten types of economic participants.

This is suggested in Matrix #3 in Table 3, in which are related along both horizontal and vertical axes ten economic role positions. Sets of interactions are suggested by the 90 possible interrole relationships. Thus, in the marketing process areas of ethical judgment arise in the relations of managers to consumers (often identified as seller-buyer relations); of managers to intermediate customers (identified as channel relations); and of managers to competitors and to others indicated.

In trade relations arise expectations quite apart from those induced by other social institutions and by cultural factors, and which also have direct bearing upon the formation of ethical standards.

TABLE 3
Matrix #3
Sets of economic relationships through which expectations affect behavior

Economic participants	*Economic participants*									
	1	*2*	*3*	*4*	*5*	*6*	*7*	*8*	*9*	*10*
1										
2										
3										
4										
5										
6										
7										
8										
9										
10										

For example, consider the question of whether a vendor, by failing to "stand behind" the quality of his products, is guilty of an unethical act. Cultural expectations of integrity, disclosure, and honesty are involved. Moreover, circumstances of a mass-market economy produce expectations that individual events be governed by policy, that personal relations be handled impersonally, and that incidental risks be assumed by the party who stands to lose least.

In addition to this, particularly in a buyers' market, vendors publicize their willingness to guarantee performance, to make refunds, and to assure satisfaction. Although these are obligations assumed by consent, they are so general in some trades that buyers may take them for granted. Thus, by experience, announced policy, and application of general social expectations, one may infer a sufficiently clear standard of behavior to assume that the ethics of responsibility in trade relations is definite.

Because of the diversity of trade policies and practices, the certainty of such an ethical standard is not so assured as the illustration suggests, or as one might hope.

Nevertheless, among the marketing participants there are highly specialized expectations that evolve, which have the character of ethical standards: expectations of the integrity and protection of distributive channels, of protection of customers against detrimental product and price changes, and of freedom to innovate and to compete.

However, there are debatable areas of interests and interactions where ethical behavior is less defined, and where courts and other authorities may have to interpret more fundamental values of the society relating to the economic process. Such areas today are found in resale price maintenance, tax exemption of cooperative enterprises, time-price differentials in consumer sales-financing, and practices that have evoked controversy over truth-in-lending and truth-in-packaging.

In summary

An attempt has been made to identify and to illustrate the manner in which ethical standards are formulated in a marketing economy. They derive from both general and technical expectations sanctioned by society, either in general or the society of small groups. With an understanding of economic and noneconomic influences upon decision and behavior, it is presumed that "rightness" in interpersonal action may be determined.

Knowledge of the problems of ethics, however, does not provide the solution to ethical problems. This poses a second requirement of a model for ethics, namely, a guide to action, presuming that the standards of action are known.

COMPLEXITY OF ETHICAL DECISIONS

Assuming that standards of ethics are determinable, managers faced with problems requiring ethical decisions and actions have no simple, single course of action.

First, not everyone is aware of or subscribes to a universal code of ethics. Therefore, decisions often necessitate superimposition of one's own standard, compromise of it, or surrender of it. These actions are not without some conflict and adjustment within one's frame of reference.

Second, in a pluralistic society not one but many expectations must be met. Therefore, resolution of what is right to do produces a balance of obligations and satisfactions. Ideally, full satisfaction of the expectations of all parties would constitute the most ethical behavior. This is impossible, for expectations are often contradictory and sometimes exceed social sanction. Therefore skill and judgment must be used to guide one in determining the point at which his own integrity can best be maintained.

Third, because marketing obligations are of both a noneconomic and economic nature, fulfilment of social expectations cannot be divorced from the economic limitations within which business decisions must be made. Thus, the complexity of determining what in a society are the standards of ethical behavior is compounded by the multiplicity of factors affecting application of the standard.

THRESHOLD OF ETHICAL SENSITIVITY

Of prime importance in application of an ethical standard to relations among economic participants is a manager's threshold of ethical sensitivity, that is, his level of interaction at which he finds within himself satisfaction in his actions toward others.

Although these levels may be identified variously, a useful classification is suggested by the stages through which the bases or standards of ethics have evolved during the past century.

Self-interest

Perhaps the lowest level of sensitivity to ethical obligation is that on which little, if any, consideration is given to the expectations of others.

This is the basis upon which it is popularly believed that most businessmen operate, seeking profit for themselves to the exclusion of others' interests. Such a description was more true of the 19th-century business manager than of today's. No obligations to competitors, customers, employees, dealers, government, or the community were acknowledged.

"Laissez-faire," "caveat emptor," and "the public be damned" were expressions of the ethics of self-interest.

This is not to say that then *no ethics existed;* after all, the standards of that day that permitted such behavior were sanctioned by society *of that day*. Individual self-interest and collective collusion characterized the "ethics of collusion," in which owner-manager interests were predominant and profit was an end in itself, rather than a measure of economic capacity to fulfill many ethical obligations.

Legal ethics

As the social conscience rose, rejection of the "ethics of collusion" took form in legislation compelling or prohibiting certain types of business behavior.

Thus emerged a threshold of sensitivity which might be called the "ethics of compulsion." The Sherman Antitrust Act was an important waymark in the formulation of legal standards—legal ethics. It illustrated the manner in which society, expressing its cultural and noneconomic values, forces or compels obligations upon business participants. With such legal formulations, there is no justification for a lower standard of action. However, laws are often a minimal standard, sometimes representing compromise in their enactment and subject to judicial review and interpretation. There are, therefore, higher bases upon which decisions may be made.

Voluntary codes

In contrast to the forms of compulsion typified by the Sherman Act, there appeared during early years of this century a movement of voluntary formulation of codes of ethics by businessmen.

Trade groups were the medium in which this commonly occurred, although individual firms sometimes stated their own ethical tenets. As these were voluntary, they represented an "ethics of compliance," that is, compliance with acknowledged obligations to various other parties in the economic process. They often presented standards where no laws applied, or elevated the legal minimum with a willingness for fuller discharge of responsibilities.

Such standards, however, being purely voluntary and societal, were also relative, arbitrary, and revocable. They represented the accepted standard of the social group, whether that group was society in general or the small group of the business community.

Conviction

Still another basis of ethical decision is that of illumined personal convictions.

One could not say that the self-interest of the 19th century was very illumined. Neither did the laws and codes of later years always evoke spontaneous compliance. However, personal convictions concerning one's duties and obligations to others in society, as they participate in the marketing processes, probably furnish the greatest encouragement for an evolving body of ethics.

Such ethics usually arise from an integrated sense of social and personal values, and from respect for law, honesty, fairness, and the like. They often bring religious concepts to bear upon business-relationship problems, interpreting men's obligation to men from the basis of men's relation to God. Concepts of divine sonship, brotherhood, stewardship, forgiveness, mercy, and the like are applied to business relationships.

Thus, an "ethics of conviction"—even of spiritual conviction—is evolved. In recent years acknowledgment of the relevance of religious convictions to business behavior has increased.

In Matrix #4 in Table 4 are shown the relationships in which managers act, and the bases upon which their decisions as to what is ethical action rest. One basis is not always equally useful, and the decision maker will move from one to another, depending upon the situation.

When in doubt concerning the adequacy of a decision, gravitation is toward higher levels of social expectation and conviction.

Balance of claims

With conscious awareness of all expectations and of the extent of his corresponding obligations, one may be forced to modify behavior in any one relationship because of the interrelationship of many claims.

TABLE 4
Matrix #4
Decision bases in management role relationships

Bases of decision	*Management relations with roles*								
	#2	*#3*	*#4*	*#5*	*#6*	*#7*	*#8*	*#9*	*#10*
Qualitative factors:									
Self-interest									
Law									
Social standard									
Conviction									
Balance of multiple claims									
Quantitative economic limitations									

Priority of some claims over others for satisfaction may be decided on the basis of such principles as rotation of claims, superiority of owner-interests in a capitalistic economy, superiority of market-interests in a market economy, national interests, legal requirements, or the demands of power blocs. Most ethical decisions do require a balancing of numerous claims.

Economic circumstances

A final basis of decision is the extent to which economic circumstances permit doing what one may feel he is ethically obligated to do.

In a private economy, one is forced to act within economic limitations. If there is no profit for a period, the expectation of owners may be denied. If working capital is low, creditors may be required to wait for payment. If costs increase, changes may be made in the product and service normally expected by the customer.

In other words, *ethical decision under private capitalism is a moral decision impelled by social sanction but modified by economic exigency.*

IMPLICATIONS

An attempt has been made in this article to examine the anatomy of marketing decisions having ethical implications.

One is concerned, first, with the manner in which "rightness" of action is determined in a given society. Standards derive from the culture, from various institutional processes and structures, and from the expectations nurtured among the economic participants. With determinable standards, one next must select a course of particular action. He is guided by the level of his ethical sensitivity, by the strength of complementary and contrasting claims, and finally in some instances by economic capacity to act.

Employment of a model for ethics such as that proposed will sharpen one's grasp of the factors involved; but until that can be achieved, he will go a long way in his ethical marketing decisions if he possesses the basic qualities of unselfishness, honesty, fairness, and sincerity.

What operational guidelines are available to aid a marketing executive in his evaluation of alternative courses of action? The author believes that it is not sufficient to merely satisfy the legal aspects of marketing decisions. The socially responsible marketing manager must also concern himself with the more difficult questions of equity, fairness, and morality.

---

19. WHAT ARE THE SOCIAL AND ETHICAL RESPONSIBILITIES OF MARKETING EXECUTIVES?*

James M. Patterson†

There is no specific, concrete guide to responsible action for marketing executives, beyond a sort of "watered-down" commercial version of the Golden Rule.

Let us face the fact that the search for a general set of rules defining the social responsibilities of marketing is misguided in principle and doomed to fail.

Instead of asking, "What are the social responsibilities of marketing?", the question might better be, *"What workable guides are available to help a marketing executive to evaluate alternative courses of action in a specific concrete situation?"*

RESPONSIBLE ACTIONS

The really difficult problem of defining *responsible* marketing actions lies in those everyday marketing activities that raise simple questions of *equity, fairness,* and *morality*—not just questions of legality. To quote from Howard Bowen's classic questions about the responsibilities of businessmen,

> Should he conduct selling in ways that intrude on the privacy of people, for example, by door-to-door selling . . . ? Should he use methods involving ballyhoo, chances, prizes, hawking, and other tactics which are at least of doubtful good taste? Should he employ "high pressure" tactics in persuading people to buy? Should he try to hasten the obsolescence of goods by bringing out an endless succession of new models and new styles? Should he appeal to and attempt to strengthen the motives of materialism, invidious consumption, and "keeping up with the Joneses"?[1]

The marketing executive faces nagging questions about the propriety of attempting to *manipulate* customers, and in particular of the ethics of using emotional and symbolic appeals in various forms of persuasive

---

* Reprinted from "What are the Social and Ethical Responsibilities of Marketing Executives?" *Journal of Marketing*, Vol. 31 (July 1966), pp. 12–15.

† Indiana University.

[1] Howard R. Bowen, *Social Responsibilities of the Businessman* (New York: Harper and Brothers, 1953), p. 215.

communication. The list of problems might go on and on, but these examples serve to suggest the type of marketing actions in question.

For those who would act responsibly, the answers to such questions are not at all clear-cut, with the "good guys" lined up on one side and the "bad guys" on the other. How, then, is the marketing executive who actually wishes to behave responsibly to find his way through the labyrinth of ethical and moral issues?

Instead of trying to give general answers to questions that have not yet been asked, the objective should be for the harassed marketing executive to frame his problem in such a way that he can solve it for himself.

Abstract general rules offer little or no guidance to a marketing executive who is concerned about the quality of the tire he is forced to produce if he is to make a profit in the $12 price-line, or about the extent of headquarters intervention into the internal operations of his company's franchised dealers. What he needs is an approach, or way of thinking about these issues, which will help him to determine whether this particular decision with respect to product quality or that particular form of intervention is in some sense "wrong" or "unfair."

This search for the responsible course of action is not a problem unique to business and marketing. It is central to all areas of social thought and action. Consequently, the marketing executive might profitably borrow approaches and insights from other areas.

Three obviously relevant areas immediately come to mind: *ethics, law,* and *political theory*—ethics, because "right" conduct is a central concern; law, because it attempts to administer justice by means of specific case decisions; and political theory, because of its traditional concern with power and its regulation.

ETHICS

As a branch of philosophy, ethics has been concerned for centuries with standards for decision making and right conduct. Consequently, one would expect ethical writings to be an important source of guidance to the marketing executive in determining responsible courses of action.

Unfortunately, though, the connection between ethics and policy is not quite so clear-cut as one would wish. In fact, so long as ethics is looked to for answers, the decision maker remains in the difficult position of having to apply abstract ethical principles to specific concrete situations which seldom if ever quite fit the general definition.

Take, for example, the moral commandment, "Thou shalt not steal." Is it stealing for a marketing executive to accept a gift from a supplier? The marketing executive is forced to resort to "common sense" to guide his decisions.

However, Wayne A. R. Leys, in an important book on ethics, argues that if policy makers were to read philosophical ethics for critical or deliberative questions instead of conclusive answers, they would correct many sources of bad judgment.[2] He approaches ethics much as John Dewey did—not so much as a command to act in a certain way, but as a tool for analyzing a specific situation.[3] In other words, right and wrong should be determined by the total situation and not by the rule as such.

Here are some "deliberative questions," representative of those Leys derived from some of the different systems of philosophical ethics.

A. *Utilitarianism:*
   1. What are the probable consequences of alternative proposals?
   2. Which policy will result in the greatest possible happiness for the greatest number?

B. *Moral Idealism:*
   1. Is the practice right? Is it just? Honest?
   2. Does the policy put first things first?
   3. Can you will that the maxim of your action should become the universal law?
   4. Are you treating humanity as an end and not merely as a means?

C. *Instrumentalism:*
   1. What will relieve the conflicts and tensions of the situation?
   2. Does the proposed solution anticipate consequences in the larger environment as well as the immediate situation?

In effect, Leys would have us abandon the principles-approach in favor of the case-approach. This may not be bad advice. Perhaps if the marketing executive were to ask similar deliberative questions about a proposed policy, he too would find them of value in defining the responsible course of action. He might ask, for example, "Would it be desirable if *all* firms adopted this practice?"

LAW

In his attempts to determine the responsible courses of action, the marketing executive should also consider law as a potential source of guidance.

In an important book, Edmond Cahn notes that judges, under the official guise of deciding technical legal issues, are frequently required to assess moral interests and to resolve problems of right and wrong.[4] Thus, he concludes that the great body of case law should be regarded as a rich repository of moral knowledge that is continually being reworked and refined.

---

[2] Wayne A. R. Leys, *Ethics for Policy Decision* (Englewood Cliffs, N.J.: Prentice Hall, Inc., 1952).

[3] John Dewey and Charles Tufts, *Ethics* (New York: Henry Holt and Co., 1932), p. 310.

[4] Edmond Cahn, *The Moral Decision* (Bloomington, Ind.: Indiana University Press, 1955).

One section of Cahn's book, dealing with what he calls the "Radius of Loyalty" is especially relevant to the marketing executive in his search for workable guides to responsible action:

> The most valuable moral lesson the law can teach concerning loyalty (responsibility) is the lesson of relations. . . . The duty always remains a function of the relation. . . . By the same token, there can never arise in anyone's moral life an indefinite, unlimited duty of loyalty to any one creature or institution. Loyalty—however light or intense it may be—always has reference to a defined and specific relation. . . .[5]

Those familiar with the distinction between the liability of a common carrier, an ordinary bailee, and a trustee will recognize this "relational" principle in action. Perhaps this "lesson of relations" can also be applied to marketing.

Clearly a customer is related differently to a firm than is an employee, or a supplier, or even an audience member who watches a sponsored television show. For that matter, even different customers are likely to have different relationships with a firm. If responsibility is in fact a function of a *specific relationship* involving a *specific kind of transaction,* then a more precise definition of the exact character of a customer relationship might help to clear the air of nebulous admonitions to management to act responsibly.

Another approach for the marketing decision maker was developed in an earlier book by Cahn.[6] In *The Sense of Injustice* he notes that over the years the frustrations attending the traditional search for abstract justice nearly led to its abandonment.[7] He further notes that were it not for the "sense of injustice"—that sympathetic reaction of outrage, horror, shock, resentment, and anger—society would be left entirely without empirical guidance in its search for a path to justice. He continues:

> Why do we speak of the "sense of injustice" rather than the "sense of justice"? Because "justice" has been so beclouded by natural law writings that it almost inevitably brings to mind some ideal relation or static condition or set of perceptual standards, while we are concerned with what is active, vital, and experimental in the reactions of human beings. Where justice is thought of in the customary manner as an ideal mode or condition, the human response will merely be contemplative, and contemplation bakes no loaves. But the response to a real or imagined instance of injustice is something quite different; it is alive with movement and warmth in the human organism.[8]

It follows that the responsible marketing action is the one that does not arouse the executive's "sense of injustice." Often when a time-worn

[5] Ibid., pp. 151–52.

[6] Edmond Cahn, *The Sense of Injustice* (Bloomington, Ind.: Indiana University Press, 1949).

[7] Ibid., p. 13.

[8] Ibid., p. 13.

trade practice is looked at in this light, one can see that it is not "fair," and this means that reform can be instituted. The change in the grading of items for export so that they now conform to domestic standards is a classic example of how an established practice is changed to reduce the "sense of injustice."

POLITICAL THEORY

The third example comes from the area of political science.

Over the years political theorists have been concerned, among other things, with devising ways to subject potentially arbitrary power to the "Rule of Law," that is, to ensure that discretionary governmental power will be exercised responsibly.

Granting the differences in degree, this concern is quite similar to the concern of those who seek to ensure that discretionary market power will also be exercised responsibly. And it is demonstrable that *structural* limitations on potentially arbitrary power work better than *substantive* limitations.

Take, for example, the Anglo-American constitutional experience. Minimum reliance was placed on substantive limitations, that is, on generalized prescriptive commands of the "thou shalt not" variety, while maximum reliance was put on an intricate set of structural "checks and balances."

Of course, there is a Bill of Rights; but much more important have been such structural limitations as the separation of certain key powers among the various branches of the federal government, the reservation of other powers to the several states, and the creation of a representative government which consciously reflects the variety and diversity of interests affected by governmental power. *In fact, the success of the Anglo-American experience is much more due to emphasis on structural rather than substantive limitations.*

The success of this structural approach argues strongly for its application in the realm of private power. Instead of attempting to specify elaborate codes of conduct, the wiser strategy would be to attempt to develop a set of structural limitations on private power, to ensure that it will be exercised responsibly, that is, in accordance with the legitimate purposes of society.

But this may not be as easy as it sounds. For example, the concept of separation of powers may have no application in the private sphere. And of course, it is not at all clear what structural forms are appropriate for recognizing the legitimate interests of the various constituencies affected by the firm's marketing decisions—or for that matter, which constituencies ought even to be recognized.

Still, we are not entirely without structural precedent in the private sector. Several structural limitations have already been developed which give various constituent interests a "say" in the determination of those corporate policies which vitally affect their own interests. Collective bargaining, for example, structurally recognizes the interests of the employee constituency in corporate decisions relating to the terms and conditions of employment. Similarly, General Motors' dealer councils give structural recognition to the franchised dealer's interests in certain GM distribution policies.

But clearly the prime example of a structural limitation in the private sphere is *market competition.* Certainly competition is by far the most important and most pervasive structural limitation on the exercise of private market power.

And yet this is not an altogether effective limitation; and a certain amount of potentially arbitrary discretion remains. In fact, it is this element of freedom from competitive control that raises the whole problem of business responsibility in the first place.

SOME IMPLICATIONS

If competition worked perfectly, by definition there would be no discretion in the marketplace, and therefore no need for the businessman to bother thinking about which course of action is the responsible one. However, an element of market power persists in all markets; and even the most vigorous enforcement of antitrust laws would be unlikely to increase the effectiveness of competition to the point where marketing decisions would be controlled in every detail.

Certainly attempts should be made to improve the performance of competition as a structural limitation on potentially arbitrary corporate discretion. In fact, effective competition is much to be preferred over substantive limitations in the form of government-imposed codes of conduct. The marketing executive ought to try to improve the effectiveness of *the structural limitations of competition*, simply to forestall potential impositions of *substantive limitations by government fiat!*

But even beyond improving market competition as a structural device for reflecting the interests of customers in the marketing decisions of the firm, and thereby making the decisions more "responsible," nonmarket structural arrangements are needed to reflect those interests the market fails to register.

For instance, customers' interests in the firm's marketing decisions might be partially recognized by the voluntary appointment of a representative "Customer Review Board," which would consider and react to most proposed marketing decisions. At minimum, this would provide the firm with a useful "sounding board" for testing proposed courses of action.

It might also be possible to select a representative sample from a firm's customer list, and then to use survey techniques to "tap" these customers' opinions as to contemplated marketing actions. This, too, would serve as a source of guidance in management's search for responsible marketing practice.

In neither case, however, would management be bound to abide by the opinions of the customer group. Still, if there were negative reactions from a representative group of customers, management would find this helpful.

The important point is that structural limitations on potentially arbitrary power have been so eminently successful in the public area that their application in the realm of private power deserves careful consideration.

This proposal for dealing with a problem of social and ethical responsibility in marketing has been a mere "prologue." The most important problems remain.

Clearly, the possibilities of developing new structural arrangements that will effectively recognize customers' legitimate interests in the marketing decisions of the firm have only begun to be explored. And of course, the actual workability of the ethical and political approaches in specific cases remains to be tested.

The role and responsibility of private enterprise is being challenged by many socially aware organizations. It is essential that managers give increasing attention to the balance between economic goals and social responsibility. The author suggests that the social contract, or the implicit understanding of relationship among business, government, and the public, is being fundamentally altered.

---

20. CHANGING THE SOCIAL CONTRACT: A ROLE FOR BUSINESS*

Melvin Anshen†

Among the problems confronting top corporate officers, none is more disturbing than the demand that they modify or abandon their tradi-

* Reprinted from "Changing the Social Contract: A Role for Business," *Columbia Journal of World Business*, Vol. V (November-December 1970), pp. 6–14.

† Columbia University.

tional responsibility to devote their best talent and energy to the management of resources with the goal of maximizing the return on the owners' investment.

This demand takes many forms. It may appear as pressure:

to withhold price increases to cover rising costs;
to give special financial support to black ghetto properties and businesses;
to provide special training and jobs for the hard-core unemployed;
to invest in equipment designed to minimize environmental contamination by controlling, scrubbing, or eliminating industrial process discharges into air or water;
to contribute generously to the support of charitable, educational, and artistic organizations and activities;
to refuse to solicit or accept defense and defense-related contracts;
to avoid or dispose of investments in countries where racial or political policies and practices offend elements of the citizenry;
to provide for "public" or "consumer" representation on boards of directors;
to make executives available to serve without compensation on public boards or other nonbusiness assignments.

The common element in all these pressures is their departure from, even contradiction of, the economic considerations which have been regarded as appropriate criteria for determining the allocation and use of private resources. They challenge the thesis that decisions taken with a view to maximizing private profit also maximize public benefits. They deny the working of Adam Smith's "invisible hand."

This cluster of pressures is not limited to alleged deficiencies in the traditional elements of management decision making. It also raises fundamental questions about the intellectual ability of business managers—reflecting their education, experience, and norms of behavior—to respond adaptively and creatively to new goals, new criteria for administering resources, new measures of performance.

It would be comforting to conclude that the emergence of these pressures at this time is a temporary phenomenon, stimulated by an unpopular war, the dramatic juxtaposition of affluence and poverty in society, expectations for living standards rising faster than perceived gains, massive urban decay, and similar causes. It may be closer to reality, however, to suggest that society is approaching and fumbling with a basic redefinition of the role and responsibility of private enterprise.

REDEFINITION

At least two underlying developments support this view. One is the visible achievement of the private enterprise system, its extraordinary success in applying science and technology to resources under skilled management. The popular recognition of this record cannot fail to stimulate disturbing questions about ways and means of directing this great wealth-creating power to the removal of poverty, of degraded and degrading urban and rural living conditions, indeed of all gross economic and social inequities.

The second development is the widespread recognition, contrary to the bulk of earlier economic and psychological prediction, that general, if less than universal, affluence does not lead only to a simple, insatiable desire for more economic goods. It leads also to concern about what is beginning to be called the quality of life, in a sense that includes other than economic values. In the popular phrase of the moment, growth in GNP is not a sufficient measure of social performance.

One way of comprehending the whole development is to view it as an emerging demand for a new set of relationships among business, government, noneconomic organizations, and individuals. Some such set of relationships, of changing character and composition, has existed throughout recorded history. Without some implicit and broadly accepted design for living together, man's existence with his fellow men would be chaotic beyond endurance.

Philosophers and political theorists have observed the persistence and the necessity of this organizing concept. They have even coined a useful descriptive phrase for it: "the social contract." They have noted that the contract is fundamentally implicit in nature, despite the fact that men have often tried to convert implicit to explicit expression through decrees, constitutions, and bodies of law. The explicit expressions have all turned out to be temporary, limited, in some way inadequate. Whenever a need has been sensed for redefining the terms of the contract, this has been done. On occasion, the remedial action has been wholesale, revolutionary, as in the case of the Soviet Union and China. At other times, as in the United States, remedy has been piecemeal and gradual, through reinterpretation of the enduring constitution. Today, in many parts of the world, there are varying pressures for a reformulation of the implicit social contract as it affects traditional institutions, including the goals and responsibilities of both private business and public agencies.

If this is indeed what is occurring, managers should try to understand the development. They may not like it, but neither did most managers familiar with the economic and social environment of the 1920s like some of the changes introduced in the next decade under the rubric of the New Deal. Whether the prudent management response is determined to be opposition, adaptation, or influence over change, it will lack purpose and force if it is grounded on raw emotional revulsion.

Of all the "givens" in any management decision setting, the terms of the social contract are the most far-reaching, powerful, and inescapable. A manager does not have to like them, but he does have to learn how to live with them. In the course of learning this, he may also develop some ability to influence them in ways that may tilt the balance in favor of conditions friendly to continued vigorous economic and social progress and against constraints and the emasculation of incentives.

The ultimate determinant of the structure and performance of any society is a set of reciprocal, institutionalized duties and obligations which are broadly accepted by its citizens. The acceptance may be described as an implicit social contract. Without such a contract, not less real or powerful for being implicit, a society would lack cohesiveness, order, and continuity. Individuals would be confused about their own behavior and commitments as well as about their appropriate expectations with respect to the behavior and commitments of the private and public institutions which employ them, service them, and govern them.

It is not the Federal Constitution with its related legal, administrative, and judicial actions which defines and supports society in the United States. Rather, it is the underlying set of assumptions which created an environment in which the Constitution could be drafted and accepted, and in which all that followed that acceptance could be permitted to occur, including the continuous interpretation and amendment of the Constitution to reflect broad new views and conditions.

DEVELOPMENT OF THE SOCIAL CONTRACT

The concept of the implied social contract is an old one in Western civilization. It found early expression in the writings of the Greek philosopher Epictetus. It was central to the intellectual system developed by Thomas Hobbes in the first half of the 17th century. Without such an implicit contract, he observed, man faces the terror of anarchy, for the natural condition of man is "solitary, short, brutish and nasty." Hobbes used his concept to rationalize the power of the state to compel obedience to the terms of the implied contract. A few decades later, John Locke converted this view of compulsion as the lever to the view of consent as the lever—the consent of the citizens to a relationship of reciprocal duties and obligations.

In the next century, Jean Jacques Rousseau expanded the idea into an intellectual system in which each member of society entered into an implicit contract with every other member, a contract that defined the norms of human behavior and the terms of exchanges and tradeoffs among individuals and organizations, private and public. His view even provided for handling disagreements about ends and means. The implied social contract, he wrote, stipulated that the minority would accept the decisions of the majority, would express its opposition through legitimate channels of dissent, and would yield before proceeding to rebellion. To Rousseau, therefore, the act of rebellion signified not what it appeared to be on the surface—a rebellion against the ends and means favored by the majority—but rather a rejection of the very terms of the contract itself.

Most recently, the fundamental thrust of such a book as John Kenneth Galbraith's *The New Industrial State* challenges the terms of the implicit social contract that defines, among other things, the function and role of private enterprise in today's society, the popular view of the responsibilities and performance of private corporations and the network of reciprocal relationships among corporations, government, and citizens. Galbraith's description of the enterprise system is distorted and incomplete, but his perception of the fundamental contract and its pervasive influence is accurate.

The terms of the historic social contract for private business, now coming under critical attack, are brilliantly clear. They existed for more than a hundred years with only minor modifications. Indeed, they acquired a popular, almost mythic, concept which purported to define a set of institutional arrangements uniquely advantageous for the national well-being, superior to all alternatives.

THE OLD RATIONALE

These contractual terms were an outgrowth of interlaced economic, social, and technological considerations in which the economic issues were overwhelmingly dominant. Economic growth, summed in the grand measure of gross national product, was viewed as the source of all progress. The clear assumption was that social progress (including those benefits associated with ideas about the quality of life) was a by-product of economic progress and impossible to achieve without it. Technological advance both fueled economic progress and was fueled by it in a closed, self-generating system.

The engine of economic growth was identified as the drive for profits by unfettered, competitive, private enterprise. Natural and human resources were bought in an open market and were administered in the interest of profit maximization. Constraints were applied only at the margins and were designed either to assure the continuance of the system (as in antitrust legislation and administration) or to protect those who could not protect themselves in the open market (as in legislation prohibiting child labor, assuring labor's right to organize or restraining deliberate injury to consumers). These and similar constraints were "the rules of the game," a suggestive term. The rules protected the game and assured its continuance as a constructive activity.

The implicit social contract stipulated that business could operate freely within the rules. Subject only to the constraints on conduct imposed by the rules, the responsibility of business was to search for and produce profits. In doing this competitively, business yielded benefits for society in the form of products and services wanted by consumers who earned the purchasing power to supply their wants by working at jobs created by business.

The social gains were viewed as so great that there was never any serious question about the costs of the system that were thrown out on society. For most of the period (until the cataclysm of the 1930s), there was no strong public demand that private firms absorb any share of the costs of unemployment or of retired workers. For an even longer period (until the last few years) there was no strong public demand that private firms carry any share of the costs of environmental contamination. The contract stipulated that business was not responsible for these and similar costs. It said that the specific and sole responsibility of business was to provide relatively stable economic growth. As long as business produced this growth, the only costs it had to carry were the internal costs of acquiring resources in the market and using them to produce and sell goods and services to the market. The external costs of the system were not even recognized as costs. They were not accounted for. When they were evidenced in the form of extreme personal hardship for individuals and groups, they were met by private charity, or they were not met at all.

Beyond the concept of social costs, the contract stipulated that private business had no responsibility for the general conditions of life or the specific conditions in local communities. The unresolved problems and strains of industrialized urban living were seen by none but a handful of radicals as in any way a proper concern of business firms or their managers.

Although there was a long history of efforts by individuals and groups to remove racial discrimination, for example, there was no strong public demand until recently that private business accept responsibility for eliminating discrimination within firms, much less for deliberately changing hiring policies in accordance with noneconomic criteria, or for modifying lending policies to minority businesses and individuals in order to accept risks previously assessed as economically unrewarding.

The terms of the contract were so visibly defined by national norms of acceptable business behavior that they were rarely questioned by responsible managers. The relatively few and weak critics of some of the contract terms were identified by managers and even by themselves as radicals or revolutionaries interested not in reforming the system but in destroying it. This intellectual posture inhibited constructive criticism from within the system by impugning the patriotism, if not the rationality, of dissenters. One dangerous result has been to constrain flexible adaptation to dynamic economic and social changes which have been the inevitable by-products of advanced industrialization, urbanization and, broadly viewed, demonstration of the feasibility of universal affluence.

It is getting late, although not too late, to substitute cool reason for hot emotion. Today's managers have a good grasp of the critical importance of adapting to economic and technical change. However, most managers have a dimmer perception of the meaning and power of social change, particularly of those aspects of social change that bring into question the traditional goals, strategies, and values of business organizations.

All the implications of evolving social dynamics for central elements in the social contract cannot be forecast with confidence. If nations are to have constructive adaptation rather than destructive revolution, it will be important to identify and think creatively about the emerging demands for revision of the contract. They are not all bad or inevitable. But surely the first step in adapting economic needs to social needs and the reverse—to separate good from bad, feasible from impossible—is dispassionate appraisal of the directions in which the principal demands are moving our society.

THE CONCEPTUAL SHIFT

The most dramatic element for business in the emerging new contract is a shift in the conceptual relation between economic progress and social progress. Until recently, the primacy of economic growth as the chief engine of civilization was generally not seriously questioned. Some of its unpleasant or wounding by-products were, to be sure, superficially deplored from time to time. But they were accepted by most people as fundamentally inevitable and were appraised as a reasonable price to pay for the benefits of a steadily rising gross national product. As a result, the by-products were rarely studied in depth, their economic and social costs were not measured—indeed, little was done even to develop accounting techniques for tooling such measurement.

Michael Harrington's book, *The Other America,* with its quantitative documentation of the existence of an unacknowledged poor nation within a rich nation, could strike with genuine shock on the mind and conscience of many professional and managerial leaders in public and private organizations. The facts of urban decay and the implications of trends projected into the future were not analyzed and reported in terms that would permit a realistic assessment of their present and future costs. Nor, certainly until the outbreak of mass riots in minority ghettos, was there penetrating consideration of the relation of social disturbance to continued economic progess.

While much remains to be done in scientific research and analysis of the side effects of economic progress, the accumulating formal and informal documentation has begun to influence the set of general ideas that constitute the terms of the contract for business. The clause in the contract that stipulated the primacy of economic growth, and thereby gave a charter to free enterprise within broad rules of competitive economic behavior, is now widely challenged. It is becoming clear that in the emerging new contract, social progress (the quality of life) will weigh equally in the balance with economic progress.

COSTS

Such equality foreshadows some drastic revisions in the rules of the game. As one example, it will no longer be acceptable for corporations to manage their affairs solely in terms of the traditional internal costs of doing business, while thrusting external costs on the public. Since the 1930s, of course, some external costs have been partially returned to business firms, as in the case of unemployment compensation. But most have not, and this situation is on the edge of revision. This means, as is even now beginning to occur, that the costs associated with environmental contamination will be transferred from the public sector to the business firms which generate the contamination. It also means that corporations whose economic activities are judged to create safety hazards (from automobiles to atomic power plants) will be compelled to internalize the costs of minimizing these hazards by conforming with stipulated levels of acceptable risk or of mandatory manufacturing and performance specifications.

To be rigorously correct, it should be noted that industry's new cost structure will be reflected in its prices. Purchasers of goods and services will be the ultimate underwriters of the increased expenses. But a moment's reflection on the supply-demand charts that sprinkle the pages of economics texts will demonstrate that a new schedule of supply prices will intersect demand curves at different points than formerly. This may lead to a changed set of customer purchase preferences among the total assortment of goods and services. What is implied is not a simple pass-through of newly internalized social costs. The ultimate results will alter relative market positions among whole industries and, within industries, among firms. Choices from available options in short-term technological adjustments to the new contamination and safety requirements and in long-term pricing strategies to reflect higher costs will, in the familiar competitive way, determine success or failure for a number of companies. Some interesting management decisions lie ahead.

The internalization of traditional social costs of private operations is the most obvious of the changes that will follow on striking a new balance between economic and social progress. More subtle, and eventually more radical, relocations of responsibility can be foreseen. The complex cluster of socioeconomic problems associated with urbanization, population shifts, and the needs of disadvantaged minorities are already overwhelming the administrative capacities, probably also the resources, of city, county, and state governments. Evidence is accumulating that the public expects private business to contribute brains and resources to the amelioration and resolution of these massive strains. History suggests that such expectations will be transformed into demands.

VULNERABLE RESPONSES

Some imaginative business leaders are beginning to recognize that a passive response to such pressures may be dangerous. They see that a society in upheaval may accept disastrous political remedies roughly equivalent to the nostrums of medical quacks. Quite aside from humanitarian considerations, they see the self-interest of private enterprise in initiating local remedial programs and in participating in the formulation of plans for joint public-private remedial programs on the national level. These early responses are visible in scattered corporate efforts to do something about training and jobs for the hard-core unemployed, financing for ghetto construction and manufacturing, and management counseling for minority businessmen.

Despite some masking statements, most of these responses are not economic ventures of the kind traditionally associated with commitments of private capital. If they were genuine investments, the volume would surely be much greater, and they would have been made before the social strains became as explosive as they now appear. They must therefore be viewed as quasi-philanthropic commitments made in the effort to relieve intolerable distress and preserve a relatively peaceful environment for the private enterprise system.

As long as commitments remain of this character, they are vulnerable to the demonstration of their inadequacy, much as the programs of private charity proved inadequate to cope with the demands of the early 1930s. The social distress of the cities and many of their inhabitants contains at least as large a charge of dynamite in today's affluent economy as did massive unemployment overwhelming the resources of private charity in the great depression. One can predict with some confidence, therefore, that business initiatives must be forthcoming on a scale that dwarfs commitments associated with the familiar scale of charitable contributions. Alternatively, society will use the instruments of legislation and taxation to compel corporations to make contributions of management skills and financial resources far beyond anything known hitherto. This type of development was precisely what led to the New Deal legislation of the 1930s. The problems of fundamental dislocation are more spectacular now, and the remedial measures are likely to be larger.

Such a development will involve a major revision of the terms of the social contract for business. It strikes at the central concept that the job of private business management is to maximize profit. It portends a redefinition of the nature and scope of the management responsibility and of profit. The changes inherent in this forecast define a revolution in management thinking and practice that may be fairly described as beyond anything in the history of modern business.

Few managers are prepared by training and experience to conceptualize the structure and performance of private enterprise within the terms of a social contract of this character. But then few nonmanagers have any better preparation. The whole apparatus from grand design to simple bookkeeping needs to be thought through. The creative manager will be substantially motivated to push into all aspects of the problem, his motivation being fueled by consideration of the alternatives.

The most dismal of these alternatives for both economic and social progress is the total substitution of public for private goals, strategies, and actions—what President Eisenhower once presciently described as the effort to achieve the security of the inmates of the penitentiary. In such a transformation, the dynamism of private business initiatives and of consumer dominance of the market system would disappear, and with them, if the examples of the socialist states mean anything, the political liberties and personal freedoms of the citizens of a democracy. Short of this extreme, one can readily visualize large-scale transfer of economic activities from the private to the public sector, accompanied by bureaucracies that inhibit experimentation and risk assumption.

These are profoundly unpleasant prospects. But the powerful pressures now being experienced for fundamental revision of the contract for private business suggest that it is not going to be possible to maintain the status quo intact against the thrust of change. The economic and social values of the enterprise system can be preserved only through a flexible adaptation of those elements of the system which have either contributed to extreme public discomfort or have found no ready avenues for alleviating the human and physical decay of our times. This adaptation is more likely to be constructive and workable if those who understand and respect the energy of the business system advance into the problem and share in the design of its solutions. There are many would-be architects who start their work in ignorance, or even contempt, of the business system. However disturbing their rhetoric, it is their ignorance, not their animosity, which is the true danger.

MANAGEMENT CONCERN

If the thrust of this analysis is generally on target, the principal lesson for private management is clear. It must participate actively in the redesign of the social contract. There can be no greater danger than to permit the new rules to be formulated by either the small group of critics armed only with malevolence toward the existing system or the much larger group sincerely motivated by concern for ameliorating social ills but grossly handicapped by their ignorance of the techniques and dynamism of private enterprise.

The record of recent public efforts to revise some of the rules of private business behavior (as in grocery product packaging, consumer credit terms, air and water contamination, and automobile safety) suggests, however, that business firms and their managers will not be allowed to participate in revising the rules if they volunteer their assistance only after their demonstrated resistance to any change has been overcome.

The experience of the American Medical Association is illuminating on this point. Decades of official opposition to any public program of financial assistance for the medical needs of the aged created such widespread distrust of the AMA's motives that some of those professionally best qualified to design an effective and efficient Medicare program were denied a share in the drafting. Not their competence but their intentions lacked credibility. If business leadership is publicly committed to a general defense of the status quo in the face of rising discontent with significant elements of prevailing economic and social conditions, then managers who have the technical competence to make valuable inputs will not be allowed to contribute even marginally.

FOR EXAMPLE

A review of two of the areas in which thoughtful, concerned managers can make creative contributions to revision of the terms of the contract will suggest both the complexity of the problems and the richness of the opportunities. Environmental contamination is a good example. Within a very few years, the subject has moved from the domain of a small number of specialists in natural and human ecology to the stage of broad public concern. President Nixon gave it major treatment in his 1970 State of the Union message. Legislation has been enacted at every level of government, and more is proposed. In one way or another, the thrust is toward transferring a social cost back to the business firms which contribute to the contamination through their manufacturing operations or the performance characteristics of their products.

These actions are being taken in ignorance of the magnitude and specific incidence of the costs. This is matched by an almost equal ignorance of the costs and effectiveness of available technologies for suppressing or removing the sources of contamination. Finally, there is minimum legislative and administrative experience with the variety of cost transfer instruments which include taxes, incentives, and direct charges. The results are practically guaranteed to be chaotic and inequitable.

If the posture of corporate management ranges from opposition to passive acquiescence, the total attack on the problem is likely to be grossly inefficient, and the ultimate costs for industry and its customers are likely to be substantially higher than necessary. Only by open recognition of the total problem in all its complexity, open acceptance of responsibility for its creation, and open expression of a desire to bring business knowledge and technical competence to bear on the analysis of complementary and alternative solutions will corporate management establish a posture that will entitle it to a ticket of admission to the redesign of this element of the social contract. And only in this way will there be a reasonable chance of developing solutions that are technically effective, economically efficient, and socially equitable.

WHERE TO BEGIN

A good place to begin would be the uncharted jungle of cost estimates. We need concepts and techniques for measuring and accounting for the real costs of environmental contamination. We need to build a body of reliable information about what the costs are in all their complexity, where they originate, where they impact. We also need to evaluate present and potential technologies for suppressing or removing contaminants, along both engineering and economic parameters. Using history, experimentation, and game theory, we need to study the relative effectiveness of all types of cost transfer instruments, both inducements and penalties. One might speculate that the conclusion will be in favor of applying a variety of devices, each fitted to a specific set of technical and economic circumstances, rather than a single instrument. But this is a foresighted guess, not a basis for public policy determination.

A second area where business competence can make a contribution is the cluster of problems associated with poverty in the midst of plenty, unemployed or underemployed minorities, and urban decay. Less clearly defined than the contamination issue, this area possesses much greater potential for violent disruption that could mortally shred the fabric of our society. If this occurs (and there are too many recent examples of limited local disruptions to be comfortably skeptical about the possibilities ahead), many of the environmental conditions essential for the private enterprise system will disappear. There can be little doubt that what would follow would be an authoritarian, social-service, rigid society in which the conditions of production and distribution would be severely controlled. In such a setting, the dynamism, creativeness, and flexibility of the economy would disappear, together with all the incentives for individual achievement in any arena other than, possibly, the political.

It is not easy to project with confidence how private business might move effectively into this area while retaining its fundamental profit orientation. One interesting possibility is to transfer the concept of the defense contractor to the non-defense sector. The brute economics of low-cost urban housing, for example, may rule out unsubsidized, business-initiated investment. Not ruled out, however, is business as contractor, remodeler, and operator under negotiated or competitive-bid contracts. There has been limited experimentation in arrangements of this type, in housing, education, urban systems analysis and planning and other fields. Freer exploration in diverse circumstances and in public-private relationships might discover an attractive potential for alleviating and removing major causes of gross social discontent while retaining a large degree of private initiative and the familiar web of revenue-cost relationships. The true social costs remaining, representing the layer of subsidies that may be found necessary to absorb the remaining expenses of an acceptable ground level of general welfare, could then be allocated through the tax system.

This is obviously not the only possibility in sight. Business has made only a few limited experiments in the application of incentives. More extensive analysis and trial might suggest at least the special circumstances in which this tool could effectively supplement or supplant the public contractor device. A third possibility is suggested by the concept embodied in Comsat—the mixed public-private corporation. Other options, including combinations of the foregoing, await imaginative creation.

The incentive for business management to enroll as a participant in the general exploration of ways and means for removing the cancerous growth in the vitals of society is classically selfish. Somehow, this cancer will be removed. The recognition is spreading rapidly that its continuance is intolerable. Some of the proposed or still-to-be-proposed lines of attack may be destructive of other elements in society, including the private enterprise system. Management is in a position to contribute rational analysis, technical competence, and imaginative innovations. The interests served by continuing the enterprise system coincide here with other social interests.

These and comparable innovations imply for private managers a willingness to think about new economic roles and social relationships that many will see as dangerous cracks in the wall of custom. It is not unreasonable, however, to suggest that we are considering nothing more adventurous than the explorations and commitments that managers have long been accustomed to underwrite in administering resources. The only significant difference is that the stakes are higher. In place of the marginal calculus of profit and loss, what may be involved is the preservation of the civilization that has created such an unparalleled record of wealth and growth.

b.

Business and the quality of life

How DOES the "quality of life issue relate to marketing?" The phrase, "quality of life," is frequently discussed in terms of national social goals. But also involved in the quality of life are the concerns demonstrated for the rights of others through the behavior of individual consumer-citizens and business firms. Every member of society shares in the collective responsibility for the quality of life. One important contemporary business question concerns the specific responsibilities of businessmen for improving the quality of life.

Society is demanding a better quality of life; business is expected to listen and to respond to this demand. There is little question that public expectations of business responsibility to society are increasing compared to the level of performance expected in the past. However, there is little common agreement as to the extent and ramifications of this involvement. It is unrealistic to require business to be totally responsible for improving the quality of life. However, business, through cooperation with other groups in society, each group working in its area of expertise and specialization, can be effective in improving the quality of life.

The quality of life issue is a practical one relating to business self-interest. First, it is to the advantage of business to respond to social problems, especially those caused by business, before they reach acute proportions. Second, the self-interest of business is best met over the long run when public interest is paramount; a weak society cannot support strong business indefinitely. Third, the quality of life concept represents additional business opportunities through the conversion of society's needs into profitable business ventures.

Some of the implications for marketing of the quality of life issue emerge from the articles in this section. They range from the broader concepts of the quality of life issue to concern with more specific areas of business and the arts and business and environmental crises. In the first article, Drucker discusses the demands, importance, and implications the quality of life issue presents for the business community. In the next article, Henderson describes the new consumer demands and their impact upon marketing and the total business community. Gingrich then comments on the relationship of the business community to the arts. Quinn contends, in the last article, that environmental improvement offers new and profitable markets for industry.

Has business, in the past, demonstrated sensitivity for societal needs? Can business, in the future, continue responding to society's increasing demands? Business must act and react as business. Social considerations are mandatory, but they must be handled in a "business sense."

---

21. BUSINESS AND THE QUALITY OF LIFE*

Peter F. Drucker†

I.

In the late 1940s and early 1950s, the American automobile industry tried to make the American driving public safety-conscious. Yet when Ford introduced cars with seat belts, sales dropped so catastrophically that the company was forced to abandon the whole idea. But when 15 years later the American driving public suddenly became safety-conscious, the car manufacturers were sharply attacked for being "merchants of death."

Similarly, a good many electric power companies tried for years to get the various state utility commissions to approve of their use of low-sulfur fuels and of cleaning devices in the smokestacks. The commissions refused again and again, with the argument that the public was entitled to power at the lowest possible cost, insisting that neither a more expen-

---

* Reprinted from "Business and the Quality of Life," *Sales Management*, Vol. 102 (March 15, 1969), pp. 31–35. Note: This article first appeared in the book, *Preparing Tomorrow's Business Leaders Today*, Peter F. Drucker, ed. (Englewood Cliffs, N.J.: Prentice-Hall, Inc., 1969).

† New York University.

sive fuel nor capital investment to clean the smoke would be permitted in the rate base. Yet when eventually air pollution became a matter of public concern, the power companies were roundly berated for "befouling the environment."

Ever since the advent of the "miracle drugs," which occurred in the 1940s, the medical profession has been urging the drug companies to respect the independence and knowledge of the physician and not, by word or deed, to interfere in his complete control of the relationship with public and patient. Similarly, the druggists have been demanding that the drug companies respect their "professional integrity" and continue to compensate them as if they, rather than the drug companies, were still the compounders of medicines. And yet the same physicians are now attacking the drug companies for making it possible for the slipshod physician to overprescribe highly potent drugs. And the public tends to hold the drug companies responsible for the "spiraling costs of medical care," even though drugs are the only component of medical bills the cost of which has risen less than the general level of prices.

For 20 years, there has been a campaign to get private businesses to take part in defense production. Businesses that did not bid on defense work have been atacked in Congress, in the press, and in public as unpatriotic. Yet even though the profits on defense business are less than half what the same companies can earn on nondefense business, defense contractors are being criticized for "profiteering" on defense business. And companies that accepted defense contracts under great government pressure find their recruiters chased off college campuses and their offices picketed.

And these are only a few examples of many.

II.

When we suddenly realized after the urban riots of 1967 how close we were to explosion and civil war in the black ghettos, the very groups who had always been most contemptuous of business and of the free enterprise system turned as one to the large corporation as the ultimate resource, if not the savior, of the cities. Business is now expected to create overnight a large number of jobs for the least skilled and least trained people in the ghetto and to make employable (and to employ) the very people whom government policy has kept on permanent welfare rolls as "unemployable."

Even staunch believers in free enterprise have long treated low-cost housing, primary and secondary education, and transportation as governmental concerns. Yet as government is proving itself increasingly unable to manage the city, traditional "liberals"—and even a good many "leftists"—now cry for business to take over these functions. It was the late Robert Kennedy, rather than the National Assn. of Manufacturers, who proposed that the rehabilitation of the slums be taken on by business.

The Black Power militants want to make education competitive, with the individual parent deciding whether the task money available for the schooling of his children should go to the public schools or to private institutions designed and run by the country's major corporations. Columbia University's Frank Tannenbaum, who made his name as a fervent apostle of salvation through industrial unionism, proclaimed in the Spring 1968, issue of the *Journal of World Business* that the multinational corporation was "the last best hope" and the only foundation of a peaceful world order. New York's Mayor Lindsay (according to the New York *Times* of May 11, 1968) now wants big business to take over obligations which the welfare agencies were originally created for, that is, to "adopt" whole ghetto neighborhoods—to the point where business, Mayor Lindsay suggests, should make sure that there is a man in the house to look after the Negro family.

It is not my purpose to discuss these specific demands on business and businesses. In any event, the list could be extended indefinitely. What matters is that these demands illustrate a major change in the social environment of business and in society's expectations from business and businessmen. Our society now expects business and its senior executives to take responsibility for the health of society in addition to its traditional accountability for economic performance and results. Society now expects business and businessmen to look ahead and to anticipate the social problems of tomorrow. It expects business to be able to solve these problems when no one else can, if not to prevent their emergence in the first place.

Traditionally, business has been held responsible for quantities: for the supply of goods and of jobs, for costs, prices, wages, hours of work, and standards of living. Now business increasingly is being asked to take on responsibility for the quality of life in our society.

The traditional responses of businessmen and of academicians to such demands have been "public relations" and the "social responsibility of business." These responses are not so much inadequate to meet these new expectations as they are irrelevant to them.

Public relations is concerned with the question whether a business or an industry is "liked" or "understood." Public relations would therefore be worried, because Black Power advocates blame the "profit motive" for the ghetto, and they presumably like business just as little as they like any other part of the "white establishment." But what really matters is that the Black Power leaders expect business to perform miracles in respect to ghetto employment, ghetto education, ghetto housing; they expect these miracles virtually overnight. The relevant questions are: Can business tackle these huge problems? How? Should it tackle them?

These are not questions which public relations is equipped to handle.

Similarly, public relations was not able to anticipate the problems of automotive safety and air pollution, or problems of the drug and defense industries. In each of these cases, business is in trouble today in large part because it was so very receptive to yesterday's public opinion and did such a good job in its public relations. The great sensitivity of the drug industry to its "publics"—the physicians and the druggists—is a good case in point, and a major reason for the troubles the drug industry finds itself in today.

What has always been meant by "the social responsibility of businessmen" is the way businesses and businessmen spend spare time and spare cash. In a good many cases, the words "social responsibility" were really little more than another way to say "good works." "Social responsibility" meant "Lady Bountiful." But even at its most serious, social responsibility was concerned with events outside of and separate from the day-to-day conduct of business. It was a restraint on business. It never implied responsibility for society and for the quality of life in it.

The new demand is, however, a demand that business and businessmen make concern for society central to the conduct of the business itself. It is a demand that the quality of life become the business of business. The traditional approach asks: How can we arrange the making of cars (or of shoes) so as not to impinge on social values and beliefs, on individuals and their freedom, and on the good society altogether? The new demand is for business to *make* social values and beliefs, create freedom for the individual, and altogether produce the good society.

"The quality of life"

In one way these new expectations are dangerously unrealistic. It is silly to believe, as a great many people seem to believe today, that business is *the* institution of our society and that business is, therefore, the appointed keeper of our society.[1] The fact is, rather, that every major task of our society is today being discharged in and through an organized and large institution such as the university or the hospital, the government agency, the armed services, the labor union—and, of course, business as well. Each of these must be held fully as accountable as any other for "the quality of life" of our society. Business has a distinct impact on society, distinct capabilities and characteristics, and distinct opportunities. But it is not unique, not the only institution, let alone the only one with impact on the society and the community.

At the same time, it is clearly to the self-interest of business and businessmen to accept this responsibility for the quality of life in our

[1] A good example of this fallacy is Professor J. K. Galbraith's recent book, "*The New Industrial State*" (Boston and New York, 1967).

society and to build it into businesses and into the vision of senior executives. This is, of course, particularly true for the large corporation.

The quality of life in our society is involved with the self-interest of business for three reasons.

First, the penalty for neglecting this area is so very high. Whenever there has been the kind of crisis which the automobile industry had in respect to automotive safety, the public utilities in respect to air pollution, the drug industry in respect to medical care, or the defense contractors in respect to defense pricing and procurement, the penalty imposed in the end on business has been high indeed. Such a crisis always leads to a scandal in the end. It leads to Congressional inquisition, to angry editorials, and eventually to the loss of confidence in an entire industry and its products by broad sectors of the public. And finally, punitive legislation always follows. The fact that the public today sees no issue is not relevant. Indeed it is not even relevant that the public today—as it did in every single one of the examples above—resists actively any attempts on the part of farsighted business leaders to prevent a crisis. In the end, there is the scandal, and then business is in the pillory.

On the other hand, the public always in the end accepts an intelligent solution for such a crisis if business works conscientiously to design one. This has been the experience of the Committee for Economic Development (CED) in its 20 years of existence, and of any other business or industry which took responsibility for a crisis and brought to bear the knowledge, the competence, and the seriousness of its best people.

It is, in other words, definitely to the self-interest of business to anticipate social problems, especially those which will be generated by the activity of business itself. And usually these problems can be anticipated. It is not hindsight to say that we should have known that there would be a problem of automotive safety; everyone in the automobile industry knew this 20 years ago. It is not hindsight to say that we should have done something about the smoke from power company smokestacks; everyone in the public utility industry has known this for 20 years. That the "miracle drug" drastically changed the practice of medicine and made yesterday's pharmacist obsolete, everyone in the drug industry has known for at least 15 years. And everyone in the defense industry has been saying for 20 years that our defense regulations, written for "temporary emergencies," were increasingly inappropriate for the realities of a permanent, preventive defense establishment. It was, in other words, predictable 15 to 20 years ago that every one of these problems would become an "issue" in which business would be attacked and penalized. There was only the question how soon this would happen.

A second, even more important reason why responsibility for the quality of life is to the self-interest of business is the obvious fact that a healthy business and a sick society are not compatible. Healthy businesses require a healthy, or at least a functioning, society. The health of the community is a prerequisite for successful and growing business.

Better to anticipate . . .

This is, of course, not at all new. Sixty years ago this was obvious to such men as Julius Rosenwald and Theodore Vail, who built Sears Roebuck and the Bell Telephone System, respectively. Indeed Rosenwald, the "city slicker," went so far as to invent—and for years to support single-handedly—the County Agent system through which the work of the land-grant colleges first became effective in raising agricultural productivity and with it the farmer's standard of living and purchasing power.

The only new aspect is the demand that business anticipate today what society's central problems will be tomorrow. But to try to do this is better than to wait till the problem is upon us in full force.

Finally, the quality of life of our society should be a tremendous business opportunity. It is, after all, always the job of business to convert the needs of society into profitable business opportunity. It is always the job of business to convert change into "innovation," that is, into new business. And it is a poor businessman who thinks that "innovation" refers to technology alone. Social change and social innovation have throughout business history been at least as important as technology. After all, the major industries of the 19th century were, to a very large extent, the result of converting the new social environment—the industrial city—into a business opportunity and into a business market. This practice underlay the rise of lighting, first by gas then by electricity, the streetcar, and the interurban trolley, the telephone, the newspaper, and the department store, to name only a few.

Yet the demand that business take responsibility for the quality of life of our society is a dangerous demand. It needs to be thought through carefully. Shooting from the hip and ad hoc response to yesterday's headlines can only cause havoc. There is grave danger that businessmen will be found inadequate in their vision, that is, that they do not address themselves to the full scope of these demands. This would make business appear irrelevant to society. There is also a danger that business will tackle things it cannot do, or tackle things the wrong way. This leads to failure and to disappointment with business. Yet the cry of "Let business do it," is heady wine even for sober heads. It may not be the sincerest form of flattery, but is a most insidious one.[2]

[2] A good example of this is Mayor Lindsay's idea that business should "adopt a neighborhood in the ghetto." This is simply another version of something we have tried before with signal failure, namely, community paternalism. This is exactly what the textile industry of New England did in the 1830s when Lowell, Mass., was a "model town"—and the result was, 30 or 40 years later, deep bitterness which has not yet died down. Patrons of the neighborhood were exactly what

III.

This whole area will undoubtedly occupy us for many, many years to come. But some guidelines for the approaches to it can already be discerned.

The first thing to say is that business cannot behave like anything else. It can only behave like business. And this is the right way for it to behave.

What this means is that business is an economic institution entrusted with responsibility for the most productive employment of the communitys' scarce economic resources. If it is untrue to this trust, it is untrue to itself and to the community. It also is not competent, as a rule, to do anything else. This is what businessemen are trained for and tested in. They are likely to perform well only if the tasks can be organized in terms of economic rationality.

Business must be business

Specifically, this implies that profitability must be the yardstick for business activity in respect to the quality of life fully as much as it has been the yardstick for business activities in respect to the quantities of life. "Profitability" is simply another word for the economic employment of economic resources. While not a perfect yardstick by any means, it is the only one we have. What is not profitable is subsidized. And businesses, as such, have no right to hand out subsidies—they are trustees for the community's economic resources. Experiments business can support; research and development business must support. Philanthropy business may engage in, up to a point. But in its main thrust, business must behave as a business, that is, must apply economic rationality to whatever it is doing.

Another implication is that business must put to work its specific strength: the market test. The great strength of business as an institution is not that it "makes a profit" but that it is under an objective outside test of performance. The great strength of business as an institution is that it can go out of business if it does not perform. No other institution has any such measurement nor is under such discipline. This is the reason that we now call for business to tackle the problems of the city which no other institution so far has been able to solve. This is the reason, of course, why the communist economies today are all getting back to profitability and the market test—without them there is no measurement of performance and, therefore, ultimately no performance.

the social worker and his community welfare agency were designed to be, and their failure is a major cause of our present discontent. In other words, there is need to think through what the problem really is and how it really should be tackled, rather than sloganeering and flag-waving, which makes for impressive headlines and good "public relations," but for serious trouble a little later on.

Second, business needs to organize for its concern with the quality of life the way it organizes for any other new and dynamically changing area. It needs to organize its "R & D" for society and community fully as much as it has been organizing its "R & D" for technology.[3] Business has to organize itself to anticipate the issues, the crises, the problems, and the opportunities which tomorrow will bring in society and community. Today's public opinion is largely irrelevant for this, just as yesterday's technology is not too relevant for tomorrow's new products. Where we are likely to go, and above all, where we should be going, are the major questions. For business will have to be ready with the answer when the public finally catches up with the question. Otherwise it will be held to blame for "the mess."

Finally, we know in a general way that responsibility for the quality of life means three kinds of "products," that is, three approaches to the problems of the community:

1. The first and most desirable is an approach in which a "problem" can be converted into an opportunity for profitable competitive business. I would not rule out the possibility, for instance, that the drug companies, had they gone to work on the problem, might have come up with a solution which might have made the dependence of the physician on drugs he does not understand into a highly profitable business opportunity for the pharmaceutical industry.

The best example of such a solution is the automobile industry. We take the secondhand car for granted. But it actually is a solution to what otherwise would have become a serious social problem. While we worry about housing for the poor, we do not worry about transportation for them; we know they have available serviceable automobiles, at least in the United States. But these they only have because the people who buy new cars willingly take a loss which in effect subsidizes the buyer of an old and used car. Could we not, for instance, work out a similar approach to the housing problem? Unless they are able to buy cheaply the used but highly serviceable goods of the affluent, poor people have never been able to get capital goods of decent quality at a price they can afford. That this is not entirely speculation may be indicated by the fact that "mobile homes" are already the largest single segment of the American housing market, and the fastest growing one.

2. But where a problem cannot be converted into business opportunities, business must then ask: What *regulation* is needed here to enable this problem to become accessible to private, competitive, and profitable business? What standard has to be set by public authority? Automotive safety, for instance, had to be imposed by government regulation once

[3] One approach towards this is the new function of "public affairs" that has lately come into fashion, though this is still only too often simply a new and fancier name for the old "public relations," if not for political lobbying.

it had proven impossible to convert it into a competitive advantage, that is, once the American public had shown clearly that it was not willing to pay a premium for it (or indeed, to purchase it altogether). Otherwise the irresponsible and opportunistic will always drive out of the market the responsible and farsighted business. Regulation, in other words, is not an alternative to competitive business. In many areas it is a prerequisite to it. What is needed, however, is a universal standard which applies to everyone and which creates equal burdens as well as equal opportunities for everyone. At the same time it has to be a standard which accomplishes the needed public purpose at a minimum economic cost. Increasingly it is these public regulations that determine the productivity and with it the competitive position of a country in the world economy. Increasingly, therefore, there is need for a solution which provides the right standards without impeding productivity or imposing costs. And this only businessmen can work out.

3. Finally, if no such regulation can be worked out to create the conditions for competitive business enterprise, the public policy that would enable business to tackle a problem should be thought through. What subsidies might be needed, what guarantees, what forms of public financing or of tax relief and so on would enable business to become effective in a given area, e.g., public education or low-cost housing?

This is a dangerous area. Businessmen are rightly suspect when they discuss the subsidies they should be getting. Yet subsidy is necessary if business is to take over areas in which the market mechanism cannot possibly perform for the time being. It should always be the aim of such a solution therefore to stimulate the creation of a market and of a working market mechanism.

This means that subsidies, if needed, should be open. They should be payments of government rather than hidden charges on the community or on the consumer. The goals and objectives should be clearly spelled out, and the results should be evaluated in relation to them in a constant performance review. There should be a definite time limit set for any such subsidy with renewal the exception rather than the rule. Every economist knows the reasons for these safe-guards (and every politician tries to conceal them). It would be singularly unwise for business not to emphasize them, and not to insist on them.

Needs and profits

No less an authority than George Champion, the chairman of the Chase Manhattan Bank (and by no means a "liberal") recently pointed out in the *Harvard Business Review* that many of the "problems" of the city actually offer opportunities for major new industries and new profitable enterprises. I too am hopeful that most of the needs of society and community today can be converted into profitable business opportunity—as were the needs of community and society a century ago. But even if it should turn out that many of them need government and cannot be satisfied through the market mechanism, there is need for business and businessmen to concern themselves with them. The alternative is simply too costly. Business, it is now clear, is both going to bear the blame and pay the price for the inability of other institutions to handle these problems adequately.

Altogether perhaps it might be said that these problems—even that of the black ghetto—are not primarily problems of "failure." It is only because we now take it for granted that the economy can provide the quantities of life that we are becoming conscious of our shortcomings in respect to the quality of life. It is only because business has done such a good job in its traditional areas that it is now, even by its least friendly critics, expected to concern itself with the quality of life in our society.

Corporations possess vast resources and occupy positions of great power in our society. Because of their broad impact, corporations must develop an appreciation of society's needs that will be satisfied not solely by more products but by responsible and concerned behavior in and out of the marketplace.

---

22. REDEPLOYING MARKET RESOURCES TOWARD NEW PRIORITIES: THE NEW "CONSUMER DEMAND"*

Hazel Henderson†

Let me begin by briefly reviewing what I consider and what many other speakers at this conference have already described as America's emerging social values. They might well be termed the "postindustrial values" espoused by a growing number of our more affluent, politically

* Reprinted from the address "Redeploying Market Resources toward New Priorities: The New Consumer Demand,'" given at the White House Conference on the Industrial World Ahead, Washington D.C., February 8, 1972.

† Director, Council of Economic Priorities.

influential citizens who are disenchanted with many of our existing institutions and priorities, but for the most part still believe that their objectives can be reached by restructuring business and government machinery through constitutional means. They include environmentalists, militant consumers, students and young people, middle and upper income housewives newly activated by the consciousness of the women's rights movement or the boredom of suburban life, the public interest lawyers, scientists, engineers, doctors, social workers and other politicized professionals, the joiners of extrapolitical organizations such as Common Cause, the activist stockholders, and the various crusaders for "corporate responsibility."

The new "postindustrial values" of such groups are to a great extent needs described by humanistic psychologists Abraham Maslow, Erich Fromm, and others as transcending the goals of security and survival, and therefore less materialistic, often untranslatable into economic terms, and in turn, beyond the scope of the market economy and its concept of "homo economicus." They constitute a new type of "consumer demand," not for products as much as for lifestyles, and include yearnings, which Maslow referred to as "meta-needs," for meaning and purpose in life, a closer sense of community and cooperation, greater participation in social decision making, as well as a general desire for social justice, more individual opportunities for self-development and more options for defining social roles within a more esthetic and healthful environment.

Ironically, these new values attest to the material successes of our current business system and represent a validation of a prosaic theory of traditional economics which holds that the more plentiful goods become, the less they are valued. For example, to the new "postindustrial consumers," the automobile is no longer prized as enhancing social status, sexual prowess, or even individual mobility, which has been eroded by increasing traffic congestion. Rather it is seen as one component of a mode of transportation forced upon him by the particular set of social and spatial arrangements dictated by an interlocking group of powerful economic forces embodied by the auto, oil, highway, and rubber industries. Such a consumer has begun to view the automobile as the instrument of this monolithic system of vested interests and client group dependencies, which has produced an enormous array of social problems and costs including decaying, abandoned inner cities, an overburdened law-enforcement system, an appalling toll of deaths and injuries, some 60 percent of all our air pollution, and the sacrifice of millions of acres of arable land to a highway system that is the most costly public-works project undertaken by any culture since the building of the Pyramids and the Great Wall of China!

It has become expedient of late for business spokesmen to excoriate such views as these held by such new consumers. At best, they are seen as esoteric, at worst, un-American: but certainly a luxury not affordable by the average American family, let alone those living in poverty. And yet it must be acknowledged that these views are increasingly validated by the realities of environmental degradation, decaying cities, unemployment, continued poverty in spite of a climbing Gross National Product, and other visible evidence of the shortcomings of current social and economic arrangements. At the same time, some of these "postindustrial values" are surprisingly congruent with some of those values being expressed by the poor and less privileged. Some of these groups, whether welfare recipients or public employees, less powerful labor unions or modest homeowners and taxpayers, seem to share the same demand for greater participation in the decisions affecting their lives and disaffection with large bureaucracies of both business and government. For example, we have witnessed the very real suspicions of the labor movement expressed in the charges that President Nixon's New Economic Policy was tailored much more to the liking of business interests than it was to labor. Similar charges were made by consumers, environmentalists, minorities, and the poor concerning the unfairness of tax credits "trickling down" from business rather than "trickling up" from some form of consumer credits to create instant purchasing power. Further, environmentalists found themselves agreeing with labor and minorities that human service programs, which also tend to be environmentally benign, should have been expanded rather than cut; and that a federal minimum income program is more needed than ever because it would create purchasing power for instant spending on unmet basic needs, such as food and clothing, as well as permitting the poor greater mobility to seek opportunities in uncrowded areas, thereby relieving the overburdened biosystems of our cities. Or to recast the disenchantment with our automobile-dominated transportation system, we may note the very different but equally vocal objections of the poor. Some 20 percent of all American families do not own an automobile. For the poor, many of them inner city residents, the cost of even an old model is prohibitive. This decreases their mobility and narrows their job opportunities, while the decline in mass transit and increased spatial sprawl permitted by wide automobile use worsen the situation. The highway-building spree is too often experienced by poor and minority groups as the callous driving of roads for white suburbanites through black and poor neighborhoods. This in turn permits even more of the cities' remaining middle and upper income taxpayers to flee urban problems for greener pastures.

Therefore, although it is possible to dismiss these "postindustrial consumers" as irrelevant, and indeed they may well be less of a market for consumer goods, they nevertheless represent a new and different challenge of vital concern to corporations. Even though they are no longer willing to perform the heroic feats of consumption which have heretofore been successfully urged upon them by massive marketing barrages, their opinion-leadership roles and trend-setting lifestyles will continue to influence traditional consumer tastes as they have in the new anarchism and casualness in clothing fashions, the popularity of bicycling, the trends away from ostentatious overconsumption toward more psychologically rewarding leisure and lifestyles, reflecting the astounding growth of encounter groups and other activities associated with the human potential movement. In addition, their "meta-needs" will express themselves in increasingly skillful political activism and advocacy as they continue to find in their more holistic concepts greater congruity between their own goals and the aspirations of the less privileged. Furthermore, their growing confrontations with corporations over their "middle-class" issues such as the environment and peace, have led them to discover the role of profit-maximizing theories in environmental pollution and the role of the military-industrial complex in defense expenditures and war. These insights, together with their awareness of their own privilege and their acceptance of guilt and concern for social injustice are leading to the kind of convergence with other socioeconomic group interests so much in evidence in the movement for corporate responsibility.

Many of the corporate campaigns have been equally concerned with peace, equal opportunity in employment, pollution, the effects of foreign operations, safety, and the broadest spectrum of social effects of corporate activities. Typical was Campaign GM, which simultaneously sought representation on General Motors' board of directors for minorities, women, consumers, and environmental concerns. The same convergence is evident in the newly formed Washington-based Committee to Stop Environmental Blackmail, composed of labor unions, including the United Auto Workers and a cross section of environmental groups, who are pledged to stand united in the face of a growing number of corporations who attempt to prevent implementation of pollution control laws by raising fears of unemployment, plant shut-downs or even relocating in more "favorable" states or other countries. Both labor unions and environmentalists view such tactics as more often power plays and bluffing, or poor management than bona fide cases of corporate hardship.

Similarly, environmentalists and unions have worked together to reduce in-plant pollution and the ravages of such occupational diseases as black lung, or in fighting the wholesale destruction of small farms, open lands, and streams through the excesses of strip-mining. This convergence is also visible in the comprehensive manifestoes and social critiques of theoreticians, whether in the movements for civil rights, peace, women's liberation, or environmental and consumer protection. Most of these critiques tend to explain war, racism, sexism, and all forms of social and environmental exploitation as being interrelated and stemming from current patterns of power and distribution and their roots in prevailing economic and cultural assumptions. This growing understanding of the political nature of economic distribution has naturally focused on the dominant economic institution of our time: the corporation and its political as well as economic role. Nothing displays the political power of our large corporations more vividly than their own managements' concepts of the corporation as power broker, mediating the interests of virtually all other constituent groups in the entire society! Such an all-encompassing role is traditionally ascribed to popularly elected governments in a democratic system such as our own, rather than to private, special purpose organizations. Such acknowledgment by both businessmen and their critics in the corporate responsibility movement, of overriding social power of the large corporation points up the fallacy of Dr. Milton Friedman's argument that corporations do not have the right to make social decisions, but only maximize stockholders' profits. The reality is that corporations in pursuing their profit motives, regularly makes ipso facto social decisions of enormous consequence.

One might conclude, therefore, that if our corporations remain as powerful as they are today; and many business analysts believe that this power in the multinational corporation will soon dominate or even supplant that of many nation states; then we might also expect it to collide more extensively with that of other social forces. This will lead to unprecedented challenges to corporate activities based on traditional economic theories, greater numbers of confrontations with citizens radicalized as they are more closely affected by corporate efforts to expand, apply new technology, increase production, or move into new areas such as large-scale agri-business operations with specially severe social repercussions. It is to be hoped that these confrontations, whether boycotts, picket lines, or politicizing annual meetings and proxy machinery, will eventually find civilized channels for expression, and will lead to new structures of social mediation as envisioned in my article, "Toward Managing Social Conflict," in *Harvard Business Review* of May-June 1971. In addition, technology assessment will surely advance beyond today's rudimentary stage, which is often no more scientific than the intuitions of citizens who have lain down in front of bulldozers and so passed political judgment on scores of new power plants and highways in the past few years. As technology assessment methods improve and become democratized and institutionalized at every level of government by public demand, we can expect that these former areas of management prerogative will give way to a more open, consultative public decision-making process. Similarly, we may also expect the fruits of currently stepped-up funding will produce workable sets of social indicators of human well-being, as well as better documentation of social and environmental diseconomies generated by current production. These indicators must collect both *objective* data on depletion of resources and other environmental "capital," the social health and welfare costs passed on to taxpayers by corporate automation, relocation, or various standards for employee occupational health and product safety; and the *subjective* data concerning states of relative satisfaction with "quality of life" as perceived by the citizen. These might be based on polling techniques, or monitoring citizens' complaints funneling into government agencies or city halls, and using them as inputs into social indicators of the gap between expectation and performance of government, as demonstrated by Dr. Ezra Krendel, professor of economics at the University of Pennsylvania's Wharton School of Business and Finance. (See my article "The Computer in Social Planning," *MBA*, December 1971.)

As macrolevel social indicators are developed and begin to reformulate and enhance the accuracy of current narrowly defined economic indicators, the information that individual companies base their decisions upon will also change. As social and environmental costs are factored into the Gross National Product, company decisions will be framed in terms of a much more slowly growing "Net National Product." As these externalities become more explicitly quantified and publicly disseminated, there will be further pressure to internalize these formerly unacknowledged costs of production and add them to the market price of products. This will change the definition of profit to apply only to those activities which create real added wealth, rather than private gain wrung from social or environmental exploitation. At the microlevel, community groups are already asking their local chambers of commerce penetrating questions concerning their euphoric "development" plans. Some communities already demand that exhaustive cost/benefit analyses be prepared on a broad range of development options, including the option of *not* developing at all. Through citizen pressure, such need-oriented projects as The U.S. Soil Conservation Service's stream channelization program and their justification by distorted "cost/benefit analyses" will be exposed as fraudulent.

The inevitable result of all this reassessment of economic concepts and quantification methods will be the popular realization that economics is not much more than a set of unacknowledged assumptions parading as a "value-free" hard science. This realization will further politicize economics and one would expect to see the growth of "public interest economics groups" to join those in public interest law and science. Such groups will eventually find foundation and other institutionalized support as citizens' groups learn that they must have their own economist present testimony on the diseconomies of one-way bottles to counter the testimony of the container companies' economists at public hearings. Similar insights will lead to demand for interest-group representation on all governmental economic decision-making bodies, such as the Federal Reserve Board, the Treasury, and the President's Council of Economic Advisers, which consumer, environmental, and minority groups have already sought to expand, so as to include member economists representing their interests.

For the corporation, there will be similarly stepped up demands for interest group representation on their boards of directors or "public interest directors" as suggested by many corporate critics. It is also likely that other corporate publics, particularly stockholders, consumers, and environmentalists, will organize themselves into coherent negotiating blocs and engage in annual bargaining with corporations just as labor unions do today.

Meanwhile, efforts are now underway on Wall Street to broaden traditional security analysis to cover the social and environmental performance of corporations, following the pioneering work of New York City's Council on Economic Priorities, of which I am a director. The council's bi-monthly *Economic Priorities Report,* which counts among its subscribers a growing list of banks, brokerage houses, mutual funds, and other institutional and individual investors, publishes comparative information on the social impact of corporations in various industry groups in five key areas: environment, employment practices, military contracting, political influence, and foreign operations. The need for this type of corporate analysis is highlighted by the fact that there are now no less than six new mutual funds whose stated purpose is to invest only in those companies with superior social and environmental performances.

Also, a recent study presented at the annual meeting of the Financing Management Association by Dr. John T. Marlin and Joseph H. Bragdon Jr. based on an in-depth study of pollution in the pulp and paper industry by the Council on Economic Priorities, disputes the widely held contentions that (1) pollution control is achieved only at the expense of profits, and (2) that pollution control is a close function of prior profitability. On the contrary, it was shown that many companies with superior environmental performance also showed superior profitability. Four possible explanations were advanced, including better management; lower cost of capital which a favorable corporate image can sometimes command through marginally higher stock prices and lower borrowing costs; and lower operating costs in labor, health insurance, maintenance, taxes, and particularly in the cost of pollution control itself, when it is an integral part of the design of manufacturing equipment, rather than added later. Indeed, Dow Chemical Company claims that it expects to profit from its pollution control program. All of this suggests that U.S. capital markets are becoming more sensitive to socially related aspects of business performance, and that social performance ratings sheets on companies will be as common in the future as are those rating traditional performance today.

If this kind of future domestic environment is a likely scenario for the U.S. corporation, then it will have to change considerably in order to maintain its current broad mandate; or embark on a restless search overseas for short-run advantages in politically and economically prostrate nation states willing to provide sweated labor and resources, and a blank check to pollute. Some U.S. corporations, driven by profit-maximizing imperatives, are already eyeing such less-developed nations, and Japan has already declared its intention to transfer its own labor-intensive, high-energy, polluting industries to such areas of the world. Corporations choosing such a strategy will surely gain their short-term, narrowly defined profit objectives, but they will incur social and environmental debts which will eventually lead to further social conflict both in the United States and in international relations. Meanwhile U.S. labor unions, fearing the further export of jobs, are themselves going multinational, and the consumer and environmental movements are gaining strength in the industrialized nations of Europe and in Japan. Therefore, let us assume that companies will refrain from such a destructive course and instead attempt to modify their policies and practices so as to bring them more into harmony with emerging social goals and the diminishing resources of the ecosystem on which they and society ultimately depend.

One of the most vital and farreaching new corporate strategies must be that of learning to live with the new definition of profit and the internalizing of the full social and environmental costs of production. This will alter markets and production as it more rationally assigns such costs to the consumer, rather than the taxpayer. For instance, it is highly likely that in face of the coming energy squeeze, current promotional rates for electricity will be restructured to include external costs and remove subsidies from heavy users, such as the aluminum industry. One outcome would be the wholesale replacement of aluminum in many consumer products, another might be the disappearance of the throw-away aluminum can. Another consequence of such a more realistic definition of profit would be the discontinuance of many consumer items whose production was only profitable with formerly hidden social or environmental subsidies; and, as resources become scarcer, the gradual replacement of high energy/matter input goods with low energy/matter input goods, and the continued growth of services in the public and private sectors that is already evident. All of this may be initially inflationary while readjustments are occurring, and may cause many American products to face even stiffer competition in world markets. However, this is disputed by Prof. James B. Quinn of the Amos Tuck School of Business Administration in the *Harvard Business Review*, September-October 1971. Quinn believes that the new environmental costs will eventually be sold as "value added" in products; that the new pollution control processes will result in raw materials savings, and that while foreign competition may initially cause some disruption, this may be offset by rising ecological awareness in other nations, added exports from a growing domestic pollution control industry, and other factors.

In view of such conditions, it would seem that the only possible areas for future profits will be in three general areas: (1) *Better energy-*

conversion ratios. For example, we will no longer be able to afford the thermal inefficiencies of the current generation of light water nuclear fission reactors or the internal combustion engine. It is now becoming clear that adding pollution control equipment, such as cooling towers, or catalytic converters on cars, may on a total-energy basis, leave us with a tradeoff. Only by developing inherently more efficient energy-conversion systems, such as fuel cells or nuclear fusion, can we hope to achieve actual economy and environmental benefits. (2) *Better resource management and rehabilitation.* Production loops must be closed by recycling, but probably not in the current mode of volunteer recycling of bottles and cans, because it does not constitute a valid negative feedback loop for the container industry and permits them to continue externalizing the severe costs of collection. (3*a*) *Better "market failure research" into those areas of our economy where there are unmet needs for basic consumer goods but inadequate purchasing power.* This group of some 10 million families with incomes of less than $5,000 per year, as well as those with annual incomes between $5,000 and $10,000 per year, represent one of the greatest challenges to our business system, requiring conceptual breakthroughs as farreaching as the invention of consumer credit. Federally underwritten home mortgages or the G.I. Bill's massive investment in human resources—all these families, even those below the poverty line or on welfare, have explosive aspirations for better housing, education, vacations, and consumer goods which are so pervasively flaunted by advertising and mass media.

One obvious strategy for corporations is to support an adequate national minimum income, not only for humanitarian reasons and to prevent further erosion of our human resources and equalize the unfair distribution of welfare costs among our taxpayers; but also to irrigate our economy with instant and much-needed purchasing power. For those families in the annual salary range between $5,000 and $10,000, corporations and labor unions alike should explore the strategies of building purchasing power by broadening capital ownership and dividend incomes. This broadening of corporate ownership by cutting employees in on "a piece of the action" after the style of Louis O. Kelso's Second Income Plan Trusts, has already proved effective in many corporations and has also reduced labor strife and increased motivation. These employee stock ownership trusts permit corporations to finance new capital equipment with tax-deductible dollars, while apportioning out newly issued shares representing the expansion to the workers, without payroll deductions. Corporate activists, such as the Minneapolis-based Council for Corporate Review, have also proposed that SIP Trusts be used as a financing tool in helping defense-oriented corporations achieve the necessary conversion to civilian-oriented production so that employees' security need not be tied to production of weapons.

(3*b*) *Better "market failure research" into those areas where indi-*

vidual consumer demand is inoperable unless it can be aggregated, i.e., the potentially enormous public-sector "markets" where the backlog of unmet group consumer needs is greatest, for such services as mass transit, health care, clean air and water, education, retraining, parks, and all kinds of public amenities. Many of these needs might well become coherently aggregated with a little corporate support of the necessary political activities of coalitions of potential consumers now working to underpin them with government appropriations. And yet many companies, blind to these new market opportunities, continue to oppose such citizens' efforts and even lobby against mass transit or clean air, because they still identify with past vested interests in old, rapidly saturating markets.

If corporations can lobby to procure government contracts for military and space products, they can also learn the methodologies of the new multistage public-sector marketing. Companies interested in developing new markets in the public sector must first contact citizens organizations pushing for new priorities in public spending and assess which new needs they might be best equipped to serve. Only these grass roots coalitions of potential consumers can create enough genuine political steam to capitalize these new economic activities, and corporations must learn to see these groups as indispensable allies instead of enemies. The companies must then determine the citizen's expectations for the performance of the new public sector goods and services and together begin formulating the design criteria and functional goals, with the companies providing technical and other supporting services to develop more detailed plans. Some companies, such as Northern States Power Company in Minnesota, have instigated this kind of community consulting process in the location of a new power plant.

These processes are particularly vital in such areas as the design of mass-transit routes and facilities, so as to include the greatest number of riders. Then the size and shape of the total market must be measured by extensive polling and interviewing with additional monitoring of "little" magazines and underground media to flag new expectations. New technology for social choice is now in the experimental stage which has proved capable of increasing citizens' motivation and participation in articulating such new demand, assessing options, and formulating community goals, and then has been used to analyze and profile the resulting feedback. For example, using computers and television, we might model all the alternatives for a town's transportation mix and assess outcomes for such options as (1) do nothing and permit continued ad hoc growth of highways and auto use, (2) make more provision for safe paths for short trips on foot or bicycle, (3) build mass-transit line for high-density areas with feedforward from potential riders as to routes, (4) start a dial-a-bus-on-demand system with computerized dispatching, or (5) designate open lanes for express buses on major freeways so as to lure commuters out of their cars with the faster trip. All the variables can be plotted and simulated on television as "games" and audience feedback can be profiled to change the plotting of the diagrams on the screen as the "votes" are recorded. Currently, corporations hoping to serve the incipient mass-transit market are circling and waiting, or developing expensive hardware designs which they will try to put across with lobbying efforts—rather than becoming involved with all the clamoring civic groups demanding such facilities—so as to learn their needs and thereby design systems that they will use.

Finally, corporate marketing men should begin to sell these groups of potential consumers on the merits of their systems or services, and then join with them in lobbying efforts to pass the legislation or bond issues necessary to create the market for these big-ticket items. This was the way that the pollution control market developed in response to the consumer demand already expressed through political channels. The fledgling firms in the field put some of their marketing dollars together to back trade association programs of providing speakers and film strips to inform civic groups of the technology available for the cleanup; thereby raising enthusiasm for appropriations and bond issues, and often bringing discreet third-party pressure on the recalcitrant companies to purchase the needed equipment.

Market failure research is the corporations' equivalent of social indicators of broader consumer demand and subjective states of satisfaction. Its goal is to keep producing corporations informed of social shifts in closer to real time so that new product development can be more rationally based on faster and more accurate information on genuine consumer needs. This is a reversal of the current corporate tendency to develop products with their own capabilities in mind, and then market them with million-dollar advertising campaigns of saturation-bombing of American braincells. We need only look at the proliferation of drugs and toiletries where the packaging and the promotion represent more cost than the product, and in some cases, such as the marketing of analgesics, it has become necessary for the merchandisers to invent a new disease like "the blahs" in order to push the product. The annual advertising overkill of some $20 billion is now itself producing diminishing returns, as the mounting public backlash shows. Environmentalists sue for free air time under the Federal Communication Commission's Fairness Doctrine to counter the distortions and nonsense of corporate image ads claiming concern for the environment, which have been dubbed "eco-pornography." Champions of children's rights to protection from televised hucksterism, such as Boston-based Action for Children's Television, are effectively advocating an end to all advertising on children's programs.

Meanwhile the real needs wait. The ripest public sector market is for mass transit, which will need massive infusion of federal, state, and local funds. The aerospace companies' heads are still in the clouds, trying to push monorails and hovercraft; the riders are ready to begin now, where we are, with mounting the effort to divert funds for express bus routes, open lanes on freeways, jitneys for congested inner cities, upgraded subways and commuter trains, and fast airport-to-center-city transit. The grass roots coalition is in place: environmentalists, inner city dwellers, suburban commuters, public health groups, the aged and infirm, and all the others disenfranchised by current transportation patterns, as well as the workers who see tomorrow's job opportunities. They are waiting for the companies to show an interest, to start earmarking those wasted advertising dollars to build public support for the new priorities, and to offer citizens the support they so desperately need in shifting the old system and its client dependencies into a new and more productive pattern. Another ripening public-sector market is in waste disposal of all kinds. Some companies are beginning to think creatively about how to handle this massive problem, and General Electric has offered an interesting proposal for large regional waste-handling "utilities" which would separate and recycle every salvable component and then incinerate the remainder to produce usable energy for heating. Other opportunities await in housing, health, environmental control, communications, and human development. But business must learn to play by the new rules: real, not false, profits, technology assessed by human and environmental criteria, with full public participation in design and accountability in its operation.

The new consumers are not Luddites, they are realists. They do not reject technology, because current population levels in industrialized nations clearly preclude such a course. Rather, they seek an end to the gross, wasteful, "meataxe" technology which has characterized our receding industrial age. They envision a second generation technology, more refined, miniaturized, and organically modeled along biological analogies. Buckminster Fuller calls this process of doing more with less "ephemeralization." For instance, we might de-emphasize the high-energy transportation side of the coin of human interaction and increase the communications side. This could mean decentralizing of population into smaller, more organic sized communities, managed locally by cable-TV based "electronic town meetings" and all linked into nationhood by mass media. Likewise it might mean decentralizing corporations by breaking them up into more functional units as we learn more of the growing phenomenon of "diseconomies of scale." Smaller production units, while somewhat more costly, can be offset by lower transportation, distribution, and inventory costs. It could also mean a renaissance of grassroots capitalism, with small entrepreneurial groups providing local daycare and other community services, or cooperatives for cable TV or apartment building ownership and operation.

Lastly, the new consumers understand that just as computers and mass communications can be used to manipulate people's buying habits or intimidate them politically by government surveillance and databanks; so they can be used to rewire the individual citizen back into the central nervous system of the body politic through electronic town meetings, instantaneous polling, and eventually voting in referenda, modeling public problems and issues, as the very hardware of participatory democracy. Reformulating our concepts of "capital," "return on investment," and "resources" will help us see that all such uses of technology to inform our citizens and improve public decision making are more profitable than, for example, government funding of the development of machinery to automate tobacco harvesting, which has served to worsen rural unemployment and increase migration into already overcrowded inner cities. The new consumers are aware how narrowly based economic decisions control current allocations of resources and that large corporations and the business system in general is a predominant force in our society and much of the rest of the world. Therefore they also understand that they must deal with it and work within it because they are, in reality, within it and a part of it. But they also believe that with sufficient creative, vigorous, and uncomfortable public pressure, the productive forces within capitalism can be adapted to the needs of the immediate present as well as the next two decades, and redeployed away from their current preoccupation with our "death-industrial complex" toward a new "life-industrial complex."

What is the relationship between the arts and the modern corporation? How can this seemingly unique relationship grow and prosper? The author explains that the concepts of relevance, recruitment, and respect will be influential in this ongoing relationship.

---

23. THE ARTS AND THE CORPORATION*

Arnold Gingrich†

That business and the arts are not natural enemies is a latterday discovery. Before the 1965 publication of the Rockefeller Panel Report, *The Performing Arts: Problems and Prospects,* there was little general awareness of any useful relationship between business and the arts, and it was certainly not a topic of frequent discussion.

* Reprinted from "The Arts and the Corporation," *The Conference Board Record* (March 1969), pp. 29–32.

† Esquire Magazine.

The keynote address of a 1965 New York Board of Trade luncheon, "Is Culture the Business of Business?" marked the first recognition by the business community that there was a growing trend toward corporate support of the arts. At this affair, awards were given to 12 companies for activities in the arts, and to three companies for contributions to the environment through architectural accomplishments. An Arts Advisory Council was formed within the membership of this hundred-year-old Manhattan institution, and an awareness began to spread around the corporate world that the arts are a central, rather than a fringe, aspect of that society of which business now sees itself as an integral part.

Due largely to the revelations of the Rockefeller Panel Report, some sense of interdependence between business and the arts began to take on general currency. Before the year was over, something of a movement could be discerned.

By the next year, when the Twentieth Century Fund study, *Performing Arts—The Economic Dilemma,* by William J. Baumol and William G. Bowen, served to reinforce the growing realization that the arts could not be expected to be "a paying proposition," the movement had gained evident impetus. In the spring of '66, at a conference jointly sponsored by the New York Board of Trade and *Esquire* magazine, Theodore Sorenson sounded the keynote that "the business of business is America." The concept of corporate citizenship that had up until that point largely justified corporate support of the arts in the narrow terms of "enlightened self-interest" began to be broadened, on the basis that "what's good for America is good for business."

To the rather passive corporate role of purely donative support of the arts, there was added the consideration of more active involvement, tending to the enlistment of the arts as an ameliorant of urban stresses in the short-term or tactical view, and as an enhancement of the quality of life in the community in the long-term view. The scope of the New York-based Board of Trade "Business and the Arts" awards was enlarged by adding *Esquire*'s "Business in the Arts" awards, in which the degree of community involvement is a determinant, quite apart from consideration of amounts of money or either size of the company or of the community.

Some idea of the momentum of the movement came with the realization that while it had taken some digging to come up with a dozen logical recipients of the Board of Trade's 1965 awards, the judges of *Esquire*'s 1966 awards had close to 200 nominations in hand.

By 1967 there were so many companies engaged in arts-related activities across the land that it was no longer possible for the judges to confine themselves to 20 selections. They had to enlarge the number, by the addition of Honorable Mentions, to 44.

Thus, a practice that had seemed unusual only a few years earlier was becoming regarded as commonplace.

But the real breakthrough came as the result of another Rockefeller activity. In 1966, at the Fiftieth Anniversary Conference of the National Industrial Conference Board, David Rockefeller called for the creation of a committee to stimulate corporate support of the arts, and in the fall of 1967 the Business Committee for the Arts was established under the chairmanship of former Secretary of the Treasury Douglas Dillon and the presidency of G. A. McLellan. It is comprised now of almost 100 business leaders across the country who participate by invitation.

This development was as important as the New York Board of Trade's pioneering move in the field just a couple of years earlier. Both concepts sprang from within the business community. It could now, with BCA established, be said that the business and arts phenomenon, already remarkable for the speed with which it had caught on, was gaining national momentum.

According to the National Industrial Conference Board, civic and cultural causes together received only 3 percent of corporate contributions a decade ago; now the total for the arts alone is 3 percent. But that is nowhere near enough.

All figures in the national picture of the arts needs are at best good estimates. The Rockefeller Panel Report estimated the annual dollar gap between income and outgo of the performing arts alone as being between $40 and $60 million, but all subsequent studies have indicated that even the higher of the two figures was considerably low. However, every study points to the growing income gap and the critical financial needs of the arts. Furthermore, national figures are not necessary to make the point of need to any businessman involved with an organization struggling—as almost all of them are—for survival.

The 1966 New York Board of Trade Conference posited as a goal that business allocate to the arts one half of 1 percent of the tax-deductible giving, and thus raise the level of corporate support of the arts to around $250 million yearly, a more than tenfold increase.

Although corporate contributions of all kinds may be taken on a tax-deductible basis up to a total of 5 percent of income, it has been noted that while such corporate contributions have been rising, their increase has been simply a reflection of rising corporate income, not of an increased *percentage* of income. Corporate philanthropy has remained approximately 1 percent, despite a 50 percent rise (from around $530 million in 1962 to $800 million in 1965) in the amount of giving. There have been some spectacular examples of business gifts to the arts in recent years. American Export-Isbrandtsen Lines gave the Metropolitan the cost of a new production of "Aida." Eastern Air Lines gave a half million to the Metropolitan Opera in 1967 for a new production of Wagner's *Ring* cycle. TWA gave $150,000 to help meet the overseas touring expenses of the New York Philharmonic in 1969. These examples—outstanding as they are—are almost insignificant in raising the share of corporate contributions to the arts, when measured against the rise in corporate giving as a whole.

Even the available figures are subject to some guesswork, since most breakdowns of charitable giving lump "civic and cultural" together. Contributions in these fields rose, between 1962 and 1965, from 5.3 percent to 8.3 percent of all corporate giving. This has since led the National Industrial Conference Board to subdivide the category in its figures.

Money is in any case only a part of the story of business and the arts. That aspect of the relationship, the whole question of *support,* can be comparatively passive. The question of *involvement* is the active side and, undoubtedly in the long run, the more fruitful for both partners. For it presupposes not that one gives and the other takes, but that they enrich each other, while doing much for the community they share.

In all probability the level of business support of the arts will not rise to the indicated optimum unless and until a greater degree of business involvement with the arts brings it about as a natural consequence, rather than as a result of high-pressure fundraising or the earnest exhortations of high level do-gooders.

Businesses will be of a lot more help to the arts when their interest is volunteered rather than drafted. The businessman who involves his business with the arts because his own interest has been quickened by them, is likely to bring about a much deeper and more lasting relationship than the one who is dragooned into paying them lip service and giving them no more than token support. In fact, without such involved men, it is doubtful that the business and the arts relationship would ever have become more than a biological sport, a rare and atypical phenomenon.

The status of the business and the arts movement today is in the stage of simple arithmetic, whereas tomorrow and sooner or later thereafter it may achieve the successive levels of geometry, trigonometry, and calculus. Today it is simple enough and in a sufficiently early stage to be fairly well summed up in a new set of Three R's.

The first of these Three R's is Relevance. Art has become more relevant to our daily lives than was ever true in the past. Not only is art in all its forms and many new guises much more readily and widely available to all of us. Also there is more and better art in our lives today through the advertising and merchandising forces which have come to realize the effectiveness of beauty as a business tool, with the result that, particularly of late, business and the arts have been brought closer together.

The second of these Three R's is Recruitment. Today's young men of talent and promise can no longer be taken for granted as logical prospects for recruitment into the ranks of business. It's a common phenomenon for the businessman to find that his son today not only looks on his business, but also on the town where that business is conducted, with disdain. He'd much rather do something interesting, in and of itself, in some place far enough away to enjoy the glamour that only distance confers.

One answer to this reluctance of youth to look on both business and the old hometown with any but a jaded eye is to try to invest both with some of the glamour that rubs off from involvement in the arts. One of the most revealing and significant sections of the Rockefeller Panel Report cites instances where there was a direct ratio between the ease of recruiting talent for business enterprises and the presence of cultural attractions in the community.

The third of the new Three R's is perhaps less immediately self-evident. It is Respect. There's a new respect for the arts, as well as a new respect for education, in many businesses today. The ranks of management are increasingly filled by men who have either been educated to an interest in the arts and a respect for them, or acquired it as collectors or even as practitioners.

Much of the genuine interest in and respect for the arts that has come to permeate management levels as a logical concomitant of "the culture boom" may be taken simply to stand for the new emphasis on arts and creativity which has characterized the sixties, in contrast to the emphasis on science and research that was the counterpart in the fifties. It is this which has tended to give the arts and all appeals connected with arts projects a new respectability in the executive suite. Even those occupants who still have neither interest nor appreciation now would pause before admitting the fact.

So call it Respect, or call it Respectability. It amounts to the same thing, because there's a certain and growing bandwagon aspect to the current involvement of business with the arts.

While it would be fatuous to propound that artists and businessmen, as a whole and as a class, have overnight fallen into an ecstatic state of brotherly love, still it would be equally wide of the truth to state that they still look at each other like strange bulldogs. There is still far to go, but the 1965 discovery that business and the arts are not natural enemies is leading toward their cooperation for the betterment of America.

On the immediate and short-term basis, the forecast for the weather ahead could well be "partly cloudy to cloudy, with bright intervals," even though the long-range outlook is beyond a doubt very good.

Contributing to the cloudy aspect of the short-term outlook is the fact that the prospect of substantial government aid, hailed with such fanfare just a few years back, has gone into momentary eclipse. The Yahoo congressman may well be a vanishing breed, but the day of his extinction is not yet arrived.

Also a factor is the crisis aspect of the urban problem, with the unrest in the cities conferring a higher priority on the emissary of an organization concerned with better jobs and training programs for nonwhites than any that can be realistically expected currently to be accorded someone attempting to raise money for the arts. The one exception on that front, of course, is the time-honored tactic of "If you can't lick 'em, join 'em," in the form of working up arts programs purely on their value and virtue as ghetto-condition palliatives and ameliorants. This is bad even when it's good, as the arts should be able to stand up on their own and be counted as among the positive attributes to overall community enrichment, and not snuck in disguised as tranquilizers of turbulence.

In the long run, the role that the arts must play is one of helping to make life more tolerable for us all, by relief of some of the stresses and strains that make modern living equally hard on the nerves and tempers of rich and poor.

Can a free society maintain both high standards of affluence and a clean environment? Is the private enterprise system capable of providing those elements of "an improved quality of life" which represent public, rather than private, demands? Will industry be able to meet its environmental demands and still maintain its competitive international position? These questions are considered by the author. He concludes that whether the new public markets present an opportunity or threat to business depends largely on the responsiveness of business leadership to the new public demands.

---

24. NEXT BIG INDUSTRY: ENVIRONMENTAL IMPROVEMENT*

James Brian Quinn†

The often strident cries of the "environmentalists" have raised a fundamental challenge to the private enterprise system. Questions like these are basic concerns for all:

Can a free society have both a high standard of individual wealth and a clean environment?

* Reprinted from "Next Big Industry: Environmental Improvement," *Harvard Business Review*, Vol. 49 (September-October 1971), pp. 120–31.

† The Amos Tuck School of Business Administration, Dartmouth College.

Is the private enterprise system capable of providing those elements of "an improved quality of life" which represent public—rather than private—demands?

Can industry meet environmental demands yet maintain its capacities to compete internationally?

I believe private enterprise cannot only meet the challenge but thrive on it. To do so, however, requires some basic rethinking of the whole environmental issue. The following ideas are basic to this reconceptualization:

1. The demand for environmental improvement offers opportunities to nearly all types of companies to share in huge untapped primary markets.
2. Properly developed, these markets will create economic growth, which can pay for many of the environmental improvements sought.
3. Much of what appears to be "the national cost" of environmental improvement really represents new markets created by unfilled public demands.
4. Business and public policy should focus on: (*a*) developing these markets rationally, and (*b*) minimizing the real overhead costs of environmental improvement, i.e., unproductive bureaucracies, improperly established standards, unnecessary dislocations, and ineffective public expenditure systems.
5. It is not enough to approach environmental improvements as a "business responsibility." Fair and well-enforced national regulations, sensibly developed public-market mechanisms, and fiscal policies which support intended growth and investment patterns will be essential.

For purposes of this discussion, I use the term "environmental improvement" in its broad sense—to include not only such matters as cleaner water and air but also safer highways, healthier communities, and a better educated population.

CREATING PUBLIC MARKETS

Our private enterprise system has developed the capacity to satisfy almost immediately the most detailed demands of any consumer, household unit, company, or institution in which a single authority can make purchasing decisions and has independent access to funds. But the system has been considerably less adept at developing and filling demands for public consumption and investment—hospitals, schools, water supplies, sewage systems, roads, parks, airports, waste disposal systems, and so on. If such public markets *could* be developed by private enterprise, however, they would provide exciting growth opportunities for many industries and simultaneously ameliorate many pressing social problems. For example:

> To clean up a river—and the shorelines and beaches it affects—requires sewage treatment plants, heat transfer units, cooling towers, waste and by-product processing units, improved storm drain and sewage systems, sophisticated monitoring apparatus, and so forth. These, in turn, create supplier markets for steel and metal products, construction equipment, pumps and treatment equipment, meters, switches, wire, electronic controls, construction materials, glass, ceramics, plastics, and chemicals in profusion.
>
> A national commitment to make adequate health care available to all U.S. citizens would require expenditures of over $120 billion per year in the late 1970s. A network of regional hospitals, local diagnostic centers, rural clinics, medical schools, special care units, and medical extension services would have to be built and equipped. Enormous new markets would be created for medical and dental equipment, hospital supplies, prosthetic and corrective devices, laboratory equipment and supplies, construction materials, and sanitary materials. These, in turn, would lead to expanded demands for chemicals, plastics, textiles, basic metals, metals fabrication, production and construction equipment, measurement and test equipment, and so on throughout industry.

These two simple examples suggest that demands for "a cleaner environment" or "a better quality of life" could create new or expanded markets for almost every industry—no matter how basic. Exhibit 1 presents some informed forecasts of the size of these and other major public markets. Because of the dominant influence of political factors, one cannot attest to the accuracy of the forecasts, but all estimates indicate that the markets will be huge.

How do public markets come into being? They may be produced by (*a*) aggregating individual demands through public expenditures, and/or (*b*) forcing individual actions through regulation or tax policy. Let us examine each of these forces in turn.

Aggregating demands

In some—but by no means all—cases, government bodies have to aggregate and dispense funds to purchase items individuals cannot afford. Refuse, sewage, transportation, education, recreation, and public safety systems would all fall in this category.

Can such expenditures result in net growth for society? Some traditional economists might argue that tax-financed public expenditures only transfer funds from one source to another—and consequently cannot

EXHIBIT I

Estimates of public markets, 1970–1975 (in billions of dollars)

	Direct annual expenditures	*Primary data source*
Medical and health services	$70–$120	*Predicasts,* First Quarter, 1971.
including: Hospital construction	2– 3	*Engineering News Record,* January 1971.
Medical equipment and supplies	3– 5	Standard Research Institute, *World Market for Nonpharmaceutical Health Products,* Long Range Planning Service Report, 1969.
Education systems	80– 103	U.S. Department of Commerce, Business Defense Services Administration, *U.S. Industrial Outlook,* February 1971.
including: Educational construction	5– 6	*Engineering News Record,* January 1971.
Educational equipment and supplies	7– 10	Diverse sources.
Roads and highway construction	10– 15	*Predicasts,* First Quarter, 1971.
Sewage treatment and sanitary systems	5– 10	Council on Environmental Quality, *Environmental Quality,* 1970.
Solid waste disposal systems	4– 10	*Environmental Quality,* 1970.
Subsidized housing starts	3– 10	*President's Report on National Housing Goals,* 1970.
Air depollution—automotive	4– 5	U.S. Department of Commerce, *Automotive Fuels and Air Pollution,* 1971.
Air depollution—fixed source	2– 5	U.S. Department of Health, Education, and Welfare, *The Cost of Clean Air,* 1970.
Airport development	1– 2	Federal Aviation Agency, *The National Aviation System Plan,* 1970.
Mass transit systems	1.0– 2.0	*The Economist,* March 27, 1971.
Water supply systems	1.0– 1.5	*U.S. Industrial Outlook,* February 1971.
Industrial water depollution	0.5– 1.0	*Environmental Quality,* 1970.
Air-control facilities and equipment	0.25	*The National Aviation System Plan,* 1970.

provide net growth. But past experience does not support this view. For instance:

The railroads and canals of the 1800's—built with large public contributions—expanded markets and lowered distribution costs for all.

In recent years publicly financed interstate highway systems and subsidized aircraft development have stimulated the growth of public travel, trucking, airlines, transportation fuels, and other related industries.

The U.S. space program created a whole new market never previously conceived.

Even wars—man's most uneconomic and tragic expenditures—cause temporary economic booms. (Military programs are superimposed on the basic demand system of society. Hence they call forth more resources, production, and employment. Although uneconomic in terms of values produced, such programs do represent responses to felt needs in the society at the time.)

Environmental improvements could have a similar effect. Economic growth occurs whenever a society begins to commit energies and resources to fulfill "felt needs" beyond those it has been able to or willing to fulfill in the past. Almost all society's needs—beyond minimum food and shelter—are psychologically based. People need vacation homes and skis because they *think* they need vacation homes and skis. Similarly, as people begin to *think* they want an improved environment, this demand can be converted into a series of new markets. These markets merely require public—rather than private—action to aggregate and channel the resources needed to satisfy the demand.

Although the American consumer seems to have an extremely high capacity for absorbing ever more intricate trinkets, many consumer markets are approaching saturation—with growth essentially linked to population growth. By contrast, markets for improved public well-being seem remarkably unsaturated. Exhibit II suggests that consumers are ready to spend much more in these areas. In addition, most forecasts show nondefense public expenditures increasing at a more rapid rate than private consumption (see Exhibit III). In fact, public markets probably offer the fastest growing primary markets of the next two decades. The real problem is to develop these markets so they contribute to national growth and well-being and do not become endless "resource sinks" without significant social gain.

Potential of regulations

Properly administered, government regulations and standards can expand market opportunities. Obviously, the television and radio industries could not have developed without standardized signal patterns, regulated frequency allocations, and safety regulations for receivers. Railroad

EXHIBIT II
Forecasted personal consumption (in billions of dollars)

	1970	*1980*	*Annual growth*
Medical care	$48	$113	8.9%
Education & research	10	21	7.7
Personal care	10	20	7.2
Religious & welfare	9	18	7.2
Recreation	39	76	6.9
Housing	92	177	6.7
Personal business	35	66	6.5
Transportation	79	146	6.3
Foreign travel & others	5	9	6.1
Household operation	88	158	6.0
Clothing & accessories	62	109	5.8
Food & tobacco	141	247	5.7

Source: *Predicasts,* Third Quarter, 1970.

EXHIBIT III
Selected macroeconomic forecasts (in billions of dollars)

	1970	*1980*	*Annual growth*
Gross national product	$978	$1,890	6.8%
Personal consumption	617	1,160	6.5
Durables	90	160	5.9
Nondurables	264	464	5.8
Services	268	536	7.4
Gross private investment	136	288	7.8
Residential structures	30	76	9.7
Nonresidential structures	35	72	7.3
Producer's durable equity	68	125	6.3
Government purchases	221	1,980	7.0
Federal	100	155	4.5
Defense	76	100	2.7
Nondefense	23	55	8.9
State and local	121	278	8.7
Disposable personal income	684	1,260	6.3

Source: *Predicasts,* Third Quarter, 1970.

growth required standardized rail guages, car sizes, coupling heights, and agreed-upon time zones. In both cases, individual companies had to change practices that initially appeared to be in their own self-interest, but they ultimately gained because their total markets expanded. Similarly, regulations of the Food and Drug Administration and the Department of Agriculture forced all companies to meet product quality and safety standards that some producers found objectionable. But such regulations helped create the consumer confidence that was essential to mass markets for most packaged foods, drugs, and household products.

Can this pattern also apply to currently proposed social and environmental regulations? I feel it can. Consider the following possibilities:

When the 1966 Highway Safety Act regulations were implemented on automobiles, unit costs undoubtedly increased slightly to cover seat belts, turn signals, dash padding, and collapsible steering columns. But the relative price effect of these items was so small that primary demand for transportation could not have shifted significantly toward nonautomotive modes. The initial impact on the industry was probably a slight delay in average repurchase cycles. However, increased profits from all the safety items (which no individual company would have dared to force unilaterally on all its customers) could easily outweigh such losses. Seat belt, padding, and vinyl cover suppliers undoubtedly increased their sales and profits. And the social costs of injury and death appear to have been reduced.

When electric utilities install air and thermal depollution equipment, their rate bases need to be increased (to maintain their return on investment), thus allowing higher prices, dollar profits, and taxes. Power use for installed capacity is quite insensitive to small price changes, especially in the power-short East, where pollution is worst. Consequently, power companies, construction groups, and depollution equipment suppliers all gain (and pay increased taxes). And jobs are created in the area, with corresponding multiplier effects on all household and consumer items—including electric appliances.

More stringent radioactive emission and waste disposal standards—which recent cases indicate nuclear producers can already meet—would increase confidence in the atomic power plants and thus expand the market for them.

Safety regulation of dangerous family articles like power mowers, snowmobiles, power boats, and trailers could enhance unit values and expand markets for responsible producers.

In short, the net effect of government regulation can be to express, through political processes, fragmented demands that individual consumers cannot effectively express in the marketplace. Proper regulation can create new primary markets which contribute to national growth in the same way as a new product innovation. Just as television satisfied a latent demand for visual home entertainment, safety and depollution devices can fulfill latent demands for personal health and other intangible "qualities of life." Effective regulations simply aggregate these demands to a sufficient level to call forth the productive resources needed to satisfy them.

Needless to say, all government regulations affecting products and services do not create new market opportunities. They certainly do not if standards are developed, administered, or enforced in an illogical or haphazard manner. The point is that the *potential often exists* for regulation to increase total market opportunities, rather than to hinder or thwart real economic growth. But government and industry action is necessary to bring out this potential. I will suggest some approaches later.

COSTS VERSUS MARKETS

Clearly, improved environmental quality and public services are not free. What portion of proposed expenditures consists of self-supporting new markets? And what portion is really an increase in national overhead?

There is no question that each sewage treatment plant, air scrubber, or cooling tower represents a cost to its owners—as opposed to dumping waste into the environment. This is why so little action has been taken in the past. How, then, can depollution be anything but an added cost to society?

The same question could have been asked when the automobile was introduced. The automobile required an increase in the unit price of vehicles. It demanded that the public pave roads. It called forth traffic control systems and increased police forces. It substituted expensive petroleum for cheap hay as fuel. It caused the demise of carriage, harness, and accessory suppliers. It filled hospitals with the injured, cut short productive lives, and made bereaved families instant paupers. The physical damage done by automobiles was so extensive as to require a whole new insurance industry. And highway departments and government regulatory bodies were necessary to cope with the changes it wrought.

Yet people wanted flexible transportation. And—despite the undoubted social costs of accidents and pollution—the production of automobiles and the public services to support them greatly expanded jobs, incomes, and product demands for almost all industry. Today more than one person in four is employed directly or indirectly as a result of the automobile industry.

Similarly, environmental improvement can create self-sustaining domestic markets for better health care, housing, education, transportation, or depollution systems. If people really want such benefits, they must be willing to pay for them just as they would pay for hair styling, mod clothes, or snowmobiles.

But can the values of growth more than offset the overhead costs of (*a*) collecting and dispensing needed funds and (*b*) regulating industrial practice when necessary? Assuming that our society has underemployed human and fiscal resources, each additional person employed in a new or expanded industry creates (as we know from past experience) three or four new jobs in service and support industries, including retail and wholesale trades. If each of these people and their employers are paying taxes, it is not hard to see that the additional revenues from these groups alone could pay for the overhead costs of their industry—and, indeed, for a large portion of the new services themselves.

Add to this the employment and innovative effects of a generally higher demand level, and enough expansion could occur to exceed *all* of the costs of new public markets. (This point could be verified with more quantitative economic analysis, but that would require another whole article.)

Under the specified conditions, the industries serving public markets become self-sustaining. Buyers pay the full cost of the benefits they receive, and the new industries do not become a drain on other sectors. It is plain fallacy to state that if people choose to spend part of their incomes on parks or health, this will somehow increase the cost structure for steel or chemicals. Even when the regulatory approach is used—for example, in depollution—buyers, not producers, ultimately pay the cost of services demanded. Producers actually have an opportunity to sell a product with greater value added; i.e., their product *plus* environmental improvement—just the kind of opportunity most are normally seeking.

The growth process just described is not immutable, of course. Two assumptions are vital: (*a*) the demands expressed through public purchases or pressures must be stronger than those substituted for; and (*b*) there must be some slack in the economy, i.e., some underemployment of people and capital. Otherwise the new industry would merely take away from one or more existing ones, and no real growth would result. But even when resources are limited, the public can increase the value (or utility) it receives—if it substitutes marginally important public purchases for less desired private consumption.

Note, however, that added capacity usually *is* available. There are unemployed people who want and are able to work. There are employees who, with training or better management, could become more productive. Investments could be made in new technologies that would free employees for work in other areas; and so on. So long as conditions like these are present, the environmental-improvement industry can add to GNP as other new industries have in the past.

Sizing up the costs

Actually the nation is already absorbing many costs that would be eliminated or reduced with environmental improvement. Inadequate medical care now means that people die earlier, are unnecessarily debilitated, or are cared for by people whose efforts do not show up in the national accounts. Polluted riverbeds and estuaries cause reductions of fishing, recreation, and housing-development potentialities that may be greater than depollution costs. Air pollution leads to physical plant depreciation, acidification of soil, cleaning bills, personal discomfort, and deteriorated health. And inadequate air traffic systems cost millions of dollars in personal delays and extra equipment operating costs, not to mention human life.

All of this is little comfort to the company, community, or individual who must suddenly pay the cost of a new depollution system. If a unit has capital, it could presumably devote its funds to purposes that yield more direct and shorter term gains. However, as suggested earlier, many companies—including some prime producers of toxic effluents in the air—could pass depollution costs along, with little or no negative impact on profits. And many basic processing companies have found that they actually save money when forced to innovate in response to environmental controls. To illustrate:

American Cyanamid Company is using new processes in Polk County, Florida that return ecologically harmful and unsightly phosphate strip mines to usable purposes, yet reduce costs by as much as one third.

Dow Chemical Company recently reported that to date it has almost always found ways to lower costs when it improved effluent controls.

In many industries *primary* demand is relatively unchanged by small industrywide price changes—although similar price shifts by any one producer could cause a substantial shift in *selective* demand. In such cases, minor cost increases caused by depollution or safety regulations—applying to all producers—could be passed along in prices with a negligible impact on individual producers. Even in industries with higher depollution costs, demand shifts may be limited if there are no feasible substitute products or if functional competitors' costs increase by a similar amount.

Nevertheless, there will be some very real costs as society shifts its energies to environmental improvement. What are they? The following seem to be most important:

1. *Lower growth in private demand* for certain goods and services will undoubtedly occur in the short run. Companies providing these items must either run harder or suffer. Total injury from substitution will depend on the rate public markets built up, the real strength of marginal private demands, government fiscal policies affecting total economic growth, and time lags in shifting people into the new industries.

2. *Displacement costs* can hit individual companies or communities hard. For example, marginal companies in small towns may lack the capital needed to meet new regulations. And if these companies are forced out of business, costs to both owners and communities can be very high.

3. *Small price changes* may seriously affect some industries' primary demand. This occurs when another product or service can be easily substituted for the one in use—for example, coal for oil in power plants. In these cases sizable industrywide displacements could result from increased investments or operating costs due to new standards. In time, this displacement would be absorbed by the growth in the industries with the substitute products or services. Still individual losses and short-term changeover costs would be real.

4. *Government bureaucracies* could become an expensive result of environmental-improvement programs. Unfortunately, past experience with regulatory and social expenditure groups has often been discouraging. Well-intentioned bureaus frequently acquire a growth syndrome quite independent of their function. In some cases, this only results in inefficiency. In others, agencies cease performing their intended services or regulatory functions and merely consume the funds appropriated for these ends. Some bureaucratic efforts—like public housing or welfare—actually turn out to be counterproductive. Unlike displacement costs in industry, where one's loss eventually becomes another's gain, bureaucratic costs can be both high and permanent.

Softening the blow

The first three costs are merely characteristics of a market economy undergoing a demand change. If we really mean to have a market economy, the consequences of shifts to public demands should be accepted in the same vein as private consumption shifts. And the temporary distress these changes create can be relieved in familiar ways, such as stretching out the impact of the change, providing temporary tax relief, imposing short-term quotas, or helping communities injured by industry displacement. All of these have long been standard tools of public policy.

But, as soon as possible, such supports should be dropped so that each industry and company is competing on its own merits and absorbing its full costs. Society must ultimately pay—through higher prices, if necessary—for the added demands it places on producers. In a market economy the impact of these choices should be distributed through industry by the price mechanisms, with each company and industry absorbing the full cost of its existence.

International competition poses some special problems. For example, although the depollution industry could become self-sustaining on a domestic basis, individual producers' costs could increase vis-à-vis competitors in foreign countries with lower environmental standards. Foreign products shipped into the United States would, of course, be subject to U.S. product-standards (e.g., automobile safety). But lower production costs—from more lax pollution standards—could allow equivalent foreign products to enter with a price advantage. And U.S.-made products would face similar price disadvantages in most overseas markets. The net impact on U.S. balances of trade and payments would undoubtedly be negative in the short run.

The problem is very real and should not be minimized. Still, it is mitigated by several factors. For one thing, a number of important U.S. companies overseas have production bases that can help them to relieve these cost disadvantages. For another, some of the industries most affected by environmental-improvement costs—for instance, electric utilities and basic process industries—are either not large exporters or are insulated from foreign competition by high transportation costs. Also, many important exports—like high technology products—should be relatively unaffected by environmental costs unless basic materials represent a high percentage of their cost. Finally, some U.S. antipollution devices and processes should become highly salable exports in themselves.

Another alleviating factor is that foreign countries too are becoming highly sensitive to ecological needs. Effluent charges have long been used along the Rhine river. Great Britain is now implementing a program for cleaning up the Thames and other rivers by means of better effluent control; Italy has drafted legislation that will control the pollution of its inland water systems through the construction of purification plants; and Sweden now requires new plants to incorporate the latest technology for pollution control. There are many other such examples.[1] Actions like these will certainly help equalize international competition.

Nevertheless, some U.S. industries will doubtless need temporary quotas, tax relief, or other protection. Multinational agreements on "offsets" for relative pollution standards seem too difficult to achieve within the time span needed.

RESTRUCTURING MARKETS

In this country, there has long been a demand for improved refuse, sewage treatment, transportation, medical, educational housing, and recreational systems. More recently the public has demanded industrial water, air, effluent, and safety systems. However, these demands have not been converted into effective markets that producers can sensibly anticipate and serve. No one can now predict exactly how these markets can ultimately be best structured.

But, then, who in 1890 could have predicted the radio and television networks, chains or supermarkets, refrigerated home storage capacities, automotive transportation linkages, ubiquitous credit institutions, and federal quality control systems that now underlie our mass marketing structure? Business and government leaders invented or evolved these

[1] See Theodore Swanson, "Europe Cleans House," *The Lamp,* Spring 1971, p. 38.

institutions and devices—with many uncertainties and conflicts in viewpoints—as the demands and dynamics of society permitted.

In many ways today's public market mechanisms are as undeveloped as consumer mass marketing was in the 1890s. But given a proper outlook, industry and government can together develop needed solutions—just as they evolved the social innovations that permitted mass private markets. Let us examine some of the main problems and most encouraging current trends.

New political units

Precinct, town, county, and state units provide the electoral base for politicians and the funding base for taxation. But the boundaries of these units bear no relationship to today's public purchasing or regulatory problems. For example, water depollution may require consistent policies for a multistate river basin; air pollution abatement may require coordination on a broader regional basis; a regional hospital system may involve a large number of other local political entities; and so on. Our traditional political units complicate the processes of: (*a*) obtaining popular support for taxes needed on a regional level; (*b*) standardizing systems, components, and building specifications to achieve scale economies; (*c*) developing administrative units to oversee and/or manage regional expenditures; and (*d*) setting priorities among programs at a regional or national level.

But recently a new level of quasi-governmental "authorities" has evolved to coordinate action on specific functions or problems throughout the areas they affect. These authorities include river basin commissions, air quality agencies, regional transportation commissions, emergency service coordinators, port authorities, and so forth. An average of more than 25 such authorities now exists in each Standard Metropolitan Statistical Area (covering all towns with more than 10,000 people) in the United States.

Although not completely effective now, these regional bodies may eventually provide a much needed decision mechanism for many new public markets. The big questions are whether they will be properly funded and whether they can force a reasonable degree of uniformity and coordination on local political units. If Congress uses these regional bodies to enforce national standards, and channels the bulk of its environmental funds through them, they could have enormous impact. They could create the most profound change in U.S. governmental structure in two centuries. Many county and state regulatory and purchasing functions could diminish in importance or disappear. And new mechanisms would be necessary for people to adequately express their preferences on priorities for the regional authorities themselves. This poses formidable problems.

Improved political practices

Political decisions often seem to be keyed more to creating local headlines or maintaining power positions than to solving problems. Legislators frequently support this year's flashy ideas—the ones with high current visibility or emotional content—while prosaic tasks with a higher payoff limp along. These fads often move too rapidly and inconsistently for industrial suppliers to risk development funds on them or to effectively plan other needed responses.

The problem is especially perplexing in new fields of government action like this one of environmental improvement. For a company to make the required long-term commitments, it needs some real assurance of long-term consistency in government regulations or fiscal support. Some answers to the latter may lie in trust funds, effluent fees, and fee-for-service pricing by public corporations. Although still experimental, such devices could provide relatively independent long-term financing for specific environmental improvements. Such funding, effectively administered through professional regional authorities, could eventually decentralize public-spending decisions to the degree needed to assure rational public markets.

Poorly formulated political standards have also been counterproductive. For example:

Many informed observers feel that Congress' decision to move 1980 auto exhaust standards ahead to 1975 was made with inadequate recognition of some very serious technological problems faced by manufacturers. It may well be technically unfeasible to meet these standards without prohibitive price increases or solutions that markedly *increase* fuel consumption. Automotive company protests were ignored because Detroit had lost credibility during its earlier protests against pollution standards.

Similarly, the National Highway Safety Administration's much discussed goal of "passive survivability" in 50 mile-per-hour head-on-collisions did not result from a careful analysis of the causes of death and disfigurement in automobile accidents. A high percentage of deaths and injuries from other causes could undoubtedly be eliminated at much lower cost—for example, through drunken driver regulation. The appropriate question—whether it is worth the marginal cost to move from alternative safety levels to passive 50 mile-per-hour head-on-collision protection—does not seem to have been explicitly asked.

Actions like these erode the confidence of all parties and make rational progress difficult. Companies become defensive and will promise nothing in the fear that politicians will always demand more. Government agencies become frustrated by company intransigence and confused as to whether standards are real or merely strawmen. And the public becomes cynical as promised standards are never met or enforced.

Political factors will always enter regulatory and public expenditure decisions. But more thoughtful business leadership could (*a*) anticipate and avoid many crisis situations, and (*b*) actively stimulate programs that offer growth in markets and public well-being. I will comment again on these issues later.

Better public management

Ineffective administration and poor planning have often overwhelmed well-intended public programs. Early public housing programs are a case in point. Individual programs often destroyed more existing housing than they created. Currently the negative "second order consequences" of fertilizer, insecticide, "green revolution," superhighway, and welfare programs have been astonishing.

There is a great need to manage public expenditure programs better. Especially, new methods must be developed to measure the overall performance of regulatory and purchasing agencies and their subunits. Without such measures public administrators must follow costly, detailed contracting and internal control procedures that make it difficult to pinpoint responsibility and remove all efficiency incentives from contracts or operations. Of course, higher caliber, professional, and technical managers are essential to cope with planning, evaluation, and organizational problems at all agency levels. But entirely new institutional forms and management approaches are also needed to streamline regulatory and public purchasing agencies and to free them from undue political influence on their decisions.

WHAT CAN BUSINESS DO?

Now, what can business executives do—in their own self-interest—to help achieve the needed changes?

Posture and attitude

First, public markets and environmental controls must be approached as major strategic issues and not be relegated to back-bench decision makers. These issues pose some of the most critical opportunities and threats facing private enterprise in the next few decades. As such, they require companywide—if not industrywide—perspective and action. If companies do not respond to public demands effectively, the prerogatives of private enterprise can be swept away or drastically changed here as elsewhere. The threat is real. But so are the opportunities. As Henry Ford II said:

> The successful companies of the last third of the twentieth century will be the ones that look at changes in their environment as opportunities to

get a jump on the competition. The successful companies will be those that anticipate what their customers, their dealers, their employees and their many other publics will want in the future, instead of giving them what they wanted in the past. . . . These are the companies that will earn the highest profits for their stockholders by discharging their responsibilities to the society.[2]

Second, today's public demands cannot be dismissed as fads. They result from fundamental changes in population concentrations and affluence that will continue into the future. As one set of public problems is "solved," these and other forces will create new demands, which in turn will create new industries.

These new industries—to the extent that they add to production—will, of course, create some negative consequences. But, since their central purpose is to improve environmental quality, their net impact on the environment should be positive. However, in any complex system involving energy, manpower, and resources, there are likely to be some unpredictable consequences which may themselves create new challenges.

There is nothing "socialistic" about these challenges. Any sensible scheme to satisfy them will leave essentially all production—and most technological—choices in private hands. But public groups must set the performance specifications and aggregate the resources to express public demands. To be effective their activities need aggressive business participation and support. Too often business groups—because of traditional thinking—have resisted legislation that could be in their own as well as the public's interest. To illustrate:

Oil companies put up a powerful defense against the gasoline taxes that became the Highway Trust Fund. Yet this fund opened incredible growth opportunities for the industry.

Ethical pharmaceutical companies have generally opposed Medicare and other national health insurance plans. Yet such plans would expand drug markets to include people who could otherwise not afford pharmaceutical products. The companies claim their customers—the doctors—do not favor such plans. But one wonders which brands doctors could prescribe if they opposed a stand taken by the Pharmaceutical Manufacturers Association. The companies also fear price regulation resulting from government-controlled plans. But there are many approaches to nationwide health insurance—such as specified minimum health insurance for all employees—which require only limited direct federal intervention on behalf of the medically indigent. Such programs would seem a "natural" for pharmaceutical industry support.

Third, the notion of "business responsibility" alone will not solve current social problems. To gain short-term profits, some companies will always cut corners, struggle against safety or pollution regulations, and

[2] *The Human Environment and Business* (New York: Weybright and Talley, Inc., 1970), p. 63.

dogmatically resist public expenditures for health, education, or environmental quality. Some managements must lead the way—as many have in the past—to support social programs and to surpass all imposed environmental standards. Their leadership is absolutely essential to (*a*) create the favorable political environment so necessary for all business, (*b*) stimulate and restructure public markets to serve new public demands, and (*c*) develop standards that are economic and effective throughout industry.

Marketing and credibility

Developing public markets requires a consistent, long-term program. At the outset the company must identify where its own best opportunities lie. For consumer product companies this may merely involve promoting their product *and* its safety or environmental benefits. Public utilities may sell both their direct services *and* cleaner air or a less cluttered skyline. Other companies may need careful input/output or other analyses to see how larger public markets could benefit their particular operations, so that each can then select the few significant public opportunities it can most sensibly influence.

The next step may be to stimulate a deeper public awareness of what could be done. Depending on the status of public and political perceptions, fairly low levels of advertising and public relations may be adequate at this stage. The power of such efforts in the public sector seems generally underestimated (even though employed effectively in the past by space and defense contractors).

The average person now spends more time in contact with TV and other media than in any other waking activity except his job. And these media are prime creators of personal values. If even a small percentage of media messages emphasize public needs, people could be vastly influenced. No single company has to dilute its product message appreciably, provided that others in the industry are working in the same direction. Interestingly, last year's enormous dissemination of environmental concern was probably achieved more by sponsored TV programs—news and otherwise—than by any other single force. The same power can be used to stimulate other public demands.

Once these demands begin to crystallize, more direct political action is possible. Responsible politicians have more latitude for action. And, if a company or industry has built up its public credibility and has a thoroughly thought-out position on key features of needed legislation, it can effectively lobby or participate in decisions covering public markets or regulation.

Such a program would have eased the problems of the automobile industry. Despite the substantial technical work the industry had done on environmental questions, the companies did not adjust automobile designs to mitigate growing public disenchantment with air pollution and accident costs. As political pressures built up for regulation, managements became increasingly defensive and emphasized the difficulty or impossibility of improved performance. Their intransigence gave their opponents added opportunities for attack. Public impatience increased. The industry lost credibility. And political activists forced more stringent regulations than would have been necessary.

Setting standards

In the environmental sphere, development and enforcement of effective standards are the keys to progress. What specific approaches should industry support in its—and the public's—interest?

1. *Nationwide standards uniformly enforced are essential.* Otherwise, some local groups may lower standards or not have the political will or power to enforce them. Such situations create competitive inequities that reward those who act most irresponsibly. National standards also help build aggregate demand for depollution devices and systems, enabling some suppliers to achieve economies of scale, lower depollution costs, and create the jobs, tax revenues, and growth that could help pay for environmental improvement.

2. *Standards should be set well in advance.* Except in emergency cases like severe mercury contamination, standards should normally be announced at least three to five years before their effective date, and broad guidelines should be projected for a decade ahead. Only then can company and town managers minimize total costs by efficient planning of utility and plant locations, process changes, product designs, fund raising, and capital commitments.

Responsible towns and companies can be badly hurt when they make costly investments to meet one set of hastily enacted standards only to encounter new standards requiring additional processes which could have been incorporated at lower cost in their initial equipment. Further, short lead times mean that neither supplier nor regulated companies can pursue promising technological options that would take some years to develop.

3. *Performance specifications should be used whenever possible.* Material, practice, or product specifications freeze design and innovation. But functional or performance specifications can express the results desired. Managers can then choose the lowest cost method for achieving these results, given the particular resources and processes available. Performance standards also encourage the research, innovation, and competition that can minimize total safety and depollution costs for society.

4. *Federal fiscal policies should be pointed toward the maintenance of total economic growth during the changeover period to help absorb displacements and short-term profit drains.* Such measures combined

with carefully phased introduction of regulations could allow many industries' overall growth rates to more than offset substitution losses from minor differences in depollution costs among functionally competitive industries. Protective quotas, subsidies, or tariffs should only be established in extreme cases and for limited periods. Otherwise U.S. industry runs the risk of provoking protectionist reprisals in other countries and of weakening itself by continued reliance on artificial government supports.

5. *Healthy regulatory agencies are essential for equity and progress in environmental control.* But they must be kept to minimum sizes, be exceedingly well staffed, and be open to public scrutiny and policy review. Each major environmental agency should have the support of a competent technical laboratory system, like those of the National Bureau of Standards or the Environmental Science Services Administration to provide technical expertise comparable to that of the industries regulated.

Legislation establishing regulatory agencies should define the physical goals to be accomplished along with fixed dates for achievement. And performance against these targets should be monitored, at least annually, through public reports. The entire mission of each agency should be reviewed and explicitly revised every five years to recognize the fact that environmental needs will constantly change.

CONCLUSION

Needed practices and institutional changes will only come about if an influential segment of industry acts vigorously and consistently in its long-term self-interest. The essential actions must come from the very top of the organization. If taken in time, such actions can be effective. As Peter Drucker said:

> Whenever the leaders of an institution anticipate an impact and think through what needs to be done to prevent it or make it acceptable, they are given a respectful hearing by the public and the politicians. This is particularly true of business. Whenever business leaders have anticipated an impact of business and have thought through its prevention or treatment, their proposals have been accepted. Whenever they have waited until there was a "scandal" and a public outcry, they have been saddled with punitive regulation which, only too often, has aggravated the problem.[3]

Top executives may have to make some critical changes in marketing attitudes and management controls to give public-market programs needed momentum. New-product efforts toward environmental improvement may need special long-term recognition and support at the corporate level—such as Carborundum and other companies have already

[3] *The Age of Discontinuity* (New York: Harper & Row, Inc., 1969), p. 203.

begun to give them. And current profit and return-on-investment standards in operating divisions may need adjusting to allow the long-term investments in research, marketing, public relations, lobbying, and public action programs that help build their public markets. Further action may be needed to insure that middle managers do not cut regulatory corners to increase short-term profits. Companies seeking to build public markets will have to accept—and even encourage—environmental control over their own operations.

The public will not clean up dumps and sewage spills unless industries control their effluents. And both water and air depollution campaigns are integrally intertwined with other demands for better overall health care and recreational opportunities. These cannot be separated from transportation, open space, and housing demands, which in turn relate to traffic control, urban development, and other public-service commitments, including education. In short, these huge markets interlock and grow together—and whether they grow to become opportunities or threats depends on how industry responds to them.

Every new public demand for environmental improvement represents an unexploited primary market. Companies must take positive action to convert these demands into viable opportunities. Properly developed, such markets can be financed from the economic growth they permit; they need not create massive social overheads, as so many people assume. But, improperly developed, they can become tax sinks, regulatory nightmares, and bureaucratic potholes that sap the resources of our whole society. The choice is largely up to business leadership.

C.

Governmental impact on the marketplace

What is the most efficient balance of power between government and business in our complex inter-dependent socio-economic system? Experience has indicated that free market mechanisms, alone, may not be sufficient to ensure a proper balance between profit motives and social concerns. Governments are taking a more active role in helping to reshape marketplace processes. How much governmental intervention will the market system require to ensure this proper balance? How much intervention will be accepted by society in view of the fact that regulations limit freedoms? The amount of acceptable intervention will depend upon the interaction of business and consumers in their efforts to achieve a socially desirable environment.

Given that government will be active in the reorientation of business goals, what form might this involvement take? Federal laws have delimited the scope of business practices by excluding those activities considered detrimental to society and corporate competition. In the future, this philosophy of government intervention may be altered. It may no longer be practical to merely delimit business behavior to protect the consumer, and competitor, from social or environmental degradation. These problems do not lend themselves to the same decision making rules as those facing the regulators of the market system in the early 1900's. Hasty delimitation may indeed severely limit the ability of business to respond to matters of environmental and social inequities. What will be required is an ongoing process of social feedback between the consumer-public, government, and business to ensure that the free enterprise system is capable of dealing efficiently and effectively with these problems.

This section opens with an article by L. L. Stern providing perspective on some issues relating to firm size and merger policy. Narver then summarizes the economic and social costs and benefits of a more stringent merger policy, past merger policy enforcement patterns, and the financial performance of mergers. Cohen discusses the use of behavioral science research not only for the establishment of standards for protection from advertising abuse, but also for the amendment of present regulations. Grether discusses the responsibility which business has toward the market. Completing this section, L. L. Stern points out limitations of government and business in consumer protection efforts and the possibilities of self-regulation.

The following article reports on the most recent debates concerning market structure, corporate size, and the effect of these variables on competition. In addition, the author describes areas of research that will facilitate the evaluation of mergers. With this information future market conditions can be enhanced by the most efficient and effective public policy decisions involving merger impact!

---

25. PERSPECTIVE ON PUBLIC POLICY: COMMENTS ON THE "GREAT DEBATE"*

Louis W. Stern†

Essential reading for individuals interested in antitrust policy is the transcript of the seminar discussion entitled "Are Planning and Regulation Replacing Competition in the New Industrial State?" held before Subcommittees of the Select Committee on Small Business of the U.S. Senate.[1] It repeats, verbatim, the much publicized "Great Debate" between Professor J. K. Galbraith; Professor Walter Adams of Michigan State University; Dr. Willard Mueller, chief economist of the Federal

* Reprinted from "Perspective on Public Policy: Comments on the Great Debate," *Journal of Marketing*, Vol. 33 (January 1969), pp. 32–39.

† The Ohio State University.

[1] "A Seminar Discussion of the Question: Are Planning and Regulation Replacing Competition in the New Industrial State?" Hearing before Subcommittees of the Select Committee on Small Business, United States Senate, 90th Congress, First Session (Washington, D.C.: U.S. Government Printing Office, 1967). The seminar was convened as a result of the provocative issues which J. K. Galbraith raised in his book *The New Industrial State* (Boston, Mass.: Houghton Mifflin Company, 1967).

Trade Commission; and Professor Donald F. Turner of Harvard University, then Assistant Attorney General of the United States.

As the protagonist, Galbraith made a number of highly significant and meaningful observations about antitrust policy which the other members of the seminar attempted to refute. It is the purpose of this article to examine several of Galbraith's observations in the light of current marketing thought and developments and to show why the arguments raised by the other seminar participants may be out of phase with what is actually taking place in the marketing of highly differentiated[2] consumer goods.

Even though some of Galbraith's perceptions have been amended or modified to aid the presentation of this writer's views, the basic thrust of many of his beliefs has been maintained throughout. Specifically, this article deals with the importance of (1) economies of scale, (2) innovation, and (3) mergers, as each of these relates to the extent and kind of competition in the United States and to the viewpoints of federal agencies and economists about competition.

From the transcript of the seminar, Galbraith's primary thesis can be boiled down to two points which he stressed repeatedly. The first, in his words, can be stated as follows:

> To be big in general and big in an industry is by far the best way of influencing prices and costs, commanding capital, having access to advertising and selling resources, and possessing the other requisites of market power . . .
> If a firm is already large it is substantially immune under antitrust laws. If you already have the basic requisite of market power, you are safe.[3]

The second, which incorporates the first point for emphasis and contrast, is:

> If a firm is already large, it has as a practical matter nothing to fear under antimerger provisions of the Clayton Act. It will not be demerged. . . . But if two medium-sized firms unite in order to deal more effectively with this giant, the law will be on them like a tiger.[4]

Although there may be some quarrel with Galbraith's use of colorful phrases to overstate or distort a dialectic, it is very possible that he has, in truth, told it "like it is."

FIRM SIZE AND ECONOMIES OF SCALE

The fact that large corporations dominate the industrial scene is certainly not a fresh insight; Berle and Means' study published in 1932

[2] For the FTC's operational definition of "differentiated consumer goods industries," see Willard F. Mueller, "The Celler-Kefauver Act: 16 Years of Enforcement" (Washington, D.C.: U.S. Government Printing Office, 1967), p. 29 and p. 30 fn.

[3] "A Seminar Discussion . . . ," Hearing before Subcommittees . . . , p. 7.

[4] Ibid., p. 8.

proved this conclusively.[5] The major issue is whether or not this giantism, with its concomitant economic concentration of resources and markets, is warranted. Dr. Adams, as one of the participants to the Debate, stated, bluntly and honestly, that Galbraith

> offers little evidence to demonstrate that Brobdingnagian size is the prerequisite for, and guarantor of (1) operational efficiency; (2) invention, innovation, and technological progress; and (3) effective planning in the public interest.[6]

If Galbraith had been able to show a positive correlation between firm size and the above three measures of welfare and then demonstrate cause-and-effect relationships, he might have silenced Dr. Adams somewhat. However, the weight of evidence gathered to date shows, rather conclusively, that in most producer and consumer goods industries large size is not a prerequisite for operational efficiency in the sense of achieving economies of scale *in production.* Production economies are achieved on a plant rather than on a company basis. Large firms generally have several plants whose economies can be matched by smaller firms each operating only one optimally sized plant.[7]

On the other hand, the evidence is not at all conclusive with regard to economies of scale in marketing, which includes selling, buying, transporting, and storing, as well as numerous facilitating functions such as marketing research and financing. Surely, the term "operational efficiency" can be expanded to include expenditures for marketing, which, in many industries, account for close to 50 percent of all costs making up the final price to the ultimate consumer.

Admittedly, there is contradictory evidence related to economies of scale in selling, promotion, and distribution. On the one hand, Bain states:

> It appears possible that there is an important category of concentrated industries—those selling highly differentiated consumer goods in situations where nationwide sales promotion is the superior alternative to the firms—in which distribution economies of increased firm scale in a sense justify much larger scales of firm and higher degrees of concentration than production economies alone would.[8]

---

[5] A. A. Berle, Jr., and G. C. Means, *The Modern Corporation and Private Property* (New York: Commerce Clearing House, Inc., 1932).

[6] "A Seminar Discussion . . . ," Hearing before Subcommittees . . . , p. 13.

[7] For specific examples, see John M. Blair, "Analysis of Divergence Between Plant and Firm Concentration," Hearing on Economic Concentration, U.S. Senate Subcommittee on Antitrust and Monopoly (Washington, D.C.: U.S. Government Printing Office, 1966); National Commission on Food Marketing, *Studies of Organization and Competition in Grocery Manufacturing,* Technical Study No. 6 and *The Structure of Food Manufacturing,* Technical Study No. 8 (Washington, D.C.: U.S. Government Printing Office, 1966).

[8] Joe S. Bain, "Advantages of the Large Firm: Production, Distribution, and Sales Promotion," *Journal of Marketing,* Vol. 20 (April 1956), p. 345.

On the other hand, Simon has argued, relative to advertising:

There is no piece of conclusive evidence to support the general belief that there are economies of scale in advertising.[9]

Although Simon admits that his hypothesis regarding the nonexistence of economies of scale in advertising for one product may have biased the choice of literature he cited, his careful study is convincing enough to leave considerable doubt about the subject. There is, however, little doubt in this author's mind, at least, that businessmen had best begin supporting studies exploring such scale economies. Findings from these studies, if positive, might produce a significant justification for the existence of giants, assuming such economies can be linked to "operational efficiency" in the economist's sense of the term. On the other hand, if the objective in marketing is to eliminate uncertainties, specifically to tie buyers more tightly to sellers, then any economies of bigness which enable marketers to accomplish this objective are, from an economist's perspective, doubly suspect because they increase the "monopoly power" of sellers.

It is obvious that many of the above statements relate to firms in consumer goods industries. In some respects, it is difficult to carry Galbraith's argument to producer goods industries. The reason for this is that Dr. Mueller, in a careful study of 16 years of enforcement of the Celler-Kefauver Act, has shown in bold relief that concentration has declined in producer goods industries over the time span studied and that the enforcement of antimerger law may have been instrumental in bringing about that decline.[10] Mueller is quick to admit, though, that concentration has increased in consumer goods industries, and especially in those industries where goods are highly differentiated, as shown in Table 1. Significantly, he points out:

The best available evidence suggests . . . that economies of large-scale production, invention, and innovation are less important in consumer goods industries than in producer goods industries. The apparent reason for the growing concentration in consumer goods manufacturing is to be found in the advantages of large-scale promotion and distribution.[11]

Mueller made the same point during the Debate.[12] Although one might quarrel with his assumption regarding invention and innovation, the second sentence in his statement is undoubtedly correct and the question may again be raised—"Are there economies of scale in promotion and distribution which enhance operational efficiency?" For the time being

[9] Julian L. Simon, "Are There Economies of Scale in Advertising?" *Journal of Advertising Research,* Vol. 5 (June 1965), p. 19.

[10] Mueller, "The Celler-Kefauver Act: . . . ."

[11] Ibid., p. 31.

[12] "A Seminar Discussion . . . ," Hearing before Subcommittees . . . , p. 22.

TABLE 1
Number of industries and value of 1963 shipments, by level of concentration between change, 1947 and 1963

Type of industry	Number of industries	Number of industries in which 4-firm concentration—			Number of industries in which 8-firm concentration—		
		Increased 3 percentage points or more	*Changed less than 3 percentage points*	*Decreased 3 percentage points or more*	*Increased 3 percentage points or more*	*Changed less than 3 percentage points*	*Decreased 3 percentage points or more*
Total	213	81	46	86	95	50	68
Producer goods	132	38	32	62	44	38	50
Consumer goods	81	43	14	24	51	12	18
Undifferentiated	28	10	7	11	14	5	9
Moderately different	36	21	5	10	23	6	7
Highly different	17	12	2	3	14	1	2

	Shipments in 1963		Distribution of shipments					
	Value (millions)	*Percent*	*Percent*	*Percent*	*Percent*	*Percent*	*Percent*	*Percent*
Total	$175,721	100	35	20	45	44	18	38
Producer goods	103,854	100	21	22	57	27	24	40
Consumer goods	71,867	100	54	17	29	68	10	22
Undifferentiated	12,258	100	26	12	62	36	4	60
Moderately different	28,089	100	55	23	22	70	14	16
Highly different	31,520	100	65	13	22	78	8	14

Source: Bureau of Economics, Federal Trade Commission, based on data in "Concentration Ratios in Manufacturing Industry 1963," Subcommittee on Antitrust and Monopoly of the Committee on the Judiciary, U.S. Senate, 89th Cong., 2d sess.

at least the question is begged; or, among some antitrust lawyers operating on the government side, assumed to be answered in the negative. Neither action is excusable.

Innovation and technological progress

Adams' second welfare issue, as stated above, relates to the question of invention, innovation, and technological progress. Time and again the antagonists returned to this point to harpoon Galbraith, and time and again they brought up the case of the basic oxygen furnace that was introduced in the steel industry by McLouth Steel, a relatively small competitor, in 1954. It is true that the steel industry is a producer goods industry and that previously the reader was notified that Galbraith's arguments were weak here. But if Galbraith had retorted that invention is not innovation and that innovation determines commercial success, he might have been able to thrust the harpoon back. In the Schumpeterian sense, the capitalist becomes an innovator only when he receives rewards for *bringing to the market* a new process or product. Thus, the act of innovating goes well beyond that of inventing.

For example, it makes little difference that McLouth was the first to incorporate the basic oxygen furnace into its production facility; the measure of success in this and similar cases should be whether, post-adoption, McLouth was significantly better able to bring its products to market. The road to fortune is strewn with great inventors who lacked the marketing skill and the entrepreneurial genius to capitalize on what they discovered. And even though U.S. Steel and Bethlehem were ten years behind McLouth in adopting the basic oxygen furnace,[13] such products as cold rolled steel and steel bars are physically undifferentiated; as a result, the quality of one company's personal selling effort versus that of another might well be the determining factor in getting the sale, assuming identical prices. Thus, even in the steel industry, it might be possible to uncover the significance of promotion and distribution as a determinant of long-run success. Certainly, McLouth's actions were laudable, but in the cold light of reality its actions did not markedly alter its standing in the competitive structure of the steel industry.

The whole question of innovation and technological progress is another issue that is fraught with emotion. Just what constitutes innovation and technological progress is highly debatable. Is a new type of extruded and puffed breakfast cereal, successfully brought to market, an innovation? Is the stainless steel razor blade an innovation? In the latter case, what happened to the Wilkinson Sword Edge Blade? It is still to be found in distribution, but, as was predicted in an earlier article by the

[13] "A Seminar Discussion . . . ," Hearing before Subcommittees . . . , p. 21.

author,[14] its presence is being swamped out by competitors with superior promotional funds and distribution systems. Thus, long-run success in innovating may very well depend on the resources available to firms to bring the product to market and to emphasize, ad infinitum, the qualities of the innovation.

A study by Buzzell and Nourse describes in detail the investment made by large grocery manufacturers to stimulate the innovation process.[15] A few selected statistics from their study give some notion of the investment required. For product categories isolated by them, it took an average of 37 months *per product* from first activity (usually research and development) to achieve full distribution.[16] Average expenditures *per product* for research and development and for marketing research were $68,000 and $26,000, respectively. For seven "pioneering" products (defined by Buzzell and Nourse are those basically different from *any* product previously on the market), the figures were $127,000 and $76,000.[17] The average net negative contribution *per product* during test marketing operations, exclusive of costs for plant and equipment, amounted to $248,000. For pioneering products, the figure rose to $592,000.[18] Furthermore, only by the end of the third year of full distribution did a majority (61 percent) of the new products break even.[19] It is not necessary to belabor the point; the cost of innovation in these food processing industries is very high. Coupled with the high failure rate for new products, it is not difficult to see why such industries are highly concentrated; the resources required to compete successfully provide an extremely high barrier to entry, assuming that the potential entrant wishes to market branded merchandise.

Innovation requires, for the most part, administrative skill and capital. It is not merely the process of invention. And innovation has become inherent in the fabric of competition in American consumer goods industries. Certainly, there are examples of relatively small firms that have been able to innovate successfully. But Adams, Mueller, and Turner have ignored the realities. This fact is never more evident than when Mueller, during the Debate, cites the late T. K. Quinn, former vice president of General Electric. He shows where Mr. Quinn acknowledged that small companies invented many of the electrical housewares now on the market but he also quotes Mr. Quinn as stating that

[14] Louis W. Stern, "Management Insights Through Historical Perspective," *Business Topics*, Vol. 12 (Summer 1964), pp. 47–54.

[15] Robert D. Buzzell and Robert E. M. Nourse, *Product Innovation in Food Processing: 1954–1964* (Boston, Mass.: Division of Research, Graduate School of Business Administration, Harvard University, 1967).

[16] Ibid., p. 107.

[17] Ibid., p. 111.

[18] Ibid., p. 112.

[19] Ibid., p. 129.

The record of the giants is one of moving in, buying out, and absorbing the smaller companies.[20]

Why did the small companies sell out? Why do the large manufacturers dominate many of the product lines in this industry? The answer seems obvious—while the smaller companies had (and have) inventive skills, they do not have the resources to innovate. This argument was reinforced by Kaplan, Dirlam, and Lanzillotti in their classic pricing study.[21] And given the mode of competition in consumer goods industries, with its emphasis on innovation, product differentiation, and superior distribution systems, it is also obvious that concentration will continue to increase. The odds on the small firm succeeding with its invention are small, at best, at least over the long term.[22]

One cannot credit the above argument to Galbraith, and perhaps he would not want credit for it. His basic stance is that the market is dead; this author's is that the response to gaining access to and maintaining one's position in the market has changed. It is no longer a classical response derived from fluctuations of supply and demand and based on price, but rather a response to demand in a buyer's market using other means as well as price to meet the demand.

Galbraith implicitly recognized, however, the importance of the marketing manager in the technostructure, even though the recognition is given with a shudder of disapproval. But Adams and Turner, especially, seem to ignore the technological nature of the marketing process, as well as the technological progress that has been made in the last two decades by the massive corporation in bringing its goods successfully to market. It appears to be in the economist's psyche (Turner is an economist as well as a distinguished lawyer) that the term "technology" does not apply and should not be applied to marketing management. Bartels has already examined the term "technology" as it might be applied to marketing;[23] and if such a discourse is not enough, one might compare the marketing curricula at leading graduate schools of business in 1950 with those of today to discern the technological revolution taking place. Although no major studies have been undertaken in this regard, it is likely that there is a positive correlation between the technological progress in marketing in the business world and size of firm.

In sum, size may be a requirement of the type and method of competition as it is presently constituted in consumer goods industries. The

[20] "A Seminar Discussion . . . ," Hearing before Subcommittees . . . , p. 20.

[21] See A. D. H. Kaplan, Joel B. Dirlam, and Robert F. Lanzillotti, *Pricing in Big Business* (Washington, D.C.: The Brookings Institution, 1958), p. 264.

[22] The case history of "All," a low-sudsing laundry detergent, provides an excellent example. See Spencer Klaw, "The Soap Wars: A Strategic Analysis," *Fortune*, Vol. 67 (June 1963), 122 ff.

[23] Robert Bartels, "Marketing Technology, Tasks, and Relationships," *Journal of Marketing*, Vol. 29 (January 1965), pp. 45–58.

larger the firm, the more likely its chances of success because of the availability to it of capital and managerial skills. It is also possible that the increasing concentration in these industries may be justifiable, in an economic sense, if one could prove the existence of economies of scale in marketing.

Extending Galbraith's thesis

With regard to the first point of the Galbraith arguments—"if a firm is large, it is substantially immune under antitrust laws"—it is possible to go the next step and state that if a firm is large, its size may further its ability to compete and thereby *enhance* competition (viewed from a businessman's perspective as intensive rivalry in winning customers). If three or four giants are battling it out in the area of product differentiation, it is likely that their efforts to succeed vis-à-vis one another will have more profound effects on the industry than if competition is among several smaller firms in the fringe, none of which has the capital resources and manpower skills to attract attention in the message-saturated, oversold environment in which they want to compete.

This view of competition is seldom apparent in the policies of the federal agencies, the decisions of the Supreme Court, and the thinking of economists, including Adams, Mueller, Turner, and Galbraith. But Galbraith recognizes the realities while one often receives the impression that the others with whom he is debating are still holding fast to some notion of a classical economy. In this respect, business is not a "dirty" word, but marketing is; for the term "marketing" as distinct from "business" often implies manipulation (in a derogatory sense) through the use of persuasion on the part of sellers to create consumer demand.

Therefore, if we are to seek to achieve the type of competition desired by Adams, Mueller, and Turner, it is logical to argue that outside of cases of economies of scale in production, large size is not entirely justifiable. We can only return to a more classical system where smaller units compete against smaller units, for it is in situations of atomistic, as opposed to oligopolistic, competition that price tends to become the primary regulator of the market. Assuming for the moment the correctness of this stand—and certainly this is the basic stand of the enforcers of the antitrust laws—it is imperative that the antitrust agencies undertake a vigorous policy of breaking up the large firms extant in consumer goods industries. Given the present realities, there is no likelihood that price competition will become the dominant policy of the large firms in these industries and, as stated previously, economies of scale in production can be reached rather rapidly with relatively small outputs from individual plants.

Here, then, is the gist of the "charade" as explained by Galbraith and expanded upon by this author. Economic concentration of a wide variety of markets was uncovered quantitatively by the efforts of the

TNEC in 1939. Studies published by the TNEC showed that a small number of large firms, both in absolute and relative terms, accounted for major shares of the sales of many U.S. consumer goods industries.[24] However, with few exceptions, the federal agencies and/or the courts have permitted these large firms to remain large (or to grow even larger via internal growth) and have, since World War II and especially since 1950, been content to try to prevent additional concentration in various lines of trade by restricting the merger activity of these firms.[25] For example, despite the fact that the agencies fought the General Foods-S.O.S. merger, they have taken no visible steps to "break up" the General Foods Corporation which existed prior to the S.O.S. acquisition and which is economically stronger now than it was then, even after netting out the effects of the S.O.S. merger. It has been reported that the Justice Department is "ready to go" with a suit relative to breaking up General Motors. The probabilities of the case actually being brought to court are, however, very slight.[26]

Thus, there is a tremendous inconsistency in public policy as it is applied to consumer goods industries. If one accepts the arguments spelled out earlier—that large size may be correlated with an ability to compete, defining competition as it is and not how economists might like it to be—then one might be willing to give this blessing to large firms because they seem to be the most viable competitors in our society. But if one wants to see a different mode of competition emerge, he should urge the dissolution of the large firm. Federal policy lies somewhere in between—in limbo—for it will not bless the large firm, but at the same time will not condemn it. In this respect, the antitrust laws take on the character of a charade so long as the federal agencies and Congress fail to come to grips with the realities of competition.

MERGER POLICY AND CONSUMER GOODS

Given the existing state of competition which is primarily nonprice in nature in many highly concentrated consumer goods industries, and given the fact that concentration is increasing in them (as Mueller has so ably documented), what should be the policy of our federal government with respect to mergers in these industries? It is entirely likely that, if there are economies of scale in marketing, firms such as General Foods, General Motors, and Procter and Gamble have already achieved them for specific product lines. Therefore, an increase in the size of these firms through horizontal mergers would have no beneficial effect

[24] See W. L. Thorp and W. F. Crowder, *The Structure of Industry*, TNEC Monograph 27 (Washington, D.C.: U.S. Government Printing Office, 1941).

[25] See *Federal Trade Commission* v. *Procter & Gamble Co.*, 386 U.S. 568 (1967) and *General Foods Corp.* v. *Federal Trade Commission*, 386 F. 2d 936 (1967).

[26] See "Anti-trust Bombshell: Proposed Suit Against GM Poses Peril for LBJ," *Wall Street Journal* (October 31, 1967), p. 1.

on competition or on social welfare in general. The Federal Trade Commission and the Justice Department have, implicitly at least, held to this line of reasoning; their posture toward horizontal mergers by the giants is clear and seemingly correct. Borden and other large dairy firms have been prohibited from merging horizontally for several years now, and the rule that applies to these firms has been applied, explicitly and implicitly, to other large firms in other consumer goods industries. Given their present size, these firms can innovate and progress technologically without adding additional firms via the merger route.

On the other hand, what about the firms outside the oligopolistic core of the top three to six firms in many consumer goods industries? Can they compete successfully with competition as it is, against the giants with their capital resources and managerial talents? If one wishes to promote competition, isn't it logical to assume that countervailing power must be developed among the smaller firms in any given industry? If competition takes the form of product differentiation, efficient distribution, and product innovation, how can the small firms effectively enter into this competitive arena if their resources are limited?[27] Some of these firms take the private label route, but this path is unstable and risky, at best.[28] If other small or medium-sized firms wish to "do battle" with the giants, they will probably have to merge together or form alliances or cooperatives of some sort in order to amass the requisite capital and talent. The answer to their problem seems to lie in the merger route, and thus mergers among the smaller firms in highly concentrated consumer goods industries should be encouraged. The net result should be more, not less, competition. Crossland has observed that proponents of the Celler-Kefauver Amendment desired to create a tool to prevent all mergers having anticompetitive effects but at the same time recognized that many mergers would stimulate rather than impede competition. He quotes the 1955 *Report of the Attorney General's National Committee to Study the Antitrust Laws* as follows:

> Acquisition may provide socially desirable consequences insofar as "it increases efficiency in production and distribution or enables a smaller company to strengthen its competitive position and thereby compete more effectively."[29]

Galbraith states bluntly that "if two medium-sized firms unite in order to deal more effectively" with the giants, "the law will be on them like a tiger." Although such an argument is appealing from a sensational

[27] See, for example, *Economic Report on the Manufacture and Distribution of Automotive Tires,* Staff Report to the Federal Trade Commission (Washington, D.C.: U.S. Government Printing Office, 1966), p. x.

[28] See Louis W. Stern, "The New World of Private Brands," *California Management Review,* Vol. 8 (Spring 1966), pp. 43–50.

[29] Hugh J. Crossland, "Clayton Section 7: A Critical Appraisal of the Supreme Court's Antitrust-Antibigness Complex in Merger Litigation Since the Brown Shoe Case," *Wayne Law Review,* Vol. 11 (1964–1965), p. 761 fn and p. 748.

viewpoint, the author could find little evidence to support this claim relative to consumer goods industries. After studying numerous cases, it was possible to find only a few in which this kind of issue has been raised. The Von's case is one,[30] but in this situation the merger took place in a market that would be typified as monopolistically competitive or, at worst, mildly oligopolistic. The largest firm in the market shared only 8 percent of the total grocery sales in the defined territory. Small firms could compete satisfactorily without merging; there was little need for additional countervailing power. The Brown Shoe case follows much the same pattern.[31] Thus, with the exception of a case involving two Philadelphia banks[32] and the Chrysler-Mack Truck case,[33] there is no documentation that the federal agencies or the Supreme Court have been antagonistic to mergers among relatively smaller firms attempting to compete in highly concentrated industries. Turner's statement is extremely pertinent here:

> There are, of course, instances where companies are indeed extremely small and it would be ridiculous to attack them if they were proposing to merge. And we have hosts of examples of that. There were various mergers of smaller companies in the automobile industry. They were not attacked by the Antitrust Division and I do not think anybody had the idea they should be attacked.
> But that was a case where it was so clear that the companies were operating under severe disabilities and that, if there were any prospects for them to survive, merger was one of the ways they could.[34]

There is, however, a real potential danger in the federal agencies' misinterpreting the recent court decisions (for example, Von's, Brown Shoe). It is imperative that these agencies understand that there is likely to be a significant difference between competition in an industry which is *already* highly concentrated and one which is not. A proposed merger by smaller firms in the former situation may serve to enhance competition, even though the net result from a structural perspective may be to increase concentration among the 20 largest firms in the industry once the merger is allowed. Structural measures per se tell little about the extent of competition in an industry, although they do give some evidence as to the mode of competition.

Merger policy relative to small and medium-sized firms should not

---

[30] *United States* v. *Von's Grocery Co.*, 384 U.S. 270 (1966).

[31] *Brown Shoe Co.* v. *United States*, 370 U.S. 294 (1962).

[32] See "Law Versus Logic," *Wall Street Journal* (February 29, 1968), p. 14.

[33] Although not a merger between two small firms, the logic of increasing competition through merger was violated in *United States* v. *Chrysler Corporation*, 232 F. Supp. 651 (D.N.J. 1964). General Motors, Ford, and International Harvester controlled about 85 percent of the truck market at the time. A proposed merger between Chrysler (with about 7 percent of the truck market) and Mack (with about 1 percent) was not allowed by the district court. Management argued, in vain, that the proposed merger would promote competition rather than lessen it.

[34] "A Seminar Discussion . . . ," Hearing before Subcommittees . . . , p. 44.

only be undertaken with the aim of insuring survival, as indicated by Turner above; it should also be pursued with the aim of furthering competition. And because competition is primarily nonprice in nature in many consumer goods industries, it seems necessary that the federal agencies assume a supportive role and thereby encourage mergers among smaller firms in situations of high economic concentration. Even though the Galbraith argument does not always pertain to the case of consumer goods manufacturers, if we accept at least some of his notions about the way competition exists, it is important that public policy reflect the need for more viable competitors to countervail the power amassed by the giants—that smaller firms be permitted *and* encouraged to attempt to seek some of the economies of scale in marketing that may exist. The Von's case should be interpreted by the federal agencies as a situation where merger would not necessarily increase competition, but it should also be interpreted as an exception, given the concentration levels in other market areas both in grocery retailing and for many of the consumer goods industries.

RECOMMENDATIONS AND CONCLUSIONS

It is obvious to the author that there is considerable merit to be found in Galbraith's position during the Great Debate. Although there is not agreement with some of his rationale for coming to his conclusions (for example, the author does not hold with his stance that the market is "dead"), Galbraith sees competition "like it is" and not how it might be if this planet could be reshaped. The federal agencies appear to have passively accepted competition "like it is" in consumer goods industries; for any number of reasons, they have not "broken up" the giants. The American Tobacco case took place over two generations ago; there has not been another case like it affecting consumer goods manufacturers since then. Therefore, if large firms with tremendous capital and managerial resources are going to be allowed to continue to exist, and if these resources permit them to compete most effectively in bringing their products to market and keeping them there, the federal agencies *must* then actively redefine their view of competition to make it more compatible with reality.

At the same time, these same federal agencies must make it known that mergers among smaller firms in highly concentrated consumer goods industries are to be encouraged. The resources held by the larger firms must be matched at least to some degree by the smaller, if the smaller firms are going to countervail and hopefully enhance their standing in the competitive struggle. These agencies have been relatively permissive with respect to such mergers, but permissiveness is not enough. What may be called for by such units as the Small Business Administration is to aid and abet such mergers.

From a managerial perspective, should the federal agencies decide to hold to the original position they have paid lip service to and go with a vengeance after the giants in the consumer goods industries, there appears to be one main line of defense open to the giants that has not been pursued with enough vigor. There must be some highly scientific studies undertaken to discover whether or not economies of scale actually do exist in marketing—in product development and innovation, in advertising and sales promotion, in personal selling, and in physical distribution. Such studies will require that the major companies open their books to economists and that the economists apply their techniques without encumbrance. Such studies are long overdue and should be initiated by industry at the earliest possible moment, for it is likely that Galbraith's arguments and similar ones, including this one, will be instrumental in stirring the agencies to action.

What is the impact of antitrust merger policy on marketing policies and practices? Does the present trend towards larger and more complex conglomerates offer real economics for the buying public? Will increasing corporate size lead to greater economics of scale? Present merger policy and legislation is reviewed with suggestions for maintaining a suitable marketing environment for consumer and industry alike.

---

26. SOME OBSERVATIONS ON THE IMPACT OF ANTITRUST MERGER POLICY ON MARKETING*

John C. Narver†

This article attempts to put into perspective the question of the impact of antitrust merger policy on marketing by summarizing some concepts of the firm, data on the current merger movement and enforcement patterns, and evidence suggesting the apparent low *real* productivity of many large mergers. The author hopes that this article can contribute to the understanding of a complicated topic, if only by pointing to the high ground which may serve as marshalling points for ultimate systematic analysis.

* Reprinted from "Some Observations on the Impact of Antitrust Merger Policy on Marketing," *Journal of Marketing*, Vol. 33 (January 1969), pp. 24–31.

† University of Washington.

THE MEANING OF IMPACT ON MARKETING

There is little in our enterprise economy that is not to some extent related to marketing, if we regard marketing as encompassing all the supply and demand activities related to the transfer of title to goods and services in intermediate or ultimate markets. For present purposes, however, the focus must be limited. The "impact on marketing" in this assessment of merger policy will be limited to two substantial aspects of marketing: (1) the product markets of firms, and (2) the purchase alternatives of consumers. With respect to firms, this paper considers the impact of antitrust merger policy on marketing's contribution to the present value of the firm. Specifically, the relevant question is the extent to which merger policy has affected the real productivity of marketing.

For consumers, who at least in principle are sovereign in our form of economy, the obvious question is whether merger policy has enlarged the number of substantive alternatives. The ensuing discussion applies equally to intermediate customers and ultimate consumers; however, the term "consumer" will be used for convenience. The meaning of "substantive alternative" is largely subjective, for each consumer's unique experiences filter his perception of the relative want-satisfying ability of goods and services. In general, there are substantive alternatives when there are various combinations of price and nonprice emphases among offerings in a market. However, rather than wrestle with more precise, arbitrary definitions, the concept of substantive alternative will be left at an intuitive level. This analysis merely will indicate the market contexts in which substantive differences are *likely* to be more numerous.[1]

THE ROLE OF MARKETING AND MERGERS IN THE PERFORMANCE OF THE FIRM

The objective of this section is to place marketing and mergers within the framework of the objectives of the firm. In general, management seeks to maximize the present value of the firm, that is, the present value of its future earnings. The present value of a firm is the market value of its outstanding common stock, a value dependent principally on the firm's expected future earnings and the capitalization rate. Typically, firms with steady increases in earnings per share have higher present value.

Marketing can increase the firm's earnings per share by effecting either real or pecuniary economies. These two economies are easily distinguish-

[1] Two texts paying some attention to marketing and the maximization of alternatives, on *both* the demand and supply sides are E. A. Duddy and D. A. Revzan, *Marketing: An Institutional Approach* (McGraw-Hill Book Company, 1953); and Wroe Alderson, *Marketing Behavior and Executive Action* (Homewood, Ill.: Richard D. Irwin, Inc., 1957).

able by breaking marginal cost into its component parts. The marginal cost of engaging in marketing, or any specific aspect of it, is elementally:

$$MC = P_v\left(\frac{1}{MP}\right)$$

where P_v is the price paid per unit of a variable input and MP is the marginal product of the input, that is, the change in total output produced by an additional unit of input.[2]

A real economy is an increase in MP. It is described as "real" because it is based on a *technological* relationship between inputs and outputs—specifically, each unit of input yields an increased amount of output. The concept of real economies is completely general—the inputs, for example, may be units of labor, advertising, or market research. Real economies are social economies because only they directly release scarce resources for employment elsewhere in the economy. With P_v constant or increasing proportionately less than increases in MP, it is clear that MC will decrease.

Pecuniary economies with respect to inputs are simply reductions in P_v. With respect to output markets, pecuniary economies are revenues exceeding the cost of all factors of production, including a normal return on equity. Market power, defined as selling price exceeding marginal cost including profit, is the name given pecuniary economies in output markets. On the input side, with M constant or decreasing proportionately less than P_v, MP will decline. A pecuniary economy, whether effected in input or output markets, is necessarily a private economy, and only possibly a social economy; for unless a pecuniary economy begets real economies in the firm or elsewhere in the economy, it remains strictly a private saving. A pecuniary economy becomes a social economy when the proceeds from the former produce an increase in MP such as, for example, the probable effect of investing in higher quality inputs or more effective organization of the inputs.

The acquisition of Clorox by Procter & Gamble provided Clorox with both real and pecuniary economies. First, because Procter received quantity discounts in advertising rates, it could purchase units of advertising in behalf of Clorox at a lower price per unit than Clorox could alone. Moreover, Clorox conceivably could acquire other types of marketing inputs such as personal selling and physical distribution at lower per-unit prices by "buying" them from Procter at the lower cost provided by Procter's vastly larger scale. The pecuniary economies probably far outweighed the social economies in this merger, a point stressed by the Federal Trade Commission in its complaint that this merger would prob-

[2] The basic theory of production and cost, curiously absent in most analytical marketing texts, is found in any intermediate price theory book; a treatment exceptional for its detail and clarity is C. E. Ferguson, *Microeconomic Theory* (Homewood, Ill.: Richard D. Irwin, Inc., 1966), Chapters 6–8.

ably raise entry barriers to anticompetitive levels in the liquid bleach market.[3]

For Clorox, one real economy—similar to an external economy—was the increase in *MP* of all Clorox's marketing inputs resulting from Procter's market position. The merger in effect yielded Clorox an outward shift in its product demand curves, but the demand increase required *no* increase in Clorox's inputs. Procter's products, with their established brand loyalty and presence in virtually every supermarket and grocery store, were in effect the products to which Clorox's products could be tied. Thus, Clorox, through its association with Procter & Gamble, required in principle no additional inputs to realize increased push through the channels as well as increased goodwill-pull by consumers. Also, to the extent Clorox could absorb any idle capacity in Procter & Gamble's marketing operations, Clorox would realize through this joint-product relationship an increase in *MP*. On the other hand, the mere spreading of overhead costs is not an economy, although obviously any department not charged or not charged proportionately for inputs used, enjoys a reduction in *MC*.

In the contemporary literature on acquisitions, mergers which increase earnings per share are said to produce "synergy"—the postmerger whole is greater than the sum of the parts. Synergy in a merger is typically measured by the effect of the merger on earnings per share. An alternative measure is the effect on the price per share of outstanding common stock. The measures are approximately equivalent, except that risk is accounted for in the stock price. For present purposes, it is more useful to focus on synergy in terms of earnings per share.

Mergers may produce synergy in either or both of two ways: (1) through a *valuation* effect concomitant with the combining of independent firms into a single surviving firm; and (2) through *operations* of the postmerger firm. The valuation phenomena, which are strictly pecuniary gains, we shall call "financial synergy." The synergy generated through operations, a result of either or both pecuniary and real economies, will be called "functional synergy." Some elements of financial synergy will be discussed briefly, since this concept requires additional comment.

Financial synergy

In a merger it is possible for the earnings per share of the acquiring firm to increase in the complete absence of functional synergy, if its price/earnings multiple exceeds that of the acquired firm. Moreover,

[3] For reference to the reduced P_v for advertising see *Trade Regulation Reporter* (Commerce Clearing House), paragraph 16,673, p. 21,579 ff; and see also the Supreme Court decision upholding the Commission, and maintaining the distinction between private and social economies, *FTC* v. *Procter & Gamble*, 386 U.S. 568.

the acquiring firm's present value increases if the market continues or increases its expectations of future earnings. Thus, if the market does not revise downward the price of the acquiring firm for having acquired a firm discounted at a higher rate, the former upon boosting its earnings per share will also heighten its present value. Many of the glamour firms today—namely, some of the merger-prone conglomerates—have benefited from acquiring low price/earnings firms. The intensity of a booming conglomerate's halo cast over the acquired firm and market alike has induced continued low capitalization rates yielding high price/earnings multiples.[4]

Price/earnings imbalances are one but not the only means by which a merger may create financial synergy. For many reasons, firms may be underpriced, thereby representing a "bargain" to the buyer. A firm's resources may be underpriced either absolutely or relative to the acquirer, the latter implying that opportunity for financial or functional synergy is not fully reflected in the purchase price. Tax opportunities (loss carry-overs) are other financial reasons for merger which can yield a gain, quite aside from functional synergy.[5]

Moving from this review of the role of marketing and mergers in the overall performance of the firm, the enforcement patterns in merger policy and some implications for impact on marketing will be considered.

SECTION 7 AND MERGER ENFORCEMENT PATTERNS

How has Section 7 of the Clayton Act, the merger law, been implemented in terms of the types of mergers and sizes of mergers most frequently attacked? First, it is necessary to define the different types of mergers. A horizontal merger is one in which there is a high substitutability of supply or demand, a vertical merger is one in which there is a potential or actual supplier-customer relationship, and a conglomerate merger is any merger which is neither horizontal nor vertical.

Conglomerates may be usefully divided into three categories: product extension, market extension, and pure conglomerates. In product-extension acquisitions the acquiring and acquired firms are substantially related, either or both in production and marketing. Market-extension mergers are those in which the acquiring and acquired firms sell the same product or products, but in different geographic markets. So called

[4] The real productivity of pure conglomerates is an important question that even Wall Street analysts cannot answer. See, "Time of Testing for Conglomerates," *Business Week* (March 2, 1968), pp. 38 ff; *New York Times* (January 28, 1968), Section 3, p. 2 ff; and "Looking for a New Yardstick," *Business Week* (August 29, 1966), p. 119.

[5] The bargain aspects of mergers are well treated in W. W. Alberts and Joel E. Segall, *The Corporate Merger* (Chicago, Ill.: University of Chicago Press, 1966), especially Chapter 11.

pure conglomerates are those in which the two firms are virtually unrelated except for common ownership.

The primary emphasis: Manufacturing and large firms

Through June 1967 (the first 16½ years of the 1950 amendment to Section 7), the Department of Justice and the Federal Trade Commission issued 206 merger complaints involving 801 acquisitions. Of the 206 corporations against which complaints were filed, approximately 80 percent were in manufacturing and mining.

From 1950 through June 1967, the two agencies concentrated their enforcement activity in manufacturing and mining, and focused very substantially on *large* acquiring firms, that is, assets exceeding $10 million. Specifically, in this 16½-year period, 94 percent of the 162 mining and manufacturing corporations whose acquisitions were challenged were firms of this size. Among all acquisitions in which the size of the acquired firm was known, 67 percent had assets in excess of $10 million. Thus, in terms of merger complaints, the enforcement of Section 7 to date has emphasized (1) manufacturing and mining, (2) acquiring firms larger than $10 million assets, and (3) acquired firms (in two out of every three instances) exceeding $10 million assets.[6] The explanation for the emphasis on large mergers is perhaps obvious: large firms more frequently have market power and thus acquisitions by or of them more frequently have anticompetitive implications.

Type of large merger challenged in period 1951–66

The two enforcement agencies, in the period 1951 to 1966, challenged in total about 10 percent of the number of all large mergers in manufacturing and mining (Table 1). Over half of the acquisitions challenged were horizontal—representing 27 percent of all large horizontal mergers. The remaining mergers challenged divided about evenly between vertical and conglomerate. Two other facts are important: only 3 percent of all large conglomerate mergers and *no* pure conglomerates were challenged. Of course, complaints are not the whole of enforcement. In addition to the complaints issued, there have been Supreme Court decisions plus guidelines issued by the agencies that will be carefully considered by firms contemplating merger.

Horizontal mergers. Armed with strong Supreme Court horizontal-merger precedents, the two enforcement agencies have indicated they will challenge virtually any horizontal merger which increases concentration or entry barriers in a moderately concentrated or rising-concentration market.[7]

[6] Willard F. Mueller, *The Celler-Kefauver Act: 16 Years of Enforcement*, A Staff Report to the Antitrust Subcommittee, Committee on the Judiciary, House of Representatives (October 16, 1967), Tables 3 and 4.

[7] See *Brown Shoe* v. *U.S.*, 370 U.S., 294; *U.S.* v. *Philadelphia National Bank*,

TABLE 1
Large Acquisitions (acquired firm $10 million assets or larger) in manufacturing and mining, percent challenged and distribution of challenges, by type, 1951–1966

Type of large merger	*Percent of each type challenged*	*Percentage distribution of challenged acquisitions*
Horizontal	27.0	53.0
Vertical	17.0	26.0
Conglomerate	3.0	22.0
Product extension	2.0	11.0
Market extension	19.0	11.0
Pure conglomerates	0.0	0.0
All large mergers	10.2	100.0

Source: Willard F. Mueller, *The Celler-Kefauver Act: 16 Years of Enforcement,* A Staff Report to the Antitrust Subcommittee, Committee on the Judiciary, House of Representatives, October 16, 1967, Table 5.

In principle, horizontal mergers are those most likely to yield functional synergy; thus, this strict merger policy against large horizontal mergers *may* affect marketing's profit contribution. However, what are the foregone *real* economies in precluding a large firm from acquiring a competitor? For a large firm, is functional synergy—especially real economies—more profitably attained by a horizontal merger than by internal investment? Until these critical questions are answered there is no necessary profit implication stemming from the fact that large firms in many markets cannot acquire a competitor. This point will be further discussed in a later section.

Vertical mergers. The Supreme Court declared that Brown Shoe Company's acquisition of Kinney, a merger combining a shoe manufacturer with 4 percent of U.S. production and a shoe retailer with 1.6 percent of all retail shoe store sales, was illegal on vertical as well as horizontal grounds. The reasoning in large part was based on the fact that the industry had experienced a series of vertical mergers, and Kinney was the largest remaining individual shoe retailer. The Department of Justice *Guidelines* are equally firm against vertical mergers which foreclose a substantial market share to buyers or suppliers.[8]

From *Brown Shoe* and pronouncements of the two agencies, current

374 U.S. 321; *U.S.* v. *Von's Grocery Co.,* 384 U.S. 270; and *U.S.* v. *Pabst Brewing Co.,* 384 U.S. 546; Department of Justice "Merger Guidelines" (May 30, 1968); and FTC, *Enforcement Policy with Respect to Mergers in the Food Distribution Industries* (January 3, 1967).

[8] See *Brown Shoe* v. *U.S.,* 370 U.S., 294; *Guidelines,* same reference as footnote 7; and FTC, *Enforcement Policy with Respect to Vertical Mergers in the Cement Industry* (January 3, 1967).

merger policy clearly precludes many vertical mergers by or of large firms. But again, the frequent illegality of vertical mergers by large firms has no *necessary* implications for real economies. This point is deferred to a subsequent section.

Conglomerate mergers. The pattern in Table 1 understates the merger policy with respect to product-extension mergers, for in 1967 the Supreme Court handed down its decision in *Procter & Gamble-Clorox.*[9] This decision increases the probability that the agencies will challenge any product-extension merger in which: (*a*) the acquiring firm has both the resources and experience for product differentiation, (*b*) the acquired product is differentiable and already a leader, and (*c*) the market of the acquired product is moderately concentrated with medium-to-high barriers to entry. Many product-extension acquisitions of consumer products approximate these conditions. Other focuses in product-extension merger policy are on the elimination of potential competition and anticompetitive reciprocity.[10]

But of all the theories of probable anticompetitive effects of conglomerate mergers, elimination of potential competition is the theory perhaps best supportable theoretically and empirically, as well as most explicable to managers. Both the Justice Department and the FTC have taken increasingly strong stands against mergers which eliminated potential competition with respect to concentrated markets.[11]

In the recent Procter & Gamble-Clorox decisions and policy statements by the enforcement agencies, there are bases for precluding product-extension mergers which eliminate potential competition in markets already moderately concentrated or tending to concentration, or which through intrafirm resource allocation raise already moderate entry barriers. As a result, product-extension mergers in certain contexts are foreclosed to many large firms. As with horizontal mergers, however, there may be only minimal cost, for what is precluded may not be necessarily the most profitable avenue to functional synergy.

To summarize, horizontal, vertical, and product extension mergers are in varying degrees increasingly foreclosed to relatively large firms in concentrated or high-barrier markets; whereas, to date, pure-conglomerate mergers are still unconstrained by Section 7. The impact of government merger policy with respect to large firms will be considered next.

---

[9] *FTC* v. *Procter & Gamble,* 386 U.S. 568.

[10] See *Foremost Dairies, Inc.,* FTC Docket 6495; *The Borden Co.,* FTC Docket 6652; *Beatrice Foods Co.,* FTC Docket 6653; and two Supreme Court cases which have considered the elimination of potential competition, and one, the issue of reciprocity. See, respectively, *U.S.* v. *El Paso Natural Gas Company et al.,* 376 U.S. 651, and *U.S.* v. *Penn-Olin Chemical Co., et al.,* 378 U.S. 158; and *FTC* v. *Consolidated Foods Corp.,* 380 U.S. 592.

[11] See *FTC* v. *Procter & Gamble,* 386 U.S. 568, 580–581; *Merger Guidelines,* same reference as footnote 7; FTC *Enforcement Policy with Respect to Product Extension Mergers in Grocery Products Manufacturing* (May 15, 1968); and John C. Narver, "Supply Space: An Elaboration of Potential Competition," *Proceedings of the American Marketing Association,* August 1968.

SOME EVIDENCE OF THE IMPACT ON MARKETING

Changing patterns among large mergers

From the preceding summary of the relative strictness of government merger policy on types of mergers, one would expect the percentage of horizontal, vertical, and product-extension mergers to decrease somewhat and the percentage of pure conglomerates to increase among all large mergers. These implications are borne out in part in Table 2, which shows the percentage distribution of large acquisitions in manufacturing and mining.

ABLE 2
ercentage distribution of large acquisitions (acquired firm assets exceed $10 nillion) manufacturing and mining, by type of merger, 1951–67

Type of merger	*1951–54*	*1955–58*	*1959–62*	*1963–66*	*1967*
orizontal	37.0	28.0	17.0	15.0	8.0
ertical	12.0	16.0	18.0	15.0	8.0
onglomerate	51.0	56.0	65.0	71.0	84.0
Product extension	37.0	47.0	39.0	52.0	61.0
Market extension	6.0	4.0	8.0	5.0	1.0
Pure conglomerate	7.0	5.0	17.0	14.0	22.0
Total	100.0	100.0	100.0	100.0	100.0

Source: Willard F. Mueller, *The Celler-Kefauver Act: 16 Years of Enforcement*, A Staff Report f the Antitrust Subcommittee, Committee on the Judiciary, House of Representatives, October 16, 967, Table 7 for 1951–66 data and Bureau of Economics, FTC, for 1967 data.

Table 2 does not of course indicate the absolute magnitude of large mergers, which have increased from a mere 9 in 1951, to 101 in 1966, to 170 in 1967.[12] In light of the persistent increase in the total of large mergers, the percentage distribution in Table 2 permits some additional inferences as to the impact of merger policy. The increase in product-extension mergers as a percentage of all mergers is probably primarily due to two facts: (1) many horizontal and vertical mergers, the types believed most likely to yield functional synergy, are precluded; thus, product-extension mergers, perceived as the next best merger avenue for functional synergy, increase; and (2) the potentially adverse policy on product-extension mergers, coupled with the full impact of *Procter & Gamble-Clorox* (1967), have yet to take full effect.

The data in Table 2, in conjunction with the continued increase in large mergers, suggest that large firms perceive some profits in merging

[12] Bureau of Economics, FTC, for the 1967 figure. The complete data on large mergers, but with a lower preliminary figure for 1967, are published in FTC, *Large Mergers in Manufacturing and Mining, 1948–1967: Statistical Report* (May 1968).

regardless of the particular type of merger. Thus, the data in Table 2 are consistent with the posited concept of *financial* synergy discussed in a previous section, for firms can gain simply from merging. With merger policy discouraging many economically related mergers because of probable anticompetitive effects, the merger movement rolls on by shifting into less related and even virtually unrelated mergers. The polar extreme, of course, is the pure-conglomerate merger, which by definition is one with virtually no marketing and production relationships. Unlike other mergers, increases in earnings per share in *pure*-conglomerate mergers came largely from financial synergy, although some functional synergy from pecuniary economies in the capital market and real overhead economies, is a distinct possibility.

Scale economies, profitability, and mergers

Suppose that merger policy, in stressing probable anticompetitive effects in markets, continues to be strict toward large horizontal and vertical mergers and also establishes a stringent policy on many product-extension mergers. What is the *real* (input productivity) effect on the firm and society, if antitrust policy substantially precludes a large firm from merging into related areas? Or from merging in *any* area? The bulk of the evidence to date suggests that a strict merger policy directed toward large firms would sacrifice relatively few real economies in marketing, production, or elsewhere in the firm; moreover, not only would the real costs be small, but the social gains potentially large, for large firms would have to grow by internal investment which, to the extent that it adds capacity to a market, is growth that is necessarily procompetitive. Mergers, of course, also may increase competition, but in contrast to internal growth, this result is problematic rather than automatic.[13]

In many industries the most efficient scale of operations is relatively small. One analysis of 20 manufacturing industries concluded that in the majority of the industries, firms exceeded the minimum-size efficient scale—the smallest output level yielding lowest average costs—in one or more of the three areas of production, sales promotion, and physical distribution. Furthermore, the study found only relatively small multiplant or overhead economies.[14]

In Congressional hearings on market concentration, the testimony from scholars and industry witnesses was largely to the effect that small to medium-sized firms are frequently as or more productive, efficient, and inventive than much larger firms. On the basis of real productivity,

[13] The procompetitive character and social desirability of internal growth are widely recognized in the antitrust literature and cases. See, for example, Carl Kaysen and Donald F. Turner, *Antitrust Policy* (Cambridge, Mass.: Harvard University Press, 1959), p. 135; and *U.S.* v. *Philadelphia National Bank*, 374 U.S. 321, 370.

[14] Joe S. Bain, "Advantages of the Large Firm: Production, Distribution, and Sales Promotion," *Journal of Marketing*, Vol. 20 (April 1956), pp. 336–46.

the optimal scale is typically smaller, and in some industries considerably smaller, than the largest firms.[15]

The net-profit performance of the 1,000 largest manufacturing firms provides further evidence that beyond some point profitability does not *substantially* increase with size. In 1966, the 1,000 largest U.S. manufacturing firms earned 13.4 percent on equity; whereas, the average in that year for all U.S. manufacturing corporations was 13.1 percent. In 1967 the profit on equity was 11.8 percent and 11.4 percent respectively. These data suggest that in U.S. manufacturing there is increasing profitability to scale, at least up to some point.[16] Obviously, increasing profitability may be due to pecuniary economies, real economies, or both. But whatever the reason or reasons, the 1,000 largest manufacturing firms on the average earned higher profits on equity than the remaining corporations in manufacturing.

The generally higher profitability of the 1,000 largest manufacturing firms, however, apparently does not hold throughout all manufacturing industries. In 1966, 7 of the 19 major industry groups in manufacturing revealed a higher total-industry profitability than that earned by the members of the 1,000 largest firms in those industries. There were similar results in 1967. In the latter year, 11 of the 19 major industry groups had a total-industry profit on equity higher than that of the representatives of the 1,000 largest.[17] Thus, there is a general tendency across all 19 major industry groups for the 1,000 largest to earn a higher percent return on equity than the all-corporation average. However, within various major groups—the majority of major groups in 1967—the members of the 1,000 largest did not earn a higher return on equity than the industry average.

Moreover, there is mixed evidence of the relationship between profitability and size *among* the 1,000 largest firms. An investigation of 21 2-digit and 3-digit SIC manufacturing industries for 1966, consisting of 715 of the 1,000 largest firms, revealed no strong positive relation between asset size of the firm and profits on equity. In fact, large firms' profit/equity performance in 13 of the 21 industries was *negatively* correlated to the asset size of the firm.[18]

[15] See *Hearings on Economic Concentration,* Subcommittee on Antitrust and Monopoly, Committee on the Judiciary, U.S. Senate, 89th Congress, 1st Session, especially Part 3, *Concentration, Invention, and Innovation;* and Part 4, *Concentration and Efficiency.* For a less technical discussion, see George J. Stigler, "The Case Against Big Business," in Edwin Mansfield, *Monopoly Power and Economic Performance* (New York: W. W. Norton and Co., 1964).

[16] *News Front* (May 1967), p. 46; (August 1968), p. 38.

[17] Ibid.

[18] Of the 13 negative correlations, 2 were significant at the .05 level, and none of the positive correlations was significant. For a study which found increasing profitability among large firms, largely explained by capital market pecuniary economies and barriers to entry, see Marshall Hall and Leonard Weiss, "Firm Size and Profitability," *Review of Economics and Statistics,* Vol. 49 (August 1967).

Data pertaining to the 1,000 largest manufacturing firms suggest that in several industries beyond some point there *may* be *decreasing* profitability to scale. This can be shown by total-industry profitability exceeding that of the 1,000 largest, as well as negative assets-profitability correlation among the 1,000 largest firms. This tentative conclusion is consistent with the frequent observation that the long-run average cost curve for most firms is "L" or even slightly "U" shaped.[19]

With respect to the profitability of merging, there is some evidence that mergers are no more profitable, and perhaps less profitable, than internal growth.[20] Merging firms may fail to improve their earnings for several reasons, ranging from an absence of any further exploitable economies to management incompatibility and other postmerger administrative problems.[21] For whatever the reason, it is clear that in many instances a merger is not the most efficient means for a firm to enter a new market or to enlarge its current market shares. Obviously, if entry barriers are high, entry into the market by internal investment may be difficult. However, surely a prospect for acquisition in such a market is cognizant of this fact and, if rational, will capitalize his full future earnings to the acquirer. The seller may even hold out for a sizable premium.

An excessive premium paid in a merger will, of course, reduce earnings/share unless offset by the financial and/or functional synergy. Two students of mergers agree that firms desiring to enter profitable industries usually find it less expensive to enter *internally* than through merger.[22]

Impact of merger policy on consumers

The impact of merger policy on consumers is measured, in principle, by the changes the policy brings in the number of substantive alterna-

[19] For example, see Joe S. Bain, *Industrial Organization* (John Wiley & Sons, Inc., 1959), Chapters 5 and 9; and *The Structure of Food Manufacturing*, National Commission on Food Marketing, Technical Study No. 8 (June 1966), pp. 61–104.

[20] John Bossons, *et al.*, "Mergers for Whom—Managers or Stockholders?," Workshop on Capital Market Equilibrating Process, Working Paper No. 14 (Graduate School of Industrial Administration, Carnegie Institute of Technology, 1966), Table 7. The study is summarized in *Business Week* (September 17, 1966). Also seen Eamon M. Kelly, *The Profitability of Growth through Mergers* (University Park, Pa.: College of Business Administration, Center for Research, The Pennsylvania State University, 1967).

[21] See John Kitching, "Why Do Mergers Miscarry?," *Harvard Business Review*, Vol. 45 (November-December 1967), pp. 84–101.

[22] William W. Alberts, "The Profitability of Growth by Merger," pp. 286–87, and Michael Gort, "Diversification, Mergers, and Profits," pp. 43–44, in *The Corporate Merger*, W. W. Alberts and J. E. Segall, editors (Chicago, Ill.: University of Chicago Press, 1966). Also, Donald J. Smalter and Roderick C. Lancey, "P-E Analysis in Acquisition Strategy," *Harvard Business Review*, Vol. 44 (November-December 1966), pp. 85–95.

tives from which the consumer may choose.[23] "Substantive alternatives," defined at the outset of this paper, include *both* offerings in which price is the principal variable and offerings emphasizing nonprice elements. As mentioned, the issue turns on perceived differences, and each person's perception is unique. Thus, indirect means must be used to assess the effect of merger policy on consumer alternatives.

Theory indicates and observation confirms that when rivalry among firms in a market is vigorous—when competition is active—there is a greater variety of offerings than under most quiescent conditions. The absence of intense rivalry, either among the firms already in the market or the lack of potential or new entrants to goad competition, is reflected in excess profits. Empirical investigations confirm theoretical predictions that in the presence of certain other market-structure characteristics a high concentration of sellers tends to be associated with high profits. The polar extreme, of course, is the pure monopolist.[24]

The evidence does not indicate that all concentrated markets lead a quiet life and earn excessive profits, nor does the evidence necessitate a conclusion that completely unconcentrated markets are the ideal for consumer alternatives. The investigations merely suggest that, on the average, high concentrations of sellers are less likely than moderately concentrated markets to provide substantive alternatives to consumers.

What has been the impact of merger policy on market concentration, and thereby on consumer alternatives? Specifically, the critical question is the extent to which merger policy has curtailed further increases in market concentration, or actually reduced concentration by prohibiting horizontal mergers—an action which clearly lessens concentration in growing markets.

Trends in market concentration differ between producer goods and consumer goods. In the period 1947–63, generally speaking, the 4-firm level of concentration declined in producer goods industries, whereas it rose in consumer goods industries. These counter movements offset each other, leaving the overall average level of 4-firm sales concentration in markets relatively unchanged.[25]

Antitrust policy, and in particular that pertaining to mergers, constitutes but one determinant of the level of concentration in a market.

[23] A consumer focus for antitrust is argued, for example, in Kenneth S. Carlston and James M. Treece, "Antitrust and the Consumer Interest," *Michigan Law Review*, Vol. 64 (March 1966), pp. 777–800.

[24] For a comprehensive treatment of market structure-performance relationships, see Norman R. Collins and Lee E. Preston, *Concentration and Price-Cost Margins in Manufacturing Industries* (Berkeley, Cal.: University of California Press, 1968); see also H. Michael Mann, "Seller Concentration, Barriers to Entry, and Rates of Return in Thirty Industries, 1950–1960," *Review of Economics and Statistics* (August 1966), pp. 296–307.

[25] Willard F. Mueller, *Status and Future of Small Business*, Hearings before the Select Committee on Small Business, U.S. Senate, 90th Congress, 1st Session, 1967, p. 479 and Fig. 8.

In some markets merger policy can significantly contribute to a leveling or even lessening of concentration:

> Postwar trends in market concentration support the hypothesis that in producer goods industries antimerger policy has created an environment preventing increases in concentration in some industries and encouraging decreases in concentration in others.[26]

However, in consumer goods markets, merger policy and other economic factors have had a less deconcentrating impact:

> Although horizontal merger policy almost certainly has slowed the growth of concentration in many consumer goods industries, the prevention of horizontal mergers alone has not provided an adequate remedy to the problem.[27]

Product differentiation and large-scale promotional activity account for some of the increases in market concentration among consumer goods. Conglomerate mergers may be another reason for rigidities in market structure, for while they do not immediately change concentration, these mergers may nevertheless alter the market structure facing more specialized firms. In some markets, the presence of a large conglomerate may induce smaller, less diversified firms to compete less aggressively out of fear of retaliation; similarly, under certain conditions, a conglomerate may raise entry barriers.[28]

Antitrust merger policy has probably increased the substantive alternatives to consumers by facilitating, directly or indirectly, lower concentration and lower entry barriers. However, the impact has not been equal across all markets, and the direct impact is virtually unmeasurable.

CONCLUSIONS AND IMPLICATIONS

Merger policy, stressing probable anticompetitive effects, has focused primarily on relatively *large* mergers. If the present pattern of enforcement continues, large horizontal, vertical, and product-extension conglomerate mergers will be increasingly difficult for many large firms in concentrated markets.

Empirical evidence suggests that *in general* the real cost to marketers (firms) of a stringent large-merger policy is low, for real economies apparently are largely exhausted in numerous industries at relatively small to moderate scale. The evidence on profitability and scale indicates several industries in which the minimum cost scale is relatively large. One

---

[26] Mueller, *The Celler-Kefauver Act:* . . . , p. 30, and Ibid., pp. 457–65 for the effects of merger policy in the daily industry and food retailing. Pertaining to vertical mergers, see for example, FTC, *Enforcement Policy with Respect to Vertical Mergers in the Cement Industry* (January 3, 1967).

[27] Mueller, The Celler-Kefauver Act: . . . , p. 31.

[28] The market-structure implications of conglomerate mergers are discussed in John C. Narver, *Conglomerate Mergers and Market Competition* (Berkeley, Cal.: University of California Press, 1967), Chapters 5–7.

must distinguish between real and pecuniary economies: pecuniary economies are not necessarily an economy to society; whereas, real economies have immediate social value, for as resource productivity increases, they free scarce resources for employment elsewhere in the firm or the economy.

A procompetitive merger policy is strongly *for* economies and *for* growth. Such a policy says merely that in some market circumstances, because of probable anticompetitive effects, a firm must grow internally rather than by merger. In addition, the evidence suggests that internal investment is in many cases a more profitable avenue of growth for the large firm. For society as well, internal investment is generally preferable. In adding capacity, internal growth is immediately procompetitive; whereas, the procompetitiveness of many mergers is more problematical.

Marketers, logically, cannot object to a policy which requires the firm to grow by meeting the test of the market. If, in the face of competition, a firm grows by internally investing in product development and channel improvement, any resulting growth is the *justly earned* reward for successfully meeting the test of the market. If a firm needs additional capital and if the capital market, upon assessing the earning ability of the firm, provides the needed funds, the firm again has successfully met the market test. In principle, a firm in a market economy is like an office seeker in a democracy; he must meet the test of the voting place both as to capital and output. By contrast, mergers through financial synergy may increase earnings per share yet represent neither an affirmation by the market nor a real economy. To the extent that firms' growth in earnings per share results largely from acquiring a firm with a lower P/E, one cannot logically argue that a policy requiring growth substantially through internal investment raises society's real costs. Large firms have access to the capital market, and, therefore, the internal investment option is always open. Moreover, from all social standpoints, internal growth should be encouraged.

The real productivity that genuinely is a part of much of marketing and which benefits consumers and businessmen alike has been virtually unharmed by antitrust merger policy. Furthermore, it would appear that an even more stringent *large-merger* policy would not likely affect real marketing economies. The present merger policy in conjunction with growing markets undoubtedly has helped enlarge the substantive alternatives open to consumers. Taken as a whole, current merger policy has produced and should continue to produce social benefits outweighing social costs.

The Federal Trade Commission regulates advertising for the protection of the consumer; it also examines the adequacy of the criteria which underlie the regulatory process.

Is it possible for the consumer treated as "economic man" to be adequately protected from advertising abuse? This article illustrates that the current research on "behavioral man" can help plug the gaps in present regulatory policies.

27. THE FEDERAL TRADE COMMISSION AND THE REGULATION OF ADVERTISING IN THE CONSUMER INTEREST*

Dorothy Cohen†

It is the purpose of this article to review the present means by which the Federal Trade Commission regulates advertising for the protection of the consumer, as well as the adequacy of the criteria which underlie the regulatory process. Further, it is suggested that additional measures be taken that would increase the effectiveness of the advertising regulatory process.

In implementing its responsibility to regulate advertising for the protection of consumers, the Federal Trade Commission has developed informal decision criteria. In broad terms, the Commission's judgments have been consistent with an "economic man" concept of consumer purchase behavior. It views the consumer as an informed, reasoning decision maker using objective values to maximize utilities. This is essentially a normative concept.

The basic assumptions of the Commission's regulatory design or criteria are maximization of the consumer's utilities and rational choice. A necessary ingredient to fulfill these assumptions is full, accurate information. The Commission, therefore, protects the consumer by identifying and attacking information which is insufficient, false, or misleading. These deficiencies are uncovered by relating the objective characteristics of a product, as determined by the Commission, to its advertising representations.

The Commission, therefore, operates under the legally and economically acceptable premise that the consumer is to be assured full and accurate information which will permit him to make a reasoned choice in the marketplace. Nonetheless, examination of the results of the Com-

* Reprinted from "The Federal Trade Commission and the Regulation of Advertising in the Consumer Interest," *Journal of Marketing,* Vol. 33 (January 1969) pp. 40–44.

† Hofstra University.

mission's activities utilizing this concept reveals the existence of several gaps in its protection. For example, the poor are not always protected from excessive payments because of lack of information about true cost or true price. The health and safety of the consumer are not always assured, since information concerning the hazards of using particular products is not always available. The belief that added protection is needed was reinforced by a report of the Consumer Advisory Council to President Johnson which states "that although this is an era of abundance . . . there is also much confusion and ignorance, some deception and even fraud. . . ."[1]

The need for added protection does not necessarily suggest discarding the Commission's regulatory framework, because a more effective structure currently does not exist. The elimination of the present regulatory design would in fact create a void in the consumer protection network. It does suggest, however, that steps should be taken as a basis for stronger protection in the future. The current movement to improve regulation through stressing full disclosure, while serving to eliminate some deficiencies, is not sufficient.[2] The Consumer Advisory Council's report, for example, in summarizing the outlook for the future, observes:

> Technological change is so rapid that the consumer who bothers to learn about a commodity or a service soon finds his knowledge obsolete. In addition, many improvements in quality and performance are below the threshold of perception, and imaginative marketing often makes rational choice even more of a problem.[3]

Full disclosure of pertinent facts is one step in improving the protection network. Additional steps are needed to assure that the consumer understands the significance of the facts. It has been noted, for example, that the consumer is selective in his acceptance of information offered. This selectivity is due, in part, to a difference between the objective environment in which the consumer "really" lives and the subjective environment he perceives and responds to.[4] The consumer reacts to information not only with his intelligence, but also with habits, traits, attitudes, and feelings. In addition, his decisions are influenced significantly by opinion leaders, reference groups, and so on. There are predis-

[1] *Consumer Issues '66,* A Report Prepared by the Consumer Advisory Council (Washington, D.C.: U.S. Government Printing Office, 1966), p. 1.

[2] See *The J. B. Williams Co., Inc.* and *Parkson Advertising Agency, Inc.* v. *F.T.C.,* 5 *Trade Regulation Reporter #72,182* (Chicago, Ill.: Commerce Clearing House, Inc., August 1967); and several aspects of truth-in-packaging and truth-in-lending legislation.

[3] *Consumer Issues '66,* A Report . . . , p. 6.

[4] Herbert A. Simon, "Economics and Psychology," in *Psychology: A Study of a Science,* Simon Koch, ed., Vol. 6 (New York: McGraw-Hill Book Co., Inc., 1963), p. 710.

positions at work within the individual that determine what he is exposed to, what he perceives, what he remembers, and the effect of the communication upon him.[5]

It has been noted that appeal to fear (emphasizing the hazards of smoking or of borrowing money) may not deter the chronically anxious consumer, nor will it necessarily protect his health or pocketbook. Valid communications from a nonauthoritative source may not be believed, whereas questionable communications from an authoritative source may be readily accepted. Thus, the extensive use of "sufficient" truth may take on an aura of nonbelievability and be rejected. Attempts to avoid conflicting evidence may result in ignoring the information completely.

The Commission's efforts to provide the consumer with economic information concerning value are not completely effective, since the consumer does not measure value in economic terms alone. Brand loyalties create values in the eyes of the consumer as does the influence of social groups and opinion leaders within these groups. His desire to attain certain levels of aspiration may lead the consumer to be a "satisficing animal . . . rather than a maximizing animal,"[6] that is, one who chooses among values that may be currently suitable, rather than those which maximize utilities. In order for the Commission to improve the consumer protection network, it must reflect an understanding of the behavioral traits of consumers.

Adapting the regulatory design to handle behavioral traits is no easy task. An examination of a behavioral model of consumer performance reveals the existence of many intervening variables, so that the creation of standards for this nonstandardized consumer becomes exceedingly difficult. Moreover, current knowledge of the consumer as a behavioralist is far from complete. Indeed, the feasibility and success associated with the practical uses of this model are dependent upon future research.

It is, therefore, recommended that attention be directed toward current and future research in the behavioral sciences to devise means for amending the advertising regulatory framework. This would lead to improvements in the communication process and the elimination of protection gaps. The application of behavioral characteristics to the regulatory model is not intended as a panacea, but is a suggestion for improving some regulatory ailments. In broad policy terms the Commission can initially do little more than establish closer contact with the consumer and analyze behavioral data which may be relevant to the regulation of advertising. Suggestions for improved administrative procedures are limited to applications of current behavioral knowledge of the consumer. Future research may suggest more precise administrative action,

[5] Joseph T. Klapper, "The Social Effects of Mass Communication," in *The Source of Human Communication,* Wilbur Schramm, ed. (New York: Basic Books, Inc., 1963), p. 67.

[6] Simon, "Economics and Psychology," in *Psychology:* . . . , p. 716.

for increased knowledge of the consumer's buying behavior should lead to the development of more effective mechanisms for his protection.

RECOMMENDATIONS

The following specific recommendations are suggested as guidelines for future governmental activities relative to consumer advertising.

Bureau of Behavioral Studies

A Bureau of Behavioral Studies should be established within the Federal Trade Commission (similar to the Commission's Bureau of Economics) whose function would be to gather and analyze data on consumer buying behavior relevant to the regulation of advertising in the consumer interest.

Consumer complaint offices

The Federal Trade Commission should establish "consumer complaint" offices throughout the United States. One method of gathering more information about the consumer is to provide closer contact between the Federal Trade Commission and the public. Complaints about advertising abuses may originate with consumers, but these have been at a minimum; and lately the Commission has accentuated its industry-wide approach to deceptive practices. Although the industry-wide approach is geared toward prevention and permits the FTC to deal with broad areas of deception, it minimizes the possibility of consumer contact with the Commission. In 1967, awareness of this fact resulted in an action in which the Commission's Bureau of Field Operations and its 11 field offices located in cities across the United States intensified its program of public education designed to give businessmen and consumers a better understanding of the work of the agency.[7]

If the Commission is to operate satisfactorily in the consumer interest, it must develop a closer relationship with consumers. Most consumers are still uncertain about the protection they are receiving, and the Federal Trade Commission appears to be an unapproachable body with little apparent contact with the "man-on-the-street."

Consumer complaint offices would identify the Federal Trade Commission's interest in the consumer and act as a clearing house for information. Consumers could be informed about steps to take if they believe they have been deceived, what recourse is open, and how to secure redress for grievances. The Commission could secure evidence about deception direct from consumers. Moreover, the complaints of these private individuals might be based on noneconomic factors, permitting

[7] Federal Trade Commission, *Annual Report*, 1967, p. 67.

clearer delineation of the behavioral man and the ways in which he might be protected.

Priority of protection

The Federal Trade Commission should establish a definitive policy of priority of protection based on the severity of the consequences of the advertising. While appropriations and manpower for the Federal Trade Commission have increased in recent years, they are still far from adequate to police all advertising. Therefore, the ability to protect is limited and selective. In its recent annual report the Commission did indicate, however, that it had established priorities:

> A high priority is accorded those matters which relate to the basic necessities of life, and to situations in which the impact of false and misleading advertising, or other unfair and deceptive practices, falls with cruelest impact upon those least able to survive the consequences—the elderly and the poor.[8]

Nevertheless, in the same year the Commission reported that approximately 20 percent of the funds devoted to curtailing deceptive practices were expended on textile and fur enforcement (noting that the Bureau of Textiles and Furs made 12,679 inspections on the manufacturing, wholesaling, and retailing level).[9]

Priority may be established in two ways. First, it may be considered relative to the harmful consequences of deceptive advertising. This approach could suggest, for example, that the Federal Trade Commission devote more of its energies to examining conflicting claims in cigarette advertising than to examining conflicting claims in analgesic advertising (which seems to focus on the question of whether one pain reliever acts faster than the other). Exercising such priorities might accelerate the movement toward needed reforms (such as the current safety reforms in the automobile industry) by pinpointing the existence of inadequately protected consumer areas.

A second method of establishing priority could be to delineate the groups that are most susceptible to questionable advertising. This is where the behavioral model may play an important role. Sociologists are trying to discover common aspects of group behavior, and research has disclosed that each social class has its own language pattern.[10] Special meanings and symbols accentuate the differences between groups and increase social distance from outsiders.[11]

---

[8] Ibid., at p. 17.

[9] Ibid., at pp. 30 and 81.

[10] Leonard Schatzman and Anselm Strauss, "Social Class and Modes of Communication," *American Journal of Sociology*, Vol. 60 (January 1955), pp. 329–38.

[11] Tamotsu Shibutani, "Reference Groups as Perspectives," *American Journal of Sociology*, Vol. 60 (May 1955), p. 567.

Disclosure of special facets of group behavior should be helpful to the Commission in designing a program of protection. As noted earlier, the poor cannot be adequately protected by the disclosure of true interest rates because their aspirations may provide a stronger motivating influence than the fear of excessive debt. Knowledge of the actual cost of borrowing would offer no protection to the low-income family which knows no sources of goods and credit available to it other than costly ones. Nor would higher cost of borrowing deter the consumer who, concerned mostly with the amount of the monthly payment, may look at credit as a means of achieving his goals. In fact, the Federal Trade Commission concluded, in a recent economic report on installment sales and credit practices in the District of Columbia, that truth-in-lending, although needed, is not sufficient to solve the problem of excessive use of installment credit for those consumers who are considered poor credit risks and are unsophisticated buyers.[12]

The problems of the poor extend beyond the possible costs of credit. They include the hazards of repossession, the prices paid for items in addition to credit costs, and the possibility of assuming long-term debt under a contractual obligation not clear at the outset. It is possible that behavioral studies may disclose a communication system that would be a more effective deterrent to the misuse of credit than the disclosure of exorbitant interest rates. Until then, the Commission should give priority to investigations where the possibility of fraudulent claims, representations, and pricing accompany the offering of credit facilities to low-income groups. For example, advertisements of "three complete rooms of furniture for $199.00, easy payments" continue to appear despite the Commission's ruling that "bait and switch" tactics are unfair. Thus, the possibility exists that the low-income consumer may be "switched" to a much more expensive purchase whose costs become abnormally high due to the exorbitant interest rates included in the "easy payments." In its monitoring and review of advertising the Commission's staff should give precedence to investigations of such "bargain, easy payments" advertising, since much of it is especially designed to attract the low-income groups.

Improvement of the communication process

The consumer's cognitive capacity (the attitudes, perceptions, or beliefs about one's environment) and its effect on the communication process should be reflected in designing advertising controls so that the inefficient mechanisms can be improved or eliminated.

Currently the concept of full disclosure is being expanded as the major means of offering the consumer additional protection. This is par-

[12] *Trade Regulation Reporter* #50,205 (Chicago, Ill.: Commerce Clearing House, Inc., July 1968).

ticularly evident where the objective is to dissuade the consumer from the use of or excessive use of a product or service. Little attention is paid, however, to determining whether the selective consumer is taking note of these disclosures.

An examination of behavioral man reveals that he is less "perfect" than economic man. His values are not based on objective realities alone, nor are his choices always what may be objectively considered as best among alternatives. In legislative design the regulatory authorities should come to grips with the question of whether protection of the consumer includes "protection from himself." There are indications that the latter concept is considered a legitimate area for regulatory activities—as evidenced in legislation affecting cigarette advertising and in some elements of the truth-in-lending and truth-in-packaging bills.

While questions may be raised about the legitimacy of interfering with the consumer's "freedom of choice," there is evidence that the methodology devised for this interference is deficient. In the current regulatory design, the proposed method of securing these different kinds of protection is the same, although the kinds of protection offered to the consumer may differ. For example, the consumer is currently protected against deceptive advertising by laws requiring that he be provided with truthful disclosure as to the product and its features. Where authorities believe that the advertising claims of certain products or services should be minimally used or completely avoided, the consumer is again protected by nondeceptive "full disclosure" as to the product and its features. Yet a quick review of consumer behavior and persuasibility reveals that a strategy designed to change or dissuade must, of necessity, differ from a strategy designed to reinforce. The consumer may be quite willing to accept information which supports his beliefs or preconceptions and yet be unwilling to accept evidence which refutes these same beliefs. Moreover, research has disclosed that adherence to recommended behavior is inversely related to the intensity of fear arousal. Intense fear appeal may be ineffective since it arouses anxiety within the subject which can be reduced by his hostility toward the communication and rejection of the message. It has also been noted that the tendency toward dissonance reduction can lead to failure to understand the information disclosed. Thus "full disclosure" cannot be a completely effective control mechanism when its main purpose is to protect the consumer from using a particular product or service, for the consumer may simply ignore these disclosures.

Based on current research, one approach the Commission might take toward an improved program of dissuasion would be to reinforce the negative information through an authoritative source, such as the Commission itself. Although the agency has a number of publications—*Annual Report, News Summary, Advertising Alert*—none of these is specifically geared to provide the consumer with information. A monthly report to consumers, initially available at "consumer complaint" offices, might serve as an effective mechanism for denoting the existence of hazardous products, excessive claims, questionable representations, and so forth. Specifically, this report could detail information of particular interest to consumers concerning advertising abuses that had been curtailed, cease and desist orders, questionable advertising practices currently under investigation, and so on. It is also suggested that this printed publication occasionally be supplemented by reports through a more pervasive medium—television.

It is not recommended that the Commission become a product-testing service, since the latter implies governmental control over competitive offerings and could place excessive restrictions on freedom of choice. Instead the report is to be considered a communication device, designed to insure that consumers take more note of available information on the premise that the information emanates from an authoritative governmental source.

Behavioral criteria

The Federal Trade Commission should use behavioral as well as economic criteria in evaluating consumer interest. Subjective as well as objective claims should be examined in determining whether a "tendency to deceive" exists. Due to insufficient knowledge of consumer behavior, an accurate blueprint for defining products in terms of consumer choice is not available. Future research may present more precise propositions about consumer behavior which would facilitate the development and implementation of behavioral criteria. However, currently there are areas wherein the adaptation of behavioral factors in establishing criteria for advertising regulation may provide for more adequate protection in the consumer interest.

Assuming it were possible to provide the consumer with complete information based on economic criteria, the individual may still be unable to exercise informed choice. A recent report by the National Commission on Food Marketing stated: "Given complete price information, the help of computers and all the clerical help needed, it is impossible to say which retailer in a particular community has lower prices."[13] Moreover, as noted earlier, individuals do not choose on the basis of price appeal alone.

Advertising today, to a great extent, stresses noneconomic or promotional differences. Products are denoted as being preferred by groups, individuals, society, motion picture stars, sports leaders, and the average man. Since consumers may make their selections on the basis of these

[13] *Organization and Competition in Food Retailing, Technical Study No. 7*, a report prepared by the National Commission on Food Marketing (Washington, D.C.: U.S. Government Printing Office, 1966), p. 169.

promotional representations, adequate protection requires that advertisements be subject to as close an examination for deceptive representation as they are for deceptive price claims.

Insufficient emphasis has been placed in the advertising regulatory design on the importance of testimonials in influencing consumer choice. In the examination of the selective consumer it has been noted that his choice is influenced by a desire for group membership and by the opinion of leaders within these groups. It has also been noted that the consumer engages in selective exposure and selective perception, suggesting that when the consumer finally does accept an "opinion leader," the latter exerts significant pressure on the consumer's choice.

The use of testimonials in advertising takes account of this fact of consumer behavior, but the regulatory design does not. Those who are deemed to be opinion leaders and dominant members of groups are selected and paid for their "testimonials." Moreover, where the selected figure does not perform well, for example, on television, an actor is used to replace him. The consumer may be deceived into believing an "opinion leader" is evaluating a product or service. These opinions may be used by the consumer to substantiate the suitability of this particular item in his own value structure.

Currently, the basic legal requirement is that testimonials be truthful. However, if someone declares that he prefers "Brand X," validation of this statement is necessarily subjective. Adequate consumer protection requires more stringent regulations which should extend into evidence of truthfulness of this testimonial and disclosure as to the way in which it was secured. It is suggested that in using a testimonial no substitute attestors be allowed; and if payment has been made for the endorsement, the advertisement should so state. If evidence is available that the individual does not use the product (such as a cigar recommendation by a non-cigar smoker), his testimonial should not be permitted.

SUMMARY

In its efforts to protect the consumer against advertising abuse, the Federal Trade Commission has developed a protective network in the consumer interest primarily based on economic standards. There are gaps in this protection network, which result from the fact that the consumer does not appraise his interest solely in economic terms. Rather, the consumer develops patterns of buying behavior that reflect the influence of noneconomic values and the individual's cognitive capacity. The Federal Trade Commission should take cognizance of this "behavioral" man in its consumer interest activities.

It is recommended that the Commission become more familiar with and establish closer contact with the consumer through a Bureau of Behavioral Research, consumer complaint offices, and through the distribution of consumer publications to disclose advertising irregularities. In addition, it is recommended that the Commission adapt regulatory criteria to current knowledge of the behavioral man in order to assure that federal regulation of advertising is accurately functioning in the consumer interest.

Does a conflict arise when a firm attempts to maintain its profitable market position while it is striving to be socially responsible? The author cites the need for a strong market system, coupled with an adequate competitive position. He sees these as necessary prerequisites for the establishment of an effective long-term social involvement.

---

28. BUSINESS RESPONSIBILITY TOWARD THE MARKET*

E. T. Grether†

In recent years, there has been a rising crescendo of discussions of the social responsibility of business in general and, particularly, of large corporations. Currently, the combination of social, economic, and political problems and of crises at home and abroad has increased both the tempo of the discussions and the urgencies of the demands upon business leadership. Obviously, such discussions are of high significance because of the important roles of business in general and, especially, of great corporations in our society. Throughout the polemics, there is, on the one hand, a continuing drumbeat of criticism of business leadership for its failure of adequate response to the needs of our times, i.e., for being too parochial, self-serving, and narrow in its outlook and in its drive for profits, growth, and security. On the other hand, there is both a rising recognition and exhortation that "it has become imperative for business to undertake social responsibilities on a major scale."[1]

* Reprinted from "Business Responsibility toward the Market," *California Management Review* (Fall 1969), pp. 33–42.

† University of California, Berkeley.

[1] William C. Stolk, chairman of the Committee for Economic Development, at the annual meeting of the National Association of Business Economists, *Management Review,* 57 (December 1968), p. 43.

Business and the social system

Any given enterprise, small or large, so it is stated also, should see itself as a subsystem or series of subsystems imbedded in the total social system.[2] In order to plan properly in its own interests, but especially in the interests of society as a whole, business management should develop the interests and capacity and background to think in a grand, total social systems framework. That is to say, business managers must in a sense become philosopher-leaders in order to make their long-range planning and short-run operations truly relevant, meaningful, and socially acceptable.

I agree, of course, that everyone in our society, including business executives of great corporations, should explicitly, if possible, and at least intuitively, think and react in relation to the broader totality of social forces and relations. This is another way of saying that we should behave rationally and try to think logically, try to see both the parts and the whole, and, especially, try to see the parts functioning in the whole.

During the war, when repairmen were scarce, a philosophy professor colleague of mine at the University proved to his wife's satisfaction and surprise that this type of thinking even has a payoff around the house. Their washing machine had broken down; the repairman, located after a long search, lacked competence for the job of repair. So the philosopher, observing this failure, excused himself, went to his study, and put his head in his hands, and thought about the machine as a system. In a few minutes, he returned and told the repairman what to do to make the machine operational again. Last summer at our lake place, when the motor in our boat failed, a neighbor, who is a self-taught mechanic, after two hours of tinkering, got things working again. I observed that, as he removed and adjusted parts, he kept saying to himself, "Now, what is the philosophy of this?" He was thinking and tinkering in a systems sense.

But thinking logically about the closed mechanical systems of household washers or motorboats is immeasurably and, in fact, inconceivably different than trying to do the same thing for our open, modern society as a whole. Regardless of the quality of the intellect, or the breadth of background, the results will be enormously influenced by the vantage point and the *Weltanchauung* and biases of the thinker, despite all pretenses to the contrary. Usually, the thinker must either try to strip off the complexities of reality by exposing only a few selected elements or basic processes or a skeletal framework, or start from a given nexus and move out into the complex relationships and go merely as far as he is able. For most persons, the penetration into the complexities of

[2] See, e.g., D. Votaw and S. P. Sethi in *CMR* (Fall 1969).

the total system will be very superficial except, perhaps, intuitively. On the contrary, a great, diversified corporation has an extraordinarily wide number of nexuses into these complex relationships.

As my colleague, C. West Churchman, has remarked, however, "There is bound to be deception in any approach to the system" and to the solution of systems problems. Even so, I agree with Churchman that, while we are both deceiving and perceiving, "we have to maintain the contradiction, or else we allow ourselves to be overwhelmed by the consistent."[3] There is nothing in the constitutional protections of our democratic society that would guarantee full consistency; on the contrary, our democratic federal system with its mechanism of checks and balances and combinations of centralization and decentralization in decision making both allows and makes for some inconsistencies.[4] The same observation applies to the functioning of our economy and society in general.

To state this is not to be antiintellectual or antirational, but merely realistic and pragmatic. We must all do the best we can; regardless of our limitations and failures, we must continue to seek rational solutions and to relate to a broader play of forces than that of our own situation or intuition, even if we cannot understand the play. But it is important to always have a defensible base from which to relate to broader social functioning, especially in endeavors to influence social values and goals. It is suggested here that the appropriate base for business enterprises to enter the grand arena of society and social responsibility is through the market system.

Business and the market system

The initial and typically major normal responsibility of business, especially in terms of its legitimacy, is to perform acceptably as an efficient business enterprise in production, manufacturing, marketing, the provision of services, and so on. In this country, with our private property base and freedom of choice in production, selling and buying, and the requirement of competitive regulation and discipline ("the rule of competition"), it is of utmost importance to maintain an acceptably effective general market system with its myriads of subsystems. This general system and its subsystems are the coordinating and responsive mechanisms for the host of private, decentralized choices, preferences, and decisions. The competitive market system in our society is the social alternative to an enormously complex, centralized state or other bureaucracy.

[3] C. West Churchman, *The Systems Approach* (New York: Delacorte Press, 1968), p. 229. Churchman also notes that the management scientist in his models "forgets many things: basic human values and his own inability really to understand all aspects of the system, and especially its politics." (p. 228).

[4] E. T. Grether, "Consistency in Public Economic Policy with Respect to Private Unregulated Industries," *American Economic Review*, 63: 2 (May 1963).

The general market system and its subsystems represents an incredibly complex set of relationships—so much so, that economists in order to try to explain and interpret these complexities have developed formal models in highly simplified terms. Only under the extreme assumptions of static, general equilibrium are certain hypothetical workings and performance results disclosed. Everyone, of course, recognizes that real world conditions depart widely from the assumptions of static, general equilibrium. The primary value of the hypothetical static systems is to isolate basic or fundamental forces and performance results for the purposes of very general economic policy and appraisal. Actually, the standards so developed may be misleading and harmful if they depart too largely from achievable performance. Currently, very exciting experiments are under way with computerized models. An enormous vista may be in process of being disclosed in terms of more realistic, complex analyses and, hence, achievement.

All societies, socialist, communist, or capitalist, use market mechanisms to some extent, but in our society a viably acceptable general market system is mandatory for the majority of economic decisions, unless we wish to give up democratic, decentralized free choices among genuine alternatives and replace market discipline by direct governmental regulation or operation. A substantial proportion of our economic activity is now performed entirely or partially outside the market system, and the remainder is under continuing public and private constraints and adjustments, subsidy and subsidy-like differential treatment, or public utility or quasi-public utility regulation. Consequently, a strong view has appeared and is widely accepted that the market is dead, or at least so near its demise that it is necessary now to appraise the performance of business enterprises through tests of social performance instead of or in addition to the price, cost, profit, and efficiency tests of the competitive market.[5]

This view is especially strong on the part of those who look at our economic society in terms of the economic position and functioning of great mature corporations—AT&T, General Motors, Du Pont, General Electric, and IBM. The viewers are so impressed by the economic and market power, continuing growth and stability, and earnings of such giants that all else in economic society falls sharply away and only the high peaks stand out against the skyline. The viewers from below see only these peaks and their massive height and not the two thirds to three fourths of the varied land mass above which the peaks stand. The viewers, also, tend to see only the highest peaks and not the more numerous foothills, often in widely different economic and market situations.

[5] See, esp., John K. Galbraith, *The New Industrial State* (Boston: Houghton Mifflin, 1967), and A. A. Berle, *The American Economic Republic* (New York: Harcourt, Brace, & World, 1963).

But the great corporations are not the totality of our economic society. Within the group of the largest 50, 100, or 500, there are enormous variations in economic and market power, earnings, and the degree to which the compulsions of the market are immediately effective. Contrast, for example, great railroad and steel companies with IBM and the other enterprises in the computer industry, soon to be the largest industry in this country.

All business enterprises and especially the giants should be expected first to test and demonstrate their legitimacy in terms of effective, intelligent participation in the competitive market system. A grasp of the nature and functioning of the enormously complex interrelations of the market system is the most appropriate base for business management to view the incomprehensibly more complex relations and values of the total social system. Understanding the multiple relationships of the enterprise in the functioning of the market system as a whole in itself thoroughly tests analytical mettle and ability and willingness to think broadly and greatly. Unfortunately, we cannot simply assume in general that an "invisible hand" will guide free choices and free responses in the manner allegedly posited by Adam Smith. It is worth noting, too, that this expression in Adam Smith was not, in fact, given the same role in *The Wealth of Nations* as appears from the accumulative impacts of the commentaries over the years. Furthermore, it is not generally known that Adam Smith spoke also of the "great society."[6]

MULTIPLE RELATIONSHIPS

Market structure analysis

It is entirely feasible for business, no matter how small or how large, to analyze systematically its nexus or the numerous multiple linkages with the market system and subsystems. Usually, the best initial approach is through a so-called market structure analysis, which is in the direct line of descent from the partial equilibrium (industry) analysis

[6] The reference to "an invisible hand" appeared in a discussion of the use of capital in the support of domestic industry as follows: "By preferring the support of domestic to that of foreign industry . . . he intends only his own gain, and he is in this, *as in many other cases,* led by an invisible hand to promote an end which was no part of his intention" (italics added). *The Wealth of Nations,* Bk. IV, chap. 2.

The reference to "a great society" is as follows: "The third and last duty of the sovereign or commonwealth is that of erecting and maintaining those public institutions and those public works, which, though they may be in the highest degree advantageous to a *great society,* are, however, of such a nature that the profit could never repay the expense to any individual or small number of individuals, and which it, therefore, cannot be expected that any individual or small number of individuals should erect or maintain" (italics added). *Ibid.,* Bk. V, chap. 1, pt. III.

of classical and neoclassical economics. Under this approach, the market structure of each product, product line, department, division, subsidiary, or what not, is first analyzed separately.

As the label suggests, market structure analysis begins with the definition and delimitation of a market—product-wise or area-wise, usually both. In its most elementary use, it examines chiefly the number and size distribution (market share and concentration) of both sellers and buyers, the conditions of entry into the market, actual or potential, in relation to the basic demand and production characteristics of the products. The analysis of the actual and potential conditions of entry leads into a detailed examination of the technology of production and nature of marketing organization, including channels (vertical structures) of marketing. The analysis of the demand factors or setting includes not only the amount of demand, but its growth and expansibility and the cross-elasticity of demand among competitors. Highlighted always is the character and importance of product innovation and differentiation. Strong product differentiation at any given time represents a barrier to entry and is considered by some scholars to represent the most important single class of barriers.[7]

In all market structure analysis, unique special factors are isolated in addition to the standard ones involved in every search. A complication, especially in relation to large, powerful organizations, is that market structure and market conduct (policy and decision making) interact. Only in the simple models of pure and perfect competition is there a simple, direct, linear, predictable relationship between structure, conduct, and performance. In more complex situations, especially in competition among the few (oligopoly), it must be assumed that the price, product, market organization, market channel, selling, and so on, policies of one firm become the action parameters for other firms. It must be assumed, too, in the dynamics of market competition that these action parameters will be under constant adjustment in the moves and responses, aggressive and defensive, of the market competitors. Consequently, the proper interpretation of competition requires both cross-sectional, structural portrayals and trend studies.

In all cases, of course, the basic production technologies and demand factors provide a framework and setting for the analysis and interpretation of the play, or the strategy and tactics. Market structure analysis in economic analysis is an endeavor to bring to bear the realistic elements, dimensions, and action parameters of actual markets in the endeavor to explain, predict, and appraise behavior and performance. The primary focus and interest of economic analysis is on performance; there is no reason, however, why the focus for a business firm should not also be upon its own policy and decision making. In economic analysis,

[7] See, esp, J. S. Bain, *Barriers to New Competition* (Cambridge, Mass.: Harvard University Press, 1956, 1965).

the degree of concentration and of actual and potential entry rank high for purposes of interpreting performance results. For business policy and decision making, these dimensions or elements would be given very specific formulations and would be supported by the analysis of multiple action parameters.

Market structure analysis is often relatively simple for small, local, or regional enterprises, or even for national enterprises (as tire and beer manufacturers) with only one or a few clearly definable, well-established products. It becomes much more complicated for large, diversified enterprises operating in national and multinational markets. But in these complex cases, it is feasible and should, in fact, be an essential tool under the present legal system and economic climate both for internal operating purposes and for longer range planning. In fact, such analysis is almost mandatory now for compliance with antitrust enforcement. In recent years, antitrust cases have increasingly involved issues of market structure and of structural adjustments. There appears to be a definite shift away merely from regulation in terms of the abuse of market power to an endeavor to affect, also, the structural sources of such power, especially in merger cases under revised Section 7 of the Clayton Act.[8]

A very significant by-product of market structure analysis is the disclosure of the variety of competitive expressions. Frequently, the structures of local and regional markets are highly diverse; hence, there is no single, simple, homogeneous national market. The character of the competition, the number and market share of competitors, the nature of competitive interactions, and so on, usually tend to vary among geographical areas. Rarely does a national firm enjoy the same market share or position uniformly throughout the United States or abroad. Obviously, marketing policies must be able to adjust flexibly in relation to geographical variations—a most difficult problem sometimes for national firms nowadays under a contradictory variety of federal and state regulations.

THE CONGLOMERATES

Synergism

Another by-product of market structure analysis can be the analysis of the synergistic effects. The problem is to measure or at least to interpret the degree to which various products and product lines, or functional activities, or units of operation under one banner aid or strengthen

[8] For an excellent rationalization of this approach, see C. Kaysen and D. F. Turner, *Antitrust Policy: An Economic and Legal Analysis* (Cambridge, Mass.: Harvard University Press, 1959). For a summary of cases to 1967, see J. F. Brodley, "Oligopoly Power Under the Sherman and Clayton Acts—From Economic Theory to Legal Policy," *Stanford Law Review*, XVIX:2 (January 1967), pp. 287–366.

each other through joint economies, shared expertise, picking up organizational slack, backward vertical integration, use of common marketing channels and enterprise and trademark goodwill, and so on. The absence of synergism suggests that the corporation is merely a holding company for discrete units or an investment operation justified only by the acquisition of bargains or for achieving tax advantages, or a device for the improvement of the consolidated price/earnings ratio for stock market purposes through the acquisition of enterprises with lower P/E ratios. Undoubtedly, the most solid, successful organizations involve a balanced combination of investment, competitive market, and synergistic benefits, whether in growth by internal expansion or through acquisition and merger. Very likely, the recent decline in stock market valuations of some conglomerates reflects their weakness in generating substantial synergistic effects.

Market structure analysis, hence, is particularly important for the increasingly diversified and conglomerate enterprises. On the one hand, it will provide the setting for appraising competitive functioning, product by product, subsidiary by subsidiary, division by division, and so forth. Even more important, it would indicate how and to what extent these performance results are affected by the interrelations and interdependencies as between products and administrative units, horizontally or vertically, within the organization.

It is of highest importance from a general economic point of view to know whether resources as allocated within a corporation are being used efficiently. A sizable proportion of economic resources now is allocated either directly by government or from within the internal resources of corporations, and not through the market. It is important from a social standpoint to know whether such allocations are equivalent to competitive market allocations. Usually, the best evidences are the competitive alternatives for use which can often be measured by using market prices for internal transfer pricing and accounting. The conglomerates will perform most usefully if they become vehicles for increasing the use of resources in the areas of higher profit and, hence, for shifting resources from areas of lesser effective to more effective application. It is likely that focus upon the short-run price/earnings ratios for stock market purposes may produce just the opposite results. As yet, no one can speak with full assurance.

COMPLEXITY OF STRUCTURE

Classical models inadequate

Although, as noted, market structure analysis is in the direct line of descent from neoclassical, partial (industry) equilibrium analysis, it must break out of the confines of this intellectual format. Classical models were conceptualized in terms of homogeneous staple products and large numbers of market participants with price as the central equilibrator of the supply and demand forces. Nowadays, in many fields especially outside the staples, it is essential to think of the totality of interacting competitive variables or action parameters and, often, of small numbers of sellers and buyers or of highly mixed situations. It is essential, also, to think in terms of rapidly moving technologies throwing off a continuing stream of new ideas, new products and processes, and cost-reducing procedures. Consequently, at a given time, a single or simple price factor is no longer the only or perhaps even chief action parameter. Instead, a large number of variables or action parameters are in processes of interaction in the moves and responses of enterprises. Consequently, too, the bands in the spectrum between the poles of monopoly and competition and, especially, in competition among the few, rather than the many, become the focus points of much competitive analysis.

The wide prevalence of oligopoly, and the simple presumption in much of economic theory, and in public policy, that market concentration reduces the effectiveness of the use of resources while making for higher prices, has probably done more than anything else to focus attention upon market structures. But answers cannot usually be found from the theoretical results of simple formal models.[9] Furthermore, unlike the classical model of partial equilibrium, it will not always be possible, in fact, to relate the firm and all of its products directly to the definable industry or industries en route to the total market system; although, more often than not, it is likely this can be done, at least loosely. This is not to say that competition is not present as an effective force, but merely that the force cannot be estimated through a simple classical-industry model. Recently, I sat with a group of financial analysts in discussions of enterprises in the fields of high and rapidly moving technology. Even though firms and their highly innovative products, including unexpected by-products, often could not be classified clearly into a known industry or product categories, there was always specific awareness of at least several active or potential competitors. Frequently it is essential to envisage competition in much more elusive, but no less effective, guises than the simple industry price models of classical competition and the simple definition of the relevant market of orthodox antitrust.

CONTRAINDICATIONS

Now, it may be stated in rejoinder that my proposal is either (1) too difficult for useful application, or (2) is being done already by

[9] See N. R. Collins and L. E. Preston, *Concentration and Price-Cost Margins in Manufacturing Industries* (Berkeley: University of California Press, 1968) for a summary of previous empirical work and for the most recent extension of cross-sectional empirical analysis.

all large, successful corporations with professional staffs, including economists, either overtly or by intuitive judgment. As to the first charge, usually market structure analysis is not excessively difficult or onerous, and it is all the more necessary when it appears tenuous or almost impossible, or when it must be adapted because a product market is not clearly definable. In some, perhaps a high proportion, of instances in which a clear-cut industry–market structure is not definable, it will, however, be possible to discover the competitors, actual or potential, perhaps outside the recognized industry, if there is one. This type of adaptation is becoming increasingly important in antitrust enforcement. And, as to the second charge, it is earnestly suggested that intuitive judgments be replaced, or checked, or sharpened by explicit frameworks and tools of analysis and, above all, that the results of such an analysis be used to demonstrate the multivariate nature of complex competitive functioning in many situations, especially under rapidly changing technologies.

THE USES OF MARKET POWER

The great corporation and the market

But suppose that market structure analysis discloses that the enterprise is the beneficiary of a series of interrelated areas of such high market power, so well protected as to be almost free of the market, or at least from the type of competitive pressure that would force price reductions with their general benefits to buyers and to the community. This, of course, is the Galbraithian view concerning the present position of the great mature American corporation. In such a situation, if it ever really exists over an extended period of time in the form stated, the responsible parties in the leadership of the corporation, as a manifestation of their broader social responsibility, would hopefully still cast their lot with the national economic policy of competition, even though it might sometimes call for structural or policy adjustments in order to enhance competitive compulsions. In other words, the corporation would declare its basic allegiance to a national antitrust enforcement program or, if you wish, its loyalty to the market and competitive market system.

It needs to be noted that this is a problem only of the stance of large, powerful corporations and not of the mass of small enterprises whose chief means of subverting the market—collusion—is clearly taboo. It is of interest, however, to the small and weak because they too hope to grow big and powerful and not find their way barred by the vested, excessive market power or exclusionary, restrictive policies of those who have arrived. There should be genuine, independent alternatives for choices for buyers at all levels and in all situations, under acceptably effective competition.

A thoroughgoing market structure analysis would also provide a basis for measurable, or at least judgmental, interpretation of economies of scale or other synergistic effects, in addition to the enhancement or maintenance of market power. All experience to date in public policy suggests that significant economies of scale would usually be protected in order to preserve efficiencies and economies. If, under given circumstances, competition is not deemed to provide and cannot be expected to provide adequate discipline, it might be socially desirable to create a special form of regulation, perhaps even quasi-public utility status.[10] It would seem preferable in almost all cases, if at all feasible without sacrificing important economies of scale, to make structural or policy adjustments in order to enhance competition, both from the point of view of the enterprise and of society. The market system could become balkanized by a series of areas of special jurisprudence or partial removal from the system.

AN OPEN SYSTEM

It is likely, however, that some large corporations would prefer other alternatives to structural or policy adjustments, including the French-type close working relations between Big Government and Big Business as dominant bureaucratic oligarchies. In a sense, this is the wide door that Galbraith holds open for business; although he is not too explicit, it seems clear that big business would inevitably become absorbed within the governmental apparatus and sanctions. Its performance would be judged in terms of social performance standards established by government and not by market. Gradually, perhaps imperceptibly, but surely, the corporations would be transformed into bureaucratic arms of the government to provide goods and services as required. It would be only a short and, perhaps, meaningless step to direct governmental operation, or at least partial ownership by the state, as in some European countries.

Envisage, in contrast, the alternative of participation under an effective, open, competitive market system in which competitive discipline and functioning, except during times of great emergency and crisis, is protected, nurtured, and recognized as paramount by both business and government. Efficiency in the competitive production and marketing of goods and services and in serving the free choices of consumers and other buyers would be the initial, and usually the primary, test of acceptable social participation and performance.

[10] Gardiner C. Means, who for many years has stressed (1) the separation of ownership and control in modern big business and (2) administered pricing, has proposed a new category of "collective enterprises" under special legislation midway between the private enterprise and public utility categories; *Pricing Power and the Public Interest: A Study Based on Steel* (New York: Harper and Brothers, 1962).

Corporations, however, would be subject to changes in social values, for these would be influential throughout the open flexible market system, in the preferences and choices of buyers at all levels. Corporations themselves, of course, would be influencing these social values and their impacts in the great system of interrelationships. It is contended by some, of course, that this is the most critical issue of all because of the dominance of large corporations and their alleged management of demand, and their impacts upon social values through both an overemphasis on goods as such and upon the wrong goods. "Our imbalance . . . threatens us with a society where comforts accumulate while human potentialities decay."[11]

Insofar as this social judgment has merit, it would seem preferable to place regulatory constraints on production and marketing and sales promotion rather than to bring corporations directly into the governmental complex. But in the use of such controls, governmental authorities must be able to distinguish clearly between regulations that merely constrain, or mold, but do not subvert or destroy competitive expressions. A most sensitive area is that of "puffing" competitive wares. There is already an abundant number of actual and potential controls over clear-cut misrepresentation and falsehood, but there is often an uneasy line of distinction between explicit deceit and falsehood and the impressions created by legal puffing. When health and safety or other specific injuries are at stake, it should be preferable to provide or adjust or strictly enforce existing regulations or their common-law interpretations, rather than to subvert or replace competition.

BUSINESS ATTITUDES

Resisting social change versus creative participation

There is always the possibility that large and powerful corporations will use a portion of their resources to resist social and political change because of strong and, perhaps, mistaken preferences for the status quo. For years, the public image, rightly or wrongly, of the National Association of Manufacturers was of this sort. This type of stance, often in the name of the maintenance of capitalism or free enterprise, is easily interpreted as a shirking of social responsibility or of standing in the way of progress. It must be recognized, too, that an expression of clear-cut fealty for an effectively competitive market system could be so interpreted and believed to be merely another guise for the defense of the status quo. Hence, it is of utmost importance that the pro-competitive stance be clearly understood and interpreted in relation to national anti-trust policy and our changing social values.

[11] R. T. Averitt, "American Business: Achievement and Challenge," *Daedalus* (Winter 1967), p. 74.

Consequently, too, the pro-competition stance should be supported by the appropriate evidences in general, and in particular situations, of recognition of public and social interests and responsibility beyond the specific, narrow business confines of an individual firm and of effective participation under the competitive market system. The simplest and most direct opportunities for participating in social programs and for demonstrating social responsibility occur in the case of industries and firms whose operations inherently create social hazards or undesirable environmental changes, but where control or solution usually requires group action and/or public intervention and regulation. Obvious examples are stream and water pollution, air pollution, the effects of the use of pesticides, and highway safety. All involved members of the business community should be crying with one voice and far in advance of crisis demands for careful study and appropriate, private and federal, state, or local action in such areas.

Recently, a national magazine reported that Missoula, Montana, in its lovely, natural setting at the confluence of rivers and valleys, had become the No. 2 air pollution center of the United States. Regardless of the truth of this allegation, it would seem that the Missoula forest product enterprises and local and state authorities should have long since foreseen this emerging problem and have taken the appropriate private and public remedial actions. In situations in which a single firm is dominant in a community, this conclusion is even more pertinent and obvious. In fact, in some instances, business firms should be and often are more farsighted and socially responsible than the chambers of commerce or industrial development associations that try to lure them to a given location. Of course, in these situations, the local community gains often are so high, since the local plant is a source of tax revenue to provide lush support for local community facilities, employment, and benefits to owners of scarce resources, especially land, that there is a tendency to disregard possible community liabilities.

Similarly, businesses have a vital stake in education at all levels, in crime prevention and law enforcement, in the employment of minorities and of handicapped persons, in effective urban transportation, in the alleviation of poverty and the maintenance of a high level of employment and of prosperity, and so on. In these and other instances, the business stance at the very least should involve the encouragement of study programs and recommendations for action rather than resistance or lagging behind.

PRIMARY RESPONSIBILITY

Summary observations

Of course, business enterprises, large and small, should have a high sense of social responsibility and awareness. But their initial and primary responsibility is to produce and distribute goods and services efficiently in competition, taking full advantage of advancing technologies. Most small or medium-sized enterprisers are no better qualified and, in fact, may have weaker qualifications for social and political leadership than other members of the community. Years ago, when I was making some business trend studies in San Francisco, a small jobber remarked, "Well, I guess this sort of thing is O.K. for you, but I am so busy just keeping going day by day that I haven't time for it."

The state of affairs of great corporations with competent, professional staffs, public relations counsel, lobbyists, short- and long-range planning, and so on, of course, is entirely different. But, even in these instances, the initial and primary responsibility is competitive efficiency in providing goods and services and in the organization and use of resources. The ready-made vehicle for proving the case is acceptable competitive performance in offering genuine, independent alternatives for choice in competitive markets. Hence, private enterprises, large and small, should, above all, attempt to understand the workings of and give full support to the competitive market system. From this basis and through the multiple linkages into the general market system, individual enterprises can or should delineate first the areas and issues of direct responsibility arising of their own activities. When the activities of business enterprises directly help create an economic or social problem, as air or water pollution, or environmental change, they have a very direct responsibility and opportunity to participate in efforts at solution. The solution sometimes may even have a profit payoff as in the case of petroleum refineries now able to recover hydrogen sulfide and ammonium for commercial products instead of sending them up the stacks into the air.

THE PROPER PERSPECTIVE

Rarely, however, can a single firm alone, even a General Motors, provide an appropriate, general solution. This observation is even more true of issues of broad, social concern such as the alleviation of poverty, the employment of minorities, providing education for all, and the multiple facets of the urban and population crises. In these instances, the proper stance should be to support and participate in bona fide objective studies, governmental hearings, and other worthwhile efforts to find solutions. Many business firms, of course, have done this and are doing so through programs of research and of study as under the aegis of the Committee for Economic Development, the National Industrial Conference Board, the National Bureau of Economic Research, the Brookings Institution, and innumerable research grants to universities and other research agencies. Above all, business and especially great corporations can no longer afford to be considered merely as defenders of the status quo and protectors of their own vested interests. Daring, imaginative leapfrogging into the future with all its risks is greatly to be preferred. Undoubtedly, too, the solution of social problems will provide enormous business opportunities directly, or under governmental incentive programs.[12]

But it is equally important for all other participants in our democratic society to see and appraise business and business responsibilities in proper perspective. There is a risk that criticisms of business and insistent cries for greater social responsibility and leadership may produce inappropriate political reactions. It is becoming increasingly evident that, in the foreseeable future, we shall have inordinate and increasing needs in this country, and even more so in other countries, for the efficient and enlarging production of the supply of goods and services. Public and private needs, especially for services, now far surpass our abilities to fulfill them—despite the views to the contrary. It could be calamitous if we inhibited our technological know-how and drives in the face of such insistent demands. It is of utmost importance for us to enhance, not weaken, our productive capacities and, insofar as is feasible and reasonable, direct our technological drives toward the areas of enormous social needs, including educational and health facilities and services.

CONCLUSIONS

Business enterprises, including great corporations, meet the test, both of social performance and of competitive market performance, when they first fulfill the requirements of the open competitive market system. From this basis of performance and the comprehension of these broad interrelations, business can and should participate with government, labor, education, and all other elements of our society in the search for better political and social solutions, but without arrogating to itself the exact nature and direction of social action. Inevitably, large, diversified national and multinational corporations interlinked so broadly and deeply at so many levels carry very heavy social responsibilities. They, above all, must be solidly based, however, in the efficient, competitive production of wanted goods and services. From this base, they have innumerable vantage points and linkages for broad, creative social interpretation and participation in efforts at solution and amelioration.

Private and public policies and interactions along the lines prepared here do not require a sharp break with the past or departure from the most basic tenets of our form of society. Likewise, their orientation is so pragmatic in terms of the general social systems framework as

[12] As I write these words on March 8, 1969, I note a story in today's San Francisco *Chronicle* about an experimental teaching program at the junior high level in which computer hardware is used. According to the story, "the curriculum is written, planned, and supervised by Lockheed Corporation of Sunnyvale, which believes that a systems approach to learning works."

to protect both from (1) becoming lost in the mists of metaphysical, social ideologies, and from (2) excessive expectations as to what individual enterprises alone can accomplish even with the utmost goodwill and desire. Inevitably, there must be broad participation with government and in community programs.

Consumer protection is a sort of tripod affair, involving business, government, and the public. If business is to keep the tripod in balance, self-regulation must grow accordingly. What are the limitations of government and business in consumer protection efforts? Can industry self regulation effectively deal with social issues?

---

29. CONSUMER PROTECTION VIA SELF-REGULATION*

Louis L. Stern†

Consumerism, like marketing, is becoming a broadened concept.[1] It encompasses "health services, public utilities, transportation, and automobile safety, and urging consumer representation, consumer education, and antipoverty programs."[2] The new consumerism includes concern for distortions and inequities in the economic environment and the declining quality of the physical environment.[3] Mary Gardiner Jones expressed it this way:

> What is new today about consumerism is the fact that consumers' concerns today are much more directly focused on the human values and environmental considerations involved in today's economic decisions than they are on the

* Reprinted from "Consumer Protection via Self-Regulation," *Journal of Marketing*, Vol. 35 (July 1971), pp. 47–53.

† Wayne State University.

[1] Philip Kotler and Sidney J. Levy, "Broadening the Concept of Marketing," *Journal of Marketing*, Vol. 33 (January 1969), pp. 10–15.

[2] National Goals Research Staff, *Toward Balanced Growth: Quantity with Quality* (Washington, D.C.: U.S. Government Printing Office, 1970), p. 133.

[3] George S. Day and David Aaker, "A Guide to Consumerism," *Journal of Marketing*, Vol. 34 (July 1970), pp. 12–19.

more strictly "economic" problems of obtaining the highest quality goods at the lowest possible price.[4]

Accordingly, it has been suggested that during the 1970s the Federal Trade Commission (F.T.C.) will "by an imaginative, vigorous interpretation of this broad language (Section 5 of the F.T.C. Act) take cognizance of every type of business practice which offends the current social mores."[5]

It is generally agreed that consumerism is here to stay. This is the implicit assumption or explicit conclusion of the business community. In the words of the Chamber of Commerce of the United States,

> But whatever the causes, it is of paramount importance to recognize that the consumer movement is well established and is likely to gain strength in coming years.[6]

Therefore, attention is now turning toward various forms of response to the consumer movement. Indicative of this direction is the creation of the Consumer Research Institute by the business community to objectively study consumer problems and evaluate alternative responses. Listed below are examples of questions that are being raised concerning organization, techniques, and policies:

1. Is it socially wiser to accept the present state of consumer dissatisfaction than to pay the cost of reducing consumer dissatisfaction?
2. Can industry reform itself without government pressure?
3. Which is likely to be most effective and economical, Better Business Bureaus, trade association complaint bureaus, or corporate divisions of consumer affairs?
4. Should consumers be encouraged toward self-protection through class action suits?
5. Can public policies be market tested?
6. What is the best positioning of consumer representation?
7. Can consumer education suffice to eliminate market abuse?

The following basic issue underlies these questions: What should be the role of private versus government effort to protect consumers? Buskirk and Rothe stated that, "The relative role the government will play, and that which industry should play, is a critical aspect in the resolution of the consumerism issue."[7]

---

[4] Address by Mary Gardiner Jones, Federal Trade Commissioner, before the Manufacturing Chemists Association, New York, November 25, 1969.

[5] Address by Joseph Martin, Jr., General Counsel, Federal Trade Commission, at a conference sponsored by California Business Seminars, Inc., Los Angeles, California, September 23, 1970.

[6] Chamber of Commerce of the United States, Council on Trends and Perspective, *Business and the Consumer—A Program for the Seventies* (Washington, D.C.: Chamber of Commerce of the United States, 1970), p. 10.

[7] Richard H. Buskirk and James T. Rothe, "Consumerism—An Interpretation," *Journal of Marketing*, Vol. 34 (October 1975), p. 63.

Because consumer issues will be attended to in one way or another, government versus private regulation is a vital subject. This article addresses itself to that subject. It examines the difficulties of private and public regulation and suggests means of improving both. It interprets consumer interests in the broad manner indicated above.

GOVERNMENT REGULATION

There are several objections to government regulation. One objection is that it may lead to further and repressive regulation. Regulations seldom fade away; instead, they proliferate. As each refinement or clarification comes into force, business ingenuity probes to discover the minimum requirements necessary for compliance. Then new regulations are formed to close the loopholes which have been found. The process continues with additional and ever more confining rules until innovation is choked and business operating costs are increased. In short, government regulation tends to become progressively intrusive and destructive of incentive.

A second objection to government regulation concerns lack of uniformity of application. Differences from case to case in interpretation of regulations may appear inexplicable and inequitable. Perhaps worst of all, they are unpredictable. On the other hand, uniform application of regulations without consideration of individual circumstances also raises objections, especially from small firms.

Regulations are sometimes unevenly enforced. Because the F.T.C. and the Department of Justice have limited resources, they cannot hope to prosecute all violators of the law. The F.T.C., which is the principal government agency concerned with consumer protection, receives a small budget ($19.5 million in 1970)[8] in comparison to the job it faces. Moreover, the size of its staff is decreasing relative to the size of the U.S. economy. Merely to keep pace with the growth of disposable personal income since 1962, the F.T.C. would have needed a staff of 2,000 people by 1970 compared to the 1,270 people it actually had.[9] In addition, the F.T.C. has assumed new responsibilities under the Fair Packaging and Labeling Act (1966) and the Consumer Credit Protection Act (1968). The relatively few F.T.C. investigators have time to observe only a small proportion of the total number of firms, products, markets, and transactions.

Uneven enforcement is certain to be regarded as unfair if the prosecuted actions were committed in response to competitive necessity. Compound a sense of unfairness with suspicion that government agencies

[8] From an address by Mary Gardiner Jones, Federal Trade Commissioner, before the Sixth Biennial World Conference of the International Organization of Consumer Unions, Baden/Vienna, Austria, June 29, 1970.

[9] Ibid.

are more interested in developing the dark areas of the law than in enforcing the lighted areas equally, and objection to government regulation is to be expected.

A basic objection to government regulation is that the F.T.C. functions as both prosecutor and judge. Since the commissioners direct the thrust of agency effort and authorized the issuance of complaints, it is unrealistic to expect them to rule impartially when the cases are argued.

There are other criticisms that are raised. Regulatory actions often take many years to conclude. Sometimes regulatory action is not initiated until the objectionable behavior has been terminated. In addition, the F.T.C. is charged with lassitude, cronyism, and incompetence; with responding only to business and Congressional pressure groups; failure to aggressively detect consumer abuses; and failure to allocate its energies toward really important issues.[10]

Government regulation is a mixed blessing. It serves to represent public ideals. It serves to clarify, define, and make explicit acceptable and unacceptable norms of conduct. It is simultaneously a last resort and a precipitator of action. In addition, it is insensitive, inept, and burdensome. It is fashioned by compromise and twisted by interpretation.

SELF-REGULATION

Self-regulation is an obvious alternative. It is repeatedly called for by businessmen and government authorities.[11] However, what does experience show? Until the passage of the Fair Labeling and Packaging Act (1966), the food industry did virtually nothing to eliminate package-size proliferation or higher-priced large "economy" sizes. The gasoline industry promoted a wide variety of contests or sweepstakes in some of which the winners were controlled geographically or chronologically.[12] The detergent industry had to be forced into developing biodegradable detergents, then pressured into removing phosphates and enzymes from their products. The automobile industry produces useless

[10] Edward F. Cox, Robert C. Fellmeth, and John E. Schulz, *'The Nader Report' on the Federal Trade Commission* (New York: Richard W. Baron, 1969). See also "The Regulators Can't Go On This Way," *Business Week*, No. 2113 (February 28, 1970), pp. 60–73; and Louis M. Kohlmeier, Jr., *The Regulators; Watchdog Agencies and the Public Interest* (New York: Harper and Row, 1969).

[11] Significant articles in this area include Robert B. Hummer, "Antitrust Problems of Industry Codes of Advertising, Standardization, and Seals of Approval," *Antitrust Bulletin*, Vol. 13 (1968), pp. 607–18; H. Richard Wachtel, "Product Standards and Certification Programs," *Antitrust Bulletin*, Vol. 13 (1968), pp. 1–38; Harvey J. Levin, "The Limits of Self-Regulation," *Columbia Law Review*, Vol. 67 (March 1967), pp. 603–42; and Jerrold G. Van Cise, "Regulation—By Business or Government?" *Harvard Business Review*, Vol. 44 (March-April 1966), pp. 53–63.

[12] See *Investigation of "Preselected Winners" Sweepstakes Promotions*, hearings before the Select Committee on Small Business, House of Representatives, 91st Congress, 1st Session, 1970.

bumpers of variable heights. Sixty percent of the commercial AM and FM radio stations and 35 percent of the commercial television stations do not support the code of the National Association of Broadcasters.[13]

The record is *not* as one-sided as the listing above. If space permitted, an industry-by-industry analysis might be attempted, but value judgments would still be involved. In any event, it is difficult to discover the whole truth of a company for industry situation. Pollution is a case in point. The public relations field has jumped on the antipollution "bandwagon" to such an extent that a substantial credibility gap exists.[14]

Nevertheless, it can be said that many individual companies and various associations have undertaken proconsumer activities. These activities range from the proposal of codes "that acknowledge business responsibility to protect the health and safety of consumers, improve quality standards, simplify warranties, improve repair and servicing quality, self-police fraud and deception, improve information provided consumers, make sound value comparisons easier, and provide effective channels for consumer complaints,"[15] to concrete actions to implement such goals.

But voluntary action is seldom adequate. No matter how willingly some companies may observe voluntary guidelines, there are other companies that must be coerced to observe them. The other companies may not pull an industry to their level of ethics, but neither are they so few, or so insignificant, that they can be ignored. In fact, "It isn't just the fringe operators who are guilty, . . . it is too often the nation's most reputable companies."[16]

Enforceability

To be meaningful, self-regulation must be enforceable and industry-wide. It must punish or prevent violations of regulatory norms. To do so requires collective action in the form of a boycott against the offender (if he refuses to reform). But boycotts in restraint of trade are illegal under the Sherman Act regardless of how meritorious or beneficial the motives or results may be. In fact, the courts are so dogmatic on this point that the Supreme Court of the United States proclaimed:

> Even if copying were an acknowledged tort under the law of every state, that situation would not justify petitioners in combining together to regulate and restrain interestate commerce (in order to prevent copying).[17]

---

[13] Maurine Christopher, "Work Added by New Guidelines Strains NAB Codes' Resources," *Advertising Age* (March 15, 1971), p. 93.

[14] See E. B. Weiss, "Management: Don't Kid the Public with Those Noble Anti-Pollution Ads," *Advertising Age* (August 3, 1970), p. 35; and Stanley E. Cohen, "Anti-Pollution Claims May Prove Pandora Trouble Box for Advertisers," *Advertising Age* (September 14, 1970), p. 110.

[15] National Goals Research Staff, *Toward Balanced Growth: . . .*, p. 143.

[16] "The Editorial Viewpoint," *Advertising Age* (March 30, 1970), p. 14.

[17] *Fashion Guild* v. *F.T.C.*, 312 U.S. 457, 458 (1941).

One cannot help but feel that the Sherman Act needs to be amended by Congress or judicial interpretation to permit meritorious restraints of trade. If amended by Congress, the determination of which restraints are meritorious should be left to the F.T.C. and the courts. The procedure would be to require prior approval and periodic reapproval of proposed restraints by the F.T.C. If, after open hearings, the F.T.C. cannot distinguish between meritorious (from the public's point of view) restraints of trade and self-serving restraints of trade, then surely the restraints are not of much consequence to begin with. If a half-open door policy toward restraints of trade complicates the enforcement task and increases court loads, so be it. That is the price for freeing private energies on behalf of consumer interests. Self-regulation cannot be fully effective without enforcement power.

PRODUCT STANDARDS

One of the most common areas of self-regulation is product standards. Because of recognition of their potential for public gain, several thousand voluntary product standards are now in existence. Product standards may concern safety or healthfulness, size and style variations (thereby reducing production and distribution costs and consumer confusion), or quality or performance. Product standards are least desirable in the latter role since consumer needs and preferences vary the most in this respect and can alternatively be served by mandatory informative labeling.[18]

The principal danger of product standards is that they may slow product improvement and innovation, or deny reasonable product alternatives to consumers. (In addition, producers may tend to manufacture the minimum quality possible consistent with meeting the standard.) These effects, in turn, may restrict market entry and lessen competition, thus protecting the dominant producers and the status quo rather than consumers' interests. On the other hand, even though product standards are formed solely in the consumers' interests, even safety, they cannot be enforced by collective action. For example, an association of gas pipeline companies, gas distributors, and gas appliance manufacturers adopted a seal of approval for appliances. Safety of operation was a primary criterion in granting the seal of approval. Although the case was clouded by the use of additional test criteria and allegedly discriminatory testing procedures, the court's decision centered upon the refusal of the association to supply gas for use in nonapproved appliances. The boycott was declared illegal (if proved to exist) regardless of consumer peril.[19]

---

[18] Louis L. Stern, "Consumer Protection Via Increased Information," *Journal of Marketing*, Vol. 31 (April 1967), pp. 48–52.

[19] *Radiant Burners, Inc.* v. *Peoples Gas Light and Coke Co.*, 364 U.S. 656 (1961).

The law bends over backward, so to speak, to protect competition regardless of the immediate consequence to consumers. Accordingly, voluntary standards are only as effective as the willingness of industry members to accept them and the extent to which consumers rely upon them. Naturally, the least ethical producer is least likely to be bound by a voluntary standard, and the industry is more or less helpless to do anything about it. The best the industry can do in concert is to attempt to persuade buyers to accept only products conforming to the standard and to persuade the government to make the standard mandatory. Members of the industry may unilaterally attempt to force the deviant firm into line, but they run the risk of being accused of implicit agreement in doing so.

Is there a way out of the dilemma of trying to protect consumers in the short-run while preserving the long-run benefits of freedom? In the writer's opinion, the answer is to: (1) provide maximum consumer involvement in the writing of product standards; (2) provide for automatic review of standards at frequent intervals; (3) permit the sale of products not conforming to the standards provided that the nonconforming products are labeled with the relevant standards and the manner and extent to which they do not conform to those standards; and (4) *permit collective action among firms to boycott any firm whose products conform to neither the industry standards nor the labeling requirement.*

Health or safety considerations might require that some standards be conformed to without exception. In most cases, however, the proposed privilege of deviating from product standards would guarantee the right to innovate. It would also enable firms to better serve specialized market segments for which the standards might be inappropriate. The fact that deviations from product standards would have to be prominently labeled would place some products at a competitive disadvantage for the sake of improved market information. However, the extent of the disadvantage would be limited by the merits of the deviation from the standard and the extent to which consumers felt a need for relying upon the standard.

PROMOTIONAL PRACTICES

Promotional practices are of equal or greater importance to consumer welfare than product standards. Hence, as with product standards, self-regulation is both prevalent and contentious, and the issue again becomes the purpose and effectiveness of such self-regulation.

Promotional practices raise questions of (1) amount (waste, competitive barrier, omnipresence); (2) cultural effects (media control, social values, unbalancing of competition between private goods and social goods); (3) function (to inform or only persuade); and (4) taste. Even the basic principle that consumers should not be deceived, though readily agreed upon, is disputed in interpretation. For example, how many readers would agree with various members of the F.T.C. that: (1) it is unfair or deceptive to withhold useful information (such as gasoline octane ratings, automobile mileage per gallon, or product test life); (2) irrelevant or emotional appeals are misleading and deceptive; and (3) promotional claims are deceptive unless proven? Three successive presidents of the United States have proclaimed the right of consumers to be informed, yet manufacturers do not acknowledge and fulfill a corresponding obligation to provide information—certainly not negative information.[20]

Nonperception

Aside from being constrained by the Sherman Act, the difficulty of self-regulation of promotional practices is two-fold: On the one hand is nonperception, and on the other it is nonresponsibility. The first problem is simply a failure to perceive any injustice in questionable practices. For example, a soap manufacturer may distort a competitor's test marketing program. He may arrange with a wholesaler to buy up a sufficient amount of the test product to inflate the sales measurement. Simultaneously, he may adopt the test product advertising theme and begin to implement it nationwide. As a result, the competitor may be falsely encouraged to "go national" with the new product. Since most of the huge introductory promotional expenditures will be incurred at the start of the campaign, a large loss will be sustained before it becomes apparent that the product is failing. If the product does succeed, its success will be minimized and undermined by the preemption of the copy theme. The perception problem is that both companies may regard these occurrences as simple competitive gamesmanship.

Another example of misperception (by buyer and seller) is the claim of price reductions or performance advantage "up to" a stated amount. Advertisers are well aware of the legal requirement to be objectively honest in advertising. Furthermore, it is illegal to make statements which by themselves are true, but which, when taken as a whole, are likely to deceive.[21] Yet literally true "up-to" statements which probably convey the impression that the price-cut or performance-gain to be expected by the buyer is of the "up to" amount are widespread. Whether such statements are deceptive could easily be resolved through appropriate research. It illustrates the potential value of a government-funded insti-

[20] For alternative concepts of information see same references as footnote 2, pp. 139–40.

[21] *Bennett* v. *F.T.C.*, 200 F2d 362; *P. Lorillard Co.* v. *F.T.C.*, 186 F2d 52.

tute to study consumer behavior and the impact of advertising and marketing upon society.[22]

The point is that there are many advertisements and marketing practices in general that are objectionable to many people, but which raise no compunctions among some sellers. Such abuses as the advertisement in poor taste, the unsolicited merchandise, the engineered contest, the shrinkage of package weight, the unsubstantiated claim, and the negative-option sales plan are all defended by sellers who perceive no wrong in them. Their insensitivity may be profit-motivated or philosophical, but in either case it is not conducive to effective self-regulation.

Levitt suggests that a primary reason for businessmen's insensitivity to social responsibility, even though it may be in their long-run interest, is their total commitment to achieving day-to-day profit maximization.[23] The blindness caused by "keeping one's nose to the grindstone" is exacerbated by a steady diet of "chauvinistic pattern" from business journals written according to what their editors think businessmen want to hear. Other observers have suggested that businessmen's nonperception of the social environment is due to the narrow direction of consumer research toward improving product, package, and promotional appeals; in short, their research has been too sales-oriented.[24]

Nonresponsibility

The second aspect of the problem of promotional practices is nonresponsibility; that is, sellers recognize the wrong but accept no responsibility for it. A classic case is beer and soft drinks. With society becoming ever more concerned about waste disposal, these two industries are selling more of their product in nonreturnable glass containers. Thirty-six percent of all glass shipments in 1969[25] were for nonreturnable bottles of beer and soft drinks compared with 7.5 percent of such shipments in 1959.[26] The beverage industries, including liquor and wine, but excluding milk, are responsible for 50 percent of all glass container waste.

When companies are confronted with this abuse of social interest (which is aggravated by consumption of beverages away from home), they reply that they are only serving the public's preference for nonre-

[22] See Dorothy Cohen, "The Federal Trade Commission and the Regulation of Advertising in the Consumer Interest," *Journal of Marketing*, Vol. 33 (January 1969), pp. 40–44; and "Nobody Understands Marketing Economy, Sen. Moss Says; Proposes a New U.S. Institute," *Advertising Age* (February 15, 1971), p. 14.

[23] Theodore Levitt, "Why Business Always Loses," *Harvard Business Review*, Vol. 46 (March-April 1968), pp. 81–89.

[24] For example, see Peter F. Drucker, "The Shame of Marketing," *Marketing/Communications*, Vol. 297 (August 19, 1969), pp. 60–64.

[25] *Modern Packaging Encyclopedia* (New York: McGraw-Hill, Inc., 1970), p. 19.

[26] *Modern Packing Encyclopedia* (New York: McGraw-Hill, Inc., 1961), p. 41.

turnable containers. To their way of thinking, it is the public's responsibility, not theirs. (The cigarette industry uses the same rationale, although additional factors are involved.) Indeed, the responsibility is shared by consumers as individuals and through their governments, however, the first responsibility belongs to the bottlers. Just as producers have a concerted interest relative to consumers in lobbying activities, so, too, producers have concerted responsibilities.

Businessmen who reject the concept of social responsibility may do so in order to maximize profits, or because they feel a lack of mandate from society to take specific actions. That the profit consideration may be declining in importance is indicated by the statement of B. R. Dorsey, president of Gulf Oil Corporation, who declared that " 'maximum financial gain, the historical number one objective' of American business, must move 'into second place whenever it conflicts with the well-being of society.' "[27] The second reason, namely, the lack of public mandate, may also be overcome; that is, a concern for democratic process may be upheld, via attitude research. However, a deeper question remains: Should the attitudes of an ill-informed and untrained public be controlling?

ALTERNATIVES

Although the line between nonperception of wrong and nonacceptance of responsibility may be difficult to distinguish, the absence of effective self-regulation is clear. Why? One reason is that self-regulation is stymied by the Sherman Act barrier against collective use of pressure upon offenders. Only the removal of the legal barrier to enforceable self-regulation will provide the necessary test of whether enforceable self-regulation can obviate the need for more government regulation.

Resistance to the idea of enforceable self-regulation is based upon fear that self-regulation may be perverted to industry benefit at the expense of consumers or prospective competitors. This fear can be allayed by requiring prior F.T.C. approval of proposed regulations and periodic reapproval. Such fear can be further allayed by including a counter balance to the possibility of business or political influence over the F.T.C.'s judgment. This counter balance would include:

1. Separation of the prosecuting and adjudicating functions of the F.T.C., and placing the latter function under a newly established system of trade courts;[28] and

[27] Reported by Alfred L. Malabre, Jr., "The Outlook," *Wall Street Journal* (March 22, 1971), p. 1.

[28] See "F.T.C.'s Elman, in Parting Shot, Advocates 'Radical Structural Reform of Agencies,' " *Wall Street Journal* (August 12, 1970), p. 4.

2. Providing competitors, consumer organizations, and other government agencies the right to seek injunctions from the above trade courts against any form or application of self-regulatory activity which is deemed unfair or socially harmful.

A significantly lesser form of self-regulation would be for trade associations to attempt to prosecute offenses under existing law. This approach might include the initiation of trade practice conferences in order to spotlight questionable activities within the industry and generate trade practice rules or guides. There are three major weaknesses to this approach. First, although the F.T.C. Act broadly prohibits unfair methods of competition and unfair or deceptive acts in commerce, it does not authorize private suits. The Lanham Act does authorize private suits, but applies only to false descriptions or representations in commerce. Second, while Congress could authorize private suits under the F.T.C. Act, neither this Act nor the Lanham Act reaches the potential of enforceable self-regulation for implementing social responsibilities. For example, as currently interpreted, neither law interdicts the sale of hand guns, "high-powered" cars, or telephone solicitation. Third, industries tend to have a "live and let live" attitude. Companies with high ethical standards seldom are inclined to report, much less take action against, the dishonest or offensive members of an industry.

CONCLUSION

The more technology advances, the more deeply will marketing become involved in social issues. The argument that business has no responsibility but to satisfy consumer wants is an open invitation to government regulation. In the short run, consumers to not always fully comprehend the private effects of their wants (witness disbelief of smoking hazards) let alone the social effects (say of D.D.T., nonreturnable containers, or private urban transportation). Nevertheless, reality cannot be denied, and wisdom eventually prevails. When business does not accept social responsibility in fact as well as in survey response,[29] public regulation is eventually forced upon it.

Self-regulation cannot repeal human nature, and a free enterprise system cannot survive without a vigorous profit incentive. On the other hand, neither can a free enterprise system remain healthy if "the responsiveness of a firm to the consumer is directly proportionate to the distance on the organization chart from the consumer to the chairman of the board."[30] What is needed is a greater sensitivity to changing public demands upon business.

[29] See Arthur M. Lewis, "The View from the Pinnacle: What Business Thinks," *Fortune*, Vol. 80 (September 1969), pp. 92–95, and 207–8.

[30] Address by Virginia Knauer, Special Assistant to the President for Consumer Affairs, before the Federal Bar Association, Washington, D.C., September 1970.

In order to harness the potential of self-regulatory effort, the Congress, the F.T.C., and Department of Justice must make enforcement possible when it is clearly in the public interest. However, the opportunity for enforceable self-regulation by no means assures unqualified success for this approach. A continuing threat of increased government regulation will always be necessary to make self-regulation work. Government regulation, in turn, needs consumer advocates to make it function effectively. Hence, consumer protection is a sort of tripod affair. If business is to keep the tripod in balance, self-regulation will have to grow accordingly.

The more educated society becomes, the more interdependent it becomes, and the more discretionary the use of its resources, the more marketing will become enmeshed in social issues. Marketing personnel are at the interface between company and society. In this position they have a responsibility not merely for designing a competitive marketing strategy, but for sensitizing business to the social, as well as the product, demands of society.

Bibliography

1. Beerle, A. A. "Corporations and the Arts," *Saturday Review*, November 4, 1967, p. 35.
2. Brower, Michael, and Little, Doyle. "White Help for Black Business," *Harvard Business Review*, May 1970, pp. 4–16.
3. Burman, Jeffery. "The Birth of a Black Business," *Harvard Business Review*, September-October 1970, pp. 4–19.
4. Burney, D. "Antitrust and the Relations between the Economy and Government," *Conference Board Record*, August 1969, pp. 21 ff.
5. "Business Fights Pollution and the Nation's Profits," *Nation's Business*, Fall 1970, pp. 29–30.
6. Commoner, W. S. "Vertical Mergers, Market Powers and the Antitrust Laws," *American Economic Review*, May 1967, pp. 254–65, 269–72.
7. "Companies Lend Their Expertise to the Arts," *Business Week*, May 15, 1971, p. 102.
8. "The Company and the Arts," *Duns Review*, July 1965, pp. 40–41, 62–67.
9. Connor, J. T. "The Changing Pattern of Business-Government Relations," *Conference Board Record*, May 1971, pp. 23–26.
10. Day, John W. "Closing the Credibility Gap in Environmental Control," *Business Management*, June 1971, pp. 29ff.
11. "The Environment, A National Mission for the Seventies," The editors of *Fortune* magazine, October 1970.
12. Erpf, A. G. "Interface: Business and Beauty," *Columbia Journal of World Business*, May-June 1967, pp. 85–90.
13. Etzel, M. J. and James, D. L. "Can Government Regulation Replace Market Orientation?" *Journal of Retailing*, Winter 1971–72, pp. 14–23.
14. Forbes, M. S. "Business and the Arts," *Forbes*, April 15, 1963, pp. 11–12.
15. Garvin, W. J. "The Small Business Capital Gap: The Special Case of Minority Enterprise," *Journal of Finance*, May 1971, pp. 445–57.
16. Grether, E. T. "Galbraith versus the Market: A Review Article," *Journal of Marketing*, January 1968, pp. 9–13.
17. Harrington, M. H. "Politics of Pollution: Why Are Corporations Cooperating?" *Commonwealth*, April 17, 1970, pp. 111–14.
18. "Helping Negro Business Prosper," *Nation's Business*, August 1968, pp. 50–53.

19. HENDERSON, HAZEL. "Should Business Tackle Society's Problems?" *Harvard Business Review*, July-August 1968, pp. 77–85.

20. KAPOR, A. "Business-Government Relations Become Respectable," *Columbia Journal of World Business*, July 1970, pp. 27–32.

21. KASSARJIAN, HAROLD H. "Incorporating Ecology into Marketing Strategy: The Case of Air Pollution," *Journal of Marketing*, July 1971, pp. 61–65.

22. LINDSAY, F. "Management and the Total Environment," *Columbia Journal of World Business*, January 1970, pp. 19–25.

23. LONDON, PAUL. "Channeling Business Expertise to Black Entrepreneurs," *Management Review*, December 1968, pp. 58–63.

24. MCLELLAN, G. A. "What's Good for the Arts Is Good for General Motors," *Industry Development and Manufacturer's Record*, January 1970, pp. 3–6.

25. PARKER, DANIEL. "To Improve the Conditions of Life for Everyone Everywhere," *Columbia Journal of World Business*, July 1968, pp. 19–26.

26. "Poetry Is Alive," *The Economist*, September 27, 1969, pp. 58–59.

27. "Pollution and the Profit Motive," *Business Week*, April 11, 1970, pp. 82+.

28. "Putting Blacks in the Black," *Nation's Business*, December 1968, pp. 58–63.

29. PUTZELL, E. J. "Antitrust and Long-Range Planning," *Conference Board Record*, June 1971, pp. 33–35.

30. ROGERS, W. D. "Antitrust: How Far Does the Writ Run?" *Columbia Journal of World Business*, March 1971, pp. 46–50.

31. "The Seeds for Black Capitalism," *Business Week*, November 15, 1969, pp. 40–42.

32. SICILANO, ROCCO C. "A Piece of the Action," *Nation's Business*, March 1970, pp. 56–59.

33. SPATER, G. A. "New Mission for Business," *Saturday Review*, February 28, 1970, pp. 29–31.

34. STANS, MAURICE H. "Businessmen Must Participate in Solving Social Problems," *Commercial and Financial Chronicle*, February 12, 1970, pp. 16–20.

35. TAKAYAM, A. "Behavior of the Firm Under Regulatory Constraint," *American Economic Review*, June 1969, pp. 255–60.

36. WAJTUSIAK, JOANNE. "In Support of the Arts, Companies Know What They Like," *The Conference Board Record*, January 1970, pp. 62–64.

37. WAYS, MAX. "How to Think About the Environment," *Fortune*, February 1970, pp. 98–102, 160, 162, 165.

38. WILLIAMS, D. N. "Autos: Can Good Faith Beat Bad Air?" *Iron Age*, May 13, 1971, p. 55.

4 SOCIAL INTERFACES OF THE MARKETING MIX

THE MARKETING MIX concept emphasizes the complexity and total firm involvement necessary for sound marketing decisions. The marketing mix has traditionally faced various internal and external constraints. These constraints in the internal area include: financial status, manufacturing capacity, and traditions of the firm. In the external area, constraints include competitive actions, government regulation, and the consumer.

The components of the marketing mix are now being reexamined in response to the expanding influence of consumerism within the socio-economic system. This reexamination includes a "cost-benefit analysis" of the impact of the firm's product on the public. This examination of product strengths and weaknesses reflect the perspectives of various groups including those of consumer groups and advocates, private citizens, public officials, students and practitioners.

This evaluation of the social relevance of marketing mix components has raised two principal issues. The first is the necessity for the existence of the mix components; the second is a method for the regulation of those components that are both necessary and vital.

The first issue, the necessity for the actual existence of the marketing mix, has both opponents and proponents. Opponents suggest that these components may actually be wasteful of society's time, energy, and resources, that they are a nuisance to the public, contributing to noise and visual pollution problems, and that they are unnecessary, in their current state, for a society of intelligent consumers. They thus conclude that the marketing mix components should either be altered in their current state, or that they should be eliminated. Proponents, while acknowledging some wastefulness on the part of marketers, illustrate the importance of these components to the functioning of the marketing system, and the necessity of these marketing mix components for intelligent purchase decisions on the part of consumers.

Debate concerning the second issue, a method of regulation of these components, has suggested two principal alternatives for the current system. The first of these is increased and more stringent government regulation. Proponents of this alternative cite the need for uniform standards for industry, and for uniform incentives to comply with these standards. Opponents to the increased governmental regulation alternative predict more regulation would lead to limiting marketplace sovereignty and individualism.

The second alternative for a method of regulation is self-regulation within the industrial system. This would entail, for example, a code of ethics for advertisers, or standards for fair warranty agreements. Proponents of this alternative argue that the marketplace would be allowed to function normally and that those who know the limitations and capabilities of the industry could best set reasonable standards. Opponents argue that the consumer would be excluded from policy decisions which ultimately affect him, and that these standards could not be effectively and uniformly enforced.

a.

Product-services

In 1962, President Kennedy proposed four basic rights of consumers. They are:

1. Right to safety.
2. Right to be informed.
3. Right to choose.
4. Right to be heard.

The result of President Kennedy's message was to focus national attention on the subject of consumer rights. Two of these, the right to safety and the right to choose, deal specifically with the product-services component of the marketing mix. In this area, the main issues being reexamined by the consumerist forces are the safety of the product while in use, effects of the product's use such as contributing to environmental pollution, effects of the manufacturing of the product such as the employment or destruction of natural resources, availability and ease of obtaining services for the product after purchase, and the availability of a variety of differentiable products within a particular classification.

Cracco and Rostenne, in this section's first article, discuss the concept of a socioecological product and the implications of it for marketers. Following this is an excerpt from the Final Report of the National Commission on product safety concerning product risk to consumers. Fisk offers some guidelines for business to develop and improve their warranty programs. Gardner then attempts to describe the relationship between the product package and shopper behavior. Concluding this section McLaughlin points out the necessity for a thorough consideration of consumer desires.

Daily "consumption" of environmental pollutants has helped shape the modern consumer, viewed as a total person with new maturity and self-discipline, and concerned with the interests of others as well as his own use satisfactions in his consumption decisions. This phenomena is leading to the development of socio-ecological priorities and products. What is the strategic implication of this new concept of "total product" for business and marketers alike?

30. THE SOCIO-ECOLOGICAL PRODUCT*

Etienne Cracco†
and Jacques Rostenne‡

Independence is a concept of the past; interdependence is the name of the game. Gone is the proud, selfish, and independent user, someone exclusively interested in those products and services he or his immediate family might personally use. He voted with his checkbook; if he wanted a product he paid for it; if he did not want it he left it alone. This aloofness and noninvolvement is rapidly fading way. People today are discovering that air, water, space, time, and privacy are scarce commodities and that they are forced to share in the consumption of each and every product being bought and used by any individual in the society, if not in the entire world. They are forced to accept the noise of neighbor's motorbikes, the polluted river created by the upstream papermill, the junk of discarded cars, the foul smell of passing automobiles, the exhaustion of natural resources. Such daily "consumption" shapes a new man, the consumer, different from the traditional user. This emergent consumer perceives the total product differently, forcing upon business a new concept of product which can best be described as socioecological. The implications of these new concepts are far reaching. They necessitate new company objectives, thus modifying ideas about market, consumption, and product, and compelling marketing strategies to be socially and ecologically oriented.

Obviously, the modern consumer recognizes that he derives advantages from the consumption of all the products the modern society has to offer him, for example, a better standard of living, more fulfilling jobs,

* Reprinted from "The Socio-Ecological Product," *MSU Business Topics* (Summer 1971), pp. 27–34.

† Ecole des Hautes Etudes Commerciales, Paris, France, and Maitre de Conferences, and Catholic University of Louvain, Belgium.

‡ University of Sherbrooke, Quebec, Canada.

more leisure time, more mobility, and a higher life expectancy. Nevertheless, the modern consumer is beginning to feel that he is paying too high a price for these amenities; he is increasingly unwilling to allow others to "use" products, the existence or operation of which causes him some form of physical or psychic discomfort. By joining with other consumers of the same opinion and by becoming extremely vocal, the consumer has succeeded in imposing his veto on the existence of a few products (such as the SST) and certainly has succeeded in modifying many, many others.

To the user, a product is the right of ownership or use of a bundle of need satisfaction composed of form, place, time, and ownership utilities. Generally this definition is applied to a physical object which can perform a certain task the result of which is agreeable to the owner or user. It is important to note that the traditional user measured the satisfaction produced by a product only in terms of the intended output: he saw the product as a well-defined, finite object with little or no linkages with the environment. In summary, the user viewed himself essentially as an independent component of society whose consumption neither affects, nor is affected by, other users and who aims at satisfying his needs, wants, and desires.

The modern consumer realizes that all products have unintended outputs, some good, some bad. For instance, in order to produce a car it is necessary to have factories which create employment, this being a positive although unintended output of the production of a car. On the other hand, factories create water pollution problems, another unintended, and this time negative, output. Because he realizes that unintended outputs are always present in the creation of a product, the consumer tends to reject the traditional definition of product and to accept a new one (see Table 1). The latter takes into account the effect of the existence and marketing of a product on the user, on other individuals, on groups, and on organizations, all of which are inseparable components of society. The crucial difference between the user and the consumer lies in the consumer's awareness of the fact that products have intended as well as unintended outputs. The consumer also differentiates himself from the user in that he recognizes that although the intended utilities built into the product are generally positive and are intended for his personal use and enjoyment, the unintended utilities can be negative as well as positive and can affect a far greater number of people. Unintended utilities can take various forms: direct (increased mobility) or indirect (exhaustion of mineral resources), intense (air pollution) or rather marginal (the noise of a dashboard clock). Utilities can be created before the product is brought into existence (employment in automotive parts manufacturing which precedes the existence of the car); it can be created in conjunction with the product (employment as gas station attendant); or, at a future time, it can flow from the fact that the product has been produced and marketed (junk dealer).

TABLE 1
The traditional and the new consuming society

	Traditional concepts	*Consuming society's concepts*
Product	Bundle of need satisfaction.	Sum of all positive and nega tive utilities which must b accepted by society as whole in order to allow th satisfaction by users of a cer tain bundle of needs, wants or desires in a certain way.
Consumption	Act of using a product.	Act of ratifying the existenc or marketing of a product.
Consumer	Individual who uses a product in order to satisfy his needs and wants.	Society which consumes i order to satisfy needs, wants and desires.
Market	Aggregate of users.	Aggregate of individuals an pressure groups, members o the society, which elects t use its right of consumptio in order to maximize satis faction.

Source: Etienne Cracco and Jacques Rostenne, "La Société Consommatrice," *La Revue Commerce,* June 1971, p. 22.

THE SOCIO-ECOLOGICAL PRODUCT

If, for example, we look at the total system of which the car is a part—rubber plantations, oil fields, refineries, manufacturers, new cars, roads, service stations, pollution, noise, mobility, junk—it is clear that no part exists separately from the others. They must be considered as one entity, a total product which encompasses all the elements of the system from nature back to nature and which also takes into account the effects upon the entire social structure. The overriding components of this system are the time, physical, psychic, and social dimensions of the socio-ecological product.

TIME DIMENSION

At any point in time a product is the sum of its component parts, the existence of which was caused by the decision to create the product. This notion of backward causality is essential to understanding the fact that all the activities which precede the creation of a product are part of it and, therefore, all the utilities, positive and negative, which result are also part of the socio-ecological product. The very existence and use of a product means, necessarily, there are intended and residual outputs, either of which, in turn, may have desired or incidental consequences. It is unfortunately true that where there is a new car there will be junk. This forward causality notion (essentially the backward

FIGURE 1
The ecological cycle

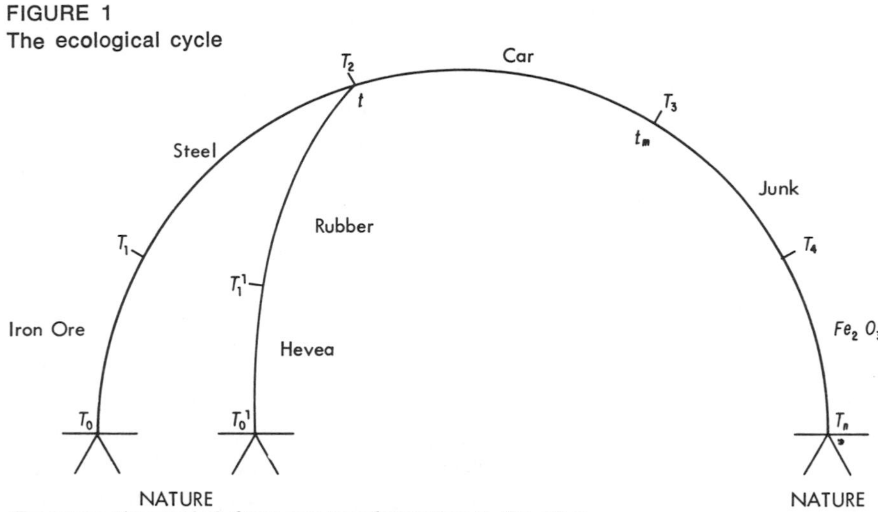

T = macro time period, from one transformation to the other.
t = micro time period, within one transformation.

causality notion viewed from another vantage point) allows us to regard the socio-ecological product in its macro time dimension. This dimension is a continuum, starting with the interaction of raw materials from nature and ending with their return to that state (see Figure 1).

The macro time dimension can be subdivided into micro time periods. Each micro time period corresponds to the time span from one transformation along the ecological continuum to the next. For instance, in the case of the automobile we would have, among others, the micro periods of nature to steel, steel to sub-assembly, new car to junk, and junk to nature, this list being by no means exhaustive. Each micro time period is a time dimension in itself, all other dimensions of the socio-ecological product—physical, psychological, and social—are tied to and evolve in relation to it. Utilities, in an objective sense, are created by the product as defined within the boundaries of each micro time period (the macro utility is related to the sum of the micro utilities), but various other considerations are involved. The maximization of the performance of all the components of a system does not guarantee that the performance of the system is maximized. In fact, it is possible that an attempt to increase the performance of one of the links of the system will decrease the overall system performance.

The accepted concept of total product, defined as a "bundle of need satisfaction" composed of form, place, use, time, and ownership utilities, is too limited a concept to enable maximization on the macro level. It views the total product's time span of existence as limited to the moment of purchase, although some attempts have been made to include a postpurchase dimension in the concept. This conceptual limitation can lead to macro suboptimization, as seen in the following example. Let us say that two transportation systems, one a car-based the other a mass system, both of which represent a different socio-ecological product, are being evaluated under the more limited "total product" conceptual framework. It is possible that the one which creates the fewest macro utilities and the highest socio-ecological cost (the car) may be chosen if the decision is made considering only the situation at the point of purchase. That is the point at which the user evaluates the utilities he expects to derive from riding a car versus riding a mass transit system. At that point, the car promises each individual a maximum of mobility and psychic satisfaction and offers the society a tremendous economic and social leverage by providing greater job opportunities and higher standards of living. If, however, the analysis is made using the socio-ecological product approach, all utilities created in all time periods, T_0 to T_n, will be considered. Such factors as traffic congestion due to the increase in private car traffic, increased pollution, and exhaustion of natural resources make clear that the mass transit system is more desirable.

The time dimension thus becomes the most important dimension of all. Resources are limited and it is obvious that products that are capable of satisfying needs, but at the same time have a short, nonuseful existence, are preferable to those which, not being reabsorbable, continue to tie up resources while not fulfilling any needs. A product should be reintegrated into nature or into another production cycle as soon as the utilities created by that product become negative or socially unacceptable. This concept is the product life termination concept. An example might be the annual automobile inspection in some states and in many European countries. Cars must have a minimum level of workability and safety; if defects are found, the owner has to return with the defects repaired, otherwise he cannot drive his car. Similar requirements in air and noise pollution levels for automobiles could be added to mechanical inspection, and beyond a certain level of potential pollution and mechanical danger a car might have its life terminated. This might force car manufacturers to produce a car, perhaps a disposable one, built in such a way that all its parts would have approximately the same expected useful duration. Obviously the car would have to be recyclable. The advantage to the user lies in the fact that he would always have a car at the peak of its capability. The cost might very well be higher, but the overall socio-ecological cost would probably decrease.

PHYSICAL DIMENSION

The socio-ecological product also has a physical dimension: the shapes taken by the product during its time dimension. The physical dimension is traceable to the nuts and bolts or any physical elements which are created for, used in, or in conjunction with, the satisfaction of the bundles of needs involved. In speaking of the time dimension we mentioned two levels of approach, the macro and the micro. The micro level corresponds to the time span from one transformation to the next, the macro to the sum of all the micro periods. The notion of physical dimension follows the same pattern; from one transformation to the next we are partly dealing with the traditional, microstatic approach to product definition. From the sum of all the micro components emerge the true physical dimensions of the product. It is important to note again that the concept of physical dimensions can only be understood when seen in conjunction with the time dimension and in a systemic approach.

The systemic approach is necessary because the physical dimension concept considers as part of one and the same product all the elements of a system which have to exist, over space and time, to allow the satisfaction of a certain need in a certain way. If we analyze the total system from the vantage point of its primary intended output, for example, the car, we can differentiate between several types of elements in the physical dimension. First, we have the component parts, all the generations of components and subassemblies which are brought together to form the car itself. Second, we have the enabling components, which are entire systems, exemplified by the roads and service station system. Finally, we have all the physical by-products and rejects created by the system as it is built and operated to produce the utilities expected of it. All this residue must be accounted for and recycled, which can only be done at a certain cost. This cost can be translated into a certain amount of negative utility, and, therefore, it becomes clear that the residue is part of the socio-ecological product.

In order to better grasp the concept of physical dimension in the socio-ecological product it may be helpful to consider it as an aggregate of interrelated and interconnected transvections as defined in the Aldersonian sense,[1] with the reservation that Alderson's transvection spans the distance from production to purchase while the physical dimension is more like the multidimensional "ecological transvection." For instance, roads, cars, refineries, gas stations, and so forth, are part of a unique physical product since all must exist in order to permit the operation of any of the parts. Moreover, it is clear that some coexist over space while others are sequential over time (for example, oil extraction, refineries, gas stations, air pollution). To these we must add the rapidly increasing disenchantment with the internal combustion engine and all the other expectations, doubts, and misgivings attached to certain other aspects of the system, such as the fears of ecological disaster presented by the Alaskan pipeline. The micro element of the physical dimension

[1] Wroe Alderson, *Dynamic Marketing Behavior* (Homewood, Ill.: Richard D. Irwin, 1965), pp. 86–87.

truly reflects the traditional product concept and all the traditional rules apply. Value is given in function of remaining economic life; it is dependent upon reliability of the parts and new technological developments. Approached in this manner, the physical dimension is seen as a declining function over time. Some exceptions do exist—as time goes by the physical properties of wine could improve—but these types of goods are rather the exceptions confirming the rule.

PSYCHIC DIMENSION

The total product also has a nonphysical, psychic dimension. This dimension is similar to the others in that it evolves, changes, and modifies itself along the time dimension. The main elements of the psychic dimension are all the successive sets of expectations, images, and psychic satisfactions related to the product as it goes through its existence cycle and as the needs it satisfies change. The traditional approach also incorporates the notion of psychic dimension but, again, it takes a static view. In the traditional analysis a car would have an image and a set of expectations at the moment of purchase decision. We postulate that a car factory has an image, as does a new car, a used car, and an abandoned junk car, all of them different and relevant in the mind of the modern consumer making a decision about whether to allow the manufacture and use of this car, which is a farther ranging decision than the decision to buy or not to buy. In an economy of abundance such as ours, where the intended outputs of products must be diversified by other than physical differences, the psychic element becomes increasingly important and accounts for an increasing part of the product itself. The ratio of physical utilities over purely psychic types is diminishing rather rapidly. It is interesting to note that, barring the emergence of some form of "psychic pollution," the increased importance of the psychic element in the socio-ecological product may well result in a reduction of the ecological costs of fulfilling needs.

SOCIAL DIMENSION

Finally, the total product has a pervasive social dimension due to the all-encompassing linkages of all other dimensions and their relationship to all the aspects of the social structure, the economy, and, last but not least, the very balance of the ecological system.

Clearly, the whole society and everyone in it is affected over time and space by the production, marketing, and consumption of any given product. That production involves allocation of scarce resources, manpower, capital, and time, and these factors have first-, second-, and fourth-order repercussions which, as a result, involve everyone and provide each of us with positive and negative satisfactions. In that sense it can be said that the product has a social dimension. No longer is it sufficient to insure that the intended output of a product will satisfy its user; it is now necessary to insure that the entire spectrum of utilities will be desirable or at least acceptable to society. Since the consumer and the user are no longer one and the same, it becomes necessary to update the approach to marketing planning.

Society can be viewed as an aggregate of individuals, groups, and organizations which have in common the fact that they are willing to make their views about a product known and are willing to pressure the rest of society into taking steps toward forcing products to be consistent with their desires. Groups may be either favorable or unfavorable to a certain product because the types of utilities they may derive from it can differ widely, ranging from employment in its manufacture to being outraged by the symbolisms imbedded in the product. The amount of power they have and the amount of dissatisfaction they are willing to tolerate become important factors in determining the shape of the product. Ideally a socio-ecological product should be developed on the basis of the following principles:

1. Maximizing positive utilities.
2. Minimizing negative utilities.
3. Maximizing the positive spread between both.
4. Limiting the amount of negative utilities produced to a level below the threshold of unacceptability to any relevant consumer.

MARKETING IMPLICATIONS

What are the strategic implications of this new concept of total product? We must admit that most are still emerging, although certain aspects appear to be quite well defined.[2]

[2] It is already possible to incorporate this "firm-consuming society" within a general mathematical framework (see below). This formula illustrates the fact that the traditional utilities we try to provide through our marketing strategies have macro and micro time dimensions which, in turn, have an impact on the physical, psychic, and social dimensions of the total product. Time becomes an overriding factor in developing a marketing strategy.

If we let

Fy = physical dimension
Psy = psychic dimension
S = social dimension
t = micro time
T = macro time
$P1$ = place utilities
F = form
O = ownership
N = moment at which the product is reintegrated into nature or into another production cycle
m = moment at which a new transformation occurs,

then, to optimize U,

$$U = \sum_{T=0}^{N} \sum_{t=0}^{m} (Fy, Psy, S)_{P1,F,O}.$$

First, marketing will have to become system and time oriented. A firm must look at all the components of the socio-ecological product and how they affect society and the environment. Because of the macro time dimension involved, a firm will have to evaluate the socio-ecological impacts over the macro time period which is much longer than the one within which the product released its intended utilities. Optimization will involve the complex problem of maximizing the benefits to be derived from the entire socio-ecological product over the entire macro time period.

Second, today's marketing is user-centered. Firms attempt to satisfy at a profit the user's needs, wants, and desires even when these conflict with social needs and wants or when the satisfaction of these individual necessities create ecological imbalances. Marketing will have to reorient its priorities (see Table 2), and the maintenance of the equilibrium

TABLE 2
Changing marketing priorities

Traditional priorities	*Socio-ecological priorities*
Individual	Environment
↓	↓
Corporation	Society
↓	↓
Society	Individual
↓	↓
Environment	Corporation

must become the first and foremost rule upon which the decision to create or market a product will depend. A firm's success will be evaluated not only on the basis of profit but also on the basis of social contribution of which profit is merely one part. The second priority will be that the product must enhance social utilities without creating unacceptable levels of socially undesirable side effects. The third priority may be to satisfy the desires of the individual user, but this must be subject to the limitation of the very stringent constraints imposed by the first two. The levels of tolerance of society toward undesirable products is gradually declining and this is becoming a key factor in proper product and marketing development planning.

Third, today the desirability of a product is judged as a function of the amount of intended utilities it can create for the user. Marketing will have to consider that the consumer can also influence the fate of the product although he is not a user. Therefore, products will have to be developed to maximize the positive surplus of utilities over the macro time period for individuals, groups, organizations, and society, which represent users and consumers. The maximization of utilities will not be sufficient because it may be associated with a high level of negative utilities. The maximization of the positive surplus is itself an insufficient condition because it is possible that the negative utilities produced could be higher for some groups of consumers than the maximum threshold of acceptable utilities. In this case, the group of consumers could certainly express its right of nonconsumption through social, legal, or economic pressure aimed at modifying or barring the production or marketing of the product under consideration.

Fourth, prices must be related not only to the micro time dimension but also to the dimension and to the total socio-ecological product. For instance, since the socio-ecological cost of a transit system based on private cars is higher than one based on buses, prices of cars will be increased in order to internalize some of the costs possibly incurred later in the macro time. Prices at any given time along the micro time dimension become a strictly managerial decision. The important point is that the sum of the prices paid at each transformation should be equal to the socio-ecological cost and that prices at any given time should make the socio-ecologically economic alternative competitive. Shifting ecological costs to an earlier period is feasible only if the proper fiscal legislation is enacted; as a result, governmental intervention in the area of marketing should tend to increase.

Fifth, any product development strategy evolving from these considerations would take into account that quality of life is a substitute for quantity of material welfare and that a firm's selection of inputs reflects the socio-ecological impact of their use. A firm would take its marching orders not only from product users but also from society as represented by pressure groups such as environmentalists, consumers' associations, governmental agencies, and so forth. In some ways, the result is a partial loss of the user's sovereignty to the "consuming society."

Sixth, today promotional efforts concentrate upon the user of a product, with the exception of some long-run institutional advertising. It will become necessary to "sell" the socio-ecological product to all individuals, groups, and organizations who can potentially be affected by the product and who therefore will have to participate actively or passively in its consumption. The type of promotion directed at such segments may differ tremendously since the expected utilities derived are different. The timing of the promotions must vary because all groups will not be affected simultaneously. The promotional emphasis will differ because the utilities under consideration may be crucial to some and marginal to others. Nevertheless, all groups must be identified, the effect of the product on them must be hypothesized, and their attitudes and expectations must be judged in order to allow for proper promotional planning. The complexity of the task is apparent, but it is necessary.

Finally, a firm's responsibility will expand far beyond the present legal limits of the corporation. It will become legally liable for everything done in response to its demand for component parts; it will be responsible for the effects of the enabling subsystems upon the ecology and society; and accountable for the costs and other burdens attached to recycling the resulting elements of the socio-ecological product. Because all firms involved in the production and marketing of a socio-ecological product will have joint and inseparable responsibilities, it is expected that channel coordination and integration will become prevalent.

These are but a few of the more obvious implications. On the other hand, the gradual acceptance of the notion of socio-ecological products probably will allow a new set of marketing strategies to develop. Hopefully these will be better adapted to the needs of the modern consumer, who exerts his right of consumption not only through purchase but also through ratification (open or tacit), or rejection, of the existence and marketing of the socio-ecological product. This evolution of the marketing concept also will help to bring about an era of heightened maturity and self discipline in consumption where "no one can have *all* of what he wants, so that everyone may have *some* of what he wants," as expressed by Archie K. Davis, president of the Chamber of Commerce of the United States.

How are "unreasonable hazards" of products defined? How can the consumer be protected from products which may be harmful to health and safety? This report documents the extent of deaths and injuries caused by household products. It recommends the establishment of standards and procedures for new products in a proposed Consumer Product Safety Act.

---

31. PRODUCT RISK TO CONSUMERS*

National Commission on Product Safety

The primary charge to the National Commission on Product Safety was to "consider the identity of categories of household products . . . which may present an unreasonable hazard to the health and safety of the consuming public."

Annual estimates of the National Center for Health Statistics of the

* Condensation of pp. 9–36 from the final report of the National Commission on Product Safety (Washington, D.C.: Superintendent of Documents, June 1970). The condensation was prepared by Norman Kangun and originally published in *Society and Marketing An Unconventional View,* Harper and Row (New York, 1972), pp. 58–71.

Department of Health, Education, and Welfare (DHEW) and the National Safety Council for injury in and around the American home indicate 30,000 persons killed, 110,000 permanently disabled, 585,000 hospitalized, and more than 20 million injured seriously enough to require medical treatment or be disabled for a day or more. . . . Most of these casualties are associated with consumer products. Costs to the economy and to individual consumers and manufacturers run to billions of dollars annually.

The role of specific products is, however, difficult to define. The estimate of 6,200 killed by home fires and 1.3 million injured by burns received at home leaves open the question of cause: matches, stoves, wiring, fabrics, or cigarettes?

Home falls kill about 12,000 a year and injure 6.9 million, but again the precise causes are uncertain: high heels, loose treads, rough floors, flimsy ladders, worn stairs, slippery floors, torn carpets, alcohol?

Every hour of the day, on the average, household hazards in America kill three victims. For every one they kill, more than 1,000 suffer injuries. The injuries restrict activities of about half of the victims and force a third of these to take to bed to recover. A tenth of the bedridden require hospital care.

Injuries around schools and vacation homes or in recreational areas add to these numbers substantially.

Injuries at home account for more than half of the total that do not involve transportation. The total injured at home is more than four times as many as those injured on highways, more than twice as many as those injured at work. Deaths on highways, however, are double those at home.

The most dangerous years are below age 5. Approximately 7,000 children under 15 die each year in home accidents—a death toll higher than that of cancer and heart disease combined. More than 2 million children every year are injured while using bicycles or playground equipment.

In the lowest income groups, household risks injure far more women than men, but above the middle-income line, men are injured more.

About a third of the deaths from household hazards occur in kitchens and living-dining areas. Stairs account for about one in every twenty deaths from household hazards, and slightly fewer deaths occur in the bathroom. Falls figure in half of these deaths, fires or suffocation in a third, poisoning in about one in twenty.

Such numbers unfortunately convey no sense of the agony and mortification of the victims and their families. We were deeply moved by accounts of individual lives destroyed or blighted by defective household products.

Rather than direct our energies toward developing new estimates of total injuries, we chose to study a number of household product hazards in depth. The data presented in the following pages come from four primary sources:

1. Public hearings.
2. A survey of injuries treated by U.S. physicians in April 1969.
3. Continuing surveillance of injuries seen in emergency rooms of fourteen hospitals near Washington, D.C., and Memphis, Tennessee.
4. A survey of product liability insurance claims from April to June 1969.

EVALUATING HAZARDS

In assessing individual hazards, we studied data relating frequency, severity, duration, and sequelae of injury to the frequency and degree of exposure to the product. Other variables we looked at were the degree of inherent risk, the essentiality of the product, and the feasibility and approximate cost of safety improvements.

We also considered whether there were acceptable alternatives for a hazardous product; effects on the product of aging and wear; the contribution to hazards of defective maintenance and repair; exposure to instructions or warnings; influence of product advertising on behavior; the extent and forms of abnormal uses of the product; effects of storage, distribution, and disposal; and characteristics of the persons injured, including age, sex, skills, training, and experience.

UNREASONABLE HAZARDS

Beyond the foregoing guidelines for defining "unreasonable hazards," we believe that no completely satisfactory definition is possible. Prof. Corwin D. Edwards of the University of Oregon has presented an excellent statement which supplements our guidelines:

> Risks of bodily harm to users are not unreasonable when consumers understand that risks exist, can appraise their probability and severity, know how to cope with them, and voluntarily accept them to get benefits that could not be obtained in less risky ways. When there is a risk of this character, consumers have reasonable opportunity to protect themselves; and public authorities should hesitate to substitute their value judgments about the desirability of the risk for those of the consumers who choose to incur it.
>
> But preventable risk is not reasonable (*a*) when consumers do not know that it exists; or (*b*) when, though aware of it, consumers are unable to estimate its frequency and severity; or (*c*) when consumers do not know how to cope with it, and hence are likely to incur harm unnecessarily; or (*d*) when risk is unnecessary in . . . that it could be reduced or eliminated at a cost in money or in the performance of the product that consumers would willingly incur if they knew the facts and were given the choice.

Risks that are unreasonable by this definition of unreasonableness seem . . . to be common.[1]

In products we examined, we found evidence of substantial neglect of the consumer's right to safety, although in a few situations we were impressed by effective governmental action or the concern of conscientious manufacturers.

Although the categories of products described below . . . illustrate risks to the American consumer which we believe are unacceptable, there may be equally unacceptable risks in products we have not dealt with in depth. . . .

While we prefer to emphasize positive recommendations for the future protection of consumers, we find that within each of the categories discussed in the pages immediately following, there are makes, models, and types of products which constitute "an unreasonable hazard to the health and safety of the consuming public" within the meaning of our mandate.

COLOR TELEVISION SETS

On New Year's Day 1966, the Fassero family of Springfield, Illinois, after a day of watching TV programs in color, turned off the set and went to bed. During the night, Mr. Fassero found the living room in flames, attributed to a fire in the TV set. The house was gutted. Mrs. Fassero was disabled. Her mother died of the effects of the fire.

Battalion Chief E. D. Gutierrez of the Ventura County (California) Fire District, reported that a 1967 fire which burned to death four children, their father and grandmother, was traced to a nonmetallic sheath cable overheated by a short circuit in the high voltage of the family color TV set.

Even when personal injury does not result, a TV fire can cause extensive property damage. A blazing TV set in Alliance, Ohio, reportedly started a fire at 3 P.M., November 18, 1969, destroying the interior of the home of Paul J. Baughman.

On January 3, 1969, a color TV set owned by Thelma Turner in Wilberforce, Ohio, started a fire which destroyed most of the belongings of nine families for a loss of $160,000.

Because the exact cause of a fire is difficult to prove, investigators cannot always be sure when a TV set is responsible. Surviving witnesses, however, have reported how some TV fires began.

Among the 85 million TV sets in the United States in 1969, including about 20 million color sets, about 10,000 sets caught fire. Most of the fires were in color sets: The incident rate for color versus monochrome was found to be on the order of 40 to 1.

[1] Corwin Edwards, Testimony, National Commission on Product Safety Hearing (March 4, 1970).

Our estimate is based on data on fires compiled in New Hampshire, Illinois, and Oregon and on our spot check of those major cities which record specific sources of fires. Oregon, which had been averaging about fifty TV fires a year for the period of 1966–1968, reported a marked increase to 175 for 1969. On the basis of the state data alone, an official of the National Fire Protection Association estimated more than 7,000 TV fires a year. Estimates of the International Association of Electrical Inspectors indicate almost as high a number of fires.

We cannot say how many such fires cause extensive damage, although all were serious enough to be reported. About half were contained within the set. Much of the data concerns components not sold for several years, but still in use.

The reason for the higher rate of fires in color sets is that they require up to and sometimes more than 25,000 volts. If conductors in the set are not well insulated, the high voltage forces a short circuit. Resistance to this flow of current builds up temperatures to the flaming point.

Operating temperatures of color sets are in the 110°–115°F range. Heat generated in normal circuits in some sets changed the properties of wax insulating coating around the high-voltage transformer, so that it broke down. This form of insulation has since, for the most part, been replaced by a more durable, less combustible silicone rubber.

Improperly dressed wire, another weakness in insulation, can be avoided either by 100 percent inspection and correction or a method of assuring full dressing and insulation of component connections.

The spread of fire is enhanced by the present use of flammable paper or cardboard to enclose capacitors; flammable lubricants; accumulation of dust around components; frayed leads; and closely packed circuitry. Other components considered to be potential fire sources are the deflection yoke around the cathode-ray tube, automatic tuning devices, printed circuit parts in the chassis, the AC switch, and ceramic resistors.

As soon as we alerted TV manufacturers to the fire data, the Electronic Industries Association launched a crash program to review and upgrade its safety standards. At the same time, the industry initiated a uniform method of recording data. Underwriters' Laboratories, commenting on the efforts of the EIA ad hoc task force's proposed new standards, observed, "It is our opinion that materials which will not burn should be used wherever possible."

An independent review of industry standards by Tracor, Inc., Austin, Texas, found that the EIA-recommended standards, though an improvement, were still

> . . . not adequate to eliminate this [fire] hazard because they permit the time-phased existence of a flame and the use of materials which will support combustion. . . .

It is within the industry's grasp to make . . . [a tenfold] improvement in a few months with respect to TV fire safety.[2]

GLASS BOTTLES

"I will be blind in one eye for the rest of my life because of a defective glass bottle." The testimony of 14-year-old Sharon Jackson of Chicago tells the tragic potential of exploding glass bottles.

The Federal Trade Commission considered the hazard presented by exploding glass bottles for three years in a series of interdepartmental memoranda culminating in a decision to ask what the Interstate Commerce Commission thought. Although Commissioner Philip Elman urged a meaningful investigation, the FTC decided to concur with the ICC's conclusion that

> . . . the current efforts of the industry as to adequacy and suitability of the glass container for beer and soft drinks are adequate. We believe that the safety record is sufficiently good as to not warrant Federal regulation and control over the design criteria of beverage bottles, regardless as to whether jurisdiction exists.[3]

The FTC staff memorandum dated February 3, 1967, which contained the recommendation adopted by the Commission, included the following:

> Promulgation of standards would not, it is believed, be the answer . . . . If it were the answer, in all probability the industry would have voluntarily, long ago, revised its standards. . . . It is believed that should the Commission gratuitously go further in this instance, it may well eventually be placed in the position of having opened Pandora's box with no apparent way to reclose it.[4]

Contrary to these judgments, we find that glass bottles used for carbonated beverages present an unreasonable risk to consumers. When one of these bottles fails, the glass under internal pressure bursts into splinters. Because of this pressure, bottles of carbonated drinks are more hazardous than those containing inert beverages.

Although explosions are the most dramatic cause of injury from glass bottles, they are not the most common. Insurance companies reported more claims related to glass bottles than to any other consumer product.

---

[2] Tracor, Inc., *Evaluation of Standards Applicable to Television Fire Hazards*, Report No. 69-1015-U, prepared for NCPS (January 1970); Tracor, Inc., 27 *March 1970 Revisions to TR69-1015-U*, (April 1970).

[3] George A. Meyer (Interstate Commerce Commission, Bureau of Operations and Compliance), *Letter to Joseph W. Shea* (Federal Trade Commission) (November 3, 1966).

[4] Garland S. Ferguson (Division of Food and Drug Advertising), "Exploding Glass Bottles," *Memorandum to Federal Trade Commission* (February 3, 1967).

Of closed claims reported for three survey months, 17 percent concerned glass bottles, a frequency almost three times as high as the next ranked product. Responses to our inquiries from the six largest bottlers indicate that 5,000 to 7,000 injuries are reported annually. Hospital records confirm that glass bottles consistently rank high among products connected with injuries treated in emergency clinics.

Of the 430 closed cases on bottle injuries reported by insurers, 80 percent required medical treatment. These sometimes involve loss of vision, disfigurement, or permanent disability.

Children under 15 received more than a third of over 1,700 injuries related to glass bottles and containers, according to hospital emergency room surveillance reports.

In more than a third of the injuries investigated, our staff found the product at least partially at fault, and in 29 percent wholly responsible.

In 1968 the soft-drink industry filled about 30 billion glass containers. Of these, more than half were returnables, but thin-walled disposables have gained rapidly in recent years.

These billions of bottles, simply by their numbers, create a problem. Even if only a small proportion is defective, the number of incidents is large.

Although the industry blames explosions on consumer misuse, bottles have been known to burst while standing on a shelf. Whatever percentage may be laid to quality control flaws, many explosions occur during ordinary use. The industry should anticipate routine stress on bottles, including reported minor impacts when they are checked at the counter, carried, or placed in a refrigerator.

The industry maintains that a glass bottle in prime condition will never fail without abuse. But in ordinary use, scartches or bruises weaken the structure, which becomes increasingly more fragile. The phenomenon of static fatigue permits stresses to accumulate so that a damaged bottle may explode from internal pressure or minor impact long after the primary damage.

At present there is no industrywide standard regulating bottle-wall thickness or permissible number of trips for returnable bottles. The three standard tests most relied upon during production have not measured such critical factors as proper distribution of the glass or the ability of the glass to withstand impact, although these factors are analyzed by some producers during design. Subsequent to our hearing, the manufacturers' trade association began examining the feasibility of new tests to accomplish these purposes.

It may prove necessary to increase the amount of glass used in one-trip bottles. Because of their thin sidewalls, the disposables are weaker than the returnable bottle and are less likely to survive even slight impact.

Tests performed during the manufacturing process are required by the industry standard at most only once every two hours. As bottles come off the line at a rate of some 100 per minute, more than 10,000 may pass between test samples. At the bottling plant, bottles are inspected visually as they pass at a rate of approximately five per second. This procedure cannot detect hairline cracks, fractures, scratches, and other defects.

According to evidence presented by Joseph J. Tomassi, Jr., former vice-president and general manager (International Division) of Canada Dry Corp., major bottling companies are sometimes under pressure to reduce their quality-control standards and use lower-quality glass. For example, because of periodic shortages of glass, inferior bottles have been accepted, filled, and sent out to the consumer.

Virginia Knauer, Special Assistant to the President for Consumer Affairs, has pointed out that, unlike returnable bottles, disposable bottles cannot be recycled. They are nondegradable. The remnants or fragments litter the land and cause a high proportion of lacerations.

Reduction of risk lies in a new container strong enough to resist breaking or bursting and which can be burned, dissolved, or recycled. Until then, a minimum standard for bottle-wall thickness is critical, and quality assurance by bottlers as well as by manufacturers will continue to warrant close scrutiny.

ROTARY LAWN MOWERS

On the first warm Saturday in spring, hospital emergency room crews expect a parade of patients holding a bloody towel around a lacerated or amputated hand or foot. On opening day of the grass-grooming season, the rotary power mower begins its work of trimming lawns, fingers, and toes. About 70 percent of the injuries from power mowers are lacerations, amputations, and fractures that result from the cutting and crushing action of the fast whirling blade.

In addition, there are high-velocity ejections of wire, glass, stones, and debris that can puncture vital body parts.

Thomas Cohiles regularly cut two or three lawns in his hometown of Marysville, Calif., to earn pocket money. One day in September 1965, Tom stood nearly thirty feet from a friend operating a power mower. As the machine turned sharply right, a rock hurtled from the discharge opening and struck Cohiles' right eye. Today, that eye is blind.

Injuries from power mowers have increased in proportion to the numbers and use of these machines. A Public Health Survey study in 1960 estimated there were 55,000 to 80,000 injuries from power mowers. In 1969, the Department of Health, Education, and Welfare estimated the annual rate of injury was 140,000.

Although mower hazards are properly of serious concern to manufacturers, one-quarter of the 216 models we examined did not comply with the industry's own consensus safety standards, notwithstanding a self-certification program under which the models professed to meet those standards. Referring these findings to the Federal Trade Commission, we were informed by Chairman Casper W. Weinberger that

> . . . the Commission believes that government action is needed to ensure the promulgation of adequate safety standards and effective procedures for the enforcement of such standards, with the result that only those power lawn mowers which have been tested and found to meet the prescribed safety standards will be offered for sale to the public.
>
> However, since legislation may be the most appropriate method for dealing with this problem, the Commission has decided to await the recommendations of the National Commission on Product Safety before taking further action in this matter.[5]

While the industry standard, ANSI B71.1, was apparently too rigorous for noncomplying manufacturers, it offers insufficient protection to the consumer. According to testimony, the large discharge chute permits mowers to throw out debris at a variety of heights and angles. On the other hand, if the opening is small, wet or juicy grasses clog it, and the clogged machine tempts the operator to remove the grass with his fingers while the blades whirl by. When the operator starts the motor, his feet may be near the unguarded blade at the chute or he may be exposed to missiles hurled through the aperture.

Measurements for shielding, specified by the standard are related to the blade at rest, although at high speed the tip of some blades turn in a lower plane. The permissible blade tip velocity of 19,000 feet per minute was challenged as too high.

Most injuries are associated with speeding rotary blades which strike several times when the operator reaches under the housing, pulls the machine over a foot, or picks at grass clogging the discharge opening.

Missiles thrown by the rotary blades strike bystanders as well as operators. The blades hurl such debris as pebbles, nails, glass, and wires like shrapnel fifty feet or more, no matter how carefully a lawn is policed before mowing.

Of 12,726 cases of injury reported to us by physicians, 418 were linked to power mowers in two weeks of April 1969—topping the list of products causing injuries. A survey of insurance companies covering closed claims placed power mowers sixth as a cause of claims for injuries.

About 27 million power mowers are in use. Yearly sales exceed 5 million. More than 90 percent of power mowers use the rotary blades.

Both popular and professional literature has reported the hazard for years. Senator Warren G. Magnuson, the National Safety Council, and

[5] Casper W. Weinberger (chairman, Federal Trade Commission), *Letter to NCPS* (May 1, 1970).

the Outdoor Power Equipment Institute have called attention to misdesign and misuse.

Nevertheless, many users apparently have not learned to cope with the hazards or with the idiosyncrasies of certain models. For example, the blades on certain models continue to whirl while the clutch is disengaged to stop forward movement. Adding to the confusion, the placement and movement of parts and controls are not standardized.

User error is predictable. One victim lost parts of two fingers upon reaching under the housing to tighten the blade; he neglected to stop the motor. Others, working up or down a grade, lose control and part of a foot. Operators should mow at right angles to a slope and never on a steep grade.

Following our study of the hazard, the Outdoor Power Equipment Institute acknowledged:

> Compliance with the existing B71.1—1968 standard by the industry generally is questionable;
>
> The existing . . . standard is not adequate;
>
> Manufacturers self-certification is not a satisfactory program;
>
> There is no check on compliance with the standard by users of the triangular safety seal, and no penalty for noncompliance.[6]

The Institute launched a "crash program" for improvement in September 1969, but by April 1970 had no definitive proposals to report on revision of the existing standard. Instead, it issued interpretations of ambiguities in the existing standard and notified the industry that after June 30, 1970, all power lawnmowers must have independent laboratory certification of compliance with that concededly inadequate standard.

A newly designed OPEI label will certify compliance with a uniform testing procedure that has been adopted as an official interpretation of the ANSI B71.1 Standard. A 1970 revision of that standard is planned.

The effect of these steps in protecting the consumer will, however, depend ultimately on the quality of the new mower standard and compliance by manufacturers.

Cornell Aeronautical Laboratory has suggested that the hazard of the rotary blade might be eliminated by designing a machine with a two-surface shearing action operating about a vertical shaft at a low rotational speed. A private designer demonstrated to us a model of a power reel mower which would be relatively safe, with the claim that the price and performance are competitive with the rotary mower. The testimony was not rebutted.

Unless the conspicuously deficient safety standard for rotary mowers is corrected, federal intervention is called for to require adoption of less hazardous designs and possibly recall or reconstruction of hazardous mowers currently in use.

---

[6] Harold K. Howe (OPEI), *Letter to NCPS* (Sept. 15, 1969).

TOYS

"A child has to experience some minor injuries, some minor experiences of trauma in order to learn," according to the Child Safety Consultant of the National Safety Council.

We do not concur.

The U.S. Public Health Service estimates that toys injure 700,000 children every year; another 500,000 a year are injured on swings and 200,000 on slides. At least 22 parents are suing the manufacturer of an Etch-a-Sketch toy for lacerations suffered by their children from broken glass panels. In Philadelphia alone, at least 13 children put the wrong end of a Zulu Gun into their mouth and inhaled darts into their lungs. A Little Lady toy oven for young girls had temperatures above 300°F on the outer surface and 600°F on the inside. There are no voluntary industrywide safety standards for any of these products.

Such hazards led us to recommend legislation which the Congress enacted as the Child Protection and Toy Safety Act of 1969, amending the Federal Hazardous Substances Act to cover electrical, mechanical, and thermal hazards from toys or other articles for children.

Injuries from toys often result from predictable misuse. A child can be expected to put the wrong end of a blowgun in his mouth and to dismember a doll to expose sharp pins that hold the arms and legs.

Statutory law has been no more successful than common law in reducing undue risks in toys. The Federal Hazardous Substances Act, as amended by the Child Protection and Toy Safety Act of 1969, gives the Food and Drug Administration of the Department of Health, Education, and Welfare authority to declare toys or other articles intended for children to be banned hazardous substances. But in our Interim Report we characterized the amendment as a "standby" measure only, adding we were not then "prepared . . . to endorse the processes, enforcement procedures, or underlying philosophy of the Federal Hazardous Substances Act." The act does not provide for mandatory standards of safety for toys or for proscriptive restraint of hazards before the toys are marketed.

Among the toys presented at congressional hearings as evidence of the need for the 1969 amendments were: the Rapco Castright Metal Casting Set which reaches temperatures of 800°F on the cooking surface and 600°F on the sides as well as the Empire Little Lady Oven and Etch-a-Sketch toy already described.

According to Consumers Union, all these toys were on the market in March 1970—two months after the new act took effect—with the same or similar hazards. The shipping carton containing the Etch-a-Sketch toy bears a caution about the glass, but there is no warning on the toy itself. The manufacturer of the Casting Set says that he has corrected the hazards and relabeled the packages to say, "Not intended for children's use; for teenagers and adults." But Consumers Union found that newly purchased samples bore no such legend and had pictures of children playing with the sets.

In 1966, one of the largest manufacturers of toys stopped selling a successful bazooka toy, at $7 to $10 each, upon learning that it deafened the playmate of a user. The firm employs 300 engineers but did not anticipate this danger.

Nearly 6 million Zulu Guns were sold before the maker installed a safety device to prevent inhalation of the darts. Those without the device remain on the market.

In Philadelphia 18 stores removed from sale a rattle that had 7 needle-sharp spikes beneath the cardboard and plastic covering, after congressional hearings had alerted the public to the hazard.

The Hazardous Substances Act was passed originally because of such toys as crackerballs—small torpedoes that looked so much like candy that youngsters exploded them between their teeth.

One company offered for sale by mail "200 Explosive Formulas," including a recipe for nitroglycerin. Two boys in Cleveland, Ohio, were maimed when fireworks, produced by using a mail-order formula, exploded.

In 1968, retail toy sales reached an estimated $2.5 billion. The toy industry has not demonstrated the ability to police its own members or develop adequate industry standards. The Toy Manufacturers Association cannot in any event control nonmembers, including importers.

Many retailers are in the position of Charles W. Veysey, president of the F. A. O. Schwarz toy store, who states:

> We can't take every toy and break it apart. We carry 12,000 different items. There are between 150,000 and 200,000 toys on the market to choose from. We have to rely on the manufacturers' integrity.[7]

Representatives of toy manufacturers, testifying on the Child Protection Act, favored a provision for formal hearings on hazards rather than informal hearings, for reasons discussed in our section on federal law. Congress authorized the secretary in his discretion to use either procedure.

Toys as a product category included a significant number of unreasonable hazards when we filed our Interim Report in February 1969. Our investigators found in December 1969 that neither the interest created by congressional hearings nor passage of the Child Protection and Toy Safety Act had significantly reduced the hazards. They found some of the specific items mentioned in the Boston hearings available on store shelves:

[7] Stanford N. Sesser, "News from Toyland," *New Republic* (December 20, 1969), p. 13.

Dolls still have pins to hold their hair ribbons on, little girls can still bake their own cakes in their own electric ovens, a little boy can make a design with his glass screen Etch-a-Sketch toy—and run the risk of sketching a permanent scar design somewhere on his body. . . .[8]

The inadequacy of an all-or-nothing banning provisions of the Federal Hazardous Substances Act, described in our chapter on "Lessons of Federal Law," leads us to conclude that children will continue to be exposed to unreasonably hazardous toys unless regulatory methods are improved.

CONCLUSIONS

Product safety is an open-minded affair. Familiar products require periodic restudy. New products may need guidelines for safety. Consequently we suggest authority for special standards and procedures for new products in our proposed Consumer Product Safety Act.

We do not recite tales of horror for their emotional effect. It is our purpose to indicate the variety and ubiquity of consumer product hazards. The nation must be constantly alert to their significance, their cost, their changing character, and to means of preventing them.

It has been our purpose to identify these hazards but we cannot forbear mention of ways of moderating undue risks. While we have hardly exhausted the subject we believe that surveillance, field inquiries, and adequate safety standards may discover methods of protection to be found in the original concept, in the design, in systems of assuring quality throughout production, storage, and distribution, in information for the consumer and repairman, and in methods of disposal or recycling of the product.

STUDY QUESTIONS*

1. Why does the Commission begin its paper with statistics for injuries and deaths around the home? Do the statistics obscure or emphasize the statement of the thesis?
2. Distinguish between "reasonable" and "unreasonable" hazards.
3. In the categories of products cited in the paper which contain unacceptable risks to consumers, it is commonplace to find that the industry either has no internal safety standards, that existing standards are lax, or that member firms do not adhere to industry safety standards. Why? Is self-regulation likely to be an effective remedy? Under what conditions might self-regulation be impossible?
4. Should decisions relating to public health and safety be delegated solely to producers and/or distributors?

---

[8] Larry Schott (Chief, Investigation Unit, NCPS), "Survey of Hazardous Toys and Suspected Dangers," *Memorandum to Commission* (December 8, 1969).

* Prepared by Professor Norman Kangun.

5. Do you feel that consumer education is the answer to reducing and/or preventing injuries? Why or why not? What part should marketers play in consumer-education programs?
6. What accounts for the failure of the market to reduce unreasonable risks in consumer products? Is the failure of the market also a marketing failure?
7. Write a paper in which you assume an audience of representatives from the television, glass-bottle, power-mower, and toy industries, and argue for government intervention in the establishment of performance and/or design standards for their products. What counterarguments are you likely to have to come to grips with?

Warranty service is often a neglected aspect of the total product offering. As a result, government agencies are taking actions to protect consumers from ineffective warranty programs. The author discusses guidelines which will assist business in developing and improving their product warranty programs in conjunction with consumer needs.

---

32. GUIDELINES FOR WARRANTY SERVICE AFTER SALE*

George Fisk†

The recent decision of General Motors to call back 4.9 million cars to check for safety defects was estimated to cost the company 50 million dollars in addition to the time and inconvenience to which GM customers would be subjected.[1] GM's dramatic callback announcement may have been made with an eye to forestalling government controls such as the bills introduced into the Senate of the United States by Senators Magnussen and Hayden calling for truth in warranty legislation.[2]

The GM recall move underscores the fact that everything that moves breaks down sooner or later. With over 800 million traffic vehicles and major appliances in use, individual warranty programs will not follow

* Reprinted from "Guidelines for Warranty Service after Sale," *Journal of Marketing*, Vol. 34 (January 1970), pp. 62–67.

† Syracuse University.

[1] "The Week in Review," *The New York Times* (March 2, 1969), p. 9-E.

[2] *The Federal Household Appliance Warranty Act*, U.S. Senate, 90th Cong., 1st sess., S. 2728 (December 6, 1967).

exactly the same plan because service facilities and consumer use patterns vary from product to product. Nonetheless, there is an urgent need for manufacturers and distributors to try to find warranty guidelines to assure adequate service after sale. This paper is one effort to provide such help.

It is easy to ask, as many indignant consumers do, why manufacturers and their distributors do not provide more adequate warranty services.[3] Walker Sandbach, executive director of Consumers' Union reports that warranty complaints are among the most numerous and bitter of those received by C.U. He reports over 5,000 letters of complaints annually concerning written warranties. Firms such as Zippo Cigarette Lighters and the Whirlpool Appliance Corporation have attempted to use warranty performance to build solid reputations for quality products. A large number of firms—perhaps a majority—have neither consistent warranty programs nor consistent policies for servicing their products after sale.[4] During his term as president, Lyndon Johnson advised firms holding these views to assure customers that guarantees and warranties meant what they said and said what they meant. He implied that government would act if businessmen did not. Today, the Magnuson and Hayden bill has considerable support from angry consumers who, although they have been winning court cases for a long time, have lacked direct means for protecting their rights as buyers.[5] Mounting support for the consumer movement leads many a businessman to ask what he can do to assure consumers of adequate service in the event that his products fail in the consumer's hands.[6]

A POSITIVE PROGRAM

The programs of firms that have used warranty service to build consumer preference demonstrate that American industry can convert consumer complaints into successful marketing strategies. To do so will require more than proclamations of intent, however. If for no other reason than to prevent legislative overkill, industry must seek to apply the same intelligence to service after sale that it now applies to wooing the customer in the first place. Four guidelines are proposed here as instruments for meeting the social responsibilities of marketing as well as for assuring a continuing customer interest: warranty integrity,

[3] "Marketing's Credibility Gap," *Sales Management*, Vol. 101 (June 15, 1968), p. 25.

[4] *New York Times* (June 15, 1964), p. 48, col. 2.

[5] *Report of the Task Force on Appliance Warranties and Service*, Special Assistant to the President on Consumer Affairs (Washington, D.C.: January 8, 1969), p. ii.

[6] "The Good Is Often Overlooked, So It Is with Appliance Men," *Home Furnishings Daily* (March 5, 1968).

education of the consumer, product quality control, and service on demand. The Whirlpool Corporation, for example, has cut its complaint/sales ratio to a relatively low 20 percent in seven years using a coherent warranty program based on some of the concepts described here.

WARRANTY INTEGRITY

Most manufacturers and distributors issue written warranties. A majority attempt to live up to the provisions of their warranties but a substantial number of firms use warranties as legal disclaimers of responsibility.[7] To avoid misunderstanding, more attention should be given to the way prospective purchasers interpret written warranties. An unambiguous warranty states not only the details of what is covered but also:

1. The name and address of the guarantor.
2. The length of time each phase of the guarantee or each major component is covered.
3. Who can file for a claim.
4. What conditions the claimant must fulfill.
5. What proportion of the cost must be covered by the person making the claim.
6. What parts and types of damages are not covered.
7. When and how the guarantor will fulfill his obligations.

Consumers know that some manufacturers offer stronger warranties than others. Weaker firms tend to offer more comprehensive guarantees than their more successful rivals. Since most businessmen believe that customer satisfaction builds brand loyalty, they are behaving inconsistently if they permit consumer hostility to be directed against an explicit but effectively worthless warranty. The first step in bridging the warranty "credibility gap" is to tell the truth to consumers as they understand it and not as the corporation's legal department would like it to be. If the warrantor fails to deliver according to the customer's expectation, the credibility gap widens, and when large numbers of consumers become aware of the fact that they have suffered the same kinds of losses, the consumer protectionist movement gains support for additional legislation. Consequently, warranty integrity is more than a pious assertion of intent; it is a necessary precondition for customer goodwill and continued freedom of action in the business community.

"Unconditionally guaranteed," "money-back guarantee," and "life-time guarantee" are terms often used to conceal the fact that component or accessory parts are not included in the seller's guarantee, that labor

[7] Same reference as footnote 5, pp. 4, 39–47. See also *Staff Report on Automobile Warranties*, Federal Trade Commission (Washington, D.C., 1968).

costs are not guaranteed, or that the fitness of the product for use is explicitly disclaimed by the seller. Repetition of unsatisfactory experiences based on these kinds of intentional deceptions have led articulate consumers to press for a change in warranty regulations. Even businessmen with the best intentions find it difficult to know how customers will interpret their warranty statements. Therefore, these ambiguous phrases are to be eschewed as vigorously as efforts to include the items previously mentioned in a written warranty are to be encouraged in warranty programs.

The first guideline in establishing warranty policies is to tell as much of the truth as the consumer needs to know to keep his warranty in force, and not as little as he is willing to believe in order to buy. If it is necessary for a seller to include a service contract tie-in to validate a warranty, the buyer has a right to know about this condition before he seeks to file a claim. If the warranty applies to the original purchaser only, subsequent buyers also have a right to this information. If the warranty is intended to apply for the design life of the product, the buyer should be explicitly informed that the *product* life, not the *buyer's* life, is the relevant time span. If there are other limiting conditions, the buyer has a right to know them.

CONSUMER EDUCATION PROGRAM

Perhaps as many as 80 percent of all consumer claims for warranty service may not be necessary. It is not that consumers are stupid, but they seldom read the operating instructions that accompany their purchases, or obey these instructions faithfully even when they know them. For this reason, some in-warranty service activity should include explicit consumer training in the use of the products purchased. In one instance a housewife complained that her new car would not go. After an 18-mile journey over back mountain roads, the dealer whom she telephoned found that the reason was an empty gas tank. Similar complaints from people who fail to turn on motors, add oil to new engines, or observe other operating instructions, are responsible for needless warranty calls. The pretesting of warranties, using warranty readership analysis, can lead to improved operating instructions so that the consumer understands not only her obligations under the warranty but also what is necessary to make the appliance operate effectively.

Since most humans learn by experience rather than by study, an effective warranty education program can capitalize on periods in the use-cycle when the customer is psychologically receptive to suggestions on how to use a product. Housewives are eager to learn how to use equipment when they have just paid for new appliances, but not after self-doubt about the wisdom of their purchase sets in. At the time of purchase it is often possible to use a simple slide film presentation of the product in use. The same film may be repeated when a repair call is needed to restore the product to use the first time. Home demonstrations by public utility representatives, repairmen, or mechanics can be highly effective. Although instruction manuals and decals are helpful, customers frequently fail to read them. Consequently, visual instructions in color may be preferable to an enclosure or to the fine print that adorns the inside wall of a cabinet. The firm that conducts readership tests on its operating instructions and warranty provisions is a rarity indeed, but such studies can be helpful in determining what information customers will attend to, what questions they have that are unanswered by instruction manuals, and what instructions they misinterpret in a way that damages their new purchases.

PRODUCT IMPROVEMENT

Premature failure in use is a prime cause of customer disenchantment with new products. Industry representatives sometimes argue that at the price per pound at which U.S. products are to be sold to compete with imports, multiple inspections for critical parts and subassemblies are too costly. Such claims are frequently made without the benefit of cost-effectiveness analysis.[8] Were the tradeoff values of research and development programs, inspection programs, and quality control programs to be compared to the costs of legal defense, customer brand switching, and costly callback programs, the advantages of improved quality control might often be sufficient to offset the increased costs.

From the standpoint of the disenchanted consumer, it is not the price per unit of output but per period of trouble-free use that counts. If, for example, a U.S. tire costs half the price of a European radial tire delivered in the United States, it is not cheaper if it must be replaced in one-third the time while the European product is still safe and delivering excellent gas mileage. The high quality of the products marketed by small foreign firms, which have been eroding the U.S. market share underscores the significance of the loss due to brand shifting in a number of industries ranging from automobiles to textiles.[9]

Two avenues of improved quality are especially deserving of closer attention by management: product redesign cycles and assembly inspections. In evaluating the cost-effectiveness of lax quality control against high quality control and redesign, a systems analysis of costs and benefits can improve allocation decisions with respect to the maintenance of parts inventory, the frequency of complaints on performance failures,

---

[8] Stephen Upton, Walker Sandbach, and Fred Prince, "Warranties, Guarantees and Service After Sale," taped dialog, *A New Measure of Responsibility for Marketing*, June 1968 Conference of the American Marketing Association, Philadelphia, Pennsylvania.

[9] *Wall Street Journal* (June 5, 1969), p. 1.

and the desirability of model changeovers. European manufacturers, for example, are not addicted to annual model redesign. Thus, they are able to stock repair parts even though their production runs are smaller than their American counterparts. Products which are redesigned annually require immense parts inventories compared to products which are redesigned only when a technological improvement warrants change. Annual or biennial redesign also prevents repairmen from discovering and correcting performance defects as rapidly as the designers make new mistakes. For example, a decline in sales of one outstanding electronics product can be traced to the fact that a basic component of this expensive machine is no longer manufactured. This situation developed because under the warranty the component is termed an "unwarranted auxiliary part" for which the manufacturer assumes no liability. At least some consumers are irked by this not uncommon practice even if the producer's interest in cutting costs through reduction of inventory is understandable.

While it is true that the consumer demand for novelty gives dealers something to sell, the tradeoff in many consumers' minds between dependability and variety does not necessarily favor variety to the degree that American marketing men have sometimes assumed. If dependability were not a valued product feature, Volkswagen and Rolleiflex, Wilkinson's Blades, and Electrolux Vacuum Cleaners would not enjoy the American sales they do.

If annual model changeovers are necessary to sustain sales, several choices remain open with respect to warranty policy. A producer can indicate that the warranty coverage is more limited on annually redesigned models, or he can charge a premium for a service contract based upon frequency of repair records and current hourly rates for repairmen. If consumers could register their choice between time-tested models under a cost-free warranty and annual changeover models with a labor service charge for in-warranty service, it might be possible to discover the tradeoff point at which proponents of new design would willingly choose dependable performance in preference to annual model changeovers plus labor charges for warranty services.

Improved assembly and inspection routines can also reduce in-warranty service calls by raising quality. Extending standard assembly times, reinspection of parts and assemblies, reduction of the proportion of allowable defects in parts inspections, setting closer tolerances on moving parts, and using higher quality primary materials are techniques quite well known to industrial engineers.

No socially responsible firm can advocate salability despite social costs such as death and injury on the highways and in the home. (Marketing men need not dictate a level of quality that is detrimental to serviceability if engineering can define for the marketing department an equation for optimality of salability and serviceable quality.) What products businessmen cannot warrant at prevailing competitive prices they are ill-advised to sell. The temper of the times dictates a more prudent social policy than "marketability at any price" on the part of sellers whose volume philosophy has gone unchallenged for many years.

SERVICE

The core of any warranty program ultimately lies in the quality of the maintenance and repair services that can be offered to customers. Inferior postwarranty service calls can induce needless brand switching. In addition, a backlog of uncompleted service calls can depress the level of market penetration for products ranging from television to garbage disposal units. One explanation for unsatisfactory service is the inadequate compensation and training of service technicians. It is commonly believed that more repairmen are leaving the retail service field than are entering, and that crash training programs to create "tube jockeys" capable only of hit-or-miss replacement tactics are simply adding to the number of unserviced appliances awaiting repair. The BLS estimates that there are 200,000 "appliance repairmen" with an annual attrition rate of 10,000, but the main problem is believed to be quality of service.[10]

To obtain qualified service personnel, industry has to foot the bill although some help is available from government. Recognizing this situation, most trade association apprenticeship proposals for training new appliance technicians depend on Department of Labor funds made available through the Manpower Training Act. However, programs dependent on federal aid could easily collapse under the impact of congressional budget cuts. The training of inner city youths in service technician careers will require a sustained level of dedicated cooperation between municipal and state government on the one hand and manufacturers and distribution agencies on the other. Uncle Sam cannot deliver the quality and volume of training required to solve industry's appliance technician manpower shortage problem without industry help. Cooperation with the Department of Labor is necessary and desirable for pilot projects, but the dominant training role should be assumed by industries whose customers have a right to the service they are promised in written warranties.

Many firms such as RCA, GE, Carrier, and Whirlpool maintain technical training centers where their appliance technicians can periodically update skills needed to assure competent performance.[11] Recruiting and

[10] "The Servicer's Problems: How the Trade Groups Are Solving Them," *Merchandising Week*, Vol. 100 (July 1, 1968), pp. 8–9, esp. p. 9. Also same reference as footnote 5, pp. 178–79.

[11] See for example, Stephen E. Upton, *Customer Services Division*, A Serviceways Recap (Benton Harbor, Michigan: Whirlpool Corporation), n.d.

training new service technicians takes a lot of time and money to assure mastery of technically difficult repairs. Refresher courses stressing design changes are also needed for already proficient repairmen. The implied scope of such programs makes it necessary to hire full-time service training directors to do the job effectively. In many firms this could force a reexamination of present payroll allocations. However, if business cannot voluntarily provide the quality of repair and maintenance service demanded by the increasingly sophisticated equipment it puts on the market, the government will have little alternative but to impose licensing and inspection programs such as already are in force in Connecticut, Indiana, Louisiana, and Massachusetts.

For example, California has a licensing system under which bill-padding and faulty diagnosis can be traced. New York is considering such a step after tests by Consumers' Union showed wide variations in the quality of diagnosis and in prices for replacing an inexpensive tube in a color TV set. The Louisiana Motor Vehicle Commission requires auto companies to pay the same rate for warranty work as the dealer charges for routine customer service. Since the first step in fair pricing is competent diagnosis and repair, only professional supervision can assure that the quality of repair services will meet these exacting requirements.

Subtle pricing issues also arise in connection with warranty terms. In the first place there is the question whether a producer should be held responsible for replacing components he does not make, such as light bulbs and switches, or whether the consumer should be forced to pay for the manufacturer's assembly and inspection mistakes by paying for the labor required to complete a repair. Reputable manufacturers are in some cases reimbursing dealers at the regular work rate for work performed in fulfillment of warranty contracts.[12]

Sales of separate service contracts with the same characteristics as insurance policies are finding growing markets among producers of complex products such as color TV's and washing machines. If the machine functions properly, the customer is out of pocket for the costs of the service contract; if the machine is defective, the dealer charges the manufacturer for routine customer service. If the customer requires such service, she gains by the amount that the service charge exceeds the cost of the warranty contract. The fairness of such a system has been challenged on the grounds that the customer is forced into a lottery in order to enjoy use rights already promised by the warrantor. Some firms therefore are now promising to fix anything that goes wrong during the warranty period but including an average warranty service charge in their retail selling price which discounters cannot safely undercut without withholding the warranty as an element of the transaction. If

[12] Same reference as footnote 8.

the favorable results attained by these firms were widely duplicated, additional government legislation would be irrelevant.

CONSUMER SATISFACTION: KEY TO SUCCESSFUL WARRANTY PROGRAMS

Customer satisfaction with products in use provides the clue as to the effectiveness of the warranty program. Despite great efforts made in preparing training materials and conducting seminars, classes, and workshops for their service technicians, customer service audits are required to find out how well the training has been applied. Customers seldom complain in a way that commands the attention of top management. In fact, only a fraction of customer dissatisfaction is expressed in complaints: brand switching and store patronage changes are more frequent expressions of dissatisfaction than is letter writing or telephone calls to dealers.

One of the few studies directly attacking the problem of customer satisfaction was conducted by Better Homes and Gardens.[13] When asked if they followed the warranty requirements specified by the manufacturer, 84 percent of the new car owners queried replied in the affirmative. In other words, 16 percent did not. Of the group that followed warranty requirements, 56 percent were "generally satisfied" while 34 percent were partly or not at all satisfied, and 10 percent had no warranty work performed. Among the 16 percent of the new car buyers that failed to follow the manufacturer's warranty requirements, a few said it cost too much, but a striking 43 percent of those that did not follow manufacturer's warranty programs admitted to apathy and indifference by such statements as "didn't remember to take the car in at required intervals," or "too much trouble to keep up warranty." Among these individuals who don't squawk about defective warranties, a surprising proportion are in families in which the household head has done graduate work at a college or university.

The Better Homes and Gardens study also showed that consumers distinguish between the manufacturer's warranty and reputation and the dealer's reputation for service.[14] In fact, the reliability of the dealer was chosen as the most influential factor by an increasingly larger proportion of consumers in each successively higher age category, possibly reflecting the accumulative effects of experience. If other studies support the Better Homes and Gardens data, it could be inferred that while consumers take a long time to become conscious of the warranty programs supporting their use of appliances and durables, they would choose continuous serviceability in preference to initial design advantages.

[13] *Better Homes and Gardens Consumer Questionnaire* (Des Moines, Iowa: Meredith Corporation, 1968), pp. 91, 92, and 107.

[14] Ibid., p. 107.

CONCLUSION

The burdens for servicing goods under warranty are multiplying rapidly. With the rate of increase in automobile population outstripping that in human population, and with over 800 million appliances in use in the United States, the short-run advantages of using warranties as a come-on to make sales hardly seems worth the price that industry will be forced to pay as a result of the popular outcry against malpractices. Following the warranty program guidelines outlined here can stimulate repeat sales and word of mouth recommendation by satisfied customers. Such guidelines can aid in designing advertising and promotion campaigns, in pricing repair services, wording the warranties themselves, and making adjustments either at no cost to the consumer or on the basis of a service contract charge. If manufacturers individually and collectively do not recognize the legitimate claims of consumers, there is ample evidence that the Congress, regardless of which political party is in power, may be obliged to do so as the result of mounting public frustration with haphazard warranty service after sale.

The self-service mode of shopping has resulted in the package becoming more important to the consumer as an information source. The author indicates that both shopping behavior and the package-shopper relationship must be studied before additional packaging regulations are imposed. He considers three recommendations which will facilitate the elimination of deceptive practices.

---

33. THE PACKAGE, LEGISLATION, AND THE SHOPPER*

David M. Gardner†

In the last few years, such terms as "deceptive packaging," "mislabeling," "short weights," "nonexistent price reductions," "false advertising," and "truth-in-packaging" have become all too common in the field of marketing. The concern has been that potentially unethical practices

* Reprinted from "The Package, Legislation, and the Shopper," *Business Horizons,* Vol. II (October 1968), pp. 53–58.

† University of Illinois.

lead to confusion and the erosion of competence by the consumer in the marketplace. The result has been charges and countercharges by consumer organizations, legislators, and the marketing industry; on the sidelines is the housewife, who tends to view the industry as a usurious, unethical ogre, a view supporting her conviction that gouging middlemen are to blame for cost-of-living increases.

The most recent development is the passage of truth-in-packaging legislation by the eighty-ninth Congress. It is generally conceded that this legislation, which places considerable reliance on voluntary standards, is mild. Unquestionably, most marketing firms can live with the way it deals with the listing of ingredients for cosmetics and detergents, definition of slack fill, and labeling requirements. The new law is apt to be amended in the near future, however, for two reasons. First, it contains a phrase stating that packaging should be regulated in such a way as to "facilitate value comparison." Congress and the various regulatory agencies will soon try to define exactly what is meant by this phrase and how the idea should be implemented. Second, Senator Warren Magnuson, chairman of the Senate commerce committee in his role as champion of the unprotected consumer, is unhappy with the legislation passed by the eighty-ninth Congress and has promised to keep the subject alive in the ninetieth.[1]

The goal of present and proposed truth-in-packaging legislation is to "protect" the consumer. Unfortunately, this goal is not stated in operational terms. To do so, it is necessary to look at the shopper in the marketplace. We must have an understanding of how the shopper behaves if we are to provide a sound basis for future legislation and interpret present legislation. (For the purpose of this discussion, "shopper" will be used to describe the person who is the purchasing agent for a family.)

It is not the purpose of this article to offer moral judgment of the marketing industry or governmental bodies. It does seem appropriate, however, to offer a way of thinking about the relationship between the shopper and the package.

IMPORTANCE OF THE PACKAGE

Truth-in-packaging legislation is based on the assumption that consumers are not getting the most value possible for their money due to misleading or inadequate information. Presenting misleading or inadequate information is judged to be a deceptive practice.

To understand the basis for this assumption, is is necessary to look back one generation. Self-service is a rather recent innovation in the

---

[1] "House Is 'Adamant,' so Senate Accepts Mild Package Bill," *Advertising Age*, XXXVII (Oct. 17, 1966), p. 1.

marketing of consumer goods; in addition, fewer choices for products and brands were offered one generation ago. The usual relationship in the marketplace was between the salesperson in the store and the shopper, who, for the most part, relied on the salesperson's judgment and recommendations. In many cases, the merchandise was measured out to order in front of the shopper.

We have moved away from this type of "personal" merchandising and now emphasize self-service. Self-service has both a cause-and-effect relationship to deceptive packaging because of the attention that now must be given to the package. Instead of a salesperson-shopper relationship, we now often have a package-shopper relationship. The information that was once passed on to the shopper by the salesperson must now be transmitted by the package and its label. If any deception exists, it is now easily documented.

In short, given the absence of salespeople, the package itself has now become a crucial marketing element. The intense competition in most grocery product markets has led many manufacturers to introduce an array of adjectives and labeling practices designed to induce the shopper to buy a particular product. Such descriptive phrases as "the giant pound" and "generous servings for a family of four" produced confusion and skepticism in many shoppers. Any issue of *Consumer Reports* or the mailbox of any congressman contains complaints about the packaging practices of the grocery products industry. This, coupled with complaints in other areas of consumer interest, has led Congress to pass "consumer protection" legislation of which the truth-in-packaging effort has been most notable.

This article attempts to give some structure to this rather undefined area of shopper-package relationships by advocating a realistic view of the shopper in the marketplace, by offering a partial checklist against which to evaluate present and future regulations, and a definition of deception in packaging.

SHOPPER IN THE MARKETPLACE

Two distinct views of the shopper in the marketplace can be used to understand the shopper and to form the basis for legislation. The underlying assumptions of each view would produce different types of legislation.

In one view, the shopper evaluates all purchases on a price/quantity basis. The view implicitly assumes that brands are of little or no importance and that the shopper is operating independently of any environmental influences. Therefore, the act of paying additional money is judged to be irrational—whether it is intended to gain the perceived benefits of a branded good, the convenience of a smaller package, or the advantage of a "nondrip" syrup container. That shoppers do not use the price/quantity relationship in many purchase decisions is the finding of 46 studies conducted by the Creative Research Associates.[2]

Shoppers do seem to perceive values in products other than "most for the least." Not too many years ago, for example, a large cereal company lost a substantial part of the cereal market because of the shape and size of its packages. Therefore, any legislation or interpretation based on this view of the shopper will be based on a rather narrow and static understanding. The result is apt to be legislation and rulings that tend to put emphasis on clear statements of weight so that price/quantity comparisons can be made readily.

The second view is one offered by Wroe Alderson, who suggests that the shopper is engaged in problem solving with primary emphasis on replenishing or extending an assortment of goods needed to support expected future behavior.[3] The shopper is a problem solver, not in the sense of getting the most units of breakfast cereal for the least amount of money, but finding that particular breakfast cereal that will be most apt to satisfy the family. This view also holds that an individual item cannot be evaluated on a price/quantity basis; attention must be given to the total assortment of goods into which the item will fit. The assortment of goods that an individual or family assembles is based on the particular values of that individual or family, values determined by reference groups, perception of social class, education, income, influence, and the nature of the assortment. This view is primarily concerned with the quality of the assortment. Cost certainly enters into the decision process, but not necessarily as the most important variable.

This view is more complete and accurate. It takes into account the fact that the shopper is buying items to support a way of life, and "getting the best buy" has entirely different connotations than under the first view of shopper behavior. Any legislation or interpretation based on this view of shopper behavior is apt to be more difficult to write because it must be general, rather than specific. The legislation is more apt to set up rules of reason and guidelines rather than specific do's and don't's because of the shopper's concern with the "quality" of an assortment of goods, rather than a price/quantity concern for a single item.

SHOPPER-PACKAGE RELATIONSHIP

The shopper-package relationship is basically one in which the package, by its shape, color, size, label, and price, gives information to the shopper, who evaluates the information and considers the possibility

---

[2] Irving S. White, "The Perception of Value in Products," in Joseph W. Newman, ed., *On Knowing the Consumer* (New York: John Wiley & Sons, Inc., 1966), p. 92.

[3] Wroe Alderson, *Dynamic Marketing Behavior* (Homewood, Ill.: Richard D. Irwin, Inc., 1965), pp. 144–46, 155–59.

of extending or replenishing an assortment. The evaluation process, which ultimately results in an assortment of goods, is the product of various influences. All of these make up the need-value system of the shopper. In the absence of a salesperson, the package must convey the information to be evaluated. The shopper evaluates the information against the needs of the family with the goal of increasing the quality of the assortment of goods.

The information conveyed by the package is both *objective* and *subjective*. Objective information is a factual description of contents, and its weight, volume, and price; subjective information is offered by the brand name, color of the package, size and shape of the container, and design of the label. (There is a very good commonsense argument that price, in many circumstances, is also subjective information.) This type of information is subjective in the sense that it is affected by the biases and background of the shopper.

More specifically, then, how does a shopper decide whether an item should be added to an assortment? A family (or individual) over time tends to value certain groups, certain ideas, and certain objects more highly than others, and to build an assortment of goods that fits this need-value structure. This structure has a specific influence on the assortment of goods and the package-shopper relationship and determines for the shopper whether an item will add quality to an assortment. For instance, a family that values being "modern" will select a different assortment of goods than will a family that values traditional behavior. Therefore, the "modern" family would be quite apt to add frozen dried chicken cubes to its assortment or even a prestuffed and seasoned turkey. The "traditional" family, however, would be less apt to have either in its assortment of goods.

This article adopts the commonsense position that a package's subjective information conveys an image to the shopper. The shopper, in the process of problem solving, decides whether the image "fits" with the need-value system of the family. If it does, the brand is apt to be added to the assortment. Keep in mind, however, that certain objective information, like calorie content or extremely high prices, could override the decision for addition.

The most important fact about the evaluative process is that the information transmitted by the package is filtered or understood by the shopper on the basis of previous contact with a social group and the anticipated contact with this group. The process is also affected by culture, education, experience, and the physiological makeup of the shopper. The accompanying figure shows this relationship. The information transmitted by the package is seen in a selective way by the shopper. This means that, because of the need-value system of the shopper, certain words take on value loadings, certain shapes and sizes of containers look larger and more attractive, and certain adjectives denote social

Shopper-package relationship

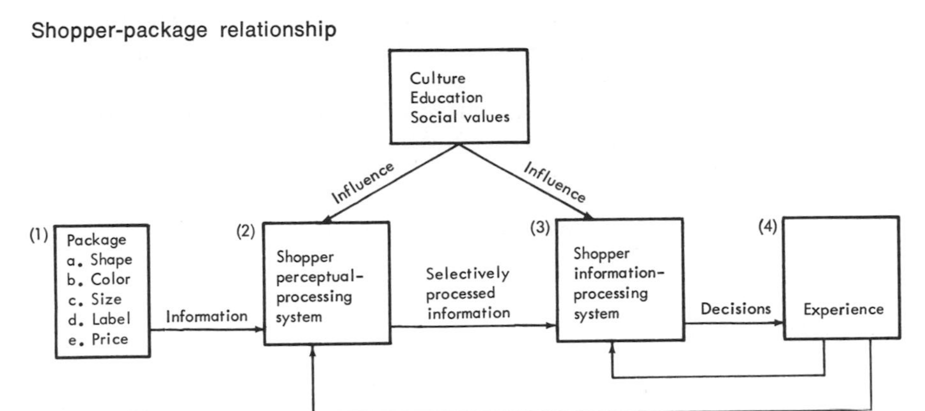

and cultural approval. The information is evaluated, and decisions are made on the basis of the evaluation. An item is purchased if it will make the assortment of goods more complete in the view of the perceiver, not what it actually does in fact. Experience with a brand or product alters the perception and understanding of future package-shopper relationships.

In replenishing or extending an assortment of goods, a shopper acquires certain brand loyalties but may be induced to alter these loyalties in case of poor experience with a previous purchase or because a package of another brand contains information in the form of shape, color, price, and so on that makes it appear to fit into the assortment of goods. We are primarily concerned with the situation where a shopper alters brand loyalties based on perceptions that produced the feeling that the quality of the assortment would be enhanced, but, in fact, is not.

Given this brief look at the shopper-package relationship, we can now advance a definition of deception in packaging:

> Shoppers purchase an item because they anticipate it will enhance the quality of their assortment of goods. Therefore, if any package transmits information in any form that induces the shopper to purchase, and the value of the item adds less quality to the assortment of goods than expected, then deception in packaging exists.

Note that this definition is quite general—necessarily so. Each package must be examined on an individual basis in relation to the context in which the information will be perceived by the shopper. For this reason, this definition is not meant to include potential deception in packaging.

Based on the preceding discussion, a partial and necessarily general checklist is offered to evaluate present and future legislation and interpretations.

Have all the relevant influences on shopper behavior been taken into consideration? Has the influence of culture, experience, education, and so on been taken into consideration?

Is the legislation based on an understanding of the individual shopper, or an aggregation of consumer behavior in the macro sense?

Is the emphasis placed on an individual item and its price/quantity relationship, or on the item as it fits into a total assortment of goods?

What assumptions about perception and meaning of information to the shopper are being made? Are they realistic or normative?

RECOMMENDATIONS

The understanding of the shopper-package relationship advocated in this article leads to three recommendations. First, the legislation passed by the Eighty-ninth Congress, if understood to be concerned with deception in objective information, is certainly a valid piece of legislation. However, I would strongly recommend that further attempts be stopped at once by Miss Betty Furness, the executive branch of government, well-intentioned congressmen such as Senator Magnuson, and organizations such as Consumer Union to facilitate value comparison by reducing or eliminating the subjective information conveyed by packages. This must be done until we are able to document and understand the value of the subjective information to shoppers, and base any further legislation on how shoppers actually do behave, rather than on how we would like them to behave.

The second recommendation follows from the first. It is imperative that the federal government in its assumed role of consumer protector set out to study in detail each phase of the shopper-package relationship shown in the figure. This will not only form an important foundation for potential legislation, but will aid consumer good firms in better understanding the shopper-package relationship and hence help them become more efficient. Much of the necessary information for such a study already exists in the files of private firms and in a wide collection of academic papers. However, for various reasons, the information is not public or not readily useful. Therefore, the federal government must take the initiative and provide the framework and motivation for such a study.[4] The actual study can be conducted by private firms and the academic community. One important caution, however, allowance must be made for incorporating and evaluating new evidence as it becomes available. This study must *not* be the study to end all studies.

The final recommendation is directed at Congress itself. Any legisla-

[4] Two possible frameworks for this type of study are in existence. For this particular study, modifications would be necessary, but they do represent a point of departure. They are: Alan R. Andreasen, "Attitudes and Customer Behavior: a Decision Model," in Lee E. Preston, ed., *New Research in Marketing* (Berkeley, Calif.: University of California Institute of Business and Economic Research, 1965), pp. 1–16; and John A. Howard and Jagdish N. Sheth, "The Theory of Buyer Behavior," mimeographed, Graduate School of Business, Columbia University, 1965.

tion should contain provisions that make it mandatory for the appropriate regulatory body charged with administering truth-in-packaging legislation to make its rulings and interpretations based on actual consumer behavior evidence, rather than on a normative view that characterizes shoppers as evaluating all purchases on a price/quantity basis.

Marketers have professed that "the consumer is king." The consumerism movement provides evidence that not all consumers agree they have been well treated by business. The author illustrates that only a more thorough consideration of consumer desires can unite the two groups into a closer relationship.

---

34. THE CONSUMER-BUSINESS PARTNERSHIP*

Frank E. McLaughlin†

If a "PARTNERSHIP" for nutrition, health, and safety exists at all, I'm afraid it does not fit easily into any of the classifications or definitions of the standard law dictionary. In fact, there are many who believe that the only worthwhile objective of business is profit and that the businessman has no social responsibility in the fields of public health, nutrition, and safety. That does not sound like the joint effort—joint benefit criteria of a partnership does it?

The point has been made valid no doubt, that the concerns and orientation of industry are generally of a short-term nature. Marketing professors Buskirk and Rothe illustrate this point in the October 1970 *Journal of Marketing* in their comment.

> Top management's insistence on quarterly and annual budgeting performance may force operational management to make short-run decisions detrimental to the consumer because the impact of such decisions will not be reflected during operational management's tenure in that position. Consequently, when a product revision is needed, the response may be increased advertising and promotion expenditures rather than the more appropriate effort.

---

* Reprinted from "The Consumer-Business Partnership," *Food Drug Cosmetic Law Journal* (December 1970), pp. 519–24.

† President's Committee on Consumer Interests.

Standing in the way of a partnership relationship is the historical and still popularly advocated marketing theory that the "consumer is king," an adequate defender of his interests with a life and death power over the business enterprise represented by his dollar choice. At war with this concept and, therefore, at war with the partnership image is the belief that 20th-century techniques of advertising and promotion create an irrational demand unrelated to more important needs of the individual: That business in a "Pavlovian" exercise is stimulating artificial demand rather than discovering real need. As stated by Morton H. Broffman, president of Morrell & Company in an October 1970 speech before the American Meat Institute:

> While the modern marketer may concede that some consumer behavior is irrational, he regards as legitimate any need that is not antisocial, whether the consumer already is aware of it, or if he responds to it only when it is called to his attention.

The other side of that coin is seen in Dorothy Sayers' statement: "A society in which consumption has to be artificially stimulated in order to keep production going is a society founded on trash and waste . . . "

Working against the partnership relationship is the widely discussed consumer ignorance of economic and marketing factors. Professor James Carman, speaking of widespread economic illiteracy, asked: "How can one react logically to a radical, new idea for structuring our economic system and economic institutions when one does not have a basic understanding of the working of the present system?" Rephrasing the question one might ask, how can there be a partnership when one party doesn't understand the business?

The same lack of understanding is attributed to government. Writing in the November issue of *The Chief Executive* on this subject, Mr. J. V. Clyne of Canada wrote: "Tax reforms, changes in the unemployment insurance act, proposals for the control of foreign ownership, etc., often containing impractical and visionary ideas, can be put forward by men of good will but with little real understanding of the impact of their ideas on business." I recall reading something similar about certain proposed "cents off" and food standards regulations on this side of the border.

And then, of course, there is the argument that the consumer is not a full partner because someone inside or outside of government is always presuming to speak for him. Recently, I spoke at an industry meeting where a marketing professor singled out certain congressmen and senators for vigorous criticism as "consumer activists" representing only themselves and not consumers. It would seem that there is quite a distance between the schools of government and business on his campus.

Mr. Broffman of Morrell and Company argued that "Some spokesmen (for the consumer) tend to have no awareness of higher costs, and the possible unwillingness of consumers to pay more for the value received by a given protective measure."

If there is a partnership, it is a partnership which has seen continuous polarization throughout the last decade over issues of proof of drug efficacy, the adequacy of the average American's diet, scope of color additive preclearance authority, the role of food standards in advancing the interest of the consumer—the list goes on and on. The list is likely to face expansionary pressures in the 70s on the questions of extrapolation of lower animal test results to man, premarketing standards for medical devices and cosmetics, "imitation" versus "traditional" foods, and other issues which we can but dimly perceive at this time.

What kind of partnership are we talking about anyway?

Partnership of necessity

In keeping with the "equal time" posture I have set above, I would like to give you a few relevant comments on the subject of this "partnership" made last month by Mr. F. Ritter Shumway, president of the Chamber of Commerce of the United States.

> Our triumphs and accomplishments have helped make America what it is. And our mistakes and our shortcomings have also had other impacts. We can glory in the one, and try to remedy the other, but the good as well as the bad are the unerasable evidence that business is embedded in the social as well as the economic fabric of our nation. Business can no more live apart from society than society can live apart from business. We interact constantly with other great American institutions. Education, government, the family, and labor, among others, are as much a part of our social and economic environment as air, water, and land comprise our physical environment. Each of these insitutions has responsibilities toward all the others and to the society we all belong to.

To paraphrase, consumers, industry, and government participate in a partnership of necessity.

What does the consumer expect of this partnership? At a minimum he wants the rights that three successive presidents and the American marketing system have affirmed. I refer to the right to be informed and to be heard, i.e., the right of communication. One of the reasons that President Kennedy's 1962 consumer statement struck a responsive chord with the business community is that the basic premise of the American marketing system is discovering and responding to the consumer's needs. Of course, rights to choose and to safety go with the right of communication, but without communication, discussions of relative safety and relative degree of choice are academic.

Talk of credibility gaps, age gaps, and information gaps is very fashionable these days. Recently, Mr. Herb Cleaves of the General Foods Company gave a speech about the "consumer gap." The message of consumerism in the 70s is symbolized by a bridge recognized thus far by only a few. The fact that editors and publishers of newspapers in the early 60s began paying reporters to cover consumer-related topics on a full-time basis has nothing to do with the desire of newspaper management to reduce the size of the unemployment rolls. Consumer columns in a paper sell newspapers. Consumer topics on TV and radio swell the size of the audience and bring in new sponsors. Inexpertly perhaps, but inexorably nevertheless, an increasingly better educated American consumer is bridging the interest gap. He has communicated that mood to the media and to others.

The old catch words like "nutrition won't sell" and "safety won't sell" are beginning to sour in the mouths of marketers. "Service won't sell," they said until words like "We service what we sell" and "the set with the works in a drawer" began to make the cash registers sing.

"Stressing warranties is negative selling" they said. The simplification and liberalization of warranties now underway are rapidly changing that statement.

"People don't care about environmental issues" they said, but women's groups writing in to the government for lists of the phosphate content in detergents just keep writing and city councils keep placing environmental issues on their agenda.

Words like "extrapolation," "ecology," "persistent pesticides," "food additives," "functional bumpers," "unit pricing," and "code dating" are becoming a part of the everyday vernacular.

I expect that at least five more studies will be done showing that unit pricing and code dating are unusual, unneeded, costly, and possibly fattening, but the handwriting on the wall was read clearly by Mr. Cleaves when he said ". . . if Mrs. Jones wants to know the unit price of what she buys, and the nutritional content, and how long it has been on the shelf, it won't infringe our God-given right to do business to tell her, right on the label . . ."

The appeal to right of information will in short be so powerful that, wonder of wonders, the consumer will undoubtedly be told the price of what she is buying.

The interest in consumer issues and the growing sophistication of the consumer have not been lost on legislators either and the events of this last session of Congress, where much was debated and little enacted, will no doubt become grist for the election mill of '72.

Even the dignified corridors of the National Archives building have been penetrated by the growing interest and awareness of the consumer. Perhaps you missed the notice, but the December 1 issue of the *Federal Register* carries a proposal that all documents be accompanied by key word identification and head note. The notice explained in part: "Over the years many persons have pointed out the *Federal Register* is a difficult document for the average laymen to use. Comments and criticisms have increased in the recent past in direct proportion to the growing interest in consumer affairs." It just may be that the government will begin to take some pains to explain what it is about.

Generally, what does this partial bridging of the interest gap by consumers mean for government and business?

I think it means, among other things, that the combination of increased education, greater exposure to mass media, and growing sophistication of consumers is forcing an alteration of the two-handed game of regulators versus the regulated. I think there is a growing and demonstrable disenchantment with the job that independent and old line agencies have done as stand-ins for and representatives of consumer voters.

I think it means that government and industry will be forced, for the first time, to turn briefly away from the substance of a particular key issue and do some agonizing over the procedure for bringing the issue to a public forum or public opinion registering mechanism for consideration. Opening up the decision-making process may have either of two effects for the government administrator, namely, presenting him with evidence that his proposed decision does not have public support, or presenting him with insulation against pressure from private interest groups to change his proposed decisions.

By the above, I do not mean that issues of great economic, health, or safety import which have not been supported by public argument and subjected to public scrutiny should be dumped on the committee system on Congress for resolution. There are limits on the ability of Congress to expose flaming issues to reasoned debate for the correct period of time.

It is now time to talk in specifics.

I think that this new partnership for nutrition, health, and safety that is emerging means in part the following:

If the Delaney amendment has deficiencies, those deficiencies and any suggested remedies should be proposed and discussed openly.

If the concepts of imitation, traditional, and standard foods are to be replaced, then the public should be let in on the replacements which are contemplated as well as the potential health and actual economic effects of the replacements.

If the merits of premarket standards for cosmetics and medical devices cannot, in the months to come, be discussed openly, then the partnership must accept the inevitability of the winds of fate and the uncertainty of pressures acting upon Congress.

Whether on the front pages of newspapers or through more protracted and orderly avenues, the public will be educated to the limitations of lower animal chemical studies.

If we do not carefully use existing sources of information regarding public nutritional understanding, we may well be putting the cart before the horse in a horse race of nutritional labeling claims.

In short, I think this "partnership" of necessity will be changing the way business is conducted.

Mr. Lelan F. Sillin, Jr., president of Northeast Utilities, made the same point a good deal better than I have in the November issue of *The Chief Executive* when he wrote: "People are telling us over and over again, in some cases violently, that they want and demand a participatory role in shaping the events that affect their lives."

All of us, in the utility business and in society at large, are in serious trouble unless we can build a constructive bridge of understanding leading to a reconciliation among government, business, and people in the communities we serve.

b.

Communications

Two consumer rights, the right to be informed and the right to be heard, have a direct influence on the communications component of the marketing mix. Within this area consumers are demanding that business firms provide them with specific information concerning product contents, uses, restrictions, and claims, and that this information be validated by facts and independent studies.

Consumers are also demanding that business firms listen to them and their complaints and desires, and that firms seek out such information. Consumers desire an effective two-way communications channel between firms and themselves. This channel, if properly utilized by the firm, could lead to quicker reactions to consumer communications and complaints. Such action may also help the business community avoid further governmental intervention.

Greyser, in the first article of this section, presents an adapted and augmented version of his testimony to the Federal Trade Commission concerning recent social criticism of advertising and marketing. Following this, Capitman attempts to develop standards or ethics for the advertising industry. Next Ward suggests the importance of assessing the relative impact of television advertising on children learning to be consumers. In the concluding article in this section, Blankenship calls for expansion of the consumer research function from a one-way to a two-way communication channel between the consumer and the corporation.

What is really known about advertising's social impacts? How sophisticated or defenseless are consumers in their ability to screen advertising content that comes their way? Rather than allowing the consumer's interest to be represented by business or consumer advocates, the consumer's own voice should play an important part in the making of public policy decisions regarding advertising's role in society.

---

35. ADVERTISING: ATTACKS AND COUNTERS

Stephen A. Greyser

The fall 1971 Federal Trade Commission hearings on "modern advertising practices" have raised new questions and issues regarding the impacts of advertising in our society. Included are such matters as advertising's persuasive abilities, the truthfulness of its content, its tastefulness, and its cultural impacts of our values and lifestyles.

Most readers' familiarity with these issues and their related allegations signals the fact that such criticism of advertising is hardly a new phenomenon. However, the current wave of critical comment seems more strident and pervasive—much akin to advertising itself. It is reflected in less favorable attitudes toward advertising on the part of businessmen and the public. Further, such criticism is often accompanied by recommendations for regulation which bid to inhibit some of advertising's most cherished practices, perhaps most notably that of puffery and exaggeration which to some represent the poetic essence of advertising but to many critics seem little short of outright fabrication.

The public policy proposals and rulings accompanying the criticism have in turn spawned further industry self-regulatory efforts. Particularly in view of the spate of external and internal regulatory activity, this is an appropriate time to make a systematic examination of the social impacts of advertising. More specifically, let us consider certain questions:

What do we really know about advertising's social impacts?

Is there a sensible overall structure for considering them?

Can we explain the misunderstandings over them that divide advertising's advocates and critics?

Most important for businessmen, what are the implications of the criticisms and the resultant regulatory actions and proposals?

In this Special Report, I shall address myself to these specific ques-

---

* Reprinted from "Advertising: Attacks and Counters," *Harvard Business Review*, Vol. 50 (March-April 1972), pp. 22–36.

† Harvard Business School.

tions; but, first, I shall mention some background facts to set the historical perspective for the accompanying discussion.

HISTORICAL PERSPECTIVE

An extensive review of historical critiques of advertising leads me to four observations:

First, as we have already noted, questioning of advertising—and indeed of the whole selling process—is not new. Centuries of commentary from economists, businessmen, philosophers, and others have treated its uses and abuses, its virtues and vices.

Second, assessments of advertising, particularly its social aspects, have deep ideological roots. And, as with all ideological matters, the debate is often very heated. One's conclusions are closely linked to one's subjective value judgments about how the marketplace works and what kind of a society ours should be.

Third, as knowledgeable advertising and marketing executives realize, any appraisal of advertising must recognize that it cannot be viewed in total isolation. After all, it is but one—albeit to the consumer the most common—of numerous forms of marketing communications, including personal selling, packaging, point-of-sale materials, and sales promotion (such as coupons and premiums). Further, advertising is but one in the constellation of elements that constitute the familiar marketing mix—including price, product policy, distribution, and others—which every successful marketer must develop and adjust for his products and brands.

Fourth, the bulk of the positive commentary on advertising has its foundation in its economic accomplishments, while the bulk of the criticism of advertising has been based on its social impacts. For example, in studies of the public's and businessmen's attitudes toward advertising, its economic roles receive generally strong approbation (even from those who are unfavorable to advertising), but its social consequences are criticized and aspects of its content are questioned. Thus it should not be surprising that my comments addressed primarily to advertising's social effects will focus on issues wherein advertising may often be portrayed essentially in a rather negative cast.

I mention these background facts in order to underscore the need for further understanding—on the part of public policy makers, marketers, and critics alike—of how (*a*) the strategies and techniques of advertising fit into broader corporate and marketing planning, and (*b*) the marketplace mechanism really works.

SOCIAL ISSUES

Let us turn more specifically to the complex issues involved in an appraisal of advertising's social effects. Exhibit I represents an attempt

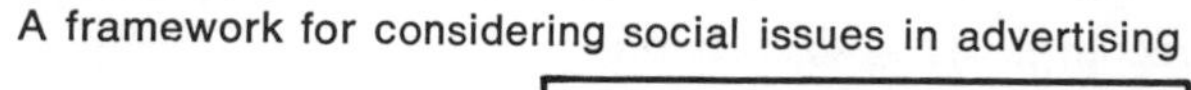

EXHIBIT 1
A framework for considering social issues in advertising

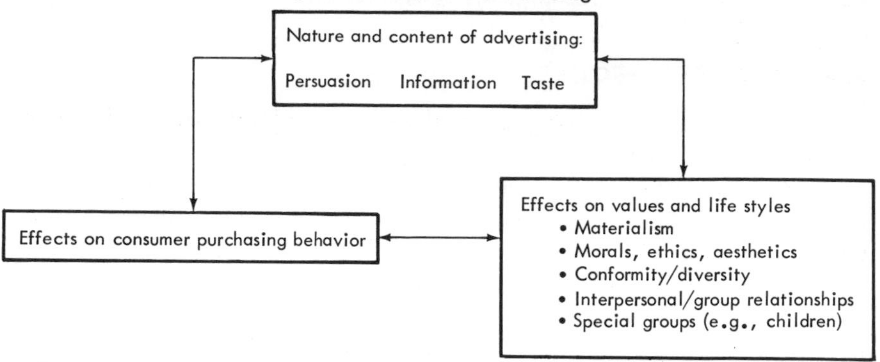

Source: Adapted from Chapter 4 of *Appraising the Economic and Social Effects of Advertising*, a monograph prepared by Michael Pearce, Scott M. Cunningham, and Avon Miller under the direction of Robert D. Buzzell and Stephen A. Greyser (Cambridge, Mass.: Marketing Science Institute, 1971).

to structure and help organize our thinking about the principal social issues. The two-way arrows reflect the interrelationships among these areas.

In this section of the article, I shall concentrate on the nature and content of advertising, including the important dimensions of its *persuasive powers,* its *information content,* and its *taste aspects.* Then, I shall consider the social effects of advertising on consumer purchasing behavior, particularly its broad impact in our *values and lifestyles.*

Persuasive powers

Many social critics have tried to separate the persuasive aspects of advertising from the informative aspects. Such a separation is, in my view, a false dichotomy since the objective of all advertising is to influence one's thinking or buying. For analytic purposes one may say that a particular advertisement may use more exhortation and less detailed information, but the objective is the same. Indeed, persuasion—in religious, legal, interpersonal, political, or commercial settings—is deeply ingrained in the fabric of our society.

But is it socially acceptable to persuade in behalf of some ends and not others (e.g., cigarettes, natural fur coats, the U.N., military recruiting), under some conditions and not others (e.g., when the consumer economically cannot satisfy his desires), and so on?

The increasing diversity of our society, and the increasingly vigorous affirmation of such diversity by subgroups, make me think it unlikely that we can reach strong public consensus on what "good ends" are. Thus, while there may be some agreement on the conditions under which commercial persuasion is more or less appropriate, to lay out the specific criteria on which to base such judgments (and who should make them) is difficult, if not impossible.

A practical example of this difficulty can be seen in the cases arising under the Federal Communications Commission's "fairness doctrine," through which free broadcasting rebuttal time is made available for "anti" advertising on controversial issues. The District of Columbia Court of Appeals recently ruled that the Friends of the Earth, an environmental protection group, had the right to counter gasoline and automobile advertising. It is easy to point to the extremes to which such rulings could go. Almost any product could be considered dangerous or controversial by some critics—e.g., chewing gum (effect on teeth), alcoholic beverages (excessive drinking), foreign cars (U.S. unemployment). If the fairness doctrine is to be more broadly applied, rather than using case-by-case judgment alone, we need advance guidelines.

Underlying a substantial amount of the criticism of advertising's persuasive powers is an assumption that advertising is extremely powerful. Indeed, attitude surveys show that both the public and the private sectors attribute considerable power to advertising in affecting consumer needs and wants. Many an advertiser, as he viewed the wreakage of a product failure which had heavy advertising support, has wished that this were so. The myth of the defenseless consumer is one of the most enduring outputs of the social critics of advertising.

Yet a substantial body of consumer behavior research tells us that the consumer is hardly a helpless pawn manipulated at will by the advertiser. We know, for example, that almost all consumers are very selective in what advertising they pay attention to, perceive, evaluate, and remember—let alone act upon. This process on the part of the consumer not only varies considerably with the characteristics of the individual, of the product and brand involved, and of the ads in behalf of those products and brands; but it also often varies for the very same individual under different buying circumstances, e.g., for inexpensive versus expensive products.

In the same way that advertising's power is disputed, much effort has also been expended to define consumer "needs" and "wants," and further to separate "genuine" from "artificial" needs and wants. For example, Arnold Toynbee thought that three categories could be defined: (1) needs (minimum material requirements of life), (2) genuine wants (which "we become aware of spontaneously, without . . . Madison Avenue"), and (3) unwanted demand (created by advertising).[1]

The problem is one of deciding what represents a requirement of life at a given point in time for a given society. When and how does, say, a telephone, a car, a radio, or a TV set go on an "official list"?

[1] See *America and the World Revolution* (New York: Oxford University Press, 1966), pp. 144–45.

For example, who decides, for whom, whether and when an underarm deodorant is a "genuine" want or not? (A genuine need is perhaps easier to judge.)

Short of the marketplace itself, I find it hard to envision—other than in matters of health and safety—a workable democratic modus operandi for deciding what should and should not be manufactured, marketed, and advertised. My comments on these basic issues are not intended to settle them; but they are intended to suggest their very insolubility.

All of the foregoing discussion raises questions of consumer sovereignty—a credo subscribed to by marketers and their critics alike. Marketers will say that the consumers certainly are kings and queens, and the many unsuccessful advertising campaigns and product failures bear this out. Critics will argue that true consumer sovereignty is a myth because the playing field and rules are established by marketers rather than by more objective and less commercially circumscribed individuals. I shall treat this point later in commenting on how the marketplace works.

Information content

Any consideration of advertising content leads us directly to the matter of truth and deception. While we know that the public has a high tolerance of puffery in advertising, the atmosphere in recent years has become one of increasing public skepticism in regard to whether advertisements generally present a true picture of the products advertised. This growing skepticism is shared by the business community. This background, typified by the frequently heard phrase, "That's just advertising," is best reflected in the Admiral Corporation's headline for its recent campaign: "Admiral is having a *real* sale."

Nonetheless, at the same time that we have seen growing skepticism, we have also consistently seen evidence that the public thinks the standards of advertising are improving. The explanation: the public is asking for higher and higher (absolute) standards in commercial communications.

Where can public policy bite in? By recognizing various subcategories of truth,[2] each of which calls for a different level of concern. Here is an array:

Literal truth. Is the claim substantiable?

Although on the surface the matter of claims substantiation seems straightforward enough, in fact it is far from clear-cut. For example, there are research questions about the kinds of tests (the size of a test sample of a product or of people) that warrant results to be considered definitive, how much "more" or "better" constitutes a valid claim,

[2] Subcategories developed in conjunction with Alice E. Courtney (York University), and in part from the work of Christopher Gale (University of Virginia), *Truth in Advertising: The Consumer View*, unpublished HBS doctoral thesis, 1970.

and so forth. There are also questions about whether claims central to the product's performance should have stronger (methodological and statistical) support than minor claims, and under what conditions design modifications call for retesting of a claim.

My argument here is not to shrink from seeking to have advertising claims substantiated (in fact, 90% of businessmen agree on this). Rather, it is to point out some of the difficulties associated with even such an ostensibly straightforward matter.

True impression. Despite literal truth, is the impression true?

Here we are in much deeper water, for "impression" raises questions of what goes on in a "reasonable" person's mind. Nonetheless, some useful dimensions of this subcategory can be identified, most notably that of the suppression of relevant information.

For example, does the claim pertain to all models? Is the advertised "special" in only very limited supply? Yet in considering "true impression," should we ask the advertiser to reveal—at his own expense—a host of reservations and caveats about his product? (Rare indeed is the brand which is not stronger than competition on some dimensions and weaker on others.)

Traditional adversary procedure, as in the law, would argue that an advertiser should not have to subsidize the dissemination of information counter to his own interest. In the instance of health warnings about cigarette smoking, public policy has deemed otherwise.

Discernible exaggeration. Aside from the absence of literal truth, is the exaggeration or puffery discernible as such? Here, again, we must concern ourselves with the notion of a reasonable man. All of us presumably would agree that people who actually believe a specific soap powder can truly "make their washing machine ten feet tall" need a different kind of help than can be provided by the FTC. But where does one draw the line?

False impression. Whether deliberately, or not, does the ad actually include material that suggests a false impression (in contrast to suppressing information)—i.e., material that has the capacity to deceive?

Ads which imply uniqueness, ads with distorted demonstrations, ads which present unsupported "best buys," and the like fall into this territory. Substantiation can help. But it is in this territory that the creative freedom to develop imagery via words and pictures clashes with literalness. Allusions and romanticization are the core of advertising for many mundane products. (After all, how legitimately excited can one get over a floor wax?)

Advertisers see regulatory efforts in this area as presaging external dictation of which selling points (not just how to express them) may be used. Indeed, some critics see regulation here as a wedge to attack the promotion of psychological differences (rather than just functional differences alone) between brands. Drawing the line between "discernible exaggeration" and "false impression" is to me the toughest judgment in the zone of advertising content.

One category not on this list is *irrelevance*—that is, regardless of the truth or true impression, does the ad address itself to what consumers want to know? Ads that may be irrelevant represent a category that in my view does not warrant regulation. Many, for example, might agree that the piano manufacturer's advertising which emphasizes that it is the *heaviest* piano is addressing itself to something not germane to the typical consumer. The reader, I am sure, can cite ads and ad campaigns that he considers stupid, aimed at the "wrong" consumer, and the like.

However, the fact that a manufacturer wishes to spend money to promote his products with a message or in a way that may well be ineffective lies in the realm of business judgment. Both business and government should be interested in preserving every opportunity for good or bad business judgment to be exercised (and properly rewarded) in the marketplace.

Associated with such assessments is the question of who may be misled—people not in the market for the product, inexperienced buyers, those with little education, children, and so on. Further, is the result of the false impression on the consumer's part simply that—an impression or idea that she or he is capable of making allowances for *before* he decides to buy.

Or is the result a buying decision that is a bad one in terms of the consumer's own buying criteria? (Note that there may be several "best buys" in a given product category!) Finally, is the effect of a bad buying decision large or small financially, or is it a matter of health or safety?

All these questions must at least be asked, in order to assess where the highest payoffs are for the public in terms of focusing limited regulatory resources (be they government or industry). Although the questions are complex, many are susceptible to consumer research that is methodologically relatively straightforward.

Restoring the marketplace seems to be the clear intent of the FTC's principal remedial thrust, "corrective advertising." Under this plan, a certain percentage of advertising for a company whose past advertising has been ruled deceptive must consist of public admission of the company's past guilt. Proponents also feel that such a public confessional represents a stronger deterrent than the penalty of a fine. (Opponents construe corrective advertising as akin to wearing a scarlet letter.)

The notion of rectifying in consumers' minds the damage wrought by deceptive advertising raises new questions for regulators beyond those just cited. Interestingly, these are questions about the effectiveness of ads and campaigns not dissimilar to those asked by advertisers and their agencies themselves. Despite the amusing spectacle during the FTC's Firestone hearings (the first case on corrective advertising) wherein advertising people claimed relatively little effectiveness for advertising and its critics claimed much effectiveness, public cases in which we try to learn the impact of a particular message on consumers' minds promise to uncover more knowledge about the impact of advertising.

Taste aspects

Considerable criticism has also been expressed over the taste aspects of advertising content, or what has been referred to as the manner rather than the matter of advertising. Again, based on what the public says, let us try to dissect the most common criticisms:

Moral concern over the product itself (e.g., personal hygiene products, liquor, cigarettes).

Objections to the occasion of the ad (e.g., lingerie ads shown on early evening TV, too many ads together).

Objections to the appeals employed (e.g., use of sex or fear).

Objections to the techniques of advertising strategy (e.g., campaign intensity, excessive repetition of the claim and/or the ad, silliness of presentation).

All these elements can lead to general consumer irritation. But there are only a few black-and-white areas in consumer annoyance with advertisements. The many variations stem from individual life situations (e.g., men reacting adversely to ads primarily addressed to women), to one's use of the products advertised and preference for the brands advertised, as well as to one's individualized style of pursuing happiness via fantasy.

Needless to reiterate, the problem of positing broadly acceptable general standards of taste for advertising, or even situational standards, is difficult. Again, to use smoking as an example, the implied association of sexual attractiveness and smoking has long been criticized; but what about the current use of fear in antismoking campaigns?

Values and lifestyles

Of all the social issues involving advertising, the broadest have to do with its impact on values and lifestyles. Unfortunately, as one might suspect, it is in this area that value judgments are most rife, and hard data are least in existence. Hence, rather than review the rather flimsy evidence in detail, let me lay out the major issues and questions involved.

The overriding question in this area is whether advertising *creates* or *reflects* the values of society. Most observers implicate advertisers and marketers, to some extent, not as creators of values but as exploiters of values which exist at or just below the surface. Hence they perceive that advertising not only tends to reflect values, but that it also is one of the leading edges that can reinforce and accelerate them. Unfortunately, there are virtually no specific examples cited that can be linked demonstrably to advertising-marketing alone. Thus, although advertising has certainly played a part in the growing usage of new feminine hygiene products by helping to make their use more acceptable, the existence and success of such products seem to reflect general social trends toward more openness about one's body and its sexual functions.

Attempts to connect advertising with materialism seldom recognize anthropological evidence that analogies to our society's use of products for ego-enhancement have existed in almost all primitive cultures. Likewise, there are many opinions as to whether advertising adversely affects our moral-ethical-aesthetic standards, but there is no empirical evidence. Once again, different views of what those standards are and should be, and the wide variety of institutional influences that affect them, make it highly unlikely that advertising's effect on them can be isolated.

The same problem pertains when we consider conformity and diversity: much opinion and lots of value judgments, but no data. A marketer might argue that product proliferation offers greater opportunity for diversity. A critic might argue that having products with large shares of the market creates conformity.

In the area of interpersonal and group relationships, there seems to be more substance than in some of the other areas just cited. The portrayal of women and of ethnic groups in ads has been a topic of concern and complaint. For example, ads in which women are portrayed in a particular manner may individually be defensible in terms of management's view of the majority of its market.

Yet the cumulative effect of all such ads (for a given brand, product, or in general) may not reflect present-day roles of women.[3] Value judgments are distinctly involved—e.g., should ads show society as it is or as someone (the advertiser?) thinks it should be? However, this is an area where notions of fairness can be brought to bear and where research can presumably help identify the impact of such ads on the "learning process" of those exposed to them.

The subject of the learning process leads to my final area of questioning of advertising's social impacts—namely, its impact on special groups, including among others the poor, the less educated, and children. In all cases, the key issue seems to be whether or not advertising exploits the relative lack of sophistication of these people. (For children there is the added question of whether advertising teaches them socially unacceptable values—whatever those may be.)

Inexperienced buyers, especially children, are typically in the process of acquiring rather than changing their ideas and values. Thus far this

[3] For an interesting analysis of this subject, see Alice E. Courtney and Sarah Lockeretz, "A Woman's Place: An Analysis of the Roles Portrayed by Women in Magazine Advertisements," *Journal of Marketing Research* (February 1971), p. 92.

kind of learning—or, in the critics' view, perhaps narcotization—has unfortunately been the subject of too little research. At this point, however, it should be clear that the impact of advertising on special groups is a matter of great concern and seems to lend itself to empirical research more so than most issues in the area of values and lifestyles.

TOWARD RESOLUTION

We have examined some of advertising's major zones of social impact. What now can be done to try to understand them better and to try to resolve the conflict over them?

Better understanding

Because almost every issue involving advertising's social effects is steeped in one's own value judgments about everything from what constitutes marketplace morality to the nature of our society, I believe it is essential that one separate his judgments of advertising's *power* and *capabilities* from his assessments of the *rights* and *wrongs* of that power. That is, one's appraisal of whether an allegation about advertising's influence is true or false should be separated from one's value judgment as to whether—if the allegation were true—this would be a good or bad thing.

In my mind, unless and until one separates these assessments, one is doomed to the illogical process of an analysis whose sequence moves from conclusion back to evidence, rather than the reverse.

A broad illustration of this concept rests in the increasing practitioner emphasis on segmentation (in product development, advertising message development, and media selection) as a way of providing more specifically designed products to targeted groups of interested consumers. Experienced marketers and advertisers use refined research that permits the analysis and delineation of such segmented markets. They do this not only on the basis of traditional demographics but also on consumer attitudes, interests, lifestyles, and so forth in order to do a better job of identifying and reaching the kind of people at whom the product and advertising message should be aimed.

My point: Is this increased efficiency in marketing and advertising to be construed as *response* or as *control*? As better service to the consumer? Or, conversely, as yet another manifestation of advertising's Svengali-like capabilities bending unsuspecting consumers to its will? The answer: It all depends on your point of view, your value system, and your idea of how the marketplace works.

One's model, explicit or implicit, of how the marketplace works goes far in explaining one's attitude toward advertising and its role. The concept of marketplace models basically involves the interface between marketers and consumers, including how advertising works in terms of the consumer behavior it is intended to affect as well as how that influence occurs.[4]

From the mouths and pens of commentators on advertising, I discern three different overall models:

1. ***Manipulative.*** A critic's model that portrays marketing's role as basically that of persuading/seducing less-than-willing consumers to buy. Consumers are seen as pawns struggling in an unequal battle against their adversaries, the marketers, who use advertising as an important and powerful one-sided weapon.

2. ***Service.*** A probusiness model that (*a*) portrays as successful marketers only those who serve consumers best and (*b*) predicts failure for those who do not so serve. Consumers are seen as rather more intelligent and less seduced than in the manipulative model. A credo of the service model is: "Consumers cast their ballots at the cash register every day . . . and besides, we know what they want via market research." Advertising is seen as helping to facilitate choices made by consumers who generally know what they want.

3. ***Transactional.*** A model derived from communications research that portrays the marketplace relationship in more of a give-and-take fashion. Consumers trade time and attention to advertising for the information and entertainment in the ads; consumers trade money for products that provide them with functional and/or psychological satisfactions. The transactional model posits a somewhat sophisticated consumer, at least in terms of his or her individual buying criteria.

At this juncture, I would invite you to try to define your own model of the marketplace via a self-administered test of your thinking. Thus:

What is your basic view of how the marketplace mechanism operates?

What really constitutes "consumer needs" and "rational" choice?

How intelligent are the choices made by the typical consumer?

Where does the emphasis lie between adversary and friend in the marketer's role toward the consumer?

How does advertising work?

What is the perceived "seduction quotient" in advertising?

How sophisticated or defenseless are consumers in their ability to screen the advertising and its content that comes their way?

After you have determined your marketplace model, then ask yourself whether your model grows from your view of how consumers do behave or your view of how consumers should behave. I suspect that how consumers should behave is the premise for what most critics of advertising and marketing believe, whereas how consumers do behave perforce is the premise for what most marketers believe. From answering the fore-

[4] For a more detailed treatment of this concept see Raymond A. Bauer and Stephen A. Greyser, "The Dialogue That Never Happens" (Thinking Ahead), *HBR* (November-December 1967), p. 2.

going questions, you should be able to understand why you view certain issues regarding advertising's social impacts as you do.

Remedial actions

Where does all this lead? First, to some sense of comfort that we can at least sort out the issues, even if we are unlikely to resolve very many of them. Second, despite the problems of providing answers to the many difficult and sometimes amorphous questions I have been posing, there seem to be some directions for remedial action. Naturally, the consideration of such directions involves the inevitable balancing of present admitted imperfections of the marketplace against the probability of improvements under new administrative procedures. In my own view, one can try to separate those areas in which calibration of the system is involved from those areas that call for restructuring of the system. Each observer may, of course, have his own definitions for what constitutes the former and the latter.

Attempts to treat problems of truth in advertising or advertising to children seem generally to be in the area of calibration. In contrast, attempts to decide for the consumer as to whether products or brands should be advertised (or sold) at all seem generally to be in the area of structural revision. The likelihood of achieving some public consensus for the former seems greater than for the latter.

Further, the former would seem to be less risky in terms of upsetting a system that has generally worked rather well and that is more likely to bear short-term fruit. The latter would seem to call for more of a "grand design" growing from difficult consensus on value-laden matters and to take much longer to assess the results. Also, while calibration would certainly lead to modifications in advertisers' planning processes, in some ways advertisers might find that such mandatory activity may be beneficial, as I shall note momentarily.

In terms of recommended remedial action, the many questions that arise from examining even a single area such as "truth and deception" suggest that a variety of analyses—and resulting remedies—would apply to different situations. One can envision a spectrum of remedial actions: claims substantiation, affirmative disclosure of relevant negatives, preclearance of advertising (as in health and safety), post hoc corrective advertising (as is now being run in Profile bread ads), free counter advertising (e.g., antismoking, antipollution).

But, even then, an advertiser's efforts will be difficult to judge without some advance guidelines. For example, one snowmobile manufacturer has been running a campaign claiming his product is "tougher seven ways." Should the substantiation of these seven ways be done, say, in every ad or cumulatively in a series, in each medium where the campaign appears or cumulatively across all media, or in some other manner?

These questions apply whether the regulatory vehicle lies inside or outside the advertising industry. Many people, especially within the industry, are optimistic that new self-regulation procedures of the National Advertising Review Board (NARB) in the realm of advertising content can work effectively. I share their hopes and think that in many ways the very existence of the procedures will be beneficial. For example, some advertisers may not "push the line," knowing that they may be called to account.

Nonetheless, for several reasons, it is hard to believe that the NARB procedures will result in stilling criticisms of advertising content. First, expectations (particularly from critics) regarding advertising content may be elevated unrealistically. Second, even though the procedures may not address matters of taste, much of the criticism of advertising stems from concerns over taste. (In late January, the NARB stated that it would extend its interests to areas of "taste" and "social responsibility.")

Further, in an increasingly diverse society, common acceptable standards on matters of taste are ever more unlikely. In short, one man's fantasy is another's annoyance, one man's bad taste is another's amusement, one man's threshold of intolerance for a particular theme or ad is another's threshold of awareness.

Whether or not the NARB seeks to treat these issues, they are likely to remain as part of what might be seen as an irreducible minimum of continuing complaints about advertising. For one inherent problem is that most advertising in the mass media, especially TV, has an opportunity for exposure to many more people than may be real prospects for the product or brand. Thus, in the light of improved targeting of products and messages, annoyance and offense over advertisements may well increase in the near term despite the new procedures.

What can *advertisers* do amidst this welter of complex issues and questions? Unfortunately, no simple and effective prescription is at hand. Perhaps the most important implication from all of the foregoing is that advertisers will have to evince much more advance sensitivity to possible criticism. More than ever before, conscious concern for the customer—and even the noncustomer—is necessary, for one's image if not for one's sales. The age of accountability for advertising, heralded by consumerism's rise in recent years, means that marketers and advertisers will have to live the precepts of consumer orientation which their predecessors of the 1950s and 1960s may have only talked about.

How does this manifest itself specifically for advertisers? By demanding that before every advertising theme and message is used, it be viewed through the lens of the prospectively critical consumer. This "devil's advocate" filter must also be applied to specific advertising claims. Here are the kinds of questions that must be asked:

Is the claim testable?

Is a competitive claim of superiority defensible in terms of normal use and/or in terms of extraordinary but reasonable use?

Does the claim apply to all models in the product line or just to some?

Can the message be misinterpreted by a reasonable person?

Because of these questions, as Leo Burnett Company's Seymour Banks has suggested, copy testing must go beyond its typical emphasis on communicability and comprehension to discern miscommunication and incorrect comprehension on the part of consumers. Companies will have to be concerned with turning off these negative dimensions, in addition to their traditional interest in turning on the positive ones.

Another zone for company action is that of the tone of its advertising—its stridency, aggressiveness vis à vis the consumer, and the like. These irritation factors, along with the total amount of advertising, are in large part responsible for what I see as an erosion in the general reservoir of public goodwill to all of advertising.

Some advertising people honestly believe that noisy attention-getting devices and irritation in advertisements result in more selling effectiveness. Consumer research has shown that advertisements for one's favorite brands are considered far and away more informative and enjoyable than ads for one's less preferred brands.

By the same token, consumers consider the ads for their nonpreferred brands far more annoying and offensive than the ads for their preferred brands.[5] This is based on attitude (not effectiveness) data and is thus only a strong correlation, with the causal direction not established.

However, a clear suggestion which emerges is that pleasantness and effectiveness in advertising can go hand in hand. Is it too much to think that those of the "annoyance school" can be taught by their colleagues to trade off some effectiveness for an improvement in public goodwill?

Much of the preceding discussion is concerned with the difficulty of tight judgments on these regulatory issues. However, the egregious offenders can typically be identified. And here is where industry efforts will be watched closely. If the industry—with or without government stimulus—fails to move decisively against the "bad apples," today's atmosphere portends grief for not just them but for nonoffending advertisers as well.

My final suggestion may be particularly difficult to swallow. Advertisers are going to have to learn to live in a world of more attention, more criticism, and more regulation. How they calibrate their own be-

[5] See Raymond A. Bauer and Stephen A. Greyser, *Advertising in America: The Consumer View* (Boston: Division of Research, Harvard Business School, 1968), Chapter 9.

havior can affect the pace and intensity of the attention, criticism, and regulation.

What can more *information* do for us? Although a lot of money is already being spent on research into advertising's effects, it is allocated almost exclusively to research for improving the effectiveness of advertising for particular brands or products, not for its broader societal impacts. Why this glaring paucity of research-based knowledge on the social aspects of advertising? In part, it is because no commercial cause is served by such research; thus funds are hard to come by. In part, it is also because of the inherent difficulties of conducting meaningful studies in this area; many input variables would have to be controlled and measured simultaneously, and ideally the researcher would virtually need two identical societies—one with advertising and one without it—for observation over time.

Even then, because of the aforementioned predominance of value judgments, one's assessments of advertising's social impacts may be unchanged by new data. For example, if it could be definitely shown that advertising resulted in a 10% increase in sexual permissiveness, would this be a benefit or a disservice to society? Cardinal Cooke and Hugh Hefner might have different answers.

In light of these problems, what practical contributions can research make to our deliberations? Obviously, research into the issues can not only help us define and articulate the subissues that seem to lie all around us, but can also serve as a handmaiden to a clearer understanding of just what these social impacts of advertising comprise. This article has sought to do some of this here. More important, though, field research can provide practical consumer inputs to help answer specific questions, such as the extent to which different kinds of presumed "truth" problems are in fact problems.

As a student of consumer behavior, I believe strongly that the consumer's own voice should play an important part in the making of public policy. Note that I say the consumer's *own* voice, and not the consumer as represented by business (through its commercial interpretation of marketing research) or consumer spokesmen (typically without much input from consumers).

Along this line, even with today's use of consumer research in copy testing, I foresee the further use of such research by regulatory agencies (and the courts) in trying to resolve issues of "consumer impressions." New questions spring to mind almost at once as to what constitutes proper criteria for "valid research" and "meaningful findings" about the state of consumers' minds.

More than ever before, now is the time for us to let information replace intuition in public policy making about advertising and marketing. I emphasize this for businessmen, critics, and public policy makers alike.

When is advertising misleading? When is it against the public welfare? When is it in good taste? Standards of behavior need to be established to answer these questions. The author describes the need to eliminate deceptive advertising on moral grounds and not merely as a response to public pressures. New moral standards may be more effective than the legal structure in reducing misleading advertising.

36. MORALITY IN ADVERTISING—A PUBLIC IMPERATIVE

William G. Capitman†

The Clearwater River, fifty miles upstream from Potlatch Forests Incorporated pulp and paper mill, is, as *Newsweek* put it, "a scene of breathtaking natural beauty." The Potlatch people apparently agreed; they photographed it, added the caption *It cost us a bundle, but the Clearwater River still runs clear,* and ran an ad. But at the plant site, and downstream from the picture location, Potlatch pumps fresh water in from the stream and pumps out forty tons of suspended organic wastes. Simultaneously, Potlatch exudes some 2.5 million tons of sulfur gasses and 1.8 million tons of particulates into the air. The implication that the river, as shown in the ad, was the creation of Potlatch is belied by the subsequent photos, never shown in the ads, taken of the situation at the plant and below it. Says *Newsweek:* "When an enterprising local college newspaper editor pointed out the discrepancy between ad copy and reality, the company responded by cancelling all corporate advertising." Other such incidents and the growing concern throughout the country with questions relating to the social responsibility of corporations all point to the need for a new view of the morality of advertising.

What do we mean by morals in advertising and how can we approach the question? Is all advertising and are all parts of a given ad to be subject to the same rules and standards of morality? There is a need for discussion and assessment of the moral state of advertising now, as well as the establishment of guidelines and rules for the future.

Theodore Levitt, in his article "The Morality (?) of Advertising," has performed a valuable service in raising the discussion of the role

* Reprinted from "Morality in Advertising—A Public Imperative," *MSU Business Topics* (Spring 1971), pp. 21–26.

† Center for Research in Marketing, Inc.

of advertising in our society to a new level of abstraction. The article provides a framework for considering the question of advertising morals in particular, and business morality in general. Despite his thoughtful consideration and the development of a rationale for a conception of advertising morality, the argument in its totality is likely to lead down some blind, and even unprofitable, alleys. Levitt conceives of the roles of advertising and packaging as being much the same as those of art and poetry, in that they all help create the symbolic and anticipated world rather than simply reflect reality. "I shall argue that embellishment and distortion are among advertising's legitimate and socially desirable purposes, and that illegitimacy in advertising consists only of falsification with larcenous intent," Levitt says. He believes the common purpose of art and advertising is to "persuade."

Levitt's distinction is a nominal one: "Commerce, it can be said without apology, takes essentially the same liberties with reality and literality as the artist, except that commerce calls its creations advertising, or industrial design, or packaging. As with art, the purpose is to influence the audience by creating illusions, symbols, and implications that promise more than pure functionality."

ART AND ADVERTISING

This argument presents serious problems. Although one can generalize similarities by using the word *persuade,* it seems to me that such a formulation evades and justifies rather than clarifies the issues. There is a sharp distinction between what the artist and the company are being persuasive about. The artist, broadly speaking, is concerned with convincing people that his conception of reality is worth considering. He does not regard what he is doing as reality, or even as the only way to perceive reality. His purpose is to bring new insights by trying new forms, and his work becomes art when it communicates some level of his differentiation to others, even though objective interpretation may arrive at conclusions different from his intentions. One cannot question the facts that there are fads and fashions in art; that internal artistic politics and mores often have more to do with an artist's success than the quality of his work; or that the artists, if they are to be fully devoted to their life's work, must live by selling their accumulated product. Still, it is only in terms of the need to market and sell his product that the artist can be seen as trying to persuade in anything like the sense *persuasion* is used in advertising.

What advertising does is use the tools of art, both visual and verbal, for a totally different purpose. Its object is to convince someone to act in a specified way and in a specified area. Business clearly has revealed its understanding of this intention through various efforts, such as persuading people to act by engaging their unconscious. A few years ago James Vicary experimented abortively with subliminal advertising.

This process communicates messages the recipient is not conscious of receiving, and operates by evading the individual's censors in order to reach and effect basic and perhaps instinctual elements in the human make-up. By so doing, the person affected presumably would feel an uncontrollable impulse to buy the product without ever having been conscious of being exposed to the persuasion.

This key difference in function between art and advertising cannot be disregarded lightly. It results in the development of a different set of standards and criteria by which we judge the merit of a painting or a poem on the one hand, and a package or an advertisement on the other. If we are to talk of advertising morality, we must take this into account.

There are other distinctions that must be made between advertising and art: the former is institutionalized, the latter is not. Advertising, for the most part, is a corporate effort, while art is a highly personalized, individual effort. Advertising, regardless of its artistic merit, is terminated if it is not successful in persuading people to act, a criterion which can be measured by sales. Art is not so terminated or measured and, in fact, the work of an artist may never have an influence in his own time. Art and art forms are more or less effective techniques of selling regardless of the artistic merits of the persuading construct. Advertising's function is to operate immediately. Its artistic aspects usually are buried in volumes of the "100 Best Advertisements" of one year or another; there is no necessary relationship between advertising persuasiveness and artistic merit.

ADVERTISING: SYMBOLS AND SYMBOLISM

If advertising is seen as using the techniques of art for affecting a different sort of persuasion than does art, what then can we say about advertising morality? One point of departure is to begin to discuss the broader effect of advertising on the polity, and whether or not such effects are legitimate, or "good." It seems important to me to discuss the world of symbolism which advertising creates and which the public uses. Cigarette advertising is a case in point. From the inception of the use of tobacco, certain elements in the society have regarded use of the product as immoral. The consequences of smoking were seen as destructive, morally speaking, and diverting from propriety. Cigarette smoking soon became a mass activity nonetheless. Since the U.S. Surgeon-General's report, there has been an accumulation of evidence that cigarette smoking has a direct and negative effect upon the physical well-being of an individual. One of the first successful attacks was made upon cigarette symbolism when government and public pressure forced cigarette advertising on television to be removed from time in which children might view it. Cigarette manufacturers also were pushed to remove from their advertising any implications and suggestions that there are *social* and *sexual* advantages to be gained from smoking which might appeal to the immature. The restrictions were based on the impropriety or immorality of the advertising, rather than any "fraudulent claim" made with "larcenous intent."

MORALIZING SEEMS FRUITLESS

Moralizing about the very existence of advertising seems to me fruitless. One might just as well moralize about the existence of evil, pornography, automobiles, detergents, or telephones. Morality is concerned with what is "good" or "bad" in human behavior, not with the existence of artifacts. In C. P. Snow's *The New Men,* his protagonists argue about the morality of developing atomic energy, in which was implicit the danger of human destruction. The question of morality had to do with the obligations of the human beings and human institutions that would employ this new force. If there was a moral conclusion to be arrived at, it was that human beings had the obligation to use the artifacts which they created for "good" rather than "evil" purposes, and that it is not moral to divorce oneself from the consequences of one's behavior.

The moral questions raised about advertising, then, are not related to its existence—it is a humanly developed artifact—but, rather, to its consequences. Whether embellishment is good or bad depends upon the consequences of that embellishment, both in commercial and noncommercial terms, and making that determination is not so simple as it sounds.

In the first instance, it is a simple-minded economistic error to assume that a product is only a physical thing. Levitt properly points out that "symbolic" satisfactions are provided by products and that these are a vital part of the role that a product plays in our society. But symbols really are shorthand statements about reality, and they too can lie about reality and about a product. The fact that they are symbols do not make them any less subject to moral objection. Just as they can lie, however, they can be truthful, and perhaps even more truthful about the essence of a product than a simple informative statement. So the fact that advertising is symbolic is not the essential problem of advertising morality.

Several years ago, in expression of the role of advertising as a symbol system, I described advertising as having a reality of its own and having a special effect upon the realities of the consumer's life. However, I did not exclude the possibility that advertising was *more* than simply a symbol system. It is, in fact, in toto, a *communication* system which, like other such systems, operates on a variety of levels. One level is the communication of factual information about the product. It requires considerable effort to regard price, as stated in an advertisement or on a package, as having only a symbolic meaning. *All* advertisements have this factual or informational element in their matrix.

IMPLICATION AND EMBELLISHMENT

One of the great temptations to an advertiser and his agency is to turn these facts into symbols, or to at least manipulate the factual elements so that they do not mean quite what they say. There is extensive usage of this process of implication in advertising, ranging from suggestions that products are more effective than they actually are to implications in a photograph (as in the Potlatch-Clearwater River incident) that the corporation is engaged in activities that enhance the beauty of the environment when, in fact, it is not. This sort of implication always deals with apparent facts about the product or the producers and usually arises from the corporate conception of what the consumer wants to believe about a purchase. The implication usually concerns the desirable consequences of purchase in a factual or performance sense.

This manipulation is of a different order from the symbolic aspects of an ad or package which imply that what might be called social and environmental benefits will accrue to the user, and about which one might expect a choice. Thus, for example, the factual elements relating to deodorants have to do with their ingredients, their performance, and their price. The environmental elements have to do with sociality, status, insecurity, and so forth. Sometimes environmental elements are closely allied to performance. The performance of a deodorant can be perceived as the process of providing security in social situations. In this instance the symbolic meanings of the product becomes more important to the consumer than do the factual elements. However, this does not provide a basis for dodging moral consequences. Factual statements in an advertisement, those relating to ingredients, physical performance, and price, never can be embellished without becoming lies.

MISLEADING ADVERTISING

This is not to say that a fact cannot be presented forcefully and dramatically, which often is done by using symbolism. For example, for some years proprietary drug products of various forms presented performers as physicians in their ads. The purpose of this was to present dramatically the qualities of the product in an environment that symbolized authority and, specifically, medical authority. But the practice was stopped by the FTC because it was misleading; it implied that doctors were, in fact, recommending the products being advertised.

The process of producing an advertisement is of interest when we talk about morality, for in most corporations, and in most decisions, the extent to which one will embellish a fact in an advertisement or a package is a legal question rather than a moral one. The question is whether the various institutions which act as censors of the corporation—the FTC; the television stations, which are themselves under the eye of one agency or another; the legal system—will let the corporation have its way. The question of consequences in the marketplace is seldom considered, other than some broad conception of public acceptance, but the parameters of that acceptance almost always are seen as broader than the legal limitations. Some corporations tend to believe that they can sell sows' ears as silk purses insofar as their ability to move the public is concerned. It is not moral considerations that prevent them from doing so, but anticipated legal consequences.

People object to misleading advertising only because they expect to believe it. If advertising really were being approached as cynically as studies suggest, there would be no concern with misleading ads but a sense of wonder at honest ads. The dismay over advertising is related to its factual distortion rather than the fact that it is not symbolically true. There is no clear evidence that symbolism offends, although there is considerable latitude in taste and fantasy. It would appear that the public is ready to distinguish between facts and symbols, and feels free to have opinions about the latter. However, facts presented according to conventions as being true are a different matter. It is only by testing or by prior knowledge that the consumer can determine whether the facts are untrue or misleading.

Specific problems of morality regarding facts arise over time. A manufacturer may produce and advertise a product which in all respects and by all known standards contains safe ingredients and does what it promises to do. Subsequent investigation may reveal that one of the ingredients could be dangerous, or that the product has unexpected side effects either on the user or on the environment although the producer had no way of knowing this beforehand. Further, it might be posited that new facts are slow in disseminating among the public. Disregarding for a moment that there may be agencies that will force the company to do something about the products, what steps can be taken and what moral questions arise concerning the continued advertising of the product after it has been exposed as harmful or misleading? There are several possibilities: the company can stop advertising and withdraw the product; the company can use its advertising to disseminate the new information and continue to market the product; it can disregard the new facts and continue to advertise as before.

The moral question is whether one action or another is right or wrong, good or bad in terms of its consequences as they affect the various parties. A moral decision would be one in which self-interest is secondary, but in which one acts on the basis of a principle, and one examines the consequences of so acting. Another aspect of a moral decision will involve the fact that what is good for one group may be bad for another. For example, the decision to stop advertising and withdraw a product has consequences for the employees, the distributors, and the consuming public. The problem for moralists then becomes one of balancing the greater good against the lesser evils. It was much easier to make these decisions when the clear-cut rule existed that the actions of a purchaser in the marketplace were totally his own responsibility. However, caveat emptor has been much revised. It only had meaning if one could assume the perfection of the competitive system and equality of power and knowledge on the part of both buyer and seller. In a situation in which we know that competition is notably imperfect and where, for the most part, knowledge and power are clearly out of balance between buyer and seller, new versions of old moral principles once again come into play.

REALITY AND FANTASY

If we turn to what I have termed the environmental or social aspects of advertising—what Levitt sees as the symbol world of advertising—some of the subtler difficulties of moral issues are revealed. In the first instance there is clearly a range of symbolic devices and meanings used in advertising. One might broadly distinguish between symbols of reality and fantasy. Conceive of the two as on a continuum, at some point of which the two merge or overlap. Symbols of reality involve clear portrayals of more or less real situations in which social consequences accrue as a result of the use of a product or service. The social consequences are identifiable with the real life position of the viewer, either in terms of his own experience or other social experiences. Fantasy, on the other hand, is a clear portrayal of unreality—like the man from Glad appearing on the scene, magically, to solve a sandwich-packaging problem—but it may be symbolic of a real situation at one level or another.

Many critics of advertising tend to regard symbolism as one of its greatest faults. Ralph Nader, for example, asserts that much of advertising is designed to "evoke and provoke the emotions and weaker instincts humans are often prey to" and, in effect, it "strips" the consumer of his "sovereignty" in the marketplace. Such an opinion reflects a conclusion about the effectiveness of symbolism in advertising and about the ability of the consumer to deal with this symbolism. In addition, it also means we have decided that consumers have neither the intelligence nor discriminatory power to differentiate between fact and symbol given a fair opportunity to do so; that symbolic values are not real values; and that the satisfactions involved in product choice and purchases are confined to the physical parameters.

If this view of the human condition in the United States is accepted, we must then conclude that anything other than the starkest reality and functionality is immoral in advertising, or packaging, or product design. At its best, such a decision means that beauty or decorativeness have no place in marketing, and this is inevitably contrary to the ethos of a better quality of life. Such a conclusion might please those who wish to retail the essentials of the Puritan ethic in American life, but it will not correspond to the aspirations and desires of a rather sophisticated populace.

GOOD TASTE OR MORALITY

One must distinguish between taste and morality in considering these elements of environment. Good taste is not a moral issue. Rather, it seems to be related to social class, education, values, and other societal and personal factors. The question of the taste level of advertising is an issue that needs consideration, but it is, in most respects, separate from the issue of morality. Again, the moral question regarding the use of symbols or symbolism in advertising is related to the good or bad consequences of the symbolizing or the truth or falsehood of the symbol as used in this context. These moral questions about symbolism are, at one level, at least closely tied to the levels of morality and hypocrisy in the system as a whole. The issue, for example, of whether or not to use nudity in advertising is confused by the equivocal nature of public moral standards on nudity.

Advertising, however, tends to treat this matter not as a moral but as a sales issue. One goes as far as one can in using nudity, where it is regarded as appropriate, but the consideration is whether or not it will cause a negative or positive response among one's market. If one can go a little beyond conventional standards and thereby offend only a few, but titillate many, the morality of nudity is only a sales, and perhaps a taste, issue rather than a moral one. The moral aspects, in the last analysis, will depend upon one's personal or institutional conception of the moral nature of nudity. If one's personal morality says that nudity is bad in this context, but one nevertheless uses nudity *because* it is morally bad, because it is titillating, because it attracts attention, then one clearly and consequentially has committed a moral breach. Therefore, when dealing with symbolism in advertising and the morality of the use of specific symbols, motive is indeed an issue as is objective effect.

This is not merely a question of counting angels on the head of a pin. Moral questions can have broad social consequences. For example, for years advertising has developed a set of conventions regarding social stereotypes. Working-class people and old people are funny; to be middle class is a virtue, middle-class people are beautiful, and they live in suburban houses surrounded by things; ordinary poor people do not exist; Negroes are invisible and are menials, and so forth. In effect, an image of the society and its inhabitants has been created which is untrue and perhaps dangerous; in my conception it is immoral. There is an obvious need to change this for moral reasons, not simply in response to public pressure.

The basis of all morality is the concept that adherence to a commonly held moral code is good for everyone, in the short as well as the long run. There are two difficulties here. First, we are not clear about our moral code, and it is changing. Second, we have established a different set of strictures for the operation of business. A faulty set of theories has separated business and other institutions from normal human activity, and a legal structure has been created that treats business as incapable of morality. Instead of morality, there is the rather flimsy and incomplete web of the law. *Ad hoc* regulations must be made to keep business within bounds because the human beings who run business institutions are creatively seeking new ways to get around these strictures. At the end of World War II we discovered in the Nuremberg trials a new concept of a soldier's morality. A human being no longer could claim immunity on the grounds that he was obeying an order from a superior; the act that he was commanded to do had to be moral and proper. This issue has been raised again in regard to My Lai and Vietnam. If we can change so ancient a code as that of military obedience, we also can look upon the role of business, and individuals involved in it, in a new way. We can evolve new moral standards for behavior which, in the long run, may be more effective and meaningful than the imperfect legal structure.

The social-psychological impact of television advertising directed at children is subject to controversy. Advertising for children has educational implications as well as promotional ones. The author analyzes the nature and extent of television advertising directed at young children and suggests responsible short- and long-run policies necessary for the consumer learning process.

---

37. CHILDREN AND PROMOTION: NEW CONSUMER BATTLEGROUND?*

Scott Ward†

Television is the candy the child molester gives your kids.
—FCC Commissioner Nicholas Johnson

---

* Excerpted from Marketing Science Institute, Working Paper, November 1971.
† Harvard Business School.

The Consumer isn't a moron; she is your wife.
—David Ogilvy (*Confessions of an Advertising Man*)

If we can assume that Ogilvy includes our children as consumers, these two quotations are at the heart of a new and stormy issue: marketing practices which affect children. The controversy centers around television advertising, the chief promotional vehicle which advertisers have traditionally used to reach child audiences. In 1970, for example, marketers spent $75 million on network sponsorship of television programs for children. Eight companies—primarily breakfast cereal and toy companies—account for about half of this three-network total.

CONSUMERISTS' ATTACKS

Recent events testify to the importance of the issue of advertising for children:

1. A primary area of concern during the Federal Trade Commission's hearings on modern advertising practices, held during fall 1971 was "The Impact of Television Advertising on Children."
2. Several proposals have been advanced for changing advertising practices which affect youthful audiences. Robert Choate, who attacked alleged "empty calories" in breakfast cereals, advocates self-regulation. He urged the Television Code Review Board to set limits on the number of commercials per hour during children's programming time—and limits have recently been imposed. Choate also argues that vitamin commercials be banned, and he hopes to compel advertisers of products containing sugar to warn audiences of possible tooth decay which may result from consumption.
3. The section on Child Development and the Mass Media of the "White House Conference on Children" has proposed to the president that commercials during children's programming be clustered. Other sweeping changes are proposed to "defend the public interest in the media."
4. Boston-based Action for Children's Television (ACT) acknowledges parents' responsibility to monitor the amount and kind of television their children see, but insists that broadcasters (meaning marketers as well as actual network and local broadcasters) "are responsible for providing a certain amount of creative children's programming with no exploitative commercialism . . . monitoring what is put on the air, and for setting sensible limits on the kinds of programs (which broadcasters feel) are acceptable for a child audience." Previously, ACT filed a formal petition with the Federal Communications Commission to remove all advertising during children's peak viewing times, and to compel stations to carry a minimum of 14 hours of children's programming per week.

Lost revenues resulting from the advertising ban would be made up to networks and to local stations via tax breaks.

CORPORATE RESPONSES

Individuals within the business community have employed various tactics to respond to criticism of advertising practices affecting children. Some companies which advertise directly to children via network or spot television have dropped sponsorship of Saturday morning television—the major battleground of the controversy—and now buy early weekday evening prime time. A major toy company shifted $8 million advertising billings in this manner. Nielsen data indicate that the new media strategies may be wise in any case, since children watch even more during early weekday evenings than on Saturday morning, except for very young children. Other family members are also more likely to watch during evening times, so advertising reaches not only children—purchase influencers—but also parents, who are ultimate purchasers for most goods advertised to children.

More recently, the TV Code Review Board of the National Association of Broadcasters amended the code to reduce by 25 percent the time devoted to commercials and other nonprogram material during weekend television programs designed mainly for children. This means that the amount of nonprogram time in children's programs shown between 7:00 A.M. and 2:00 P.M. on Saturdays and Sundays will be reduced from 16 minutes to 12 minutes per hour.

Some within the business community have chosen to do battle with the critics. For example, when the FTC hearings on modern advertising practices were announced, the president of the National Association of Broadcasters commented that the agency did "not trust the American people to make up their minds in determining what products they want to buy." A major trade publication responded with an editorial suggesting that, if there is something wrong with programs and advertising directed at children, the blame should rest with parents, since they have ultimate control and responsibility for their children's viewing habits. Such assertions may have a cathartic effect on those who make them, but they probably do little to de-escalate the rhetoric and foster constructive solutions to the controversy.

Some companies have responded by incorporating educational and socially desirable themes in product advertising aimed at children. Breakfast cereals are now sold in the context of messages about ecology, for example. A few companies have provided funds for programs on public television—notably "Sesame Street." A slide at the conclusion of the programs is all the exposure the company gets. Still other companies have supported consumer education programs which are administered through school districts.

Finally, the Subcouncil on Advertising and Promotion of the U.S. Commerce Department's National Business Council for Consumer Affairs includes several top-level executives who are studying possible business responses to the "children's advertising" controversy.

ISSUES

A characteristic of many "consumerism" controversies is ineffective communication between businessmen and their critics. Both sides start out with markedly different assumptions concerning the issues and with erroneous perceptions of how the "other side" perceives the issues. The result is a series of "dialogues that never really happen."

Issues concerning advertising addressed to children are no exception. Figure 1 lists three basic issues in the controversy, and presents each

FIGURE 1
How businesses and consumerist groups view each other's positions on children and advertising

The issues	*Corporations are perceived as believing:*	*Consumerist groups are perceived as believing:*
Advertising influence on children	There is nothing wrong with attempting to influence children to buy, or attempt to influence their parents to buy, advertised products.	Advertising to children is morally wrong.
	Children are rarely influenced by advertising anyhow.	Advertising exerts great influence on children, who lack sophistication to objectively evaluate commercial messages.
Advertising techniques	If advertising is not judged as misleading by government regulatory agencies, it may be broadcast.	Standards for evaluating advertising techniques are sealed to adult judgment; children cannot fairly evaluate commercial messages.
Ethics of advertising to children	Children are consumers; they represent an important market. Selling to children is necessary to maximize profits.	Advertising to children is inherently distasteful and unethical.
	Advertising to children supports the mass media.	

side's perception of the other side's beliefs about the issues. Thorough understanding of each of these issues is a necessary first step in designing effective corporate solutions to the controversy. Some evidence is available from recent research on each of these issues. Let us turn now to an analysis of the issues and the research evidence which may clarify each one.

Revealing data about the *actual* effect of commercials are provided by three studies, which dealt with children themselves. Two studies focused on 5- to 12-year-old children's perceptions, explanations, and judgments of television commercials. Data are based on group and personal interviews with about 100 middle-class Boston area children. Some key findings concerned:

1. ***Perceptions of commercials.*** Children in all three age groups studied (5–7, 8–11, 11–12) could identify the term "commercials," but kindergarten children showed some confusion. Perceptions and awareness of what commercials are became more accurate and elaborate with age. The youngest children, for example, were likely to define commercials with such comments as: "they interrupt the show" and "they come between shows so actors can change their clothes." Some older children, on the other hand, defined commercials in terms of the concept of sponsorship, thus demonstrating more accurate and complex understanding.

2. ***Understanding the purpose of commercials.*** Kindergarten children exhibited no understanding of the purpose of commercials, but by second grade, about two-thirds of the children in the sample showed some understanding of commercials' intent. Fourth to sixth graders showed clear understanding through such comments as: "commercials try to get you to buy things" and "they pay for the show."

3. ***Discrimination between programs and advertising.*** While children found it difficult to give verbal descriptions of the differences between programs and commercials, the data suggest that discrimination between programs and commercials increased with age. Some minimal discrimination was apparent in the remarks of younger children: "Programs have more people than commercials"; "Commercials are shorter." Between second and fourth grades, however, discrimination becomes clear. Some children said: "Commercials are designed to sell, programs to entertain."

4. ***Classes of products recalled.*** Kindergarten children spontaneously recalled food product advertising (they are frequently exposed to it); second graders often recalled toy ads; fourth graders frequently mentioned cleaning products; no consistent pattern of recall could be identified for sixth graders. The different classes of products recalled reflect the different interests of the various age groups, perhaps also the different roles they are learning. The interest of some children in advertising for cleaning products, for example, may suggest that they have become interested in adult roles and in products associated with those roles. Overall, however, food advertising was the predominant product category recalled, reflecting the fact that food products are heavily advertised during children's viewing times.

5. ***Complexity of recall.*** The content of children's recall of commercials becomes increasingly complex with age. Youngest children may recall only a random image—for example, "there were two hands with gook on them." Older children's recall is multidimensional and coherent, and the oldest children were more abstract, focusing on characteristics of commercial techniques rather than on descriptive elements of ads.

6. ***Liked and disliked commercials.*** Younger children frequently said they liked a commercial because they liked the particular product advertised. Older children, however, like commercials which are entertaining—particularly humorous ads. On the other hand, most children in all age groups dislike commercials which are seen as not entertaining; comments such as "dull," "there are too many," "boring," characterize disliked ads. Only a few of the older children said they disliked some commercials because they didn't believe the claims made. Yet, when the children were asked if "commercials always tell the truth," over 60 percent of the younger children said "yes" or "sometimes," but 75 percent of the older children said "no."

In general, these exploratory research findings suggest that children are not defenseless victims of advertising, although younger children's perceptions, judgments, and explanations are less sophisticated than older children's. If the data from children themselves tend to refute critics' charges of advertising's potency among children, the somewhat jaundiced and cynical nature of their responses should not be reassuring to advertisers who are directly concerned with promotion to children, or to marketers generally, who will advertise to these same people when they become adult consumers.

A final study provides data with equally sweet and sour implications for marketers. Five to twelve-year-old children were observed to pay less attention to commercials than to programming. (See Figure 2) "Tuning out" may be regarded as a form of "defense," further refuting the critics' argument that advertising is a "powerful influence." While the marketer may be pleased with any finding that undermines his opponent's argument, he can hardly be pleased with the finding itself. The logic of justifying children's advertising on the basis of the finding that children often "tune out" commercials is highly tenuous indeed.

One further observation about children's attention to commercials deserves mention. Figure 3 shows the attention levels of three age groups toward advertising for household cleaners and cosmetics. Attention dropped sharply for children over eight years when such commercials interrupted programming. However, five- to seven-year-olds exhibited a slight *increase* in attention to commercials in these categories. A possible explanation is that young children learn about adult roles (homemaker) and skills (use of cosmetics) through advertising. Such learning is a kind of influence which would seem to be desirable, even to many critics. Whether advertisers intend it or not, exposure to advertising is one input in the complex, long-term processes by which children

FIGURE 2
Percent of children paying full attention to programs and to commercials for food products

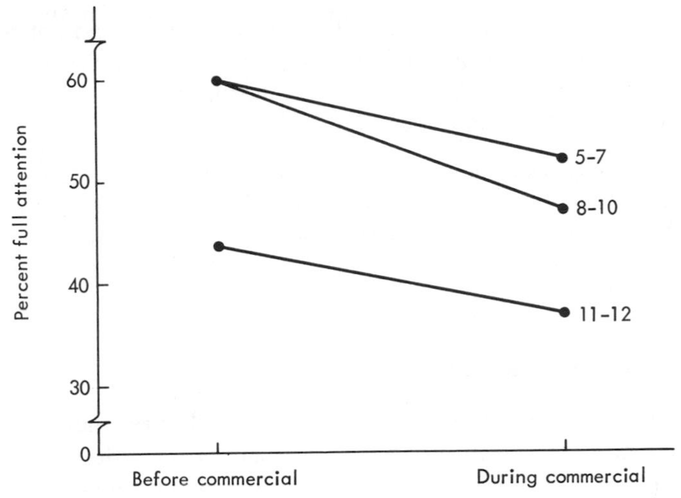

FIGURE 3
Percent of children paying full attention to programs and to commercials for household cleaners and for cosmetics

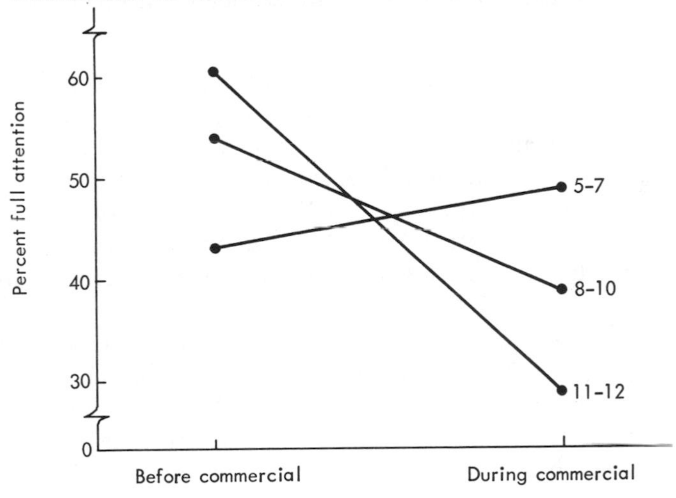

acquire attitudes, skills, and knowledge important to their development as effective and satisfied adult consumers.

Advertising techniques

The assumption underlying some criticism of children's advertising is that children are rather easily misled by certain commercial techniques. The argument suggests that adults can identify "puffery" in advertising, and respond accordingly, but that children may not be able to.

In a speech in which she cited survey results from a study of mothers' attitudes toward children's advertising, FTC Commissioner Mary Gardiner Jones summarized the kinds of themes and techniques which mothers find desirable and undesirable:

> Mothers accept and welcome commercials that "teach" children such things as good hygiene and good eating habits . . . The complaints, according to this survey, centered around misrepresentations of the products, manipulation of the child, and the stress and strains imposed on low-income mothers by their children's demands created by the commercials.

CONFRONTING THE ISSUES

Marketers whose promotional efforts involve children have two basic alternatives: they can wait for the critic's attack and then respond, or they can anticipate the critic. Either way, their policy should have three objectives:

1. To respond effectively to problems raised by critics;
2. To meet specific marketing objectives;
3. To help make better informed, more satisfied consumers in the long run.

The third objective reflects concern with what children learn from exposure to advertising (and other forms of promotion) and how this learning influences adult attitudes and responses to advertising. Marketers who advertise to children have several responsibilities. They must meet their own current marketing objectives, but they also have a responsibility to the children with whom they communicate and to the marketers who will attempt to communicate with them when they are adult consumers.

Several courses of action are open to marketers concerned about actual or potential criticism. Some have been tried, others have not. (See Figure 4 for a summary of the advantages and disadvantages of each.) The defensive strategies which until now marketers have relied upon almost exclusively have not been particularly successful.

"Stand and fight"

The cathartic effect of attacking proposed changes, shifting the blame to parents, insisting that television needs the revenue in order to support children's programming, and so forth, momentarily deludes marketers into believing that they have met the challenge of their critics, but they soon discover that their arguments have had little real impact.

FIGURE 4
Marketer response to the children's advertising controversy—Tactics

Tactics	*Advantages*	*Disadvantages*
A. Defensive 1. Ignore controversy.	No short-term costs.	Potential long-run problems. Consumerism costs hard to measure.
2. Stand and fight.	Cathartic.	Historically ineffective.
3. Withdraw: *a*) Use less obtrusive media.	Takes focus off of television "hotbox."	Costly; may be impractical. Reduce revenues for children's shows.
b) Change target to mothers.	Blunts aspect of controversy since child audiences less involved.	May be impractical, less effective.
4. Open on new fronts: *a*) Link with unattackable themes, causes.	Accentuates positive efforts.	Insufficient tactic alone. May not reduce criticism.
B. Positive 1. Short run: *a*) Sponsor quality shows.	Effectively meets key criticism although definition of "quality" needed.	Quality shows still hard to find, especially at local station level.
b) Pretest with mothers.	Allows marketer to anticipate criticism. Shows concern for ad impact. Useful information for design of future promotional programs.	Some added research costs.
2. Long run: *a*) Consumer education for children.	Provide context for children to "receive" ad exposure. Useful for self-regulation efforts. Contribution to better informed, more satisfied adult consumers.	Costly. Will require careful research in design and evaluation.

No matter how correct the marketers' position might be, such tactics have always been interpreted by critics as "defensive" and "self-righteous," and they do not contribute to effective solution of problems.

"Withdraw"

The most visible strategy to date has been the shift of advertising billings to family viewing hours. Nielsen data indicate that 2- to 5-year-old children watch an average of 3.2 hours of fall Saturday mornings (8:00 A.M.–1:00 P.M.) and 6- to 11-year-olds watch 2.6 hours, but both age groups watch about 3.5 hours per week during the 5–7:30 P.M. week-day evening slot. Thus, marketers may reach children even if they don't advertise on Saturday mornings, which is often the focus of critics' attacks. Still other media buying strategies allow marketers to direct their messages almost exclusively to mothers. Some marketers, such as Fischer-Price toys, have been doing this all along.

Advertisers may find that they have simply brought their critics with them to the new time slot. A more serious consequence is the damage that will be done to children's programming if advertisers shift billings away from children's primary viewing times, or to other media. This consequence does not seem to be understood or anticipated by the critics.

"Open on new fronts"

Some advertisers have supplemented their marketing efforts with activities aimed at achieving public goodwill. Two major breakfast cereal companies sponsor "Sesame Street," and one of them donates funds to support a consumer education project. A variation on this strategy is to incorporate relevant, topical, instructional themes—such as ecology—with children's advertising. While these activities meet some critics' objections by providing useful "teaching," they are not adequate by themselves.

NEW AMMUNITION

Taking the offensive in the children's advertising controversy may well prove to be more effective than relying on such defensive tactics as doing battle with critics, fleeing the scene, or simply opening on new fronts.

Short-range tactics

Any marketer who wishes to respond effectively should be concerned first with the quality of the programming he sponsors. Criticism of children's advertising is invariably mixed with criticism of children's programming. *The Wall Street Journal* reports that the Federal Communications Commission "has received over 80,000 letters asking action for more and better children's shows with fewer ads." Network advertisers can choose to sponsor only quality programs, but spot advertisers buy time on the basis of how many children in specific age groups a local station can deliver at a given hour of the day. Consequently, they may find themselves "sponsoring" low-quality programs available in local stations. The result, according to the critics, is guilt by association.

Not even advertising's most severe critics are so preoccupied with advertising that they will not agree that there has been a shortage of prepackaged "quality" children's programming. The situation at the network level is rapidly changing, however, because commercial broadcasters, taking note of the critical and popular success of "Sesame Street," have incorporated the key ingredients of that program—an instructional orientation combined with fast-paced action—in their own programming for children. A problem does remain for the national spot advertiser who wishes to buy in several major markets, but has no effective control over the quality of programming originating at the local level. In addition, the opportunity for spot buying within and around network-oriented "quality" children's shows will decrease as the NAB TV Code stations accept new limits on the amount of nonprogram time they are allowed.

A possible solution for advertisers is to support locally originated quality programming. There are many people—college students, local talent—who would welcome the opportunity to design and product children's programs, if they had sponsorship. Local stations, which are increasingly interested in community involvement and original productions, would welcome these efforts. Local programs which proved extremely successful might provide models for network programming. Finally, advertiser support of local efforts would generate a great deal of favorable publicity.

Once marketers have found quality children's programming to sponsor—either existing productions or locally originated shows—they should measure the effects of this programming. That is, advertisers should conduct on-going, small-scale research, designed to monitor children's responses to these programs.

Just this sort of research has been done for "Sesame Street," the widely acclaimed production of the Children's Television Workshop. Any program as popular and as highly praised as this is bound to attract some criticism, and "Sesame Street" has had its share. But the most effective antidote for this criticism has been the data showing that children who watch the show—whether "culturally deprived" or not—learn more and faster than children who do not watch it.

"Sesame Street" used Educational Testing Services to conduct its "monitoring" research, but advertisers need not go this far to demonstrate their concern for the quality of the programs they sponsor. Even a modest amount of continuous research would provide enough information about children's responses to programs to gauge whether instructional or entertainment objections are being met, and to alert local producers to the need for modifications in programming.

A second short-range tactic for marketers who advertise to children on either a network or spot basis is to pretest commercials among groups of mothers. Most advertisers run copy tests to predict the impact of appeals on children. But very useful data could be provided by recording mothers' reactions to children's commercials.

Marketers were caught rather flat-footed at the recent FTC hearings, when no "child marketers" could produce any research data other than copy tests conducted with children. If marketers argue that mothers must be the watchdogs for their children's television viewing, it is surprising that they have ignored the possibility of conducting a systematic appraisal of mothers' opinions about children's advertising and using this information in the design and executions of children's promotional campaigns. Systematic research among mothers could provide marketers with a criterion for evaluating alternative advertising messages designed for children. On-going copy testing among mothers would enable them to identify the particular themes and techniques which mothers find acceptable or unacceptable.

Long-range tactics

Most parents—even most critics of children's advertising—will accept the proposition that marketers may advocate their products via the mass media. Most would also give implicit consent to promotional efforts directed to their children, if, in return, marketers would sponsor quality programming and take the necessary steps to see that consistently high standards were being maintained. But the bargain would also require some limits on the techniques and tactics of advertising. "If you give my kid good, useful programs, I'll let you advertise to him, *as long as you're reasonable.*"

If the industry hopes to be allowed to regulate itself, it will have to begin doing some pertinent research. Advertisers have done a poor job of self-regulation, as the critics point out, because advertising to children has been based on "what works." Critics perceive a lack of concern on the part of marketers for the particular characteristics of children as an audience, and as a market. Clearly, children *are* a special audience. Yet virtually no industry research into the characteristics of this "special audience" has been concerned with providing a basis for self-regulation. Recently, however, one industry representative pledged a major study of how children acquire consumer skills and how advertising enters into this process. There can be little doubt that a research effort initiated by industry for the express purpose of providing a basis for self-regulation will be more effective than righteous indignation and useless wind sprints as a means of forestalling government-imposed regulation.

Another long-range tactic is education. The disillusionment might never set in, if, along with the commercials, children were given a simplified but straightforward introduction to the purposes of advertising and the criteria which should be used to evaluate it. Specifically, marketers should get into the business of consumer education for youngsters, primarily through support of instructional television programs designed to provide children with a context in which to receive, evaluate, and use advertising and other forms of promotion. This kind of education would help children learn to evaluate their wants carefully and to consider alternative means of satisfying them.

Marketers and their critics would probably agree that most Americans are "poor consumers." Businessmen argue that many consumerism issues arise because of uninformed consumer decisions. More educated consumers should make fewer mistakes in buying and fewer mistakes will mean greater consumer satisfaction. Because education is most effective during the formative years, marketers would do well to provide their own inputs to the process by which children acquire knowledge, skills, and attitudes related to the consumer role. The limited research cited above suggests that children develop somewhat cynical attitudes toward commercials at a fairly early age.

By giving children a perspective on marketing promotion, consumer education programs would counter criticism, i.e., that children cannot fairly evaluate commercial messages. Such programs would also enhance the implicit "bargain" with parents, which allows marketers to exercise their right to advertise within the American system of commercial broadcasting in exchange for quality programming and "fair" advertising techniques.

To summarize, the issues surrounding the "children's advertising" controversy are complex and emotional, but not insoluble. Marketers can ignore the controversy, argue with critics, use less obtrusive kinds of promotion than television advertising, appeal to mothers instead of to children, or attach themselves to "socially desirable" themes and activities. None of these strategies, however, is as effective as taking the offensive. In the short run, marketers should take greater care to sponsor only quality programs. Secondly, they should pretest children's commercials with samples of mothers. Mothers do not object to all advertising, and even welcome some types of messages. The wise children's marketer would not rest comfortably with having demonstrated his concern over the impact of his advertising messages, but would go on to use mothers' objections and suggestions as a basis for changes in future children's promotions.

Finally, in the long run, marketers should be more concerned with processes of consumer learning. Research into these processes could provide a sound basis both for industry self-regulation and for marketer-initiated consumer education programs for children. Such efforts, in turn, would counter a key criticism of children's advertising, reinforce the implicit "bargain" with parents, and contribute to the development of more skilled, and perhaps more satisfied adult consumers.

As a result of changing social values and expressed consumer activism, consumer research must now provide a two-way channel of interaction between the consumer and the firm. The author contends that consumer research should not only facilitate the marketer's awareness of consumer wants and needs, but should in addition provide the consumer with an opportunity and channel to assess the marketers performance from the consumers perspective.

---

38. POINT OF VIEW: CONSUMERISM AND CONSUMER RESEARCH*

A. B. Blankenship†

Consumerism is having a massive impact on our society, not least of all upon consumer research. It is time that those of us in the business sit back and study (or worry) about how we had better be reacting.

For the audience of this publication, there is no need to define consumerism, or to talk about its impact upon society generally. The Ralph Naders have done this dramatically for us. They have pretty definitely shown us that business does not understand the consumer. That goes for the consumer researcher, too, who ought to know better. Consumer research is supposedly *the* channel for communication from the consumer to business. But we in consumer research, unfortunately, may understand neither the consumer nor his viewpoint.

Interest in the consumer is not new to consumer research. Most codes of ethics for researchers who deal with the consumer say—and have

* Reprinted from "Point of View: Consumerism and Consumer Research," *Journal of Advertising Research,* Vol. 11 (August 1971), pp. 44–47.

† Bowling Green State University.

for some years—that anonymity is guaranteed, that no one else will ever get the name of a respondent, that no respondent will ever be followed up for nefarious purposes such as sales or sales promotion. The codes all pretty well agree that it is unethical to mislead the respondent into believing that he is responding to a survey when in fact the survey approach is being misused to try to sell him an encyclopaedia, magazines, or some other item.

But these ethical points merely scratch the surface. If consumer research indeed provides the communications link between consumer and marketer, it had better do more than provide this minimal kind of protection for the consumer in its contact with him. Consumer research should be in the forefront of the drive for a better communication between consumer and marketer.

Consumerism is affecting and will affect consumer research in three ways: the kinds of people questioned, the treatment of people questioned, and the kinds of information obtained.

KINDS OF PEOPLE QUESTIONED

In the first place, the lower socioeconomic groups are going to be included far more often in commercial surveys than in the past. The marketer has usually taken the viewpoint that these groups are not really part of his market, and can be avoided in his survey work. But the inner-city people are not going to permit themselves to be discounted all that readily. They are part of the public, and this public is increasingly demanding a right to be heard, even though it may not be able to afford to buy higher priced products as often as its more well-to-do friends.

In Canada, where I have practiced marketing research, one particular research company was approached by a government agency that had plans to offer a public utility sort of service. The particular agency knew that the service would not be available for many years to other than major urban areas, and that only the income groups above the lowest could afford it. Yet plans for the survey, for political reasons, had to include smaller communities, and include the lower economic classes. There was too much chance that someone in Parliament might come across the specifications for the study and make political hay. The same risk is increasingly present in commercial studies as the chance for government review is increasing.

Another point: consumerism means that we are going to have to concentrate more on the consumer than on the purchaser. We know that for many product categories, the housewife is the buying agent for the family. But today's and tomorrow's consumers are not limited to the housewife; they include other members of the consuming family as well. As consumer researchers, we are going to have to include those untapped consumers more regularly in our surveys. The manufacturer is going to have to be as much interested in consumption as in purchase. Again, in Canada, a major buyer of consumer research advised a research firm that for the purposes of dealing with the government, the research company should start asking consumer-oriented questions, not just purchaser-oriented ones.

TREATMENT OF RESPONDENTS

Most of us have followed the general rule that we should be honest with respondents. We should be candid, not mislead them. Yet the question can be raised as to whether we have been sincere about this. Too often, we have taken the position that if our efforts don't really damage the consumer (respondent), they aren't really all that bad. It is all right to mislead the consumer if we don't hurt him. Let's be honest with ourselves: that is merely saying that the end justifies the means. It won't do in today's consumer environment.

Recently, a research firm was found carefully marking identification numbers on questionnaires in invisible ink. The purpose was to identify those on the mailing list who sent back questionnaires, to enable a second mailing to nonrespondents. In the accompanying letter, the recipient was told that no identification was necessary, and it certainly wasn't; it was already there, but without his knowledge! The rationale was that it would not hurt him, and that it was designed only to help do better research. But the real point is that the means was being justified because of the end, which was honorable. To its credit, the firm immediately changed its policy on the use of invisible ink.

There are other ways in which researchers kid the consumer. Take the projective test, where the purpose is, as all of us know, something the consumer hasn't the slightest idea of. We use it to measure personality characteristics, or to delve into reactions the consumer has no way of knowing he is revealing. In the name of consumerism, are we justified in using such techniques?

What about psychographics? Here the respondent answers questions which, when analyzed in a pattern, provide us with a psychological profile of the individual. The respondent is not aware of the purpose of the questioning, nor that his personality may be appraised through his responses. Are we justified in asking such questions without his knowledge of their intent?

What about physiological tests which reflect emotionality, such as measuring the respondent's blood pressure, sweat activity, pupillary size? While these techniques may not be used all that much, this does not lessen the ethical issue. The respondent is typically not told the purpose of the measurement and does not understand it. If we don't explain it to him, we are misleading him.

Yet another case: the simulated product test. You know what we are talking about here—the so-called product test in which the identical product is tried by the respondent except for variations in characteristics which really have no influence on their quality. You may ask a person to taste two cups of coffee, which are absolutely identical except that one is darker than the other. The tester glibly describes the difference in taste, aroma, and all the rest. The objective may be fine: to determine the influence of color in marketing a coffee. But we have kidded the consumer in our testing procedure by implying that there are differences in the two coffees.

Then there is the free-draw question, as used by Schwerin and others. In this technique—used as a measurement of brand preference—the respondent is told that there will be a free-draw question—sometime after the study—and that he may win it. He is to indicate which brand of toothpaste, for instance, he would want if he happens to make the $5.00 jackpot. Or he may be told that this draw is made for the purpose of repaying him for his cooperation. This is certainly not the whole story. Why do we give any reasons at all? This is simply more misleading of the respondent.

If the respondent begins to get tough with us because of our abuses of him, consumer research is in for trouble. An ugly spectre is beginning to raise its head in terms of consumer response to surveys. Some disadvantaged people have been surveyed so often on actual or potential programs designed to aid them that they are beginning to demand payment for their time. Why should the interviewer be paid for the time it takes her to converse with the respondent if the respondent is not also paid?

We don't know the answer to this. We can comment only that if this movement catches on—and we fear that it might—it will drastically reduce the number of consumer surveys. Surveys will become so excessively expensive that they will become a real luxury. The consumer will end up with less ability than ever to get his message across to the marketer. The consumer research industry needs an advertising or public relations campaign directed at consumers to let them know the advantages to them in cooperating in studies, but only if the industry *is* convinced that consumer research is for the good of the consumer. Let's admit that we all sometimes have our doubts.

One thing consumer researchers are going to have to do is to start spending some time, money, and energy on finding out what the consumer likes and dislikes about contacts with him. How many times does he remember having been questioned. Does he feel that he is questioned too frequently? Does he resent being questioned at all? Why?

Does he feel that it is all right, or not all right, for the questioner to ask the kind of questions he asks? What about his feelings about questions concerning income, age, and other things he may feel are personal and perhaps none of the questioner's business?

Why do those who refuse to be questioned do so?

It is surprising that consumer researchers have not started to ask the consumer about issues as important as this. Aren't we risking alienation of the consumer toward consumer surveys?

KINDS OF INFORMATION OBTAINED

There is going to have to be an increasing emphasis on the kinds of information obtained from the consumer; the information will have to be increasingly in terms of the consumer's interest. Up to now it has been mainly in terms of the marketer's interest.

Consider some examples of consumer research. Perhaps the first—because of its ubiquitousness—is the consumer product test.

What about the consumer product test designed to test two products, one with a lower-priced ingredient, or a lower-quality ingredient, where the only hope of the marketer is to learn that the consumer cannot detect the difference, so that the manufacturer can make more money by making the substitution? This is not an infrequent form of consumer product testing.

Or, what about the simulated product test (mentioned earlier), where the only purpose the manufacturer has in mind is to modify the product in a valueless way because it will subconsciously offer more appeal to the consumer?

Most consumer product tests cover only a short time period. The respondent's first reaction may not be held over a longer period. This means that in the consumer's interest, the short-term product test should probably extend into the continued-use test that we all know.

Consumer studies of packages and labels must markedly change their direction. And it is up to the research firm to take the lead here.

There is going to have to be less emphasis on which is the more appealing package, and more stress on the ease of understanding amount of contents, price per ounce, quality, and how to use. Ingredients will have to be made specific, so that the diabetic, for example, knows whether or not he can safely use the product. The consumer research industry is going to have to lead the way in determining what consumers want in the way of standard package sizes and weights, and what is desired on the label.

Name research (for a brand) is occasionally undertaken. Now, with the consumerism drive, it must be undertaken more cautiously. Is there any chance that the name is misleading? Example: Eiffel Tower, as a brand name for a spray deodorant, could have a lot of consumer appeal. If it also suggests, perhaps misleadingly, that it is a French product, then the name is not good from a consumer viewpoint. And this is the sort of questioning that must now—in the name of consumerism—be included in name testing.

Advertising research, too, must change. It is still fine to use consumer research to predict which advertising approach is more likely to sell the brand, but that is not enough—not by any means.

The marketer—to satisfy consumer requirements—is also going to have to measure a host of elements he has never bothered with before. The researcher will have to measure relative acceptance or rejection of the claim. (Acceptance of the old weasel: It's toasted! must be measured if it is to be a modern claim.)

The advertisement must also be tested, for consumerism, in terms of its general acceptance. If it is annoying, in terms of being boring, irritating, or downright annoying, the pressure of consumerism should suggest changes in the ad.

Finally, the advertisement should say something that is informative. The research conducted on the advertisement should determine whether the advertisement says anything that will really help the consumer make a choice.

There is one last point on the kinds of information to be obtained from the consumer. If business and industry are to cater to the consumer, they must learn more about consumer reaction to basic areas such as pollution, life quality, and the like. It is not enough to say that industry in general must do this. It is up to the individual business producer to measure it in terms of what the public expects of him.

LOOKING AHEAD

In the past, consumer research has concentrated on those aspects of consumer reaction that the marketer wanted to hear about. The fields of interest were those dictated by the marketer.

In these days of the consumer, the emphasis is changing, and must change rapidly. The consumer research function must not only provide a channel for the marketer to learn what he wants to know from the consumer, but should also provide a channel to give the consumer a chance to tell the marketer what he wants from him.

In short, consumer research must become a two-way communications street between marketer and consumer. If it doesn't, consumer research could die.

C.

Distribution

WITHIN the distribution mix component, two main issues are being evaluated. The first is the availability of products and services to the consumer, or the consumers right to choose, and second is the responsibility for recycling of the product or its package after use.

In this first area, criticism has been principally leveled at marketers operating within ghetto or inner city areas. These critics cite evidence; higher prices, less selection within a product category, fewer services offered by the retailer, and less modern facilities as presenting problems different from those encountered in other elements of the retail structure.

Criticism concerning the second issue, recycling of the product or its package, has stemmed from the current environmental crises. Questions arise as to who is responsible for how the product is used. Whether the persons actually using the product bear the responsibility, or whether the manufacturer should not offer products or packaging potentially dangerous to the environment presents an area of further concern.

Zikmund and Stanton open this section with an article dealing with recycling as a channels-of-distribution problem. Next, Wall provides a systems approach to improve the effectiveness of marketing programs directed at low-income neighborhoods. Sturdivant then proposes a program to revitalize the economic structure of ghetto areas. Concluding this section, Goodman reports results of his study dealing with the purchasing patterns of low-income families.

The recycling of solid wastes is a major technological goal. However, reversing this flow within existing distribution channels presents a serious marketing challenge. The author describes two basic problems inherent to the recycling process: that of consumer motivation, *and* channel conflict and cooperation.

39. RECYCLING SOLID WASTES: A CHANNELS-OF-DISTRIBUTION PROBLEM*

William G. Zikmund† and William J. Stanton‡

In 1970 every American threw away approximately five and one-half pounds of solid waste (industrial construction, commercial, and household) each day, which amounts to a ton a year. This daily disposal rate is predicted to increase to eight pounds by 1980.[1] The escalation of public concern over environmental issues has, to an increasing extent, led government officials, business leaders, and conservationists to seek a solution to the problem of solid-waste pollution. One ecologically desirable technique for the disposal of trash is recycling. Simply stated, recycling consists of finding new ways of using previously discarded materials.

The recycling of solid wastes is being recognized as a tenable solution to cleaning up the cluttered environment. Scientists view recycling as a substitute for the declining supply of natural resources. Technology has responded to the recent interest in recycling with many new and sophisticated techniques capable of turning solid wastes into basic raw materials.

Although science and technological innovations are necessary aspects of recycling, the task of alleviating solid-waste pollution may be treated as a marketing activity; that is, the marketing of garbage and other waste materials. If it is a marketing function to distribute products and to add time and place utility to products, then, theoretically, it should make no difference whether the product is an empty, used beer can

* Reprinted from "Recycling Solid Wastes: A Channels-of-Distribution Problem," *Journal of Marketing*, Vol. 35 (July 1971), pp. 34–39.

† University of Colorado.

‡ University of Colorado.

[1] "Cash in Trash? Maybe," *Forbes*, Vol. 105 (January 15, 1970), p. 20.

or a full one. More specifically, recycling is primarily a channels-of-distribution problem, because the major cost of recycling waste products is their collection, sorting, and transportation. The American Paper Institute estimates that over 90 percent of the cost of recycling paper is the cost of distribution.[2]

This article discusses the major alternative channels necessary to handle the waste materials created by the ultimate consumer, and identifies some of the major marketing problems involved in the recycling of these waste materials.

CONCEPT OF THE "BACKWARD" CHANNEL

If recycling is to be a feasible solution to the trash problem, there must be some means to channel the waste materials to the firm for future reuse. However, marketers have traditionally examined the channel of distribution starting with a producer; that is, a channel of distribution is the vehicle which facilitates the flow of goods from producer to consumer.

Recycling, on the other hand, is unusual from a marketing standpoint, because the ultimate consumer who recycles his waste materials must undergo a role change. The household consumer who returns his old newspapers and used bottles is the *de facto* producer of the waste materials which eventually will be reused. Thus, in this case the consumer becomes the first link in the channel of distribution rather than the last. The unique circumstances of recycling present an interesting marketing situation.

Recycling waste materials is essentially a "reverse-distribution" process. Reverse distribution is facilitated by a "backward" channel which returns the reusable packaging and other waste products from the consumer to the producer; it reverses the traditional physical flow of the product.

Conceptually, reverse distribution is identical to the traditional channel of distribution. The consumer has a product to sell and, in essence, he assumes the same position as a manufacturer selling a new product. The consumer's (seller's) role is to distribute his waste materials to the market that demands his product.

There is a practical difference, however, between the traditional channel and the "backward" channel. The consumer does not consider himself a producer of waste materials. Consequently, he is not concerned with planning a marketing strategy for his product—reusable wastes. Thus, for analytical purposes the recycling of waste materials will be considered as the reverse distribution of the original product, and the flow of the product from the consumer to the producer will be treated as the manufacturer's "backward" channel.

[2] Walter P. Margulies, "Steel and Paper Industries Look to Recycling as an Answer to Pollution," *Advertising Age,* Vol. 41 (October 19, 1970), p. 63.

REVERSE DISTRIBUTION: TYPES OF BACKWARD CHANNELS

One of the prime considerations in recycling household wastes is returning the waste product to a manufacturer for reuse. One of marketing's important roles is to determine the most efficient channel of distribution necessary to move the trash to the firm that will technically recycle the materials. The nature of the product and the nature of the market are as important in the determination of the backward channel as they are in the selection of the traditional channel of distribution. Thus, there is not an ideal channel that will typify all recycling efforts. The backward channel used to recycle an automobile is not likely to be the same channel used to recycle a glass bottle. However, some generalizations may be made about various backward channels, since a number of channel patterns are evident.

Direct backward channel—consumer to manufacturer

Perhaps the simplest contemporary recycling attempt is exemplified by the plan of the Glass Container Manufacturing Institute (GCMI). Waste glass—known as a "cullet" in the industry—can supply 30 percent or more of the materials required to make new bottles. To obtain empty bottles and jars from the public, the manufacturer-members of GCMI have established approximately 100 bottle-redemption centers at glass container manufacturing plants in 25 states.[3]

It is doubtful that the modern consumer will make the effort to return his waste products directly to the manufacturer. The selection of any channel must consider the ultimate consumer's needs, and it is unlikely that the modern consumer, accustomed to convenience, will exert any substantial effort to recycle his trash. The GCMI's recycling plan places the burden of recycling on the consumer. This innovative attempt to recycle glass is still in the "production-orientation" stage of development.

Backward channel with an atypical intermediary

The absence of a middleman causes the consumer a number of inconveniences. Ecologically concerned civic and community groups which are sponsoring paper drives and community clean-up days are an important link in the reverse-distribution process because they are performing the middleman's function in the backward channel.[4]

Considering the low prices paid for waste materials and the high

[3] Walter P. Margulies, "Glass, Paper Makers Tackle Out Packaging Pollution Woes," *Advertising Age*, Vol. 41 (September 21, 1970), p. 43.

[4] See "Does Ecology Sell?" *Sales Management*, Vol. 105 (November 15, 1970), p. 20; and Walter P. Margulies, "Aluminum Industry Is Already Hard at Work against Pollution," *Advertising Age*, Vol. 41 (November 16, 1970), p. 64.

cost of reverse distribution, it is not surprising that these organizations are the prime collectors of discarded newspapers, beer cans, and other waste materials. The collection and distribution of trash is a worthwhile venture for these associations because of the volume of their operations. It should be noted that the normal business costs are absent in paper drives and clean-up days because expenses such as labor and collection vehicles, are donated by the associations' membership. Since the main activity of these organizations is not the collection of waste materials, their performance of the middleman's reverse-distribution function tends to be sporadic. Even if community action recycling programs are conducted on a regular basis, it is not realistic to assume that they will be adequate to recycle the mountains of household wastes which will be generated in the coming years.

Backward channel with traditional middlemen

Past recycling efforts used the traditional channel of distribution as the backward channel. Although recycling was not their major function, these intermediaries cooperated because the system was extremely convenient for the producer.

The recycling soft-drink bottles for a deposit provides a familiar example of one of the major attempts to recycle waste products and to reuse them in their existing forms.[5] This backward channel is literally the reverse of the normal channel for soft drinks.

During the 1930s and 1940s, packaging and wholesaling in the soft-drink industry was tied to the system of cycling the returnable bottle. The returnable bottle was desirable from the bottler's point of view, because every reuse reduced the "manufacturing" cost per bottle.

If this was the case, how can the steady growth of one-way bottles and cans be explained? Today, returnable bottles represent less than 50 percent of the soft-drink industry's business because both retailers and consumers resisted the returning and handling of empty bottles.[6] To maximize their profits, supermarkets emphasize the efficient utilization of space. Storing and handling empties was an additional task that retailers were not willing to assume. Consequently, supermarkets influenced bottlers to introduce soft drinks in one-way bottles in 1948.[7]

One-way containers increased the bottler's manufacturing cost, and the consumer was required to bear the additional cost of throw-away bottles and cans. The response in the marketplace demonstrated the

[5] See "Will Returnables Make a Comeback?" *Business Week* (October 31, 1970), p. 25, and Sanford Rose, "The Economics of Environmental Quality," *Fortune,* Vol. 81 (February 1970), p. 184.

[6] "Packaging Advances Promise Much but Environment Dampens Outlook," *Soft Drink Industry,* Vol. 49 (Mary 27, 1970), p. 1.

[7] Robert K. Rogers, "Soft Drink Industry's Progress Paced by New Developments in Packaging," *Soft Drink Industry,* Vol. 49 (July 17, 1970), p. 17.

consumer's willingness to pay a few cents more for the convenience of one-way containers.

Indirect backward channel using trash-collection specialists

Various trash-collection specialists have developed to satisfy the consumer's need to dispose of his garbage and other solid wastes. In the past, the channel for recycling some household wastes included the "old rag and junk man" who served as a recycling-middleman specialist. By calling on homes and purchasing waste products such as rags, used papers, and discarded metal items, he provided both a service and a small-income source to consumers. However, he was part of a subsistence economy and a depression era. As people became more affluent, they preferred the convenience of throwing away their wastes. Moreover, his collection and processing costs were rising. Thus, the "old rag and junk man" largely disappeared because his role in the marketing of trash ceased to provide a sufficient service to household consumers or a profit to himself.

A contemporary waste-disposal specialist is the garbage or other trash collection agency—either a private contractor or a unit in a municipal service system. At one time, these agencies made no attempt to recycle the wastes; they simply carried the rubbish to a city dump. Today, many trash-collection agencies function as a link in a backward channel which recycles household wastes into landfill, power (via incineration), fertilizer, and other uses. The buyer of the trash (possibly after it has been sorted into basic materials) may be a power plant, a metals company, or a fertilizer company.[8]

Obviously this channel is convenient for the household consumer; he simply discards his rubbish into one or more trash cans. However, trash collection by an intermediary specialist is probably not the answer to the recycling channel problem. Unsorted trash used as landfill soon will exhaust available dumping sites. Trash sorted into various basic materials (e.g., glass, paper, and steel) for recycling increases the costs of these materials, although technology in this area is making significant progress.[9] Sorted materials (e.g., glass bottles), frequently are too damaged to be reused in original form. Incinerated trash poses air pollution problems.

THE PROBLEMS OF RECYCLING

The development of effective backward channels should greatly facilitate recycling. However, in order to reach this goal, at least two major

---

[8] See "Turning Junk and Trash into a Resource," *Business Week* (October 10, 1970), p. 64; and "Aluminum Peddles Its Own Recycle," *Business Week* (*January* 30, 1971), p. 21.

[9] "Gold in Garbage," *Time*, Vol. 97 (February 1, 1971), p. 61.

tasks must be accomplished. First, the ultimate consumer must be motivated to start the reverse flow of the product. Second, a greater degree of cooperation has to be achieved among channel members than is likely to occur under present conditions.

Consumer motivation

The greatest barrier to recycling household solid wastes is the consumer himself. The experience of the beer and soft-drink industries indicates that consumers have become accustomed to the luxury of convenience packaging and a throw-away economy. The purchase of 44 billion nonreturnable beverage containers each year provides rather strong exemplary evidence that the consumer's cooperation will not be easy to obtain.[10]

The crux of any recycling plan must be to motivate the consumer to sort and return his waste products. Existing financial incentives such as a bottle deposit are not likely to elicit his cooperation. An appeal to a sense of civic duty or social responsibility so far has proven to be of momentary value, with little lasting effect.

In recognition of the fact that the present free-market system may not result in the recycling of consumer trash, various forms of government intervention are being tried to motivate consumers. Some legislators view packaging taxes and the banning of one-way containers as possible means of stimulating consumers to initiate the reverse distribution process. Some places (e.g., Bowie County, Maryland; South San Francisco, California; and British Columbia) have already passed laws restricting the sale of nonreturnables.[11] The President's Council on Environmental Quality has recommended promoting the idea of recycling bottles.[12]

These attempts to force the consumer to recycle his trash are attacking only a symptom of the problem. The real problem is the consumers' throw-away lifestyle. It probably will be a monumental task to change these attitudes, but it must be done before household solid wastes can be efficiently reused.

Channel conflict and cooperation

Retailers and other middlemen must be willing to cooperate with the manufacturers if reverse distribution is to operate effectively. Generally, traditional middlemen in the backward channel have not been anxious to cooperate with recycling attempts, because it has not been

---

[10] "Does Ecology Sell?" *Sales Management,* Vol. 105 (November 15, 1970), p. 20.

[11] Ibid.; and "Bottlers, Makers of Throwaway Cans Active in Ecological Programs," *Advertising Age,* Vol. 42 (March 1, 1971), p. 62.

[12] "New Federal Programs May Strengthen Efforts to Guard Environment," *The Wall Street Journal,* Vol. 176 (October 27, 1970), p. 1.

profitable. The last 20 years in the soft-drink industry illustrate that retailers may resist recycling in order to utilize their space more efficiently. Consider the costs incurred by the outlet which collects waste materials from the consumer. The retailer must count or weigh the waste products, pay the consumer for his efforts, and store the materials for delivery to the manufacturer or another party in the backward channel.

No matter how delicately recycling is handled, conflict is inevitable in a backward channel. The middleman is an independent force, and he has the freedom to set his own objectives. Thus, he will need an additional incentive to participate in reverse distribution. A financial incentive may be adequate, but will the economics of recycling provide enough money to induce the middlemen's support? Making products from new resources has been economically more feasible than recycling, because existing channels are not designed to recover and reuse old household products.

These middlemen will probably have to commit themselves to a higher order of social responsibility and a longer range perspective than they customarily consider. They may have to become one of the cases Rosenberg and Stern envision as being malign for channel participants, but benign for the society at large.[13] It is questionable whether such a societal commitment can be reasonably expected from existing middlemen in traditional channels.

FUTURE OUTLOOK

The recycling of solid wastes is a major ecological goal. Although recycling is technologically feasible, reversing the materials flow in channels of distribution presents a significant challenge. The existing distribution system is designed to move products from the producer to the consumer. Existing backward channels are primitive, and financial incentives are inadequate. Most traditional middlemen recycle trash only as a sideline. Yet today, societal pressures and dwindling natural resources are forcing consumers to market their trash, even though the price paid for solid wastes is low, and the cost of collecting and processing these materials remains high.

New institutions

"A society, like any other open system, is an adaptive mechanism which responds to the demands of its environment. As it responds, a certain amount of internal adjustment, a large amount which is unpredictable, and the consequences, which are even less predictable, takes

[13] Larry J. Rosenberg and Louis W. Stern, "Toward the Analysis of Conflict in Distribution Channels: A Descriptive Model," *Journal of Marketing*, Vol. 34 (October 1970), p. 45.

place."[14] Existing institutions must adapt to their environment or new institutions will arise to perform the job which is not being completed.

One new institution which may evolve in the reverse-distribution process is a *reclamation or recycling center*. In essence, this would be a modernized and streamlined "junkyard." These centers would be placed in locations convenient to the customer who would be paid an equitable amount for his goods. The recycling center, unlike the junkyard, would have a high turnover of wastes, because its prime goal would be the efficient collection and sorting of basic raw materials, rather than passively waiting for a buyer to purchase junk. If recycling centers perform some minor processing before shipping the basic raw materials to the various manufacturers, the centers might be very profitable operations.

If the recycling center is not convenient enough for the ultimate consumer, perhaps a modernized "rag and junk" man might work for the center, and periodically collect sanitized containers each containing the basic wastes (e.g., glass, paper, and aluminum). The consumers' use of garbage compactors and glass crushers could also enhance the economic feasibility of this operation.

Supermarket chains recycling their used cardboard packaging materials often employ *brokers* to negotiate sales to paper mills.[15] Brokers specializing in the recycling of trash could provide a useful service for small reclamation centers which may evolve into a significant institution in a backward channel.

To aid the recycling efforts of existing middlemen in traditional channels, *central processing warehousing* systems may develop to store trash and to perform limited processing operations on these waste materials. Existing middlemen typically have very limited space available for storing trash, and transportation is likely to represent a major portion of total recycling costs.

Packaging design and materials

As part of their management of solid-waste disposal, marketers will have to reconsider the role of packaging in their marketing mix. The promotional benefits of superfluous packaging (such as shadow boxes) and the convenience factor in packaging (such as vegetables packaged in plastic cooking bags inside of cardboard boxes) will have to be reevaluated in terms of the ecological problems they cause. Marketers could reduce the quantity of trash and facilitate the recycling of used packages through actions such as (1) building reuse value into the package (a jelly jar becomes a drinking glass); (2) avoiding unnecessary

[14] Raymond A. Bauer, "Social Responsibility of Ego Enhancement," *The Journal of Social Issues*, Vol. 21 (April 1965), p. 50.

[15] "They're Finding Gold in Their Trash Bins," *Chain Store Age*, Vol. 45 (January 1969), p. 18.

packaging (does an aspirin-bottle package have to be placed inside a cardboard box package?); (3) using materials which are degradable or which simplify recycling (the metal ring remaining on a glass bottle after a twist-off cap is removed causes a problem in the recycling of the bottle); and/or (4) placing a message on the package reminding the consumer to dispose of his trash properly (don't be a litterbug).

Reverse distribution as part of marketing strategy

From the viewpoint of marketing management in a firm, reverse distribution should be treated as another ingredient in the market mix. As such, the success of any firm's recycling attempts will be contingent upon the marketing strategy employed. Educating the consumer via promotion, for example, will affect the consumer's willingness to use a firm's backward channel.

Management should recognize that waste products may be recycled in different ways:

1. The waste product may be reused in its existing form. For example, a Pepsi bottle is returned to the Pepsi bottler and reused as a Pepsi bottle.
2. The waste product may be reused as a raw material in the manufacture of additional units of the same product. For example, the aluminum from empty beer cans may be reused to make new beer cans.
3. The recycled waste product may become a different product, as when oil and tar are produced from old tires, or when organic wastes are converted to fertilizer.

The major factors in the selection of traditional channels of distribution are the nature of the product and the nature of the market. These factors are equally important in the selection of the backward channel, because the bulk and weight of the waste materials, and the types of buyers and sellers will significantly influence the nature of the backward channel.

Each marketer contemplating the recycling of his product will have to choose one distribution strategy from a number of alternatives. The brewers of Coors beer, for instance, may wish to recycle their own beer cans exclusively. It is also possible that Coors' recycling strategy would have the backward channel return empty Budweiser beer cans which would then be reincarnated into Coors cans.

The type of reverse channel a company selects may influence the raw materials it purchases. A strategy of exclusively recycling waste products through traditional middlemen could provide the manufacturer with control over his sources of raw materials, thereby freeing him of dealings with some suppliers. In addition, the firm's environmental and ecological image may be enhanced if recycling is done by outlets identified with the manufacturer.

Role of government and public policy

In their role as citizens, people in the United States are demanding a cleaner environment, but when acting as consumers they have not been sufficiently motivated to help clean up that environment by recycling their trash. The result of this role conflict will undoubtedly mean an increase in the government's influence on a company's marketing policies with respect to recycling and reverse distribution. Previously, the article referred to a packaging tax and other local and state limitations on nonreturnable packaging. In addition, a bill was recently introduced at the federal level to ban the manufacture and sale of nonreturnable containers because they pose a threat to public welfare and the environment, and because they represent a high-cost form of litter and solid-waste management.[16] As Weiss observed, "When government moves in this radical new direction, can industry, can marketing, look in the other direction?"[17]

CONCLUSION

Predicting the future is difficult, but knowledge of society's needs helps us to know the general direction of the changing environment. One focus of the 1970s seems to center on the reduction of pollution in our environment. The environmentalists who see recycling as the solution to the problem of solid-waste pollution must rely on marketing's help; technology alone is not enough. Lavidge has observed that "as it [marketing] matures, as it broadens in function and scope, marketing will become increasingly relevant during the 70s to the fulfillment of man. And as the impact of marketing on society increases, so does the social responsibility of marketing people."[18] Recycling waste materials is part of marketing's growing responsibility.

[16] U.S. Congress, House, 91st Congress, 2nd Session, H.R. 18773.

[17] E. B. Weiss, "The Coming Change in Marketing: From Growthmanship to Shrinkmanship," *Advertising Age*, Vol. 42 (February 1, 1971), p. 63.

[18] Robert J. Lavidge, "The Growing Responsibilities of Marketing," *Journal of Marketing*, Vol. 34 (January 1970), p. 28.

Marketing to the low-income segment requires special emphasis on distribution policy. A systems approach is designed to improve the effectiveness of marketing programs directed at low-income neighborhoods. The author states that more research focused on low income groups is needed. He contends that cultural and credibility gaps must be bridged. Most importantly, the successful marketer in a low-income area must translate his image from "them" to "we."

---

40. MARKETING TO LOW-INCOME NEIGHBORHOODS: A SYSTEMS APPROACH*

Kelvin A. Wall†

Because it is generally agreed that marketing in the low-income segment needs improvement, a review of current levels of performance and isolation of these by functions is useful. This process provides a clearer picture of the interrelationships of marketing functions as they affect low-income consumers.

Any analysis of this marketing problem is complicated by the fact that low-income family buying patterns tend, in general, to be determined by neighborhoods. These neighborhoods are composed of a "sizeable complement of individuals who differ in one way or another from the neighborhood norm. Nonetheless, even these people tend to conform to their own group behavior patterns."[1] Marketers should, however, carefully appraise their tendency to draw conclusions from the characteristics of a single segment or neighborhood.

I. LOW-INCOME DEFINITIONS TODAY AND TOMORROW

My definition of low-income segment, purely on a dollar basis, has to be arbitrary, because of the differences in spending power at different cost of living levels in various parts of the country. Also, both the aspiration level and the life cycle are variables difficult to pinpoint.

For purposes of this study, this author considers families earning $5,000 or less annually as components of the low-income segment. By this standard, over 19 million families were low-income in 1960, nearly 41 percent of the total United States population at the time.[2] It is esti-

* Reprinted from "Marketing to Low-Income Neighborhoods: A Systems Approach," *University of Washington Business Review* (Autumn 1969), pp. 18–26.

† Georgia Institute of Technology.

[1] Alvin Schwartz, "Study Reveals 'Neighborhood' Influence on Consumer Buying Habits," *Progressive Grocer*, April 1966, pp. 269–72.

[2] *United States Census*, 1960.

mated that by 1970 approximately 7 million white families and 2 million black families will still be below the $5,000 income mark, a substantial decrease from the 19 million families in 1960. The median income by 1970 will be $9,600; however, the Bureau of Labor Statistics estimates a comfortable living cost of $9,200 for urban dwellers. A little less than half the population will fall below this mark, with 11.6 million white and 3.9 million black families below $7,000.

Marketing to low-income neighborhoods demands a consideration of central city population statistics. By 1970, it is estimated that whites will show a decrease of 2 million, and blacks an increase of 3.3 million, in these areas. Close to 58.9 million people will live in these areas, with blacks representing 20 percent of the total.[3] Much emphasis has been placed on the nonwhite urban poor in this country; yet, in 1960, 10.7 million white families in urban areas were in this category as compared with 5.5 million blacks.[4] Even in the central cities of these metromarkets, poor whites outnumber blacks by 1.2 million people.[5]

Of all white families earning over $5,000, the percentage of two wage earners per family ranged from a low of 44.3 percent for the $5,000–$7,000 group to a high of 75 percent for the $12,000–$25,000 group. Most of the 10 million-plus white families earning under $5,000 have only one wage earner per household.

II. INFLUENCE OF LIFESTYLES ON MARKETING

Figure I presents a schematic representation of a systems approach to marketing for low-income groups. A number of socioeconomic characteristics and lifestyle factors encourage such an approach. Briefly, these are as follows:

1. Increased central city low-income population.
2. Low-income groups have experienced a greater increase in income than their cost of living.
3. Their neighborhoods primarily consist of small outlets in which consumers purchase frequently and in small units.
4. Community organization exerts pressure for faster economic and social changes.
5. Lifestyle of consumers is need-oriented, peer-directed, income-limited, mobility-inhibited, and isolated from the rest of the city.
6. Low-income families are heavily concentrated by region and within the city.
7. A unique communications network exists within the community or neighborhood.

[3] "Changing American," *U.S. News and World Report*, June 2, 1969, p. 69.

[4] "Forgotten Men: The Poor Whites," *U.S. News and World Report*, November 27, 1967, p. 76.

[5] "Most U.S. Income Found Inadequate," *The New York Times*, November 18, 1968, p. 38.

FIGURE 1
A systems view of marketing in low income neighborhoods

Sociological-economic characteristics	*Marketing implication*	*Marketing functions or functions affecting marketing*
Increase center city low-income population as middle-class outmigration continues	Low-income segment more important to most major consumer goods marketers and in-city retailers.	Distribution/physical sales coverage Advertising coverage Product and package mix Package size mix Wholesaler/jobbers
Greater increase in income of low-income group than cost of living	This part of the total market will exercise more influence because of increased income and rapid population growth. Competition for their dollars will intensify.	New products New outlets Sales coverage Distribution/physical Product, package, package size mix Advertising coverage
Neighborhoods have small outlets Consumers purchase small units	Maximizing sales or profits requires different marketing and sales strategy because of different outlet mix and purchasing patterns.	Distribution/physical sales coverage Dealer promotions Product, package, package size mix Sales promotion Retail store audits
Community organization pressure for social and faster economic changes	Mass urban marketers, both retailers and manufacturers, will either respond to these pressures voluntarily or be forced to respond through direct economic action against them.	Product or service quality Existing outlets New outlets Employment practices Personnel training Advertising content Advertising media Public relations Sales promotion Joint ventures New distributors

Some of the lifestyle patterns of low-income consumers are unique in either degree or kind. These patterns, when interrelated with consumer behavior, can be linked to a number of critical marketing functions, such as distribution, merchandising activities, product mix, packaging mix, advertising programs, sales policies, and dealer relations activities. These various marketing functions tend to interrelate in response to the unique environment of the low-income neighborhood.

"The low-income consumer is a block dweller, who sees himself as part of his immediate environment and neighborhood, rather than a part of the city in general. His peer relationships are close in this limited environment, and as a consumer, he is strongly motivated to shop

FIGURE 1 (continued)

Sociological-economic characteristics	*Marketing implications*	*Marketing functions or functions affecting marketing*
Life style Need-oriented Peer-oriented Mobile-inhibited Income-limited Isolated from rest of city	Both retailers and other marketers faced with wider differences in consumer motivations and behavioral patterns between low-income consumers than with any other combination of income groups.	New products Merchandising policies Outlets—old and new Copy platforms Sales promotion Fashion/styling/colors Music Advertising media Retail store audit Market research Public relations Distribution
Low-income families heavily concentrated by region and within cities Density increase with low-income Low-income whites Low-income blacks (both important factors)	The problems and the needs of low-income people are more similar than unique or distinct among subgroups. The amount of money they have to spend and their relationships with the total community are, in general, their two most important problems.	Sales promotion Point-of-sales Advertising media Copy platform Music Package size Product mix
Communications Neighborhood outlet-part of communications network Conversation topics limited How as important as what is said Metaphoric and anecdotical Peer group network	Conventional media can and do bring messages into the low-income areas, but these are considered messages from the "outside" and the impact is questionable since their form and language are different from those of the low-income group.	New media New copy Sales promotion Point-of-sales Music Public relations Outlets

within these confines."[6] "The poor consumer is less psychologically mobile, less active, and more inhibited in his behavior than well-to-do customers. The stores he considers for possible purchases are always small. The poor people more often buy at the same store."[7] "A comparison of shopping habits of middle-class and working-class women shows . . . fewer lower class regularly shop in the central business district. The low-income white housewife shops in 'local' stores. The working man's wife or the low-income white wife most frequently prefers to shop in a local and known store."[8] Because of this narrow territorial

[6] Unpublished report, "The Low Income Study," 1969.

[7] David Caplovitz, *The Poor Pay More* (New York: The Free Press, 1963), p. 49.

[8] Lee Rainwater, Richard P. Coleman, Gerald Handel, *Workingman's Wife* (New York: Oceana Publishers, 1959), pp. 163, 164.

view, product availability is an important factor in the marketer's distribution system in low-income areas. Add to this the fact that low-income consumers make frequent shopping trips for small package sizes, and you can see the importance of delivery frequency or frequency of sales calls and other sales management policies. Along with product availability, the type of outlet that dominates low-income neighborhoods should also be considered.

III. REACTION TO COMPANY POSTURE

Community relations have only a minor influence on immediate sales in market segments other than the low-income group. However, such secondary issues as employment policies toward minority groups are particularly important to low-income blacks, and strongly influence their purchasing behavior.

"A company which advertises in Negro media, contributes to the United Negro College Fund, and employs Negroes is perceived as being concerned with the welfare of Negroes, and therefore is entitled to special concern and patronage." Edward Wallerstein, of The Center For Research and Marketing, went on to state that "Negroes tend to believe that a company which advertises in Negro media will be fairer in terms of its employment practices than most companies . . . further, our respondents said that they would tend to switch to the products of the company which advertised in Negro media."[9] Because blacks look more favorably on companies which advertise in black media and employ blacks, the marketing man is operating in a climate of increasing intensity. As Thomas F. Pettigrew predicted in 1964, "Negro protests will continue to grow both in intensity and depth," and "will increasingly attract larger proportions of low-income Negroes and shift from status to economic goals." He further stated, "a more intensive use of local and national boycotts of consumer products will be made."[10] His statements clearly indicate the interrelationship between sound community relations efforts and employment practices and sound marketing programs as they effect low-income blacks.

Recent organized boycotts have intensified these attitudes. The physical isolation caused by segregation in housing, either by income or race, has compounded marketers' problems. Another factor is the low-income consumer's "lack of mobility, both physical and psychological."[11] Car ownership is low, and parking space is scarce. This means that besides the general tendency of low-income people to stay within their neighborhoods, there are fewer opportunities for them to travel outside this en-

---

[9] "Negro Boycott Could Have Serious Lasting Effect on Sales, Study Shows," *Advertising Age,* September 30, 1963, p. 38.

[10] Thomas F. Pettigrew, *A Profile of the Negro American* (Princeton, N.J.: D.

[11] David Caplovitz, *The Poor Pay More,* p. 49.

Van Nostrand Co., 1964), pp. 197–99.

vironment. Therefore, marketing performance in low-income areas must be measured by the success—or lack of it—of retailers in these neighborhoods.

IV. MEETING THE ADVERTISING CHALLENGE

The problem of communicating to residents of these neighborhoods offers a challenge to a variety of marketing and marketing-related functions. Advertising strategy, both from a copy platform and media planning standpoint, is as much affected as sales promotion and point-of-sale activities. One reason why the variety of selling activities needs to be tailored to low-income consumers is the uniqueness of their lifestyle patterns, including their language and communications patterns and attitudes toward advertising.

The language of this group is *concrete*. They are "less verbally oriented than better educated groups, and their interpersonal exchanges involve smaller amounts of symbolic linguistic behavior."[12] Their day-to-day conversations are less abstract and have less conceptualization. They deal primarily with concrete objects and situations. The fact that they generalize less and are less reliant on the intellectual process than on observations often renders some sophisticated advertising and sales promotion efforts of major marketers ineffective.

To fully appreciate the burden that advertising communications must carry into low-income neighborhoods, one should remember that advertising must function as a persuasive vehicle that stimulates the desire to consume. The educational function that advertising performs in this regard is important. Many low-income housewives, both white and black, look to advertising to fulfill an educational role. Nearly 12 million United States adults have less than a sixth grade education, with 2.7 million never having attended school at all. More than 23 million never completed grade school.[13]

Low-income consumers' preference for certain types of models also affects commercial communications. In the case of white blue-collar wives, "advertising which is people-oriented is much more meaningful than . . . advertising that communicates a highly technical, impersonal or objective atmosphere."[14] A study conducted by Social Research asserts that "the safest route to high rewards from the Negro audience is to be found in advertisements which feature Negroes exclusively."[15] Natu-

[12] Lola M. Irelan, ed., *Low Income Life Style* (Washington, D.C.: Department of Health, Education and Welfare, August 1967), p. 72.

[13] "The New Market," *Harvard Business Review*, May-June 1969, p. 61.

[14] Rainwater, Coleman, and Handel, *Workingman's Wife*, p. 153.

[15] *Negro Media Usage and Response to Advertising*, Social Research, Inc., April 1969, Study No. 3621, p. 4.

rally, this preference should be considered in decisions concerning media, types of advertising, and sales promotions programs.

V. BRIDGING CULTURAL AND CREDIBILITY GAPS

Understanding the behavior patterns of residents of low-income neighborhoods requires a clear understanding of their attitudes toward the world outside their environment. They often consider it hostile, and think in terms of "we" and "them." "The lack of effective participation and integration of the poor in the major institutions of the large society is one of the critical characteristics of the culture of poverty."[16]

Although it is difficult, a marketer in a low-income area must translate his image from "them" to "we." "Supermarkets operating in disadvantaged areas do not enjoy the confidence of their customers . . Negroes believe that they are treated as undesirables or untouchables . . . there is a definite credibility gap between what the food chain says they are doing for ghetto residents and what these people think is being done." Both white and black ghetto residents have more complaints about their local food stores—"prices are high, service is bad and unfriendly, stores are dirty, and lighting is inadequate."[17]

Both marketers and retailers are faced with a number of problems. In the case of the marketer, has he made certain that the items that appeal most to low-income consumers—the items that fit best into their lifestyle—are available in the right package sizes? And, are products continuously available for a consumer who has a more frequent shopping pattern than the average?

The preconditioning done by the marketer affects the retailer and the consumer. The retailer who has the right variety of merchandise, meaning the merchandise most appropriate to the needs of the low-income community and most readily accepted by that market, will greatly improve his image. Since the food chain store has a poor image among this group, the responsibility of the marketer is more critical. Consequently, such functions as merchandising policies, distribution and sales activities, as well as community relations and public relations functions, are key factors.

VI. BETTER RESEARCH IS SORELY NEEDED

The marketing executive who relies on information derived from his own life experiences is usually handicapped when faced with the problems of marketing to low-income groups, because their lifestyle is quite different from his middle-class one. Nor can he rely on usual sources

[16] Oscar Lewis, "The Culture of Poverty," in *Man Against Poverty: World War III*, Berstein, Woock, eds. (New York: Random House, 1968), p. 264.

[17] "Poor Still Don't Trust Chains," *Chain Store Age*, February 1969, p. 63.

to help him to narrow his informational gap. It is "acknowledged that most market research is now focused on middle and upper income people, but there is increasing awareness of the need to focus more marketing attention on those in low-income groups."[18] A. C. Nielsen and other store audit services usually do not have a large enough sample in this segment to produce reliable data.

These combined factors clearly indicate a need for a systems approach to dealing with the low-income segment. Example: The systems of small outlets, that is, outlets that have a small physical space limitation, are interlocked with the fact that merchants operating them usually have limited financial resources and management skills. Both their physical and financial limitations usually allow these retailers to purchase only limited quantities at a given time. If the manufacturer's delivery frequency cannot fit these limitations under which retailers operate, product availability and dealer goodwill become critical problems, accentuated by the low-income consumer's propensity to buy often and in small units. To attack the problem of product availability, it is necessary to deal with several marketing functions, such as frequency of delivery, credit policies, and merchandising and display facilities. Changing a single marketing function probably would not be effective.

VII. SUMMARY

A list of factors which led to the conclusion that there is a need for a systems approach to improve the effectiveness of marketing programs directed at low-income neighborhoods includes the following:

1. Marketing administrators responsible for share of market in the major urban centers must look at how their total system is working in this part of their sales environment.
2. While consumers in low-income neighborhoods are increasing their income more rapidly than their cost of living, they still have limited education and income. These two factors influence a number of marketing functions differently than for other income groups.
3. Lifestyle differences tend to prevail and marketers are forced to respond with a different marketing mix. Factors such as varying product or packaging mix policies are required.
4. Finally, the concentration of low-income families in certain regions of the United States and within certain parts of cities is likely to continue. Communications problems to this group, because of educational differences, will continue to be a challenge for progressive marketers.

Low-income neighborhoods will continue to be a problem to marketers who have not adjusted their total system to this segment's needs.

[18] "Lavidge Says Market Researchers Must Focus on Minorities," *Advertising Age*, May 26, 1969, p. 45.

APPENDIX A

Residential patterns for whites and blacks

	Whites		*Blacks*	
	1960	*1970 (est.)*	*1960*	*1970 (est.)*
Central cities	48,800,000	46,800,000	9,800,000	12,100,000
Suburbs	55,700,000	74,400,000	2,900,000	4,400,000
Small towns and other nonfarm areas	42,500,000	49,400,000	4,600,000	5,100,000
Farms	11,800,000	7,800,000	1,510,000	1,100,000
Total United States	158,810,000	178,400,000	18,900,000	22,800,000

Source: 1960, U.S. Census Bureau: 1970, projections by USN&WR Economic Unit, based on census data.

White Americans increased by 19.6 million, or 12.3% in the 1960s, while Negro Americans increased by 3.9 million, or 20.6%.
Central cities lost an estimated 2 million whites and gained about 2.3 million blacks.

APPENDIX B

Income trends for the United States

	White families		*Black families*	
Yearly income	*1960*	*1970 (est.)*	*1960*	*1970 (est.)*
Under $3,000	7,800,000	3,000,000	1,900,000	1,000,000
$3,000–$4,999	8,100,000	3,900,000	1,000,000	900,000
$5,000–$6,999	10,000,000	4,600,000	600,000	1,000,000
$7,000–$9,999	8,700,000	11,100,000	300,000	900,000
$10,000–$14,999	4,600,000	13,900,000	200,000	700,000
$15,000 plus	1,600,000	9,700,000	20,000	400,000
	Whites		*Blacks*	
Persons living in poverty*	27,500,000	13,600,000	10,500,000	6,400,000

*Single persons or members of families with incomes below officially designated "poverty" levels, set at $3,060 per year in 1960 and $3,358 in 1968 for a nonfarm family of four.

Sources: 1960, U.S. Census Bureau; 1970, projections by *United States News and World Report* Economic Unit, based on census estimates through 1968.

Income gains are dramatic for both white and black families. Median income for black families has doubled since 1960, to an estimated $6,500 in 1970. Median income for white families rose 65 percent, to $9,600.

The poorest segments of our society are being served by the least efficient segments of our distribution system. The author proposes a necessary program to revitalize the economic structure of these areas.

41. BETTER DEAL FOR GHETTO SHOPPERS*

Frederick D. Sturdivant†

However remote and unreal the newspaper photos of large numbers of looters carrying furniture, groceries, appliances, and other merchandise through the streets of many of this nation's major cities may seem, their message for U.S. business is profound. "Such poverty as we have today in all our great cities degrades the poor," warned George Bernard Shaw in 1928, "and infects with its degradation the whole neighborhood in which they live. And whatever can degrade a neighborhood can degrade a country and a continent and finally the whole civilized world. . . ."[1]

Over the past two years an epidemic of this contagious disease has struck with great violence in Los Angeles, New York, Rochester, Chicago, San Francisco, Newark, Detroit, and other large U.S. cities. There is the threat of more riots to come. A major share of the responsibility for halting the epidemic and preventing further assaults on the structure of society rests with the business community.

No informed citizen questions the presence of large numbers of people living in poverty in the United States. Indeed, most Americans have tired of the debate which attempts to quantify and measure a state of existence that is too qualitative and miserable to be measured precisely. Many companies have participated in private and governmental programs by hiring and training individuals from disadvantaged areas.[2] In fact, efforts to deal with the dilemma of the underskilled and unemployed have represented the major thrust of the business community's

* Reprinted from "Better Deal for Ghetto Shoppers," *Harvard Business Review*, Vol. 46 (March-April 1968), pp. 130–39.

† University of Texas.

[1] *The Intelligent Woman's Guide to Socialism and Capitalism* (Garden City, N.Y.: Garden City Publishing Co., Inc., 1928), p. 42.

[2] See Alfonso J. Cervantes, "To Prevent a Chain of Super-Watts," *HBR* (September-October 1967), p. 55.

commitment to the War on Poverty. In some areas of high unemployment such programs have led to significant improvements in local conditions.

While few would question the importance of training and employing the disadvantaged, a fundamental point is generally ignored. *The most direct contact between the poor and the business community is at the retail level.* The greatest opportunity to assist and to revolutionize the daily lives of the poor rests in the retailing communities serving poverty areas.

While it is a great step forward to create jobs for the unemployed or to train men for better-paying jobs, such improvements can be nullified when the worker and members of his family enter the marketplace as consumers. Very little may be gained if they are confronted with a shopping situation that generally offers them higher prices, inferior merchandise, high-pressure selling, hidden and inflated interest charges, and a degrading shopping environment. Such conditions are closely related to the frustrations that have produced the spectacle of looted and burned stores throughout the nation.

A TALE OF TWO GHETTOS

The first of the terribly destructive and bloody Negro riots took place in the south central section of Los Angeles in August 1965. In the aftermath of the nearly week-long Watts riots, which seemed to set the pattern for subsequent revolts around the country, it was apparent that retail establishments had been the primary target of the rioters. Of the more than 600 buildings damaged by looting and fire, over 95% were retail stores. According to the report of the Governor's Commission on the Los Angeles Riots, "The rioters concentrated primarily on food markets, liquor stores, furniture stores, department stores, and pawnshops."[3]

Manufacturing firms and other kinds of business facilities in the area, which in many cases contained valuable merchandise and fixtures, were virtually untouched, as were public buildings such as schools, libraries, and churches. Not one of the 26 Operation Head Start facilities in the Watts area was touched.

Even a cursory survey of the damage would indicate that a "vengeance pattern" might have been followed. The various news media covering the riots reported many interviews which revealed a deep-seated resentment toward retailers because of alleged exploitation. The possibility that the rioters were striking back at unethical merchants was reinforced by the fact that one store would be looted and burned while a competing unit across the street survived without so much as a cracked window.

[3] The Governor's Commission on the Los Angeles Riots, *Violence in the City—An End or a Beginning?* (Los Angeles, December 1965), pp. 23–24.

In the fall of 1965, facts and questions like these prompted a two-year study of consumer-business relations in two disadvantaged sections of Los Angeles:

1. As the center of the Los Angeles riots, Watts was an excellent place to begin the study. Consumers and merchants were very willing to discuss their experiences and to explore the causes of the riots. Civil rights groups and merchants' organizations were eager to cooperate with an "objective" research effort which would vindicate their respective points of view. In effect, there were a number of advantages in studying the conditions in Watts while the rubble still littered the streets and participants in the destruction were seeking to be heard.

2. But Watts by itself was not sufficient for an objective investigation. The basic retail structure of the area had been virtually destroyed, and it was impossible to contact many of the merchants who had been burned out by the rioters. In addition, feelings were so intense on both sides that the danger of distortion was greatly magnified. Since the population of the area was heavily Negro, the investigation might have become a study of exploitation of this minority rather than an analysis of the relations between business and the poor in general. Therefore, a second study area was selected—a disadvantaged section of the Mexican-American community in east Los Angeles.

In each area, more than 25% of the population fell below the government's $3,000 poverty line. In addition, each area had high unemployment (7.7% for Mexican-Americans and 10.1% for Negroes), a high incidence of broken homes (17.2% for Mexican-Americans and 25.5% for Negroes), and the many other household and community characteristics which are associated with ghettos.[4]

Over a period of two years, more than 2,000 interviews were held with consumers and merchants in these two poverty areas, numerous shopping forays were conducted, and price-quality comparisons were made with stores serving the more prosperous sections of Los Angeles and surrounding communities. Although there were a number of interesting differences between the findings in the two areas (the differences were based for the most part on cultural factors), the evidence points to two basic flaws in local retailing which were present in each of the areas:

1. The prevalence of small, inefficient, uneconomical units.

2. A tendency on the part of many stores to prey on an undereducated and relatively immobile population with high-pressure, unethical methods.

These findings, I believe, apply rather generally to the retail segments

[4] California Department of Industrial Relations, *Negroes and Mexican-Americans in South and East Los Angeles* (San Francisco, July 1966). These data understate both the income and unemployment problems since they cover the entire area and not just the poorest sections analyzed in this study.

serving disadvantaged areas in U.S. cities. Let us look at each of them in more detail.

INEFFICIENT "MOMS AND POPS"

One of the cruelest ironies of our economic system is that the disadvantaged are generally served by the least efficient segments of the business community. The spacious, well-stocked, and efficiently managed stores characteristic of America's highly advanced distribution system are rarely present in the ghetto. The marvels of mass merchandising and its benefits for consumers normally are not shared with the low-income families. Instead, their shopping districts are dotted with small, inefficient "mom and pop" establishments more closely related to stores in underdeveloped countries than to the sophisticated network of retail institutions dominant in most of the U.S. economy.

With the exception of one outdated supermarket, no national or regional retailing firms were represented on the main street of Watts before the 1965 riots. Following the riots, when 103rd Street was dubbed "Charcoal Alley," not even that lone supermarket remained. On Brooklyn Avenue, the heart of the poorest section in east Los Angeles, one found such establishments as Factory Outlet Shoes, Nat's Clothing, Cruz Used Furniture, Villa Real Drugs, and Chelos Market, ranging in size from 315 square feet to 600 square feet. Of the 175 stores in the shopping district (this figure excluded service stations), only 5 were members of chain organizations, and 2 of these firms traced their origins back to a time when the neighborhood was a middle-class district.

Lacking economies of scale and the advantages of trained management, the "moms and pops" muddle through from day to day and, in the process, contribute to the oppressive atmosphere of such neighborhoods. Their customers generally pay higher prices, receive lower-quality merchandise, and shop in shabby, deteriorating facilities.

Inflated prices and . . .

The most controversial of these conditions is pricing. The phrase, "the poor pay more," was popularized by Columbia University sociologist David Caplovitz's widely read book with that title.[5] Unfortunately, in addition to being an eye-catching title, it describes reality. While the small, owner-operated stores do not have a monopoly on high prices in the ghetto, they contribute significantly to the inflated price levels. Consumers in Watts, for example, can expect to pay from 7% to 21% more for a market basket of 30 items if they shop for groceries in one of the small local stores than would a family shopping in a supermarket

[5] New York: The Free Press, 1963.

in affluent Beverely Hills. Similar or even greater price differentials prevail in most merchandise categories.

Comparative pricing analyses of the disadvantaged areas and the more prosperous sections in a city are very difficult to make because of quality differences. When national brands are carried by a ghetto appliance dealer, for example, he generally stocks only the lower end of the line. Retailers in higher income areas usually concentrate on the middle and upper price ranges of the product line. Furthermore, off-brand merchandise tends to make up a substantial part of the ghetto dealer's line. Since these lines are not carried in other areas, direct price comparisons are impossible. In food stores, the problem is particularly acute with respect to meat and produce items. Commercial grades of meat are generally carried by ghetto stores, and visual comparisons reveal major qualitative differences in the produce carried, but precise measurements of these quality distinctions are impossible.

Depressed looks

The physical setting also does little to enhance ghetto shopping. Resentment over the appearance of stores is deeply felt in Watts. I have encountered many reactions like these:

"The manager of that grocery store must think we are a bunch of animals," charged one middle-aged Negro woman with whom I talked. She continued, "The floors are filthy, there are flies all over the place, they handle our food with dirty hands and never say thank you or nothing that's nice."

Commenting on the shabby appearance of the stores on 103rd Street, one young Negro activist said, "The merchants don't give a damn about Watts. They take our money back to Beverly Hills and never spend a cent fixing up their stores."

While such changes are influenced by emotion, the reasons for the bitterness become understandable when one takes a walk down "Charcoal Alley" with its many vacant lots, one dozen or so vacant stores, two thrift shops, six liquor stores, one dime store, one drugstore, one pawnshop, one record shop, one appliance-dry goods store, and a few bars. Although the number and variety of stores along Brooklyn Avenue in east Los Angeles is greater, 53% of the stores are more than 20 years old and have had no apparent improvements made since their construction. Of these stores, 6% are in obvious need of extensive repair and remodeling.

PARASITIC MERCHANTS

While the deteriorated condition of shopping facilities obviously does little to attract shoppers from outside the area, the ghettos do act as magnets for high-pressure and unethical merchandisers who become parasites on the neighborhoods. Take New York, for example. Because of the predominance of parasitic merchants in the ghettos of Manhattan, Caplovitz describes business communities there as "deviant" market systems "in which unethical and illegal practices abound."[6]

The parasitic merchant usually deals in hard goods and emphasizes "easy credit." He stocks his store with off-brand merchandise, uses bait-switch advertising, offers low down payments and small installments, employs salesmen who are proficient at closing often and fast, and marks up his merchandise generously enough to assure himself of a very good return for his effort. Again, direct price comparisons are difficult because of brand differences, but Exhibit I reflects the higher prices paid by

EXHIBIT 1
Ghetto shoppers pay more for appliances

	Price		
Product	*Watts area*	*East L.A. area*	*Control area*
1. Zenith portable TV (X1910)	$170	—	$130
2. Olympic portable TV (9P46)	$270	$230	—
3. RCA portable TV (AH0668)	$148	—	$115
4. Zenith portable TV (X2014)	—	$208	$140
5. Emerson portable TV (19P32)	$210	$200	$170
6. Olympic color console TV (CC337A)	—	$700	$630
7. Zenith clock radio (X164)	—	$42	$19
8. Eureka vacuum (745a)	—	$35	$30
9. Fun Fare by Brown (36" free standing gas range)	—	$200	$110

Note: Prices for items 1–4 are averages computed from the shopping experiences of three couples (Mexican-American, Negro, and Anglo-White) in three stores in each of the three areas. The three couples had nearly identical "credit profiles" based on typical disadvantaged family characteristics. The stores located in the Mexican-American and Watts areas were selected on the basis of shopping patterns derived from extensive interviews in the areas.

Items 5–9 are the only prices obtainable on a 24-item shopping list. One low-income Anglo-White couple shopped 24 randomly selected stores in the disadvantaged areas.

All prices are rounded.

ghetto shoppers compared with store prices in a middle to lower-middle class suburb of Los Angeles.

[6] Ibid., p. 180.

Data gathered on markups further confirm the presence of exploitation. The major furniture store serving the Watts area and its unaffiliated counterpart in east Los Angeles both carried Olympic television model 9P46. This model wholesales for $104. The retail price in the Watts area store was $270, a markup of 160%, and $229.95 in east Los Angeles, a markup of 121%. The latter store also carried a Zenith model number X1917 priced at $269.95, or 114% above the wholesale price of $126.

Are such substantial markups justified because of the higher risks associated with doing business in a ghetto? It would seem that such risks are more than offset by the interest charges on the installment contract. The rates are highly volatile, but never low. A Mexican-American couple and a Negro couple with virtually the same "credit profile" shopped a number of furniture and appliance stores in the two disadvantaged areas as well as stores in the middle-class control area. An "easy payment" establishment serving south central Los Angeles applied the same high-pressure tactics to both couples, who shopped for the same television set. The retailer charged the Negro couple 49% interest on an 18-month contract, while the Mexican-American couple really received "easy terms"—82% interest for 18 months!

Charges of this magnitude go well beyond any question of ethics; they are clearly illegal. In California the Unruh Retail Installment Sales Act sets the maximum rate a dealer may charge on time contracts. For most installment contracts under $1,000, the maximum service charge rate is 5/6 of 1% of the original unpaid balance multiplied by the number of months in the contract. Accordingly, the legal rate for the television set selected by the two couples was 15%.

While it is true that most ghetto merchants do not exceed the legal limits, their customers still pay higher credit charges because of the inflated selling prices on which the interest is computed.

How they get away with it

Parasitic merchants are attracted to disadvantaged areas of the cities by the presence of ill-informed and generally immobile consumers. Operating from ghetto stores or as door-to-door credit salesmen, these merchants deal with consumers who have little understanding of contracts or even of the concept of interest. Given their low-income status, one dollar down and one dollar a week sounds to the buyer like a pretty good deal. The merchants are not at all reluctant to pile their good deals on their customers with the prospect of repossessions and garnishments.

Comparative shopping outside his own neighborhood would, of course, provide a ghetto resident with a vivid demonstration of the disadvantages of trading with the local merchants. Unfortunately, the idea of comparing prices and credit terms is little understood in the ghetto. And for those residents who can appreciate the advantages of comparative shopping, transportation is often a barrier. In Watts, less than half of the households studied had automobiles. The public transportation facilities, which are inadequate at best throughout the city of Los Angeles are archaic. Infrequently scheduled, time-consuming, and expensive bus services are of little value to the area's shoppers.

In east Los Angeles, the Mexican-Americans have greater mobility; 73% of the households studied had an automobile, and bus services were better than in Watts. The Mexican-Americans also have relative proximity to modern shopping facilities. However, there are strong cultural ties that encourage residents to forgo shopping advantages offered in other areas. They choose, in effect, to be reinforced continually in the existing cultural setting by frequenting stores in the disadvantaged area where Spanish is spoken. Whether for reasons of transportation problems or self-imposed cultural isolation, the local merchant enjoys a largely captive market.

SHUNNING DEPRESSED AREAS

Not all merchants in disadvantaged areas are there for the purpose of exacting all they can from a neighborhood of undereducated and poor consumers. As noted before, many of the small shops offer their customers higher prices and lower quality because of inefficiency, not by design. The great villain, say the retailers, is the cost of doing business in disadvantaged areas. For example, it is said that small merchants normally cannot afford insurance protection. Of the merchants interviewed in Watts, fewer than 10% had insurance before the riots. Retailers in slum areas have always paid higher insurance rates. According to California's insurance commissioner, rate increases of 300% following the riots were not uncommon. In this respect, the riots throughout the country have only magnified the problem of good retail service, not relieved it.

Since so few small merchants attempt to insure their businesses, the major effect of the abnormally high rates is to deter larger organizations from investing in ghetto areas. An executive responsible for corporate planning for a retail chain would be hard pressed to justify building a unit in Watts or east Los Angeles when so many opportunities and excellent sites are available in fast growing and "safe" Orange County (in the Los Angeles area). A parallel could be drawn with building in the South Side of Chicago as opposed to the prosperous and rapidly expanding suburbs on the North Shore, or in virtually any central city slum area contrasted with the same city's suburbs. Large retailers not only are frightened away by insurance costs, but also point to personnel problems, vandalism, and alleged higher incidences of shoplifting in disadvantaged districts.

This is not to suggest that there are not profits to be made in such areas. Trade sources, especially in the supermarket industry, have pointed to unique opportunities in low-income neighborhoods.[7] The managements of supermarket chains such as Hillman's in Chicago and ABC Markets in Los Angeles admit that, while there are unique merchandising problems associated with doing business in depressed areas, their profit return has been quite satisfactory. It might also be noted that companies that do a conscientious job of serving the needs of low-income consumers are highly regarded. For instance, interviewees in Watts were virtually unanimous in their praise for ABC Markets. Perhaps the most dramatic affirmation of the chain's position in the community came during the riots: not one of the company's three units in the area was disturbed during the week-long riots.

My interviews with executives of Sears, Roebuck and Co. and J.C. Penny indicate that these companies have been slightly successful in adapting to changing conditions in transitional areas. Those of their stores located in declining neighborhoods have altered their merchandising programs and the composition of their work forces to adjust to the changing nature of the market area. The result has been profits for both firms.

Yet, in most cases, such opportunities have not been sought out by large retailers, but stumbled on; they have been happily discovered by older stores trying to readapt themselves in areas where the racial and economic makeup is changing. New stores are built only in trading areas where the more traditional competitive challenges are to be found. As one executive said, "Our target is the mass market, and we generally ignore the upper 10% and the lower 15% to 20% of the market." The upper 10%, of course, can be assured that Saks Fifth Avenue, Brooks Brothers, and a host of other such firms stand ready to meet their needs. The poor, however, are left with "moms and pops" and the easy-credit merchants.

A WORKABLE SOLUTION

Most critics of business-consumer relations in disadvantaged areas have called for legislation designed to protect consumers and for consumer education programs. Indeed, laws designed to protect consumers from hidden and inflated interest charges and other forms of unethical merchandising should be passed and vigorously enforced. Consumer economics should be a part of elementary and secondary school curricula, and adult education programs should be available in disadvantaged areas. However, these approaches are hardly revolutionary,

[7] See, for example, "Supermarkets in Urban Areas," *Food Topics*, February 1967, pp. 10–22.

and they hold little promise of producing dramatic changes in the economic condition of the disadvantaged.

A crucial point seems to have been largely ignored by the critics and in the various bills introduced in the state legislatures and in Congress. This is the difficulty of improvement so long as the retailing segments of depressed areas are dominated by uneconomically small stores—by what I call an "atomistic" structure. Indeed, many legislators seem eager to perpetuate the system by calling for expanded activities by the Small Business Administration in offering assistance to more small firms that do business in the ghettos. Another common suggestion is for the federal government to offer low-cost insurance protection to these firms. This proposal, too, may do more to aggravate than relieve. If the plight of the ghetto consumer is to be dramatically relieved, this will not come about through measures designed to multiply the number of inefficient retailers serving these people.

Real progress will come only if we can find some way to extend into the ghettos the highly advanced, competitive retailing system that has so successfully served other sectors of the economy. To make this advance possible, we must remove the economic barriers that restrict entry by progressive retailers, for stores are managed by businessmen, not social workers.

How can these barriers be removed?

Investment guarantee plan

Since shortly after the close of World War II, the federal government has had a program designed to eliminate certain barriers to investment by U.S. corporations in underdeveloped countries. In effect, the government has said that it is in the best interest of the United States if our business assists in the economic development of certain foreign countries. In a number of Latin American countries, for instance, the program has protected U.S. capital against loss through riots or expropriation. The investment guarantee program does not assure U.S. firms of a profit; that challenge rests with management. But companies are protected against the abnormal risks associated with building facilities in the underdeveloped countries. If a guarantee program can stimulate investment in Colombia, why not in Watts or Harlem?

I propose a program, to be administered by the Department of Commerce, under which potential retail investors would be offered investment guarantees for building (or buying) a store in areas designated as "disadvantaged." A contract between the retail firm and the Commerce Department would guarantee the company full reimbursement for physical losses resulting from looting, burning, or other damages caused by civil disorders as well as from the usual hazards of natural disasters. In addition, the contract would call for compensation for operating losses sustained during periods of civil unrest in the area. To illustrate: A Montgomery Ward store established in the heart of Watts would, under this program, be insured for the book value of the establishment against damages caused by natural or human events. If the firm emerged from a period of rioting without suffering any physical damages, but was forced to cease operations during the period of the riots, Montgomery Ward would be compensated for operating losses resulting from the forced closure.

Costs and restrictions. The costs to a company for an investment guarantee would be minimal in terms of both financial outlay and loss of managerial autonomy. An annual fee of 0.5% of the amount of insured assets would be charged. There is no actuarial basis for this rate; rather, the fees are charged to cover the costs of administering the program and building a reserve against possible claims.

There would be no restriction on either the size of the investment or the term of the guarantee contract. The contract would be terminated by the government only if the firm violated the terms of the agreement or if the economic character of the area improved to the point that it was no longer classified as disadvantaged.

In addition to paying annual premiums, the participating companies would be required to conform to state and local laws designed to protect consumers (or minimum federal standards where local legislation is not in effect). A participating retailer found guilty of violating state law regarding, let us say, installment charges would have his contract terminated.

In effect, the ethical merchandiser would find no restrictions on his usual managerial freedom. So long as he abided by the law, his investment would be protected, and he would have complete freedom in selecting his merchandise, setting prices, advertising, and the other areas of managerial strategy.

Enlarged investment credit

The guarantee program would offer the manager maximum discretion, but it would not assure him of a profit. The guarantee phase of the program merely attempts to place the ghetto on a par with nonghetto areas with respect to investment risk. The final barrier, the high costs associated with doing business in such areas, would have to be offset by offering businesses enlarged investment credits. Credits of perhaps 10% (as compared to the usual 7% under other programs) could be offered as an inducement to outside retailers. Firms participating in the guarantee program would be eligible for such investment credits on all facilities constructed in disadvantaged areas.

The more generous investment credits would serve as a source of encouragement not only for building new facilities, but also for expanding and modernizing older stores that had been allowed to decline. For example, the Sears Roebuck and Penney stores located (as earlier mentioned) in transitional and declining areas would be likely targets for physical improvements.

Key to transformation

Perhaps the most important characteristic of the investment guarantee and credit program is the nature of the relationship that would exist between the government and the business community. The government is cast in the role of the stimulator or enabler without becoming involved in the management of the private company. The program is also flexible in that incentives could be increased or lowered as conditions warrant. If the investment credits should fail to provide a sufficient stimulus, additional incentives in the form of lower corporate income tax rates could be added. On the other hand, as an area becomes increasingly attractive as a retail location, the incentives could be reduced or eliminated.

If implemented with vigor and imagination, this program could lead to a dramatic transformation of the retail segment serving ghetto areas. While size restrictions would not be imposed, the provisions of the program would be most attractive to larger retail organizations. Thus, the "atomistic" structure of the retail community would undergo major change as the marginal retailers face competition with efficient mass distributors. The parasitic merchants would also face a bleak future. The study in Los Angeles revealed no instance in which a major retail firm was guilty of discriminatory pricing or inflated credit charges. In addition, the agency administering the investment program could make periodic studies of the practices of participating firms, and use these investigations to prod companies, if necessary, to assure their customers of equitable treatment.

CONCLUSION

No one program will solve a problem as basic and complex as that of the big-city ghetto. A variety of projects and measures is needed. While the program I propose has great potential, its promise is more likely to be realized if it is supported by other kinds of action to strengthen local businesses. For instance:

Various "activist" groups have been bringing pressure on unethical retailers. In Watts, some limited efforts have been made to boycott retailers who do not conform to a code of conduct that has been promulgated. In Washington, D.C., a militant civil rights organization, ACT, has launched a national campaign to encourage bankruptcy filings by poor merchants; it has devised an ingenious scheme that could deal a severe blow to parasitic retailers.

In Roxbury, Massachusetts (a part of Boston), Negroes are organizing buying cooperatives. Such cooperatives have limited potential, but many people believe they can compensate for at least some of the problems of smallness and inefficiency which plague "mom and pop" stores in the area.

Some corporate executives are trying to help Negro businessmen develop managerial knowhow. Business school students have recently got into this act, too. A group of second-year students at the Harvard Business School, with the financial backing of The Ford Foundation, is providing free advice and instruction to Negroes running retail stores and other firms in Boston. The instruction covers such basic matters as purchasing, bookkeeping, credit policy, tax reporting, and pricing.

Some large stores are reportedly considering giving franchises to retailers in ghetto areas. Assuming the franchises are accompanied by management assistance, financial help, and other advantages of a tie-in with a large company, this step could help to strengthen a number of local retailers.

Some of the large-scale renewal projects undertaken by business have, as a secondary benefit, introduced residents of run-down areas to progressive retailing. In the 1950s, a 100-acre slum section of south Chicago was razed and turned into a 2,009-apartment community with a shopping center. In the shopping center were branches of various well-known organizations—Goldblatt's Department Store, Jewel Tea Supermarket, Walgreen Drug Stores, and others. Similarly, if a group of Tampa business leaders succeed in current plans to rebuild part of Tampa's downtown business district, such leading stores as Macy's, Jordan Marsh, Bon Marche, and Sears, Roebuck plan to open branches in the new buildings. In both cases, residents of the poor areas adjoining the shopping sections would be able to take advantage of progressive retailing.

Projects like the foregoing would be welcome allies of the program proposed in this article. For this program, despite its many great advantages, will not be easy to carry out. The major retailers attracted to disadvantaged areas will face many challenges. Studies will have to be undertaken to help them adapt successfully to local conditions. Creative and imaginative managers will be needed at the store level.

The new program should be good for retailers from the standpoint of profits. In addition, retail leaders should derive a great deal of satisfaction from demonstrating that U.S. enterprise is capable of contributing significantly to the solution of the major domestic crisis of the twentieth century. An efficient and competitive retail community in a ghetto would certainly discourage ineffective and unethical store managers in the area. And while the new program would not solve all of the problems of the nation's cities, it could do a great deal to reduce the injustices suffered by the poor and to eliminate the bitterness that feeds the spreading civil disorders.

Are low-income families victims of high prices in ghetto markets? How well do lower income shoppers perceive price and other differences among stores? The author answers these questions and provides thoughts for additional areas of research in low-income markets.

---

42. DO THE POOR PAY MORE?*

Charles S. Goodman†

Recent BLS studies attempting to determine if food chains were charging higher prices in low-income areas than in other parts of the same city found that this frequent allegation was not supported by evidence in any of the several cities studied.[1] The same studies noted, however, that small independent stores as a class tend to have higher prices than the supermarket chains and that small independents represent a large proportion of the store population in low-income areas. This observation and the wide publicity afforded allegations of high prices being charged by stores in low-income Negro areas have led some people to conclude that the poor pay more for their food than those of greater means. Thus Caplovitz' findings that New York poor families paid higher prices than the well-to-do for consumer durables were believed to hold for food as well.[2] Such allegations cannot be fairly appraised without knowledge of the purchasing practices of the

* Reprinted from "Do the Poor Pay More?" *Journal of Marketing,* Vol. 32 (January 1968), pp. 18–23.

† University of Pennsylvania.

[1] "Retail Food Prices in Low and Higher Income Areas: A Study of Prices Charged in Food Stores Located in Low and Higher Income Areas of Six Large Cities, February, 1966" in *Special Studies in Food Marketing* (Technical Study No. 10, National Commission on Food Marketing. Washington: GPO, 1966), pp. 121–44.

[2] David Caplovitz, *The Poor Pay More* (New York: The Free Press of Glencoe, 1963).

families involved, including particularly the stores which are *actually patronized* for a major part of food purchasing by these groups.

An opportunity to test the hypothesis that the poor pay more for food and to explore their purchasing behavior was presented when the Philadelphia City Planning Commission was faced with the need of determining the desirability of including new supermarkets in redevelopment areas. In the belief that such a policy might be needed to overcome an unsatisfactory high-cost retail food situation, provision was made for inclusion of such a market in the West Mill Creek Redevelopment program. The presence of such an ordered plan of change of retail facilities furnished an opportunity to study current purchasing practices of residents and to note changes that emerged with the introduction of the supermarket. This article summarizes the "before" situation. It deals with the following questions:

Do the poor pay higher prices for food than the well-to-do? If so, why?

What kinds of stores do lower-income families patronize and why?

To what extent do lower-income families use various services such as credit and delivery from stores and home delivery by routemen?

How well do lower income shoppers perceive price and other differences among stores?

NATURE OF THE STUDY

Two related surveys were conducted in the summer of 1965: (1) a consumer survey of food purchasing practices, and (2) a study of prices prevailing in 12 stores used by these consumers.

The survey area

The survey area encompassed (*a*) the West Mill Creek Urban Renewal Area, a 120-acre project based on selective rehabilitation, demolition, and redevelopment; (*b*) the Philadelphia Housing Authority's Mill Creek Public Housing Project comprising 444 dwelling units; and (*c*) an unredeveloped area similar in many respects to the West Mill Creek area lying east of that area and north of the Mill Creek Project. (Figure 1)

There are no large or modern food retailing facilities within the survey area. As part of the redevelopment program, a new food supermarket is to be installed at 48th and Brown Streets in what is at present the mixed industrial-residential section. The location is about one-half block from the site of a slaughterhouse demolished in redevelopment. It will be closer to virtually all of the residents of the area than any existing outside supermarket.

FIGURE 1.
Map of survey area. (West Mill Creek redevelopment area within heavy black line)

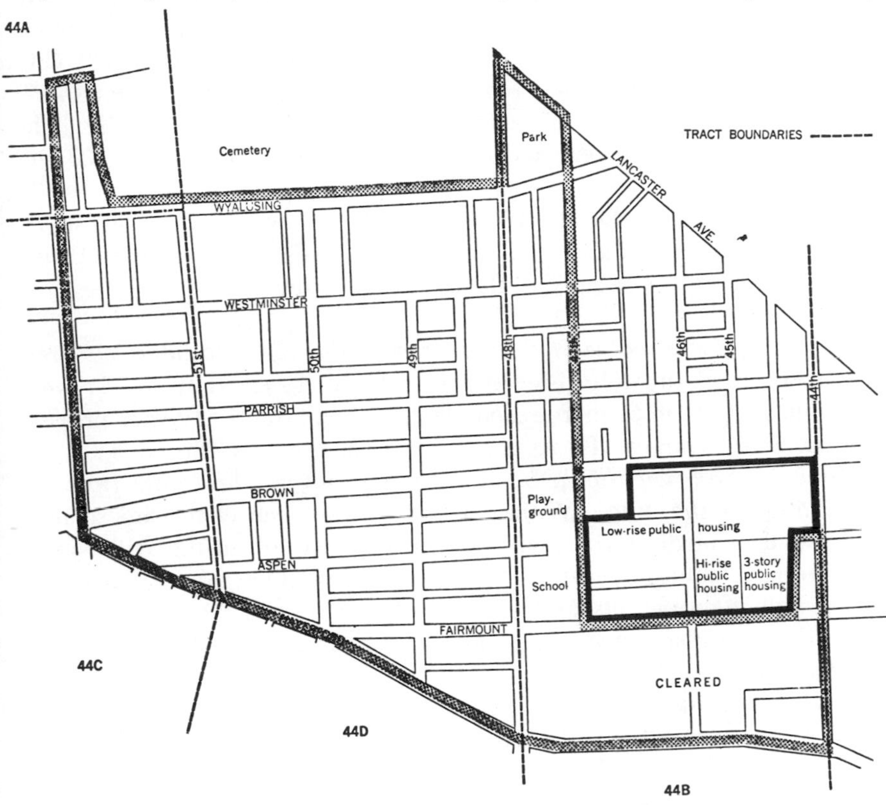

The consumer survey

The food purchasing practices of residents of the survey area were obtained through field interviews. Because location within the area was considered likely to affect the stores which would be patronized, a 20% sample was drawn from each of the 79 blocks. A random starting point was selected for each block and every fifth dwelling unit thereafter selected for interview. The total sample consisted of 651 units. Repeated call-backs were used to obtain responses from those not at home on the initial visit. A total of 520 usable interviews were obtained.

Respondents were asked a series of questions about the store in which they did most of their food shopping. In addition, questions were asked about other stores sometimes patronized to determine respondents' perceptions of store services, quality, and prices.

The respondent group. Reflecting the predominantly Negro character of the area, only 6% of the respondents were white. Based on the 1959 median family incomes for the tracts involved, the completed interviews were: 18.5% in tracts in the eighth decile, 42.3% in tracts in the ninth decile, and 39.2% in tracts in the tenth decile of all tracts in the City of Philadelphia. Demolitions and public housing construction since 1959 may or may not have altered these relationships significantly. The median family income reported by respondents was between $4,000 and $5,000.

Classification of stores. In addition to being classified as supermarkets or nonsupermarkets, all stores were assigned a code indicating their location with reference to the area being studied:

Zone A—Stores within the boundaries of the 160-acre interview area. There are approximately three dozen of these stores, of which 21 were mentioned by three or more respondents as being used as either primary or secondary sources. There are no supermarkets in this area.

Zone B—Stores within a band extending out one-half mile from the boundaries of the area. Within this area are seven chain supermarket outlets, some medium-sized independents as part of an old string-street development along Lancaster Avenue, and a number of smaller stores. All of the supermarkets and eight of the nonsupers were reported by three or more respondents as being used as either primary or secondary food sources.

Zone C—Stores more than one-half mile from the boundary of the area. Eight stores beyond the one-half mile band were listed by three or more respondents. All were chain supermarkets.

The price survey

A study of basic food prices was conducted to determine the relative prices paid for food items by families included in the study and to determine if there were differences in food costs dependent on the store or type of store at which a family primarily shopped either from choice or from necessity.

Selection of stores. Prices were sought from three types of stores: supermarkets, medium-sized independent stores, and small corner (mom 'n pop) stores. The stores selected for pricing were those which the consumer survey indicated to be the most commonly patronized within each of these classes. All of the supermarkets and two of the four medium-sized independents were located outside of the consumer survey area but within one-half mile of its boundaries. The remaining two medium-sized independents and all of the corner stores were within the survey area itself.

Selection of items and determination of prices. The foods priced were the 72 items used by the Pennsylvania Department of Public Welfare in its pricing work. This list is divided into 11 nutritional classes (for example, milk and milk products, leafy green and yellow vegetables, fats and oils). Department of Welfare weights were used to obtain an average price for each class for each store.

Conversion to market baskets. Weighted prices for nutritional groups were converted to food baskets through the use of the table of nutritional standards used by the Department of Welfare. This table sets forth the quantity of a nutritional class deemed adequate for a person of a given age and activity group; for example, 12 ounces of leafy green and yellow vegetables per week for a girl aged 13 to 15.[2] A market basket was calculated for each of three hypothetical families.

SHOPPING PRACTICES

Stores used for principal shopping

Despite the availability of a large number of small stores within the survey area, more than 92% of the residents went outside of the "A" zone for their principal grocery shopping. As may be seen in Table 1, 420 (81%) of the 520 families did their principal grocery shopping

TABLE 1
Type and location of store used for principal food shopping by 520 families

	Number of families		
Location	*Supermarket*	*Other store*	*Total*
Survey area "A"	0*	40	40
Fringe area "B"	336	49	385
Outside "C"	84	11	95
Total.	420	100	520

*No supermarkets in survey area.

at chain supermarkets, all of which lie outside the area. Another 60 (12%) went outside the immediate area to patronize other stores. Of these 60 families, 33 patronized one or the other of two medium-sized independents in zone "B," whose prices were studied and found to compare favorably with those of the supermarket chains.

Eleven of the 40 families who did their principal grocery shopping

[2] The Dept. of Welfare table used was adapted from "Food Plan at Low Cost," Household Economics Research Division, Agricultural Research Service, U.S. Department of Agriculture, March 10, 1959.

within the "A" zone used Max & Jeanne's, a store which our price survey found to be the lowest priced of the 12 stores studied. No more than a half dozen of the other 29 families used any one store as its principal food source. Presumably these few families placed a high value on store proximity.

Transportation used in shopping at principal store

Fewer than one half of the families walked to do their regular shopping at their principal store. Automobiles were used by 45%; an additional 14% used public transportation. As might be expected, the automobile was used more commonly where the store is more remote, although even a few patrons of stores within the "A" zone reported using one.

A surprising finding is that one seventh of the repondents, or one fourth of those not using autos, used public transportation for principal food shopping, chiefly in patronizing supermarkets in the fringe "B" zone. Use of public transportation tended to be highest in tract 44C, reflecting the availability of bus service on 52nd Street and the distance to the nearest supermarkets.

The use of an automobile was also affected by income. About three fifths of those with family incomes in excess of $5,000 used cars. Less use of a car was made by lower income groups, but even at the lowest income level—under $2,000—an automobile was reported as being used by nearly one fourth of the respondents.

The use of automobiles, and even more emphatically the use of public transportation, for food shopping reinforces the statement made earlier that families in this area exerted effort and some expense to go outside their immediate neighborhoods for food sources they regard as suitable.

Attitude toward store principally shopped

Respondents were asked their reasons for shopping primarily at the stores which they named. In addition, they were asked to suggest ways in which the named stores could serve them better, thus providing an indication of areas of dissatisfaction.

Reasons for shopping principal store. Price (52%), quality (42%), and location (28%) were the reasons most frequently stated for patronizing a particular store. The most commonly mentioned reason differed among the patrons of different stores. Thus, price was the reason given by more than 75% of the patrons of Litt's, Max & Jeanne's, and A & P, while quality was most frequently mentioned by Penn Fruit customers, and location by patrons of two small "A" zone stores.

Ways in which principal store could serve better. In-store service factors, especially check-out speed, were mentioned nearly twice as often as product and price factors and about 2½ times as often as the spatial factors, for example, convenience of location or delivery. Some three fifths of the respondents had no suggestions for improvements and were at least overtly satisfied. Differences in response by income levels were minor.

When asked how stores other than their principal sources could serve them better as their secondary sources, those interviewed mentioned improvements in products and price factors more frequently than they did in evaluating their principal sources (20% as against 10%). In-store service factors were of minor importance (noted by 6.4% as against 17.2%).

Other sources of food products

In addition to the store principally shopped, two other types of food sources were examined: vendor home delivery (peddling) of milk and bakery products, and the use of one or more stores for secondary shopping.

Home delivery of milk and bread. The extent to which home delivery dairy and bakery systems were used is related directly to a family's need for fill-in purchases during the regular shopping interval.

Only 29% of the families obtained milk from a home delivery route, and fewer than 8% obtained bakery products at the door. The use of home delivered milk is lowest in the under $3,000 income class and in the 36–45 age brackets. The purchase of bakery products from a route man does not seem to be income- or age-related.

Additional stores sometimes used. In addition to being selected as primary food sources by more than four fifths of the respondents, supermarkets receive important mention as "other" stores used. Indeed, 45% of the respondents mentioned a supermarket first when asked about other stores used.

Supermarkets are rarely used for fill-ins. Ordinarily they serve as alternative stores for weekly shopping trips. More than 94% of those who mentioned a supermarket as their first choice among secondary sources purchased at the named supermarket once a week or less, most commonly less. The principal reasons given for the selection of such stores were prices or specials (50%), location with reference to home or travel (18%), and quality (18%).

About two fifths of the residents used small stores in the "A" zone as secondary sources. Of those who visited these stores, 37% used them for small or emergency type items. Another 18% used them for bread and milk only, while 5% used them for meat, poultry, or fish, and 15% for one or two other types of items. Less than one fourth of the patrons reporting use of these stores obtained as many as three types of goods from them. For the majority of residents these stores are thus used as supplementary sources after one or possibly two supermarkets are used for main supplies. The fill-in character of purchases from these stores is also attested by their frequent use. Nearly one half of the users of this group of stores made purchases three or more times per week from them.

In sharp contrast to the reasons for using supers, the overwhelming reason for the use of "A" zone stores is convenience of location. Eighty-three percent state this as their reason.

Nonsupermarkets outside of the "A" zone (except those used as the principal food source) are most heavily used for perishables. Eighty nine (55%) of the 163 persons reporting use of a nonsuper outside the "A" zone as a secondary store used the store solely for meat, fish, or poultry. Quality is stated to be the principal motive for patronizing these stores (39% of mentions), followed by prices or specials (33%), and location (19%).

Use of delivery and credit services offered by stores

Both credit and delivery services are available in the area, but their usage is limited.

Delivery services. Although some of the nonsupermarkets in both the "A" and "B" zones offer delivery services, less than one fifth of the residents of the area ever make use of them. In fact the total (18%) is not much larger than the number (14%) who, lacking an auto for food shopping, use public transportation. Daily or other frequent deliveries by the gorcery boy appear to be a thing of the past in this area. Even among the 18% of the families who used delivery services at some time, only about one in eight used it as often as twice per week.

Charge acuounts. Little use of charge accounts is made by residents of the survey area if what they report about themselves can be relied upon. The allegation that lower income groups are forced to buy groceries on credit does not seem to apply to this area. Only 1% of the respondents used charge accounts regularly, although an additional 4% reported using them occasionally. In addition to the very small usage of charge accounts, only 13% of the residents believed that such service was available.

PRICE DIFFERENCES, PRICE PERCEPTIONS, AND STORE OFFERINGS

Price differences among stores

Prices of three of the four medium-sized independents averaged below those of the supermarket chains. As Table 2 shows, one of the inde-

TABLE 2
Prices, by stores

Store	Price index (A & P = 100)		
	Family #1 man 21-40 woman 21-40 boy 10-12 child 7-9	*Family #2 man 21-40 woman 21-40 child 4-6 child 1-3*	*Family #3 man 65+ woman 41-64*
Supermarkets			
A & P	100.0	100.0	100.0
Food City	101.8	101.4	101.1
Penn Fruit	103.4	103.0	103.1
Acme	103.7	103.7	103.8
Medium-sized independents			
Max & Jeanne's	92.8	92.8	91.8
Litt's	95.2	95.2	94.0
Eddie's*	98.2	98.1	97.5
Lee's	107.2	107.2	106.9
Small stores			
Cy's†	101.6	101.9	101.4
Miller's	105.5	105.7	105.0
Frank's	107.8	107.8	107.5
Orlando's‡	114.3	114.4	114.5

*Produce not carried.
†Processed, but no fresh meat carried.
‡Eggs not carried.

pendent stores, the promotionally oriented Max and Jeanne's had prices about 7% below those of the A & P. Two other stores, Litt's and Eddie's, were observed to have prices below but close to the A & P level. The prices of the remaining medium-sized independent, Lee's, were substantially above those of the supermarket chains.

Prices in the small stores were found to be somewhat higher, but here again differences among stores within the group were observed to be greater than differences among the groups. On the one hand, Cy's prices compared favorably with those of Penn Fruit and Acme although higher than A & P, Food City, and three of the medium-sized independents. At the other extreme, Orlando's prices were substantially higher than those of any other store studied.

Relationship of price differences to patronage

It was reported above that four out of five residents of the survey area used one or more of the supermarkets as their principal shopping sources for food. Of those who did not, the largest numbers used Litt's,

Eddie's, or Max & Jeanne's as their principal source. Prices in all of these stores compare favorably with those in the supermarket chains. In contrast, despite the fact that Lee's is located near the center of the survey area and is 2,400 feet from the nearest supermarket, not one of the more than 500 respondents reported it as their principal shopping store. Perhaps it may be concluded that Lee's relatively high prices outweigh the convenience afforded. The survival of the high-priced small stores would appear to rest on their use of milk, bread, soda, and emergency items rather than as principal food sources.

Price differences and shoppers' perceptions

The failure of residents to use the local stores seems to reflect their perceptions as to these stores' relative prices, although they may also reflect other considerations such as inferior quality, attitudes, or promotion.

Respondents were first asked whether there were differences in prices among stores in the area. No comparison of specific stores was requested, though stores were often named. The 439 (85%) who indicated that differences did exist were then asked to indicate the store(s) that had higher and lower prices.

Most respondents (266 cases) consider supermarket prices to be lower than those of other stores. In 21 cases, on the other hand, independent stores were believed to offer lower prices than supermarkets. In 12 of these 21, the lower-priced store named was one of the three stores priced which, according to our price study, had lower prices than A & P.

Respondents who made comparisons among specific independents most often indicated as the low-priced store Max & Jeanne's, Eddie's, or Litt's; these are stores which were found to be competitively priced. Twenty-four of the 31 respondents comparing independents named one of these three as the lower priced store.

In the cases in which respondents compared prices of two supermarkets covered in our pricing survey and showing price differences in excess of 1%, their opinions agreed with those of our pricing survey in 24 cases and disagreed in five cases.

It seems clear that both in their shopping behavior and in their responses to questions shoppers perceive significant price differences quite well.

Item coverage of stores

Although none of the stores carried all of the 72 items priced, the supermarkets generally carried most of them. Every super offered complete coverage in at least eight of the eleven nutritional classes and at least 70% coverage in each of the remaining classes.

Max & Jeanne's, the low-priced independent, also had full coverage in eight classes and at least 75% in each of the others. Litt's and Lee's coverage was slightly lower.

Coverage of the other stores was more limited. Eddie's—meat market turned superette—carries no produce. The smaller stores had important gaps. In some cases lines were so limited that a consumer relying entirely on such a store would have no oppprtunity to buy a substantial proportion of the items listed. Orlando's, the store with the highest prices, had full coverage in only two of the eleven classes and less than 70% of the listed items in seven classes.

SUMMARY OF FINDINGS

1. Because they shop at competitive stores, going outside their residence area to do so if necessary, the poor do *not* pay more for food in this area.
2. Despite the large number of small stores within the area, all but a small fraction (less than 8%) of the residents go outside their immediate vicinity for their principal food shopping. With few exceptions, they go to supermarkets (81%) or to competitively priced, moderate-sized stores (8%). Automobiles or public transportation are used to accomplish this.
3. Price and quality far outweigh location as a stated patronage factor.
4. Most families patronize more than a single store. The second store chosen is more likely to be another supermarket or competitively priced independent outside the residence area than a local convenience store.
5. Local convenience stores are used almost entirely as supplementary sources of emergency items or for frequently purchased perishables such as bread or milk. For these latter items, convenience stores take the place of more costly route delivery sources. Less than 6% of the families use a convenience store as their principal food source.
6. Shoppers' perceptions of the relative levels of prices of different stores are generally good, not only as between stores of different types but also as among stores of a given type.

FURTHER RESEARCH NEEDED

This study dealt with an area considered to be sufficiently low income to need public housing and extensive redevelopment efforts. Nevertheless, the median family income of $4,000–$5,000 might be considered by some to be too high to represent truly poverty-stricken areas. Further studies might well seek to determine if similar behavior patterns exist in neighborhoods with even lower incomes and in other cities. Further studies might also consider one or more areas in which travel to outside stores was more difficult than found to be the case here.

The price comparisons made in the present study were based on those posted, or, where unposted, those quoted by store operators. Further studies may be needed to determine if the quoted prices are those actually charged in the course of daily business and whether they are uniform among customers.

Further studies are needed to sharpen our knowledge of other aspects of differences in store offerings. In particular, it would be desirable to have appropriate measures of and adjustment factors for differences in product quality, especially for meats and produce. While quality evaluation was not a serious handicap in this pilot study, a more extensive study should make provision for de facto quality evaluations and for appropriate adjustments, including adjustments for trim of meats and freshness of produce. There is also a need to provide appropriate indices of service quality, in particular the adequacy of assortments to meet different types of consumer needs. Low coverage ratios suggest not only that the store does not provide for the varied needs of the customer, but also that the customer may find it necessary to accept substitutes having lower utility per dollar of cost, or to incur additional effort or cost to go elsewhere.

Finally, there is an important need to determine how redevelopment programs affect both the behavior and the welfare of consumers. In particular it should be determined how changes in housing and retailing facilities affect how families in these neighborhoods meet their food needs, and how well retailing serves them. Closely related to this is a need to determine how changes in retailing facilities affect the operations of ambient stores.

Bibliography

1. BACKMAN, JULES. "Is Advertising Wasteful?" *Journal of Marketing,* January 1968, pp. 2–8.
2. BECKER, BORIS W. "The Image of Advertising Truth: Is Being Truthful Enough?" *Journal of Marketing,* July 1970, pp. 66–67.
3. BOGART, LEO. "Where Does Advertising Research Go from Here?" *Journal of Advertising Research,* p. 21.
4. DARNEY, ARSEN J., JR. "Throwaway Packages—A Mixed Blessing," *Environmental Science and Technology,* April 1969, pp. 328–33.
5. GEYSER, STEPHEN A., AND RIECE, BONNIE B. "Businessmen Look Hard at Advertising," *Harvard Business Review,* May-June 1971, p. 162.
6. KOTTMAN, E. J. "Truth and the Image of Advertising," *Journal of Marketing,* October 1969, pp. 64–66.
7. LEVITT, THEODORE. "The Morality (?) of Advertising," *Harvard Business Review,* July-August 1970, pp. 84–92.
8. "Planned Obsolescence—Is It Wrong, Is There a Better Way?" *Printer's Ink,* May 19, 1961, pp. 23–31.
9. "Truth in Ads Is the Advertiser's Job," *Advertising Age,* January 25, 1971, p. 16.
10. WEISS, E. B. "Advertising's Crisis of Confidence," *Advertising Age,* June 26, 1967.
11. WHEATLEY, JOHN J., AND GORDON, GUY G. "Regulating the Price of Consumer Credit," *Journal of Marketing,* October 1971, pp. 21–28.
12. ZALTMAN, GERALD, AND VERTINSKY, ILAN. "Health Service Marketing: A Suggested Model," *Journal of Marketing,* July 1971, pp. 19–27.

Editorial postscript

THE DEVELOPMENT OF SOCIAL MARKETING

THE MARKETING ENVIRONMENT in the world's developed countries tends to be characterized by relative affluence, accelerated progress, intensified competition, and increased governmental control over business activities. The market process has long been dominated by the dictates of consumer satisfaction, profit maximization, and government control. Currently, a broader view of the social responsibility of the firm has developed that is expanding the concept of marketing. There is increasing concern with environments, values, ethical issues, the quality of life, and other societal dimensions. As a result, marketing managers are recognizing the extent and implications of society's long-run wants and needs. They also recognize the necessity of providing initiative for studying long-run consumer welfare and for responding to society's well-being.

Marketing is currently in the process of evolving from a business function to an important social force in society. Marketing is now recognized as one of the major controlling factors of socioeconomic growth and a social instrument through which a standard of living is transmitted to society. Thus, business in general, and marketing in particular, should be conceived of as more than an economic organization. They should also be viewed as a social subsystem working within a total social system. In this context, marketing cannot be confined to business activities alone. Its dimensions are being shaped and extended in a continuously changing environment.

The discipline of social marketing is emerging as a result of such changes in the businesses' external environment. Social marketing considers more than economic goals in the appraisal of marketing performance. Social marketing presents not a threat to, but many opportunities for, marketing management. It affords the challenge of increasing the quality of life and offers new potential for innovation and growth.

An affluent society tends to become less concerned with tangible goods and material possessions. It tends to become more interested in such thrusts as ecology and cultural inventories. The social costs of products are given increasing attention. Such social goals as health, safety, and education are being reexamined as areas of concern for both business and society at large. Business-government relationships are being reassessed, and new organizational forms and focuses are being developed so that social goals may be achieved. It is in the interest of business to operate in a healthy environment. As a result, social audits and indicators of social contributions by business take on rich meaning.

The readings in this book have focused on marketing in a social setting. Such topics as the conceptual foundation of social marketing, consumerism, social and ethical marketing responsibility, quality of life, the business-government interface for the benefit of society, and the social costs of the basic marketing components have been considered. These readings are presented, not in the spirit of providing answers, but rather to raise some significant questions and to provide a base for stimulating discussion.

CONSUMERISM

Consumerism is now more than a movement. It is a fact of life for corporations, both domestic and foreign. Consumerism is a long-run force influenced by rising social expectations and social unrest. Although the term "consumerism" has many definitions, in all cases consumerism implies an undercurrent of consumer dissatisfaction, a need for greater business concern, and the desire for change and improvement in the marketing system.

Consumerism has gained increasing political and government support. A White House office of consumer affairs with statutory status was established by executive order. Congress is considering a statutory agency for consumer protection. According to Ms. Virginia Knauer, the president's special assistant to consumer affairs and director of the Office of Consumer Affairs, the federal government expended a total of $578 million on consumer programs in 1970.

Regrettably, many businesses are still attempting to ignore consumerism, perhaps in the false hope that the consumer movement will quietly fade away. On the other hand, some progressive firms do not view consumerism as a threat. Rather they welcome the market opportunity which it presents. Some of them have already initiated their own consumer service programs and are experiencing additional profits as a result.

Communications between consumers and businesses are likely to increase in the future. The need for communication with the consuming public throughout the entire marketing channel is being highlighted. More corporations will reorganize and establish new positions and new organizational units to gather such information and translate it into meaningful action to serve consumers more efficiently and effectively.

Yet there are those who contend that only government can solve the problems raised by the consumerism movement. Others claim that only the business community free from restrictions should do so. At this juncture, it appears likely that it may be in the best interests of all sectors of society for business and government to combine forces and to pool their respective talents so as to meet consumer problems as effectively as possible.

BUSINESS-GOVERNMENT RELATIONS

Changes in social values may be among the most powerful factors in the society of the 1970s. Social value changes are being reflected in almost every aspect of our consumeristic society. What will be the social values of the 1970s and beyond? How will these changing social values influence marketing? These are among the issues that are important for social marketing.

There is currently increasing recognition that service to the consumer involves not only the personal satisfaction of the individual consumers, but also the meeting of environmental and social concerns. These concerns include: How should society organize itself to serve the public interest? Who determines the priorities of social values? How are these to be determined? What is the responsibility of corporate marketing executives? Should such issues be handled by the government? Other questions which center on how the public interest might be enhanced by new business-government relationships are also being raised.

Governments have implemented laws and regulations affecting all marketing components. For the most part, regulations have emerged because the government did not believe that business was able to develop effective self-regulation. To date, business has not been particularly successful in developing satisfactory self-regulation. This failure, combined with the new social and governmental expectations of business, suggests more government regulation in the future.

Satisfactory economic performance will no longer be considered the only criteria for evaluating business performance. It may be regarded as a minimal business achievement. Progress in the social performance area is also expected. It is part of the new social contract between business and society. Firms are now increasingly expected to evaluate the socioecological impacts of their products. This in turn may result in a reorientation of marketing priorities.

What should be the new relationships of government and business to the rest of society? It is possible that business might move toward increasing self-regulation in a manner that is in its own best interests. It is also possible that government will force business to conduct ethical operations in the way that it sees fit. It seems likely, as a result of experience, that the thrusts in the development of self-regulation will not replace the need for new legislation. Also, if business seriously takes the initiative and thus becomes an effective social partner with government, the resulting complex may result in less of governmental authority.

Internationally as well as in the United States, a shift is occurring. The government no longer is labeled as inherently undesirable, but is recognized and welcomed for its significant roles in marketing as regulator, arbitrator, stimulator, and customer. In the future, governmental agencies may play an active role in encouraging self-regulation by business. Expansion of government-business relationships can lead to the vigorous growth of the competitive free enterprise system. But it should also be remembered that it can lead to a planned economy, with freedoms drastically reduced. How this governmental business partnership develops is a matter of major social concern.

With all of the difficulties and limitations in identifying, measuring, and prioritizing social value changes, widely accepted measurements have yet to be developed. There is, however, an increasing trend to identify certain public purposes and interests, and to incorporate them with the incentives, capacities, and resources of private management. Efforts are being made in both the public and the private sectors to identify social indicators. Social indicators must be measured, prioritized, and operationalized for use in planning and decision making by the individual business and the public.

There have been experiments involving both the public and the private sector which have encouraged an interchange of executives. It may be possible to create new private-public research perspectives and programs. These could include a continuous research program to develop common goals and systematic procedures to be used by decision makers in both the public and private sector in planning for the future viability of society and for the development of its welfare.

Increasingly, government's role may be to set social and environmental standards for business. It is the responsibility of business, however, to make a contribution to the establishment of these standards in the area of its expertise. Through cooperative efforts with the government, business should be able to develop the theoretical bases and models for a more responsive social system.

MARKETING EDUCATION

Marketing is recognized as an important activity in modern business society. However, the marketing discipline has still been assigned a relatively low status both in the academic spectrum and in many businesses. This is in part a result of a lack of understanding in the mission and significance of marketing in a dynamic and highly industralized society. Marketing is not a mature discipline with a well-established body of information, theories, and principles that have been shaped and institutionalized through centuries of academic affiliation. Rather, it is a discipline and phenomenon of our century and of the American culture.

Marketing is a product of modern society. The discipline of marketing is changing from practice based on intuition and experience to a profession grounded more firmly on principles, theories, and rigorous scientific approaches. Marketing is entering a new stage of development in the seventies. Systems analysis will continue to affect the development of the marketing management philosophy and the marketing concept. In addition, the emergence of the discipline of social marketing will result in broadening the extent and the concept of marketing management.

In order to analyze dynamic business activities, executives must be concerned with economic, social, and physical structures; processes of broader perspectives. They will find it increasingly difficult to distinguish clearly between what is marketing and what is not marketing. The new concept of marketing is providing a conceptual framework for integrating such perspectives as consumer-citizen, sociomarket opportunities, and socioprofits. Pollution, ecology, resource management, consumer protection, and changing concepts of business responsibility are being carefully reexamined for their marketing implication.

As the readings in this volume indicate, the broader systems of society are characterized by the dynamics of change. It is increasingly important for marketing executives and students to develop a facility for understanding and practicing the concepts and analytical framework of social marketing. Both executives and students will be faced with problems of comprehending and operationalizing larger bodies of knowledge, effectively, in approaching the solution to social problems.

Marketing must be identified and studied as a natural area of interdisciplinary convergence. Marketing deals not only with product, place, promotion and price, but with other important, more contemporary ideas. The result of this interdisciplinary focus in marketing is a better understanding of the environmental forces discussed in this volume. The future development of a free society may depend substantially on progress in our field. Marketing is and will continue to be an essential catalytic agent in the modern consumeristic society.

As the task of marketing expands in society as well as in business, it becomes increasingly important that business education reflect these broader dimensions. Marketing education must expand its domain to include consideration and analysis of societal issues that are arousing interest in society and business. Marketing and business education in the university should emphasize an interdisciplinary or systems-based approach to the interlocking problems that threaten social welfare and man's survival.

Teaching and research at universities must be directed toward improving the quality of life, extending social welfare, and enhancing the chances of survival. At the same time, attention must be given to improving the internal performance of business operations. These are not easy tasks. They contain inherent conflicts. One of the major problems facing marketing is to achieve a better integration between social, and macro approaches on the one hand and managerial, and micro approaches to the study and practice of marketing on the other.

The business school of the 1970s will increasingly be concerned with social progress as well as economic growth. Creative thought must be given to questions concerning business's relationships to society, to government, and to the new problem of adapting corporations to changing social values and expectations. The objectives of a marketing education, both within the university and the corporation setting, must be focused to produce people who have developed a disciplined approach to meeting environmental, social, as well as managerial concerns. A considerable capacity for analysis and decision in these areas must be fostered. Management actions of the future may be evaluated in terms of their effect on social well-being and man's survival, as well as by conventional economic tests. Each businessman must understand the total dimensions of his profession including both the social and economic implications of his decisions. On the basis of this understanding, businessmen will gain an incomparable opportunity to contribute to the welfare of society. A great responsibility and opportunity rests with marketing practitioners, educators, and students in the 1970s. Meeting this opportunity will require a deeper understanding of social marketing.

AUTHOR INDEX

A

B

C

D

N–O

P–Q

R

S

T

SUBJECT INDEX

This book has been set in 10 and 9 point Caledonia, leaded 2 points. Section letters and chapter numbers are set in 48 point Baskerville; section and chapter titles are set in 24 point Baskerville. Reading numbers and titles are 14 point Baskerville Bold. The size of the type page is 27 by 46½ picas.